A HISTORY OF
YIDDISH LITERATURE

A HISTORY
OF
YIDDISH
LITERATURE

SOL LIPTZIN

JONATHAN DAVID PUBLISHE
Middle Village, N. Y. 11379

A HISTORY OF
YIDDISH LITERATURE

Copyright 1972
by
SOL LIPTZIN

Address all inquiries to:
JONATHAN DAVID PUBLISHERS
68-22 Eliot Ave., Middle Village, N. Y. 11379

Library of Congress Catalogue Card No. 79-164519
Standard Book Number 0-8246-0124-6

inted in the United States of America

PREFACE

THIRTY YEARS AGO the author, who was then chairman of the Department of Germanic and Slavic at New York's City College, recommended the introduction of courses in Yiddish language and literature at this institution of higher learning. His recommendation was met with bewilderment. Was Yiddish a language or only a jargon? Did it have a literature? These questions were asked at a time when in the very metropolis of the college more than a million spoke this language and when Yiddish literary creativity was at its peak. One professor finally volunteered the information that he had heard of a Yiddish novelist who actually produced a bestseller in English, *The Nazarene.* The recommendation was approved in 1942.

Since then, Yiddish courses have been introduced in more than a dozen colleges and universities. The prestige of Yiddish has grown so that no educated person any longer questions whether it is a language and the average reader is familiar with at least four Yiddish writers of international vogue: Sholom Aleichem, Y. L. Peretz, Sholem Asch and I. Bashevis Singer. Gradually the vast treasures of Yiddish literature are being revealed to English readers through an increasing number of translations and scholarly studies. Some of these studies have been most helpful in the preparation of the present volume.

The author wishes to express his appreciation to Thomas Yoseloff, publisher of *The Flowering of Yiddish Literature,* and to Jonathan David Publishers, publisher of *The Maturing of Yiddish Literature,* for permission to use material which formed the basis of these earlier volumes. These covered the period from Mendele to the Second World War. A projected third volume dealing with the contemporary period, and an additional volume

v

dealing with the pre-Mendele period, have not yet been completed. Meanwhile, the increased interest in Yiddish has focussed attention on the need for a one-volume historical survey of Yiddish literature. It is hoped that the present volume will meet this need to some extent.

SOL LIPTZIN

Table of Contents

TABLE OF CONTENTS—*(continued)*

TABLE OF CONTENTS—(continued)

TABLE OF CONTENTS—*(continued)*

1

OLD YIDDISH LITERATURE

Origin of Yiddish • Oldest Manuscripts • Age of Min-
strelsy • Elia Levita • *Bovo-Bukh* • *Shmuel-Bukh* •
Tseno-Ureno • *Brantspiegel* • *Maase-Bukh* • Glückel
of Hameln • *Tkhines* • Hassidic Tales • Nachman of
Bratslav • Hershele Ostropoler • Wise Men of Chelm
• Maggidim • Badchonim

YIDDISH IS A FUSION-LANGUAGE spoken by Ashkenazic
Jewry since the Middle Ages. It was fused from many components,
of which the oldest layers were Hebrew and Aramaic. It was enriched by Greek, Latin and proto-Romance words. Middle High
German is, however, its principal component, accounting for more
than 85% of its vocabulary and for its basic grammatical structure. During the formative period of Yiddish, there was no universally accepted standard for spoken German but rather a wide
variety of dialects ranging from those of the southern highlands
to those of the northern plains and the seacoast. Efforts to standardize a written language for documents of German chancelleries
and for manuscripts of epic bards and Minnesingers had little influence on Jews, whose daily contacts were mainly with tradesmen
and artisans.

The Jews who entered German-speaking territories in significant
numbers from the ninth century onwards came from France and
Italy. They brought with them their own vernacular, which consisted of Jewish correlates of Old French and Old Italian, combined
with the sacred Hebrew used in their prayers and the less sacred
Aramaic which had eclipsed spoken Hebrew even before the loss
of Jewish independence in Palestine. Coming in contact with various
German dialects, these Jews effected a fusion of these dialects with
the older language layers.

1

When Jews, ever since the thirteenth century, migrated eastward for economic reasons or were forced to flee eastward in larger numbers in the fourteenth century as a result of expulsions from Central European areas, they found themselves amidst Slavic-speaking populations and assimilated Slavic characteristics in their language pattern. Since the Ashkenazic, Yiddish-speaking Jews who settled in Eastern European provinces came from different parts of Germany, they were addicted to a conglomeration of pronunciations. Daily relationships brought about ever closer mingling of their speech habits until in the course of generations a common pattern was developed. The largest proportion of these Jews stemmed from Central German communities, a considerable proportion from Southern Germany, and by far the smallest proportion from North Germany. Hence, the fusion language that evolved contained to the largest extent characteristics of Central German dialects, especially those of the Middle Rhine region from Cologne and Frankfurt to Worms and Speyer, a region which had harbored the oldest and numerically strongest settlements. Southern German dialects, such as the Bavarian and Austrian, also had a significant impact, while the German dialects of the northern lowlands influenced Yiddish least.

The Yiddish of the Jews who had obtained a firm footing in Eastern Europe gradually became differentiated from the Yiddish of their co-religionists who had been permitted to remain in the older Central European abodes. By the middle of the seventeenth century, when Eastern European Jews fled westward before the marauding, massacring hordes of Ukrainian Cossacks led by Hetman Chmelnitzky, these differences were sufficiently striking so that one could recognize an Eastern Yiddish speech pattern as distinct from a Western Yiddish pattern. With the rise of the Enlightenment in the eighteenth century, Western Yiddish was disparaged by the followers of the influential philosopher Moses Mendelssohn as a corrupt German. Jews who mastered the language of Lessing, Goethe and Schiller avoided the use of Yiddish outside of intimate family circles or of closely knit trade groups such as the cattle-dealers of the Eifel Mountains. As a result, Western Yiddish declined precipitously throughout the nineteenth century and was almost extinct by the last third of the twentieth century.

Eastern Yiddish continued to flourish. On the eve of World War II, it was spoken by ten million Jews, about three fifths of the world's Jews. Since the eighteenth century, it had become differentiated into Lithuanian, Polish and Ukrainian modes of pronunciation. With the mass migration of Jews to the United States and Canada since the 1880's, many English expressions found their way into Yiddish. Following the rise of Israel, new-Hebrew words were added in considerable number. At the same time, Yiddish also enriched English, especially in the 1960's and 1970's when American writers of Jewish origin increasingly treated Jewish themes in their English novels, plays and essays, and when radio commentators and television personalities braided their broadcasts with picturesque Yiddish expressions. Yiddish words, phrases and proverbs also penetrated more easily into the Hebrew speech of the Israeli after the founding of the Jewish state, when earlier hostility toward Yiddish was replaced by a greater appreciation of its unique folk qualities.

Efforts to standardize Yiddish pronunciation, spelling and grammar, begun in the nineteenth century, gathered momentum after World War I. The granting of minority rights to Jews in the various peace treaties that ended this war included provisions for educational autonomy in the succession states of the Czarist and Hapsburg Empires. The increase of Yiddish elementary and secondary schools and the founding of teachers' institutes faced educators with the problem of preparing accurate, teachable texts, and cleansing the Yiddish tongue of linguistic excrescences such as the overabundance of newly imported, indigestible Germanisms, Anglicisms and Slavisms. Actors and lecturers strove for a pronunciation that would be easily understood by audiences on all continents on which they were active. Newspapers, periodicals, and printing and publishing firms looked for guidance in solving spelling problems.

In 1925, with the founding of YIVO, the Yiddish Scientific Institute, later renamed, the Institute for Jewish Research, a center became available for the discussion of literary, linguistic and lexicographical problems. It was established first in Vilna, and afterwards in New York and Buenos Aires. YIVO attracted confirmed scholars and also trained young researchers. Before long, its publications gained in importance.

By the mid-twentieth century, universities were establishing chairs and courses in Yiddish studies. The prestige of Yiddish continued to rise as scholarly studies uncovered rich treasures from its past, and as gifted writers created new Yiddish works of literary excellence. Ambitious projects, such as the nine-volume *Biographical Dictionary of Modern Yiddish Literature* and the ten-volume *Great Dictionary of the Yiddish Language,* were launched in the 1950s. Radio and television brought Yiddish programs to Jewish homes.

At the same time, the number of Yiddish-speaking persons, halved by the Nazi Holocaust, continued to decline as Jews became more fluent in Hebrew, the language of Israel, or in English, Spanish, Russian and French, the languages of the majority populations in whose midst most Jews dwelt. Despite ominous forebodings about the future of Yiddish, literary creativity was maintained at a high level and Yiddish classics were reaching worldwide audiences through the medium of translations and adaptations. Nevertheless, many more of the vast treasures of Yiddish still await translation, and the record of Yiddish literary development since its beginnings has only been partly unfolded.

The oldest surviving literary document in Yiddish, a manuscript dating from about 1382, was found in Egypt and edited in 1957 by L. Fuks. It consists of four epic poems based on biblical and Haggidic themes. Extant glosses and glossaries of the fourteenth and fifteenth centuries are of linguistic but not literary interest. They were of use primarily to teachers of the Bible who had to interpret difficult Hebrew words to their pupils.

Little has been preserved of Yiddish literature prior to the sixteenth century when the first printed books in Yiddish appeared. The earliest songs and tales were transmitted from generation to generation chiefly by word of mouth, but even when they were recorded by scribes, their prospects for survival were not as favorable as those of manuscripts in Hebrew. When Jews were expelled from their homes or forced to flee because of pillaging, bloodthirsty mobs, they could take with them only their most treasured possessions. These were more likely to include manuscripts of biblical texts or talmudic tracts than those of Yiddish tales, useful only for whiling away idle hours.

Folksongs, folk riddles, incantations and lullabies, recorded in later centuries, bear evidence of a transmission through many generations. Yiddish verse narratives, recited or chanted by merrymakers on festive occasions, must have been very popular, because they often aroused the ire of community leaders who felt that preference should be given to religious texts which would further moral conduct. Jewish audiences, no less than Christian ones, were fascinated by the exploits of Germanic heroes such as Dietrich von Bern and his armor-bearer Master Hildebrand. The former was the historic Theodoric, king of the Ostrogoths, who had become the center of many legends, some of which seeped into Jewish quarters. Stories of King Arthur and his Round Table were included in the repertoire of wandering Jewish ministrels. Side by side with Yiddish paraphrases of the Sacrifice of Isaac, the Book of *Esther* and *the Song of Songs,* there arose lengthy romances of chivalry, such as the romance of Sir Gawain and his brave son Viduvilt, adapted from Wirnt von Gravenberg's German romance *Wigalois.* The pioneering scholar of early Yiddish, Alfred Landau, who made the first detailed comparison of *Wigalois* and the manuscripts of the Yiddish *Artus-Hof,* laid particular stress on the similarities between them. His successors, Max Weinreich and Max Erik, emphasized the divergencies, the modifications which the anonymous Yiddish minstrel had to make in order to satisfy his Jewish audience.

The most popular of the knightly romances was the *Bovo-Bukh,* composed by Elia Levita in 1507-1508 and printed for the first time in 1541. This narrative of 650 stanzas in ottava rima is generally regarded as the most outstanding poetic work in Old Yiddish. Its only rival qualitatively was the *Shmuel-Bukh,* but while the latter experienced only six editions, none later than 1612, the *Bovo-Bukh* could boast of at least forty editions during the following four centuries. Levita had a great reputation among the Christian humanists of Italy, France and Germany as a Hebrew scholar and as a systematizer of Hebrew grammar, but his fame among Jews rests to no less extent upon the poetic romances he printed for less learned audiences.

Levita referred to himself in the closing stanzas of the *Bovo-Bukh* as Eliahu Bakhur, an appellation which might be translated as Eliahu the Bachelor. It may, therefore, be inferred that this wandering minstrel, unsure of bread, married comparatively late in life. He was born in 1469 at Neustadt near Nürnberg as the youngest of nine brothers. When the Jews were expelled from his native townlet and from the entire Nürnberg area, he joined the refugees who streamed southward. For a few years, after 1496, he lived in Venice, the most important commercial center of Italy prior to the discovery of America. The coming of Ashkenazic, Yiddish-speaking Jews to this Adriatic port, until then settled by their Sephardic, Italian and Levantine co-religionists, brought about a brief efflorescence of Yiddish minstrelsy. By the middle of the sixteenth century, however, the offspring of the Jewish refugees accepted the Italian speech of his neighbors, and the audience for Yiddish romances shrank. Yiddish creativity declined, and by the end of the century Yiddish books ceased to be printed in Italy.

Levita experienced many variations of fortune during his long life. He did not find it easy to eke out a bare living during his early years as an itinerant entertainer. In 1504 he exchanged Venice for the neighboring city of Padua and five years later he had to leave this war-ravaged community. He was in his forties when he came to Rome and found a patron in Petrus Egidius of Viterbo (1471-1532), whom he taught Hebrew and for whose library he copied Hebrew manuscripts, primarily cabalistic ones. For thirteen carefree years he lived with his family in the palace of this Humanist, who was elevated in 1517 by Pope Leo X to the rank of Cardinal. When Rome was sacked in 1527, however, Levita had to resume his wandering. He found work as proofreader for a Hebrew press and as a teacher of Hebrew in Venice. In his early seventies he was active in Germany, much respected by its Humanists and religious reformers, but in his late seventies he was back in Venice, where he died in 1549.

While working for a printer in Germany, he had an opportunity to print his own works, including his *Bovo-Bukh*. This poetic romance was frequently reprinted century after century. When its language became so antiquated as to be incomprehensible, and when its rhymes no longer seemed correct because of the changed pronunciation, it was rewritten as a prose narrative or translated into more modern Yiddish verse. The latest reprinting appeared in New York in 1949, and the most recent stanzaic rendering into contemporary Yiddish was made by Moshe Knapheim, and appeared in Buenos Aires in 1962.

The theme of the *Bovo-Bukh* goes back to an Anglo-Norman knightly romance of the twelfth century, whose hero was Sir Bevis of Hampton. Levita's immediate source was an Italian adaptation, in which the hero's name had been Italianized to Buovo d'Antona and which he further changed to Bovo.

The Yiddish verse epic has as its central theme the love of Bovo and Druzane. Bovo was the son of incompatible parents, an aged king and a young wife who hated her husband. Bovo's mother conspired to have his father killed while on a hunt, and she then married the murderer. Fearing that Bovo might grow up to avenge his father, the couple tried to poison him, but he eluded death and fled far from his birthplace, Antona. Merchants who discovered the tired, handsome lad asleep on a seashore transported him to Flanders and sold him to its king for whom he worked as a stable boy. When the king's daughter Druzane saw him, she fell in love with him. Soon, thereafter, the heathen ruler of Babylonia arrived in Flanders with ten thousand warriors and demanded the beautiful Princess Druzane as bride for his ugly son, Lucifer. His demand was rejected and war broke out. In the course of the fighting, the king of Flanders was defeated and carried off as a captive.

Bovo set out in pursuit on a magic horse, routed the Sultan's army, killed Lucifer, and freed the captive king, who then promised to let him marry Princess Druzane. Before Bovo could do so, however, he was enticed to Babylonia and, as the slayer of Lucifer, he was hurled into a horrible dungeon. Only after a year did he succeed in escaping. Meanwhile, Druzane, deeming him dead, had to assent to marry the knight Macabron. But on her wedding day, Bovo found his way into the knight's castle disguised as a beggar and made himself known to her. They fled and found refuge in a count's palace, where they lived happily for several months. When they learned that they were in danger of falling into the power of the angry Macabron, they escaped to an inaccessible forest. There Druzane gave birth to twins.

One day Bovo went forth to find a route which would enable his family to get back to Flanders. When he did not return, Druzane had reason to assume that he had been devoured by a ravenous lion that was prowling in the forest. She thereupon left her dangerous hiding place and set out with her twins in the direction of the seacoast, ultimately reaching Flanders. When Bovo came back to his imperilled abode in the forest and did not find his wife and children, he concluded that all of them must have fallen prey to the lion. In despair he joined a military force that was being recruited for war against his native Antona and its wicked rulers. He killed the usurper, his father's murderer, and dispatched his lecherous mother to a nunnery. He then ascended the throne as the rightful heir. After yet more adventures, he was reunited with Druzane and his children and reigned happily ever after.

When this verse romance was reprinted in prose in the latter half of the eighteenth century, its title was altered from *Bovo-Bukh* to *Bovo-Maisse*, "Maisse" being the Hebrew and Yiddish word for tale. The similarity of "Bovo" to "Bobo," the Yiddish designation for grandmother, led in the course of time to the substitution of *Bobo-Maisse* for *Bovo-Maisse* and to the use of the former expression for any grandmother's tale or old-wives'-tale, with no necessary connection to the original romance about the adventures of Sir Bovo.

Another romance in ottava rima, *Paris and Vienna,* has been ascribed to Levita on the basis of internal evidence, even though the single copy which survives lacks a title-page. It deals with the love of a knight Paris and a Princess Vienna, names unrelated to the cities Paris and Vienna. It was probably printed in 1594 in Verona and easily ranks with the *Bovo-Bukh* in quality though not in popularity.

Less important than the epic romances are two of Levita's minor poems which have been preserved in a single manuscript. These were probably written in his early Venetian years, when he had to earn his living as a roaming, rhyming entertainer, and one of them includes an attack upon a fellow-minstrel, a competitor who had inflicted hurt upon him and whom he repaid with scurrilous, biting insults.

Levita was not the equal of Ariosto or Tasso, his famed Italian contemporaries, and the knightly adventures depicted by him had no basis in Jewish reality. Though he sought to tone down the Christian symbols of his original source and to substitute Jewish customs, Jewish values and Jewish traits of character here and there, his romances could, at best, supply excellent entertainment and stimulate the imagination to romantic flights of fancy. They could not speak to the inmost feelings of his Jewish listeners as could the deeds of biblical heroes and of Jewish historical or legendary figures. Exploits of the biceps or the deft handling of a lance were not as highly regarded by Jews as were wisdom, moral courage and the sanctification of God's name through martyrdom. Women, who formed the largest part of the audience to whom courtly romances were directed, were far more entranced by the tales embedded in the *Tseno-Ureno,* the Yiddish biblical commentary which they themselves intoned in a chanting voice during each week of the year, often to the accompaniment of a copious flow of tears. However, for more than a century before the publication of the prose *Tseno-Ureno* in 1616, biblical romances in verse had become current.

The most perfect of these Yiddish religious epics was the *Shmuel-Bukh,* first printed in Augsburg in 1544, three years after Levita printed the *Bovo-Bukh.* In one of several surviving manuscripts, the next to the last stanza lists Moshe Esrim Vearba as the maker of the book. Whether "maker" meant author or copyist has been the subject of an extensive controversy. *Esrim Vearba* is Hebrew for the number 24 and the pseudonym, if it was a pseudonym, was derived from the 24 books of the Bible. Zalman Shazar, President of Israel, has sought to identify Moshe Esrim Vearba with an Ashkenazic Rabbi who was active in Constantinople during the second half of the fifteenth century, an identification which sounds convincing because of the uniqueness of this name.

The author of the *Shmuel-Bukh*, Moshe Esrim Vearba or his anonymous predecessor, had mastered the Bible thoroughly. But he was also well versed in aggadic literature and in German chivalric lore. He thus drew upon a vast treasure of folk material, which he filtered through his creative imagination.

The *Shmuel-Bukh* was composed no later than the second half of the fifteenth century. It was widely circulated in manuscript form long before it was printed. Less ambitious versified tales of Abraham and Joseph had preceded it chronologically, and a verse epic, the *Melokhim-Bukh*, dealing with events of the Book of Kings, followed it. Poetic versions of *Joshua*, *Judges* and *Daniel* were also attempted. None were of the quality of the *Shmuel-Bukh*, however, and some of the authors confessed their indebtedness to it by indicating that their verses were to be chanted in the tone or style of this grandiose epic. Its stanzaic form was similar to, but not identical with, that of the German folk epic *Das Nibelungenlied*. Its central hero was David.

The minstrel opened with an invocation, praising God for his loving-kindness. God, who inflicted punishment upon Jews when they disobeyed his commandments, also helped them when they repented and called upon him in their distress. The biblical *Book of Samuel* recorded the merciful and miraculous interventions by God in behalf of his people. With the wish that God would not forsake the Jews in their present exile and that he would once more redeem them from their misfortunes, the poet ended his introduction. He then began the narrative itself with the story of Elkana and the rivalry between Elkana's two wives—Penina, who had ten sons, and Hannah, who prayed at the sanctuary at Shiloh that she might be blessed with one. He continued with the story of the son granted to Hannah, the prophet Samuel, who was to become a renowned leader of his people and who was to anoint Saul as the first King of the Jews and, later on, David, as Saul's more illustrious successor. The author lavished his affection upon David, whose prowess he showed as stemming from God and whose aberrations he sought to minimize. David's victory over Goliath was brought about, not by his own physical mightiness, but by agility and sagacity, gifts bestowed upon him by God. In the Bathsheba episode, David was only seemingly morally guilty; in reality, he proved his unimpeachable devotion to God. He had entered into a wager with God that he could resist temptation under all circumstances even as had his forefather Abraham. When he succumbed soon thereafter to Bathsheba's naked beauty, he justified his conduct on the ground that, since God was the supreme Lord of the Universe and he himself but a servant of God, it would have been improper for the omniscient Lord to lose the wager and for the servant to win it.

With the increasing dissemination of printed Yiddish books, there was a lessening need for minstrels to recite or chant secular or religious verse romances, and for patrons, or more often patronesses, to commission scribes to copy manuscripts at great expense. Women, who were not expected to be as proficient in Hebrew as were their husbands, could acquire a knowledge of the Torah and its holy precepts by purchasing an inexpensive Yiddish translation. At first there appeared translations only of individual biblical tracts. Two translations of the Pentateuch were printed as early as 1544 by Jewish converts to Christianity. One appeared in Konstanz as the work of Michael Adam and Paulus Fagius, the other in Augsburg by Paulus Aemilius. The latter, revised by Yehuda Leib bar Moshe Naphtali Bresh, a learned Polish Jew and printed at Cremona in 1560, found a larger Jewish audience, as can be deduced from the fact that it was reprinted in Basel in 1583. Around 1590 it occurred to Jacob ben Isaac Ashkenazi (1550-1625), a rabbi of Yanova in the Polish district of Lublin, to venture beyond mere translation. His *Tseno-Ureno* supplied a running commentary, interlacing biblical passages with parables, allegories, short stories, anecdotes, legends and admonitions to ethical conduct. First printed in 1616, the book soon became a bestseller. It was reprinted at least twenty-five times before the end of the seventeenth century and many more times thereafter. It has been called the Women's Bible. Its chapters parallel the weekly portions of the Pentateuch and the weekly Haftorahs.

The title was derived from a verse of the *Song of Songs* which began with the words "Tseno Ureno Bnoth Zion"—"Go forth and see, O ye daughters of Zion." These words clearly indicated that the author had in mind primarily women as his readers. Much of his material was taken from Rashi, the most popular medieval expounder of the Bible and the Talmud, and from Bahya ben Asher ben Halawa, a distinguished biblical exegete of the thirteenth century. The erudite Rabbi of Yanova was also well acquainted with original Talmudic sources and with many authoritative biblical interpreters who preceded him. The title page of the Basel edition of 1622 gave a list of the commentators from whom he gleaned his material. His talent consisted in weaving together strands from these different sources into a fascinating, didactic book which could win the approbation of the strict moral leaders of Eastern European Jewry, and at the same time accompany women as their favorite literary and devotional text from girlhood to old age. For generations there was hardly a Yiddish home that did not possess a copy. On Saturday afternoons, mothers would read pages from it to their children and these readings helped to mold the character and values of the young, who took to heart the moral admonitions.

In interpreting the commandment "Honor thy father and mother," for example, the author elucidated that the Lord first commanded us to honor Him as the father of all mankind, and then to honor our earthly fathers who had a share in bringing us into this world. Just as one honors the Deity for His own sake and not for the sake of a reward, so one should honor parents for their own sake and not for what one may inherit from them. Furthermore, just as one honors God by giving alms and tithes, so one should honor parents by assisting them with money and providing them with food, shelter and clothing. Whosoever honors his parents is promised a long life, because aged parents are often a burden, and children who do not begrudge them their years, but rather honor them, will set a good example and, when they themselves, in turn, will attain to a ripe old age, they too will be honored, assisted and provided for by their own offspring.

The author, having women readers in mind, was especially tender when describing the behavior of the biblical matriarchs. Much was made of Jacob's wooing of Rachel, who was without blemish, and his being given Leah, who had bad eyes, the result of too much weeping. As the oldest daughter of Laban she was originally to have married Esau, the wicked older son of Rebecca, while her younger sister Rachel was to have married the kind and upright Jacob, Rebecca's younger son. Joseph's chastity received great stress. The birth of Moses and his rescue by Pharaoh's daughter were embellished with many picturesque and heart-warming details. The rewards awaiting the pious in paradise and the torments which the wicked undergo in hell were depicted vividly. Repentance was urged repeatedly. A righteous person should not put God to the test by saying "I will serve Him and will see if He will reward me." One should rather serve God wholeheartedly, regardless as to whether He allotted good fortune or ill. The virtue of charity was illustrated by many tales of kind, generous individuals. The almsgiver was urged to talk gently to the recipient of alms and not to make a display of his philanthropy. When an impoverished person was discovered who would sooner starve than accept charity, such a person should be given assistance in the form of a loan and should not be pressed to repay the loan. Giving a single penny a hundred times over was better than giving a hundred pennies at a time, because whosoever gave frequently got into the desirable habit of giving.

Beside the *Tseno-Ureno,* there circulated many other ethical tracts which served as guides for Jewesses in their religious and family life. These Musar books included the *Brantspiegel* by Moshe ben Hanoch Altschul (ca. 1540-ca. 1610), first printed in 1602. Its vogue among German communities led to the use of the word *Spiegel* in the titles of other Yiddish ethical tracts. *Spiegel* was the Yiddish term for mirror and these works sought to hold up a mirror to Jewish society. Within a few years, there were published a *Sittenspiegel,* a *Zierspiegel,* a *Klein Brantspiegel* and a *Zuchtspiegel.*

The aim of the original *Brantspiegel* was to reflect as in a mirror all the laws and precepts for an ideal, virtuous existence. Its seventy-four chapters formed an encyclopedic handbook covering every aspect of a woman's life including chapters on the difference between a good woman and a bad one, how modest women ought to behave in their homes, on decency, table manners, modesty and false pride, on the education of children, on hygiene and on how a woman should treat her domestic help. Tales and anecdotes were introduced to illustrate the lessons being emphasized but not primarily for their entertainment value.

The *Maase-Bukh,* printed in Basel in 1602, the same year as *Brantspiegel,* also sought to inculcate moral lessons by means of illustrative stories. However, its stories, culled from the lore of all the preceding centuries, occupied most of the text, while the lesson to be derived from each story was summed up as a conclusion or merely hinted at. The 254 to 257 tales included in the early editions stemmed from widely different Hebrew and Yiddish sources and were assembled and adapted by a pious Central European Jew towards the end of the sixteenth century. The largest group of stories comprised the first 157 and harked back to Talmudic narratives. A second group, embracing the tales from 158 to 182, consisted of medieval Jewish legends of the Rhenish and Danubian regions. It centered about the lives and miraculous deeds of the mystic personalities Rabbi Samuel of Regensburg (1115-1180) and his son Rabbi Judah the Pious (1150-1217), co-authors of the ethical text *Sefer Hassidim*. The third and last group contained miscellaneous tales of oriental and occidental origin, to which a Jewish flavor was added. Each story, regardless of its source, was adapted to convey a moral. Thus, a story reminiscent of *Androcles and the Lion*, related that Rabbi Samuel in the course of his voyaging between one port and another heard a terrible roaring along the coast and asked the ship's captain to return to the shore. Following the noise, he saw a frightened lion fleeing from a fire-belching panther. He rushed to the aid of the lion and put the panther to flight. The lion was grateful to his savior, kneeled down and let Rabbi Samuel ride on its back until they reached the waiting ship. When the Rabbi went on board and resumed his voyage, the lion stood on shore and kept looking at the vessel until it disappeared from sight, even as one accompanies a departing friend with long, loving gaze. From this tale, the reader could learn that even a wild beast would not harm a person who was once good to it.

The author of the *Maase-Bukh* is unknown, but the publisher or bookseller, who commissioned the book to be printed in Basel, called himself on the title page Jacob bar Abraham of Mezhritsh, a townlet in Lithuania. From him also stemmed the introduction in which he warned against the reading of romances about Dietrich von Bern and Master Hildebrand. He condemned such reading as a waste of time and to read silly, secular romances on the Sabbath was a sin. On the other hand, to read his *Maase-Bukh* would help dispel wicked thoughts and would promote goodness. Not only simple, uneducated men and women, but also scholars, rabbis and their wives could profit from his text.

The *Maase-Bukh* was frequently reprinted. Later editions added legends from the *Zohar*, the Hebrew work dealing with cabalistic mysteries. These legends told about Rabbi Isaac Luria, the sixteenth century leader of the Safad group of practical cabalists. In the *Maase-Bukh*, preachers of succeeding generations found rich material for homilies and Yiddish writers inspiration for poems, novels and dramas. An English translation by Moses Gaster, Chief Rabbi of the Sephardic communities of England, was published in two volumes in 1934.

Tseno-Ureno, Brantspiegel and *Maase-Bukh* were the three most popular Yiddish works that helped to fortify the Jewish woman of the seventeenth century in her piety. These three gave rise to a large assortment of similar printed books during this century of transition from Jewish medievalism to Jewish modernism. It was a century of physical catastrophes and spiritual tragedies that could have led to mass despair and moral disintegration for a less literate and less religiously oriented people. A climax of horror was reached in the destruction of hundreds of Jewish communities by the rampaging Cossack hordes of Hetman Chmelnitzky in the years 1648 and 1649. Not long thereafter, Jewish moral resiliency was put to its severest test by the apostasy of Sabbatai Zvi, in whom many Jews had seen the longed for Messianic redeemer from the woes of exile and who converted to Islam in 1666. Pious books in Yiddish and saintly personalities such as the Baal Shem, founder of Hassidism, spoke to the heart of the troubled masses and kindled a renewed will to carry on as bearers of God's law among mankind.

From the Yiddish memoirs of Glückel of Hameln, from the Yiddish devotional prayers ascribed to Sarah Bas Tovim, and from the Yiddish Hassidic booklets of the followers of the Baal Shem, we can trace the recovery from gloom and the revitalization of the Jewish spirit through an intensification of religious zeal.

Glückel, who lived from 1645 to 1724, stemmed from a prominent patrician family of Hamburg. When the Jews were expelled from her native town, she was only a child and when her family received permission to return to trade there she was twelve. Two years later, she was married to a Jew of Hameln, but after a year in this town of the legendary Pied Piper, she moved back to Hamburg, the Hanseatic port which offered more opportunities for business and financial enterprises. She advised and helped her husband in all practical matters even while bearing and rearing twelve children. These she later married off to members of the most prominent Jewish families of Europe. When her husband died in 1689, she was able to carry on the family enterprises successfully and to increase her wealth. After eleven years of widowhood, she married a banker of Metz and settled in this Jewish center of Lorraine. Two years later, her husband lost both his fortune and hers, and in 1712 he died. She bore her adversity with dignity. Her religious upbringing had taught her to accept whatever befell her as the will of God.

Glückel began to write her *Memoirs* at the age of forty-six, after the death of her first husband, in order to dispel the melancholy that often overtook her, and in order to acquaint her children and grandchildren with their distinguished family background. She completed writing the first five parts by 1699, before her second marriage. Then, after an interruption of sixteen years, she resumed her writing until 1719. Though primarily a family chronicle and not intended for publication by its author, the *Memoirs* unfolded a rich panorama of Jewish life in cities such as Hamburg, Altona, Hameln, Hanover, Metz, Berlin and Amsterdam. Glückel had an excellent memory, a kind temperament, a poetic gift of expression, a good traditional education, and a pious disposition. She was well versed in the legendary lore of the Talmud and had read the popular Yiddish ethical books, the *Musar*-tracts. She often made use of parables, folk tales, and stories that illustrated a moral. She was profoundly influenced by *Tkhines,* devotional prayers for women, and often echoed them in her written meditations. Her style had the charm of simplicity and intimacy and the qualities of sincerity, vividness and picturesqueness.

Tkhines, published since 1590, circulated as penny booklets and also as insertions in richly bound prayer-books. They were pious pleas to the Creator of the universe. They invoked His blessing and His help. They were chanted by women in need of spiritual sustenance who poured out their sorrow-laden hearts in phrases of anguish and contrition. They implored the Lord of Mercy to purify them of evil thoughts, to provide their family with adequate nourishment, not to let them be dependent upon their children in old age, not to shorten their span of life, and, when their end came nigh, to let death be mild and an adequate atonement for life's follies and wrongdoing. Constant references were made to the matriarchs Sarah, Rebecca, Rachel and Leah, whose righteous deeds were held up as models.

There were *Tkhines* for normal occasions, such as those to be uttered daily, or on the eve of the Sabbath before and after the lighting of candles, or on holidays in the synagogue, or on the first day of a new month, or on New Year before the sounding of the Shofar, or on the eve of Atonement Day before *Kol Nidre.* There were also *Tkhines* for special situations, such as one to be murmured by a childless woman who longed for offspring, even as did Hannah, the wife of Elkana, who prayed at the ancient shrine of Shiloh. Another was for the wife whose husband was a poor provider or an itinerant merchant exposed to daily dangers on highways and in strange places. There was a *Tkhine* to ward off an Evil Eye; there were *Tkhines* to be recited by a mother who was about to give birth, and later when she brought her son to his first school hour, and still later at his Bar-Mitzvah, and finally, at his wedding. There were *Tkhines* for worried mothers whose daughters were of marriageable age and who had not yet found a suitable mate, or whose sons had strayed from the path of learning and good deeds.

Typical of the *Tkhines* was the following, to be recited before Memorial Services for departed ancestors: "Dear, holy souls of our parents. When you dwelt on earth, you prayed that we might bring you no pain, that you should raise us to lead a virtuous life, that you should lead us to the wedding canopy, and that it be granted you to see children born to us. Do you now pray for us, your children, that we too may lead our children to the *Chupah;* that we too may live to rejoice in generations after us; that our sons be virtuous Jews, guardians of the Torah's precepts, for whom we should obtain pious Jewish maidens as wives; that our daughters perform all the commandments that the Torah prescribed for them; that it be granted us to find for them pious Jewish young men as husbands; that we have sufficient sustenance and sufficient time for prayer, and our husbands for prayer and study. Pray that we be able to educate our children in Torah and morality; that they have a good heart and a keen memory in learning Torah; that the Lord of the Universe grant us a long life in peace and joy. Pray also for all Israel that it be helped. Intercede for us and all Israel. May the Lord have mercy and deliver us from all the wicked decrees and terrible edicts. May our foes make peace with us and not oppress us. Pray that God light up our world so that we should no longer be in darkness and should be able to serve him everlastingly. And may salvation come to us speedily in our days."

The most widespread booklet of *Tkhines* was *Shloshe Shearim* ascribed to Sarah Bas Tovim, from which the above prayer was quoted. The Hebrew title denoted "Three Portals" and referred to the three religious acts obligatory for all women. The authoress lived in the latter half of the seventeenth century and in the first decades of the eighteenth. She stemmed from the townlet of Satanov in the Ukrainian province of Podolia and claimed to be a descendant of Rabbi Mordecai of Brisk. In the booklet, written in her old age, she expressed the hope that the young women for whom she composed her prayers would not be punished as she had been by having to wander unceasingly from place to place. She recalled how in her youth she had come to the synagogue bedecked with jewels, how she gossiped, laughed and jested during the divine services, and how God punished her for her frivolity and cast her forth without a permanent place of refuge. She urged her readers to take a lesson from her plight, to acknowledge their errors in time, to have mercy on widows, orphans, strangers, captives, the old and the sick.

For later generations, Sarah Bas Tovim became a mythical figure, the subject of poems and legendary tales. In a story by Y. L. Peretz, entitled *Der Zivug,* which might best be translated as "Marriages Are Made in Heaven," she was received during a snowstorm at the edge of a forest by a lonely Jewish couple who were worried about finding a mate for their seventeen-year-old son. In return for their hospitality, she left a pair of golden slippers as a gift for the future bride which heaven predestined for the son. The young man then set out in search of the girl whom the slippers would fit. After two years of wandering, he found her as a barefooted Cinderella, whose *Tkhine* for a suitable mate had also been heeded by Sarah Bas Tovim, the Wandering Jewess.

Unlike the *Tkhines,* which were directed primarily to women, the booklets about the lives and deeds of wonder-working Hassidic rabbis were meant to be read by men. An aura of mystic adoration enwrapped Israel Baal Shem Tov (1700-1760), the founder of Hassidism, Levi Yitzkhok of Berditchev (1740-1809), the most compassionate of the Hassidic leaders, and Rabbi Nachman of Bratslav (1772-1810), the most talented of the Hassidic story-tellers.

The Hassidic movement emphasized the dignity of the common man and thereby also added to the dignity of his language. It sanctioned the use of Yiddish as well as Hebrew for religious communication between man and God and between rabbi and disciple. Yiddish sayings of Hassidic sages stirred the imagination and were disseminated to the remotest Jewish hamlets. Yiddish proverbs spoke to the receptive heart far more than to the mind. Yiddish legends arose which endowed Hassidic leaders with superhuman qualities. Yiddish stories illustrated Hebrew prayers and made them more meaningful. Rabbi Nachman of Bratslav once commented: "The world says that stories are good to put a person to sleep, but I say that with stories you arouse people from sleep."

The stories of Rabbi Nachman, the great-grandson of the Baal Shem, had the widest vogue. During his short life of thirty-eight years, he succeeded in gathering a group of devoted disciples whom he exhorted to seek communion with God through ardor, song, dance and ecstasy. His many stories were often improvised on the spur of the moment in order to give vividness to his teaching. They were spread by word of mouth during his lifetime. However, some were also written down immediately in Yiddish and translated into Hebrew by his faithful biographer, Nathan of Nemirov. They were published in 1815, five years after Rabbi Nachman's death, under the Hebrew title *Sippure Massioth.* They were studied by his followers throughout later generations as religious revelations and were given mystic, cabalistic interpretations by Bratslaver Hassidim. Yet, purely as masterpieces of narrative art, they are an esthetic delight.

Their originality lies in their combination of simple folk material and mystic visions of unfathomable profundity. The reader is transported from the realm of the Arabian Thousand and One Nights to real cities like Warsaw and Leipzig. He hears of a castle of pearls atop a golden mountain but also of familiar Ukrainian forests which harbor dangerous brigands. The forces of evil are always routed in the end, but not by mighty knights encased in steel. It is rather good beings armed by their faith in God who overcome all obstacles. A Sleeping Beauty is restored to her father not by a bride-seeking prince who awakens her with a kiss but by her own brother, the Crown Prince, who cannot endure the sight of his father sorrowing for her after her disappearance. This brother survives immense dangers and overcomes repeated disappointments, year in and year out, without desisting from his search. There is an alluring suggestiveness in every one of the many incidents which can be interpreted at different levels. Is not the princess more than merely the heroine of an adventure-tale? Is she not also the embodiment of the longed-for ideal toward which one strives and stumbles throughout life and without which there would be no meaning to existence? Is not the story's emphasis upon the long road traversed and the perilous temptations encountered, rather than upon the final stage when the goal is ultimately attained, an indication that the expenditure of vital energies in the direction of the luminous ideal is far more important than the reward at the end?

The preface to Rabbi Nachman's thirteen stories stresses that not a single word is there for its own sake, that great secrets are hidden in each word, that ethical conduct can be learned and God's majestic ways discerned in the various incidents.

In *The Tale of the Wise Man and the Simpleton,* the former is always sad because he ponders too deeply and as a result he finds imperfections everywhere. The latter, in his naiveté, is always happy, content with a piece of bread, a drink of water, and a single coat which he shares with his wife. When the king sends for the two men, the simpleton asks no questions, strange as such an invitation may seem, and answers the summons to the royal court. The wise man, however, begins to ponder: why am I being sent for? What interest can a mighty monarch have in my limited wisdom when there are so many other wiser men available? Surely there must be a mistake somewhere. Perhaps there is no king in the world, for even the messenger who brought the summons never once caught sight of him but received the message from an intermediary. The wise man, therefore, decides to pay no attention to the call. The story ends with the simpleton in a high ministerial position, dispensing justice to all, and extricating his wise friend from the morass into which overmuch questioning landed him. The moral which is brought home to the reader or listener is that simplicity and integrity are finer assets than sophistication and scepticism. The path to the King of the Universe lies not along philosophic rationalization but along faith and obedience to His commands.

The Tale of the Seven Beggars is the longest and the most elaborate of Nachman Bratslaver's stories and also the most difficult to interpret. It consists of a series of tales within a tale, as in Chaucer's *Canterbury Tales* or William Morris's *Earthly Paradise*. The story which frames the others centers about two children, a boy and a girl, who are lost in a forest. Every time they are hungry and cry, a beggar appears to feed them and to bless them. Each beggar who appears has a different infirmity: one is blind, another deaf, a third a stammerer, a fourth with a crooked neck, a fifth a hunchback, a sixth without hands, and a seventh without legs. The children finally emerge from the forest and reach inhabited places. They beg for bread from house to house and from community to community. When they grow up, the guild of beggars arranges their marriage to each other. On each of the seven days of the wedding festivities, the couple recalls to mind one of the beggars who helped them during their seven days of wandering when they were lost in the woods. Instantly the beggar appears upon the scene, confirms his earlier blessing and tells the story of how he came to have his specific infirmity, which then turns out to be no infirmity at all. However, only the stories of six beggars are completed. As for the seventh, the expected concluding story, it will be heard when the Messiah appears. Then all mysteries will be revealed, including the mysteries hinted at in the earlier stories.

Not all the tales of Nachman Bratslaver were deeply serious. Some sparkled with wit and irony. Hassidim did not regard this earth as a vale of tears and did not scorn laughter. They indulged in song and dance, especially on the Sabbath and on holidays. At the Hassidic court of Rabbi Baruch of Mezhbuzh, there was even an official jester or court fool, Hershele Ostropoler (1770-1810). According to a folk legend, Hershele was called in to cure this grandson of the Baal Shem of depressive moods by making him laugh. He succeeded brilliantly. As the Jewish parallel to Till Eulenspiegel, Hershele delighted the poor and the simple-hearted with his satiric barbs against communal leaders, religious hypocrites, rich misers and pretenders to wisdom. Yiddish penny-booklets recording his pranks, tales, anecdotes and witticisms appeared posthumously and were widely disseminated. Hershele was the subject of lyrics by Ephraim Auerbach and Itzik Manger, a novel by I. J. Trunk, and a comedy by Moshe Livshitz which was performed by the Vilna Troupe in 1930.

Hershele Ostropoler was the forerunner of several folk heroes about whom entertaining legends and satiric folktales gradually accumulated. Such figures were Motke Khabad of Vilna, Efraim Gredinger of Galicia, Leibele Gottesvunder of Volynia and Yossel Loksh or Reb Yossifel of Chelm.

Motke Khabad, who lived from around 1820 to 1880, found a patron in Yudel Opatov, the rich community leader of Vilna, whom he delighted with jests and aphorisms and upon whom he exerted considerable influence in behalf of the poor. He played the role of a fool but his folly masked satiric wisdom and compassionate kindness.

Reb Yossifel was the guileless spiritual leader of Chelm, a Polish town which became for Jews, who lived there from the fifteenth century, what Abdera was for the Greeks, Schilda—home of the Schildbürger—was for the Germans, and Gotham—home of the Gothamites—was for the English. Reb Yossifel, well learned but completely impractical, believed everything he was told, since his Jews could not be anything but good. Whenever a problem arose, a solemn assembly of the burghers of Chelm was convoked, over which he presided. After listening to the exponents of varying points of view, he generally succeeded in obtaining a consensus by offering a compromise which was logically sound but which only complicated matters still further and led to utterly ridiculous con-

sequences. Finally an outsider, who was not personally involved
in Chelm disputes, succeeded in cutting the Gordian knot of complexities, and demonstrated the obvious solution which the interested persons or parties were unable to perceive. In Yiddish literature Sholom Aleichem, Itzik Manger, Jacob Glatstein and B. I.
Bialostotsky dealt sympathetically with the character of Reb
Yossifel.

On a higher level than the jesters and merrymakers were the
learned itinerant preachers and the wedding bards. The former,
known as Maggidim, spoke to the conscience of their audiences in
synagogues and called upon them to repent of their sins and to lead
a moral life which would find a suitable reward in heaven. The
latter, known as Badchonim, made wedding guests laugh and
weep by improvising rhymed verses which ranged from hilarious
reminiscences to deeply tragic recitals of Jewish sufferings in the
lands of exile.

The most famous of the Maggidim of the eighteenth century
was Jacob Krantz of Dubnow (the "Dubnow Maggid," ca. 1740-
1804). As the son of a rabbi, he was well versed in religious lore
and he early revealed an oratorical talent. His sermons attracted
large audiences and he was befriended by the Gaon of Vilna, the
greatest living Talmudic authority of the century. His parables,
which he acted out with great emotion in a voice tearful, reproving
and comforting, mingled mild and polemic humor with profound
insight. His tales illustrated biblical passages and contrasted good
and evil, poverty and wealth, Torah and idolatry, exile and a
coming salvation. Unlike lesser Maggidim, who terrified listeners
by vivid portrayals of the horrors of Gehenna awaiting unrepent-
ant sinners, he rather emphasized the joys of a coming Messianic
age and he renewed faith and hope in the hearts of old and young.
He was reputed to have met in the course of his wanderings the
philosopher of enlightenment, Moses Mendelssohn, who dubbed
him the Jewish Aesop. However, unlike Aesop's fables, which had
as their protagonists and antagonists various animals who personified human traits, the parables of the Dubnow Maggid were acted
out between human beings who suffered from human frailties and
aspired to moral rectitude.

The tradition of the Maggidim reached its peak in the nineteenth century. Some of the Hassidic leaders bore the title of
Maggid. The *Musar* movement of Rabbi Israel Salanter (1810-
1883) encouraged the preaching of the Maggidim. The most celebrated Maggid associated with this movement was the itinerant

Lithuanian preacher Moses Israel Darshan, known as the Kelmer Maggid (1827-1899). On American soil the most influential Maggid was Zvi Hirsh Masliansky (1856-1943), the beloved Yiddish orator of the immigrant Jews on New York's East Side.

The Badchonim were often no less learned than the Maggidim. Though they might be called upon to entertain on various festive occasions, their main function was to amuse guests at weddings.

A wedding in Eastern European townlets was a happy event not only for the families involved but also for the entire Jewish community. Rejoicing often extended up to seven days and took on aspects of a carnival. Though religious authorities frowned upon any expression of levity during the solemn ceremony itself, they could not restrain the populace from filling the hours preceding and those following with jest, satire and dance. Professional entertainers arose to satisfy the demand for merriment who were not subject to the requirements of dignity and piety as were the cantor or rabbi who performed the actual religious ritual. They were referred to under the title of Letz, Marshalik or Badchen.

A Letz was the Jewish equivalent of the medieval jongleur but he generally also doubled as a musician. A Marshalik (related to the English term marshal) was a master of ceremonies, thoroughly acquainted with every detail required by tradition. He supervised all arrangements dealing with the elaborate wedding procession.

The Badchen was a more pious entertainer. He rose to prominence in the second half of the seventeenth century, gradually supplanting the Marshalik and functioning as wedding bard well into the twentieth century. He combined literary skill, merriment and moralizing, and the highlight of his performance was his rhymed address to the bride before she was led to the bridal canopy.

A chair was placed in the middle of the festive room on which the veiled bride sat with all the assembled guests seated around her in a circle. The Badchen then addressed her in a chanting voice. In rhyming couplets he reminded her that she was now experiencing the most momentous event in her life, that she was taking leave of her carefree youth, and that she was about to enter upon serious marital responsibilities. He asked her to regard this day as no less holy and awesome than Yom Kippur. He urged her to turn her thoughts to God and to pray for forgiveness of her sins. He recalled the names and virtues of her departed relatives and he moved all his listeners to tears with a recital of the fleeting nature of man's earthly years. His repeated refrain was the line:

"Weep, bride, weep, willst soon under the canopy stand" (Veen, kalele, veen, vest bald unter der khupa shtehn). By the time he had concluded the many verses, the spirit of levity had yielded to grave solemnity and his rhymed address had formed a fitting prelude to the religious ritual which followed.

The most famous of the nineteenth century Badchonim were Berl Broder (1815-1886), Velvel Zbarzher (1826-1883) and Eliakum Zunser (1836-1913). These popular bards paved the way for the more sophisticated Yiddish poetry of the Maskilim and for the Yiddish drama of Abraham Goldfaden.

2

LITERATURE OF THE ENLIGHTENMENT

Haskalah • Moshe Marcuse • Mendel Lefin • Joseph
Perl • I. B. Levinsohn • Robinsonades • Heikel
Hurwitz • Aksenfeld • Ettinger • Gottlober •
Lifshitz • I. M. Dick

MODERN YIDDISH LITERATURE began with the Enlightenment and the struggle for Jewish emancipation from medieval disabilities and medieval ways of thinking. For the Jews of Central
and Western Europe the French Revolution of 1789 was the climax
of the spirit of Enlightenment which enthroned reason as the wor-
thiest guide to conduct and which destroyed the surviving vestiges
of medievalism. For the denizens of the Pale and the dreamers in
Eastern European townlets, however, the French Revolution and
the Napoleonic incursions which followed merely set in motion the
forces that were to upset the even tenor of congealed life, merely
loosened the long parched Jewish soil, merely sowed the seed for
an enlightenment that was still to sprout and that was to blossom
forth in the Hebrew and Yiddish renascence of the nineteenth
century.

There was for a long time a tendency to attribute solely to the
Haskalah—the rationalist spirit—the revival of Yiddish literature
after its decline throughout the eighteenth century. More recently,
however, Hassidism, the mystical, irrationalist movement and the
antipode of Enlightenment, has also been credited with exercising
a stimulating and reawakening influence, despite the fact that the
motivation of Hassidism was diametrically opposite to that of the
Haskalah. While the appeal of the Maskilim was to reason as
the highest authority, Hassidism sought to break the chains of

24

pure reason and to liberate the Jewish mind from immersion in the logical depths of *pilpul,* the ultraminute analysis of sacred texts. Hassidism gave free rein to the creative imagination, as in the stories of Nachman Bratslaver. It let the heart find release in lyrics of ecstatic worship, as in those attributed to Rabbi Levi Yitzkhok of Berditchev. It nourished a sense of humor as in the witty parables of itinerant preachers and the paradoxical sayings of Hassidic luminaries.

The struggle between Hassidim, the men of faith, and Maskilim, the men of reason, was waged largely in Hebrew by means of satiric epistles, prose pamphlets and versified essays. However, the need to reach a larger audience led even opponents of Yiddish to turn to the latter tongue and to feed the masses with educational propaganda mixed with entertainment.

Among the earliest Hebrew rationalists to realize the educational potentials of Yiddish were Moshe Marcuse, a physician of Königsberg, who practiced in Poland during the second half of the eighteenth century, and Mendel Lefin (1749-1826), a philosopher of Satanov in Podolia, who had become infected with enlightenment during his Berlin years in the circle of Moses Mendelssohn and Gotthold Ephraim Lessing.

In 1789 Marcuse published a popular handbook of medicine for Jewish men and women who dwelt in small, isolated communities where doctors were unavailable. To the question as to why he did not write this handbook in Hebrew, he replied that his potential readers carried on their daily activities in Yiddish and that, if he wanted to save them from charlatans who posed as healers and from mumbling old women who prescribed nostrums against the Evil Eye, he could do so only in the language intelligible to them. His book raged against the quacks who, with their unscientific remedies and magic formulae, were killing off hundreds of patients who could have been saved by simple medicines, hygienic precautions and better town sanitation. He advised against the long prevailing practice of bloodletting patients, a form of treatment which even doctors were still tolerating. He described with biting sarcasm the swindlers who impressed with their superficial piety in order to inspire confidence and whose knowledge of Latin was restricted to words such as hocus, pocus, triocus. He pleaded with parents to keep children away from disease-breeding filth and not to send them at the tender age of four to schools which could be dubbed educational dungeons. He pointed out that children too early exposed to book learning in a *kheder* from dawn to sunset became anemic and stunted in their physical growth. It would be better for such children to develop into laborers with strong bodies than into pale, sickly scholars. At least, such laborers would be able to support families instead of being supported by their wives.

In the same year as Marcuse published his medical handbook, Mendel Lefin published a tract on the natural sciences and five years later he too completed a medical handbook. However, Lefin's philosophical and scientific works were written in Hebrew. His importance for Yiddish literature rests on his biblical translations done not in the artificial Germanized Yiddish to which learned Jews sometimes stooped, but in the living Yiddish of the Ukrainian townlets. Only his translation of the book of *Proverbs* (1814) appeared during his lifetime. It aroused so great a controversy that Lefin withheld his other translations from publication. Not until 1873 did his rendering of *Ecclesiastes* appear, while his renderings of *Psalms, Job* and *Lamentations* have been lost. The controversy began in 1816 with an attack upon him by a fellow rationalist and erstwhile admirer, the irascible Tobias Feder (1760-1817), who felt that Lefin was betraying the cause of enlightenment by translating a sacred text into the language of the marketplace, and was thereby undoing much of the good work that the venerated Moses Mendelssohn had achieved by translating the Bible into pure German. Feder thundered that the sublime language of the ancient Jewish classic was being transformed into a filthy mess in order to win grace in the eyes of low class women, but even these would retreat in horror before such a product of senility and insanity. Lefin's crime, in the eyes of Feder, consisted in desecrating the beautiful German language by clothing it in the degenerate Yiddish jargon of Podolia.

Feder depicted a heavenly assembly of the disciples of Moses Mendelssohn. While they were engaged in philosophical meditation, there burst in upon them an excited disciple, Isaac Eichel, who had translated the *Book of Proverbs* into excellent German. He brought the news that a new translation of this book had just appeared in the gibberish of the peasants and that the perpetrator of such a crime was no other than one of Mendelssohn's own coterie. All were at first incredulous but, when Lefin's rendering was brought in and passed around among them, they were horrified and agreed that such a horrible monstrosity must be handed over to the flames.

Lefin's friends who rushed to his defense included Shmuel Jacob Byk (ca. 1770-1831) and Isaac Baer Levinsohn (1788-1860). The former, a patron of letters, pointed out that less than a century earlier Russian was still a language primarily of peasants, that the pedigree of German was not much older or finer, that English might with equal justification be deprecated as a jargon concocted of German, French, Latin and Greek elements. Gifted men-of-letters converted vernaculars of the common man to distinguished, refined tongues. A stylist of excellent taste such as Mendel Lefin was assisting in the refinement of Yiddish and his translation should therefore be welcomed rather than disparaged. Levinsohn, in a satiric epigram, also attacked Feder as a malicious, drunken wielder of the quill. Yet Levinsohn himself had no high regard for Yiddish. He saw it as a necessary temporary evil and hoped to hasten the day of its extinction. Nevertheless, he resorted to it when he composed the dramatic satire *The Lawless World (Die Hefker-Velt)*.

Lefin, in his attempted synthesis of faith and reason, Jewishness and Western Enlightenment, was the model for Joseph Perl, an outstanding figure among the Galician educators. Perl was born in 1773 in the East Galician commercial center of Tarnopol as the son of a rich merchant. After his marriage at the age of fourteen, he was drawn towards the mystic doctrines of the Hassidic movement then expanding throughout this Polish province. However, when his father sent him on long business trips to such larger European cities as Leipzig, Danzig and Budapest, he came in contact with German-Jewish rationalists. Mendelssohn's influence had by then spread from Berlin to Bohemian and Hungarian cities and was to reach the Galician trading center of Brody before the end of the eighteenth century. Dov Ber Günsberg, a prominent Maskil of Brody, was brought to Tarnopol for three years as a private tutor to assist Perl in acquiring the new learning. In the course of these years the mature pupil mastered German, French, Latin, philosophy, mathematics, history and natural sciences. Günsberg was succeeded by Mendel Lefin as Perl's teacher and adviser in a variety of cultural enterprises. The most important of these was the modern Jewish School of Tarnopol, founded by Perl in 1809 and directed by him until his death in 1839. This school, which became a model for others, combined secular and traditional subjects in its curriculum and prepared pupils for practical callings as well as inculcating in them a love for the Jewish past. Hassidim opposed Perl's efforts and sought to undermine his influence whereupon he retaliated by publishing satirical epistles against them under the pseudonym of Obadiah ben Petakhia.

These epistles were written in Hebrew and in Yiddish and were entitled *Revealer of Secrets* (*Megalleh Temirim*).

The 151 epistles were purported to have been written by 26 correspondents and were modeled upon the *Epistolae Obscurorum Virorum* of 1515, Latin satires which the Humanists under Johannes Reuchlin levelled against the Dominicans of Cologne with devastating effect. By imitating the stylistic mannerisms and the turgid argumentation used by Hassidim, the author pretended to reproduce letters exchanged between them. He claimed to have obtained these letters at a Hassidic court which he was able to infiltrate as the Invisible Man. The letters dealt with the intrigues of Hassidic courts, their struggle for power, their love of money, their soliciting of new recruits to their swelling ranks. The satire aroused consternation among Hassidic leaders, since some of their guileless followers believed in the genuineness of the epistles and were horrified at the apparent revelation of hidden machinations.

While the Hebrew version appeared in 1819, the Yiddish version was not published until 1937. A second Yiddish work by Perl, which also remained in manuscript form until 1937, was the satiric tale *The Greatness of Rabbi Wolf of Charnostro* (*Gdolos Reb Wolf M'Charni Ostro*). It told of the rise to power and the fall from power of a clever *melamed* who aspired to become a Hassidic wonder-rabbi and who for a time succeeded in hoodwinking a horde of followers, most of whom later deserted him for competitors with more genuine ancestral titles.

Among the Maskilim who came under the influence of Perl and Lefin was Isaac Baer Levinsohn, often dubbed the Mendelssohn of Russia because of his pioneering efforts in behalf of Jewish enlightenment in the Czarist realm. Levinsohn's satiric drama *The Lawless World* (*Die Hefker-Velt*), composed toward the end of the 1820's, was a significant Yiddish literary achievement.

Levinsohn was primarily a Hebrew writer. He evolved a theory of the Slavic origin of the Russian Jews, upon whom a corrupt Judeo-German dialect had been imposed by later immigrants from the West. At various times he called Yiddish a bastard mixture of Hebrew, Russian, French, Polish and German; a crippled organism in which there was not a single sound limb; a language which barely sufficed for simple objects and elementary concepts but which was utterly worthless for elevated discourse. He wondered why his co-religionists clung to this vile, hybrid jargon when they could use either pure German with its rich and charming vocabulary or the national tongue of their Russian neighbors. Yet he himself could not wholly dispense with the homely Yiddish of which he was inwardly ashamed. It was, after all, the best medium through which he could win mass support in his war against Jewish superstitions and communal abuses. His Yiddish satire circulated in manuscript form for six decades before it was finally published in 1888, a generation after his death. This polemic against the exploiters of the poor and the powerless took the form of a dialogue between a visitor from Lithuania and two local inhabitants of a Ukrainian townlet. The latter complained bitterly about the widespread corruption in the Jewish institutions, about patricians who increased their personal wealth through immoral manipulations, and about the injustice of impressing into military service only children of poor families.

The drafting of Jewish children for compulsory labor service from the age of twelve and for military service from the age of eighteen for a term of twenty-five years had a terrorizing and demoralizing effect upon Jewish communities. The draft was initiated in 1827 by a cruel decree of Czar Nicholas I. The impressed children were known as cantonists, since they were selectees for different cantons or training centers. Levinsohn's satire denounced the traffic in such children, pointing out that no rich boys were ever drafted. Poor boys, however, were dragged like piglets from their mother's breast in heartbreaking fashion. The kidnappers, hired by the Jewish community to ferret out such children in order to meet the imposed quota, knew well enough that parents would sell their last belongings to save their little darlings. Such children would beg their fathers and mothers to make them blind or cripples in order to escape the horrible fate in store for them as cantonists. Sodom had rearisen in Jewish townlets. Levinsohn maintained that the sick townlets could be restored to health only if their inhabitants set out to till fields and to raise cattle. Physical work was no disgrace; it would strengthen Jewish bodies and cleanse Jewish souls. The ancient patriarchs had tended flocks. Moses and David had begun as shepherds. A return to the soil, as advocated by Levinsohn, became a cardinal doctrine of many Maskilim. At first in merely lived on as a utopian vision, but later it shaped the ideology of Labor Zionism. It resulted in the founding of kibbutzim in Israel and of the collective Jewish agricultural colonies of Soviet Crimea, colonies which flourished until the Second World War.

A significant indication of the intense longing of Jews divorced from the soil for a life closer to nature was the popularity of the Yiddish narrative of *Robinsohn,* adapted from Daniel Defoe's novel *Robinson Crusoe* by an anonymous Maskil of the early nineteenth century. The full title of the narrative was *Robinsohn, the Story of Alter Leib (Robinsohn, Die Geshikhte Fun Alter Leib).* The booklet was recommended as a true and marvelous story for instruction as well as entertainment. The introduction listed ten lessons which the tale could teach its readers, lessons such as trust in Providence, faith in immortality, differentiation between good and evil, the uses of reason, the proper raising of children.

The entire narrative was put in the mouth of a wise, old merchant of Galicia, whom God had blessed with many good, pious children, grandchildren and friends. These he used to regale with fascinating stories such as that of Alter Leib, the youngest of three sons of an elderly couple. As the only one to survive, he was spoiled by his parents, and he had to go through many misfortunes before he attained to wisdom, kindness and trust in God. In his youth he succumbed to the lure of the sea and was shipwrecked. He was tossed on to an uninhabited island, while all his companions perished. In his loneliness, he turned to God as his sole comfort, and whenever he was on the verge of despair and felt that his final hour had struck, Providence intervened and came to his aid. Purified in his soul by his suffering, he learned to have compassion for all living things. When cannibals landed on his island in order to feast on foes whom they had defeated and captured, Alter Leib risked his life to save one of the captives. He named the rescued savage Shabbes, not Friday as in Defoe's novel, because the incident took place on the Sabbath. He then taught this primitive person the basic articles of the Jewish religion, thus civilizing him. Both were joined in the course of time by other castaways and ultimately were able to return to Europe. There they made an honest living as master-carpenters, content with their lot and remaining models of ethical behavior.

Robinsohn emphasized primarily those incidents and aspects of the English original which lent themselves to moralizing. The book was, therefore, not disapproved of by religious zealots who objected to other secular tales. It was frequently reprinted and stimulated the imagination of Jewish youth that dreamed of escape to islets far from their oppressive confinement in Eastern Europe.

Another Yiddish work which combined entertainment and instruction and which inflamed Jewish imagination was *Columbus,* a narrative adapted from the German of Heinrich Campe by Heikel Hurwitz in 1817 and by Mordecai Aaron Guenzburg in 1823. Hurwitz was a prominent merchant of Uman and lived from 1749 to 1822. He wrote in the spoken dialect of the Ukraine, even as did Mendel Lefin before him, and entitled his adaptation *Zaphonath-Paneah or Columbus.* In his introduction he promised his readers not only a fascinating true story but one which showed how much a human being could achieve if he used his rational faculties to the full and did not spare any exertion. Such a person could reckon with the aid of God.

Guenzburg's translation was closer to the German idiom than to spoken Yiddish. This leader of Vilna Maskilim had at first translated Campe into Hebrew, but soon realized that he could find more readers among women and also among men who were insufficiently learned in the ancient tongue. In his introduction he proudly asserted that his Yiddish rendering had been cleansed of the usual mishmash of Hebrew, Polish, Russian and Turkish words. Nevertheless, his embarrassment at having to write in the tongue of the housewives and the tailor lads manifested itself when he failed to affix his name to this, his only Yiddish publication. He merely indicated on the title page that it was done by the Hebrew translator.

Hurwitz's version also appeared anonymously and so did the later versions, published in Lemberg in 1857, based upon *Zapho-nath-Paneah,* and the version published in Warsaw in 1888, based upon Guenzburg's rendering. In 1889, Abraham Baer Gottlober wrote, in his recollections of earlier Yiddish writers, that in his young years nearly all Jews read the Yiddish adaptations of Campe's *Columbus.* "Women put aside the *Tsena-Urena,* the *Tkhines,* and even the *Bovo-Maisse* to read *Columbus.* Until that time few Jews knew that there was an America. The book *Columbus* was written in such a pure language that it could be read and understood throughout Russia, Poland, Galicia, Rumania and wherever Jews were found. My imagination bore me with Columbus on to America; I was with him on his ocean-crossing ship; I was fascinated by the American savages; and even in my sleep they were alive before my eyes."

The book disseminated the legend of America as "Columbus's Medina," a realm of marvels and mysteries, a continent whose streets were paved with gold and whose inhabitants were noble savages devoid of guile. This Rousseauan approach to American civilization, or rather lack of civilization, persisted in Jewish quarters throughout the century. In a story of 1856 by Isaac Meir Dick, a friend and townsman of Guenzburg, America was identified as the biblical land of Ophir, from which Hiram of Tyre had fetched the gold for the building of King Solomon's Temple in Jerusalem. After having been lost for many centuries, Ophir had been rediscovered by Columbus.

Dick (1814-1893) was the most prolific of the Vilna Maskilim who wrote in Yiddish in the mid-nineteenth century. However, he had been preceded in the southern provinces of Russia by Israel Aksenfeld, Shlomo Ettinger and Abraham Baer Gottlober.

Aksenfeld (1787-1866) stemmed from a prominent family of Nemirov, a center of Hassidism in Podolia, Ukraine. He began as a follower of Rabbi Nachman Bratslaver but was soon disillusioned with this movement. Engaged in business enterprises which necessitated extensive travelling, he acquired a knowledge of several languages and of the newest doctrines emanating from German and Galician centers of Enlightenment. He settled in Odessa in his thirties and his patrician home became a meeting place for literary figures. Unlike other Maskilim, he preferred to write in Yiddish rather than in Hebrew or Russian. A list of his writings compiled by him in his seventy-fifth year embraced twenty-six works. During his lifetime, however, he succeeded in publishing only a single play, *The First Jewish Recruit* (*Der Ershter Yiedisher Rekrut*, 1861). Three of his plays appeared after his death and others were being readied for publication when the Odessa Pogrom of 1871 broke out and the manuscripts were lost.

The action of *The First Jewish Recruit* took place in a Russian townlet on the day of the promulgation, in 1827, of the decree drafting Jewish young men for twenty-five years of service in the Czarist army. This decree had been touched upon by Isaac Baer Levinsohn in his indignant satire, *The Lawless World,* when its initial implementation was bitterly resented. Aksenfeld, however, made it the central theme of his tragi-comedy composed six years later. He tried to present the decree not as a cruel ukase, but as an act of grace by Czar Nicholas I. By this act the Russian ruler was placing Jews on a level of equality with the other ethnic groups in responsibility for maintaining peace and stability in the expanding realm. This was a first step in the right direction and should not be opposed.

Though the quota of the play's townlet was but a single recruit per year, the community was convulsed with fear and anger. A stratagem devised by the community leaders induced a young man to volunteer for military service and saved them the ignominy of having to draft a fellow-Jew. However, this intrigue unexpectedly backfired and brought death and tragedy in its wake.

The tragi-comedy afforded realistic insight into Jewish life of the post-Napoleonic generation. The author was a careful observer and reproduced details with meticulous accuracy. His characters were not types but recognizable individuals, each with a particular brand of folly, weakness or roguishness, but also with certain redeeming features. The dominant mood mingled humor with sadness. The climax was reached when the lively, stout-hearted Nachman was persuaded to offer himself as the townlet's recruit in order to find favor in the eyes of his beloved Frimele and when she was so overcome by shock on learning of his sacrificial deed that she collapsed and died of a broken heart. The play ended with Frimele's mother becoming insane with grief and Nachman's blind mother bewailing her lost son and his dead bride.

Aksenfeld employed everyday speech as spoken in his native Nemirov and shunned the artificial literary style which abounded in Germanisms. He directed his satire against religious fanatics and believers in superstitions. In his anti-Hassidic polemic, the comedy *The Fooled World (Der Oitzer oder die genarte Velt)*, written in 1842 but not printed until 1870, he equated a petty wonder-rabbi with a drunken, non-Jewish quack. Both were busy extracting money from all who believed in their supernatural powers and both were in the end unmasked by a clever, clear-thinking young man, who overtopped their deceptions with his own colossal deception. The author's good humor embraced deceivers and deceived and the comedy demonstrated that most people in this foolish world were gullible and wanted to be fooled.

This was also the conclusion of Aksenfeld's anti-Hassidic tale, *The Kerchief (Dos Shterntiekhel)*. An honest young man who had been deprived of his betrothed because of his apparent lack of sufficient piety turned the tables on his opponents when he later returned as an apparently rich businessman. He exposed to laughter the religious hypocrites, his former tormentors, and married the girl earlier denied him.

Aksenfeld was a reformer who used literature as a subversive instrument to undermine the petrified structure of the Jewish townlets. This was also attempted by his younger contemporary, the physician Shlome Ettinger (ca. 1803-1856).

Ettinger's most ambitious literary achievement was his realistic comedy *Serkele*, written in the 1830's, but like all his other works,

not published until after his death and then only in a pirated
edition. It was only in 1925, when Max Weinreich edited Ettinger's
work with a perceptive, scholarly analysis, that the originality of
this comedy was generally acknowledged and its author accorded
a high rank among the Yiddish pre-classical writers.

The title-heroine of *Serkele* was a strong-willed, domineering
Jewish woman who was expected not only to run her household
as wife and mother, but also to earn a living for the family by
her business talent, while her husband spent his days in the
synagogue or house of study. In the cruel struggle for existence,
she could not afford to be gentle-hearted, sentimental, morally
scrupulous. When she rose from poverty to affluence, she behaved
brutally, raged at her underlings, demoralized her own daughter
by overindulgence, and mistreated her brother's only daughter
Hinde, who had been put under her guardianship. In contrast to
Serkele, who had been distorted into an unfeminine creature by
the burdens imposed upon her in the unhealthy environment of
the Jewish townlet, Hinde was presented as the symbol of what
the Jewish woman ought to be, pure, modest, quiet, compassionate,
and honest in all her relationships. At the end, the good people
found each other, truth won over falsehood and the wicked were
punished, though not too severely. Ettinger's enlightened characters were portrayed as modern in dress and speech but traditional
in their adherence to high Jewish standards of ethical conduct.

The first performance of *Serkele* took place at the Zhitomir
school for government rabbis six years after the author's death.
Both male and female roles were acted out by the young men
who were studying to enter government service as enlightened
religious officials for the Jewish community. The chief role of
Serkele was played by the pupil Abraham Goldenfodim, who was
later, as Abraham Goldfaden, to become the father of the professional Yiddish theater. *Serkele* not only stimulated Goldfaden
to enter upon his career as dramatist, actor and theatrical entre-
preneur, but it also paved the way for his comedy, *Kabzensohn
et Hungerman,* with whose plot and characters it had many similarities. Sixty years after the first performance, *Serkele* still received an enthusiastic reception when produced by Sigmund
Turkov in Warsaw.

In addition to *Serkele,* Ettinger also wrote searing epigrams,
epitaphs, parables and fables. These fables not only conveyed a
moral, but they specifically reemphasized it by a concluding gen-
eralization. A typical fable was that of the rooster who became

angry at the farmer who once forgot to feed him on time. He therefore determined to retaliate by refusing to crow on the following morning, thus causing the farmer to oversleep. As a result, the latter concluded that the rooster had outlived his usefulness as an awakener and had him slaughtered. The fable concluded by emphasizing the moral lesson that it was better to overlook slights than to risk greater tragedies.

Ettinger and Aksenfeld paved the way for Abraham Baer Gottlober (1811-1899), who battled even more vigorously throughout his long life for the ideals of the Haskalah. Alexander Zederbaum called him the foremost missionary for Jewish enlightenment. Though his missionary objective included the transformation of the Jews of the Pale to enlightened Europeans whose language would be Russian or German, nevertheless, he could not realize his idealized goal save through communicating with the Jewish élite in Hebrew and with the Jewish masses in Yiddish.

In his childhood Gottlober had experienced the purgatory of a *Kheder*, a purgatory to which most Jewish boys were subjected at far too early an age; hence his burning desire to change the education system at the elementary school level. Learning in a *Kheder*, as depicted by Gottlober, consisted of sitting hour after hour on a long and narrow bench which extended from one end of the room to the other. With head bent almost to the knees and eyes glued to an old, torn prayer-book which lay on a shaky table, a child had to repeat after the teacher meaningless phonemes until he was in a sweat and his throat was parched, all the time trembling with fear of the teacher or the teacher's assistant, who towered above him with a cat-o'-nine tails. From this type of education, Gottlober was liberated by his father, who undertook to teach him Bible and Talmud at home and who also let him have access from the age of nine to secular works. The book which made the deepest impression upon young Gottlober was Khaykel Hurwitz's version of *Columbus*, a book which appealed to his boyhood imagination and gave him his first knowledge of the vast earth and the multiplicity of its cultures.

At thirteen, Gottlober was married off to a girl of twelve. At fifteen, he began to compose verses in Hebrew and Yiddish. At seventeen, he surreptitiously crossed the border from Russia to Galicia. In Tarnopol he became fascinated by Joseph Perl and in Brody he was in touch with young men who led him to question his own Hassidic ways. An acquaintance with Mendel Lefin's Yiddish translation of the biblical scrolls induced him to write in a similar unaffected, colloquial style. When he returned to his native town of Starokonstantin and the Hassidim discovered his heresies, they persecuted him and compelled him to divorce his wife, despite his growing affection for her and his young son. Thereafter he was a relentless foe of the Hassidim. He allied himself to Isaac Baer Levinsohn, and propagated the educational reforms of Max Lilienthal, who had been encouraged by the Czarist Minister of Education to substitute secular schools for the traditional religious ones among the Jewish denizens.

Gottlober began to teach in such a school at Kamenetz-Podolsk in 1852. He numbered among his pupils Shalom Jacob Abramowitch, who was later to become a pillar of classical Yiddish under the pseudonym of Mendele Mokher Sforim. In 1855 Gottlober was transferred to a similar school in Starokonstantin where his most talented pupil was Abraham Goldfaden, who was stimulated to compose Hebrew and Yiddish lyrics and to act in a Yiddish play, Ettinger's *Serkele*. Goldfaden then also came to know Gottlober's satiric comedy *The Canopy (Der Dektukh)*, which considerably influenced his own more successful comedies, *Schmendrik* and *The Two Kuni-Lemels*.

Gottlober's dramatic efforts had begun at nineteen with a Hebrew play, *Amnon and Tamar* and with a Hebrew translation of Friedrich Schiller's *The Robbers*. He wrote *The Canopy* before 1838. It circulated in manuscript copies for several decades and was first published in 1876 in a pirated edition without listing Gottlober as its author. Betraying the influence of Levinsohn's *The Lawless World* and Ettinger's *Serkele,* it exposed to laughter the absurdities of Jewish marriages as then arranged by parents for their immature children, and was subtitled *Two Weddings in a Single Night*. It contained autobiographic features. The most pleasant characters were the eighteen-year-old Yossele and the sixteen-year-old Fraidele who were both fond of each other. Yet their parents paid no heed to the budding love of such immature children. Yossele was promised in marriage to a half-blind, stuttering girl, whose only asset was her rabbinical lineage, Fraidele was to wed Lemel, a dull-witted, ugly cripple of irreproachable family background. Since both weddings were scheduled for the same night, Yossele succeeded in bringing about an interchange of grooms under the canopies and thus letting true love triumph. The assembled guests, unable to find a rational explanation for the interchange, ascribed it to machinations of the diabolical spirits who could effect all sorts of mischief.

Gottlober's other Yiddish writings included singable lyrics which had a wide circulation; a humorous parody of Schiller's *The Bell* under the title *The Pudding-Song* (*Dos Lied Funm Kugel*, 1863); *The Assembly* (*Der Seyim*, 1902), a satiric fable of a convocation in a forest which ended with the animals electing the lion as their monarch; and *Transmigration* (*Der Gilgul*, 1896), an extremely funny yet bitterly satiric tale of a gravedigger's encounter with a soul which had left its most recent body only a short time earlier and which remembered its former existences as a Hassid, a horse, a cantor, a fish, a tax-collector, a dog, a critic, a donkey, a doctor, a leech, a loan-shark, a pig and a broker.

Among the South Russian Maskilim, the lexicographer Joshua Mordecai Lifschitz (1829-1878) of Bereditchev championed the cause of Yiddish with polemic essays and with efforts to establish a Yiddish journal. Though these efforts were unsuccessful in the 1850's, due to a large extent to the opposition of his enlightened contemporaries, he did pave the way for the publication of the first Yiddish periodical, *Kol Mevasser*, in 1862 by Alexander Zederbaum.

In 1867 Lifschitz completed a Yiddish-German, German-Yiddish Dictionary but could not obtain a publisher. Two years later, a Zhitomir publisher undertook to print his Russian-Yiddish Dictionary. It was frequently reprinted and was followed in 1876 by his Yiddish-Russian Dictionary. In a militant introduction, he attacked the Jewish élite who preferred Russian, Polish, German and Hebrew to their mother-tongue Yiddish. His dictionaries formed the basis for later lexicographical ventures.

Far more influential with the Yiddish reading masses than the Maskilim of South Russia was the storyteller of Vilna, Isaac Meir Dick (1814-1893). He was also less militant. Dick had begun in the 1840's as a Hebrew scholar and had built up a moderate reputation among the Maskilim when in 1856 he ventured to publish anonymously his first Yiddish story, *The Recluse of Berditchev* (*Der Porush fun Berditchev*). The narrative exposed the apparent miracles of a holy man, who proved to be a conniving rascal. Within the following decade he completed at least two hundred stories. During his lifetime he composed no less than four hundred booklets, each illustrating a moral by means of a tale. He reached an audience of a magnitude unequalled by any Yiddish writer of his generation and his penny-booklets were brought by book-peddlers to the remotest townlets of Eastern Europe and were read to shreds.

In Dick's adaptation of Harriet Beecher Stowe's novel *Uncle Tom's Cabin*, which he entitled *Slavery* (*Die Shklaverei*, 1887), Tom's good master was introduced as a Jewish plantation owner. The story ended with the members of the liberated and reunited Negro family embracing the Jewish faith, merging with the Jewish community, and ultimately becoming rich merchants, some of whom were supposed to be still flourishing at the time the story was being recorded.

In 1888 Sholom Aleichem included Dick among the four giants of Yiddish literature, the others being Mendele Mokher Sforim, Y. Y. Linetzky and Abraham Goldfaden. Dick's stories, abounding in kindness and gentle humor, were designed to educate readers. He therefore often interrupted his narratives by sermonizing and stressing the lessons that could be learned from the failures, trials and successes of his characters. He sought to reconcile tradition with the demands of reason and exposed to ridicule popular follies and superstitions. He taught tolerance, generosity, and the desirability of productive labor. Avoiding a tragic ending whenever possible, he was a pioneer of the Yiddish sentimental novel, the realistic novel, and the historical novel. He broadened the intellectual horizon of his unsophisticated readers by feeding them maxims, moral anecdotes and useful information. He paved the way for Mendele Mokher Sforim, the first Yiddish writer of classical dimensions.

3

MENDELE AND HIS
CONTEMPORARIES

Mendele's Innovations • *Kol Mevasser* • Mendele's
Satires • Mature Narratives • Y. Y. Linetzky • Berl
Broder • Velvel Zbarzher • Eliakum Zunser • Michel
Gordon • Y. L. Gordon • S. S. Frug • Mark
Varshavsky • Dinezon • Shomer • Spector

THE LITERARY critic David Frishman once wrote that if a deluge were to come and destroy the entire Jewish Pale, leaving not a
shred behind, we could reconstruct it from the works of Mendele
exactly as it flourished in the first half of the nineteenth century.
Such a deluge did indeed come a quarter-of-a-century after Mendele's death, the Nazi deluge, and it did destroy the traditional
culture of the Jewish townlets together with the Jewish inhabitants. On the basis of Mendele's Hebrew and Yiddish narratives,
this *shtetl*-culture can be recovered for our historic imagination as
the vivid past of the Eastern European Jewish experience.

Mendele was an innovator in both Jewish languages. He furthered the rise of modern Hebrew prose and he laid the foundation for the new literary structure of Yiddish. He created a Yiddish style which eschewed German, Polish and Russian models
and enriched the written vocabulary with the oral treasures he
learned from the lips of simple people. He portrayed Jewish life
honestly, realistically, without embellishments and without pre-
conceptions. He painted in words what he saw since his earliest
years: poverty, filth, decay, but also poetry, joy, Messianic longings. His searing satire of intolerable conditions and surviving
superstitions stemmed from a heart overflowing with love and pity
for his people. He used his literary talent in order to educate his

39

readers; and to attack injustice in public life and misbehavior in private life. He began under the influence of his teacher Gottlober and the militant Maskilim of the mid-nineteenth century but matured to become a pure artist of an originality unequalled by any Yiddish writer before him. He discovered for Yiddish literature the splendor of natural phenomena and he gave to nature a Jewish tone and a Jewish appearance.

Mendele was born as Shalom Jacob Abramowitch in a townlet of Minsk Province. In his autobiography, he recorded December 20, 1836, as his birthday, but this date was called into question by his contemporaries who regarded him as considerably older. Six children had been born before him and others came after him. Poverty did not at first reign in the crowded household. The young boy could profit from a good traditional education. A teacher with a poetic soul opened up to him the wonderland of the Bible and stimulated his imagination, so that he was more at home among ancient Israel's fauna and flora, real and mythical, than among those of his immediate environment. The unicorn, the dragon, the leopard, the turtle-dove and the Leviathan were present in his dreams. Pharaoh and Moses, King Ahasuerus and Queen Esther occupied his thoughts more than did the rulers of his native Russia. Only as he approached adolescence did he discover the beauty of nature about him, the free green fields, the woods and hills beyond his shabby townlet, and his cramped soul expanded to embrace God's lovely world. Though this idyllic period laid the foundation for his unusually keen observation of nature, it did not last long.

When he was about fourteen, his father died and his mother had to worry about providing bread for her young children. In order not to be a burden to her, the post-Bar-Mitzvah lad left home and undertook to shift for himself while continuing to study traditional subjects with little or no guidance. While attending the Talmudic academies of Slutzk and Vilna, he had to resort to *Teg-Essen* in order to keep body and soul together. This was a form of day-boarding which persisted with but slight modifications until well into the twentieth century. Yeshiva lads who had no funds of their own were assigned to householders who volunteered to give them a single meal or an entire day's meals each week. Often such a lad could not scrape together sufficient meals for all seven days and had to go hungry part of the week, though never on the Sabbath.

When Mendele's mother remarried, he returned to his native

townlet and his stepfather's house at the edge of a forest. Amidst idyllic nature he began to sketch in Hebrew verses the impact of earth's blossoming in spring, and to communicate the secrets whispered to him by birds and trees and flowers.

At seventeen Mendele found himself attached to an itinerant mendicant who had brought reports of fabulous prosperity supposedly prevailing in Ukrainian provinces. This mendicant Avreml the Lame, misused his young companion throughout their wanderings in order to arouse sympathy for the helpless, orphaned lad and thus to stimulate greater almsgiving. After weeks of roaming through Volynia and Podolia, Mendele escaped and found his way to the home of Gottlober at Kamenetz-Podolsk. In the circle of Gottlober, he acquired a secular education and was appointed to teach in a government school. Through Gottlober's intercession, he had his earliest Hebrew article, an essay on education, accepted by the first Hebrew journal *Hamagid* in 1857. His marriage to the daughter of a prosperous merchant of Berdichev gave him the opportunity to move to that town and the leisure to devote himself for several years to further studying and writing. He soon acquired a considerable reputation as a Hebrew publicist, narrator and Maskil.

Contact with the Yiddish lexicographer I. M. Lifschitz, however, led him to question whether the exclusive use of Hebrew and the avoidance of Yiddish was really desirable. He joined Lifschitz in urging Alexander Zederbaum, editor of the Hebrew weekly *Hamelitz,* to issue a supplement in Yiddish. The first issue of this supplement, entitled *Kol Mevasser,* appeared on October 11, 1862 and Mendele's first Yiddish tale, *The Little Man (Dos kleine Menshele)* began to appear in its columns in November 1863.

Kol Mevasser was not the earliest periodical in Yiddish. As far back in 1686, a Yiddish semi-weekly, *Die Kuranten,* was published in Amsterdam. During the two years of its existence, it brought news of local interest and reports about Jewish life in other communities such as Vienna, Rome and even remote India. In Eastern Europe, *Der Beobachter an der Weichsel,* edited by Anton Eichenbaum in Yiddish and in Polish, appeared in 1823. Its forty-four issues carried official reports, foreign news, Jewish news, and business announcements. *Kol Mevasser* was, however, the first periodical with a wide circulation over a large territory and was far more influential than its predecessors. It survived for a full decade, and during its last three years, 1869-1872, was an independent organ. It helped to standardize Yiddish spelling, enriched Yiddish vocabulary with many neologisms, evolved stylistic patterns, and raised the prestige of the vernacular. Its correspondents reported on Jewish events in large and small communities in Russia and beyond Russia's borders. It reacted to non-Jewish happenings and their possible effect upon Jews, and printed articles on science, education, history, geography and literature. It sponsored activities to aid the needy. It sketched biographies of famous personalities such as Rambam and Rashi, and of Yiddish writers such as Ettinger, Aksenfeld and Gottlober, and introduced new writers, among them Mendele, Linetzky and Goldfaden.

Mendele's earliest Yiddish narratives had an educational and moral objective. He wanted to be useful to his people rather than to gain literary laurels. He was well aware in 1863, when he switched from Hebrew to Yiddish, that he was risking the literary reputation that he had already acquired. "My embarrassment was great indeed when I realized that association with the lowly maid Yiddish would cover me with shame. I listened to the admonitions of my admirers, the lovers of Hebrew, not to drag my name in the gutter and not to squander my talent on the unworthy hussy. But my desire to be useful to my people was stronger than my vanity and I decided: come what may, I shall have pity on Yiddish, the outcast daughter of my people."

Mendele's satire, *The Little Man,* castigated Jewish community leaders who were growing fat on the spoils derived from religious taxes imposed upon Jews. It was followed by a second satire in the form of a drama, *The Meat-Tax (Die Takse,* 1869), which exposed to scorn religious leaders who used the tax on Kosher meat to enrich themselves rather than to benefit their co-religionists.

Mendele's third and most effective satire was the narrative *The Dobbin (Die Klatshe,* 1873), an allegory of the Jew as the world's scapegoat. The becudgelled, overworked and undernourished dobbin was once a prince but had been bewitched and degraded to a suffering beast of burden. It symbolized the Jew, who once led a free, noble existence in his own land, but whom foes had driven forth from his native soil and transformed into an eternally wandering, eternally persecuted, and universally despised creature. Everybody rode on it, beat it, put yokes on it. Nevertheless, it retained its innate princely qualities and was morally superior to the urchins who assailed it. Mendele's dobbin did not appeal to its tormentors for mercy. It demanded justice. It claimed the same right to live as was vouchsafed to all other creatures of flesh and blood. If one creature bestowed mercy upon another, it was thereby assuming a position of superiority which was unjustified and immoral. It was asserting: I have a right to live but not you; I am, however, prepared to be gracious to you and to let you draw breath because I am good-natured or because you are useful to me.

Mendele's satires were resented by Berdichev's communal leaders and he found it advisable to move to Zhitomir and in 1881 to settle in Odessa, the Black Sea port which was then attracting prominent Jewish intellectuals. These were later dubbed the Wise Men of Odessa.

As Mendele matured, his satire became milder. His attacks upon heartless Jewish patricians yielded to compassionate treatment of their victims, the men with crippled bodies and tortured souls, the rootless waifs cast adrift and facing storms of adversity. *Fishke the Lame* (*Fishke der Krumer,* 1868-1888), his narrative of Jewish beggars, vagabonds and thieves, revealed poetic souls in hovels, angelic characters among the dregs of society, nobility shining through tattered exteriors, kindness healing brutality, and joy breaking in upon suffering. The wandering of Fishke the Lame from town to town recalled Mendele's own earlier experiences with Avreml the Lame and his meeting with an assortment of mendicants who ranged from saintly to devilish characters.

Mendele's milder humor was also evident in his uncompleted prose epic *The Wanderings of Benjamin III* (*Masoes Beniamin Hashlishi,* 1878). Though he ridiculed the impractical dreamers whose visions conjured up Jewish Utopias in distant lands, but who could not provide bread for their immediate families, his ridicule lacked venom because of his intense love for the Jewish people and his reforming zeal was subordinated to his artistic objective. Benjamin, the Jewish Don Quixote, and his neighbor Senderl, the Jewish Sancho Panza, survived intolerable degradations forced upon Jews of Tuneyadivke, the Town of Emptiness, and retained their faith in the God of Israel and in the glorious future ordained for God's people. Benjamin III, the caricature of a hero, escaped from dull, gossipy emptiness by immersing himself in books. He read wondertales of Jewish world travelers such as Benjamin of Tudela and Eldad the Danite, while letting his wife Zelda worry about supporting the household. When his imagination became wholly inflamed by the adventures of his medieval heroes, he stole forth with Senderl one morning, hoping to reach the land beyond the mysterious, turbulent Sambation River where dwelt the descendants of Moses and of the missing Ten Tribes.

The travelers never got further than neighboring Glupsk, the Town of Ignorance, where they were seized and impressed into military service. They ended by being expelled from the army by a court-martial as completely unbalanced creatures. Of their unheroic adventures, however, Mendele fashioned unforgettable scenes of humor and pathos. These characters might appear to unsympathetic outsiders to be cowardly, unworldly, lazy, and lacking in common sense, but they were basically good-hearted, honest, and not brutalized by their hostile environment. They surmounted all misfortunes and managed to keep body and soul together.

For more than a quarter of a century Mendele worked upon his longest novel *The Wishing Ring* (*Dos Vinshfingeril*) before he finally completed its third and final version in 1889. In it he portrayed the dreams, longings, experiences and disillusionment of his entire generation of pioneering Maskilim. His hero Hershele grew up in Kabzansk, the Town of Poverty, where stagnation prevailed and deformed, petrified traditions ruled every activity. Hershele felt like a bird in a cage. He dreamed of a wishing ring which would enable him to break out of his cage and would transport him to the beautiful, vast world beyond the confines of Kabzansk. From the age of thirteen he had to shift for himself. He resorted to *Teg-Essen* in the neighboring town of Glupsk and his night-lodging was a hard bench in a synagogue. The more lonely and miserable his lot, the more did he flee to dreams of an earthly paradise in which milk and honey flowed and in which angelic voices sang songs of hope, comfort, love and compassion.

After Hershele and his only friend Moishele survived an attempt by kidnappers to turn them over to Czarist military authorities as cantonists, both came under the influence of Maskilim who enabled them to obtain a secular education and to pull themselves out of the slough of their medieval townlet. Hershele saw in the Enlightenment that filtered in from Europe, the wishing ring that opened up infinite possibilities for progress and happiness. But when the pogroms of the 1880's ravaged the townlet from which he sprang, he was shocked out of his naive, rosy dreams and brought back to the dark reality of Jewish affliction. The savage massacres perpetrated by the Russians upon their helpless Jewish neighbors proved to him that universal brotherhood was a mirage or at best an ideal which had to be relegated to a remote future. His present task was to bind up the wounds of his hurt Jewish kinsmen. He was bone of their bone and flesh of their flesh. He had to take his stand with them and to give up assimilationist delusions.

Mendele's last major work was the autobiographic narrative *Shlome Reb Chaims,* completed a year before his death in 1917. Nostalgically, he recalled his childhood years before his father's death and his boyhood away from home after he was orphaned. More leisurely than in the *Wishing Ring,* he again sketched, as with a gray, tender crayon, the few joys and the many travails of a Yeshiva lad who had to scrape together meal-days at the tables of charitable families and free lodging in the hovels of distant relatives. The Mendele-style, an accurate, honest, naturalistic depiction of reality in its minutest details, and yet saturated with immense pity for all suffering creatures, here attained its utmost perfection. The tolerant wisdom of an old sage replaced the fiery wrath of the missionary zealot who had earlier castigated his people's failings so mercilessly.

Mendele was the foremost Yiddish innovator. He raised the Jewish vernacular to a refined literary language. He reproduced in artistic masterpieces Eastern European Jewish life of the nineteenth century in all its shadows and light, its horror and loveliness; Jewish types from precocious, undernourished children and orphaned waifs to pompous, heartless officials, saintly scholars and sad widows; Jewish streets, mired and bustling with noisy confusion, and houses, murky, overcrowded and yet admitting rays of happiness; the vast treasures of Jewish folklore and the deep longing of the Jewish heart.

Yitzkhok Yoel Linetzky (1839-1915) had at first a great deal in common with his contemporary Mendele, but their paths soon diverged. Both began as rebels against the Jewish establishment; both rose to prominence in the 1860's with their literary contributions to the Hebrew periodical *Hamelitz* and to the Yiddish periodical *Kol Mevasser;* both ardently espoused the cause of Haskalah and both were disillusioned with this panacea. But, while Mendele matured to become the pure artist and exerted a profound influence upon many disciples ranging from Sholom Aleichem and Chaim Nachman Bialik to David Bergelson and Shmuel Joseph Agnon, Linetzky ended as a frustrated, neglected and embittered publicist.

Linetzky stemmed from a Hassidic home in Vinitza, Podolia. Beaten and humiliated by despotic teachers who sought to indoctrinate him with Hassidic and cabalistic learning, he revolted and turned to the forbidden booklets of the Maskilim to discover truths acceptable to his logical mind. When his father, a rabbi and cabalist, discovered the boy's aberration from the strict regimen of Hassidic behavior, he sought to cure him by marrying him off at fourteen to a girl of twelve. However, the youth soon infected her with his own heretical view whereupon his father forced him to divorce her and to marry a deaf, moronic woman. Not until he was nineteen did Linetzky succeed in breaking away from his tyrannical father and the second mate imposed upon him. He escaped to Odessa, acquired a secular education, and planned to continue his studies in Germany, the wellspring of Jewish enlightenment. However, when he attempted to cross the Russian border, he was apprehended and brought back to Vinitza. There his father and the Hassidim kept a close watch over him and only in his twenty-third year did he finally free himself from their despotic yoke. He entered the Rabbinical Academy at Zhitomir and developed a friendship with his classmate Abraham Goldfaden, with whom he later shared business and journalistic projects. Both students aspired to literary laurels, at first in the sacred tongue and then, following Mendele's example, also in Yiddish.

Linetzky's most popular work was his picaresque novel *The Polish Lad* (*Dos Poilishe Yingel*). It first appeared in installments in *Kol Mevasser* in 1867, and was frequently reprinted until World War II. It was based upon his own life and the persecutions he had experienced at the hands of the Hassidim. It attacked them mercilessly. It ridiculed their strange garb, their speech, their manners, their beliefs, their brainwashing of children, their warping of sensitive souls, their neglecting their wives, their submitting unquestioningly to immoral, greedy hypocrites whom they worshipped as saints and miracle-workers.

Linetzky was a master of the picturesque, vitriolic phrase. His avalanches of invectives were coarse and often verged on the grotesque. His exaggerations and caricatures followed the militant anti-Hassidic tradition initiated by Joseph Perl and continued by Gottlober. The misanthropic attitude he displayed in his narratives was also evident in the lyrics he published under the title *The Angry Marshalik* (*Der Beser Marshalik*, 1879), a title that fitted him well. He cooperated with Goldfaden in editing one of the earliest Yiddish weeklies, *Yisrolik*, from July 1875 to February 1876. The pogroms of 1881 led him to espouse Zionism while it was still in its initial stages. In his booklet *America or Israel* (1882), he propagated the ideas of the Hoveve Zion Movement, which paved the way for Jewish colonization of Palestine.

The mid-century decades which saw Mendele and Linetzky come to the fore also witnessed the transformation of the Yiddish lyric from a linguistic medium merely of Badchonim and folksingers to a subtle literary medium, even though the more learned writers continued to prefer Hebrew. If the popularity of the Badchonim did not wane until the twentieth century, despite the rise and efflorescence of the art lyric, this must be ascribed to the triad of talented Badchonim of the Mendele generation: Berl Broder (1815-1868), Velvel Zbarzher (1826-1883) and Eliakum Zunser (1836-1913).

Broder, who was born as Ber Margolies, derived his pseudonym from his native town of Brody, the trading center in eastern Galicia. He composed songs and rhymed verses while engaged in his monotonous work of making brushes. Later, when he became a buyer for his firm, he sang these compositions at various inns where he stopped for the night in the course of his travels. In the 1860's some of his lyrics were published and thus became available to other itinerant minstrels who imitated and disseminated his texts and tunes. He preferred the genre of the verse monologue. He would begin with an introductory line such as "I, a poor shepherd," "I, a poor watercarrier," "I, a poor wagon-driver." Generally he would impersonate and act out these ghetto types, thus paving the way for the Yiddish drama of Goldfaden a decade later.

Zbarzher also stemmed from eastern Galicia. Born as Benjamin Wolf Ehrenkranz, he early came under the influence of the Maskilim of Brody and Tarnopol and composed Hebrew and Yiddish songs. When his heresies and scoffing verses roused the wrath of his townsmen at Zbarazh, he fled to Rumania in 1845. There he sang his lyrics to the accompaniment of his own melodies at inns, winecellars, tea-houses, and at the homes of rich patrons. When he discovered that fellow bards were including his songs in their repertoires without crediting him as the author, he published them in a Hebrew-Yiddish booklet, in 1865. After years of wandering and carousing, he was attracted to Vienna, where he stayed from 1878 to 1880, and to Istambul, where he lived from 1880 until his death in 1883. In the latter city, he married as his second wife Malkele the Beautiful, his longed-for beloved of many years. Itzik Manger, the last and greatest of Yiddish balladists, who was profoundly influenced by Zbarzher, romanticized this relationship of the talented, unstable bard and the idealized Malkele in a cycle of twelve verse epistles in 1937. He showed Zbarzher intoxicated by dreams, love, nature, wine and poetry, and yet aware that all forms of intoxication were but temporary palliatives that could not in the long run banish sadness and tears.

Zbarzher was the ablest forerunner of Zunser and might well have attained the pinnacle of fame reached by the latter if he had not squandered his talent in disreputable Rumanian inns and Turkish coffee-houses. Zbarzher and Zunser had much in common. They were acquainted with each other's songs and borrowed freely from each other's repertoire, even though they never met. At times they treat the same theme in an almost identical manner and it was not always easy to decide which version was written first.

Zunser was a native of Vilna and his creative life spanned more than six decades, during which he is said to have composed at least six hundred songs for various occasions, but chiefly for weddings. However, less than a quarter of these have been preserved, and for some of them the melody is no longer remembered, since Zunser was not a trained musician and did not record the music.

Zunser's boyhood was spent in poverty as a pupil of Vilna's Ramailla's Yeshiva and his youth as a braider of lace in Kovno and under the influence of Rabbi Israel Salanter's moralizing *Musar* Movement. Nevertheless, he could not avoid coming in contact with the forbidden learning of the Maskilim of Lithuania. Soon he saw in them an international brotherhood of courageous, clear thinkers. The more he read of their works, the more he was convinced that faith and reason, Torah and enlightenment could go hand in hand without detriment to each other. He never abandoned his Orthodoxy, but it was an Orthodoxy stripped of superstitious excrescences. With his lyrics he sought to bring cheer and merriment to his audiences without undermining the basic principles of their traditional faith. In his twentieth year he was kidnapped by military recruiters, even as his brother before him, and faced the prospect of a harsh quarter of a century as a cantonist. However, a few days before the military oath was to be administered to him, he was saved by Alexander II's revocation of the draft regulation that weighed so heavily upon the Jewish population.

Zunser's early songs reflected the despair of entrapped cantonists and the ecstasy of their deliverance. These songs endeared him to the common people, even if they were looked at askance by his learned associates. He sang, in simple words and catchy tunes, of the melancholy fate and the few joys of the inarticulate masses.

He answered their timid questioning of God's ways and their yearning for moral guidance in parables which they understood. He mirrored for them happier days which would surely come in God's good time and he offered them solace by painting in verse vivid Messianic visions. He castigated the petty exploiters in their own ranks and he called down the judgment of heaven upon all foes of Jews everywhere. His songs spread by word of mouth to town after town and to province after province until all Yiddish-speaking Jews were familiar with them. In 1861 his first booklet, entitled *New Songs* (*Shirim Khadoshim*) appeared and this was followed by more than fifty publications during his lifetime and thereafter. A critical, definitive edition of all his extant works was prepared by Mordkhe Schaechter and published by YIVO in 1964.

In the 1860's Zunser was primarily a Maskil, interested in enlightening and instructing his people; in aiding them to cast off outmoded habits, medieval dress, peculiar forms of behavior, and irrational communal practices. In the 1870's, after experiencing personal tragedies in the death of his first wife and all of their nine children, he became primarily a prophet of doom, admonishing his co-religionists not to venture too far on the alluring road of western enlightenment and assimilation, pointing out the dangers of overhasty Russification, warning of probable disaster which might follow too sudden and too passionate infatuation with modernism, radicalism and worldliness. In the 1880's, when his dire forebodings were realized and disaster did overtake his people, he concentrated on comforting them in their affliction and on directing their gaze toward their ancient and holy homeland, Zion, a fairer goal for their national longing than the inhospitable Czarist realm. The Badchen or Wedding Bard became the singer of the Hoveve Zion and the Bilu pioneers. His Zionist songs such as *The Plow* (*Die Sokhe*) and *Homecoming to Zion* (*Shivath Zion*) were intoned not only by the pioneers of the First Aliya but long thereafter in remotest Eastern European hamlets and in Emek Yisreel and along the shores of Kinneret.

Unable to join his young disciples in Gedera, as he hoped, when he had to flee from Russia, he made America his home in 1889. His poems of the New World mirrored the moods and the problems of adjustment faced by Jewish immigrants. These poems ranged from idealization of America as in *Columbus and Washington,* to disillusionment with American reality as in *The Golden Land* (*Dos Goldene Land*) and *The Greenhorn* (*Der Greener*). His most frequently sung American lyric was *The Peddler,* in which he urged his fellow immigrants to give up peddling and to turn to the healthier and more productive work of farming.

The transition from folk poetry to the art lyric began with Michel Gordon (1823-1890), a townsman of Zunser. Although he composed singable Yiddish poems since the 1850's, he at first circulated them in manuscript form, fearing to endanger his slender reputation as a Hebrew writer. Even when, in 1868, he finally published his first Yiddish volume, *The Beard and Other Beautiful Songs* (*Die Bort Und Datsu Nokh Andere Shene Lieder*), he did so anonymously. This volume included the lyric "Arise My People!" generally regarded as the finest Yiddish expression of the Russian Haskalah. In stirring stanzas he told the Jews that the hour had struck for their awakening from lethargy. At last they could take their place in the sun, side by side with other national groups. For their rebirth, however, they needed knowledge to supplement faith.

In a second, expanded edition, proudly published under his own name in 1889, the militant singer of enlightenment became an elegiac comforter of his generation, which had meanwhile been plagued by pogroms and expulsions. He rewrote his earlier didactic poem *The Jew in Exile* (*Der Yied In Golus*), changing his optimistic conclusion to a pessimistic one. He had come to realize that peoples and governments were not behaving more wisely and with greater tolerance toward Jews, but were rather increasing pressures and punishment. His gloom during his final years was intensified by his penury, illness, and loneliness. The world that seemed so promising in the springtime of life had disappointed him and he was being driven hither and thither as a ship without a rudder amidst jagged rocks. Death alone would bring him lasting peace.

The Yiddish poems of Yehuda Leib Gordon (1830-1892), brother-in-law of Michel Gordon, were but a minor part of his literary activity. He was primarily a Hebrew poet. When he finally did publish them in 1886, they bore the Hebrew title *Sikhath Khulin*. In an introduction, he explained that he had to use the language of the *Tseno-Urena*, sacred to his mother and grandmother, because he wanted to reach the wagonner, the porter, the innkeeper's wife and all the hard-working, simple folk. The poems were rich in social protest. He lamented his wasted youth when he could observe the changing seasons and nature's loveliness only through the dim windows of a *Kheder* in which he was kept from early in the morning until late in the evening. He lashed out at sated community bigwigs and religious pundits, who were indifferent to the woes of the poor and the widowed. Though his chief interest was in the messages he wished to convey and he did not pay the same attention to his Yiddish as to his Hebrew style, he still displayed a mastery of the Yiddish heroic couplet and the idiomatic, picturesque phrase.

Michel Gordon and Yehuda Leib Gordon paved the way for Shimon Shmuel Frug (1860-1916), who began in 1880 as a Russian poet with themes selected from biblical prophets and Talmudic legends. Not until 1888, when his Russian reputation was already firmly established, did he turn to Yiddish. Yehuda Leib Gordon then hailed him as the harbinger of a new dawn: "I am a withered leaf; you are a blossoming flower." Frug's indebtedness to Michel Gordon was expressed in two verse tributes. The first of these was composed in 1889 after the publication of Gordon's *Yiedishe Lieder* and the second after Gordon's death the following year. When Frug called his predecessor a singer of Jewish sorrows who could move stones to tears and revive the dead with his lamentations, he was also characterizing himself. He too could not write joyous songs while the moaning of pogrom victims was in his ears. Gazing upon the dead who were lying unburied in ghetto lanes and upon the survivors who were left desolate and penniless, he called upon his fellow-Jews to mitigate the mass tragedy in stanzas that ended with the refrain: "Give shrouds for the dead. And for the living bread."

Frug was born in a Jewish agricultural colony in Southern Russia. His childhood and youth amidst forests and fields were carefree and happy, but his adult years were darkened by personal tragedies, hence the nostalgic references to the past which frequently recur in his lyrics. His descriptions of nature were based on personal observation and were hence less artificial and more accurate than those of his Yiddish contemporaries. Though he wrote about all four seasons, autumn and winter were more congenial to him in his later moods than were spring or summer. He believed in the health-restoring properties of a return to the soil, but for Jews the return should be to Zion's soil rather than to the tear-stained, blood-drenched soil of Russia. His songs of Zion contrasted the heroic warriors of ancient Israel, who gave their lives in defense of their national home, with their emaciated descendants who lived in rented quarters and were evicted whenever it pleased their cruel landlords. His stirring verses in behalf of Zion inspired the early colonists who left ghetto townlets to reclaim the earth from which they had been long exiled.

Frug's songs combined honey and gall, sentimentalism and satire, Heinesque *Weltschmerz* and visions of Messianic redemption. The best of his ballads was *The Sexton's Daughter (Dem Shames's Tokhter)*, a Jewish parallel to the Greek tale of Admetus and Alcestis.

While Frug reacted to the worsening Jewish situation with elegies, Mark Varshavsky (1848-1907) sought to cheer his coreligionists with humorous songs and witty couplets to which he supplied his own melodies. These included songs of wine and merriment; songs of Zion that brought comfort and hope; songs to be intoned at the veiling of a bride before she was led to the wedding canopy, and by a father who was overjoyed on marrying off his *mezinke,* his youngest daughter. Among his dancing songs for old and young was one with the refrain "eighty he and seventy she." In it the poet reviewed the satisfying, traditional life of an old couple, surrounded by children, grandchildren and well-wishers, at peace with God and man. Instead of satirical gibes at old-fashioned ways, he emphasized their beauty and charm. His most popular song, which has been on the lips of millions for several generations, begins with the words *"Oifn Pripitshek."* Its stanzas evoke a picture of an oven-warmed classroom where a *rebbe* teaches little children the alphabet. Though the Hebrew letters are not easy to master, the effort is worthwhile, since the letters are the keys which open up the treasures of the Torah. In the ancient letters are embedded so many tears and laments, but also so much strength, the fortitude necessary to enable Jews to carry on the burdens of exile.

The sentimentalism of Varshavsky's folksongs found its parallel in the sentimental novels of Jacob Dinezon (1856-1919) and Nahum Meier Shaikevitch (1849-1905), which were bestsellers in the 1870's and 1880's.

Dinezon started out under the influence of Michel Gordon and Isaac Meir Dick. His first published work, *The Dark Youth (Der Shvartser Yungermantshik,* 1877), was the first full-length novel in Yiddish with unhappy love as its central theme. His readers, like those of Dick, were unsophisticated persons. He fed them characters that were either paragons of perfection or completely diabolical, but unlike Dick, he did not end by rewarding the hero and the heroine and by punishing the villain. On the contrary, he showed the lovable hero and the lovelorn heroine being impelled to untimely deaths, while the black egoist rose to a position of prominence and was accepted as a respectable member of the community. The emphasis on the suffering of the pure-hearted, whose tears flowed endlessly, elicited pity and abundant tears from uncritical readers. These could delve into their own fancied or actual experiences, recall their own unfulfilled youthful dreams, and picture themselves as innocent victims of wicked contemporaries. Dinezon succeeded in evoking an illusion of reality without actually depicting reality, and won the hearts of his many readers with his gentle, caressing, intimate sentimentalism. These readers numbered more than 200,000, an audience that no Hebrew writer was able to reach and that he himself failed to equal with his later novels *Even Negef* (1890), *Hershele* (1891) and *Yossele* (1899).

Dinezon's stories stressed the claims of the heart, the need for more kindness in the rearing of children, and greater freedom for young people to choose their mates. He pointed to the wreckage in human lives brought about by rigid, intolerant attitudes and he helped to arouse public opinion against the harsh pedagogical methods of the traditional *kheder*. Schools established in accordance with his newer methods made learning at the elementary level a joyous experience and were therefore often called the Dinezon Schools.

Nahum Meier Shaikevitch, who became better known under his pseudonym Shomer, was a more prolific storyteller than Dinezon. His facility was phenomenal. When in 1876 he brought a Hebrew manuscript to Samuel Joseph Finn, the editor of the Hebrew periodical *Hacarmel,* he was told that there was a greater demand for Yiddish tales. On each of the following nine mornings he then submitted a story which he had written during the preceding night, and he might have continued indefinitely if the publisher had not stopped paying for more. When Dinezon's first novel became a bestseller in 1877, Shomer was asked if he too could write long novels instead of mere booklets. Within a few months he handed in three long novels which appeared in 1879 and were followed by six more in 1880. Soon the demand for his sentimental prose romances increased to such an extent that even his prolific pen could not keep pace and a host of imitators appeared who wrote in the Shomer style and assumed similar names.

In contrast to Dinezon, Shomer reverted to the happy ending such as Dick had preferred. He wanted to entertain his readers and not to shock them. His love scenes drip with sentiment, though they never descend to luscious sensuality. He depicts the poor, honest, hardworking, beautiful seamstress who is befriended by a sympathetic beggar who later turns out to be a millionaire in disguise. He portrays Jewish Cinderellas who find aristocratic mates at the end of their exciting adventures in the realm of emotions.

Shomer gave the masses what they wanted, entertainment, suspense, humor, the marvelous and the fantastic, combined with an illusion of reality. He was the favorite writer for housemaids and apprentices, but he evoked the wrath of the intellectuals. The attack upon him which was launched by Shimon Dubnow in 1884 reached its climax in Sholom Aleichem's satiric pamphlet *Shomer On Trial (Shomer's Mishpet)* in 1888, a year before Shomer left for America. Sholom Aleichem saw him as the corrupter of literary taste and succeeded in demolishing his reputation among the literary élite but still failed to diminish his vogue.

Mordecai Spector (1858-1925) learned from Shomer the art of entertaining readers by treating them as equals and addressing them as friends rather than as ignorant pupils in need of learning or unenlightened sinners in need of verbal chastisement. Spector's plots had a sounder basis in reality than did those of Shomer. They reflected life in homes and alleys, in synagogues and even in the communal bathhouse. His characters were not above ordinary stature—simple artisans, travelling salesmen, tavern-keepers, villagers, petty merchants, housewives. They debated specifically Jewish issues of immediate concern to families and communities. Spector's language mirrored the warm, colloquial speech of the workshop and the market-place and his humor was kind and gentle. His most popular novel, *The Jewish Peasant (Der Yiedisher Muzhik,* 1884), advocated the ideas of the Hoveve Zion, the return of Jews to productive labor on the soil of Israel. In addition to long novels, Spector wrote hundreds of feuilletons, travel-sketches and short tales. He reached the height of his fame as editor of the annual *Der Hausfreund* (1888-1889) and as co-editor with Peretz and Pinski of the *Yom-Tov Blettlekh* in Warsaw in 1894. He participated in many other literary ventures of the Yiddish cultural revival in Russia before he was forced to flee to America in 1921. His short stories were translated into the principal European languages as well as into Hebrew.

Dick, Dinezon, Shomer and Spector are little read today but their contribution to the growth of Yiddish letters before the vogue of Sholom Aleichem and Peretz should not be underestimated.

They first won over masses of barely literate persons as readers of Yiddish books. The classical masters could then undertake the further task of refining the taste of the larger audience. Mendele and his contemporaries had laid the groundwork for the greater efflorescence of Yiddish after 1889.

4

PERETZ AND
SHOLOM ALEICHEM

Peretz's Life ● His Tales ● His Credo ● Sholom
Aleichem's Beginnings ● His Uniqueness ● *Tevye* ●
Menachem Mendel ● *Mottel Peise* ● Sholom Aleichem's
Humor ● His Plays ● His Vogue

YITZKHOK LEIBUSH PERETZ was the great awakener of Yiddish-speaking Jewry and Sholom Aleichem its comforter. Peretz
stimulated Yiddish creativity and weaned Jewish youth from perilous assimilationist tendencies. Sholom Aleichem brought to light
the inner dignity and the moral grandeur that was submerged
beneath the shabby appearance and the apparent submissiveness of
the Pale's denizens. Peretz aroused in his readers the will for self-
emancipation, the will for resistance against the many humiliations to which they were being subjected. Sholom Aleichem saw
in the Jews' passive endurance of humiliations imposed from
without a tactic for survival by an unarmed minority in the midst
of a hostile and often bloodthirsty majority. Peretz was both realist and romanticist. Not only did he disdain logic, but he also
delved into irrational layers of the soul and sought to set imaginations astir with visions of Messianic possibilities. Sholom Aleichem
was purely a realist who sought and discovered beauty even in
rags, hovels and deformity. Peretz was an optimist who believed
in the inevitability of progress through enlightenment, despite the
price in suffering that was generally exacted whenever the sleep
of the world was disturbed. Sholom Aleichem was a pessimist
who sought relief from despair in laughter.

Peretz was born on May 18, 1852 in the Polish townlet of
Zamosc. Though reared in an Orthodox home, he came under the

influence of Maskilim while still a youth of fifteen. Eager for secular learning, he taught himself foreign languages and the reading of numerous books in Polish, Russian, German and French enriched him with a great deal of miscellaneous knowledge and undermined his childhood faith. At eighteen he planned to escape from his native Zamosc to the larger, more enlightened center of Zhitomir, but at the last moment the tears of his mother kept him back. Soon thereafter, he was married off to a young girl chosen for him by his father, the daughter of the minor Hebrew poet and philosopher Gabriel Judah Lichtenfeld, and had to assume family responsibilities for which he was unripe. He proved a failure in his first business venture, a whiskey distillery, since his main interest was in writing and he neglected his customers. His first lyrics began to appear in Hebrew periodicals in 1875. His first published book, in 1877, consisted of Hebrew songs and versified tales written in collaboration with his father-in-law. This collaboration came to an end when Peretz divorced Lichtenfeld's daughter and in 1878 married Helene Ringelblum, whom he had ardently wooed for many months and who was his faithful companion throughout his later life. At twenty-five Peretz passed a Russian law examination which permitted him to engage in private practice as an advocate. For more than a decade he was a successful, prosperous advocate with little time for literary pursuits and not until 1888 did he enter upon his productive literary career in Yiddish. When in that year Sholom Aleichem edited and published the first important Yiddish anthology, *Folksbibliotek,* Peretz submitted to him the long ballad *Monish.* It aroused considerable interest. In verses often reminiscent of Heine, in cadences ranging from the pathetic to the satiric, this first major poem in Yiddish by the former Hebrew writer of Zamosc portrayed the tragedy of man engaged in a desperate struggle with demonic forces within himself; a struggle between his earthbound ego and his heaven-aspiring soul. The pure, pious youth Monish put up strong resistance against the lure of the demonic temptress Lilith, who in Jewish folklore paralleled the Greek Circe or the medieval Lady Venus and who appeared to him in the figure of a golden-haired maiden with a joyous, melodious, seductive voice. In the long run, however, she brought about his downfall when his fettered flesh revolted against the tyranny of his ascetic soul.

The year after the appearance of *Monish,* Peretz's license to practice law was revoked by the Russian government which suspected him of harboring revolutionary and pro-Polish sentiments.

Thereafter and until his death in 1915, he had to content himself with a subordinate position as an employee of Warsaw's Jewish community. However, his prestige as the intellectual leader of an awakening Jewish youth increased from year to year and his home in Warsaw became a shrine to which budding writers made pilgrimages from all over Eastern Europe. They brought their manuscripts to him, knowing that his approval opened the doors of publishers to them and gave them literary status. To such youth belonged among others David Pinski, Abraham Reisen, Sholem Asch, H. D. Nomberg, Peretz Hirshbein, Yehoash, I. M. Weissenberg, I. J. Trunk, Menahem Boraisha, Joseph Opatoshu, Der Nister, all of whom later became important figures in Yiddish literature.

The literary range of Peretz embraced poems, dramas, essays, travel sketches and literary reviews. But his supreme achievement must be sought in his short stories and sketches. These combined clear observations of real life with flights into romantic, mystic heavens. In his tales, visible phenomena were overtopped by higher strata of eternal truths to which one ascended via the ladder of faith or through the medium of dreams. His humble characters, such as Bontsie the Silent, Chaim the Porter, or Shmeril the Woodcutter, were not crushed by their hard tasks and endless dull routines, because they had faith in a higher reality, a more just existence awaiting them at the end of their earthly journey.

The title hero of *Bontsie Shvaig* was unnoticed by his fellowmen and mistreated by his wealthy employer. He endured in silence the deprivations and humiliations to which he was subjected until his death. In heaven, however, he ranked with the most deserving saints because there true, eternal values prevailed. Chaim the Porter, in the sketch *An Idyllic Home,* walked through the streets bent double under his load, but he could look forward to a chair in the Garden of Eden, a chair he intended to share with his wife Chane, who loved him even though he offered her so little of life's pleasures. Shmeril the Woodcutter, in the story *The Treasure,* lived in a single room with a wife and eight little children, but nevertheless resisted the temptation to desecrate the Sabbath and to run after a beckoning treasure. In consideration of his piety, he was rewarded thereafter with wealth, joy and contentment.

In the story *Beside the Dying,* Peretz depicted two contrasting characters in their hour of death. The one, Leibl Konskivoler, whose prayers resounded to heaven every morning and evening, regarded himself as a paragon of virtue and piety. In reality, he loved to accumulate wealth. Bloodstains from exploited human beings clung to his treasured coins. Hence his soul was taken from his body by the Angel of Darkness. The other was Nachman of Zbarazh, who often forgot to say his prayers but whose pitying heart went out to the feeble and the sick, to widows and orphans, to the sorrow-laden, the homeless, the tormented. When the Angel of Light offered to transport him to the radiant heavenly realm, he turned down the offer. "What am I to do there, O Angel, there where no one needs my soul, my heart, my tear of pity, my word of comfort, or my hand to lift them from the abyss?" Nachman preferred to follow the Angel of Darkness to the abode of the unfortunate, the hungry, the parched, the weary-hearted, the lost, the accursed, those forgotten by God. Even if he might not be able to help them, he could at least suffer with them and feel with them.

In the story *If Not Higher,* the Rabbi of Nemerov did not disdain to leave the realm of pure contemplation and to carry out the task of a lowly woodcutter when a poor, bedridden woman needed faggots for her stove. A sceptical Lithuanian Jew, who was told of the Rabbi's saintly reputation, set out to disprove the faith of the Rabbi's disciples in the spiritual eminence of their leader. However, when he witnessed this kind deed of the Rabbi in the silent hours of pre-dawn, he was himself transformed into a disciple of this great moral personality.

According to Peretz, simple, unsensational deeds of piety, purity and self-sacrifice were the gifts most acceptable in the heavenly abode. He exemplified this best in the story *Three Gifts,* which Maurice Schwartz in collaboration with Melech Ravitch, dramatized for New York's Yiddish Art Theater. A poor soul, whose virtues and vices balanced evenly on Heaven's scale of justice, was found to be deserving neither of paradise or hell. It was, therefore, sent back to earth with the promise that, if it brought back three gifts of extraordinary goodness and beauty, it would be admitted to paradise. The banned soul flew over many towns and villages, season after season, until it collected the three gifts.

The first gift was a bit of the earth from the land of Israel which a pious Jew, who was ready to give up his wealth to robbers, tried to keep from them. The robbers, believing the bag of earth to contain the most valuable loot, killed him to get at the bag and were bitterly disappointed at their find. The hovering soul caught a bloody speck of this earth and brought it to the window at heaven's gate.

A second opportunity came to the wandering soul when it witnessed an innocent Jewish girl condemned by German magistrates to be tied by her long hair to the tail of a wild horse and dragged through the streets until her death. The doomed girl's last wish was for a few pins. With these she pinned the edge of her dress to her feet by sticking them deep into her flesh, so that her body could not be uncovered when the horse dragged her past the crowd of onlookers. The wandering soul, who alone noticed this act of modesty just before the horse darted forward, drew a blood-stained pin from the dying girl and brought it to heaven as the second gift.

The third opportunity came years later when the soul espied a Jew running the gauntlet between two rows of lashing soldiers. When this Jew was half-way through the ordeal, a soldier struck too high and the skullcap fell off from the head of the victim. The Jew stopped short, retraced his steps to the spot where the cap had fallen and picked it up. Then he continued on, bloodstained, but with a Jewish covering on his head, until he collapsed. As he fell, the soul flew over, caught the cap, and rushed with it to heaven's gate. The portal of paradise was then opened for the poor exiled soul and the heavenly oracle commented: "Really beautiful gifts, gifts of extraordinary loveliness. They are of no practical use or material value, but their beauty is indeed precious."

Among the finest narratives of Peretz is the novelette *Self-Sacrifice*, the story of the Jewish youth Hananya who strays from the path of true learning. The study of God's Torah should be undertaken for its own sake. It should be motivated by a desire to comprehend more profoundly God's world and to justify God's acts. Hananya, however, succumbs to the temptation of showing off his knowledge and delights in refuting and confounding other scholars. His knowledge is therefore essentially negative and sinful. He pierces the Torah with verbal spears and swords, and spreads ruin and havoc everywhere. When he displays his sophistry and tricks of argumentation in a most devilishly skillful fashion and puts a fellow student to shame, he is cursed by his teacher, the head of Jerusalem's Yeshiva, who tells him: "Hananya, you can ruin an entire world. It is better that you forget your learning!" That very moment something snapped in Hananya's brain, and he forgot every word of Torah he had ever learned. To live in spiritual darkness without the light of Torah is for a Jew equivalent to damnation and hellish torture. No penance is too severe, if it can gain for a person readmittance into the realm of the learned.

But whence is salvation to come? Hananya wanders forth into exile, garbed in linen rags, with a hempen rope about his loins and a pilgrim's staff in his hand. There is as little likelihood of his soul bursting into blossom and recollecting Torah as there is of his staff blooming again and bearing green leaves. Hananya roams about in the desert, pondering mournfully on his young years that are to pass away without a ray for his darkened mind. Exhausted, he falls asleep and in a dream he is told to go to the good-hearted Reb Hiya of Safed's School of Learning and to make a full confession of his sin. There Hananya will find atonement, the staff will bloom again, and he will be spiritually reborn. Elijah the Prophet, a power in Heaven, has interceded for him. He is to be permitted to expiate his sin. He is to marry a good wife and is to die on the eighth day after the wedding. He himself is unaware of the early death in store for him, but Miriam, the daughter of Reb Hiya, learns of this decree from her father and, unknown to anyone, she undertakes to circumvent fate. She is married to Hananya. On the eighth day after the wedding, at the very moment that the staff of the penitent blossoms again and he recollects the Torah he once knew, she steals into the garden in his disguise and the poisonous snake, sent to bite Hananya, mistakes her for his assigned victim and bites her. At the heavenly Seat of Judgment the error is discovered and her soul is ordered back to her body. She refuses to return, however, on the ground that nobody can be required to suffer twice the pain of dying. She will go back only on condition that her first death is accepted in lieu of her husband's death. The heavenly host agrees and Hananya lives on to become a great sage in Israel.

Elijah, who came to the aid of Hananya on the brink of despair, is an important figure in Jewish folklore and exercised a tremendous fascination for Peretz. In several tales, this prophet was introduced as the ready helper in adversity, as the kind stranger who brings comfort to burdened hearts. In the story *The Magician*, Peretz has Elijah appear as a conjurer bringing a Passover feast to the impoverished lumber merchant Chaim-Yone and his wife Rivke-Beele when they are unable to provide it for themselves.

In another story, *Seven Years of Plenty*, Elijah offers the poor porter Tevya seven good years. These can come immediately but thereafter Tevye would revert to his poor condition, or else these

years can be given him at the end of his allotted span of life and
then he would leave this world as the wealthiest of persons. After
a consultation between husband and wife, both agree to accept
the proferred wealth now so that they could pay for the children's
schooling. When the stranger reappeared seven years later, he
was told that the couple had never regarded the wealth given
them as their own, because only what a person earned with his
ten fingers was properly his own. But wealth that came unsought
and without sweat was merely a pledge which God deposited with
a person to hold for the poor. From God's gold Tevye had taken
only a sum necessary to pay for the children's schooling, so that
these might learn God's Torah. The rest of the gold was still untouched and was available to be turned over to a better keeper.
Elijah listened to these words and repeated them before the heavenly court of justice. The court ruled that there were no keepers
on earth more suitable than Tevye and his wife. Hence, the seven
good years never came to an end for the couple so long as they
remained among the living.

Husband and wife in both Elijah tales, *Seven Years of Plenty*
and *The Magician,* are silent souls. They suffer want and hardships but they are never wholly crushed by their sad lot. They
never despair. They never avert their faces from life. They have
faith in God's world. They lack knowledge as to why they are
subjected to their troubles but they have no doubt that there is
meaning to all they are forced to endure. They try to extract a
glimmer of light out of the murky grayness all about them. They
dream of the sun that must break through the thick clouds somehow, somewhere, at some time. And Peretz rewards their faith,
their hope, their dream. He lets a dazzling ray beam upon them
and warm them. Elijah is the penetrating ray. He, the precursor
of Messiah, is the symbol of the unexpected help that may come
to those who are worthy of extraordinary assistance because they
retain faith in the fundamental justice that must prevail in heaven
and on earth, in the realm of God and in the destiny of man.

A considerable number of Peretz's sketches deal with mystics,
cabalists, and Hassidim. He recognized the importance of the
contribution made by Hassidism to Jewish survival, its elevation
of the soul, its infusion of poetry into prosaic life. He felt that the
singing, dancing and joyousness propagated by Hassidism enabled
Jews to surmount anxieties and to be invigorated on Sabbaths and
holidays for the harsh ordeals of weekdays. In the story *Between
Two Mountains,* he described a gathering of Hassidim on Simkhat

Torah, the festive day of Rejoicing of the Law: eyes sparkling, voices interweaving melodious sounds, long-robed worshippers dancing in the sunlight like carefree children. Heaven and earth seemed to join in the contagious merriment and the soul of the universe seemed to dissolve in sweet accords.

In the play *The Golden Chain*, Peretz depicted a powerful Hassidic leader, Reb Shlome, who wanted to prolong the Sabbath so that all life be an eternal Sabbath and the Messianic realm of holiness and ecstasy come into being now, rather than at the end of time. But Peretz knew full well the frailties of the human heart and the difficulty of retaining normal human beings indefinitely within higher spiritual strata. He therefore showed these persons turning away from the extreme demands made upon them by Reb Shlome and reverting to their secular pursuits. The Golden Chain of Jewishness, forged of Messianic longing, remained nevertheless unbroken and continued to be handed down the generations by Reb Shlome's descendants. According to Peretz, individuals embedded within the Hassidic brotherhood or traditional Judaism, whatever its failings, could never be as lonely, or find existence as empty and dull, as secular Jews who were wedded solely to reason, who sought merely worldly success and the full satisfaction of merely personal desires.

In the brief saga *Four Generations—Four Wills*, Peretz paints the rise of a Jewish family in affluence and outward prestige and shows that its wealth and prosperity divorced its members from their natural Jewish attachments and left them inwardly void. The more assimilated to Occidental ways they became from generation to generation, the more was their Jewish vitality sapped until their last representative was ripe for self-annihilation. He could no longer live on, for there was nothing for him to do on earth after draining to the last drop all the joy apportioned to him. He had used up everything that he needed, both things and people. His wealth was his undoing; everything it could buy he bought: the smiles of so-called friends, the kisses of red lips—and he was left barren, physically and spiritually.

In his stories, Peretz seeks the inner essence of the phenomena he describes. He ferrets out in every bit of nature, inorganic as well as organic, a sentient embodiment of spiritual traits, in every individual some relationship to universal values, in every national and religious group a unique expression of God's will. Every people is seen by him to be a chosen people, chosen by its peculiar history, geography and ethnic composition, to experience a destiny which is not identical with that of any other people. He holds the Jews to be a people, one people, even though dispersed everywhere. Willingly or unwillingly, the Jews have become a world people. Beyond its transitory and accidental traits, this people also retains common characteristics, common enduring values, a common assessment of what is good and evil, a common sense of moral responsibility. He defines Jewishness as the Jewish way of looking at things, the universal spirit as it is embodied in the Jewish soul, the viewing of the world as an organic unity bound together by a single supra-material force. "Jewishness is that which makes the Jews, in eras of national independence, feel free and enables them to fashion institutions as embodiments of their national creative will. Jewishness is, in such times, joy, ecstasy, zestful living. Jewishness is that which creates, in troubled times, institutions for defense, for preventing of danger, for protecting itself and its members. Jewishness is, in such times, a call to battle and a challenge to heroism. Jewishness is that which must in times of dependence and weakness, retreat into its shell, conserve its resources, endure in silence, and wait for better days. Then Jewishness is hope and pain, Messianic dreams and otherworldliness. Then it demands real sacrifice."

Since each literature conveys the specific culture of a people, Jewish literature must, according to Peretz, be grounded in Jewish traditions and Jewish history. It must be the expression of Jewish ideals. It must encompass the totality of Jewish life, past and present, from the radiant beginnings at Sinai, through the long night of martyrdom, to the contemporary aspirations for renewal, and even on to an envisaged prophetic future. It must present Jewishness not as static or congealed but as dynamic, evolving, embracing every aspect of Jewish thought and feeling. It must help to educate the Jewish masses, must warm the heart of every Jew, and put into his hands the means to live fully as a thinking human being. Writers must strive to bring about a Jewish renascence rather than to sow confusion in Jewish ranks by working for a so-called humanity-at-large. This greater entity, this mythical humanity-at-large, does not exist at present. Cultural groups, distinct peoples, differing civilizations are now the actors on the stage of the world. Jews did not suffer for thousands of years in order now to forget their own civilization and to assimilate to others, but rather in order to continue their own way of life, so that they might later unite with the company of mankind as equal partners, with equal rights and equal shares. This does not mean that Jews should meanwhile shut themselves up in a spiritual ghetto. On the contrary, they should get out of ghetto isolation. But they should get out not as nondescript individuals but as Jews, with their own accumulated spiritual treasures. They should interchange, give and take, not beg. Out of past memories and future hopes, irradiated by unswerving confidence in themselves and by holy faith in their moral integrity, they should continue to spin their legends and weave their symbols. The best possibility for further human development lies not on the road toward greater conformity but rather in more intensive cultural cross-fertilization. Humanity must be the synthesis, the sum, the quintessence of all national cultures, values and philosophies. "Jewish life must burst into blossom again. With the Bible as germinating seed and with folk symbols and folk legends as dew and rain, the field will sprout again, the people will revive, the Jews will rise once more to suffer anew for their truth and will reaffirm their faith in ultimate victory. The flag of a Jewish renascence must be raised again, the banner of Messiah, world-judgment, and world liberation, the symbol of a future free humanity. This is the mission of the eternal people, the world-people, a mission to be carried through in all phases of Jewish life, by the Jewish home, the Jewish school, the Jewish theater, the Jewish book, and everything Jewish."

When the Russian Revolution of 1905 roused the enthusiasm of Peretz's Jewish compatriots that at last a brighter day had dawned for them, he called attention to the pogroms that accompanied the upheaval. In his essay *Hope and Fear*, he welcomed the destruction of the Czarist regime, but he also expressed his misgiving that the oppressed Russian subjects would themselves turn into oppressors on coming into power. The victims would become bureaucrats, doling out to each citizen his portion as to the poor in a poorhouse, apportioning to each individual his assigned work as to the prisoner in his dungeon. The revolutionary regime that would introduce equality would curb individual initiative, stifle the free human will, annihilate the creator of new values, mechanize, regiment, macadamize life. It would prescribe what dreams the longing heart might indulge in. It would undertake to have all bodies well-fed, but spirits would go hungry. It would defend the equal rights of all members of the herd to the grass on the ground, but it would persecute the dissenting individual, the savior, the poet, the artist, and all who strove to ascend beyond mediocrity. Jews, as non-conformists, would be victims of such a post-revolutionary order, even as of earlier ones. Jews were cursed and blessed to be the eternally bleeding, highest-soaring expression of the divine in life. Theirs was still a long and dangerous road ahead. As the weakest of the nations, they will be the last for redemption, the last to be freed, on the day when man will rise above the all-too-earthly, when human worms will be transformed into human eagles.

Peretz was the profoundest spokesman for the Yiddish intellectuals beset by doubts, the voice of their conscience, the inspiring interpreter of their pain, idealism, disappointment and hope.

The most widely read of the classical triumvirate, however, was neither Peretz nor Mendele but Sholom Aleichem. It was Sholom Aleichem who incorporated in his writings most frequently, most clearly, and most lovingly the inarticulate desires, the unrealized dreams, the unsolved worries, and the undying hopes of the average person—not the heroic or the unusual individual, not the rebel or the saint, but the average Jew.

Sholom Aleichem was born as Sholom Rabinowitch on March 3, 1859 in Pereyaslav, a Ukrainian townlet, and grew up in the neighboring settlement of Voronkov, which he later immortalized as Kasrilevke, symbol of small town Jewish culture. In his school years he already exhibited a talent for humor and a far roaming imagination which vivified even inanimate objects. At thirteen, he lost his mother, who had been the main support of the family even while raising more than a dozen children. He then came under the influence of his grandfather, a Hassid and cabalist. At fourteen he attempted to write a novel about a Jewish Robinson Crusoe after reading Defoe's novel, and he completed a Hebrew narrative, *Bath Zion,* after reading Abraham Mapu's romantic novel *Ahavath Zion.* Thereafter he continued to practice writing poems, tales, and dramas, following the books he read. From eighteen to twenty-one, he was private tutor at the home of a wealthy landowner in the province of Kiev. He later looked upon these years as his happiest, especially since he was in love with his pupil Olga Loyev, whom he married in 1883.

Sholom Aleichem's first published articles appeared in the Hebrew periodical *Hamelitz* in 1881. He also wrote Russian sketches but these were usually rejected by editors. Yiddish became his main literary medium only after 1883, the year when Alexander Zederbaum accepted his first short story for the short-lived Yiddish *Folksblat.*

From 1881 until his marriage, Sholom Aleichem served as a government rabbinical official. After the death of his father-in-law, in 1885, he came into possession of considerable wealth which enabled him not only to engage in business in Kiev on a comparatively large scale, but also to be a patron of literature. He financed, edited and published two volumes of the Yiddish literary annual, *Folksbibliotek*, 1888-1889, which had a profound impact. In its columns were published not only important works of the classical triumvirate—Mendele's *The Little Man*, Peretz's *Monish*, Sholom Aleichem's *Stempenyu* and *Yossele Solovey*—but also contributions by Abraham Baer Gottlober, Jacob Dinezon, Yoel Linetzky, David Frishman, Eliakum Zunser, and Yehuda Leib Gordon. Before the third issue of the annual could leave the press in 1890, the editor lost his fortune through his speculations on the stock-exchange. Throughout all his later years, he never knew financial independence again. At first he tried to eke out a living through various callings but later had to depend entirely upon his pen. He was unsuccessful as insurance agent, stock broker, commission merchant, but his varied business experiences gave him rich material for his sketches. In 1891 and 1892, he wrote feuilletons and short stories in Russian for an Odessa newspaper and for *Voskhod*, the most influential Russian Jewish organ. He wrote in Hebrew for *Hamelitz* and for *Pardes*, an anthology edited by Y. H. Ravnitzky. He was, however, far more prolific in Yiddish. Throughout the 1890's he was at work on the sketches of Tevye, the Jewish dairyman who drives his rickety wagon along the road from Kasrilevke to Yehupetz and philosophizes on the nature of man and the world, and of Menachem Mendel, the man about town, who dreams of fortunes almost within his reach but who is always luckless in his speculations.

After experiencing a pogrom in Kiev in 1905, Sholom Aleichem left Russia, lectured and gave readings of his works throughout Europe and finally landed in New York in October 1906. There Jacob Adler and Boris Tomashevsky staged two of his plays but with little success. Unhappy in America, he returned to Europe and settled in Geneva in 1907. While on a lecture tour of Russia the following year, he collapsed and had to live during the next six years in various health resorts along the Italian Riviera, in South Germany and in the Swiss Alps. These were years of intense literary creativity and ever increasing fame. At the same time he was constantly engaged in a struggle against illness and poverty. Holding that laughter was a tonic for health, he continued to laugh at fate and to stimulate his readers to do likewise. Even when he wrote about sad happenings, he did so in a way as to arouse laughter.

While he was recuperating at a German Baltic resort in the summer of 1914, war broke out. He succeeded in escaping across the border to Denmark and made his way once more to America. In New York he worked on his autobiography *From the Fair* (*Funm Yarid*), despite ever severer illnesses and a ceaseless struggle for bread, until he succumbed on May 13, 1916.

In his will he requested that he be laid at rest not among aristocrats or men of wealth but among the simple, honest people, whom he always loved and who loved him in turn. Tens of thousands attended his funeral and millions mourned the passing of this greatest of Yiddish humorists. His fame continued to spread over all continents and surpassed that of any other Yiddish literary figure. On the centenary of his birth, Israel, Russia and Rumania issued special stamps in his honor and on the semi-centenary of his death, his popularity was still increasing. In Soviet Russia his tales were included in the curriculum of Yiddish schools and his plays were performed in government Yiddish theaters, as long as such schools and theaters were tolerated, and he was the first Yiddish writer whose work was reprinted in the original when the ban on Yiddish was lifted after the death of Stalin. In the United States, the musical *Fiddler on the Roof*, based on Sholom Aleichem's Tevye sketches, was a box-office success throughout the late 1960's and had reached many European stages by 1970. In Israel, Sholom Aleichem's tales, made available in the superb Hebrew translation of his son-in-law, I. D. Berkovitch, were taught in elementary and high schools. In Tel Aviv, a Sholom Aleichem House contained his archives and became a center of research for scholars. Recordings by prominent actors, radio and television performances, translations into ever more languages increased his prestige and through him the prestige of Yiddish among Jews and non-Jews.

Sholom Aleichem is unique in his combining an awareness of a tragic substratum that underpins the structure of human life with an indestructible will to extract somehow fragments of joy out of every happening. His is a laughter through tears, a stoic humor that surmounts all obstacles and disappointments. His most beloved character was Tevye the Dairyman, the symbol of the seemingly naive but actually wise Jew, hard-working, soundhearted, immaculately honest, oppressed for no obvious reason by the non-Jewish authorities, expelled from the village of his birth

but never despairing, never faltering in his submission to God's
will, even though constantly having to suppress gnawing doubts
as to the justice God was dispensing to the world and particularly
to His chosen people.

Tevye's great and little worries are both tragic and laughable
at the same time. Readers laugh with him but not at him. They
sympathize with him as he squirms to extricate himself from the
troubles heaped upon him. He helps himself in difficult moments
by recalling a biblical or Talmudic quotation, often a garbled
quotation, and his despondence yields to quiet resignation. What
if misfortune hounds him? Is not misfortune the normal lot of
mortals? To laugh at it, to remain happy under all circumstances,
is heroic and ennobling. As the father of seven daughters, Tevye
is plagued with a seemingly unending series of misfortunes but he
bears these with a gentle bowing of the head and an ironic smile.
He cannot oppose the immoral social and political order, weapon
in hand. He therefore bypasses it with his peculiar smile, which is
the outward expression of an inner feeling of superiority. He is
not the slave of his environment but its master. His faith in God
gives him the strength to weather all storms and to arrive at the
optimistic conclusion that, bad as things seemingly are, they could
after all have turned out worse. One should therefore continue
to sing the praises of the Almighty.

Tevye is always conscious of unbridgeable differences between
Jews and their incited neighbors who pogromize them, whenever
profitable, but who remain on friendly terms before and after the
pogroms. He is therefore horrified at the thought of his daughter
marrying outside of the Jewish fold, yet this blow too he has to
endure and he does so with dignity. He believes in Jews steering
clear of political subversive activities and revolutionary circles
and then has to see another of his daughters falling in love with
an anti-Czarist conspirator and ending with the husband of her
choice in Siberia. Tevye believes in the importance of family background and of middle-class respectability—*Yikhes*—and yet he
has to consent to another of his daughters marrying beneath her
social station. The world of Kasrilevke, the typical traditional
Jewish townlet, is changing rapidly and Tevye has to adjust to
new social values, but he will under no circumstances alter his
moral concepts, which stem from his biblical heritage and his
people's historic experiences. In the struggle between mind and
heart, Tevye's heart always carries off the victory. He makes a
great show of reasoning and, after his reason convinces him that

he ought to behave in a certain way, he still follows the promptings of intuition, often contrary to reason.

In the epistles of Menachem Mendel of Yehupetz, Sholom Aleichem presented another type of little man, the Jewish schlemihl and Don Quixote, the dynamic *Luftmensh,* who is always rushing about in feverish excitement, chasing after mirages which dissolve into nothingness upon closer examination, especially after wealth which seems to be around the corner and which always eludes him. He engages in speculative ventures which promise glamorous returns for meager investments and which always end in failure. Menachem Mendel is both a caricature of Sholom Aleichem's earlier self as well as a symbolic representative of the Jews of the humorist's generation who had outgrown the once stable solidity of Kasrilevke and who floundered about in the maelstrom of the larger cities and in the tumult of ever widening, unmanageable business and industrial horizons.

Sholom Aleichem taught Jews, enmeshed in troubles and goaded by a hostile environment, to laugh at the mess in which they found themselves. He depicted them living like members of one large family, gossiping and quarreling, but without venom, possessing a deep sense of responsibility and always ready to help each other in emergencies. They feel the pain of all mankind even though mankind is not interested in them. They wear gray, shabby clothes but their souls are colorful and alert, and Sholom Aleichem loved them with all their weaknesses and follies.

Most of all, he loved their children and he drew unforgettable portraits of youngsters who came like trailing clouds of glory from God's hand and who refused to grow up to see the world as adults see it. In the stories of Mottel Peise, the Cantor's son who was early orphaned, he created a boys' classic, the Yiddish equivalent of Mark Twain's *Tom Sawyer* and *Huckleberry Finn.* Mottel is carefree and innocent of guile. He loves the bright outdoors and is a friend to the calf, the goat and the cat. He never plans for a tomorrow and he does not want to adjust to respectability. He insists on being cheerful without knowing why and to find a humorous side in everything that comes to his notice. He engages in harmless pranks and cannot grasp why he is punished rather than applauded. When he becomes an orphan, he does not yield to sorrow, but finds a few bits of comfort in the midst of the grief surrounding his family. At least, he will not have to go to school for a while, his brother does not hit him during the days of mourning, his neighbors pity him and bring him gifts, his classmates envy him when he stands up like a grown-up and says *Kaddish* for his father. Hence, being an orphan does have a few compensations. His mother sheds tears when she contemplates leaving their home for distant America, but Mottel feels himself sprouting wings and flying on and on to the land of unlimited possibilities, where new-comers start as shoeshiners or newsboys and end as millionaires. He knows all about America before getting there and, when he arrives in New York, he is more at home there than all the grown-ups.

In addition to Tevye, Menachem Mendel and Mottel Peise, Sholom Aleichem created dozens of characters, men, women, children, Jews, Gentiles, patricians and peasants, all of whom are alive and from whose interactions the entire culture of the Russian Pale can be reconstructed. His satire is mild and not searing. His laughter is constructive and not devastating. He prefers to clothe his tales in the form of monologues by individuals who unburden their hearts to him and through him to his readers. He has no real villains and his heroes are heroic, not so much in their deeds, as in their quiet enduring of suffering and in their resilience which enables them to rise from defeats to ever new hope. They meet adversity smilingly even while the tears well up in their eyes. They always find an avenue of escape from despair by flight to the bright realm of dreams.

Sholom Aleichem arouses compassion for the frustrated lives of his insecure coreligionists in the Old World and he chastizes lovingly the misdirected hasty assimilation of Jews in the more affluent and more secure New World.

As a master of dialogue and as a keen observer of gestures and intonations, Sholom Aleichem experimented with drama as early as 1887. At first he began with one-act comedies, such as *The Doctor* (1887), *The Divorce* (*Der Get,* 1888) and *The Assembly* (*Die Asifa,* 1889). In 1894 he wrote his first longer play, *Yaknez,* a satire on the brokers and speculators of Yehupetz, but he could not get it published because of the Russian censor's objections. Almost another decade passed before he attempted another full-length comedy, *Scattered Far and Wide* (*Tsezeht Un Tseshpreht,* 1903). It proved to be his first successfully staged play. He then sought to dramatize scenes from his stories. An episode from his Menachem Mendel sketches served as the dramatic action of the one-act comedy *Agents* (*Agenten,* 1905). His early novel *Stempenyu* was adapted as the drama *Jewish Daughters* (*Yiedishe Tekhter,* 1905). It was staged in New York by Boris Tomashevsky in 1907 with little success and rather more successfully by Maurice Schwartz in 1929. In 1907 Sholom Aleichem completed his comedy *The Gold Diggers* (*Die Goldgreber*), which held the stage for many years, the most memorable performances being those of New York's Yiddish Art Theater in 1927 and of Tel Aviv's Habimah Theater in 1928.

The climax of Sholom Aleichem's dramatic creativity was reached in the plays *Hard to Be a Jew* (*Shver Tsu Zein a Yied*, 1914) and *The Jackpot* (*Dos Groisse Gevins*, 1916). The former play, which had been published as a novel two years earlier, was staged in 1920 by Maurice Schwartz with young Paul Muni in the role of the Christian student who exchanged identities with a Jewish student and thus discovered the hardships and discriminations with which Jews had to contend. This theme later influenced the main plot of the American bestselling novel *Gentleman's Agreement* by Laura Z. Hobson, published in 1947, a novel which enjoyed even greater popularity on the movie and television screens. *The Jackpot* provided Maurice Schwartz with one of his most artistic roles, that of Shimele Soroker, and he appeared in it from 1922 onwards. The play was also included in the repertoire of the Vilna Troupe in 1923, of the Moscow Yiddish Theater throughout the 1920's, and of the Habimah since 1932.

None of Sholom Aleichem's fictional and dramatic characters equalled the vogue of Tevye on the world's stages. The author himself, in a letter to David Pinski, called Tevye the crown of his creative career. *Tevye's Daughters* was first played as a tragicomedy by Maurice Schwartz in 1919 and then in a film version two decades later. Shlomo Michoels, the greatest of Soviet Yiddish actors, starred in the role of Tevye during Moscow performances at the height of World War II in 1943. The Habimah presented Tevye in Hebrew and Arnold Perl adapted Tevye in English for American audiences. The musical *Fiddler on the Roof* also centered the dramatic action about Tevye and his daughters, and was the first successful English musical with a subject-matter based on Eastern European Jewish life.

Sholom Aleichem anecdotes and aphorisms are retold wherever Jews congregate. He taught them how to seek liberation from pain in jest, how to get along without the plaudits of others, how to retain inner dignity and humaneness in an undignified, dehumanized world, how to attain inner happiness by following timeless Jewish folkways. With him and with Peretz, Yiddish literature comes of age.

5

EARLY YIDDISH THEATER

Goldfaden ● Lateiner ● Moshe Hurwitz ● Jacob
Gordin ● Kobrin ● Libin ● Hirshbein ● Pinski

ABRAHAM GOLDFADEN was the father of the Yiddish theater.
Until his appearance Yiddish drama was largely book drama because a Yiddish stage was non-existent. When Goldfaden first
burst upon the Jewish scene in Rumania in 1876, at the age of
thirty-six, he found theatrical activity restricted to amateur Purim
players, the monologues of Badchonim, and the improvisation of
the Broder Singers. When he died in New York in 1908, he left the
Yiddish theater a flourishing institution, a strong factor in Jewish
cultural survival, an artistic medium unsurpassed by the Broadway theater of his day.

Goldfaden stemmed from the Volynian town of Starokonstantin.
He received a good Hebrew and secular education but he was also
taught his father's trade of watchmaking so that he could support himself at an early age, if the need arose of smuggling him
across the border to Rumania to save him from impressment in
the Czarist army. When the Czarist authorities offered exemption
from military service to Jewish boys who attended special government schools, young Goldfaden was sent to such a school at fourteen and then to the Zhitomir Rabbinical Academy at seventeen.
At Zhitomir he came under the influence of enlightened teachers
such as Abraham Baer Gottlober, Eliezer Zvi Zweifel and Hayim
Selig Slonimsky. He began his literary career with the publication
of Hebrew poems in 1862 in the periodical *Hamelitz* and of Yiddish poems in 1863 in *Kol Mevasser,* the Yiddish supplement of
Hamelitz. His first booklet of Hebrew songs was printed in 1865,
his first collection of Yiddish songs, *The Little Jew (Dos Yiedele),*

73

in 1866, and his second Yiddish collection, *The Little Jewess* (*Die Yiedene*), in 1869. Badchonim and folksingers disseminated his songs far and wide.

The decade after Goldfaden's graduation from the Rabbinical Academy in 1866 was a difficult one for him. He was unhappy as a government school teacher in Crimea and Odessa and unsuccessful in various business undertakings. Journalistic ventures in Lemberg, Czernowitz and Jassy also proved to be failures. In Jassy he saw the Broder Singers acting out Yiddish songs, including his own, in wine-cellars and restaurant-gardens. The thought then occurred to him that the dramatic effect of the songs and impersonations could be heightened if these were combined with prose dialogues and woven into an interesting plot. He thereupon gathered a few singers and with them rehearsed scenarios which he himself composed. As in the commedia dell' arte, the exact words were largely left to the inspiration of the moment on the stage. The actors were given the plot, the songs, and general instructions what to talk about but not precisely what to say.

In October 1876, the first performances took place in Jassy. The audiences were spellbound by the rapid succession of actions and interspersed lyrics—an entirely novel experience. The initial success spurred Goldfaden on to project an entire series of comedies in other towns of Rumania and Russia. He engaged wandering minstrels and cantors' assistants whom he undertook to train as actors. He even dared a greater innovation: the acting of feminine roles by women rather than by men disguised as women. His native Volynian pronunciation became the standard stage pronunciation, even though the Lithuanian dialect was preferred on the lecture platform. His troupe was in great demand. With every year it expanded its repertoire, travelling throughout Eastern Europe. Soon other troupes of itinerant actors arose, either under his guidance or in competition with him. Most of these flourished and planned ever new repertoires—when suddenly catastrophe struck.

The Russian government, fearing this mass medium for stirring emotions, determined to put an end to it before it might be converted into a revolutionary weapon. In 1883, the authorities banned all performances in Yiddish, thus forcing dramatic authors, actors and producers to emigrate to other lands. Paris, London, New York established Yiddish theaters and Goldfaden himself had to follow this westward movement. In 1887, he arrived in New York. After a brief flurry of success, he encountered severe competition from producers and from text writers, such as Joseph

Lateiner (1853-1935) and Moshe Hurwitz (1844-1910), nicknamed Professor, who were even more prolific than he was.

Goldfaden found Europe more congenial and returned to produce and direct performances of his plays in London, Paris and Lemberg. He did not again cross the Atlantic until 1903 and he spent his last five years in New York.

Of Goldfaden's early plays before 1880, the most successful were *Schmendrik*, a satirical comedy which castigated the follies of ghetto life, *Kuni-Lemel*, a Yiddish parallel to Plautus' *Menaechmi* and Shakespeare's *Comedy of Errors*, and *Kabzensohn et Hungerman*, a Yiddish parallel to Molière's *Les Précieuses Ridicules*. The title heroes of these comedies soon became household words for certain Jewish types and are still familiar to Yiddish speaking persons. A "schmendrik," for example, is an individual who is stupid but not vicious, gullible but not vengeful, glad to accept the gifts of life which come unsought but easily reconciled to loss and failure. The original, one-eyed, lame, stuttering Kuni-Lemel is still present in the consciousness of elders who admonish their children and grandchildren not to become ugly Kuni-Lemels.

The comedy *Kuni-Lemel* and the melodrama *Kabzensohn et Hungerman* maintained themselves on the Yiddish stage until the close of the 1960's. A Hebrew version and a film adaptation of the former play were still box-office successes in Israel after the Six Day War.

Although Goldfaden's basic aim was to entertain, he also recognized the necessity of offering moral elevation when addressing himself to Jewish audiences. His early plays satirized, though without venom, seamy aspects of Jewish life. He rebuked elders for imposing their will upon youth with too great harshness and he rebuked youth for feeding on romantic delusions and disregarding the wisdom of their elders. When pogroms assailed Jewish communities in the 1880's however, he became guilt-stricken for having unwittingly and needlessly exposed his coreligionists to the ridicule of their Gentile neighbors. Successful performances of *Schmendrik* in Moscow in 1880 had resulted in amused Moscovites baiting Jews by calling them "schmendriks." To supply ammunition to anti-Semites was not the intent of his witty, satiric, dramatic gibes. He therefore sought to atone by more serious dramas composed during the pogrom decade. These retained the spectacular scenes and catchy tunes which had endeared him to the Jewish masses, but they also directed his audiences to seek inspiration in glorious events of the Jewish past and to dream of a Messianic Jewish future in the land of Israel.

In the romantic musical drama *Shulamith,* which he wrote on the eve of the pogroms, his transition from the earlier carefree period to his later Zionist period was already foreshadowed. In *Doctor Almasado,* his immediate reaction to these pogroms led him to project as the symbol of the Jew not a schlemihl, but rather a hard-working, wise and unselfish physician, the savior of his community in the hour of its greatest distress. The fanatics, fools and idlers of the early comedies made way in the works of the 1880's for national heroes who risked life and liberty in defense of their holy people. The most famous of these heroes, into whom Goldfaden infused new vigorous life in 1882, was Bar-Kochba, the Jewish warrior who opposed oppression with armed might in the last, desperate revolt against the Romans. Memorable scenes of the tragedy included the coronation of Bar-Kochba on Mt. Moriah at the end of the first act; his taming of a raging lion in the arena at the end of the second act; his bride Dina addressing the besieging Jewish army from the battlement of Caesarea, where she was held captive by the Romans, and then hurling herself down from the wall so that her compatriots should not be restrained from storming the fortress by fears for her safety.

If *Shulamith, Doctor Almasado* and *Bar-Kochba* called upon Jews to remember ancient splendor, prowess and glory, other plays of Goldfaden beginning with *Messianic Age (Moshiakhs Tseiten),* composed in 1887, a decade before the First Zionist Congress at Basel, and continuing to *Ben-Ami,* which had its premiere a few days before Goldfaden's death in 1908, looked toward the future and called for Jewish fulfillment as pioneer tillers of the soil in the Holy Land. The former play stressed the disillusionment which overtook Russian Jews, who had mistakenly placed their faith in the growth of the spirit of progress in the Czarist Empire, and who had been equally disappointed with their haven of refuge in America, where they had become victims to the mania for wealth. Only in Palestine did they find happiness, physical rehabilitation and moral regeneration.

The latter play, *Ben-Ami,* was to a large extent an adaptation of George Eliot's Zionist novel, *Daniel Deronda,* which had a profound impact upon Eastern European Jewish readers after its publication in 1876, and which stirred Goldfaden's imagination for decades. When the Kishinev Pogrom of 1903 ushered in a repetition of the tragic massacres of the 1880's, he was deeply disturbed by the indifference of the so-called civilized countries toward reports of brutalities against Jews. Bitterly he commented: "The civilized lands have clearly shown by their murderous silence that the wild bear acted correctly. They would perhaps also behave in the same way but they are afraid it is not proper. Anyhow, they were contenting themselves with closing their gates as quickly as possible for the wretched victims who were in flight, trying to save their lives under the light of the angels of freedom, the light of bronze statues." Goldfaden felt that heroic deeds were needed and not ineffective lamentation. His deed as a dramatist was his play *Ben-Ami*. He defined its idea as follows: "More than ever do we Jews need firm unity. All sects, intrigues, castes, caprices, party squabbles must be relegated to secondary importance. Every true, loyal Jew must strive to help with thoughts and deeds, with propaganda and organization, to save his people, to work for its liberation and independence, to rescue it from discouragement, and to pour into its bitter cup at least a few sweet drops of faith in a better future. This is the basic idea of my new drama: *Ben-Ami*."

Goldfaden's hero was a Viennese Baron, whose ethnographic studies led him to Odessa. While there, he witnessed a pogrom and was able to save a Jewish girl from the fury of the incited mob. From this girl, who was modelled on George Eliot's heroine Mirah, and from her brother Nehemiah, modelled on Eliot's Mordecai, the Baron gained deep insight into the Jewish soul. When he later learned that, though raised in a Gentile world, he was in reality of Jewish origin, the grandson of a famous rabbinical scholar of Prague, he gladly took upon himself the destiny of Jewishness with all its burdens and all its blessings. He married the girl whom he had rescued and emigrated with her to Palestine. There he hoped to train like-minded youths to be tillers of the soil and warriors for the Jewish national liberation. Incorporated in the play was a song, entitled *Salvation* (*Die Geula*), a hymn of joy for the children of Israel in days to come, a Messianic vision of the ingathering of the dispersed from all the corners of the world, a lyric expression of his faith in a Jewish heaven on the sacred shores of the Jordan and along the slopes of Sinai.

Goldfaden was not an original thinker, but he had the the talent to project on the stage the thoughts that coursed through the best minds of his generation. He did not invent his plots, but in the process of adapting them from successful European dramas and novels, he stripped them of their Russian, French, German or English characteristics and made them palatable to his Jewish audiences. The theatrical stage was for Goldfaden a replica of the stage of life. Even his supernatural characters—his demons and witches—were not merely symbols of spiritual realities, but also incarnations of beings that might be encountered in the flesh. Thus, in his popular drama *The Witch* (*Die Kishifmacherin*), Bobbe Yakhne was a living creature of malevolence and not a mere abstract personification of evil forces. Her opponent, the peddler Hotsmach, was not only an emissary of God's will, setting at naught the machinations of the wicked; he was also a vivid, lovable human being, laughable for his absurdities and adorable for his inexhaustible kindness.

Goldfaden's tragedies and comedies abounded in musical interludes. His catchy tunes and songs ranged from lullabies and dance melodies to patriotic hymns and festive choruses. Some of his lyrics, such as *Dos Pintele Yied* and *Yisrolik Kum Ahaim* have become folksongs known to millions.

Many of Goldfaden's sixty plays continued to be adapted by actors and producers and entered into the permanent repertoire of the Yiddish theater. The most notable of the adaptations were those undertaken by Itzik Manger.

To Goldfaden the theater was a medium for education and for stirring Jewish national patriotism, as well as for entertainment. He had faith in the curative power of laughter, in the fruitful mating of art and morality, in the benign union of beauty and goodness. He continued the traditions of the Maskilim, from whom he stemmed, and of the Badchonim, whose beginnings he carried on to dramatic fruition. His plays were successful because their texts and melodies, their philosophy and morality, were in harmony with the spirit of his people.

Goldfaden operettas formed the main repertoire of the early American Yiddish theater, whose beginnings go back to 1882. In that year Boris Tomashefsky (1866-1939), a cantor's son with a fine singing voice, made his debut in Goldfaden's *The Witch*. The lad of sixteen, who had been working in a cigar factory since landing in New York, instantly became the favorite of East Side theatergoers. After Yiddish dramatic productions were banned in Russia, he was joined by Jacob P. Adler (1855-1926) and David Kessler (1860-1920). These three pioneering actors became also the leading producers of the American Yiddish theater.

The demand for dramatic texts was satisfied by several writers who followed in Goldfaden's footsteps though with lesser ability. Joseph Lateiner, who arrived in New York in 1884, wrote the first full-length drama on an American subject, *Emigration to America* (*Die Emigratsie Kein Amerika*, 1886). He had become interested in the theater when he met Goldfaden six years earlier. His first play *The Two Shmelkes* (*Die Tsvai Shmelkes*, 1876) preceded Goldfaden's *Kuni-Lemel*, which it resembled. His more successfully staged play *Yente Pipernuter* of the following year starred the great actor Zygmund Mogulesco in the main role. Other plays followed in rapid succession. By 1880, the Lateiner-Mogulesco Troupe was Goldfaden's chief competitor in Odessa, but in 1883 Lateiner had to leave Russia. After a short stay in London, he devoted the following half-century to the writing and producing of about eighty plays in New York. At first he selected biblical and Jewish historical subjects but soon he turned to foreign sources, at times merely changing the names of non-Jewish characters to Jewish ones and inserting lyrics, couplets and slapstick humor.

Lateiner's chief rival was Moshe Hurwitz—"the Professor"— who arrived in New York in 1887 and soon overtopped him in prolific productivity, turning out plays and operettas that were effective as theatrical spectacles but generally devoid of literary value. Another competitor was Shomer who produced four successful plays during his first few months in New York in 1889. These three writers had an almost monopolistic hold upon the Yiddish theater and were not dislodged until Jacob Gordin (1853-1909) appeared upon the American scene in 1891.

Gordin emigrated to the New World with the intention of establishing an agricultural colony in which Tolstoyan ethical and social principles would find practical realizations. However, the need to support his large and growing family compelled him to turn from his utopian projects to more lucrative work. Upon the urging of Jacob P. Adler, he wrote his first full-length drama *Siberia*. It was staged toward the end of 1891 and with it the reform of the Yiddish theater was initiated.

Gordin adapted and originated more than seventy plays. He learned a great deal about dramatic construction by translating plays of Ibsen, Strindberg, Tolstoy, Gorky and Hauptmann, and by basing many of his own plays on excellent foreign models. He derived some of his plots from Euripides, Shakespeare, Calderon, Schiller, Gutzkow, Grillparzer, Hugo, Ostrovsky and Sudermann.

Gordin was a teacher of morals and the stage was his medium for inculcating ethical lessons. His favorite themes were the conflict of generations, the struggle between rich and poor, the strife within the family between decent and indecent behavior. The dramatist aroused nostalgia for the old ways which were disappearing in the New World as immigrants became Americanized. He moved his audiences to tears as he presented the suffering of good characters and the temporary triumph of selfish ones.

Gordin's first success was achieved with *The Jewish King Lear* (*Der Yiedisher Kenig Lear*, 1892). The play, which adapted to Jewish needs the Shakespearean theme of the ingratitude of children, attracted to the theater Jewish intellectuals who normally shunned the operettas of Lateiner and Hurwitz. The conflict between immigrant parents and Americanized children was then raging with full force in Jewish homes. Parents saw their own heartache mirrored on the stage and often brought their wayward children to the Yiddish performances so that these might learn to behave with greater consideration. Even more successful was Gordin's *Mirele Efros* in 1898, the tragedy of a Queen Lear, a strong-willed Jewish mother who ran her business and her household in imperial fashion but who, in a moment of weakness, turned over the reins to her children. These soon made it impossible for her to remain in her own home. Only years later did they recognize their folly and regret their misbehavior after they themselves had undergone much suffering. This play was a favorite with Jewish audiences for more than half a century and was revived in Warsaw and New York in the 1960's, with Ida Kaminska in the title role.

In the tragedy *God, Man, and the Devil* (*Gott, Mensh un Teivel*, 1903), strongly influenced by the Book of Job and by Goethe's *Faust*, Gordin wrestled with the problem of man's dual nature. In Hershele Dubrovner, the leading character, he portrayed a poor, pious Jew whom Satan sought to deflect from righteousness by showering wealth upon him. At the end, the devilish tempter had to confess that money could seduce, corrupt and cripple, but it could not entirely destroy the human soul. Conscience, temporarily drugged by affluence, would ultimately reassert itself.

In *Sappho* (1907), Gordin presented the emancipated woman who was prepared to follow the call of love wheresoever it might lead her, and whatsoever the consequences she might have to endure from outraged public opinion. In *Elisha Ben Abuya* (1907), he presented a male counterpart, a Jewish heretic of the second century who rebelled against traditional beliefs and who also was willing to accept ostracism and loneliness as the price for freedom to think his own thoughts and to live in accordance with his own concept of truth. Sudermann's *Magda* was the model for the former play and Gutzkow's *Uriel Acosta* for the latter.

Gordin, even as Goldfaden before him, saw in the theater an educational medium, a stimulus to thinking, and not merely a pleasant means of relaxation. His dramas presented characters that were alive, situations that were real, social issues which were vigorously debated by his contemporaries, moral dilemmas which demanded solutions. He weaned his audiences from melodramas and musical farces, he accustomed his actors to more natural acting, he raised the stage to an arena on which human wills clashed, human emotions exploded, and conflicting ideas were clarified. He ushered in the Golden Era of the Yiddish theater, paving the way for able disciples, such as Leon Kobrin (1873-1946) and Z. Libin (1872-1955).

Kobrin's early play *Minna* (1899) profited from Gordin's collaboration and his following play *Nature, Man and Beast* (*Natur, Mensh un Khaye*, 1900) echoed in its very title Gordin's *God, Man, and Devil*. Kobrin, however, moralized less and visualized more. He generally started, not from an idea or a problem, as did Gordin, but from character. He had his heroes and heroines battle antithetical forces within their own nature. He had them fight their way out of the moral dilemmas into which they were hurled, or die in the attempt. His dramatic striving reached its apex in *Yankel Boila* (1908), the tragedy of a strong, kindhearted but dull-witted Jewish youth in a Russian fishing village who was embroiled in a complex moral and emotional dilemma to which he could find no solution short of suicide. Kobrin had a keen ear for the melodies of the human heart. He projected lovers wrestling with duty, modesty, fear and pride. He showed them exultant in complete abandonment to their emotions at one moment and remorse-ridden and despairing soon thereafter. Kobrin's dramatization of nature's fierce sex claims upon man and woman was a daring innovation on the Yiddish stage. In depicting raw passions in their brutal nakedness, he had been preceded by David Pinski in Russia but by no contemporary in the New World. From his arrival in Philadelphia in 1892, he had himself experienced the harsh fate of the pioneering Yiddish generation, and he could therefore bring to the stage in vivid colors the fierceness of the factory struggles, the filth of the slums, the idealism of the strikers, and the hunger for bread and love.

Z. Libin, who emigrated from a Russian townlet to the United States a few months before Kobrin, began as a writer of short stories about Jewish proletarians, grim portraits of the anguish and tears of tenement dwellers in New York's East Side, faithful reproductions of real situations softened now and then by lyric sentimentalism. In 1900 he was successful with his first dramatic effort and this was followed by dozens of comedies and tragedies. The most popular of his serious plays was *Broken Hearts* (*Gebrokhene Hertser,* 1903). Its theme was the conflict between love and duty. It held the stages of Europe and America for many years and was filmed in 1926, with Maurice Schwartz in the main role.

With the death of Gordin in 1909, there began a decline of Yiddish drama in America, a decline which was only temporarily slowed down by the founding of the Yiddish Art Theater by Maurice Schwartz a decade later. Though many reasons have been given for this decline, the chief factor was the reduction of the size of the potential Yiddish audience because of the stoppage of mass Jewish immigration upon the outbreak of the First World War and the gradual transition of Americanized Jews to English as their normal speech. Only the heroic efforts of talented authors, composers, actors and producers enabled the Yiddish theaters to continue the struggle for survival in America until the mid-twentieth century.

Meanwhile in Russia, with the lifting in 1904 of the ban on Yiddish productions, a ban which had been in effect for two decades, drama was experiencing a revival. Plays by Peretz, Sholom Aleichem, David Pinski, Sholem Asch and Peretz Hirshbein could be staged.

The most dynamic spirit in this revival was Hirshbein (1880-1948), a dramatist of superb literary caliber and also a producer and director of tremendous energy. Hirshbein had begun with Hebrew dramas, which were published in the periodical *Hazman,* but there was no possibility of letting these resound from the boards of a theater because there was as yet no audience for Hebrew plays. The first Hebrew troupe, the Habimah, was not founded until 1917. In 1906, Hirshbein therefore turned to the writing of Yiddish plays. The earliest of these, *On the Other Side of the River* (*Oif Yener Zeit Taikh,* 1906), broke with the naturalistic portrayal of Jewish life which had characterized his Hebrew play of the preceding year, *Miriam,* the tragedy of a Jewish prostitute, and which led Reuben Brainin to confer upon him the title of dramatic poet of the cellar-dwellings. This title was, however, soon replaced by that of the Yiddish Maeterlinck because of the symbolist technique which the young dramatist came to prefer and which emphasized the communication of moods rather than the presentation of reality in lucid imagery.

Hirshbein's plays included *Earth* (*Die Erd,* 1907), in which his longing for an escape from the city to a simpler life close to nature found expression; *Contract* (*Tkias Kaf,* 1907), the tragedy of a Jewish girl whose marriage to a young man she loved was thwarted by her father who had pledged her hand to a mate of his choice— a theme which foreshadowed S. Anski's *Dybbuk,* which held the stage for fully half a century after its first performance in 1920; and *Parting of the Ways* (*Oifn Shaidveg,* 1907), in which he portrayed the emancipated Jewish woman who dared to fashion her own fate.

In 1908, encouraged by Bialik, Hirshbein organized in Odessa the Hirshbein Troupe of actors to present Yiddish dramas of high literary quality. For two years he wandered about Russia giving performances chiefly of his own plays, but also those of Sholem Asch, David Pinski, Jacob Gordin and Sholom Aleichem. In the summer of 1910 financial difficulties compelled the dissolution of the Hirshbein Troupe. The actors he had trained in ensemble playing, however, continued this tradition for a long time, and his crusading efforts were followed by the formation a few years later of the Vilna Yiddish Troupe and the New York Yiddish Art Theater.

Hirshbein's restlessness led him in 1911 to Vienna, Paris, London and New York, and in later years to world encircling journeys of long duration. In 1912 he completed the dramas *The Haunted Inn* (*Die Puste Kretshme*) and *A Neglected Nook* (*A Farvorfen Vinkel*). In them realism and mysticism were strangely intertwined. Unable to have them staged before the founding of the Yiddish Art Theater in 1918, he tried to eke out a living as a farmhand in the Catskills. In 1913 he returned to Russia but could not again take root there. On the eve of the First World War he set out for Argentina where Jewish agricultural colonies were being developed with funds supplied by Baron de Hirsch. Disillusioned after a few months, he sought to make his way to the United States but the British ship on which he sailed was sunk by a German cruiser. After perilous days of captivity, he was landed in Brazil and ultimately got to New York.

Of the plays he wrote during the war years, the most memorable was *Green Fields* (*Griene Felder,* 1916), which was later filmed. In 1918, the Yiddish Art Theater, of which Maurice Schwartz was the dynamic director, began with performances of two Hirshbein plays: *A Neglected Nook* and *The Smith's Daughters* (*Dem Schmids Tekhter*). The most successful actor in Hirshbein's plays was Jacob Ben Ami, who also starred on Broadway in 1924 in an English adaptation of *The Haunted Inn*.

Hirshbein was a supreme master of the natural dialogue, a creator of living characters with utmost economy of words. He brought back to the Yiddish stage literary quality on a level unknown since the death of Gordin. As the son of a miller, he was at his best in depicting the life of villagers and rugged characters close to the soil. The urban proletariat did not interest him. Even in his later works, written after the Communist upheaval, he preferred to deal with Jewish agriculturalists rather than with factory hands. His best novel, *Red Fields* (*Roite Felder*, 1935), depicted the post-revolutionary efforts to settle Jews in Crimean farming collectives.

It was his friend, David Pinski (1872-1959), who pioneered in bringing to the Yiddish stage the tragedy of the exploited city worker at a time when industrialization in Eastern Europe was still in its infancy. When Pinski entered upon his long literary career in 1892, Naturalism was the dominant tendency. It was the year in which Gerhart Hauptmann had scored a sensational success with his Naturalistic play *The Weavers* (*Die Weber*). Though Pinski's first play, *Isaac Sheftel*, was not completed until 1899, the influence of Hauptmann's tragedy was unmistakable.

Stimulated by Peretz, Pinski had begun as a writer of realistic short stories and had already obtained a considerable reputation in Warsaw before he settled in Berlin in 1896 and turned to drama. Isaac Sheftel, the title-hero of Pinski's Naturalistic tragedy, was a Jewish weaver with a creative urge. Mocked by his family, harassed by his fellow-workers, underpaid by his boss who grew fat on his inventions, he nevertheless put up mutely with all hardships and ill-will until the breaking-point was reached. Then, in a magnificent gesture of rage and defiance, he revolted against his lot, smashing and trampling upon the machines to which his fertile brain had earlier given birth. This destructive deed was the impulsive protest of a fettered, inarticulate individual, the desperate act of a creature at bay. It led him not to salvation but despair, drunken stupor, self-annihilation.

Isaac Sheftel was the prototype of Pinski's unheroic heroes who reacted to their cruel environment on the basis of inner urges, naked souls with a mixture of brutality and tenderness, callousness and kindness. These characters spoke the Yiddish of the market-place and the workbench, broken sentences, ejaculated phrases, repetitive monosyllables.

Pinski's comedy *The Treasure* (*Der Oitzer*), upon which he worked from 1902 to 1906, gave him an international reputation. It was staged by Max Reinhardt in Berlin's *Deutsches Theater* in German in 1910, even before it reached Yiddish audiences. It exposed to laughter the greed of the human species. A rumor that the idiotic son of the town's gravedigger had discovered a buried treasure in the Jewish cemetery led to a procession to his hovel of the dignitaries, the communal leaders, the charity officials and the ordinary people, all of whom expected to reap some benefit from their flattery of the new capitalist. When the gravedigger confessed, however, that he was completely ignorant of the treasure's precise location, then men and women, old and young, religious and irreligious, rushed out in the night to dig up the cemetery in the hope of being the fortunate ones to locate the treasure. In the process they desecrated the graves and disturbed the shrouded dead whom they delayed from getting to the synagogue for the usual post-midnight ghostly services. Pinski's laughter was without malice and his portrait of human folly had an educational and moral undertone.

Under the impact of the Kishinev Pogrom, Pinski wrote in 1903 and 1904 his tragedy *Family Tsvi*, in which he called upon Jews to undertake active resistance against their foes. If these foes denied them the right to live like human beings, they could not prevent them from facing death like human beings. To the older generation, represented by the grandfather Reb Moshe Zvi, the town's religious preacher, resistance meant rushing to the synagogue to defend God's holy scrolls against desecration by unholy hands. To the youngest generation, represented by his three grandsons, resistance had the more secular motivation, the preservation of human lives. One grandson, an adherent of the Bund, took up arms in the name of a cosmopolitan, socialist humanitarianism. Another grandson, an adherent of Zionism, did so in order to save from destruction precious lives of a segment of the dispersed Jewish people who were some day to be ingathered in their own Palestinian homeland. The third grandson, whose ideal of Russification had estranged him from his family, became disillusioned with his assimilationist panacea when anti-Jewish riots swept through the town's streets and he rushed back to the synagogue to offer help to his grandfather, the religious zealot, even though he himself had no faith in the survival of the old, beautiful Jewishness in the new century. With the death of the grandfather, the last pillar of the once splendid traditional structure collapsed. The play ended with the question: What now?

Family Tsvi had a profound impact upon pre-revolutionary Russian Jews, even though it had to be printed and circulated surreptitiously, since no censor could give it the official stamp of approval. It was performed by subversive amateur groups under great risk.

A new aspect of Pinski's dramatic activity came to the fore with *Yenkel the Smith* (*Yenkel der Shmid*, 1906), completed a few months after *Family Tsvi*. While Pinski had until then been as reticent as most Yiddish writers in the treatment of sensual love, in this play he let the lure of the flesh appear in all its intensity, fury and havoc. He did not glamorize illicit love. He was merely saddened by its prevalence and the damage it wrought in family relationships. Yenkel, the title-hero, was shown as torn between his love for his own wife and his inability to resist the spell of his neighbor's wife. The latter sought out the robust, healthy smith and exposed him to temptation, not because she was wicked, but rather because she was married to a good-natured, adoring weakling who did not answer her need for sense-intoxicating joy. In the end, the characters worked their way out of the entrapping morass of sensuality into an acceptance of family living which neither negated the joy of the flesh nor avoided moral responsibility. This play was acted more often than any of Pinski's earlier or later ones.

In *Gabri and His Women* (*Gabri Un Die Froen*, 1908), the dramatist again showed the man of strong passions wrestling with temptation and ultimately finding a way out of guilt and impurity, back to moral health and a stable marriage relationship. Pinski idealized the women who carried their burdens faithfully as wives and mothers, who penetrated with intuitive insight into far deeper layers of a man's personality than did the flamboyant adventuresses, and who were so patient, so tolerant, so dutiful, so forgiving that they offered a lasting haven to their erring husbands, a sheltering home after emotional hurricanes.

In *Mary of Magdala* (1910), Pinski dramatized the transformation of the passionate votary of Venus to an ascetic follower of Jesus, the new prophet. She, whose sensual magnetism irresistibly attracted all men and who compelled even the zealots of Jehova to succumb to her intense lure, experienced liberation from the turbulence of the flesh when she encountered the selfless, all-understanding and all-forgiving love of the Nazarene.

In *Professor Brenner,* written in 1911, Pinski centered the dramatic action about the love of an aging man for a young girl. This theme had been popularized on the European stage by three dramatists who exerted great influence upon him—Ibsen in *The Master Builder* (1892), Gerhart Hauptmann in *The Sunken Bell* (1896), and Arthur Schnitzler in *The Lonely Way* (1903) and *The Vast Domain* (1908). This theme had not been treated earlier by Yiddish playwrights because marriage between an elderly man and a young girl, if occurring among Jews, was based not upon emotional fascination but upon convenience and family considerations.

Pinski was primarily a dramatist of ideas. Just like his adored models, Ibsen, Hauptmann and Schnitzler, he too made the transition from realism to symbolism. His symbolist technique was most evident in his historical and Messianic dramas. In his play *The Mountain Climbers (Die Bergshteiger,* 1912), his symbolism verged upon the purely allegoric. The locale of the four acts was the mountain of life which we all climb. At its peak stood the inn where the innkeeper Death arranged for all who completed the difficult ascent to spend the long, peaceful night. The play voiced Pinski's irrepressible optimism, his faith that goodness conferred happiness upon all whom it touched, that just to breathe, just to pant on earth, was a wonderful experience, and that our last cry should be a cry of exultation that we were privileged to participate in life's journey, no matter how brief or dangerous this journey was.

Pinski's optimism also revealed itself in his earliest Messianic tragedy *The Eternal Jew (Der Eibiger Yied,* 1906). Though the dramatic action took place in Jerusalem on the day of the Temple's destruction by the Romans, nevertheless his stress was on the prophetic revelation that a child born during that catastrophe would be the savior who would restore the departed glory. A suddenly erupting storm, however, carried the newly born infant far away and the prophet had no choice but to wander over the earth in search of the vanished Messiah. With this one-act play the Habimah Troupe initiated its first season in Moscow in 1918. The theme was especially appropriate for the post-revolutionary year. It portrayed Jewish national death but it also held out the promise of Jewish national rebirth and liberation from foreign oppression. The year 1917, the year of the Balfour Declaration and of the overthrow of the Czarist regime, seemed to bring fulfillment of the promise. However, in the storm which blew up unexpectedly and carried off the Messiah, theater-goers, in 1918, saw a symbolic depiction of the storming pogrom-bands of Petlura that compelled Jews, after a brief year of exultation, to set out again in search of Messianic salvation. Maxim Gorky was moved to tears at the first performance and went to see the play a second and a third time. He felt the ecstasy and the deep holiness which enveloped actors and spectators alike at these memorable performances and wrote an enthusiastic report which helped to gain the revolutionary regime's support for Habimah.

Pinski's second Messianic drama was *The Mute Messiah* (*Der Shtumer Moshiakh,* 1919). Between the two world wars, he completed three full length plays about the three Messianic aspirants Bar-Kochba, Shlomo Molcho, and Sabbatai Zvi. He was also attracted to saintly personalities ranging from Rabbi Akiba to the Baal Shem, and to biblical characters from Noah to David. After settling in Israel in 1949, a rejuvenated burst of creativity came to him and in the ninth decade of his life he completed dramas of Samson and King Saul.

By then, however, there were no longer any Yiddish theaters which could stage them and Yiddish drama which had been largely book drama before the innovations of Goldfaden in the 1870's again reverted to a mere literary genre designed for readers rather than spectators.

6

AMERICAN LYRIC PIONEERS

Mass Immigration • The Social Lyric • Edelstadt •
Bovshover • Vinchevsky • Morris Rosenfeld • Liessin
• Yehoash • Rosenblatt • Rolnick • Die Yunge •
Mani-Leib • Zisha Landau • Iceland • Dillon •
Lapin • M. L. Halpern • Weinper • Moshe Nadir
• I. I. Schwartz

THE AMERICAN JEWISH population of about a quarter of a
million in 1880 had jumped to well over three million by 1917
when America entered the First World War. The new Jewish immigrants came in the overwhelming majority from Eastern Europe
and were Yiddish-speaking.

It was not the lure of adventure that led these average human
beings, who had rarely gone far from the provinces of their birth,
to undertake fabulous journeys by land and sea to a strange and
distant continent. It was need, physical, economic and ideological,
that hurled them forth from ghetto communities where stood the
graves of their forefathers and the cradle of their childhood, and
it was the American Dream that impelled them to direct their
steps westward rather than eastward and that gave them the
courage to face the perilous voyage and all the hardships of the
months and years of transition from their accustomed ways to a
totally unaccustomed new life.

Their basic need was the need for survival. Existence itself was
becoming increasingly precarious. Although individual Yiddish-
speaking Jews had found their way across the Atlantic ever since
the Colonial Era, it was only in New York that they formed a
significant group prior to the Civil War. During the Reconstruction Era, their number was increased when Jews fled from the
cholera which swept the Polish provinces in 1868 and from the

89

famine which raged in Lithuania in 1869. The next decade, which began with a pogrom in Odessa in 1871, the third in half a century, and which continued with constantly mounting pressures upon the overpopulated Pale, brought close to thirty thousand Russian Jewish immigrants to America's shores. This immigration was, however, only a ripple compared to the tidal wave that swept across the Atlantic when the panic stricken masses stampeded from Russia after the more virulent pogroms which began in 1881. Following the assassination of Czar Alexander II, mobs attacked Jews at Elizabethgrad, Kiev, Odessa, Smela, Neshin, Balta, Rostov, Yekaterinoslav, Krivorog, Nishni-Novgorod, and dozens of smaller communities, while police and soldiers looked on with indifference and even amusement.

In the autocratic state of Alexander III, the successor of Alexander II, anti-Jewish demonstrations of such magnitude and accompanied by so much violence could not have taken place repeatedly without the tolerance, if not connivance, of the highest government authorities. Jews in towns ravaged by pogroms correctly sensed that life itself was in constant danger and that lasting safety was possible only by fleeing across the border. Yet, even in communities relatively less exposed to massacres, the basis for economic survival was undermined by an epidemic of conflagrations which somehow singled out the large Jewish quarters of many towns and also by a series of legislative acts promulgated in May 1882 for the purpose of compressing the Jewish population into an ever shrinking area and into ever fewer professions and thus compelling mass emigration.

Coupled with the physical danger and the economic destitution, which acted as stimulants to emigration, there was also the idealized legend of America that had taken ever firmer root in the minds and hearts of the denizens of the Pale. The exploits of Columbus in discovering America—*Columbus's Medina*—as a haven of refuge for the oppressed were popularized in Yiddish ballads and proverbs. But there also seeped into ghetto communities an awareness of George Washington's supreme achievement in overthrowing the yoke of a European monarch and Abraham Lincoln's humane action in emancipating the victims of slavery.

Typical of the idealization of America by Jewish immigrants before their arrival on the new shores was a ballad of Eliakum Zunser, composed by him in 1889 on board ship and entitled "Columbus and Washington." Zunser hailed these two heroes as mankind's supreme benefactors, who were blessed by the unfortunate and the afflicted everywhere. The artisan, who labored honestly in Russia and yet could not make ends meet, betakes himself to the realm of Columbus and there his diligence is rewarded lavishly. The businessman, whom competitors unfairly denounced to cruel authorities and who could find no advocate to plead his just cause, escapes to the land of Washington, and there he prospers, unafraid of malice and protected against injustice. The girl, who was unmarried despite her beauty and intelligence because she lacked a dowry, sets sail for the marvelous country where dowries are unnecessary and where she soon finds a mate to her heart's desire and can live happily ever after. The embittered, despoiled bankrupt, who faced a debtor's prison, gets a new lease on hope and life when offered a chance to make a fresh start beyond the Atlantic. The actor, who was hounded by censors and plagued by capricious officials, sets out for the western Utopia where freedom of speech is assured to everyone. All these Jews and Jewesses join in blessing the navigator who opened a new world for them and the warrior who unfurled the flag of freedom for them.

Yiddish literature from the 1880's reflected the ever increasing importance of America in the thoughts and plans of the Eastern European Jews. The golden dreams of America as a modern Garden of Eden, as a heaven on earth, were, however, dissipated when the Jewish immigrant found himself face to face with the practical problems of earning his bread and adjusting himself to a culturally alien environment. American reality could not possibly measure up to the extravagant expectations of the newcomers. The reality encountered by Jewish immigrants was harsh, in fact far harsher for them than for any other immigrant group of their generation. A Scandinavian farmer could continue in Minnesota or in the Dakotas to plow, sow and reap even as he had in his native land. A German artisan could carry on his handicraft in Milwaukee even as he had in Munich or Stuttgart. A Polish miner, settling along the Allegheny Mountains, could descend daily into the bowels of the earth and cleave the rocks that yielded anthracite or iron ore without too great a deviation from the pattern of his accustomed life along the Carpathian range. But a Jew from Russia or Galicia or Rumania had to undergo a more thorough metamorphosis before he could fit into his new environment. Childhood in a *kheder,* boyhood in a *yeshiva,* youthful years spent over Talmudic tracts, or adult years as a small storekeeper dealing in penny wares, did not prepare a Jewish newcomer for the grueling life of a sweatshop toiler or the agonizing experiences of a pushcart peddler on New York's Hester Street or Chicago's Maxwell Street.

The bitter lot of this immigrant group, its poverty and destitution, the foulness of its slums and the disgrace of its cut-throat competition were often described in government reports and naturalistic novels, in essays by social workers and articles by talented muckrakers. Memoirs and biographies of articulate pioneers were replete with details of the converted cattle-ships from which thousands of immigrants were spewed out upon the Promised Land, after going through purgatory abroad, after being shuttled about from one unfriendly European community to another and after being degraded, insulted and helped by well-meaning but overwhelmed relief committees.

The reception of these uncouth, penniless, strangely-garbed aliens at Castle Garden or at Ellis Island—the island of tears—and the loneliness and starvation of the first days on the new soil were favorite themes for Yiddish story-tellers and balladists. But Yiddish writers also called attention to the spiritual beauty, the moral grandeur, the burning idealism, the Messianic dreams, and the cooperative spirit that made the life of the immigrants more bearable. The lonely individual was embedded in the group. The unemployed *greenhorn* on the verge of starvation could seek out the helping hand of a far distant relative, of a slightly less poor *landsman,* of a fellow-Jew. Though the *greenhorn,* a term of contempt to which the immigrant was most sensitive, generally shed not only his outlandish clothes, and his patriarchal beard but also his Sabbath rest, his traditional festivals, and even his God, under the impact of the cruel, grinding reality, he found a new faith in the various utopian movements which clamored for his attention. Anarchist slogans of Proudhon, Bakunin, Kropotkin and Johann Most, socialist slogans of Marx, Engels, Lassalle and August Bebel were espoused by hungry souls and recited at shop-meetings and cellar-assemblies with the same religious ardor and the same limited understanding with which in former years these Jews had intoned in the synagogues the Hebrew phrases of the Orthodox ritual. The emaciated peddler, tailor or cigar-maker was ready to give his last hard-earned pennies for the cause of a vague internationalism; he was willing to die, if necessary, for the greater good of an abstract humanity; he yearned to sacrifice himself for mankind in general, although he was unable to define this radiant objective in specific, practical terms.

It was this faith, this idealism, this longing for social justice, this striving for freedom for fellowmen, this immersion in activities for a better tomorrow, this Jewish Messianism, which saved the creatures of the slums from stupor, from depravity, from the swamp of sensuality, and which enabled them to build the great Jewish trade unions, such as the International Ladies Garment Workers' Union and the Amalgamated Clothing Workers of America, as enduring monuments of their generation's striving.

Had the talents and energy which the Yiddish intellectuals of the immigrant generation devoted to organizing, agitating and leading the underprivileged masses been channelled in the direction of self-enrichment and personal advancement, then wealth and social prestige of the highest order could have been theirs. They preferred otherwise. They poured their lives into unselfish causes. They froze on picket lines. They were felled by police clubs. They were herded into jail night after night. But they knew community of spirit, they felt the warmth of brotherhood enveloping them, they were lifted to fame by the enthusiasm of countless admirers, they glowed with inner happiness. The street corner was their arena and the soap-box their pulpit. Their spoken words were fire and their pamphlets were literary bullets. These semi-starved poets and half-baked philosophers, these amateur political thinkers and passionate shop-agitators were, in the eyes of their followers, resplendent knights of the spirit. They brought a new holiness to the masses from whom the holiness of their fathers' faith had receded far, far away. David Edelstadt (1866-1892) Joseph Bovshover (1873-1915), Morris Vinchevsky (1856-1933), Morris Rosenfeld (1862-1923), and Abraham Liessin (1872-1938) were the most influential of the early Yiddish poets whose winged verses spoke to the hearts of the immigrant masses.

Despite eloquent and oftentimes bombastic appeals for Jewish unity, the Yiddish poets could not agree on a common platform. The two main camps which commanded the homage of the radical, non-Orthodox immigrants were the Anarchist and the Socialist. Edelstadt was the principal lyric voice of the savage-throated but otherwise mild mannered Anarchists.

Edelstadt was born in Kaluga, a town not far from Moscow. Jews were not normally permitted to live in this region but an exception was made for Jewish veterans, such as Edelstadt's father, who had completed a quarter of a century's service in the

Czarist army. The lad's Jewish education was scanty; his Russian education more adequate. At eleven he began to write poems in Russian. At fourteen he left for Kiev and there he witnessed the pogrom inflicted upon its Jews on May 8, 1881. This left a lasting impression upon him. The following year, though only sixteen, he joined the Am Olam group of emigrants who set out for America in order to live a life of freedom as Jewish agriculturalists in settlements based on mutual aid. He got as far as Cincinnati, where he found temporary employment as a button-hole maker in a clothing factory. The Haymarket-tragedy of 1886, which resulted in the hanging of four Anarchist leaders who had organized a strike and demonstration of Chicago workers, convinced him that there was also a struggle to be waged in the New World for the freedom of enslaved, exploited Jews and Christians. The weapon he could wield in this struggle was the poem of protest and wrath.

Edelstadt became the lyric tribune of the Jewish immigrant toilers in their revolt against the sweatshop system. He was the pioneer literary spokesman for the revolutionary, anarchist approach from 1889, when he published his first Yiddish song until his death three years later, at the age of twenty-six. His earliest poems included *My Testament,* a stirring hymn more effective than all the closely reasoned pamphlets of his fellow-radicals. It had an international vogue and was sung in Siberian prison cells no less than in New York sweatshops and cellar assemblies. Its four stanzas were inscribed as his epitaph on his tomb: "When I die, carry to my grave the flag reddened with toilers' blood and sing my free song of the enslaved Christian and Jew. I shall hear it in my grave and shed tears for them. But when there resounds to me the clash of swords in freedom's final battle, I'll sing from my grave and lend courage to the people's hearts."

In 1890 Edelstadt was called to New York to edit the Anarchist weekly *Freie Arbeiter Stimme.* The following year, his health, undermined by his restless activities as agitator, orator, writer, editor and union-organizer, compelled him to leave for Denver's tubercular sanatorium. In a poem, written three days before his end, he begged King Death to spare him awhile so that he could attack inhumanity and tyranny with renewed energy. In vain!

Edelstadt expected a revolution to break out in the immediate future on both sides of the Atlantic. Chains and thrones would then fall beneath the workers' swords. The golden rays of freedom would light up the entire earth and a social order based on kindness and mutual aid would come into being. His ideal was a world without rulers and without tears; where no separation would be made between thine and mine; where love would not be bought and sold but would bestow happiness according to its desire; where churches and synagogues would be converted into cattle-barns; where bullets and crowns would survive only in museums; where art, science, industry would topple superstition and ignorance; where every human personality would be held sacred and liberty would quicken every brain.

Meanwhile the poet must take his place at the vanguard of the struggle against moneybags and oppressors. Edelstadt therefore sang of prevailing injustice which must be righted. There were the miners who dug the coal that warmed others, coal colored with the blood of their exploited bodies. There was the aging tailor who looked back upon many years of toil with needle and scissors and who was still unsure of bread for his hungry wife and child. There was the pale, homeless orphaned girl doomed to perish in a sea of pain and tears. The only salvation for all of them was the coming revolution. The poet warned readers not to seek in his verses the holy tones of a Homeric harp or the classical beauty of Dante. His songs did not mature in a garden of flowers but in the dark abode of slavery. They stemmed from a slave's struggle against his lord. "My muse is a proletarian muse."

Edelstadt's pitying and inflaming lyrics were modelled upon Byron, Lermontov, Nekrasov, Heine and Freiligrath, and were sung for decades. Some became transformed into folksongs with constantly changing text. The poet himself became a legendary figure and the subject of many lyric tributes. He was hailed as the prophet of man's liberation from want, as a fiery comet who lit up the night of oppression, as an ailing troubadour who roused the tired and enfeebled to rebel against their wretched lot.

Among these tributes was an elegy by Joseph Bovshover composed on the day of Edelstadt's death, an elegy that immediately established Bovshover as his successor as the poet of the anarchist radicals. Bovshover had just arrived in America from Riga. He found extreme difficulty in adjusting to a stable existence. Haunted by poverty, he reacted by penning verses which lashed out against the world's iniquities. He had begun under the influence of Heine. He felt the inspiration of Edelstadt. However, he sang not only of a proletarian revolution but also of the workers' joy and pride in the product of their labor. Tones of Walt Whitman became audible in his poems as soon as he had mastered the English tongue, and he began to write English lyrics under the pseudonym Basil Dahl. He anticipated Edwin Markham's *Man With the Hoe* with his own English poem *To the Toilers*, which he published in Benjamin R. Tucker's Anarchist journal *Liberty*, in 1896. At twenty-six he succumbed to melancholia and his creative career came to an end, even though death did not claim him until fifteen years later.

While Edelstadt and Bovshover gave literary expression to the anarchist philosophy that proved attractive to many immigrant Jews of the 1880's and 1890's, Morris Vinchevsky (1856-1932) and Morris Rosenfeld (1862-1923) propagated in their verses the socialist panacea which became dominant among the immigrant masses after the founding of the influential daily *Forverts* in 1897.

Vinchevsky stemmed from a Lithuanian townlet near Kovno. He acquired a good education in Hebrew, Russian and German. At seventeen he published Hebrew essays in *Hamagid* and came under the influence of Aaron Lieberman's socialist ideology. At twenty-one he edited a Hebrew socialist monthly in Königsberg and contributed to the German socialist press. At the same time he began to write feuilletons and lyrics in Yiddish. His career in Germany came to an end when at twenty-two he was imprisoned and banned because of his connection with Lieberman's subversive activities as defined in Bismarck's anti-Socialist laws. After a short stay in Paris, he spent the next fifteen years in London, where he was active as orator, editor, pamphleteer and poet. The first volume of his proletarian songs appeared in 1885 and were immensely popular among Jewish workers. In the British capital he came into contact with the circle of William Morris and used English as his fifth linguistic medium. In 1894 he immigrated to the United States and during the following third of a century he continued to advocate his credo of internationalism and socialism.

As a poet Vinchevsky was both militant and sentimental. He transformed abstract socialist doctrines into real, living imagery. He showed the flags unfurled, the proletarian masses on the march, the Jewish workers joining freedom's legions in the attack upon humanity's foes. His typical characters were the blind fiddler, the tattered beggar, the honest thief, the riveter's wife who gave birth in a stable, the three sisters of whom one sold flowers, another shoelaces, and the oldest herself.

Unlike Vinchevsky, who negated Jewish nationalism, Morris Rosenfeld stressed the need for a reinvigorated Jewish entity on the world scene. Unhappy in his native Lithuania, he joined the mass movement of the pogrom victims to America. But his years as a sweatshop worker in a clothing factory were very difficult and he expressed his unhappiness in tearful verses. These attracted the attention of Leo Wiener, Professor of Slavic Languages at Harvard University, who published them in 1898 together with an English rendering as *Songs From the Ghetto*. This volume established Rosenfeld's international reputation. Soon German, French, Russian, Polish and Czech translations appeared and the songs of the sweatshop poet were widely sung and recited.

Rosenfeld called himself a teardrop millionaire. His verses reproduced the whirring of sewing machines and the moaning of tired toilers who were being turned into soulless puppets serving the machines. The tone of pity dominated, pity for the child who rarely saw his father during waking hours, pity for the shopgirl seduced and abandoned by the son of the boss, pity for the pale operator whose sweat and tears soaked into the garments he sewed. The tone of revolt was less frequently audible and less genuine than that of lamentation. The tone of hope broke through primarily in Rosenfeld's songs of Zion. Voices called to him from the banks of the Jordan to return to the home of his forefathers. There he would experience a new spring and a renewal of joy. Jewish feet, tired of millennial wandering, would find rest. He prayed that the gates of Jerusalem be opened to admit him and all the suffering children of Abraham. The Hanukah lights recalled to him ancient glories that could be relived. Not always were Jews a people of mourners; only in exile had they become enfeebled and blighted. However, the fire of the Maccabees was not wholly extinguished. It could be rekindled and would flare up in heroism again when the hour struck for the realization of the long cherished ideal of a home-coming to Israel. Rosenfeld's Zionist poems lacked the concrete imagery and the sense of immediacy which his sweatshop poems, based on personal experience, possessed. His later poetry was marred by satiric and polemic outbursts, since after a decade of unrivalled fame he again felt himself neglected when younger, more sophisticated poets appeared upon the American Yiddish scene.

The transition from the pioneering Yiddish social lyricists to the younger poets who stressed individual joys and sorrows was effected by Abraham Liessin (1872-1938), Yehoash (1870-1927), H. Rosenblatt (1878-1956) and Joseph Rolnick (1879-1955). These poets paved the way for the first indigenous Yiddish literary movement in the New World, the movement of "Die Yunge," which burst upon the American scene in 1907.

Liessin began in Minsk as a revolutionary socialist with lyrics of rebellion and Messianic hope. Nevertheless he refused to accept the assimilationist cosmopolitanism fashionable among Jewish socialists. He held that Jews had not preserved themselves for so many generations in order to disappear when a more just social order would be victorious. In 1897 he had to flee from Russia. At first he was enraptured by America's freedom as symbolized by New York's Statue of Liberty, but soon, melancholy overcame him when he tramped New York's streets, lonely and lost. The founding of the daily *Forverts* provided him with an organ for the continuation of his agitation for industrial unionization and the abolition of the sweatshop system. But the apex of his career was reached during the quarter of a century when he was editor of *Die Zukunft,* the most influential Yiddish literary monthly.

Yehoash was the pen-name of Solomon Bloomgarden, who came to the United States from Lithuania in 1890 at the age of twenty. By then Peretz had already published the early lyrics of the precocious poet. A decade of hardships in New York undermined his health, and like Edelstadt before him, and Leivick after him, he sought to arrest the ravages of tuberculosis by moving to Denver. During his decade at Denver's Jewish sanatorium, from 1900 to 1910, in close proximity to death, he penned much of his finest poetry. There he also collaborated with his physician, Charles D. Spivak, in compiling a dictionary of the Hebraic and Chaldaic words used in Yiddish, defining about 4,000 such words. The publication of his collected songs in 1907 establishes his reputation as a foremost Yiddish lyricist. When his health improved, he left for Palestine in January 1914, but the outbreak of the First World War forced him to return. The narrative of his experiences from New York to Rehovoth and back appeared in 1917 in three volumes and was translated into English by Isaac Goldberg under the title *The Feet of the Messenger.*

Yehoash enriched Yiddish with songs, ballads, fables, legends, satires, travel sketches, short stories and translations of Longfellow, Lafcadio Hearn, Omar Khayyam, Dmitri Merezhkovski, and parts of the Koran. He had a keen eye for nature. He depicted the changing seasons in their many moods, love's intensity and contradictions, the struggle of reason and emotion, the alternation of divine purity and infernal sin, the pantheistic forces immanent in all things, acts and thoughts. He saw God in the whirl of suns and in the single dancing spark of moonlight on a leaf, in matter and in spirit, in creation and destruction, in life and in death. He felt God's nearness as a beacon in the night lighting up his way through labyrinthean mazes. He sensed in decay new birth and in fleeting moments everness.

Yehoash's supreme achievement was his translation of the Bible, a superb rendering upon which he worked for thirty years and which made use of the idiomatic treasures of the various dialects and of the many generations since the *Tsena Urena*. He faithfully reproduced the meaning, rhythm and tone of the original, the translucent simplicity of patriarchal dialogue, the rhapsodic tone of the victory paeans, the crashing intensity of the prophets, the melancholy calmness of Ecclesiastes, the passion of the Song of Songs, the lyric soulfulness of the Psalms.

Yehoash's concentration of all efforts on this marvelous translation, which he regarded as a holy task, deprived him of the leisure to continue with his own original poetry just when he had reached the climax of his poetic career and when he had acquired supreme mastery of the Yiddish medium as had no American writer before him. His lyric innovations, however, did inspire many lyricists, among them H. Rosenblatt, who came to the United States in 1892, two years after him, but who matured much later.

Rosenblatt did not at first display any great originality. His sentimental ballads followed the pattern of the dominant sweatshop poets, especially Morris Rosenfeld. His early songs, in their tuneful simplicity, were influenced by Abraham Reisen and were set to music by Solomon Golub and Michel Gelbart. He translated poems by Edgar Allen Poe and Oscar Wilde. Gradually he veered away from realism to symbolism, from proletarian themes to more intimate, individualistic moods. After his first years in New York and after sojourning for five years in Detroit, he settled in Los Angeles in 1921 and became the strongest pillar of Yiddish culture in this growing Pacific community throughout the following thirty-five years.

Rosenblatt discovered for the Yiddish lyric the Far West, the magnificence of California with its deserts, mountains, and sea. He retold legends of the Indians and aroused sympathy for their tribes whose free roaming throughout the Prairies was coming to an end. Some of his best poems were composed in his seventies and appeared in the volumes *The Brightest Day of Autumn (In Shensten Tog Fun Harbst,* 1953) and *Twilight (Farnakht,* 1957). In these he sang out his optimistic faith in life, his wanderings in the shadowy realm of memories, his nostalgia for his Ukrainian boyhood amidst forests and fields, his beauty-studded experiences, his gladness with the fate allotted to him. He blessed every hand that built and every heart that dreamed. He was content with God and man.

A mood of resignation such as dominated Rosenblatt's late lyrics also overcame Joseph Rolnick, but much earlier. Despite the fact that he worked for many years in a sweatshop and that he never emerged from poverty, he could not bring himself to hate abstract tyrants, wicked capitalists and villainous exploiters. Hence he remained aloof from the socialist and anarchist currents of the early Yiddish scene. He was prepared to embrace as his brothers both the good and the bad people, both the tyrants and the slaves, indeed all human beings over whom shone the health-bestowing, joy-infusing sun. He sealed his cries of loneliness in songs which he sent out into the unknown, hoping to find a receptive ear somewhere, somehow.

The typical Rolnick poem consisted of a few quatrains which fixated with maximum clarity, fidelity and simplicity a single thought or a single mood. When the thought or the mood was in any way complex, he resolved it into simpler components, into a cycle of successive lyrics that illumined it from different approaches, into a string of lustrous pearls, each of which added clarity and beauty to the whole.

Rolnick often reproduced in idyllic verses his early impressions as a miller's son in a village of White Russia. Amidst New York's brick tenements and asphalt pavements he yearned for the smell of tilled soil, the warm splash of a quiet brook, the swish of a sickle on ripening grain, the cheerful wetness of morning dew. He stood aside from literary coteries. His gentle tones about his sadness and solitude were barely audible and found only a few sensitive readers. Later on, however, he as well as Yehoash were claimed as forerunners by the more virile poets, grouped together under the title "Die Yunge."

This group commanded most attention after the social lyric had passed its crest and when the tide was turning from naturalism and social protest to impressionism and individualism. The appellation "Die Yunge" was derived from the periodical *Yugend* (Youth), published by young, newly immigrated poets in 1907. Their contributions were at first met with derision and vituperation by their elders and they were mocked as untalented upstarts, would-be aristocrats, decadents. Nevertheless, within a decade they attained to dominance on the American Yiddish scene and their influence was felt even in the Eastern European lands from which all of them stemmed.

The poets and novelists of "Die Yunge" sought to emancipate literature from sentimentalism and propaganda. They abhorred the moralizing tone which still persisted from the days of the Haskalah. Aloof from the tides of both Jewish nationalism and political cosmopolitanism, they saw art as the expression of individual sensitiveness. Accepting the slogan of art for art's sake, they de-emphasized content and strained for perfection of form. They used word-combinations, not to elucidate concepts or problems, but to communicate impressions and satiate eye and ear with images and tonal effects. They wanted to lead the Yiddish muse out of its parochial hamlet onto the world scene. In an effort to raise the dignity of the Jewish vernacular to the level of English, German and Russian, they insisted on grafting on to Yiddish neologisms and innovations of Occidental literary theory and practice. They produced original works of merit and impeccable translations of foreign masterpieces.

Their first organ, *Yugend,* was followed by *Literatur* in 1910 and by the more substantial *Shriften* from 1912 to 1926. David Ignatoff (1885-1953) was the most dynamic and controversial member of the group, and Moshe Leib Halpern (1886-1932) its most colorful. Mani-Leib (1884-1953), Zisha Landau (1889-1937) and Reuben Iceland (1884-1955) were brought to the public in the first volume of *Shriften* as best embodying the group's ideology and techniques. New writers like I. I. Schwartz (1885-1971), Isaac Raboy (1882-1944), Joseph Opatoshu (1886-1954), Joel Slonim (1885-1944), Moshe Nadir (1885-1943), M. J. Haimowitz (1881-1958), Berl Lapin (1889-1952), Moshe Bassin (1889-1963), and A. M. Dillon (1883-1934) participated in the publications, discussions and activities of the group. Hard upon the heels of the original members of "Die Yunge" came new followers such as Menahem Boraisha (1888-1949), Ephraim Auerbach (b. 1892), Benjamin Jacob Bialostotsky (1893-1962) and Zishe Weinper (1892-1957), each exploring new realms of Jewish subject matter and the American landscape. Literary cafés, centering about New York's East Broadway and Second Avenue, formed congenial meeting places, and bohemianism became a favorite affectation.

With Mani-Leib, who arrived in New York from the Ukraine in 1905, bohemianism was more than an affectation. He was a restless romanticist full of longing for the Blue Flower, an errant minstrel who played a gay tune for children and a melancholy tune for wiser grown-ups, a lover of overrefined sensations, a seeker of magic overtones and rainbow colors amidst stony tenements, a lyricist who discovered beauty in black bread and white salt, a composer of folkballads and songs of absolute simplicity, abounding in naive repetitions, lilting cadences, suggestive alliterations and assonances, a sonneteer who in his last years framed ripe insights in pure rhymes.

Mani-Leib preferred the pale moon to the dazzling sun, since the moon was silent and invited dreams. He preferred autumnal rains to spring freshets, since autumn bore the beauty of death. His favorite color was blue, the color that remained when all others died away. He depicted himself as the blue knight riding on a blue horse and the heavens as the blue hat of earth. He constantly invoked silence, for in silence there was comfort and by silence pain was purified. Silent was the night while raucous was the day. Silent was the kiss of the soul and the shadows about things, silent the stars above and the tears below.

Mani-Leib versified tales of Chelm, the city of Jewish Gothamites. For school children he sang of Yingl Tsingl Khvat, a schoolboy who knew no fear of darkness or bears, and who acquired a fiery horse on which to roam and a magic ring with which to conjure up snow when needed. He penned a cycle of poems about Elijah, the kind prophet who helped man and bird and wild beast, but especially Jews. When Vilna's Jews were snowed in and could not emerge from their houses to prepare for the Sabbath, Elijah came as savior and opened a path for them.

Mani-Leib's lyrics are eminently singable and were set to music by Michel Gelbart, Pinchas Jassinowsky, Samuel Bugatsh and others.

Zisha Landau came under the influence of Mani-Leib soon after arriving in New York in 1906 at the age of seventeen, but within a few years developed his own unique style, a mixture of exaltation and irony. Characterizing himself as half clown and half poet, he held that all life was illusion, a play of shadows. Seeking escape from the dullness of his daily grind as a house-painter, he conjured up imaginary worlds which, with consummate romantic irony, he then dissolved into thin air.

In Landau's four comedies in verse, *Nothing of Importance* (*Es Is Gornisht Nit Geshehn,* 1937), reality was turned topsy-turvy. Human beings and human relations were satirized through the masks of Pierrot, Harlequin and Columbine. Biblical and legendary figures, stripped of their saintliness, were involved in the marvelous and banal as they moved from fairyland to the contemporary scene before being whirled away to timelessness. Although Landau affected power and robustness, the word "tired" occurred far too frequently in his verses. At his best, his speech was soft, his phrases slender, his sentences suggestive rather than expressive. Although he posed as a free adventurer, he did not negate responsible living. He knew that, in spite of his theory about the poet being an unfettered personality, he, the grandson of the Strikover Rebbe, could not tear himself loose from the chain of generations.

But even in the cage of duties and laws he still found room for the freedom-loving spirit to spread wings. His most famous lyric was his joy-filled song of the Baal Shem, who found unending reasons for intoning hymns to life and expressing gratitude to life's creator.

As a pillar of "Die Yunge," Landau too sang of peacocks and nightingales, of knights and damsels, of ballerinas and fairy queens. He too pretended to welcome pain, terror, despair and exotic adventures. But in his finest lyrics, he preferred the quiet fireplace, the silence of simple souls and the calmness of normal routines.

While Zisha Landau and Mani-Leib were musicians in words, Reuben Iceland was the painter. His poetic ideal was to fixate moments of time, to solidify a scene or emotion before it dissolved in the whirl of events. He saw in the silence of objects their true immortality, and in daily life themes worthy of a poet's attention. Only rarely did he escape from his difficult existence as a capmaker in a factory to the world of intoxicating phrases and blissful imagery. All too soon he sank back into melancholy and nostalgia for a past that could never be retrieved. Of these young years in a Galician town he sang in his longest poem *Tarnov*, in which he recaptured faded fragrances and traditionally festive moods.

Iceland, arriving in America in 1903 at the age of nineteen, had participated in the plans, anthologies and theoretical discussions of "Die Yunge" from their inception. But not until he was thirty-five, when he came to know the poetess Anna Margolin (1887-1952), was he inspired to create his finest lyrics. The emotional struggles of both, before they found fulfillment in one another, were depicted by him in a cycle of twenty-two lyrics, *Of My Summer* (*Fun Mein Zumer*, 1922). In his memoirs of "Die Yunge," *From Our Spring* (*Fun Unzer Frihling*, 1954), he included a lengthy biographic sketch of this poetess who fascinated admirers on three continents with her beauty, her independent mind and her uninhibited relationships.

Among "Die Yunge," Abraham Moshe Dillon was the most helpless and most lonely. In his poems there was a longing for joy and for companionship, but his days were joyless and his only faithful companion the dog that howled in the field at night. He yearned for love but the beloved maidens he sang of were figments of his imagination. He had to content himself with being one of the quiet, suffering, little stars that light up the darkness with a few timid rays. A single slender volume of his sad poems appeared during his lifetime under the title *Yellow Pages* (*Gele Bleter,* 1919) and a few more poems were collected posthumously by his friends as a tribute to this minor but genuine lyricist.

Berl Lapin spent a restless youth in the Polish province of Grodno, in an Argentine Jewish colony, and in various communities of the Russian Pale, before he established lasting roots in New York in 1909. Though he entitled his first collection of lyrics *Sad Ways* (*Umetige Lieder,* 1910), his poems of joy far outweighed those of sadness. He preferred clarity to profundity, restrained emotions to explosive self-expression, impeccable form to sensational stylistic innovations. He wooed each word until he extracted its essential meaning, music, image. He used each word as an atom which he paired with another verbal atom and still another until the atomic word-dust took on crystalline shape and combined into an organic, living entity. He enriched Yiddish poetry with translations of Russian lyrics, Shakespeare's Sonnets, Robert Frost, A. E. Housman, Edwin Arlington Robinson, Edna St. Vincent Millay, and American hymns, including the anthem "The Star-Spangled Banner." His selected poems, *The Full Pitcher* (*Der Fuler Krug,* 1950), included his lyrics of New York, which reproduced the roar of its cavernous streets, the jungle-noises of its subterranean heart, the siren wails of its piers and ferries, the tramping of the hastening multitudes on its stony pavements. But Lapin also perceived the individual in the crowd, and the uniqueness in each member of the masses.

Far more dynamic was Moshe Leib Halpern, a controversial figure hailed by many as the most talented of "Die Yunge" and heartily disliked by others for his coarseness and irreverence. At the age of twelve he left his native Galician townlet Zlochov for Vienna. In the Hapsburg capital he came under the influence of the Viennese esthetes and dabbled in German verse. The Galician

Neo-romanticists, under the leadership of Shmuel Jacob Imber, persuaded him to use Yiddish as his more natural literary medium. His first Yiddish poems were published in a Lemberg daily before he left for America in 1908. His odyssey in the New World led him from New York to Montreal, Detroit, Cleveland, Los Angeles and back to New York. In every city he found admirers but nowhere could he gain an economic foothold. The unending struggle for bread embittered him. His verses became sardonic, his images grotesque, his language coarse, his sentiments anarchistic. Angry at the world, he joined the Communists in 1924 and wrote barbed verses for their newly founded Yiddish daily, *Freiheit*. Although lionized by them as the great proletarian poet, he refused to bend his free spirit to party discipline and left them in 1927.

His later poetry reflected his despair and rebellion against the poverty that chained him. It alternated between strident assertion of individualism and deep sympathy for the underprivileged, between robust sensualism and philosophical pessimism, between a love of life in all its aspects, and an awareness that all life was but the vanity of vanities. In protest against lyric phrase-mongers, he evolved in his two volumes, *In New York*, 1919, and *The Golden Peacock* (*Die Goldne Pave*, 1924), a most unconventional style—fierce, violent, raw, lurid and undisciplined. He seemed to delight in shocking readers with his coarseness and brutality. He played the clown and boasted of his gaiety, but his laughter and grandiloquent posture masked hidden tears. At heart he was a helpless child in the darkness, crying out to an unfeeling world. He once characterized himself as a living corpse in limbo. He blasphemed God and spat at the world. He could not sing of fragrant flowers when his nostrils were assailed by New York's gasoline fumes. He could not tarry in streets in which shopkeepers and hurrying crowds held sway. He was not welcome in the salons of the rich and he was not at ease in literary coffee-houses; he was homeless everywhere. He peered too deeply into human frailty, social lies and moral humbug. He was too proud to cavort before others as a beggarly intellectual who might be rewarded with a spittoonful of honor. Often tiredness overcame him but never resignation. He remained a non-conformist to the end of his days, refusing to compromise with social injustice and moral iniquity.

One of "Die Yunge" who had deep insight into the jagged soul of Halpern was his friend Zishe Weinper, who published a volume of reminiscences about him in 1940. Weinper stemmed from a

Hassidic family in Volynia. His father was a cantor at the court of the Rebbe of Trisk. After a traditional education up to his sixteenth year, young Weinper became interested in the new Hebrew and Yiddish literatures and began to wander from town to town throughout Ukraine and Poland in search of bread and learning.

In 1913 he landed in New York and came under the spell of "Die Yunge." Soon there gathered about him a group of poets, who thought of themselves as the youngest of the young. They included Aaron Nissenson, B. J. Bialostotsky, and Naftoli Gross. They published their earliest contributions in a magazine edited by Weinper under the revealing title *Beginning* (*Der Onheib,* 1918). However, when the editor joined the Jewish Legion to fight for a Jewish homeland, this venture came to a premature end.

Weinper's first volume of lyrics, *From Our Land* (*Fun Undzer Land,* 1920), dealt with his impressions, emotions and experiences as a legionnaire, his boundless joy as his ship neared the shores of the Holy Land, his longing for a Messiah who would lead the vanguard of Jewish redeemers, his sadness and animation amidst the ruins of Jerusalem.

Disillusioned with the British overlords of Palestine who had replaced the Turkish overlords but who did not redeem the land for the Jews, Weinper returned to the United States at the end of 1919. His year and a half in Palestine, however, remained engraved upon his mind and heart and found expression in many later lyrics and in his book *With the Jewish Legion,* published in 1942 at the height of the Second World War, when again a movement for a Jewish army was taking shape.

Weinper had, on the whole, an optimistic attitude toward life, until 1929. His gayest lyrics were his songs for children, written in the 1920's when he was a teacher in Yiddish schools. Many of these were set to music by outstanding Jewish composers and were sung on the concert stage as well as in Yiddish classrooms. Weinper's optimism, however, was subjected to heavy strain during the years of the Great Depression in America and of Nazi dominance in Europe. The carefree singer was disconcerted by the cynical tolerance of intolerance, by the prevalence of poverty amidst plenty, and by the widespread indifference to injustice toward his people.

Called upon to react in verse to the ever worsening political and social scene, he became the poet of the radical left and a moving spirit of YKUF, the Yiddish Cultural Federation, from 1938 on.

This led to his alienation from the mainstream of Yiddish letters, an alienation under which he suffered intensely and to which he re-acted vigorously in the lyric volume *Pain and Joy* (*Laid Un Fraid*, 1954). He arrived at the conclusion that not only in Judea but also in every hill and in every dale, from Birobidjan to Arizona, wherever the Jewish tongue was heard in song and lamentation, there was the holy land of Israel. He sought comfort by identifying his own striving with that of the ancient prophets in his *Poems of the Prophets* (*Poemen Vegn Die Neviim*, 1951), and in visions of grandiose natural phenomena such as he described in lyrics of the Grand Canyon and the Canadian Rockies. In vain! Weinper's unreciprocated love for the Jewish people left him disconsolate and frustrated at the end.

A harsher fate befell a poet far more talented than Weinper and hurled him from a higher summit of adulation to a profounder depth of misery and abject loneliness. He was Yitzkhok Reiss, one of the earliest members of "Die Yunge," who attained greater fame under the pseudonym of Moshe Nadir (1885-1943). Brought to New York from a small town in Eastern Galicia at the age of thirteen, he voiced his disappointment with his new environment in lyrics which began to appear in print before he was sixteen. In later years, nostalgia often overcame him for the ecstasy and dirt which he associated with Rivington Street on New York's Lower East Side, but in his earliest sketches, he emphasized only the travails of the immigrant generation and caricatured its efforts to graft townlet values on to the great metropolis.

Nadir's youthful poems, filled with *Weltschmerz*, were reminis-cent of the young Heine. He soon mastered Heine's technique of reversing the flow of emotions in the course of a lyric, of shocking trusting readers with sobering irony just as they were succumbing to sweet sentimentalism. This mixture of gentle lyricism and biting irony remained with Nadir throughout the four decades of his creative career and was reflected in his prose and verse, in his dramas and sketches, in his essays and aphorisms. Under vari-ous pseudonyms and in many literary genres, he acted the clown, the lover, the intoxicated idealist and the despairing cynic, and all his poses were assumed to be genuine. In the deepest reaches of his soul, however, he found life empty, barren of meaning, vanity of vanities.

From this abysmal loneliness and nihilistic moodiness, he fled back to the Galicia of his boyhood dreams. He roamed on to Vienna and Paris, but soon found that the beauty he sought in Europe was only a surface varnish masking a decaying civilization. He thereupon returned to New York and to Philadelphia, participated in the strident literary innovations of "Die Yunge," edited humorous periodicals such as *Der Groisser Kundus* and *Der Yiedisher Gazlen,* published his first book of erotic miniatures, *Wild Roses* (*Vilde Rozen,* 1915), and contributed lyric, philosophic sketches to the liberal daily *Der Tog.* Translating Peter Altenberg, Jerome K. Jerome and Mark Twain, he also assimilated into his own Yiddish style some of their characteristics and was soon hailed as the greatest Yiddish humorist since Sholom Aleichem.

While delighting others with the flashes of his wit and the brilliance of his paradoxes, Nadir himself was weighed down by a constant awareness of the senselessness of life and death and the transitoriness of all values and ideals. His bohemianism turned into an unnatural affectation. His laughter at all existing institutions and conventional ideas turned to bitter sarcasm. His extreme individualism prevented his becoming rooted anywhere. He yawned at the world, sneered at his contemporaries, succumbed to a philosophy of Pantagruelism, and entitled an entire collection of his lyrics *Delusions.* He confessed that tragic happenings no longer moved him since they occurred so often, women no longer impressed him since he knew too many of them too well, art was for him a beautiful word useful chiefly in salons, science pained him like rheumatism, readers were laughable jackasses, the whole world was hopelessly boring. From this universal ennui there was no escape unless one could forget oneself. But, as an egocentric poet, he could not do so. He was ever immersed in introspection, in brooding over the ebb and flow of his emotions, in analyzing the products of his thinking, the fragmentation of his ego, the dissolution of his kaleidoscopic impressions and fleeting memories. Angry at life, he still loved it in all its capricious, banal and contradictory manifestations.

Flight to Communist circles for a time brought him release from deepest pessimism. In 1922 he became associated with the Communist daily, *Freiheit,* and through its columns he directed the darts of his venomous sarcasm against all who did not share his new vision. In 1926 he undertook a trip to Russia and returned as a confirmed adherent of its Messianic gospel.

When the Communists in 1929 justified the Arab massacres of the Jews of Hebron, some of his associates on the *Freiheit* could not stomach this daily's headline "Jewish Fascists and Englishmen Make Pogroms on Arabs," and resigned as a group. Nadir thereupon attacked them mercilessly. His vitriolic outbursts against his erstwhile colleagues Menahem Boraisha, Abraham Reisen, H. Leivick and Isaac Raboy, as well as against his earlier victims Abraham Cahan, S. Niger, and dozens of prominent Jewish men of letters who eschewed Communism, were collected in three volumes in 1935 and 1936. Outraged literary critics refused to review his books and even to reply to his attacks. Not until 1939 did disillusionment with his ideal set in.

When his adored Russians entered into a pact with Hitler's Germany, then he recognized that he had been led astray by a utopian will-o'-the-wisp and sought to atone for his literary misdeeds of many years. In an autobiographic confession written in April 1940, he pleaded for understanding of his predicament: "For every drop of blood that I drew with my pen, I paid with two drops from my heart's blood. This is no excuse for all those I attacked with such blind fanaticism and my heart weeps because of my deeds." By then, he was anathema to both Communists and non-Communists.

If Nadir's early poems echoed the young Heine, his last poems were reminiscent of the dying German poet, to whom he repeatedly paid tribute and to whose fate he likened his own. Like Heine, the penitent Yiddish poet also sought to make his peace with the God of Israel from whom he had been estranged since his fifteenth year. He recognized that he had sinned against individual human beings even while he was engaged in a so-called holy war for a better humanity. He realized in the hellish flare of a world conflagration that force, bloodshed, revolution, despotism of right or left could not create a better society, but that only through a long process of education in tolerance, democracy and humanism could man ascend to a higher stage of civilization.

Broken-hearted, the most talented humorist among "Die Yunge" bade farewell to God and man in the final poems, published posthumously under the title *I Confess* (*Mode Ani,* 1944).

I. I. Schwartz, who was born in a Lithuanian townlet in 1885, the same year as Moshe Nadir, and who arrived in the United States in 1906, also participated in the publications of "Die Yunge," but always steered clear of the group's rebellious militancy. Just as in his superb translations of Bialik, Tchernikhovsky, Milton and Whitman he subordinated himself to these Hebrew and English poets, reproducing their spirit faithfully rather than imposing his own spirit upon the Yiddish text, so too in his original lyrics he preferred to let landscape, people and situations impose their will and their moods upon him. This is true also of his two longest poems, *Kentucky* (1925) and *Young Years* (*Yunge Yorn,* 1952), even though these are autobiographic in essence.

The latter poem affords an insight into the poet's childhood and youth prior to his departure for New York. It begins with his earliest memories of his Lithuanian birthplace and weaves a web of enchantment about his townlet along the banks of the Nieman. In this community Jews had been rooted for many generations, making a living as skilled craftsmen and busy trades-men. Throughout adult life, they found some time each day for Talmud study at the communal houses of learning, their preferred relaxation and delight.

Nostalgically the poet recalls the closing years of the nineteenth century when the fountain of Jewishness streamed bright, clear and fresh. Time obliterated whatever bitterness, harshness and cruelty he had experienced and left a residue of mild sadness and here and there bits of pure joy. He remembered his father, the revered rabbi, dispensing justice and learning, and his mother sanc-tifying each holiday with her special cooking and baking. As a Jewish child, he was no less familiar with the Nile of the *Book of Exodus* than with his native streams, and the warmth of Galilee was as much his as were the snowstorms of the Baltic. At thirteen, Schwartz was sent away to study at Kovno's Yeshiva. Together with half a hundred other semi-starved youngsters, he studied, from seven in the morning to nine at night, the many tomes in which the heritage of all the older generations was contained. Beyond traditional subjects, there blossomed the new Hebrew of Bialik and the Yiddish of Frug, Morris Rosenfeld and Abraham Reisen, and found a way to young hearts. Above all, the royal figure of Herzl dawned upon Kovno's youth like a ray of light in the *Galut* darkness. But the path of the aspiring poet led him westward, despite yearning for the land of the Patriarchs and the Prophets. The verse narrative ends with his parting from home and with his father's admonition: "Remain a Jew!"

Schwartz remained a Jew and a poet. Landing in America with the torrent of penniless Jewish immigrants, he soon found con-genial spirits who were seeking expression for their uniqueness in melodious songs and in the visual arts. Escaping from the knout of the Cossacks, they felt fire coursing through their veins as they stepped on the New World's blessed soil. Schwartz felt happy in their midst, since their striving was not for fortunes of gold but rather for the riches of the spirit. Unwilling to submit to the hellish sweatshops in New York's maelstrom, he wandered westward in 1918. He stayed in Kentucky for a few years and engaged in business on a small scale with his meager capital. His experiences and observations were recorded in *Kentucky*, his poetic epic of the Jewish pioneering peddler.

The honest, intelligent, persevering hero of this narrative also began by walking from town to town with a pack on his back, sleeping in haystacks and barns, until he finally found a desirable home among kind neighbors. These helped him to dispose of his wares and encouraged him to settle among them. His store, started in an abandoned shack, prospered. With his first savings, he brought over his family from Europe. As the community grew, it attracted other Jewish pioneers, a cobbler, a tailor, a capmaker. These Jewish settlers were not content to remain merely craftsmen. Restless and venturesome, they risked expansion and diversification, until their hovels became the town's department stores. Soon they felt the need of a synagogue, not only as a religious center but also as a warm communal Jewish home. With the passing of years, their children grew into adulthood, liberated from the harried sadness which had plagued the youth of the preceding generation. With frank eyes and sensitive ears, these children grasped at opportunities constantly opening up in Dixieland. They had no scruples about mating with non-Jewish neighbors and striking out on new roads. Orthodox practices no longer satisfied them. For their religious requirements they needed a pastor's sermons on Sundays and a Reform Temple with organ and choir on Saturdays. The pioneering peddler, having become a prosperous pillar of Kentucky society, saw children and grandchildren flocking about him. And when the final hour struck for him, the tired, old patriarch, he was lulled to eternal sleep by golden dreams in which were commingled Psalms of David and melodies of Dixie.

Schwartz's epic called attention to tendencies and forces in American Jewish life which were to gather momentum in later decades of ever greater dispersion beyond the Atlantic seaboard. But it was the Introspective Movement after World War I that widened still further the horizon of Yiddish poetry and brought to it innovations which were then being introduced by American lyricists writing in English.

7

YIDDISH IDEOLOGIES

The Bund ● Dubnow ● Zhitlowsky ● Nathan Birn-
baum ● Czernovitz Language Conference ● Klatzkin ●
Chaim Greenberg ● Abraham Golomb ● Nochum Shtif
● YIVO ● J. L. Cahan ● Harkavy ● J. A. Joffe
● Noah Prilutzky ● Zalman Reisen ● Max Weinreich ●
YKUF ● CYCO

THE MATURING OF YIDDISH as a linguistic medium, its
refinement by literary innovators, its strengthening by educational
networks, its nurture by philologists and academic scholars, called
forth an intense ideological debate which did not die down until
the majority of Yiddish-speaking persons were annihilated by the
Holocaust.

The various attitudes toward Yiddish were in large measure
dictated by the main ideological positions which were already
well established before the First World War and which continued
to flourish after the war. Epigones sought to adapt earlier systems
of thought to the reality of the post-war and post-revolutionary
generation and eclectics sought to effect a synthesis of the original
ideas inaugurated by the pioneering giants since the 1880's.

Among the original thinkers of the closing nineteenth century,
Theodor Herzl (1860-1904), Shimon Dubnow (1860-1941), Ahad-
Haam (1856-1927), and Chaim Zhitlowsky (1865-1943) exerted a
strong impact upon the Eastern European Jewish mind, even
though Zhitlowsky alone gave primacy to the Yiddish tongue.
The political Zionism of Herzl, which found incorporation in the
World Zionist Organization and was developed at various Zionist
congresses from 1897, came increasingly under the influence of
Hebraists and hailed the revival of spoken Hebrew as a major
achievement of the Jewish renascence. The cultural Zionists, led

112

by Ahad-Haam, were even more militant in their advocacy of Hebrew as the sole national tongue of the Jewish people. Eliezer Ben Yehuda (1857-1922), who landed in Palestine in 1881, was the first modern Jew at whose home only Hebrew was spoken and his firstborn son Ithamar Ben Avi (1882-1943) was the first child in modern times whose mother tongue was Hebrew. A generation after the latter's death, Hebrew had become the daily tongue of more than two million Jews and the normal medium in Israel for commerce and industry, literature and science, theater and radio, parliamentary debate, military command, and the games of children.

While Hebrew was undergoing a miraculous growth, helping to unify Jews who found their way to Zion, there persisted ideologies that laid stress upon Yiddish as the unifying factor in the Diaspora, or at least among Ashkenazic Jewry. The Bund, which was founded in 1897, the same year as the Zionist Movement was founded at Basel, was the principal organization which gave priority to Yiddish. Its philosophy attained notable success in Poland and the Baltic States, where its representatives could function legally after the collapse of the Czarist regime. In Soviet Russia, where Hebrew was banned soon after the Revolution, Yiddish was long tolerated and in pre-Stalin years even encouraged.

Dubnow's theories of Diaspora Nationalism sought to further the use of both Hebrew and Yiddish, while Zhitlowsky's philosophy sought to justify militant Yiddishism. Dubnow was primarily an historian and wrote chiefly in Russian. In his early years he expressed doubt that literary works of great artistic value could be created in Yiddish, which apparently had no standardized grammar and lacked the subtle nuances of Russian and German. Acquaintance with the first sketches of Sholom Aleichem convinced him of his error. In 1887 he published a glowing tribute to the budding humorist and later, in his volume *From Jargon to Yiddish* (*Fun Jargon Tsu Yiddish,* 1929), he recalled with pride his own participation for more than four decades in the evolutionary process whereby Yiddish grew from a jargon to literary and scientific eminence.

Dubnow's theories of Spiritual Nationalism and Autonimism matured in the 1890's when he lived in Odessa and was in contact with the circle of scholars and poets who later came to be known as the Sages of Odessa. These theories were best formulated in his *Letters on Ancient and Modern Judaism,* which first appeared in the Russian-Jewish weekly *Voskhod* from 1897 to 1906 and which formed the ideological basis for his ten-volume *History of the Jewish People* (1925-1929).

Dubnow began with the assumption that national types evolved from simplicity to complexity and from common material interests to common spiritual bonds. He saw in tribal unity the original national type. Out of common ethnic belongingness and the sharing of a common territory for many generations, there gradually evolved a more advanced common culture as there continued to accumulate common tendencies, habits, attitudes, beliefs, experiences, and above all an ever richer and more complex common language. This culture, linked with common economic activities, gradually brought about the formation of a unified political structure, the national state. If such a state was conquered by a superior armed might, the culture group which constituted its indigenous population became assimilated to the conquering group and fused with it. The process might take a longer or shorter time, depending upon how intense was the will of the defeated nationality to uphold its uniqueness. Where its collective will was unusually strong, it could ward off for a considerable time the danger of complete submersion or fusion. Remaining on its own territory, it could resist being swallowed up by the victors, despite the temporary loss of its political independence or statehood. The Irish, Poles, and Czechs exemplified such tenacious survival. However, there was only a single example in all human history of the survival of a people down the millennia after the loss both of its political independence and of its territory, a people no longer united by any common material factors but bound together primarily by a common faith, a common moral sense, a common spirituality. The Jewish people alone developed the strength to retain its nationality, its peoplehood, its historic uniqueness solely on the basis of spiritual and ethical factors. It was the precursor of the highest and most advanced national type, the spiritual type which no other group on earth had yet reached. It was held together by common convictions and common concepts of ultimate values. It made ever new cultural contributions, created ever new autonomous institutions, found ever new ways of maintaining its vital energies alive and functioning. It was the most stubborn of peoples. Its will to survive was indestructible. Without the protective shell of political independence or territorial stability, exposed to the ravages of hostile or at best indifferent surroundings, it persisted because it was able to evolve out of inner need its own distinguishing traits, aspirations and autonomous institutions.

Religion, according to Dubnow, was an essential aspect of this spiritual nationality but it was not the only aspect. In the many centuries when religion was the dominant force among the Christian and Moslem nations in whose midst the Jews dwelt, many ethical, social, political and philosophic facets of Jewish culture had to be shaped in religious contours. As a result, religion was not limited among Jews merely to man's relation to God but expanded to encompass the entire range of man's relations to man, to groupings of men, to peoples. Hence, a Jew who converted to Christianity could not be regarded as a Christian member of the Jewish people. By changing his faith, he also seceded from his people. Two generations after Dubnow, Israel's Supreme Court endorsed this conclusion in the famous case of Father Daniel when it affirmed that a person who was born a Jew could not claim to belong to the Jewish people after voluntarily converting to another religion.

Dubnow denied that Jews had a special mission but he did see them as a people which, in the course of millennia, had accumulated a tremendous treasure-house of experience. It had reached a level of spirituality unequalled by any other group. It had a right to be proud of its historic deeds (which included the giving of two other world religions to humanity), its present achievements, which included major contributions in many lands, and its Messianic ideals projected onto the future. It was justified in refusing to be absorbed in other nations whose culture was younger and poorer in experience. It must be allowed to grow freely on its own spiritual soil. Zionism enriched the Jewish people by adding a territorial protective covering for a sector of the spiritual nationality, the Palestinian sector. However, Zionism must not negate the viability of the other Jewish sectors. It should not negate Diaspora Jewishness by labelling it Galut and dooming it to ultimate disappearance through assimilation to the non-Jewish majority cultures alongside of which it still flourished.

Dubnow distinguished between national individualism, the right of each cultural group to develop its own uniqueness, and national egoism, the chauvinistic claim of a temporarily ruling cultural group to the right to impose its pattern of life, its language, its educational system and its religion upon minority groups. National egoism was aggressive, oppressive, imperialistic, while national individualism merely sought to conserve for its members the freedom to coexist quietly and peacefully alongside of its neighbors.

According to Dubnow, assimilation was national suicide. On the other hand, isolationism stood for exclusion from the currents of life flowing all round this ever shrinking globe. Opposing both extremes, Dubnow preached cultural autonomism, the preservation and strengthening by Jews of their historic personality. Jews were not only citizens of a particular country, participating in its civic and political life, but they were also members of the Jewish people, participating in the religious and cultural organizations and activities of their Jewish kin the world over.

Yiddish, as a medium of communication between Jews in many lands, was a strong force for Jewish cultural survival and every effort must be made to preserve it. Dubnow, therefore, lent his support to Yiddish creativeness not only in the folk vein but also in scientific research and public debate. His position was intermediate between that of the spiritual Zionists who looked to Ahad-Haam as their mentor, and the extreme Yiddishists whose spokesman was Chaim Zhitlowsky. While Ahad-Haam negated Yiddish and wanted to concentrate all efforts upon the rebirth of Hebrew, Dubnow saw Hebrew as the permanent healthy leg upon which the Jewish people stood but he insisted on retaining Yiddish, even if it be only an artificial leg and not present at the birth of this people. For, it was better to walk on two legs than to hobble on one. Zhitlowsky, on the other hand, believed in Yiddish as the main living language of the Jews. In his view, Yiddish was the healthy leg and Hebrew the artificial one. The difference between Dubnow and Ahad-Haam was, therefore, one of emphasis. Dubnow placed maximum emphasis on national and cultural autonomy in the lands of the Diaspora but did not object to Zionism as a supplementary activity, while Ahad-Haam wanted maximum emphasis to be put on the building of a national center in Palestine which would radiate Jewishness in all directions and stem the disintegration of the Diaspora centers.

In contrast to both Dubnow and Ahad-Haam, Zhitlowsky dissociated himself entirely from Zionism, political or spiritual, and from the Hebrew revival. For Dubnow, who loved Hebrew and wrote in Russian, Yiddish was precious as the embodiment of a heritage of several centuries in Europe. As an historian, however, he was aware that Jewish history spanned not centuries but millennia and was not limited to the European continent. Yiddish was indeed precious as the spoken medium of Ashkenazic Jewry but it left untouched other important sectors of Jewry. It should, therefore, be retained as an additional temporary pillar helping to uphold the Jewish structure, but this structure must be shored up by other pillars, especially the strongest one, the religious. For Zhitlowsky, on the other hand, Yiddish was the most powerful cohesive factor uniting the Jewish people and Yiddishism was an end in itself. He argued that, if the Jewish people were to obtain autonomous rights in the multinational states, such as the Russian and Austro-Hungarian Empires, and if, through a proper system of education and suitable cultural institutions, Yiddish could be elevated to the status of a literary, scholarly, national language, then the preservation of the Jewish nationality would be assured regardless of the adherence or non-adherence of Jews to a common religious tradition. According to Zhitlowsky, Jews, if they so wished, could even convert to the Christian faith and yet not suffer in their national structure. What would happen in such case would be a transformation of Christianity in the Jewish image, a modification of Christianity to conform to the psycho-physical organization of the Jewish converts. In earlier centuries the trunk of Jewishness was rooted in religion but since the Emancipation this was no longer valid. To flourish as a modern secular, free, progressive, vital organism, the Jewish people would have to reduce the religious factor to a subordinate role. Nor could they substitute a common territory as the foundation for their culture, since history had made of them a non-territorial people. Language would, therefore, have to serve as the unifying factor for their cultural striving. Jewish survival and growth required the preservation and elevation of Yiddish.

Zhitlowsky stemmed from a patrician family. In his youth in Vitebsk, he was most closely associated with his classmate S. Anski (1863-1920), best known for his later mystical play *Dybbuk*. In 1882, Zhitlowsky left for Tula, deep in the heart of Russia. There he hoped to assimilate to Russian ways and to participate in revolutionary work to liberate the Russian people. Contact with Russian anti-Semitic literature, however, brought him back to Jewishness. As early as 1884, there was born in him the desire to fight for the preservation of the Jewish national individuality on Russian territory. Early Zionism, embraced by intellectual penitents in the 1880's, did not appeal to him, since it meant flight from Russia and was a product of despair following the pogroms. He felt that the Jewish nationality could prosper far better in the lands of the Diaspora, if these lands were reorganized on a socialistic basis. He therefore, joined in socialist agitation among Jewish workers. In 1886, he planned to found a Yiddish socialist periodical and a Jewish section of the revolutionary movement, but was or-

dered to desist by the Russian leaders of his party, not a few
of whom were of Jewish origin, on the ground that such activities
would promote Jewish separatism and would impede the complete
assimilation of Jews to Russian ways. This raised in his mind the
question as to why Jews must assimilate to other nationalities.
To this question he at first could find no answer. Finally, after
years of study and research in Russia and at Swiss universities,
he arrived at the conclusion that Jewish assimilation to the majority populations was an error, because Jews were not a small percent of other peoples but one hundred percent of their own people
and had a distinct national configuration. They must, therefore,
strive for National Emancipation, for equality as a nationality
among the other nationalities on this globe.

According to Zhitlowsky, socialism would most quickly bring
about the regeneration of the Jewish national personality by changing the economic structure of Jewish society from a parasitic existence to a more normal and more useful existence as a laboring
group in agriculture and industry. Under socialism, the Jewish
workers would be redeemed both as Jews and as workers. Socialist
internationalism would not seek to abolish national units or to
knead all of them into a common dough, in order to make of them
one big loaf labelled humanity. It would, on the contrary, give
each nationality the opportunity to develop freely its own specific
group configuration for the benefit of all. Just as there would then
be neither exploiters nor exploited in the economic field, so also
there would be neither oppressors nor oppressed among the nations. Socialist internationalism would never recognize privileged
or chosen peoples. Each people had something of value to offer to
the others and something to learn and to take over from others.
Since nationalities occupying the same territory would be living
with each other in equality and amity, there would be no need for
Jews to abandon their present abodes and to emigrate to Zion.
They would rather found Jewish schools and universities and
develop Jewish cultural institutions in all the lands where their
numbers were significant. It might be desirable for them also to
have a single territory where they would form a majority, but
such a territory could be an autonomous province of Russia or any
other land. It did not have to be Palestine.

Zhitlowsky held that Dubnow's spiritual nationalism was too
tenuous a concept to attract the Jewish masses who were tired
of their abnormal status. They wanted to become a normal group

held together by a common language and by a common culture that flourished somewhere on earth and not in a spiritual limbo. Their striving was finding increased expression in Yiddish literature, a folk-literature that would attract ever more talented exponents and before long rival the finest European literatures. Yiddish must become rich in books embracing all branches of learning. Then the new generation would not have to seek its necessary knowledge among foreign peoples and tongues. It would express its feelings and thoughts in its own language. It would publish its achievements in art, science and technology in Yiddish. Through this linguistic medium, it would link together Jews of all lands, the educated as well as the uneducated. If three million Swiss could support ten universities, then eight to nine million Yiddish-speaking Jews ought surely to be able to support twenty-five universities. By becoming one of the most educated peoples, the Jews of the entire world, whether residing in Vilna, Warsaw or New York, would develop pride in their group's achievements; they would transform Occidental learning into their own forms and restore it to others enriched by unique contributions. They would be taking and giving. They would be fulfilling the prophecy of Isaiah that all peoples shall live in peace with each other and the earth shall be full of knowledge as the sea was full of water. Should an era dawn when all peoples would flow together into one unity, the ocean of humanity, then the Jews would also cease their separate existence; but until that distant future they must live as equals among equals and not accept a lesser role among the nations.

Zhitlowsky hailed Jewish intellectuals who were creating works in their own tongue. Peretz, Sholom Aleichem and Sholem Asch were conferring dignity upon the Jewish name through their Yiddish works. The struggle of the Yiddishists was a struggle for the normal, free, many-sided, rich, fruitful culture of the Jewish people, a struggle for its life, honor and prestige. Zhitlowsky, therefore, joined with other exponents of Yiddishism in 1908 to convoke a conference at Czernovitz for the purpose of clarifying the role of Yiddish in Jewish life.

The initiator of the conference project was Nathan Birnbaum (1864-1937), a Zionist pioneer. As early as 1883, during his student days at Vienna, Birnbaum had founded the Jewish fraternity Kadimah, the first student organization whose members accepted the concept of Jewish nationhood and the necessity for Jewish rebirth in its own land. From 1884 on, Birnbaum fought for Jewish self-emancipation, a slogan popularized by Leon Pinsker in 1882. When Herzl issued the call for the First Zionist Congress in 1897, Birnbaum enthusiastically joined the new movement and became its first secretary-general. In the course of his Zionist activity, he became better acquainted with Eastern European Jewry and discovered in them a dynamic people that expressed itself in its own living idiom, Yiddish. When Zionism, after the Second Congress in 1898, veered to the view that Jewish national life in the Diaspora was an impossibility and that all efforts must be concentrated on Zion, he left this movement and devoted his talents toward strengthening Diaspora Nationalism. This led him to stress more and more the necessity of bringing Yiddish, the natural speech of Eastern Jewry, to the Western Jews, so that Yiddish might become the universal Jewish tongue, rather than the more artificial, reconstructed Hebrew.

During a lecture tour in America early in 1908, Birnbaum won over Chaim Zhitlowsky, David Pinski, Jacob Gordin, and the publisher A. M. Evalenko, to the idea of a language conference. These five together, thereupon, issued an invitation to Yiddish writers and editors to meet in Czernovitz in order to discuss the standardization of Yiddish spelling, grammar, vocabulary, and other subjects of common interest. The most controversial item for consideration, however, was whether Yiddish was to be recognized as the sole Jewish national language, or as one of the national languages alongside of Hebrew, or as a folktongue used by the masses.

This last item was debated throughout most of the ten sessions and in a very heated manner. For a time, agreement seemed impossible, since the seventy participants included all shades of Jewish opinion from Zionist Hebraists to militant Bundists and such diverse personalities as Peretz, Sholem Asch, H. D. Nomberg, Noah Prilutzky, Abraham Reisen, Matthias Mieses—a brilliant historian of Yiddish dialects, Gershom Bader—editor of the first Yiddish newspaper in Galicia, Moshe Leib Halpern—the youthful poet of Galicia who was about to emigrate to America, J. Kisman —student-historian of Rumanian Jewry, and the fiery Esther Frumkin—a rebel against Czarist tyranny, a fighter for the Jewish proletariat of White Russia, later on an extreme exponent of Moscow Communism and a victim of a Stalinist purge. The skill of the presiding officers, Birnbaum and Zhitlowsky, succeeded in effecting an agreement on the proclamation of Yiddish as *a* national language of the Jewish people. But the relation of Yiddish to Hebrew was not too clearly defined, so that individuals and differing groups could retain a wide latitude of opinions.

After the close of the conference, Peretz, Asch, Reisen and Nomberg set out to tour Jewish settlements in order to win adherents for the proclaimed political, cultural and social equality of Yiddish and its desired evolution from a vernacular of the masses to a literary, scientific and national organ of the Jewish people.

The Czernovitz Conference was derided by Ahad-Haam as a Purim carnival. It was defended by Sholom Aleichem. It created difficulties for bilingual writers ranging from Mendele to Bialik. It brought to a climax the battle of ideas raging in Jewish press and literature. But its impact was enduring. It heightened the prestige of Yiddish. It stimulated translations of the world's classics into Yiddish. It encouraged research and publication in Yiddish. It led to a purification of Yiddish vocabulary. Its ideology became the basis for many educational institutions that flourished after World War I. In Poland, Hebrew and Yiddish schools came into existence side by side. In Soviet Russia, the Communist approach, implemented by the Yevsektsie with ever greater severity, called for a complete banning of Hebrew and favored Yiddish as the language of the common man. In mandated Palestine, on the other hand, the struggle of the Yishuv for the strengthening of Hebrew resulted in virulent antagonism toward Yiddish, an antagonism which only began to subside after the state of Israel came into being.

The ideologists who influenced the Jewish scene between the two world wars differed in their attitude toward Yiddish but none, not even the extreme Zionists who fought against the retention of Yiddish in Palestine, completely negated it as an instrument for Jewish survival in the Diaspora. Among the Zionists, Jacob Klatzkin (1882-1948) and Chaim Greenberg (1889-1953) gave clearest expression to the viewpoint of those who sought the Hebraization of the Jewish people but who also acknowledged the need for the preservation of Yiddish in the Galut until such time as Jews would be fully ingathered in their national homeland.

Klatzkin did not believe that Jews could survive much longer in the Diaspora. Nationalism had replaced religion as the strongest unifying force. If Jews wished to survive as Jews, they would have to concentrate their efforts upon reestablishing themselves as a

Jewish nation upon their historic soil, with Hebrew as their common national tongue. His essays, written in Hebrew and German, roused greater interest after their translation into Yiddish, since Yiddish ideologists could not be indifferent to their challenging logic.

Klatzkin equated Diaspora with Galut, exile. He held that Jews everywhere and at all times yearned for release from their anomalous existence, for a return from exile to their original homeland and for the rebirth of their own tongue. Their strong religious attachment sufficed to keep them distinct from their neighbors and enabled them to maintain themselves as a dispersed historic community with national characteristics, as a viable nation in exile. With the weakening of religious bonds since the Enlightenment, a process of Jewish de-nationalization set in. Increasingly Jews were absorbed in the various nations in whose midst they dwelt. Jewish values and ideals, such as monotheism, Messianism, optimism, absolute justice, became the common property of a large sector of mankind and offered an inadequate basis for the further survival of Jews as a distinctive group. All environments of the Diaspora became inimical to Jewish continuance, some more so and some less so. Philo-Semites sought to assimilate Jews; anti-Semites sought to eject them as a foreign body. To maintain their group uniqueness, Jews would have to will against their Diaspora environments. They would not be able to do so successfully without the hope of a renewed normal life in the future. Should the goal of national restoration in Zion be abandoned, then Jews would have to reconcile themselves to an acceptance of their various alien lands as their own fatherlands. This would be especially so in Western Europe and America, where anti-Jewish forces were not sufficiently virulent to compel Jews to remain outsiders. There the normal process of acculturation would erode Jewish distinctiveness and lead to continual decline and ultimate dissolution. But even in Eastern Europe Jews could not maintain their national strongholds indefinitely. They might be able to do so as long as the peoples about them had not yet reached national maturity. Once nationalism ripened there, assimilation would increase. Equality of rights included the right to assimilate to the majority population and Jews would undoubtedly make use of this right. They would adopt the language and culture of their host peoples. The concept "assimilated Jews" was, however, pure nonsense. It denoted a Jew who was not a Jew. It persisted only because Jews were in the anomalous position of a people without a national home of their own. Once Palestine became such a national home, Jewishness would be nationally determined. A Jew would be a person whose fatherland was Israel and whose language was Hebrew. All other persons of Jewish origin or Jewish faith who lived outside of Israel's borders, who were rooted in a non-Hebraic tongue, and who fought and died for another nationality would no longer be able to misuse the name Jew. Nor would it be forced upon them; their Jewish descent would have merely archival, genealogical interest. After the stabilization of the Jewish State, such designations as German Jew, French Jew, American Jew, would sound as absurd as German Frenchman, American Spaniard, or Russian Englishman. Jewish concentration in Israel must result in a gradual withering away of Jewish communities elsewhere. National rebirth in Israel spelled national death for Diaspora Jewry.

To those who argued that the Diaspora might be able to maintain a Jewish national existence with Yiddish as its unifying language, Klatzkin replied that, if this were to happen, two distinct groupings would emerge, a Hebrew people in Israel and a Yiddish people in the Diaspora. These would grow ever further apart until their distinctiveness would be as clear as that between Germans and Englishmen, two peoples who evolved from a common Germanic stock. There was, however, no likelihood of an evolution of a Yiddish nation anywhere, because Galut Jewry, weakened by the departure of its best sons to Israel, would not be viable.

Despite insistence on Hebrew as the only national language of the Jews, Klatzkin deprecated the struggle against Yiddish waged by some well-meaning but ignorant Hebrew fanatics. He was prepared to concede that Hebrew could never become the vernacular of Diaspora Jews, not even to the limited extent that Yiddish still was. National wisdom, therefore, dictated the preservation and strengthening of Yiddish as a bulwark against the destructive force of assimilation. Yiddish must be nurtured as the Jewish vernacular insofar as possible, in order to safeguard Jewish distinctiveness during the transition period until the ingathering of Jews in their homeland would be completed and Hebrew firmly established there. In the long run, however, the position of Yiddish was hopeless, as hopeless as the survival of Jews as Jews in the Diaspora.

Chaim Greenberg was no less militant than Klatzkin in his advocacy of political Zionism, but he was more sympathetic to the cultural forces which found their expression in Yiddish. Fluent in many languages and active as editor and writer in Russian, English and Hebrew, he was most eloquent in Yiddish both on the lecture platform and as an essayist. When the Yevsektsie, the Jewish section of the Communist Party, sought to suppress Hebrew after the Bolsheviks attained power in Russia, he resisted their efforts and mobilized influential support for this endangered tongue. But when the Histadrut, Palestine's Labor Confederation, sought in 1933 to ban public speeches in Yiddish, he vigorously opposed such a resolution and called for the teaching of Yiddish in the land of Israel.

In an essay on *Cultural Problems of American Jewry* (1930), Greenberg gave the clearest formulation to his attitude toward the language problem. He declared himself to be a lover of Yiddish, while at the same time recognizing the tragic fate of this language which was trying to maintain itself against attacks on two fronts. On the one hand, it was assailed by Hebrew, which had the sanctity of religion and of millennial historic continuity and, on the other hand, it had to ward off the inroads of the more useful languages of the Diaspora. But even as a folk language, its decline could not be arrested despite the high level of its contemporary achievements. It was no longer the spoken language of Jewish youth. It was becoming converted into a literary and academic tongue. In America, which harbored the largest concentration of Jews, it was doomed. If American immigrants of German or Italian origin were unable to retain German or Italian as the vernacular of their children against the competition of the dominant English speech, despite strong cultural bases in Germany, Austria, Switzerland and Italy, was there a likelihood that Yiddish-speaking immigrants would be more successful? Undoubtedly, language was the best vehicle for transmitting a people's values and traditions. A Jewish educational system, however, could at best hope to intensify Jewish experiences by exposing the younger generation to one Jewish language in which Jewish religious, literary and cultural treasures were imbedded. In that case, was not Hebrew to be preferred to Yiddish, if, as was apparent, the latter could not be retained as a natural, intimate, spoken tongue? As a book language, Hebrew certainly had more to offer.

Greenberg could not accept Klatzkin's extremist views which negated the Diaspora totally, and which must logically lead to the voluntary expatriation of all Jews outside of Israel, their denaturalizing themselves, if not legally then at least morally, their withdrawing themselves completely from all positions of influence in their native lands. He rather held that Diaspora Jews were bi-cultural. American Jews were culturally both Americans and Jews. Cultural dualism was not incompatible with political monism. He granted that cultural monism was certainly a more normal experience for human beings, but Jews were not granted by history such a normal group experience. There was, however, nothing disloyal about Jews proclaiming themselves to be cultural dualists; they had a right to nurture their Jewishness as well as their American-ism. Amnesia, forgetfulness of one's antecedents, was not a pre-requisite for citizenship in a democracy. On the contrary, enrich-ing one's life with Jewish content should enable a Jew to be a more wholesome personality and a more valuable member of the American community. While Jewish content could best be imbibed through Hebrew, it could also be absorbed through Yiddish and even through so-called alien tongues which were really not alien to millions of Jewish individuals.

In an address at the inauguration of a Yiddish Chair at the Hebrew University in 1951, Greenberg moved his audience with his remarks on the role of Yiddish in the past and the role it should occupy in modern Israel: "Yiddish weeps for its children. It mourns the millions of its sons and daughters, the annihilation of its heirs and spokesmen. A short while ago, Yiddish was the modest ruler of an entire empire. Without royalty or sovereignty, it ruled over millions of men, women and children. The sabras of Israel must imbibe the spiritual values of their Yiddish ancestors and the Yiddish language is one of the jewels in the crown of Jewish martyrdom."

In contrast to Klatzkin and Greenberg, Abraham Golomb (b. 1888), spokesman for Integral Jewishness, asked that linguistic primacy be given neither to Hebrew nor to Yiddish. He saw these languages as twins, supplementing each other. Both were con-tainers in which the wine of Jewishness was stored; they were not the wine itself. To make a cult of a language was idolatry. Con-tent was more important than form. A priest who mastered Hebrew and a Gentile maid who learned to speak Yiddish did not thereby become Jews. Golomb defined a Jew as a person whose daily life was interpenetrated with Jewish traditions and values. Not Zionism or Bundism, not Jewish theology, prophecy or phi-losophy were in themselves the essential ingredients of Jewish-ness. These were merely fruits of the Jewish tree. Daily rootedness in Jewish cultural habits and daily nourishment from the Jewish collective experience were needed to keep the Jewish tree strong and healthy. This collective experience included language, festivals, religious observances, family relationships, ideals carried into practice, taboos, social activities, group discipline.

Golomb held bi-culturalism to be unwholesome, and preferred maximum autonomous development of Jewish communal life and institutions. A person who participated in two cultures was, in Golomb's opinion, schizophrenic, in constant conflict with himself. Such a Jew, growing up in a predominantly non-Jewish environment, was bound to develop an attitude which Ahad-Haam called "servility in freedom." He was bound to regard the mores of the majority as more important, of a higher rank, obligatory, and his own mores as less important, unnecessary, superfluous. He would discard them if he could, if he were not constantly reminded by his neighbors of his otherness. His egophobia or self-hatred must lead him to assimilate to the majority cultures rather than to enrich his own group with the cultural products of others. Assimilation was, therefore, synonomous with de-Judaization, with the loss of one's own cultural configuration.

To stem de-Judaization, all conflicts must cease between Hebrew and Yiddish, Zion and Galut, religion and secularism. No aspect of Jewish culture should be discarded, because the excision or even weakening of any Jewish organ endangered the vitality of the entire organism. Continuity did not exclude evolution of forms or modification of content to bring these up to date with ever new realities. For example, the urbanization of the Jewish group, the change from a *shtetl*-culture to a metropolitan culture, necessitated certain adjustments. These adjustments and reforms, however, should be directed toward strengthening Jewish cohesiveness and guarding Jewish group distinctiveness. This involved greater efforts to maintain Yiddish and Hebrew, because the loss of common media of communication spelled disintegration for a people. Individuals might write about Jewishness in all languages, even as archeologists wrote about Sumerian or Hittite, but such writing by Jewish scholars in German, French, Russian, Spanish and English merely added archival material and helped to embalm Jewishness. It did not change habits of living to any significant extent.

Golomb, therefore, arrived at the conclusion that all alien languages adopted by Jews in order to integrate more successfully with other peoples brought about a decrease in Jewish cohesiveness. On the other hand, the languages Jews spoke in order to differentiate themselves from others led to the group's preservation and growth. Diaspora communities which were giving up Yiddish were becoming fossilized and incapable of future growth. Without Yiddish, the Jewish people would be fragmentized into scattered, dying remnants of a people. A people created its language and the language united the people. Hence, losing a language meant loss of peoplehood, because language was more than a mere collection of words. It was intonation, melody, logic, psychology, aroma, the storehouse of the collective memory of many generations.

Golomb devoted his creative years in Vilna, Kiev, Winnipeg, Mexico City and Los Angeles to teaching, writing and agitating for the retention of Yiddish as the international medium of communication among Jews. He founded schools and teachers' seminaries. He trained disciples to agitate for Integral Jewishness. He enriched the Yiddish vocabulary of science and psychology and supplemented his theoretical discourses with practical texts useful for classrooms. He often aroused strong antagonism, but he also found fervent followers. Wherever he dwelt, he was a pillar of strength for the Yiddish structure.

During Golomb's Vilna period in the 1920's, while he was devoting himself to training Yiddish teachers at the Jewish Teachers' Seminary, a movement arose to found an academic institute to further research and scholarship in Yiddish as an additional essential factor in assuring the creative viability of the Jewish people. The ideologists who stressed Yiddish as the principal cohesive force of Diaspora Jewry saw Vilna as the most desirable center for such an institute and it was there that YIVO flourished from 1925 until the Second World War.

The original proposal for the *Yiddisher Visnshaftlikher Institut,* which was better known under its initials YIVO, stemmed from Nochum Shtif (1879-1933), a Yiddish linguist and editor who often wrote under the pseudonym of Baal Dimion.

Shtif had begun as a Russian writer, a Zionist and a Socialist. He had helped to organize a Jewish self-defense group in Kiev after the Kishinev Pogrom of 1903. He had suffered imprisonment by Czarist authorities, had escaped to Switzerland, and had returned to Russia after the Revolution of 1905. He soon discovered that he could propagate his doctrines of Zionism and Socialism among the Jewish masses far better in Yiddish than in Russian. In 1916 he championed the cause of Yiddish in a memorable debate with Chaim Nachman Bialik, the champion of Hebrew. The following year, immediately after the Czar was overthrown, he im-

mersed himself in political activities and helped to found the
Jewish People's Party in the Russian capital.

In 1919 he abandoned politics and devoted himself solely to
Yiddish research. He published his polemic pamphlet *Jews and
Yiddish* (*Yiedn Un Yiddish*, 1919), in which he formulated the
ideology of the Yiddishists with great eloquence. He explained that
Yiddishism arose as a reaction to a century of anti-Yiddish agitation. This agitation was begun by the pioneers of enlightenment in
Eastern Europe. When these obtained their first glimpses of Occidental culture, they became aware of the backwardness of their
own Jewish people in the Czarist realm and of the low esteem in
which this people was held by its neighbors. They believed that they
could elevate their religious and ethnic group by changing its occupations to more productive ones, closer to the soil, and by changing its distinguishing speech, which they labelled a "jargon," to the
more esteemed languages of the majority populations, Polish,
Russian and German.

While the early men of enlightenment were genuinely concerned
with the plight of their people, Shtif pointed out that their children were far less concerned. These children were, to a large
extent, no longer raised in traditional schools, whose curriculum
stressed holy texts and whose language of instruction was Yiddish.
They attended government schools which stressed secular subjects
and where the language of instruction was Russian. They acquired
a feeling of superiority towards their bearded, kaftaned kinsmen.
They were ashamed to speak the Yiddish "Jargon" in public and
avoided doing so even at home. Some became careerists, interested
solely in their own advancement; others, more idealistic, were
caught up in various radical and revolutionary movements, and
were ready to sacrifice themselves for the common good, for
Russia's glory and Poland's emancipation. They opposed Jewish
separatism. They were horrified when the pogroms of the closing
nineteenth and early twentieth centuries hurled them back to their
own "benighted" people, from which they had been estranged.
Repentants among the assimilationist idealists then went to the
opposite extreme. They became fiery Jewish nationalists, espousing a return to Zion and a resumption of pre-Galut Jewishness.
They held that Yiddish, as the language which arose in Galut,
should make way for Hebrew, the language of the Bible and of
ancient Jewish sovereignty, whose renewal the Zionist Movement
would bring about. Until the resumption of sovereignty in a dis-
tantly envisaged Jewish state, the rebirth of Jewish nationalism

could best be accelerated by the renascence of Hebrew as a spoken tongue and not merely as a literary medium. Hebraists, therefore, joined Russifiers in the struggle against the "Jargon" of the people. The slogan of the intellectuals was Hebrew or Russian or Polish but by no means Yiddish. The common folk, however, continued to speak the Yiddish vernacular. The growing awareness of the dignity of the common man led to the rise of Yiddishism as a movement of teachers and writers to counter the attacks of the Hebraist visionaries and the self-hating Russifiers. Yiddishists wanted Jews to be sound personalities, educated in their mother tongue and satisfying their cultural needs in it.

The post-War treaties that followed the break-up of the Russian and Austro-Hungarian Empires guaranteed Jewish minority rights in several European countries. If Jews wanted national autonomy, they could not claim it on the basis of a common territory but primarily on the basis of a common language. "Yiddish does not have to be resurrected or implanted or strengthened. It is alive, it is deeply rooted, it is strong among the people. . . . The time has come to proclaim to the world and to ourselves: Yiddish is and will remain our language." Shtif, as spokesman of the Yiddishists, therefore called for Jewish secular schools in which all subjects would be taught in Yiddish, the natural language of Jewish children and their parents.

In 1922, Shtif left for Berlin, where he found a group of ardent disciples of Yiddish, including young Max Weinreich, who was then completing his dissertation on the history of Yiddish philology and the historian Elias Tcherikover, who was using Yiddish material for his studies of Ukrainian Jewry. Upon the urging of these and other Yiddish scholars, Shtif published a booklet in 1925 on the organization of Yiddish scholarship, in which he proposed the immediate formation of a Yiddish academy and outlined its program and principles. He pointed out that Yiddish scholars were carrying out their research without any central direction and with no coordinating organ for their publications. He singled out the achievements of Mordecai Veinger, Haim Tchemerinsky, Ber Borochov, Noah Prilutzky, Zelig Kalmanovitch, Max Weinreich, Zalman Reisen, J. L. Cahan, Jehuda Elzet, S. Anski, Jacob Leshchinsky, Mark Wischnitzer, Abraham Menes and Elias Tcherikover. Some of these scholars found themselves in Berlin in 1925 and, at a conference which took place there in August, Shtif's proposals were accepted as the basis for a Yiddish research institute which was to function from a main center in Vilna, with subsidiary centers in Berlin, Warsaw and New York. Although Shtif left for Kiev in 1926 and became the guiding spirit of the Kiev Institute for Proletarian Culture, YIVO continued to flourish in Vilna. Within a decade after the founding of YIVO, its influence spread to many lands with a sizable Yiddish-speaking population. Before the Second World War there were YIVO groups in Argentina, Austria, Brazil, Chile, England, France, Latvia, Rumania and Palestine. The apex of YIVO's Vilna period was reached at the tenth anniversary conference in 1935, which was attended by scholars from several continents. This was also the climax of Yiddishism before catastrophe struck and destroyed its base in Eastern Europe.

Meanwhile YIVO succeeded in collecting and preserving books, letters, manuscripts, diaries and priceless documents mirroring Jewish life. It rescued from oblivion the Jewish folklore of Eastern Europe, standardized Yiddish spelling, trained young scholars and published books and periodicals of value. It initiated significant projects, exhibits and conferences to shed light upon the Jewish past and present. It attracted to its ranks the historians Elias Tcherikover, Shimon Dubnow, Saul Ginsburg, Abraham Menes and Jacob Shatzky; the psychologists and educators Leibush Lehrer, Abraham Golomb, H. S. Kasdan and A. A. Roback; the economists and demographers Jacob Leshchinsky, Ben-Adir, Liebman Hersh and Moshe Shalit. Its strongest section dealt with Yiddish linguistic and literary phenomena. Its director was Max Weinreich and among his earliest co-workers were J. L. Cahan, Alexander Harkavy, Judah A. Joffe, Selig Kalmanovitch, Shmuel Niger, Noah Prilutzky and Zalman Reisen.

The principal contribution of Jehuda Leib Cahan (1881-1937) was in the gathering and publication of folktales and folksongs and in the training of researchers in Yiddish folklore. By profession a watchmaker and jeweler, he devoted his spare time throughout forty years in Vilna, Warsaw, London, and principally New York, to his avocation of folklore. He published his collection of Yiddish folksongs in 1912 and his collection of Yiddish folktales in 1931, reprinted and enlarged after his death. His *Studies in Yiddish Folklore*, edited by Max Weinreich in 1952, defined the scope of Yiddish folklore, its relation to the folklore of other peoples, and the scholarly methods which should be applied by researchers in this field. Cahan was a severe judge of the thousands of folksongs and folktales that came within his ken. He accepted only a small portion of these as genuine products of the Jewish folk-soul and constantly engaged in polemics with investigators who confused the popular products of Badchonim, Marshaliks, and theater-lyricists with the pure gold of the naive singers and the anonymous tellers of tales. Cahan disproved the conclusion of his predecessors Leo Wiener (1862-1939) in his *History of Yiddish Literature in the Nineteenth Century* (1899), and Saul Ginsburg (1860-1940) and Pesach Marek (1862-1920), in their collection *Yiddish Folksongs of Russia* (*Yiddishe Folkslider in Russland,* 1901), that the Jews of Eastern Europe, until recent generations, did not produce folksongs centering on love, a conclusion based on the assumption that early marriages arranged by parents never permitted love to ripen into problem, tragedy or ecstasy. He showed that such a conclusion could be based only on the way of life of the respectable middle class, the *Baalebatim.* Genuine folksongs, however, arose mainly among the lower classes, the artisans, the untutored masses. Among them, love often triumphed over the traditionally imposed barriers between boy and girl and, as a result, folksongs cropped up in century after century and bore witness to the unending ebb and flow of emotions, to the meeting, parting and reunion of lover and beloved.

Alexander Harkavy (1863-1939) was primarily a lexicographer. Self-educated in many languages, he came to Vilna in 1878 from his native Novogrudok in White Russia. He associated with the storyteller I. M. Dick and the Maskilim, while working as a book-keeper in Romm's publishing house. The pogroms of 1881 led him to leave Russia. He arrived in the United States with the Am Olam group led by Abraham Caspe. This group was unsuccessful in its efforts to found an agricultural colony on collectivist principles and Harkavy, disheartened by three years of strenuous work, on the verge of starvation, returned to Paris in 1885. Here he began his creative activity in behalf of Yiddish with a study which attempted an historical and grammatical analysis of the language. He demanded for Yiddish a classification as a distinct language and not as a dialect of German or as a jargon. After his return to the United States, he continued to write, edit, and translate into Yiddish. As a representative of the HIAS—Hebrew Immigrant Aid Society, he was in daily contact with Yiddish-speaking immigrants and composed for them a series of text-books, pamphlets, grammars, readers and bilingual dictionaries in order to enable them to learn English more quickly and to adjust to the American scene more easily. He translated for them the *Constitution of the United States* and prepared popular booklets on American history and American citizenship. His *Complete English-Yiddish Dictionary* was for more than half a century an important reference work for Yiddish readers and writers of the immigrant generation in America. It was frequently reprinted. His *Hebrew-Yiddish-English Dictionary* (1926) was less widely used and is now obsolete.

Judah Achilles Joffe (1874-1966) specialized in Old Yiddish. After his arrival in New York from his native Ukraine in 1891, he mastered many languages ranging from Sanskrit, Old Persian and Greek to Slavic, Germanic, Romance and Semitic. He taught Latin, Russian and mathematics and collaborated on dictionaries and encyclopedias, but his main interest throughout his long life was Yiddish. He accumulated the richest private collection of Old Yiddish texts and manuscripts which was turned over to the Jewish Theological Seminary of New York in 1960 and is most valuable for Yiddish scholars. His own research into the origin, history and development of Yiddish appeared in numerous articles from 1909 onwards. His basic study of Eliahu Levita's Yiddish works (1949) contained a reproduction of the verse romance *Bovo d'Antona* of 1541, with an authoritative introduction on the life and art of the sixteenth century minstrel. Joffe's last years were devoted to co-editing the early volumes of the *Great Dictionary of the Yiddish Language* (*Groiser Verterbukh Fun Der Yiddisher Shprakh*, *I*, 1961; *II*, 1966). *The Joffe-Book*, published in 1958 by YIVO, contained not only tributes to him but also significant articles on Yiddish philology and folklore by fifteen American, European and Israeli scholars.

Noah Prilutzky (1882-1941) began as a trilingual writer but soon showed his preference for Yiddish over Russian and Hebrew. At the Czernovitz Language Conference of 1908, he was an extreme exponent of the view that Yiddish was *the* national language of the Jews and it was only with great reluctance that he yielded to the majority view that Yiddish was *a* national language of the Jews, thus avoiding a split with the Hebraists. He edited the Warsaw Yiddish daily *Moment*, which had a circulation of more than 100,000. He was also politically active as the founder of the Populist Party during World War I and as its representative in the Polish Parliament. But his most enduring contributions were to Yiddish philology. He edited YIVO's publication *Yiddish Far Alle* and lectured on Yiddish until arrested by the Germans in 1941. They compelled him to classify the treasures of YIVO's main center in Vilna and then tortured him to death.

Zalman Reisen (1867-1941), younger brother of the poet and narrator Abraham Reisen, was a noted grammarian, linguist and literary historian. His encyclopedia of Yiddish literature, press and philology apeared first in a single volume in 1914 and subsequently in four volumes, 1927-1929. It was the main reference source in its field. Reisen was also a distinguished editor and the inspirer of the literary group "Young Vilna." His liquidation by the Soviet authorities after their occupation of Vilna deprived YIVO of one of its strongest pillars.

The ideology that underlay YIVO's projects from its inception was an acceptance of Jewish peoplehood the world over and of Jewish scholarship as a means for enrichment of Jewish life and of maintaining Jewish identity. YIVO's principal periodicals were *YIVO Bleter,* published since 1931, and *Yedies Fun YIVO,* since 1929.

When the Nazis overwhelmed Vilna, YIVO's New York branch became the main center, with the Buenos Aires branch as the most important subsidiary. The greater part of YIVO's library and archives, carried off to Germany and intended to be used for anti-Semitic studies by Nazi racial scientists, survived the War and was retrieved for YIVO's North American center. The directors of all four research sections of YIVO: Elias Tcherikover (1881-1943), Jacob Leshchinsky (1876-1966), Leibush Lehrer (1887-1964) and Max Weinreich (1894-1969) either were in America or were able to reach America's shores and to resume their productive work there. In 1941, *Yiddishe Shprakh* began to appear under the editorship of Yudel Mark (b. 1897). It dealt with problems of Yiddish usage and paved the way for the *Great Dictionary of the Yiddish Language (Groiser Verterbukh Fun Der Yiddisher Shprakh),* edited by Yudel Mark, with Judah A. Joffe as co-editor of the first two volumes, which appeared in 1961 and 1966 and defined 40,000 words out of a projected total of more than 200,000 words. In 1946 the *YIVO Annual of Jewish Social Studies* was founded for English readers, under the editorship of Shlome Noble (b. 1905).

YIVO also published, sponsored and supervised many basic books on linguistics, folklore, literature, psychology, labor, economics, demography, history and education. YIVO's exhibits, conferences, seminars and training program for Yiddish teachers and scholars stimulated and enriched the Jewish cultural scene. YIVO's collection of a million volumes of Judaica and more than two million archival items made its New York headquarters in the 1970's the most important center in the Western Hemisphere for the study of Eastern European Jewry.

YIVO's research director, Max Weinreich, became in 1947 the first professor of Yiddish at an American institution of higher learning, New York's City College. Stemming from Goldingen, Courland, Weinreich settled in Vilna after the Russian Revolution. There he edited the Bundist daily *Undzer Shtimme* in 1918 and the daily *Tog* in 1919. After completing his studies at German universities and publishing his dissertation on Yiddish philology in 1923, he returned to Vilna, taught at its Jewish Teachers' Seminary, and directed YIVO's research program in Vilna from 1925 until 1939 and in New York from 1940 to 1950. His own studies ranged from linguistics, folklore, and literary history to psychology, pedagogy and sociology. His most significant books were his *Survey of Yiddish Literature (Bilder Fun Der Yiddisher Literatur-Geshikhte*, 1928), covering the period from initial Yiddish to Mendele; *Paths to Our Youth (Der Veg Tsu Undzer Yugent*, 1935), dealing with the principles, methods and problems of research into Jewish youth; and *Hitler's Professors* (1947), published in Yiddish and English and detailing the role of German scholarship in Germany's anti-Jewish activities. His history of the Yiddish language, which appeared posthumously in 1972, was his supreme achievement.

Weinreich was also the editor of the *Thesaurus of the Yiddish Language* (1950) by Nahum Stutchkoff (1893-1965). This monumental volume, comprising over 150,000 words, idioms, phrases and proverbs, has been called the greatest achievement of Yiddish lexicography since the pioneering dictionary of J. M. Lifschitz a century earlier and facilitated the planning by YIVO scholars of the *Great Dictionary* during the 1950's.

When American universities in the 1960's and 1970's followed City College's example and introduced courses in Yiddish, YIVO's texts were used in American classrooms. The most popular text for students was *College Yiddish: An Introduction to the Yiddish Language and to Jewish Life and Culture*, by Uriel Weinreich (1926-1967), son of Max Weinreich and a professor of linguistics at Columbia University. The text, first published in 1949, went through numerous editions as Yiddish studies attracted more college students in America and was adapted in the 1970's for students in Israel whose native tongue was Hebrew. His *Yiddish-English, English-Yiddish Dictionary*, published posthumously in 1968, was the first adequate replacement for Harkavy's dictionary, which had appeared three-quarters of a century earlier and which had been out of print for decades. He also initiated and directed the *Language and Culture Atlas of Ashkenazaic Jewry* and edited *The Field of Yiddish* (I, 1954; II, 1965), studies in language, literature and folklore.

While YIVO specialized in research, YKUF—Yiddisher Kultur Farband—founded on an international scale in Paris in 1937, sought to stem the decline of Yiddish by the publication and dissemination of Yiddish belles-lettres. As the cultural voice of the radical Left, it published more than two hundred Yiddish works during the following three decades and disseminated more than half a million copies of Yiddish books. Its principal organ was *Yiddishe Kultur*, a literary monthly edited by Nachman Maisel from 1939 until he settled in Israel in 1964 and thereafter by Itche Goldberg. Closely linked to YKUF were the novelists Baruch Glasman, Zvi Hirshkan, Gershon Einbinder, the poets Aaron Kurtz, Sholem Shtern, the literary historian Kalman Marmor, and the editor Pesach Novick.

The Congress for Yiddish Culture was founded in New York in 1948 in order to strengthen Jewish manifestations in Yiddish throughout the world. Allied with CYCO, the Central Yiddish Cultural Organization founded in 1938, it published many Yiddish books and supported the oldest and most influential American Yiddish literary monthly, *Die Zukunft*, founded in 1892. Its most grandiose project, begun in 1954, was the publication of the nine-volume comprehensive *Biographical Dictionary of Modern Yiddish Literature (Lexikon Fun Der Nayer Yiddisher Literatur)*. This dictionary included more than 8,000 Yiddish writers of the nineteenth and twentieth centuries, and is an indispensable reference work for Jewish literary historians.

Buttressed by the efforts of YIVO, YKUF, CYCO, the Congress for Yiddish Culture, and by an ever increasing number of departments of Jewish studies at universities, the decline of Yiddish was slowed down, though not arrested. However, Yiddishism, as an ideology, was no longer at the forefront of discussion in the 1970's.

8

THE POST-CLASSICAL
NARRATIVE

The Peretz Circle ● Pinski ● Abraham Reisen ●
Nomberg ● Sholem Asch

THE CLASSICAL MASTERS, Mendele, Sholom Aleichem and
Peretz, dominated the Yiddish scene until their deaths during
World War I. Mendele, as the Grandfather of Yiddish Literature,
was the most revered. Sholom Aleichem, who dubbed himself Mendele's literary grandchild, was the most read. Peretz, however,
was by far the most stimulating mentor for aspiring literary
youth. From all of Eastern Europe, young men, talented and
untalented, trekked to his home in Warsaw and brought him the
first products of their pens. A word of encouragement from him
opened the doors for them to publishers and editors. His first disciples, David Pinski (1872-1959), Abraham Reisen (1876-1953),
Hersh David Nomberg (1876-1927), Sholem Asch (1880-1957),
Peretz Hirshbein (1880-1948), and I. M. Weissenberg (1881-1938),
expanded the range of Yiddish in directions in which he had
pioneered.

What Peretz meant for all of them was once formulated in a lyric
tribute to him by Reisen. The latter recalled Peretz's favorite
symbol of the Golden Chain. This precious chain of Jewish traditions lay dust-covered and forgotten, while Jewish intellectuals
were reaching out for foreign treasures and were being rebuffed
as intruders. Then came Peretz. He brought back to them their
own glittering Golden Chain and reawakened their pride in their
own heritage.

Pinski was the oldest of the Peretz disciples. At nineteen he left
Vitebsk in order to study medicine at the University of Vienna.

136

En route he visited Peretz and showed him his first short stories. Peretz immediately recognized the young man's talent and urged him to continue writing. A few months later Pinski threw overboard his plans for a medical career, settled in Warsaw, and two years afterwards won Peretz's collaboration in a publishing venture and his participation in the literary anthology *Literatur Un Leben,* and in the literary booklets *Yom Tov Bletlekh.*

Pinski wrote his first significant short story, *The Great Philanthropist (Der Groisser Mentshenfreint)*, at twenty while still a student in Vienna. His first published tales and sketches appeared in Warsaw and New York periodicals in 1893 and were followed by many more, displaying increasing maturity from year to year. Before he left for America at the age of twenty-seven, his reputation was well established as a pioneer of Yiddish proletarian literature. His early stories dealt with the struggle between workers and their employers, between parents and children, between traditional attitudes toward marriage and the new claims of the heart, especially the feminine heart, for greater freedom in love. In these tales Pinski sought to educate his readers and to win them over to socialism as the panacea for Jewish ills and proletarian misery. Though Pinski never lost his faith in enlightenment and in socialism, his writing after his twenties concentrated less on the struggle of workers against an unjust economic system than on the struggle of the Jewish individual for personal and national dignity. He became deeply involved in agitation for Labor Zionism and exercised an important influence in weaning the Jewish masses away from their infatuation with a vague cosmopolitanism and in directing their efforts toward Zionist national liberation.

Pinski's first two decades on American soil were devoted to drama far more than to fiction. This was the period when the Yiddish theater experienced its Golden Age and through his plays he reached out to large audiences in America and Europe. After World War I, when the Yiddish theater declined in influence, Pinski again devoted his major efforts to the narrative art. In 1921 he conceived the grandiose plan of sketching fictional portraits of each of King Solomon's thousand wives and thus baring the myriad aspects of the soul of woman. During the following fifteen years he completed 105 of these tales. The climax of his narrative art, however, was reached in his two long novels *Arnold Levenberg,* begun in 1919 and dealing with the German-Jewish aristocracy of New York, and *The House of Noah Edon,* written in the summer of

1929 on the eve of the Great Depression and dealing with the assimilation of American Jews of Eastern European origin. The subtitle of the former novel was *The Split Personality* (*Der Tserissener Mentsh*). Arnold Levenberg was an unheroic hero, a Jewish Hamlet, a refined, weak-willed individual torn between conflicting urges and conflicting social forces. As the youngest member of a well-established firm, he had no interest in acquiring additional, unnecessary wealth. As the scion of a patrician family, he did not care to seek a still higher social status. His grandfather had emigrated to America from Germany after the failure of the Revolution of 1848 and had raised children, and they their children, to love freedom, justice, equality, and to practice tolerance of differing views. Arnold's circle retained a love of German culture and a preference for the easy going ways of the Uptown Jews. When he came in contact with the less well-mannered but more intense Downtown Russian Jews—socialist agitators, militant revolutionaries, Zionist idealists—Arnold was attracted and disturbed by their strange thinking and behaving. His emotional life was also shaken by his contact with girls of different types, each of whom appealed to one aspect of his personality but not to other layers of his ambivalent soul. The First World War roused him temporarily out of his complacency but from his uncommitted vantage point he peered too deeply into the hypocrisy of the loud-mouthed war patriots, the pacifists turned militarists, the liberals espousing reactionary slogans, and he could not muster sufficient enthusiasm to hurl himself into any cause. He ended by going off to Europe after the war in the hope of understanding himself better when away from his usual routines. When he returned, he married none of the four girls about whom his young life had circled and who might have mired him in sensual swamps or involved him in complete devotion to Jewish and humanitarian causes. He rather chose as his life's companion a mediocre girl of his own upper middle class. Her main interest was art. At her side, he could escape from the storms of moral, political and ideological conflicts let loose in the post-War world. He could attain moderate happiness. Both would carry on a placid, sheltered existence in the ivory tower of estheticism.

In Arnold Levenberg and his circle, Pinski depicted the wealthy, overrefined, stable, passive, slightly decadent German Jews who had gone far in assimilating to American life and whose Jewish traditions were no longer sufficiently virile to enable them to play more than merely a philanthropic role in the struggle for Jewish survival, let alone rebirth.

Far more important was Pinski's second novel *The House of Noah Edon*, which was published in English translation in 1929, a full decade before it appeared in the original Yiddish. It was directed to Americanized readers whose linguistic medium was no longer the Yiddish of their immigrant fathers and grandfathers. This genealogical novel, which might be compared to Thomas Mann's *Buddenbrooks* or John Galsworthy's *Forsyte Saga*, portrayed three generations of a Jewish family which emigrated to America in the 1880's from a little town in Lithuania.

In the Old Country, Noah Edon lived as a member of a Jewish enclave in non-Jewish territory. When he arrived in America, he tried as far as possible to continue his traditional cultural life. He was a Jew whose Jewishness was enriched by his American environment and experiences. His children, on the other hand, were raised in the New World. They were Americans of Jewish background. They fell under the spell of the brighter, freer, gayer life which opened up before them, full of golden opportunities but also full of perilous allurements. They prospered and rose in the social scale. One became a wealthy businessman, another a corporation lawyer, a third a prominent physician. With each year they became more estranged from the Yiddish idiom which they spoke when they first set foot on American soil. They learned to live without God. They did not normally attend synagogue or temple on the Sabbath. Nor did they differentiate in their homes between a Friday evening and any other evening. But they did send their children to the finest schools and colleges, where these third-generation Americans could be trained to be perfectly mannered ladies and gentlemen.

When the aging Noah Edon in his sixties came together with his *landsleit*, his old cronies of the immigrant generation, all of them had but one complaint: their children and grandchildren had left them and the ancestral ways. A world had arisen that knew not God. The road which they and their forefathers had trodden for untold generations was coming to an end. They alone were left, a remnant of old men surviving as a traditional Jewish enclave in the great American metropolis, Noah's ark amidst the deluge. The youngest generation was smiling indulgently at the spectacle of the old men gathering daily in the basement of a synagogue to study *Gemora* and the strange ways of a strange people in a remote age. But, poring over the yellowed pages of a Talmud tract, these graybeards were rejuvenated. They seemed to live beyond time and space. They felt triumphant, despite the jeering laughter or the sophisticated jests directed at them, because they had the courage, the grand courage, to be true to themselves and to live in accordance with their inner needs. In the depths of their hearts, they hoped for a turning of the tide, for a return of their estranged children, for a reversion to God and to the ways of Israel. Or, if their children were too far gone, too completely immersed in the spirit of the non-Jewish environment, perhaps the grandchildren might be won back. One Friday evening, when the grandchildren of Noah Edon, after a long absence, came to spend the Sabbath eve with their grandparents, one of them confessed: "There is an emptiness in me, often despair overtakes me. I don't know why I'm living in this world. I don't know what to do with myself. My work amidst the skyscrapers is merely a way of killing time. This emptiness, this uselessness, must lead me astray, must lead me to weakness, folly and immorality. I believe religion could help me; it could fill my life with content; it could calm me."

Because these grandchildren were raised without religion, however, this insight came too late. Their splendid homes in the finest sections of the city had many books, usually arranged on mahogany shelves according to an artistic color scheme, but the Bible was not among these books. If it happened to stray there as a Bar-Mitzvah gift, it was unread and its message unheard and unheeded. These Americans of Jewish origin were no longer embedded in Jewish tradition. Each of them was a detached fragment in the body of America, living a lonely life and facing a lonely death.

Pinski's novel, completed when prosperity was at its height and when Jewishness seemed to be in precipitous decline, ended in despair, in suicide, double suicide, triple suicide. Its conclusion was as pessimistic as the conclusion of Peretz's story *Four Generations—Four Testaments*, upon which it was based. Its author held up a mirror to the generation of the 1920's, presenting a horrible object lesson. He called for a stemming of the tide of assimilation to the non-Jewish environment. He begged: don't let a generation grow up that is emptied of Jewish content. It will not be a happy generation.

During Pinski's half-a-century in New York, from 1899 to 1949, he interpreted for American Jews in many stories their long, long past; he sought for the meaning of their difficult present; he conjured up visions of their possibilities in Israel and America. He never inflamed or devastated. He always comforted and consoled.

Abraham Reisen was four years younger than Pinski but he came under the influence of Peretz at about the same time. He was only fifteen when Peretz accepted his first lyric for publication and only sixteen when his first short story appeared. Born in the Lithuanian townlet of Kaidanov, he preferred to write of the lethargic, traditional little settlements of the Pale long after he himself had moved to the larger towns of Kovno, Cracow, Warsaw and New York. He found poetry in their narrow, muddy lanes and decaying houses. He showed deep sympathy with the religious groups that resisted the incursions of modern ideas. His women remained unemancipated and rarely questioned their destiny as not quite the equals of their husbands for whom they bore and reared children and also carried most of the burden of breadwinners. His men were pious scholars who accepted life on the verge of starvation as God-ordained; petty merchants whose brief period of prosperity had long ago given way to penury; cantors and maggidim who were dependent for their poor livelihood upon the shifting whims of public opinion. Often his stories interpreted reality through the imagination of children who were imprisoned in gloomy classrooms and forced to imbibe the dry wisdom of old tomes but who yearned for the rarely experienced freedom of forests, brooks and birds.

Reisen was both poet and short story writer. His lyrics were often set to music; one of them, *Mai Ka Mashmalon,* became a folksong which moved millions with its plaintive melody. It was a pensive song of the itinerant Torah-students, thousands of whom were sent away far from home at too early an age to continue their studies at various centers of learning. Such youths had to provide for themselves while studying, but not by working. The hard bench of the synagogue served as their bed and pious families provided them with meals in the hope that such charity would be chalked up in heaven.

Trained to muse on the symbolic meaning of every phenomenon, the Yeshiva lad in Reisen's poem found that the raindrops trickling down the window panes were not unlike the tears trickling down his cheeks. The road was turning to mud and his boots were torn. Soon winter would come and he had no coat to warm him. Gazing upon the tallow dripping from the candle, he saw in its sputtering, ever dimming light, a symbol of his own life that was wasting away bit by bit and would soon be extinguished. Staring at the clock whose face had turned yellow, and whose hands were constantly moving, he realized that it was but doing the bidding of its maker, who allowed it no feeling or will of its own. Was it not a symbol of each of us, who were driven by our Maker to carry out his will and not our own? Did we fare any better, though we were born with feeling and vitality? Did we not let our youth rot away and yellow age sear us far too soon? Were we not denying ourselves the gifts of this world, while waiting and hoping for a world beyond?

Reisen was the poet and narrator of the defeated, the rejected, the timid, the hungry, the gray colorless persons whose longings and frustrations were of no interest to others. Yet each of these individuals retained a remnant of dignity and an abundance of goodness. The bent beggar who stood on the threshold and pleaded for alms with tired hand and lowered eyes was also God's creature, a member of the highest terrestrial species, the crown of the world. Reisen depicted the carpenter who built houses for others and made them tight-fitting to keep out the bitter cold of winter but who still lacked the means and leisure to repair his own little dwelling and thus to protect himself from the icy blasts of the cruel season. Reisen presented the tailor who worked day and night to ready garments for his customers but who could not afford to sew winter clothes to keep himself warm. Reisen's cobbler hammered on and on until midnight so that the shoes for the rich man's daughter might be finished on time and bread come into the house. Reisen bewailed the lot of his helpless Jewish people who could not ward off their bloodthirsty foes with weapons and who had to direct pleas for mercy and survival to these very enemies.

Reisen was a master of the short story and produced intensely dramatic effects with a minimum of words. In his lyrics he preferred simple quatrains to the more complex stanzaic forms, and the speech of the market place to the sophisticated language of the educated. He was the poet of autumn and winter far more than of spring and summer. Every raindrop was for him a searing tear. In the soughing of the wind he discerned a deep moaning at the unending misery it perceived in its course. The bent and dessicated treelets whose branches wept incessantly and shook in despair reminded him of the insufficiently nourished human beings who moved about without hope or purpose.

Reisen treated universal themes but imparted to them specific

Jewish features, choosing his similes and metaphors from Jewish activities. He attempted a synthesis of the biblical and the contemporary. He felt that the gift of mating words and tones had been bestowed upon him not to toy with in idle hours but rather to clarify concepts, to deepen insights, to dispel evil, to communicate Messianic visions, to work for universal salvation. His was a responsible calling. He did not brood on his own individual sorrow but rather buried it in the common sorrow of his people. His verses sought to emulate the rhythmic prayers of the synagogue, which were born of millennial martryrdom, intense faith, and prophetic vision. His love lyrics were devoid of cynicism and echoed the tone and imagery of the *Song of Songs*. The melody of love that floated between his timid youths and chaste maidens was the same melody that angels sang in Heaven's tent. Of each kiss a new angel was born. A single caress was like a ray of sunshine breaking in upon a dreary day or like a refreshing oasis in a parched desert. A moment of love was a moment of relief from the silence and loneliness that were ultimately inescapable.

The tales of Reisen charmed. Despite their sadness, they did not depress. His humor was mild, not bubbling; his tragedy was elevating, not devastating. Despite his adoration of Gogol and Chekhov, Pushkin and Heine, he followed primarily in the footsteps of Peretz and was his gentlest disciple.

Hersh David Nomberg was born in the same year as Reisen but began as a Hebrew writer. Only after he came under the influence of Peretz in 1897 was he persuaded to use Yiddish as his literary medium. He then roomed with Reisen and Sholem Asch and this literary triumvirate inspired each other and helped to make the Peretz circle dominant in Warsaw. Among them, Nomberg was the most sober and the most critical. His rationalism inhibited his creativity.

Raised in a Hassidic home and suddenly introduced to secular learning, Nomberg lost his anchor in faith and was tossed about helplessly on a sea of scepticism and pessimism. The characters he etched in his stories were autobiographic. Obsessed by inner uncertainty, they flaunted their superior knowledge and moral integrity. Suffering from congealed emotions and a paralysis of will, they never arrived at clear-cut decisions. Living in garrets, unnoticed by anyone, they became estranged from reality.

In *Fligelman,* the title-hero of his best-known novelette, Nomberg sketched in 1905 the portrait of an unworldly cynic, a gentle schlemihl whom life passed by and who found compensation for his loneliness in an ironic evaluation of his fellow mortals and their seeming successes. His superb knowledge of philosophic systems, however, availed him little when he had to face every-day problems. The years followed each other without leaving any residual impress upon his static personality. Even when he was in love or at least imagined he was in love, he could not sweep a girl off her feet, because his emotions, filtered through his intellect, could find no spontaneous, strong expression. Arriving at the conclusion that his days were devoid of essential meaning, he wanted to hurl himself to death from a bridge but hesitated at the last moment because a policeman was near the bridge. He, therefore, wound up not in the icy waters but in a police cell as a would-be suicide.

The Fligelman type of decadent intellectual reappeared in Nomberg's other narratives. Bender in *Flirtation* (*Dos Shpiel In Liebe*) and Schwarzwald in *Between Mountains* (*Tsvishen Berg*) were also bankrupt souls constantly retreating into an inner sanctuary when faced with the necessity to advance toward commitments. Bender, on the verge of declaring himself in love with Mania during their long walks together, never quite overcame the barrier imposed by the intrusion of his reasoning faculties, and ultimately gave up the attempt to win her, though success was in his grasp. Schwarzwald, student of philosophy, did fall desperately in love with Sonia but could give expression to his love only in timid hexameters and lacked the vitality to overcome her apparent resistance. His only friends, two artists, gave up trying to paint his portrait, for his was a dead face, lost to all hope and movement. He was a living corpse long before he fell to his death.

Nomberg's heroines were also living corpses, congealed souls, overripe, self-centered, apathetic and embittered. They too suffered from too much intelligence and too many inhibitions. They therefore remained unmarried and soon tired of carrying on the burden of existence. Felie Feinstein, the main character of the short story *Be Silent, Sister* (*Shvaig Shvester*), always had near her a little flask of cyanide poison and pictured for years the tremendous experience of imbibing it and dying beautifully. She was after all superfluous and would not be missed except by her sister who was likely to experience a dull, dreary fate like her own.

The scepticism of Nomberg was his undoing. He knew too much and experienced too little. With his logic he rent the veil of romantic illusions and discovered empty faces with flabby features behind the veil. When Peretz advised him to write in Yiddish so as to be more useful to the world, he replied: "And what if I were more useful?" Peretz explained that being more useful to the world brought a person moral satisfaction. Nomberg countered: "And if one is morally satisfied, what then? One can live and die without moral satisfaction." After a brief spurt of creativity under the aegis of Peretz, and after reaching the summit of his fame at the Czernowitz Language Conference of 1908, he devoted himself to journalism. He wrote feuilletons for Warsaw's Yiddish press, participated in politics, travelled to Palestine, Soviet Russia, North and South America, and published books on his travels. But only very few of his narratives were translated and his fame faded with his death in 1927.

By contrast, the fame of his contemporary and early roommate Sholem Asch increased from decade to decade and by the mid-twentieth century exceeded that of any Yiddish writer. This fame was well deserved, for Asch was the most talented of Peretz's disciples. His contact with Peretz began early in 1900, when the nineteen-year-old aspiring novelist made his way to Warsaw and was helped to publish his first melancholy, romantic stories. Though he remained in the Peretz circle only until 1910, the influence of the great master was enduring. As late as 1951 Asch still spoke of himself as a pupil of Peretz, who taught him that all writing must be genuine, an unceasing exploration of one's inner self.

The creative life of Asch embraced fifty-seven years, during which he completed sixty volumes, mainly narratives and dramas. His first story, *Moishele,* appeared in 1900 and his first collection of stories in 1903. His early reputation rested upon his idyllic tale *The Townlet* (*Dos Shtetl,* 1904) and his tragedy *God of Vengeance* (*Gott Fun Nekoma,* 1907).

The former was a nostalgic narrative of the beauty and inwardness of Jewish life in the small communities far from the mainstream of European culture. Asch's kind, tender approach to the townlet was immediately sensed as a great innovation, since such settlements had until then been subjects for ridicule and satire, symbols of Jewish petrefaction and superstitious resistance to enlightenment. It is true that Sholom Aleichem had directed attention to rays of light that pierced the prevailing gloom. But young Asch was the first to place a romantic halo about the despised townlets, to seek out fragments of beauty in the filth-infested streets, to concentrate on the moments of charm and poetic elevation amidst the grayness of daily existence. His was the Sabbath-tone, the holiday-tone.

Asch subtitled *The Townlet* a poem in prose. It centered about the house of the lumber merchant Gombiner, where the door was open day and night and where travelers from far and near were welcomed guests and felt at home. Unlike Sholom Aleichem's Menachem Mendel or Mendele's Benjamin the Third, Asch's merchant had his feet planted firmly on the earth. His eyes surveyed clearly the many business projects he set in motion and he was ever on the alert to make a profitable investment. At the same time, however, he was also aware that man in all his enterprises had a partner in God and he therefore never deviated from the moral principles recorded in God's holy book. When spring torrents broke up the ice and threatened to sweep his rafts of logs out to sea, he mobilized all available human resources to save as many logs as possible during the day. However, when darkness set in and the raging waters threatened to swallow everything, he showed no fear. He felt that the God of Mercy would guard the rafts overnight. Confident in the fairness of his heavenly partner, he ordered the work to be interrupted until dawn rather than to endanger human lives. God did indeed help. The ice bypassed Gombiner's rafts and he was able to bring his logs to safety.

Gombiner's business trip to his icebound lumber also brought him in contact with another merchant, whose studious lad, fresh from a Yeshiva, might make a fine mate for his daughter, and so the match was discussed by the fathers. Though the girl would have preferred the son of a Hassidic rabbi whom she had seen and admired from a distance, nevertheless she submitted to her father's wish and travelled with an entourage of relatives to meet the young man chosen for her. In accordance with the innovation of having young couples see each other before betrothal so that they might signify their voluntary acceptance of their parents' choice, the two young people were brought together for a few moments and then the engagement ceremony proceeded as a union not merely of two individuals but also of two families. The climax was reached a few months later when the entire community participated in the wedding festivities.

Asch's activity as a dramatist began in 1904, the same year as his idyllic narrative of the townlet. He completed fifteen plays during the decade preceding the First World War and six plays thereafter. In addition, several of his more important later novels, such as *Motke the Thief, Salvation,* and *Three Cities,* were adapted for the Yiddish theater. His drama, *Messianic Age (Moshiakhs Tseiten,* 1905), was his first success on the Yiddish stage and the following play, *God of Vengeance* (*Gott Fun Nekoma*, 1907), won him his largest international audience.

The theme of the former play was the longing for Messianic redemption, though each character saw this redemption in a different light. On the occasion of Reb Chanan's eightieth birthday, he and his wife called together their widely dispersed children and grandchildren in order to take final leave of them before setting out to live and die in the Holy Land. At the family gathering in the Polish-Jewish townlet the alienation of the younger persons from the traditional, ancestral ways came to the fore. Yet, each of the grandchildren pursued a Messianic objective or yearned for such an ideal. One loved primarily the soil of Poland and dreamed of a restoration of Polish glory. Another was infatuated with the cause of the proletariat and was willing to devote his entire life to their liberation from capitalistic exploitation. Still another was caught up in the Zionist enthusiasm evoked by Herzl and saw the regeneration of Jews as possible only by a pioneering existence in Palestine. The most tragic of the offspring of Reb Chanan was the grandson who had been raised without any Messianic faith. He was completely bewildered and found life purposeless and hence intolerable. At the end of the play, he cried out: "Here I'm a stranger, there I'm a stranger. I stand on the border between land and land, people and people, language and language. . . . My mother lost me at the crossroads. I don't know where to turn. To the right or to the left? So I stand at the crossroads and don't know who I am, where I came from, what is yours and what is mine. It's all the same to me, all the same." This despairing conclusion voiced the dilemma of the uncommitted Jewish intellectual during the revolutionary year 1905.

The international vogue of Asch's next play, *God of Vengeance*, was given impetus by Max Reinhardt's production in Berlin's Deutsches Theater, with Rudolf Schildkraut in the main role of Yankel Shapshovitch, the keeper of a brothel. As the father of a daughter whom he tried to preserve from the immoral atmosphere on the lower story of his house, Yankel ordered a Torah scroll to be written and placed in her room on the upper story. He hoped that the Torah's purity would ward off impurity from her. But the God of Vengeance, whom he feared, could not be bribed and brought retribution upon the sinner. When Yankel discovered that his daughter too had succumbed to the infernal temptations from which he drew his sustenance, he raged against the God who punished children for the sins of parents and he hurled God's

Torah from the upper story down to the abode of sin and horror. When Asch first read this unpublished play to Peretz, he was advised to burn it, despite its fine literary qualities. When it was played in German, Polish, Russian, French, English, Italian and Danish versions and published in the original Yiddish, Peretz reviewed it as a splendid literary work by a flaming talent but also pointed out its shortcomings. He deprecated Asch's overstraining for sensational effects and becoming too intoxicated with alien praise. He was nevertheless certain that Asch would not become a renegade but would always remain and must remain a Yiddish writer, best at home when dealing with Jewish themes. Religious circles, however, raged for many years became of the dramatist's desecration of the Torah by placing the Holy Scroll in a brothel.

Asch left Poland for his first trip to Palestine in 1907 and his first trip to the United States in 1909. In the Holy Land he was overawed by the biblical sites and memories. He felt as if he were returning to the home of his mother after a long, long absence. In sketches and short stories and later on, after repeated visits there, in his novel *Song of the Valley* (*Dos Gezang Fun Tol*, 1938), he gave expression to his admiration for the idealistic pioneers who restored new fruitfulness to the long neglected earth.

As a prominent Yiddish writer, he attended the Czernovitz Language Conference of 1908 and suggested the translation of the Hebrew classics into Yiddish. As his own contribution, he translated the *Book of Ruth,* whose gentle idyllic tone best suited his romantic, lyric temperament.

His trip to the New World resulted in a series of articles depicting the magnificence of America's natural phenomena from Niagara Falls to the Grand Canyon and California, and by contrast the cruel seamy side of Jewish immigrant life in slums, tenements and sweatshops. More important was his narrative *America* (1910), in which he described the sad lot of a Jewish child whose first attempt to emigrate to America with his mother, brothers and sister ended in failure when he was sent back to Russia by the health authorities of Ellis Island, the island of tears. However, when he ventured the ocean crossing a second time a few years later and was admitted to the land of his dreams, he was unable to adjust to its rugged ways, its heartless materialism and its dying Jewishness. In Yossele's odyssey, Asch mirrored the tragic homelessness of every Jewish person who was torn away from childhood roots in the Old Country. Asch himself was the tenth and most sensitive child of his family. His brothers and sisters, when transplanted to America, grew roots in the new soil. His heart, however, remained attached to the Polish-Jewish earth from which he sprang and the patriarchal atmosphere of his father's house. Not until many years later did he, the homeless wanderer, reconcile himself to America and appraise more sympathetically the American purpose.

In *Reb Shlome Nagid* (1913), the title character was modeled after his idealized image of his own father and the period described was the generation preceding his own when the new ideas that were to revolutionize the traditional townlets had not yet exerted their full impact. The tale, written in glowing poetic language, began with a description of the Sabbath at the home of the prosperous merchant Shlome Nagid and ended with the celebration of the birth of a son and the betrothal of a daughter. Temptations, quarrels and riots passed as clouds across the clear, eternal sky of Jewishness; momentarily they cast an ominous shadow, but in the long run the clouds were dissolved, the shadows disappeared, and the townlet continued in its normal, moral routines.

World War I broke out a year after Asch published this idyllic tale. He was forced to leave his temporary residence in France and he spent the war years in New York. His thoughts at first still harked back to his unfortunate coreligionists who were fighting on Russia's side and who were nonetheless mistreated as scapegoats after every Russian military setback. He described their suffering in short stories. But his most important works of the war years were *Motke the Thief* (*Motke Ganev,* 1917), a realistic novel of a thief with a heart, and *Uncle Moses* (1918), a novel of the hard lot of Jewish immigrants during their first years in New York.

After the war, Asch revisited Eastern Europe as a representative of the Joint Distribution Committee, which was organizing relief for the Jewish victims of the war and the revolution. He heard harrowing tales of communities, such as he had portrayed with much affection, which had gone up in flames and of tens of thousands of Jews who had been slaughtered by covetous neighbors, Cossack plunderers, Petlura's pillagers, Denikin's marauders. He saw the post-War pogroms as a repetition of events of 1848, when Hetman Chmelnitsky's hordes laid waste earlier flourishing Jewish communities. In old chronicles he read of the martyrdom of the Jews of Zlochov, Nemirov and Tulchin, when Ukrainian peasants revolted against Polish overlords and, unable to reach these absentee landowners, vented their rage upon the helpless Jewish minority. He was tempted to retell these historic events with an eye to the present. In glorifying the martyrs of the seventeenth century, he wanted to bring comfort to contemporary survivors of similar outrages. In seeking for a meaning to the suffering of earlier ancestors, he was at the same time giving his interpretation of the current Jewish tragedy. In the narrative *Kiddush Hashem* (1920), he succeeded in creating an enduring masterpiece of Yiddish literature.

Its central figure was the innkeeper Mendel, the only Jew of Zlochov, far out on the steppe of Podolia. Though living on good terms with his peasant neighbors and the Zaporozhe Cossacks, Mendel felt ill at ease because there were no Jews near him and no synagogue. The Polish aristocratic landowner, under the influence of a Jesuit priest, sought to humiliate the Greek Orthodox faith in the eyes of the Cossacks by leasing their church to the Jewish innkeeper, thus compelling them to apply to the Jew for the key which unlocked the church and to pay a fee to the Jewish collector of the tax whenever there was a christening or other religious rite. In moments of drunkenness, Father Stephan threatened Mendel with the little brothers who would some day come riding out of the steppe, liberate the peasants from the lords and the churches from the Jews, and avenge all wrongs.

Despite this ever present danger, Mendel won permission to erect a synagogue and thus to attract other Jews to this remote outpost. As the first settler, he became the Parnes or headman of the Jewish community. At the dedication of the synagogue, he married off his eight-year-old son to the rabbi's daughter. Six years later the young married man was sent off to the famed Yeshiva of Lublin, from which he returned at the age of twenty as a learned Talmudist fit for communal leadership.

The peaceful growth of the new Jewish community ended suddenly when Chmelnitzky rose up against the Poles and at the head of an army of Cossacks and Tatars advanced upon Zlochov. Its Jews wanted to stay and to defend their synagogue, but their rabbi commanded them to flee with the Torah scrolls. Jews must not risk their lives defending a structure built of stones and sticks. They must save their strength for a higher purpose, for a more trying occasion. They must preserve their lives, which belonged not to themselves but to God.

There followed stirring scenes of their flight to Nemirov, the massacre of most of Nemirov's Jews, the escape of the rest to Tulchin, and the betrayal of the Jews of Tulchin by their Polish allies who handed them over to the Cossacks in return for their own guaranteed safety. The climax was reached when the betrayed Jews were offered a chance to survive, if they would bow down before the cross. They replied with the singing of Psalms to the Lord of Israel. Their hour of sacrificial heroism was at hand. For the sake of their God, 1400 men, women and children were slaughtered that day in the orchard of Tulchin by the Cossacks. Their blood became intermingled and their souls rose up together. But not a single one of them purchased his life with the abandonment of his faith.

The theme of Jewish sacrificial heroism fascinated Asch. Repeatedly he reverted to the conflict between non-Jewish physical might and Jewish moral elevation, to the apparently temporary triumph of the armed fist and the more enduring victory of the Jewish spirit through the very act of martyrdom. He often contrasted the wicked arrogance of those who committed wrong with the simple holiness of the victims who suffered wrong. He held that death for the Sanctification of the Name—Kiddush Hashem— supplied the best testimony that Jews were unconquerable.

An episode from *Kiddush Hashem*—the startling effect produced by a Jewish girl with a Madonna-face upon her captor and her resolution to die for her faith, despite all allurements—was expanded by Asch to form the main theme of *The Witch of Castille* (*Die Kishifmakherin Fun Kastilien*, 1921).

The scene of the new tale was sixteenth century Rome, where many Jews who had fled from Spain and Portugal found a safe haven for a generation or two. Evil days came upon them, however, when Paul IV ascended the papal throne. Unable to stem the tide of Reformation which Luther and Calvin had set in motion, he vented his rage upon the helpless Jews of Rome's ghetto and heaped ever new indignities and tortures upon them. Still he could not break their stubborn adherence to the God of their fathers. Even in the cells of the Inquisition, as soon as they were released from the rack, they sang the Psalms of their ancient faith. A Venetian painter who found his way to the Roman ghetto was struck by the Madonna-like appearance of a beautiful, sad Jewess, a descendant of the aristocratic Sephardic family of Abarbanel. He modelled a Madonna altar-piece after her and, when the resemblance was noticed, a rumor spread that the Madonna had appeared among the Jews of the ghetto and was protecting them. When this report reached the Pope, he accused the Jewess of having usurped the face of the mother of Jesus through sorcery.

To test whether she was indeed the Madonna, as many insisted, he ordered that she be burned at the stake, holding that flames could not consume a heavenly being. Dying at an auto-da-fé as the Witch of Castille, she bore witness to her stern faith even as had her father before her and Jews of all centuries who would not bend the knee to the Cross.

Asch continued to enrich Yiddish literature with narratives glorifying Jewish deeds of brotherly love and quiet heroism and contrasting these deeds with non-Jewish reliance on force and superstitious arrogance. *Salvation (Der Tilim Yied)*, completed in 1932 on the eve of Hitler's rise to power and published in 1934, and the stories of *The Burning Bush (Der Brenendiker Dorn)*, completed at the height of Hitler's power and collected in 1946, contained such glorifications of Jewish ethical striving.

The hero of *Salvation* was called the Psalm-Jew because his learning at first extended no further than to an ability to interpret the Psalms. But, because of his all-embracing pity, he was like a magnet atttracting crippled bodies and starved souls. His confidence in the ultimate triumph of good infected all his followers and spread rays of sunshine upon their poor lives. By comforting others and suffering with them, he himself attained to salvation. His God was to be served with joy and compassion and the earth was to be sanctified and raised to a heaven for human beings.

The novel was not merely a narrative of the simple person who overcame human frailties and worked his way up to holiness, a light and a hope unto all who came within the range of his presence, it was also an epic of Polish Jewry of the nineteenth century, a Jewry that sought release from abjectness, servility and despair by embracing the joyous mysticism of Hassidism. Asch painted a broad panorama of this movement but at the same time he included a vivid portrait of the strange aberration of a rationalistic intrusion into its mysticism, the Brotherhood that gathered about the Rebbe of Kotzk. Intermingling warm romanticism and stark realism, the author attained in this work the highest triumph of his idealization of historic Jewish life and was hailed as the gifted defender of the Jewish way of life in the years when it was subjected to wide attacks.

The Burning Bush contained the story "Yitgadal V'Yitkadash," whose leading character submitted to the Nazis torturing his body but did not let them break his soul and accepted death by hanging rather than disobey God's commandment not to work on the Sabbath. In another story, "A Child Leads the Way," Asch retold the martyrdom of the ninety-three girls of Warsaw's religious Bnoth Jacob School, all of whom committed suicide so as not to fall into the immoral hands of Nazi soldiers. The school principal, who prepared the poison for these pupils, also readied them for the exalted moment of self-sacrifice when they would be received in heaven by the biblical matriarchs as worthy daughters of their people.

Asch was at the height of his popularity among Jewish readers when he suddenly shocked them with the first of his Christological novels, *The Nazarene*. This novel was first published in English in 1939 and was translated into many tongues but it was spurned by Yiddish publishers and did not reach Yiddish readers in the original until 1943. It involved him in unending controversies with Jews who felt betrayed in their hour of utmost need by his apparent apostasy. He, however, did not regard himself as an apostate. He saw no reason why he could not rehabilitate for Jews the saintly, compassionate Jewish Rabbi Yeshua ben Yosef of Nazareth, who had won his earliest disciples among their ancient kinsmen, who had made the supreme sacrifice on the cross for the sanctification of Jehovah's name, and whose martyrdom had been misused by the foes of the Jews as a scourge with which to whip them and degrade them. Yeshua, or Jesus, was a rabbi after Asch's own heart. He even set out to rehabilitate Judas Iscariot, whom he saw as the most wronged among the disciples of the Rabbi of Nazareth. However, during the decade of his work upon his Christological novels, *The Nazarene* (1939), *The Apostle* (1943), and *Mary* (1949), he became so deeply involved in his creative task and his imagination so deeply stirred by his sources, primarily the *New Testament*, that he soon found himself more at home in the generation when Jesus walked on earth than in his own. He himself seemed to be experiencing the very transmigration he attributed in *The Nazarene* to his hero Yochanan, the pupil of Nicodemus, a transmigration from the twentieth century to the first. While tragedy was overwhelming his contemporary kinsmen, Asch became imbued with the notion that he might serve as the precursor of the Messiah; he felt that he might be able to save from extinction the remnant that was surviving Hitler's Holocaust, Stalin's purges, and Bevin's rage, by effecting a reconciliation between the Jews and the Christian world. He genuinely believed that by enriching the accepted Jewish tradition with the hitherto unacceptable teachings of Rabbi Yeshua he would be helping his people and accomplishing a deed of great historic value. Then anti-Semitism would disappear and true brotherhood would reign between Jews and their neighbors. Unfortunately, his trilogy was ill-timed and his cosmopolitan religious ideas were drowned in the tears of Auschwitz and Treblinka.

The angry rejection of his Christological novels by most of his Jewish admirers—the critic Shmuel Niger and the poet Melech Ravitch were notable exceptions—hurt and embittered him. The adulation of hundreds of thousands of non-Jewish readers did not assuage his bitterness or take from him a sense of gathering loneliness. The triumph of Israel and the phenomenal recovery of the maimed survivors of ghettos and concentration camps revealed to him his people's resiliency even in the mid-twentieth century. So often he had depicted the stubborn adherence of Jews to their one God, and their unbreakable will to survive in their uniqueness. But, when he saw catastrophes descend upon them in his own time, his faith in their ability to continue any longer their separate historic existence had weakened. Had he, too, been the man of little trust? He had not expected the miracle of Jewish rejuvenation that was unfolding before his eyes. He was amazed by their re-emergence as a revitalized group. In the last decade of his life, he repented of his temporary loss of confidence in them. He sought to break out of his isolation from his adored Jews and to convince them of his good intentions. He resumed work on his novel *Moses,* which he had put aside during the decade of his Christological trilogy. He retold the story of the man of humility and supreme courage who led his people out of bondage and gave to them the Law by which they were to live ever thereafter.

In 1954 Asch settled in Israel. There the restless wanderer felt at home at last. There he wrote his last novel *The Prophet* (*Der Nabi,* 1955). The controversy about him began to ebb. His house in Bat Yam, a suburb of Tel Aviv, attracted Hebrew and Yiddish intellectuals who appraised him with ever increasing kindness. He was again recalled as the romanticist of the Jewish townlets which had been erased from the face of the earth but lived on in his early works. It was more difficult to regain enthusiasm for his realistic novels. Even his long trilogy *Three Cities* (*Farn Mabul,* 1929-1930), which had unrolled on a wide canvas Jewish life in St. Petersburg, Warsaw and Moscow before and during the Russian Revolution, seemed dated. His dramas no longer resounded from Yiddish stages. But, whatever the weaknesses of Asch, he did achieve what even his early mentor Peretz had failed to achieve. He poured the Yiddish word into the mainstream of

European and American culture. He made the Occident aware that in Yiddish a literature had arisen as the expression of a unique historic group and that this literature harbored works of esthetic beauty and moral grandeur. He was the first Yiddish writer of truly international vogue.

9

THE NOVEL OF
YOUNG AMERICA

Early Immigrant Storytellers ● Tashrak ● Abraham
Cahan ● Jacob Adler ● Ignatoff ● Raboy ● M. J.
Haimowitz ● Opatoshu ● Lamed Shapiro ● S. Miller

THE AMERICAN YIDDISH novel from its beginnings was not
primarily an educational medium as was the poetry of the lyric
pioneers. Its main purpose was not to agitate for various radical
causes but rather to attract readers to the Yiddish press by offering entertainment in addition to a newspaper's normal function
of imparting news. Through serialized narratives in dailies and
weeklies, storytellers could reach far larger audiences than through
published books. Besides, if an author attained popularity as a
journalist, feuilletonist or editor, he could more easily gain favor
with a publisher for his longer romances.

While a few Yiddish weeklies were available as media for fiction
before the mass immigration of the 1880's, they led a precarious
existence. Of the earliest Yiddish weekly, *Die Post,* founded in
1870 by Zvi Hirsh Bernstein (1846-1907) and edited initially by
Zvi Gershoni (1844-1897) and then by Mordecai I. Yehalmstein
(1835-1897), not a single copy has survived, an indication of how
limited was its circulation. *Die Yiddishe Gazetn,* founded in 1874
by Yehalmstein and his brother-in-law Kasriel Hersch Sarasohn
(1835-1905), was more successful and survived for more than
half a century. But it was not until 1885, when the first Yiddish
daily, the *Tageblatt* was founded, that talented writers could be
saved from toiling in sweatshops by being engaged to write short
stories and novels for the daily consumption of its avid readers,
whose numbers rose from an initial 3,000 to nearly 70,000. If the

Yiddish narratives were generally sensational, sentimental and ephemeral, blame rested with the undeveloped taste of the uncritical immigrant audience as well as the rapidity with which literary products had to be turned out.

Sarasohn, the publisher of the *Tageblatt*, was a pillar of the Orthodox Jewish sector and catered primarily to its needs. Hence the editors he attracted followed conservative traditions and avoided startling innovations in style and content. They included Getzel Zelikowitch (1863-1926), Johann Paley (1871-1907), Gedaliah Bublik (1875-1948), Israel Joseph Zevin (1872-1926) and Leon Zolotkoff (1866-1938), all of whom, except Bublik, a founder of the religious Zionist movement, Mizrachi, and of the American Jewish Congress, filled the newspaper's columns with their narratives. Zelikowitch had begun as a Semitic scholar and Egyptologist. He preferred to pontificate as a literary critic with learned reviews that displayed his extensive knowledge but his readers were more attracted to his novels, which he published under various pseudonyms and with sensational titles such as *The Bitter Female, The Pillaged Grave, Vengeance of a Corpse.* Since such novels helped to increase the newspaper's circulation, he wrote dozens of them. His successor, Paley, preferred to pen mystery novels and to adapt French novels that were full of suspense. Zevin, who became known under the pseudonym of Tashrak, wrote humorous tales of American Jewish life and mirrored tolerantly the foibles of the immigrants in such characters as Chaim the Customer-Peddler, Joe the Waiter, Simcha the Shadchen and Berl the Butcher-Boy. In addition to four volumes of selected narratives, he also published seven volumes of legends taken from the Talmud and from Hebraic folklore, two volumes of parables attributed to the Maggid of Dubnow, and stories for children. Zolotkoff, who edited the Chicago edition of the *Tageblatt*, wrote short stories and serialized novels, several of which were later circulated in book form. To the novelists of this daily also belonged the Hebrew writer Menachem Mendel Dolitzky (1858-1931), who came to the United States in 1892 and found no audience for his Hebrew lyrics and tales. He therefore had to turn to Yiddish and became very popular with his sensational novels in the Orthodox daily. Only a few of his more than forty novels were reprinted in book form. Even more prolific was Moshe Seifert (1851-1922), who had begun with essays and feuilletons in European Hebrew journals and continued with Yiddish plays and operettas after immigrating to New York in 1886. His many sentimental novels with happy endings—he is said to have written sixty-four of them—were eagerly devoured by readers of the *Tageblatt* for almost two decades.

Since this earliest American Yiddish daily catered primarily to the Orthodox community, several efforts were made by labor groups, Socialists, Anarchists, Free Thinkers, ex-Russian revolutionists, to establish a newspaper that would mirror their views and defend their interests. None succeeded until Abraham Cahan (1860-1951) came upon the scene and took over the editorship of the *Forverts* after it was founded in 1897 as the organ of the Jewish Socialists. For half a century he was in unchallenged command of its policies and attracted illustrious contributors, among whom the best story-tellers were Sholem Asch, Abraham Reisen, Zalman Schneour and I. J. Singer. Besides, he himself made a most notable contribution with his novel *The Rise of David Levinsky,* which became an American literary classic. The title hero, a Jewish immigrant who rose to the top of his industry by ruthless exploitation of his fellow-Jews, became aware at the height of his success that his luxurious life was empty of inner meaning, warmth and true values, and he looked back nostalgically upon his earlier self when he was less lonely and sad because he was then still linked to the precious moral heritage of his ancestors.

Nostalgia for the past and especially for the pre-immigrant years was an important theme of early Yiddish fiction in America. However, Jacob Adler (b. 1874), the most popular writer of humorous tales in *Forverts,* fascinated his readers far more with his weekly sketches of immigrant characters who were perfectly at home in New York and the Catskills, characters such as the housewife and shrew Yente Telebende, her husband Mendel, who always wilted under her picturesque curses, and Moishe Kapoir, who found the wrong way to do the right things and the right way to do the wrong things. Adler also wrote serious poetry until his nineties but to his adoring readers he was best remembered under the pseudonym of B. Kovner, the creator of Yente.

Narratives of great literary value rather than mere potboilers designed for daily consumption by newspaper readers were first written in America by the novelists of "Die Yunge," when these arrived disillusioned with pogrom-ridden Europe which had ejected them. The best novelists of "Die Yunge" were David Ignatoff (1886-1954), Isaac Raboy (1882-1944), M. J. Haimowitz (1881-1958) and Joseph Opatoshu (1886-1954).

Ignatoff was only twenty when he landed in New York and only twenty-two when he assumed the leadership of "Die Yunge," but the roots of his personality remained anchored throughout his life in the Hassidic earth of his parents and grandparents and in the revolutionary soil that nourished him at Kiev, where as a youth he participated in socialist agitation, lived dangerously, and suffered arrest and imprisonment. His activity as a writer, therefore, alternated between a colorful romanticism which cast a halo about Jewish traditions and a radical realism which linked him with proletarian literature.

Ignatoff's romanticism was best expressed in his *Wondertales of Old Prague* (*Vundermases Fun Alten Prag,* 1916-1920) and in his adaptations of Nachman Bratslaver's stories in *The Hidden Light* (*Dos Farborgene Likht,* 1918).

The hero of the wondertales is a simple-hearted Jew, Berl Prager, a follower of the saintly Rabbi Loew of Prague. Berl faces innumerable perils as he wanders from land to land in search of a livelihood. He emerges unscathed because of his optimistic faith that God, whose cause he champions, will not let him perish. In his first adventure, he is shipwrecked and washed ashore on an unknown land, together with a sole companion. After three days, both come to the grazing grounds of a one-eyed, man-eating giant. This monster prefers the fat Turk to the lean Jew for his first meal. Before he is ready for a second meal, Berl Prager succeeds in blinding him and in escaping under the belly of the biggest sheep.

This adventure is easily recognizable as of Homeric origin, as the story of Odysseus and the One-eyed Cyclops. However, while the Greek hero depends solely upon his own craftiness, the Jewish wanderer puts his trust in God and in the beloved Rabbi of Prague, God's emissary on earth. Berl ascribes his ingenious plan of escape to God's inspiration and the success of his stratagem to his invincible faith that a homecoming to his wife and children and to the Rabbi is vouchsafed him.

In all of Berl's adventures in the Land of Purity and in the domains of the Queen of the Sabbath, in the belly of the Leviathan and on remote battlefields, he retains his humility and piety. After his victories over the giants who threatened Sabbathland, he puts away his armor, sword and spear. He remarks that he is no bear in the forest, out to frighten people. His weapons were lent to him by a kind Providence to execute the Divine Will and to cleanse holy earth from forces of evil. After his successful campaigns, the weapons are no longer needed. He is not ambitious for worldly success nor does he yearn for fame or dominion. He rather wants to find his way back from the realm of marvels to his waiting family in Old Prague and to the circle of the Rabbi. This wish is finally granted him just before he is gathered to his fathers, among whom he can then dwell forever in celestial palaces.

Ignatoff speaks of the whole world as a tale not yet entirely told. Each of us can experience but fragments of it. In the fantastic stories of *The Hidden Light*, he therefore weaves one incident into another, without at first completing a single one. This accords with his view that no object and no event is an entity in itself but rather a part of the universal structure. At the end, however, the strands of his stories are somehow tied together into a meaningful pattern and the chaos of the world is resolved into a moral edifice.

Ignatoff's search for loveliness through art is reflected in his symbolic tales with their emphasis on purity and light. He has been rebuked for overstraining the use of the word "light" in all his writings. Light is, for him, the symbol of the Sabbath brightness sought by all who dwell in the murky mists of weekdays. It is the symbol of the clarity desired by all who roam in the realm of doubt. It is the symbol of the celestial radiance envisaged in golden dreams as the true eternal abode of the mystic essence interpenetrating the universe. It occurs most frequently in Ignatoff's parables. The best of these is *The Golden Boy* (*Dos Goldene Yingele*, 1921), a vision of the glory perceived in young days, pursued throughout life, and rediscovered by the inner eye after the sun-drenched outer eye has been blinded.

In addition to romantic tales, Ignatoff also composed significant novels of the New York he knew so well both as a shopworker and as a union organizer. However, above all his realistic descriptions of slums and tenements, there tower dream-turrets reaching up to a mystic heaven. Through the filthy streets with their stale air there still blows a breath of divine purity, and the decay of the soul is constantly arrested by an ideal of personal and national regeneration.

In the Cauldron (*In Kesselgrub*, 1918), he depicts the struggle between degeneracy and spiritual rebirth among the young Jewish immigrants. The writer Baruch, in whom Ignatoff portrays himself, is derided as a naive fool when he wants to take his group out of New York's crippling shops onto homesteads in the free spaces of the Western prairies. Nevertheless, he has a beneficent influence upon the sceptical young men and is adored by the troubled young women. All of them sense his inner goodness and are impressed by his unselfish devotion to a moral cause.

Ignatoff's fictional trilogy *Vistas* (*Oif Veite Vegn,* 1932) describes the rise of the Jewish labor movement. Revolutionary idealists, defeated in their efforts to bring about a better order in Russia and uprooted from their native land, try to grow new roots in the United States and to unite against exploitation there. The hero, Berman, is again easily recognizable as Ignatoff himself. He is attracted to radical Socialism, but also repelled by its militant atheism. He holds that human beings who do not have God in their hearts are like mirrors in which nothing is reflected. At the same time, he is isolated among religious Jews and stoned by Orthodox fanatics because of his radical social views. He strives for a synthesis of religion and Socialism, of traditional piety and cooperative idealism.

Ignatoff skillfully makes the real seem unreal and the unreal seem real. When, in words, he paints New York's Broadway on a weekday morning while workers are on their way to the shops, we see this avenue as a long river into which rivulets from side streets pour their human waves. Above this river of countless human droplets we see the gigantic skyscrapers towering, with their thousands of windows illumined by the red and golden rays of the setting sun. These skyscrapers in turn are held in leash by a titanic monster who directs their teeming industrial activities. Each human droplet, however, still retains individual features. One man is solemn and careworn, as he is borne along on the human tide, while another is smiling and self-satisfied. One girl, rushing to her shop, is pale and embittered, while another still trembles with delight, recalling kisses of the preceding night.

Ignatoff's later works include the biblical tragedy *Jephta* (1939), and the longer tragedy *Gideon* (1953). These were little read, because the militant movement he led in the early decades of the century had lost its influence by mid-century. Its young writers aged and scattered far and wide. Of these young writers, Ignatoff's most faithful disciple was the novelist Isaac Raboy, whom he called a pillar of "Die Yunge."

It was Raboy who introduced the Jewish farmer of the American prairies into Yiddish literature, even though the greater part of his life was spent among the slums and factories of New York. Born in the Ukrainian province of Podolia and growing up in Bessarabia, he yearned to escape from his Hassidic home and from the cramped townlet of Rishkon to a more natural existence in intimate contact with the soil. He found, however, that Jews were excluded from acquiring farmland and did not normally engage in health-giving, productive toil. Consorting with young intellectuals who had bright visions of catching up with modern trends of thought, he began to write at seventeen. However, when he sent his first story to Russian, Hebrew and Yiddish magazines, he received from all of them the same discouraging reply. Even his adored Bialik wrote him the single sentence: "You are absolutely without talent."

The Kishinev Pogrom of 1903 convinced his family that there was no future for Jews in the midst of hostile government officials and superstition-ridden peasants. Nor was young Raboy anxious to be drafted into the Czarist army to fight in the Russo-Japanese War, which erupted in 1904. He therefore escaped across the border and made his way to America.

In Raboy's two-volume autobiography, published posthumously in 1947, he related in fascinating detail the story of his flight from Bessarabia, his experiences en route in Lemberg, Vienna and Trieste, his arrival in Castle Garden, and his first impressions of New York's East Side. Two brothers had preceded him and six others, as well as his parents, were soon to follow.

The dream of a literary career, which he entertained, dissolved within a few weeks, as Raboy made the rounds of all the Yiddish newspapers and was everywhere rebuffed. He then had to reconcile himself to toil from dawn to dusk in a hat factory. Only during late hours of the night and in periods of unemployment could he indulge in his passion for literary expression. Not only in his first immigrant years, but also throughout most of his later years, he was forced to continue to earn his bread either at his specialty of making wire frames for ladies' hats or as a furrier. This hard toil, even while his fame as a writer spread, exhausted his strength, ruined his eyesight and undermined his health.

David Pinski, as editor of the weekly *Der Arbeiter*, encouraged the new immigrant by publishing three of his short stories. Mani-Leib, who was his neighbor, and Ignatoff, who worked in the same hat factory, recognized his talent and introduced him to the literary group they were assembling. The anthologies of "Die Yunge" became the principal medium for the publication of Raboy's narratives.

In 1908, weary of the sweatshop and the verbal acrobatics indulged in by the Yiddish literary practitioners of New York's East Broadway, Raboy followed the example of his friend Jacob J. Jaffe, afterwards Professor of Soil Sciences at Rutgers University, in giving up his factory job in order to study farming at the Jewish

Agricultural School set up near Woodbine, New Jersey, with funds supplied by Baron de Hirsch. For two years Raboy studied various aspects of agriculture and after graduating in 1910, he made his way to a ranch in North Dakota which specialized in horse-breeding.

Raboy's experiences as a farm hand supplied him with rich, original subject matter for short stories and for his longer novels *Mr. Goldenbarg* (1913) and *The Jewish Cowboy* (1942). For a time he seriously considered establishing a homestead in the prairie state. A few unpleasant incidents, however, convinced him that his neighbors, despite much good-will, could not entirely forgive him his Jewish origin. Strong family attachment and long-ing for Jewish companionship hastened his decision to return to the Atlantic seaboard. The single effort of his family to make a living as farmers in Connecticut ended in failure and doomed Raboy to a difficult existence thereafter in New York factories.

In his imagination, however, he still roamed the prairies on horseback. He cast a halo about his two years of freedom from the stifling metropolis. In his idealizing novel of the farmer and rancher *Mr. Goldenbarg,* he foreshadowed the characters and themes of his most important work *The Jewish Cowboy.* In both novels, the hero bears the name Isaac and is obviously Isaac Raboy himself. Mr. Goldenbarg is Jewish and sympathetic, in contrast to the boss of the later novel, who is non-Jewish, brutal and avarici-ous. The hero's supersensitive Jewish conscience prevents him from feeling entirely at ease among the various types of ranchers. He is consumed by a longing for Palestine. Though Mr. Golden-barg, aware of Isaac's love for his daughter, offers him the ownership of the successful ranch and a productive life on the fat earth of the prairie, the farmhand cannot renounce his dream of cultivating Jewish dunams in a Jewish homeland.

Raboy's first novel, later adapted for the stage and produced in 1926 under the direction of Peretz Hirshbein, was hailed as a pioneering work which broadened the horizon of American Yiddish literature and which introduced a new type of Jewish toiler, one whose heart went out to horses and cows, forests and prairies. Raboy's second novel *Seaside (Der Pas fun Yam,* 1918) was more sober in tone. It was based upon his family's unsuccessful venture on a neglected Connecticut farm. It dealt entirely with Jews who left urban occupations, unprepared for rugged country living, who therefore found adjustment to the rural environment very difficult, but who nevertheless held out.

Raboy's realistic novels of Bessarabia and of his grandparents'
experiences, after exchanging Bessarabia for New York at the turn
of the century, did not measure up to the quality of his last masterpiece of fiction, *The Jewish Cowboy.* Largely autobiographic and
going beyond realism, this narrative contrasted the beauty of the
prairies throughout the changing seasons with the cruelty of man
to man.

Isaac, the Jewish farmhand on a rich ranch in North Dakota,
fathoms in his boss the abyss of cruelty and duplicity to which
a person who is in the grip of greed can descend. He witnesses in
the latter's wife, an aging, lonely woman, the struggle between
hellish passion and nobility of soul. In the first Indian he meets,
he becomes aware of the injustice done to the Red Men by the
White Men, the degradation of the peaceful, trusting aborigines.
These were deprived of their broad prairies and grazing fields and
concentrated on small reservations, where a continuation of the
rich, native cultural existence to which they had long been accustomed was impossible for them. Isaac gets to know Ellen, the
girl sold into servitude by her poor parents, because they have no
other resource with which to pay for the pair of horses they need
on their homestead. He senses kindness and self-sacrificing love
beneath the girl's taciturn, morose exterior. At no time is he allowed to forget that, though he may be liked as an individual, he
cannot escape unreasoning antipathy toward the Jew in him. In
whatever work he does, he feels that he must excel excessively in
order to prove that a Jew can also engage in hard physical labor,
and in order to be accepted as an equal. When he rides a horse
or sharpens an axe, all eyes are upon him to see whether he be-
haves or does not behave as clumsily as the imaginary Jew is
supposed to behave. He wonders, finally, whether the horse he
tends would continue to respond to him affectionately if it too
knew of his Jewish origin. Throughout the year Isaac toils faithfully for his stern boss. Both seem to be getting along well with
each other. When in a moment of anger, however, his boss gives
vent to a deeply ingrained prejudice and calls Isaac a dirty Jew,
then he is almost strangled by this normally calm assistant. Isaac
returns east but not again to a sweatshop. On a Connecticut farm,
not entirely isolated from his ethnic kind, he hopes to live the
productive, healthy life of a dignified human being, one who
neither exploits others nor is himself exploited.

Raboy was a lyricist in prose. The fresh air of the prairies
courses through his novels, and the growth of the soil was de-

picted by him with ardent affection. He was, therefore, often likened to Knut Hamsun, long before he read this novelist of the untamed Scandinavian North, a comparison which became odious to him when Hamsun began his flirtations with the Nazis.

M. J. Haimowitz was far more prolific as a narrative writer than either Raboy or Ignatoff and yet only a few of his stories and novels appeared in book form. Most of his work is scattered in Yiddish periodicals. Co-editor of anthologies of "Die Yunge," he lacked the dynamism of Ignatoff and the robustness which attracts followers. A gifted storyteller, he steered clear of pure Naturalism, which he condemned as brutal, clinical and unimaginative. On the other hand, he could not lose himself in romantic visions and refused to spin out wondertales which lacked a basis in reality. He rather sought to enrich carefully observed facts by an injection of lyricism and by an emphasis on the emotional motivation for happenings. He was, therefore, drawn from the very beginning of his long career to the Impressionism of the Viennese esthetes, especially Arthur Schnitzler.

Under the influence of Schnitzler, Haimowitz tried to delve into the psychology of the modern woman and to unravel the subconscious layers of her soul. However, he lacked the light touch, the melancholy humor and the tolerant wisdom of the Viennese master. His emancipated characters were still plagued by a Jewish conscience. As a result, his radical girls of New York are less fascinating than Schnitzler's sweet Danubian maidens, and his irreligious heroes retain a dull stodginess and a censoring moral monitor even in the midst of questionable amorous experiences.

Haimowitz best portrayed himself as Levin in the novel *En Route (Oifn Veg, 1914)*. This weak-willed hero let himself be tempted by his friend's estranged wife Frieda. After considerable hesitation, he yielded to her on a wild night. When Frieda and her unsuspecting husband were about to be reconciled somewhat later, Levin stepped in to prevent their reconciliation. Upon Frieda's questioning his right to interfere and to reveal her recent past, he replied that he had a right to shield his friend from being a deceived and betrayed husband. His meddling in his friend's life in the name of absolute truth resulted in Frieda's suicide and in her husband's breaking with him. After this experience, Levin decided to return to his own wife, from whom he had been separated for seven years. When she told him, however, that she had not been entirely faithful to him during this long period of separation, he flared up in anger, and again rejected her as an unworthy mate. This double standard of morality, condoning the man's infidelity while punishing harshly the infidelity of both women, was logically indefensible. Nevertheless, Haimowitz accepted it despite its inconsistencies. He was no innovator in morals as was Ibsen, who had dramatized a similar situation in *The Wild Duck,* but merely an observer of life with its contradictions and failings. His characters were endowed with a conscience which was only partly flexible. They were never completely amoral. They lacked lustre and fire. Even famed adventurers, such as Casanova and Cagliostro in the narrative collection *Merry-Go-Round (Karusel,* 1946), were but pale imitations of Arthur Schnitzler's Casanova and Stefan Zweig's Cagliostro.

The most gifted novelist of "Die Yunge" was undoubtedly Joseph Opatoshu, who commanded a worldwide audience both with his short stories and his long historical novels.

Opatoshu traced his ancestry on his father's side to Reb Meir of Tannhausen, a sixteenth-century follower of Shlomo Molcho, the Messianic visionary who was burned by the Inquisition in 1532. This earliest known ancestor left Franconia in 1552 and settled in the Polish city of Posen. His descendants were rabbis and scholars in Hildesheim, Lask and Warsaw. Opatoshu stemmed on his mother's side from well-to-do villagers who dwelt on the edge of forests and engaged in lumbering.

In his childhood he imbibed from his mother the folklore of Polish woods and streams and from his father the stories of the Hassidic rebbes of Kotzk. During the decade following his birth, his father was active in the pre-Herzlian movement "Lovers of Zion" and composed Hebrew lyrics. At the same time that the young boy attended a Russian elementary school, the father provided him with an intensive Hebrew education at home. The growing lad came in contact with Jewish and non-Jewish playmates from all strata of society and accumulated a vast storehouse of memories upon which he later drew for stories and sketches.

Among strange acquaintances who left a deep impress upon him in his early years was a horse-thief who made a living smuggling horses across the border from Poland to Germany. This thief was killed while defending Jews who were being harassed and beaten at the market-place by their Polish neighbors. Opatoshu later depicted him in his first novel *Romance of a Horse-Thief (A Roman Fun A Ferd-Ganef,* 1917), both in the opening chapter as Eliahu Vilner, a Robin Hood who robbed aristocrats and priests but who never stole from Jews, and in the following chapters as

Zanvel, the hero with a rough exterior and a soft heart, who dreamed of respectability even while engaged in his not-so-respectable profession of horse-thievery.

At nineteen, Opatoshu left for France to study engineering at Nancy, but within a year, when his financial resources were exhausted, he had to return home. At twenty, he began to write. When he showed his first short story to Peretz at Warsaw, he was encouraged to continue.

The bleak reaction in Russia, after the failure of the Revolution of 1905, and the wave of pogroms, which brought about a mass flight of Jews from the Czarist realm, also swept young Opatoshu on to America. He landed in New York in 1907. After brief experiences as a worker in a shoe factory and as a newspaper vendor, he was able to resume his study of engineering. He attended classes at Cooper Union, while supporting himself by teaching in a Hebrew school on Sundays and during afternoon hours. His years of trying to hammer Jewish knowledge into the heads of reluctant pupils and under the supervision of unscrupulous principals and ignorant lay administrators were described by him in a novel published in 1929 under the title *Hebrew* and republished three years later under the title *Lost Persons (Farlorene Mentshen)*.

The main characters in this novel were indeed lost souls. Their prototypes were Opatoshu's colleagues, teachers in New York's Talmud Torahs. He described them as having given up earlier ideals, as having become morally corrupt, intellectually dishonest, emotionally decayed, and as having accustomed themselves to live cynically and to indulge in follies and trivial jealousies. Their pupils, in whom they were supposed to implant a love of Jewishness, grew up hating the Hebrew school, the Hebrew language and the Hebrew pedagogues, and preferring the exciting liberation of ballplaying to dull hours of bondage to a heritage unsuited to New York's raw reality.

From 1910 on, Opatoshu participated in the annuals and anthologies of "Die Yunge." His narrative of the horse-thief appeared in the 1912 anthology and aroused great interest. It introduced a new area of Jewish life, an area avoided until then by his predecessors—the underworld with its joys and dangers, its tremendous vitality, hot passions and not altogether respectable moral values.

Opatoshu's full-blooded, earth-rooted, ignorant, fearless, crafty thieves, smugglers and drunkards were far removed from the frail, impractical, heaven-gazing paupers of Sholom Aleichem or the overidealized, God-fearing patricians of Sholem Asch's romantic townlets. Opatoshu's hero Zanvel, horse-dealer and horse-smuggler, can neither read nor write, but he is resourceful in overcoming difficulties, overpowering opponents, eluding border police. He can also win the hearts of maidens, the timid daughter of a Hassid no less than the more sensual, laughter-loving types.

Opatoshu does not condemn his pariahs. His characters feel that their actions are justified according to their standard of values. If momentarily they are led astray and act contrary to their own moral code, they are sincere in their repentance and ready to atone. Though they revel in sensuality, it is for them rarely an end in itself. It is rather a stage in their personal development, a stepping-stone in their ascent to a more complete life which embraces body and soul.

Opatoshu is faithful to reality. In his many stories no word is spoken and no detail is introduced which is not in consonance with character, environment and era. Nevertheless, though rooted in realism, Opatoshu often transports his readers to an inner world in which dreams, longings, sublimated intuitions seek expression. *In Polish Woods* (1921) best illustrates his approach, his undeviating devotion to factual reality. This novel depicts the decay of a Hassidic court which is overladen with superstitious excrescences, but it also offers glimpses of fervent faith and visions of Jewish and world redemption.

This historical narrative paints the whole gamut of Jewish life in the post-Napoleonic generation, from the lowest depths of degeneracy to the highest summit where saints wrestle with God. It was translated into English, German, Spanish, Hebrew, Russian, Polish, Ukrainian and Rumanian, and thus established Opatoshu's international fame. Based upon thorough research, but also upon the author's recollections of incidents narrated to him by grandparents, granduncles and grandaunts, it unrolls a rich panorama of Polish-Jewish interrelations up to the Revolt of 1867. Mordecai, who grows up in a forest hamlet and consorts with woodsmen and fishermen, becomes the spokesman for the novelist's views on eternal and specifically Jewish problems. Mordecai's observations at the decaying Hassidic court of Kotzk form the central part of the narrative. Mordecai witnesses the death throes of a great mystic movement, the disintegration of a famous religious brotherhood, the wrestling of a mighty pillar of Hassidism, Reb Mendele Kotzker, with doubt and despair. He is also introduced to the pioneers of enlightenment, the early Maskilim, who were burrowing with the tools of logic and scepticism into the structure of traditional beliefs. Toward the end, he is fascinated by the glamorous mirage of Polish-Jewish brotherhood, which is to point the way to universal fraternity and world salvation. He, therefore, participates with Polish patriots in the movement for the liberation of his native land from Russian domination and is forced to seek safety abroad.

In a sequel to the novel, entitled *1863* and published in 1929, Opatoshu transports this hunted refugee to Paris, the center for exiled Polish patriots. There Mordecai, who can no longer retain his faith in the God of his childhood, seeks the divine in striving for universal justice on earth. He consorts with Moses Hess, Michael Bakunin and Western thinkers as well as with Polish poets and Polish apostles of the brotherhood of nations. From Parisian exile he then makes his way back to his native land as revolutionary plans explode into action. The rebellion of 1863 fails and Mordecai's father, who has also become involved, is hanged by the Cossacks. At the last moment, when Reb Abraham is led to the gallows, a doubt flashes through his mind. He was sacrificing his life for the cause of Poland, his cause and yet not his cause. He was dying for the sanctification of God's name. Which God? The Jewish or the Polish? The narrative closes with the crows flying from the still warm, dangling body of this old Jew of the forest to the prostrate corpse of a murdered Polish aristocrat and back again to the Jewish patriot.

Mordecai, wounded in battle, was kept alive by the author in order to figure as the central character of the third part of the fictional trilogy, but this third part was never written.

Opatoshu's interest was shifting more and more from the land of his birth to the New World and from the century of his birth to all the previous centuries of Jewish history. In describing the Jewish personality in its various transformations, he felt that he was also describing a universal personality, since Jews were not merely residents of a specific land but also members of a world people whose capital was Jerusalem. Jewish history was, in his opinion, the history of almost all lands on this globe in whose midst Jews dwelt for centuries and millennia. As a Jew, he was international, cosmopolitan. Sitting beside the Hudson, he saw the Jordan and the Vistula. In his imagination, he saw himself walking with Rabbi Akiva along the shores of the Mediterranean and with the Jewish minstrels in sixteenth century Regensburg. Cordova, Rome, Paris, Worms, Prague, Posen, Lublin and Warsaw lived in him no less than his birthplace, Mlave, or his more recent abode, New York. As a novelist, he was less chained to facts than were academic historians. He could intuitively apprehend the truth of an era, while scholars were obsessed by mere facts and were helpless when suffering from a dearth of recorded evidence. Fascinated by the vast vista of the Jewish past, Opatoshu held that this past was not adequately interpreted even by Graetz and Dubnow, the ablest historians. They were unduly emphasizing persecutions and martyrdom. Surely there must have also been happy aspects to Jewish existence in earlier eras, even as there were in his own era. Such happy events he set out to depict in a series of historical tales.

Opatoshu's joyous narrative, *A Day in Regensburg,* appeared in the catastrophic year 1933, when Hitler rose to power. It recalled to life the vanished world of Yiddish minstrels and merrymakers, the popular bards of the sixteenth century who sang of King Arthur and his knights or of Dietrich von Bern and Master Hildebrand. The research workers of YIVO, the newly founded Yiddish Scientific Institute, had uncovered old Yiddish manuscripts, had reprinted the earliest printed poetic booklets, and had proved that Jews were never hermetically sealed off from their non-Jewish neighbors. Opatoshu undertook to compose a fictional antidote to the gloomy chronicle of Graetz. In a stylized, archaic Yiddish, he unrolled colorful episodes of a single day in Regensburg, the happy day when one of its richest Jews, Shlomo Belaser, married off his daughter to the son of the patrician of Worms, Eliahu Margolis. For this glamorous occasion wandering mendicants from many communities in Ashkenazic territory streamed into town. They filled the ghetto streets with jest, laughter, song and dance. Famed merrymakers of Prague arrived for the festival, flutes and cymbals resounded, beer and wine flowed in abundance. Even the Prince-Elector and his retinue of knights joined in when the merriment reached its climax at the wedding ceremony. Despite gathering clouds and rumors of a threatening expulsion from the town, Jews were not to be restrained from enjoying in full measure their interlude of peace and prosperity.

The same historic era was again portrayed by Opatoshu in three scenes from the life of Elia Levita, the author of the *Bovo-Bukh* and the most talented of the Jewish romancers of the sixteenth century. The first scene showed Elia in the midst of a dispute with a fellow minstrel in Venice, whom he accused of plagiarizing one of his songs. The second scene brought him to the patrician home of a Jewish lady, who commissioned him to write a *Siddur* for her daughter in which he was to include not only a Yiddish translation of the sacred prayers but also secular songs and ballads. The third scene presented the sixty-year-old Elia as secretary of the Italian Cardinal Egidio di Viterbo, residing with his family in the palace and disturbed by the fact that his own grandchildren no longer spoke Yiddish and were consorting with Christians on too intimate terms.

Shortly before his death in 1954, Opatoshu completed his most important historical narrative, *The Last Revolt* (*Der Letzter Oyfshtand*), upon which he had worked for many years. The first volume, *Rabbi Akiva*, appeared in 1948, the year of the founding of the Jewish State, and the second volume, *Bar Kochba*, appeared posthumously in 1955. In the former the novelist deals with the preparations for the liberation of the Jewish homeland from Roman rule during the reign of Emperor Hadrian and in the latter with the revolt itself and its tragic outcome.

As the accumulated dust of ages is brushed away, Judea of the second century comes to life in town and countryside, and Jewish figures, from donkey-drivers and hermits to patricians and scholars, emerge in full-blooded vigor. Three score years after the fall of the Second Kingdom, Jews have recovered materially but still suffer spiritual hurt. While Jerusalem lies desolate, Jericho and Caesarea harbor Jewish merchant-princes who carry on large trading operations throughout the far-flung Roman Empire. Yet, even the richest families respect learning based on Torah and send their sons to the Jewish schools of Yavne and Bnei Brak. Some of these sons are also well grounded in Hellenistic lore and speak Greek and Latin as well as Aramaic. They can quote Homer, Sophocles and Virgil no less than their beloved teacher Rabbi Akiva. The heads of the prominent families counsel patience and submission to the Roman authorities. The disciples of Rabbi Akiva, however, gather arms and provisions, and prepare for the overthrow of the hated pagan regime.

In the person of Bar Kochba, the aged Rabbi Akiva finds the warrior-leader who can rouse the Jews to self-sacrificing heroism and who can outmaneuver and outfight famed Roman legions. Ultimately, however, Bar Kochba's moral flaws disappoint and estrange many who saw in him the Messiah of the House of David. His depleted forces are penned up in the fortress of Betar and their desperate resistance ends in defeat. This defeat is, however, only a temporary one, if measured on the scale of Jewish history. As long as Jews continue to survive anywhere on earth, their Messianic hope still lives on. It will accompany them throughout the ages. Just as Yochanan ben Zakai built a haven for the Jewish spirit at Yavne after the destruction of Jerusalem in the days of Vespasian and Titus, so Rabbi Joshua ben Hanina continues with Jewish learning after the catastrophe at Betar.

The novels were written during the years of Jewish martyrdom and the heroic rise of the Jewish State. They mirror, despite their historical setting, the events of the Warsaw Ghetto Revolt against the Nazis, and the resistance to the mighty British Empire and the Arab Kingdoms by the outnumbered Jews of Palestine. The novels voice faith in the survival of the Jews as a world people and of the Jewish Messianic idea as a world-saving force.

The novelists of "Die Yunge," Ignatoff, Raboy, Haimowitz and Opatoshu, were transition figures, spokesmen of the Eastern European Jewish generation which immigrated to America during the early twentieth century, a generation which believed itself to be emancipated from the religious, moral and social values of the Old World but which, nevertheless, retained these values within its subconsciousness. These writers were not alienated souls brooding over their alienation from Jewishness, as were far too many of their articulate descendants whose medium of expression was no longer Yiddish but English. They were members of a group that in its strident youth discovered the wonder of America and they voiced the group's yearning to be embedded in a meaningful Jewishness and a meaningful Americanism. They matured and enriched Yiddish literature with valuable insights into new horizons and with a few masterpieces of narrative art which are able to withstand the ravages of time.

Lamed Shapiro (1878-1948), who came to America in 1906, a few months before "Die Yunge" began to coalesce as a group, kept aloof from them. He had begun in 1904 with impressionistic short stories. Under the impact of the pogroms of 1905, he wrote his best tales. Upon these his fame rests, especially upon the story *The Cross* (*Der Tsehlem*, 1909). Like Bialik, his Hebrew contemporary, he called upon the Jews to banish fear and to resist their foes. Even if victory be not theirs, they could at least die sword in hand.

Unable to adjust satisfactorily to the New World, Shapiro returned to Warsaw in 1909 and engaged in translating the novels of Walter Scott, Victor Hugo, Charles Dickens and Rudyard Kipling. Before war broke out, he was back in New York. After the war, he settled in Los Angeles, a rapidly growing Jewish community. There he was joined by the poet H. Rosenblatt and the novelist S. Miller. Before the end of the 1920's the Pacific metropolis became a center of Yiddish letters and during the following half century it attracted many Yiddish intellectuals, ranging from Peretz Hirshbein to Abraham Golomb. In the United States, its Yiddish-speaking and Yiddish-reading population was exceeded only by New York.

Shapiro's productivity declined, however, during the post-war decade of booming prosperity and he returned to New York in 1929. There he wrote a series of stories entitled *New Yorkish* (1931), but these failed to arouse the same intense interest as had his pre-war tales.

S. Miller (1895-1958), who edited Shapiro's works after the latter's death, remained in Los Angeles for more than a third of a century. He published eleven volumes consisting mainly of short stories distinguished by keen observation and tolerant analysis of the traits, foibles, virtues and failings of his generation, which he dubbed *The Generation in Wasteland,* the title of his novel of 1951. No other writer has depicted as well as he did the Yiddish-speaking pioneers who streamed to the Western metropolis during the early decades of the twentieth century, leaving an indelible impression upon it and being themselves transformed by it. Most of the stories of the volume *Yesterday (Nekhten,* 1956), the last volume to appear during his lifetime, gave a panoramic view of the immigrants from the East, the charlatans, the saints and the ordinary men and women who were caught up in the boom-psychosis of Los Angeles during the 1920's, and who ended tragically in the years of the Great Depression that followed.

Miller repeatedly stressed the nostalgia for old-fashioned Jewishness which assailed yesterday's Jews who had wrested themselves away from their Yiddish roots during joyous, exciting, young years and, when the later sobering years set in, who found their materially successful life empty of meaning. This theme had been prominently treated in Jewish novels such as Abraham Cahan's *The Rise of David Levinsky* (1917) and David Pinski's *The House of Noah Edon* (1929). To Miller, as to his predecessors, the sum total of all the vaunted wealth in worldly possessions, as well as in so-called modern ways of thinking and feeling, added up to vanity of vanities. Only by returning to Jewish cultural traditions neglected in the heyday of success could desirable lasting values again be rediscovered.

There was no bitterness in Miller's criticism of the Jewish scene. He was a realist who depicted honestly the waywardness of his uprooted and transplanted characters, but he did not stamp them as villains. Some of his tales were gems of tender compassion. Yet, even in his satiric narratives he did not attack the pillars of the Jewish establishment with vigor or venom. He rather mingled mild disapproval with his usual kind understanding.

10

RISE OF LITERARY CRITICISM

Baal-Makhshoves ● Coralnik ● Gorelik ● Niger ●
Olgin ● Marmor ● Maisel ● Rivkin ● Litvak
● Bickel ● Literary Journals

LITERARY CRITICISM was practiced by Yiddish writers ever
since the first modern Yiddish organ, *Kol Mevasser,* was founded
in 1862 by Alexander Zederbaum. Among the pioneer literary
critics, Joseph Jehuda Lerner (1847-1907) was most prominent.
His Russian pamphlet on Israel Aksenfeld, which appeared in
1869, was the earliest significant critical work about a Yiddish
writer. It was followed by critical articles on other Yiddish writers
before he turned to his main interest, the writing of original plays
and the adaptation for the Yiddish stage of plays from French,
German and Russian sources. Another pioneer critic was the historian Shimon Dubnow (1860-1941), who, under the pseudonym
of Criticus, wrote in Russian on Yiddish literature in the 1880's
and was the earliest reviewer to recognize the genius of Sholom
Aleichem; still another was the Hebrew publicist David Frishman
(1860-1922), who from the late 1880's wrote critical essays and
reviews of Yiddish works in a polemic tone which involved him in
bitter controversies with Peretz, Nomberg and the exponents of
Yiddish ideologies. But it was not until the physician Isidor
Eliashev (1873-1924) appeared upon the Yiddish scene at the
beginning of the twentieth century that literary criticism was
accepted as a legitimate artistic genre alongside of poetry, drama
and fiction.

Eliashev, who wrote under the symbolic pseudonym "Baal-
Makhshoves"—The Man of Thought—, was the creator of Yiddish
esthetic criticism. Educated in a traditional home and in a Yeshiva
that stood under the influence of the ethical movement inspired by

175

Rabbi Israel Salanter (1810-1883), the *Musar* Movement, he found his way from his native Lithuania to Switzerland, where he completed preparatory studies for admission to the universities of Heidelberg and Berlin. After imbibing the best of European culture and graduating as a doctor of medicine, he left Berlin in 1901 for Kovno, then moved on to Riga and finally settled in Warsaw. Literary interests gradually eclipsed his interest in medicine.

In Warsaw, he came under the influence of Peretz and he hailed with great enthusiasm the efforts of the Peretz circle to strengthen Jewish national rebirth by means of creative works in Yiddish. His love of Yiddish, however, did not exclude a love of Hebrew. In a famous essay, "Two Tongues—One Literature," he preached the unity of Jewish literary expression, regardless of which language the author used. He did not share the view of his enlightened friends, or of the nascent Zionist movement, that Yiddish was a transitional linguistic medium useful for educating the masses so that they could rise in their cultural level and ultimately change to Hebrew, Russian, German, Spanish or English. He rather felt that literary works being created in Yiddish were of such high artistic calibre, and mirrored the Jewish soul so well, that even estranged Jewish intellectuals could be brought back through such works to a love of their people.

His essays on Mendele revived the flagging interest in this master of Yiddish. His essays on Peretz, Sholom Aleichem, Bialik, Dinezon and Nomberg were sensitive appraisals of established writers. No less important, however, was his impact as the discoverer and furtherer of talented new writers such as Leivick, Bergelson and the Kiev group of Soviet authors.

As a critic, Baal-Makhshoves combined both clarity of insight and the ability to recreate the mood about all of his subjects. We see them, we hear them, we taste them, we touch them, we sense the uniqueness inherent in each of their works. And he does this in a style so pleasant, so calm, so rich in imagery. For him, the critic was an essential pillar of the literary structure and especially necessary as a midwife at the birth or revival of a literary movement. He noted that Lessing in Germany, Byelinski in Russia and Sainte-Beuve in France were held in no less esteem by their contemporaries than were poets or novelists. A critic's role should not, in his opinion, be restricted merely to passing judgment, voicing approval or disapproval. It was also incumbent upon the critic to prepare the atmosphere for the reception of a new original work and to supply the sunlight so that young, good, fresh literary shoots might grow and prosper. The critic was the trumpeter who broke down the wall of indifference among prospective readers. He was the herald announcing the arrival of kings of thought. Far from being a cold inquisitor who sought out blemishes in works of art and who castigated artists for their inadequacies, he was rather himself a passionate lover of art who opened the eyes of the less discerning and the hearts of the less sensitive to the magnificence and loveliness which moved him.

Baal-Makhshoves was the Jew and the Good European. Upon the substratum of his Jewish heredity and early environment, there were superimposed Germanic and Slavic influences and, as a result, he interpreted Jewish life both as an intimate participant and as an objective observer from without. This dualism in his personality gave his essays an original flavor; a rich sympathy for the old forms of Jewish life, an awareness of their non-viability amidst the new social upheavals, a longing for a Jewish national and cultural rebirth, an emphasis upon the need for quality rivalling the dominant European groups, a stress upon both Jewish languages as necessary vehicles for intensifying Jewishness in all lands.

Baal-Makhshoves was both rationalist and sentimentalist. As he grew older, his optimistic Messianism yielded to an increasingly pessimistic and satiric appraisal of the changing social and political scene, and he gave vent to his melancholy moods in his *Ironic Tales* (*Ironishe Maaselekh*), rich in disillusioned wisdom.

Baal-Makhshoves was fascinated by the magnificent personality of Herzl. He saw in the Zionist leader a living example of the historic Hebrew who had once led an harmonious existence, as well as a dignified forerunner of the envisaged new Jew who yearned to return to a healthy existence in a regenerated homeland. He devoted three essays to Herzl upon the latter's death and he incorporated Herzlian ideas in several of his *Ironic Tales*. In one of these tales, "The Island of Shrouds," he pointed out how difficult it was for a community which was skilled in the art of dying to respond to a prophet of reinvigorated life such as Herzl.

In another tale for Purim of 1901, composed as a sequel to the *Book of Esther,* he stressed Herzl's idea of a return to the cradle of the Jewish people as the sole permanent solution to Jewish homelessness. This sequel centered about Parshandatha, Haman's oldest son. Since Parshandatha was of prodigious weight, the rope used for his hanging broke and he fell to the ground only half dead. At night he awoke from his swoon and fled to a forest.

There, in the course of time, he assumed the leadership of all the
surviving anti-Jewish families of Persia. The conspirators longed
for revenge and bided their time. As anti-Jewish sentiments arose
once more, and continued to mount, two young men, Ezra and
Nehemiah, suggested to their fellow Jews mass flight from the
Persian capital before the situation deteriorated even further.
They formed groups for the purpose of emigrating to the land of
Israel. They tried to convince Mordecai that it was far better to
hew stones and to draw water in their own land than to live
prosperously under the shadow of eternal fear of an unpredictable
tomorrow. Mordecai, however, had faith in the constitution of the
Persian realm, which guaranteed his rights. One day King
Ahasuerus, in a happy mood, offered to let Mordecai and his
people return to their native land from which they had been
exiled by King Nebuchadnezzar. But Mordecai, the great Persian
patriot, answered: "My land is the soil over which your sublime
steps float and I am your servant." Ahasuerus became angry when
he saw his generous offer spurned; he withdrew his golden scepter
from Mordecai and restored Parshandatha, son of Haman, to the
premiership. Then pogroms broke out and the streets ran red with
Jewish blood. Only the followers of Ezra and Nehemiah survived,
since they had already left the rich, prosperous capital Shushan
and were en route to the land of Israel.

Baal-Makhshoves realized, however, that in his own century,
most Jews still had to continue to live in the Diaspora and that
for them a longing for Zion and an interest in Hebrew were insufficient props to guarantee their group survival. He therefore advocated converting religious holidays into Jewish national holidays in order to meet the need of the irreligious and the intellectuals. He urged that on Hanukkah the struggle for national
liberation should be stressed and on Lag B'Omer the heroism of
Bar Kochba should be emphasized. Above all, he saw in the Sabbath the finest surviving pillar of ancient Jewish culture, the one
day each week when Jews would be purified of materialism, a day
of balm for the heart of a battered, scattered nationality. This
insight formed the theme of his most memorable essay, *The
Sabbath*.

After the Russian Revolution, restlessness overcame Baal-
Makhshoves. He wandered from one Jewish center to another,
happy nowhere. In 1917 he lived in St. Petersburg, in 1919 in
Kiev, in 1921 in Kovno, in 1922 in Berlin. Increasing fame and
increasing influence did not, however, lessen his melancholy.

Abraham Coralnik (1883-1937), who was in many respects his most talented disciple, characterized him as a critic in whom were united the traditional Judaism of the Kovno Yeshiva, the ethical culture of Slobodka, Russian education, German scientific training, Jewish nationalism and European supra-nationalism, Lithuanian acuity and Berlin wit, Nietzschean paradoxical seriousness and a Solomonic awareness that all was vanity of vanities.

Coralnick himself combined many of these disparate elements in his own personality. He too was a Good European and a Jewish intellectual, a lover of Hebrew and Yiddish, but without real faith in the future of Diaspora creativity. He was a Zionist working for Jewish renewal in Palestine and yet nostalgic for the culture of the East European Jewish townlet, a pessimist who was saved from cynicism and despair by an ironic contemplation of life, a rationalist with a yearning for mysticism.

Born in the Ukrainian town of Uman, Coralnik was able to enter the University of Kiev despite the severe quota system imposed upon Jews, but soon left for universities abroad. At Florence he imbibed the spirit of classical and Mediterranean cultures and at Berlin, Bonn and Vienna he came in contact with German romanticism and realism. His main interest was in philosophy and his doctoral thesis, completed in 1908, dealt with the philosophy of scepticism.

From his twentieth year on, he was active in Zionism. He edited the Viennese Zionist organ *Die Welt* during Herzl's last and stormiest year and he contributed to leading Russian and German newspapers and periodicals. Although he felt more at ease writing in Russian and German, nevertheless he early recognized that only through Yiddish could he reach the Jewish masses. He schooled himself to develop a Yiddish style which could communicate the profoundest ideas with utmost clarity and simplicity. But the communication of ideas never sufficed him. He also sought to clothe ideas in properly fitting moods, to transmit the aromas, overtones and feelings that accompanied living thoughts.

After the outbreak of the First World War, Coralnik came to the United States and was invited in 1915 by the newly founded daily *Der Tog* to become a permanent contributor. It was through this Yiddish organ that he reached hundreds of thousands of readers during the following two decades and helped to improve their literary taste and to direct their thinking on eternal problems and on specific Jewish matters.

In 1917 he was swept up in the general enthusiasm at the birth of freedom in Russia and returned to his native land. His enthusiasm quickly waned, however, when he saw the oppressed turning into oppressors and violence rampant everywhere. He then returned to New York a disillusioned humanist but still clinging to his love for Jewishness and for pure ideas.

Throughout his creative life, Coralnik wrestled with the question: what is Jewishness? Or, more specifically, what can Jewishness, however defined, mean to contemporary man? In an essay of 1909 on the essence and future of Jewishness, he expressed both fear that dominant trends were inimical to Jewish survival, and hope that, out of still undimmed Messianic longing, movements for Jewish salvation might yet arise. He saw such a movement in Zionism, which might offer redemption to the Jewish people and also to all mankind. In later years, as he accumulated ever greater knowledge and as ultimate answers still eluded him, he learned to content himself with illuminating fragments of the vast complex of Jewishness without seeking for a general panacea.

Coralnik's sympathy abided with the thinkers who asked basic questions and who were not content with easy, conventional answers. His heart went out to Elisha ben Abuya, the lonely heretic who wrestled with God and remained with scepticism, far more than to Rabbi Akiva, who sought compromises and temporary answers which enabled people somehow to live on. Coralnik was fond of Koheleth (Ecclesiastes), the ironic sage who smiled at the world through the mask of King Solomon. He was fond of Esdras, the prince of the Apocrypha, who wanted to know why there was undeserved suffering here below and who was not satisfied with the replies that satisfied Job.

Coralnik's essays stressed mood, atmosphere, inner rhythm. Often he wrote with a heavy heart, unsure of himself. He feared that he could not satisfy his Yiddish readers, who demanded of him definitive criteria by which they could live. He distrusted generalizations. Thinking was for him a playing with ideas, a dialogue with himself, a pleasurable technique for dissecting apparent reality and rebuilding its fragments in ever new forms. But he did not overemphasize the role of logical thinking in the realm of practical human affairs. Thinking might suffice to illuminate the uppermost layers of the soul but it could not penetrate to the deepest layers, there where multi-dimensional, super-individual, psychic abysses yawned, where maelstroms of emotional energy whirled, and chaotic, instinctive elements yearned to be encased in structures. He knew that culture included far more irra-

tional entities than rational ones. He therefore preferred the myth
and the legend to the historical fact.

Coralnik's essay on Georg Brandes revealed more of himself
and his own approach to critical writing than it did of Brandes.
While recognizing the achievements of Denmark's greatest literary critic, whose fame was then worldwide, he asserted that
Brandes failed to grasp the essence of artistic creativity. Why?
Because Brandes, who understood everything, could not leap
beyond the boundaries of mere understanding. Brandes never
lived art. For example, he understood the trappings of Shakespeare
and Goethe, to whom he devoted voluminous tomes. But the real
Shakespeare who was hidden behind the façade of the Elizabethan
stage eluded him and the real Goethe who was lonely amidst the
adulations of the Weimar Court was a mystery to him. Brandes
had a keen eye for the environment encircling an author. He saw
the candlestick upon which the candle was perched, the tallow of
which the candle was made, and even the circle of light at the edge
of the candle's flame, but he never pierced with his glance to the
innermost heart of the flame. He knew the facts but not the truth
behind the facts. He possessed sound common sense, an unbiased
outlook, a liberal temperament, but he lacked the seer's mystic
insight into the soul's irrational core.

Coralnik himself possessed this mystic insight but could only
communicate small fragments of it. He was ecstatic when he
caught a glimpse of a writer's true essence and he was sad that
he could not convey the full intensity of this ecstasy to his readers.
He sensed the radiance of beauty which poured as a flood of sunlight about him and he despaired of containing more than a
meager shimmer of this radiance within the straitjacket of words.

Coralnik loved life. He loved man and the works of man. Above
all, he loved his Jewish people. But he covered his love with a
cloak of irony. He was a sentimentalist but, because he feared
the ridicule normally heaped upon sentimentalists, he hid his
feelings behind a stylized mask.

Books opened up to Coralnik the entire past of peoples and
civilizations. Books brought him the wisdom of gifted individuals
and gave him insight into diverse patterns of experience. Books
were for him a source of strength, security, hope. He lived in
books and from them he extracted showpieces to display to his
readers.

In 1928, two decades before Melech Ravitch proposed the canon-
ization of the post-biblical treasures of Jewish learning and litera-

ture, Coralnik called for the collection of the best products of the Jewish mind and their incorporation within a single, comprehensive volume, a volume which should be revised and brought up-to-date every half century. In his essay "The Jewish Intellect," he advocated the immortalization of the spirit of the post-exilic generations within the covers of a supplementary Bible. Until the present, such tomes were prepared by individuals and bore the stamp of their prejudices and predilections. The authoritative book should be prepared by an authoritative body, by an academy of scholars, thinkers, poets and critics, since no one individual could today claim mastery of all fields of Jewish culture. This supplementary Bible should mirror the Jewish intellect in all its aspects. It should be designed not only for Jews but also for non-Jews who ought to know Jews as they really were and are. The vast material of two thousand years should be sifted by responsible, competent, learned Jewish representatives and the final product should be published not only in the Jewish national languages, Hebrew and Yiddish, but also in the major world languages.

Coralnik urged that in such a book there should be included, in the first place, the early post-exilic thinkers Josephus and Philo, the medieval poets and philosophers Yehuda Halevi, Solomon ibn Gabirol, Maimonides, Saadia Gaon, and the finest minds of more recent centuries down to Heinrich Heine, Abraham Reisen, Hermann Cohen, Disraeli, Herzl and Rathenau. Coralnik then suggested going further afield and also incorporating, within the Jewish treasury of thought, letters and experience, the products of heretics, dissenters and scientists which carry in some way the stamp of Jewishness: an *Epistle* of Paul, polemics of the Sabbatai Zvi Movement, a chapter of Moses Mendelssohn's *Phaedon*, selections from Georg Simmel, Marcel Schwob, Ludwig Börne, Spinoza, Henri Bergson, Heinrich Herz and Albert Einstein.

Coralnik could not accept the view that Jews should strive to become a normal people. He felt that Jews did not experience a millennial tragic fate unequalled by any other historic group in order to end as a normal people. Jews could not afford to become old and sated. The smile of self-contentment did not befit the Jewish face. They were chained to their past and to the land of their origin.

When Coralnik visited Palestine in 1926, he felt the land to be his. He walked along the streets of Jerusalem not as a tourist who gazes at novel attractions but as a son of the land who returned after sojourning abroad for a while. This while had lasted a few thousand years but, in the relativity of time, those thousands of years in exile were but as days. Now he was back home. He sloughed his usual ironic contemplation of scenes and wrote with unrestrained emotions of this center of his longing. Jerusalem was not for him a little Oriental mountain community, but his own history and the ultimate root of his personality. Nevertheless, he returned to the American metropolis and spent the last decade of his life raising the cultural level of his Yiddish readers with his critical articles on literature and philosophy. But the hope of a return to Zion never died within him.

Shmaryahu Gorelik (1877-1943) began, like Coralnik, as a multilingual essayist, participating in Russian, German, Hebrew and Yiddish publications. Under the impact of Herzl's death and the pogroms of 1905, he gave up his early Bundist, Socialist and anti-Zionist orientation. In 1908, he joined A. Veiter and S. Niger in editing the Vilna Yiddish monthly *Literarishe Monatshriften,* a purely literary organ in which writers of diverse ideologies could cooperate in working for a Yiddish cultural renaissance. During the First World War, he lived in Switzerland and participated in the pacifist movement centering about Romain Rolland. After the war he resided in Berlin until 1933 and thereafter in Tel Aviv.

Gorelik had a wide knowledge of European literature and, in his critical articles, he was more interested in the insights of modern writers than in their stylistic innovations. The essay was, in his opinion, an educational medium. It was concentrated spiritual energy converted into noble form, a flashlight illuminating for a brief moment dark and hidden corners of the human soul.

As an ardent convert to Zionism, he sought to tear his readers away from their drab daily pursuits and lead them to the more inspiring goal of rebuilding a national Jewish life. He loved the irrational aspects of the Zionist approach: the resurrection of an ancient tongue to new vitality, the transformation of stagnant European slum dwellers to healthy agriculturists on Oriental plantations and fragrant orange groves. He wanted Jews to grow wings, and meanwhile he carried them on the wings of his own imagination.

In his literary criticism, Gorelik distinguished between three types of literature. The first was the objective description of reality by honest, talented writers. Such writers revealed accurately what they saw. They communicated sensations and impressions. They provided esthetic pleasure. Yiddish literature, he held, was rich in such works.

The second type, a higher type, embodied in portrayed characters the ideas, moods, struggles and stirrings of the age in which the writers lived. Not content with merely reproducing the environment and surface reality, these writers had their characters engage in debates in which the conflicting currents of the social order and the deepest layers of the group soul were brought to the fore. Readers became involved more intensely and were influenced to change their own reactions and their own views of the current scene through their experiencing of literary works embodying philosophic and religious content and providing insight into the spiritual essence of a people and an era. Turgenev, Ibsen, Knut Hamsun and Romain Rolland exemplified this second type of literature for European readers, while Mendele Mokher Sforim, Sholom Aleichem and Peretz did so for Yiddish readers.

There was, however, still a third type of literature, the highest type. It included not only a reservoir of ideas dominant in a writer's generation but it also opened up horizons of a new world and envisaged possibilities for future human relationships unperceived or only dimly perceived until then. Such writers wrestled with eternal problems, with the meaning of existence itself. Having made their way up the ladder of human suffering, and having surveyed an ever expanding panorama of human experience, they sought to elevate their readers to their level of insight and to communicate moral and intellectual vistas attainable to our species if we but willed it. Goethe, Rousseau, Tolstoi and Dostoevsky represented this highest type in modern European literature. They helped the individual to understand his relationship not only to his own specific contemporary society but also to all super-individual entities regardless of space and time; they taught him how to escape cosmic loneliness, how to overcome the fear of death, how to find lasting meaning in his transient years on earth. While academic philosophers also sought answers to these eternal questions, they did so via cold logic. Great writers explored these regions through the creation of characters with whom we could identify ourselves, characters who traversed the entire gamut of emotions from despair to ecstasy, who worked their way up from the abyss of confusion to final clarity. Such literature was a reading of life at the deepest, most intimate strata of the soul. Through literary characters like Koheleth, Job, Don Quixote, Hamlet and Faust coursed the thoughts and dreams of the human species. Yiddish literature should now be ready to rise to this highest level. It had already mastered the art of depicting the collective soul of the townlet. It should now essay to depict the complex, tragic Jewish individual who leaves the shelter of the townlet and goes out into the great world beyond in order to seek ultimate meaning and fulfillment. It should deal with the Jew as man per se. Gorelick, therefore, called upon Yiddish writers to dare grandly, to enter the holy tabernacle of the highest type of literature, to incorporate themselves in lasting figures created to hand down eternal Jewish visions as an inspiration to all humankind down the generations.

While Gorelik's strength lay in his appeal to the imagination and Coralnik's in the communication of moods, Shmuel Niger (1883-1955), who for almost half a century exercised enormous influence as the arbiter of literary taste, preferred to reason with his readers and used logic as the yardstick for literary evaluation.

Niger, who was born as Shmuel Charney, was the oldest of three brothers who rose to prominence in Yiddish letters. One of them, Baruch Charney (1886-1938), became a leader of the *Bund* and acquired a reputation before his twentieth year as a second Lassalle because of his oratorical skill and indomitable courage. He participated in the Revolution of 1905 under the name of Vladeck and then retained this name when he was forced to flee to the United States in 1907. In the Yiddish literary monthly *Die Zukunft*, Vladeck found a congenial organ for his poems, feuilletons, short stories, travel sketches, drama and critical essays. He also influenced the American Jewish community as manager of the largest Yiddish daily, *Forverts*, from 1918 to 1938, as a Socialist member of New York's Board of Aldermen from 1917 to 1922 and as a founder of the American Labor Party.

Niger's youngest brother, Daniel Charney (1888-1959), began his literary career in Poland, edited Yiddish journals in post-Revolutionary Moscow, lived in Berlin from 1922 to 1934, in Paris from 1934 to 1941, and in the United States thereafter. He wrote love lyrics, travel sketches and essays, but is best remembered for his several volumes of memoirs and family chronicles.

Niger came under the influence of Hassidism, Zionism, Socialism in his boyhood, amassed a great deal of miscellaneous knowledge in his youth, participated in subversive activities against the Czarist regime and was arrested and tortured in Russian prisons. During and after the Revolution of 1905, he wrote in Russian, Hebrew and Yiddish on current political issues.

He made his debut as a literary critic in 1907 with an essay on Sholem Asch which aroused a great deal of attention. A year later, he joined Shmaryahu Gorelik and A. Veiter (1878-1919) in founding the Vilna *Literarishe Monatshriften*, a periodical which was influential in the Yiddish cultural resurgence after the Czernowitz Conference of Yiddishists.

During the First World War, when a clamor arose for new themes and new moods that would reflect the more immediate reality, Niger opposed the slogan of the modernists and insisted that the concern of great literature was not the ever changing present but rather the eternal problems of the human spirit, problems of life and death, free will and determinism, causation and purposefulness. The best of his essays of the war decade were included in the volume *Talks on Books (Shmuesn Vegn Bikher,* 1922).

In April 1919, during the conflict between Russia and Poland, Niger was sharing an apartment in Vilna together with A. Veiter and Leib Yaffe (1876-1948), when Polish legionnaires broke in, shot Veiter, and transported the other two writers to jail. After their release, due to Marshal Pilsudski's intervention after he was convinced of their political non-involvement in the conflict between the two opposing powers, Yaffe left for Palestine. There he edited Hebrew journals, wrote lyrics in Hebrew and Yiddish, agitated for Zionism as an emissary to many lands, and was killed when the Jewish Agency Building in Jerusalem was dynamited during the struggle for Israel's independence. Niger emigrated to the United States. There, during his thirty-five years in New York, he came to be recognized as the outstanding literary critic, as the spokesman for the Yiddish cultural movement. There his dictum made and unmade reputations.

According to Niger, a critic must have sympathy for every variety and every level of creative expression, provided that it was genuine expression. He must possess the traits of patience, curiosity, sensitivity, many-sidedness. A critic who could understand and react only to works of a single, specific tendency would fail to grasp even these works in their entirety. Whatever esthetic or philosophic approach a critic might himself espouse, he must not be deaf to other approaches, he must be able to acclimatize himself to all territories of the spirit, he must immerse himself in the essence of each literary personality he portrayed. His realm was not raw reality, but rather reality after it had been given a definite esthetic form by a talented, creative personality. A critic must be as objective in his judgments as was humanly possible and must be fearless in their expression. He must emphasize those books which conveyed unforgettable pleasures and enduring values.

Without such books an individual experienced only one life, but through them he experienced many lives. Books were emissaries that brought messages from all corners of the earth, from distant stars, from the wisest men of all eras. Books enriched, purified, lit up new roads to mysterious realms of being. Books deepened comprehension of the present by linking it to innumerable yesterdays and tomorrows. Books, therefore, extended our years beyond the normal span of three score and ten by revivifying the generations of our forefathers and by envisaging utopias and apocalypses of coming generations. Books also liberated us from the narrow confines of the self and opened up a boundless universe of freedom and pure delight.

Although Niger was often accused of being a dictator of taste, he himself placed little value on a critic's apportioning of praise and blame. A critic, he held, was neither an author's press agent nor a literary prosecutor. A critic was an artist in his own right, giving expression to thoughts, feelings and visions aroused in him by a literary product. He was a seeker of beauty. Having fallen under the spell of a work of beauty and having penetrated to its essence, he then showed others its basic configuration and taught others how to garner from it more joy and more wisdom.

A critic's function was primarily the interpretation of the text, its meaning, its basic structure, and only secondarily historical, psychological, or sociological analysis. Literary history, psychology, sociology were at best aids to the main purpose. They supplied a framework for a critic's elucidation of the text itself, for his penetration into the innermost world of the artist. They helped to illumine the uniqueness of a writer who brought to life characters able to outlast time and to transcend a specific spatial environment.

Niger put his theory of criticism into practice in hundreds of essays during half a century. Despite his preoccupation with Yiddish literature, he did not disparage the striving of the Hebrew writers who were reviving the ancient tongue. He was the principal advisor of the Louis LaMed Foundation for the Advancement of Hebrew and Yiddish Literature. In 1941, he published under its auspices a study, *Bilingualism in the History of Jewish Literature*. He pointed out that bilingualism was a Jewish tradition since biblical days. Parts of *Ezra* and *Daniel* were composed in Aramaic, while the other biblical books were in Hebrew.

During the Golden Age of Sephardic literature, writers and readers used both Hebrew and Arabic. In more recent centuries, Hebrew and Yiddish were used in ethical tracts, in devotional prayers, and by bilingual authors. Although some opposition to bilingualism arose from time to time, the fact remained that Jews were more often bilingual than monolingual. Both Hebrew and Yiddish were pillars that sustained the Jewish structure. Hence, the creative energies of Hebraists and Yiddishists should not be frittered away in mutual recriminations but should be utilized for the enrichment of a common Jewish culture.

Niger's contribution to Yiddish culture was best summarized by the poet H. Leivick at the critic's funeral in 1955: "Niger experienced in his lifetime all the sorrows of a Jew nowadays. More than once he shared our Jewish destiny, peering into the depths of the abyss; more than once he stood beneath the raised fist and the gun of death-dealing evil. He saw the hand of the murderer, he felt the pain of the victim; and there arose in him the clarity of great understanding, the purity of a humanistic view of the world. He learned to judge the world not according to the severity of law but according to that loftiest reason which embraces compassion, as he penetrated into the essence of tragedy, human and Jewish. To Yiddish literature, initially of small dimensions, he brought the light of reason and of genuine, sorrow-crowned humanism, the light of the restrained smile and of considerate love for our people's destiny; and then, as the power of Yiddish grew and flourished, he helped to convert it into a great tabernacle."

While Niger's authority carried great weight with most Yiddish readers, it was rejected by those who had come under the spell of Communist ideology and who saw in literature a class struggle and not primarily an esthetic phenomenon. Their spokesmen on the American scene were Moissaye J. Olgin (1878-1939) and Kalman Marmor (1876-1956).

Olgin had begun in Russia as an agitator for the Bund and as literary editor of its Vilna organ. He suffered arrest for his revolutionary activities but continued writing, lecturing, and organizing Bundist cells. He arrived in the United States in 1914. During the war years, he completed his first English work *The Soul of the Russian Revolution* (1917), and his doctoral dissertation *A Guide to Russian Literature,* published in 1920. These established his reputation in America as a scholar and literary critic. But it was as editor of *Freiheit,* the Yiddish Communist daily, from its founding in 1922 until his death, that he exerted his greatest influence. His evaluation of Yiddish writers and Jewish issues set the tone for the attitudes of American Jewish Communists and Fellow-Travelers towards them.

Kalman Marmor had a distinguished career as a Zionist before he was won over by Olgin as literary columnist of the daily *Freiheit* and as cultural director of Communist educational institutions. He participated in Zionist Congresses from 1901 to 1907. He was associated with Chaim Weizmann in the struggle against the Uganda Project. He joined Yitzkhak Ben Zvi and Ber Borochov in founding the world federation of Labor Zionists in 1907 and was the first editor of *Yiedisher Kemfer,* the American organ of this movement. After the Russian Revolution, however, he was fascinated by Communist internationalism and completed major studies on writers whom he regarded as its Yiddish forerunners, such as Aaron Lieberman, Morris Vinchevsky, David Edelstadt and Joseph Bovshover. During his years at the Kiev Institute for Yiddish Culture, 1933-1936, he prepared and edited the Soviet edition of the works of Vinchevsky and Edelstadt. When this Institute was suppressed, he returned to New York. His study on the beginnings of Yiddish literature in America, published in 1944, was a pioneering work on the immigrant writers who were active between 1870 and 1890. His autobiography in two volumes, which appeared posthumously in 1959, contained a wealth of material on the Jewish personalities with whom he was associated during his long life.

Nachman Maisel (1887-1966) was closely associated with Kalman Marmor during the latter's American period. After the death of Olgin, Maisel forged ahead as the most influential literary critic among American Yiddish radicals. He could look back upon a distinguished career as a Yiddish editor in pre-revolutionary and post-revolutionary Kiev and in Warsaw between the two world wars. He was related to the novelists David Bergelson and Der Nister, and his essays helped to establish their early fame. He founded the Kiev Farlag in 1917, which published more than a hundred Yiddish books within a few years. He edited anthologies of the Kiev Culture League and encouraged budding talents among Soviet Jewish youth. Moving to Warsaw in 1921, Maisel founded the Warsaw Culture League to further Yiddish creativity in the Polish capital and edited the *Literarishe Bleter,* a weekly which had a significant influence. He helped to launch YKUF, the international Yiddish Culture League, at its initial conference in Paris in 1937 and became the leading spirit of its American section and editor of its American monthly *Yiddishe Kultur* from 1939 until 1964. His more than forty major studies included books on Peretz, Mendele, Soviet Yiddish literature, and the nostalgic memoirs of pre-Holocaust Jewry entitled *Once There Was a Life (Amol Is Geven a Leben,* 1951). In 1964 he settled in the Israel kibbutz Alonim. There he completed his study on Chaim Zhitlowsky in 1965 and a pioneering work on the influence of foreign literatures upon Yiddish writers.

Maisel was a literary historian as well as a critic. His prose style was not distinguished. However, his fund of knowledge was enormous and he could overwhelm readers with an avalanche of facts about Yiddish writers, often based on his personal relations with them as well as meticulous research. His critical judgments were influenced by his Marxist ideology but the information contained in his essays, especially on Polish and Soviet writers, was accurate.

Boruch Rivkin (1883-1945) was a radical thinker, a prolific essayist, and a literary critic whose sympathy, like that of Olgin, Marmor and Maisel, lay with writers of social protest. Unlike them, however, he steered clear of Communist involvement because of his basically Anarchist views. Stemming from Jakobstadt, a town between Riga and Dvinsk, he joined the Bund in his youth and suffered a year's imprisonment in 1904 because of his underground activities. Upon his release, he fled to Switzerland and joined an Anarchist group. His first essays were in Russian but when he exchanged Geneva for London in 1911, he came under the influence of Rudolf Rocker, an Anarchist leader of German Christian origin, who wrote in Yiddish and edited the Yiddish journal *Dos Freie Vort* in England from 1898 to 1914. Rivkin then found a more suitable outlet for his literary and critical essays in Yiddish periodicals of the Anarchists. After immigrating to New York in 1912, he wrote exclusively in Yiddish. His principal work of literary criticism was *Basic Tendencies of Yiddish Literature in America (Grunt-Tendentsen Fun Der Yiddisher Literatur In Amerike),* begun in 1936 and published posthumously in 1948. After his death there appeared other collections of his essays, including *American Yiddish Poets (Yiddishe Dikhter In Amerike,* 1947), *A Religion for the Irreligious (A Gloiben Far Ungloibike,* 1947), and *Our Prose Writers (Undzere Prozaiker,* 1951). Rivkin believed in literature as a medium for spiritual elevation. He analyzed a poet's verses microscopically in order to extract maximum meaning from them and often he read potential meanings into them which they stimulated only in him. He adored Morris Rosenfeld and Abraham Reisen. He held Moshe Leib Halpern to be the most powerful and original lyricist of the following generation, that of "Die Yunge," towering above contemporaries in sheer genius and therefore in tragic loneliness. He hailed Chaim Grade as the most promising of the still younger poets. He was fascinated by the Messianic striving of Menahem Boraisha and H. Leivick. In interpreting literature, his main concern was to seek out evidences of Messianism and spiritualism. He held that religion and art were identical and that truth emanated from imaginative creation. Torah was art and Jewish holidays were theatrical embodiments of a drama of redemption. He wanted the Jewish man-of-letters to ennoble the Jewish people and to direct Jewish energies to Messianic goals. He did not express his philosophical concepts in an organized, disciplined, calm manner as did academic systematizers of ideas. He was rather a passionate, dynamic, mission-inspired critic of literature, religion and society. Probing deeply, he emerged now and then with brilliant flashes of original insights.

In contrast to Rivkin, whose thinking led him from Bundist socialism to anarchism and then to secular Messianism, A. Litvak (1874-1932) remained faithful to the ideology of the Bund throughout his life. For the Bund he suffered repeated imprisonment from 1896 on and exile to Siberia from 1902 to 1904. As editor of the Bundist organ *Der Varshaver Arbeiter* during the Revolution of 1905, and of Vilna journals in 1906 before his renewed imprisonment in 1907-1908, and of the St. Petersburg newspaper *Der Freind* from 1908, he continued to agitate for socialism in Russia until he was forced into exile in 1912. During World War I, he lived in New York, but upon the outbreak of the Revolution of 1917, he returned to Russia, joining the Mensheviks in their struggle against the Bolsheviks. When the latter attained to victory under Lenin and Trotsky, he was imprisoned in Moscow and in Minsk, but finally succeeded in escaping to Poland. He edited literary and socialist journals in Vilna and Warsaw. In 1925 he returned to the United States and spent his last years in New York, lecturing and writing in the spirit of the Bund. His memoirs, *Past Events (Vos Geven,* 1925), and his *Collected Works (Gezamelte Shriften,* 1945) were important sources for the history and literature of his generation. His knowledge was profound, his style lucid, his philosophy optimistic, and his argumentation logical. He was typical of the Bund leaders whose devotion and self-sacrifice inspired thousands upon thousands of Jews, old and young, to strive against incredible odds to build a better world, not for themselves as individuals, but for mankind as a whole. Their idealism was intense and their tragedy of titanic proportions. They perished at the hands of Czarist hangmen, Polish pogromists, in Soviet prisons and in Nazi gas chambers. But everywhere, in street demonstrations, in Siberian wildernesses, in ghetto bunkers and in refugee camps, they knew community of spirit and they felt the moral elevation which came from lives lived beyond self. They failed in their major objective of bringing about a socialist heaven on earth. But their failure was grandiose and their influence upon Yiddish literature was long lasting.

Shlomo Bickel (1896-1969), who emigrated to the United States in 1939, was the most influential literary critic after the death of Shmuel Niger in 1955, but never attained the dominant authority wielded by the latter. Though stemming from Eastern Galicia, he became the best interpreter of Rumanian Jewish culture before reaching the climax of his career in New York as literary columnist of the Yiddish daily *Der Tog,* as co-editor of the Yiddish monthly *Die Zukunft,* and as head of the research activities of YIVO, in the 1960's. However, during the decades preceding his American period, he was in the center of the Yiddish literary revival in Cernauti and Bucharest. At the former city he studied law after his demobilization from the Austro-Hungarian army and edited *Die Freiheit,* the weekly of Bukovina's Labor Zionists, from 1920 to 1922. Upon obtaining his doctorate in jurisprudence, he moved to Bucharest, where he practiced his legal profession and at the same time edited Yiddish literary periodicals.

The best essays of Bickel's Bucharest period were collected in his book *In Me and Around Me (In Zikh Un Arum Zikh,* 1936). His nine other volumes belong to his American period, but much of their content deals with Rumanian and East Galician Jewry. The vanished culture of the Galician town of Kolomea, where he spent his boyhood, is depicted in his two books *A City of Jews (A Shtot Mit Yiedn,* 1943) and *We Were Three Brothers (Drei Brieder Zeinen Mir Geven,* 1956). In his book of history, literary criticism and reminiscences, entitled *Rumania* (1956), he surveys the struggle for Jewish rights in that land since the 1870's, he sketches portraits of half-forgotten political, social and literary figures of three generations, he depicts the Jewish uniqueness of Bucharest, Marmoresh, Kishinev and Cernauti. In his historical novel *Family Artshik (Mishpokhe Artshik,* 1967) he recalls to life Bukovina's Jewish villagers of the mid-nineteenth century and examines the problems and legal disabilities Jews had to overcome when seeking to eke out a living among peasants.

As a literary critic, Bickel is impressionistic as well as deep-delving. He does not content himself merely with recording the facts and ideas of writers. He also frames them within their specific cultural environment and communicates the unique atmosphere about each of them. In the three volumes *Writers of My Generation* (*Shreiber Fun Mein Dor*, I, 1958; II, 1965; III, 1970), he reveals great sympathy for sceptics who harbor religious longings, for Soviet Marranos who sublimate their love for Jewish traditions in the deepest recesses of the heart, for Israeli poets who continue to create in Yiddish in completely Hebraized kibbutzim, and above all for Rumanian contemporaries with whom he shared earlier, happy years and who either perished or were scattered in all directions. His greatest admiration is reserved for Itzik Manger, whose beginnings he acclaimed and whose growth he accompanied with interpretative essays.

Literary criticism continued to flourish in the 1960's and 1970's primarily in the literary columns of Yiddish dailies and in literary periodicals with an international circulation such as *Goldene Keyt, Zukunft, Sviva,* and *Yiddishe Kultur.* Books of literary criticism and literary reminiscences continued to be published on all continents but increasingly in Israel. Among their authors were Jacob Glatstein, Glanz-Leyeles, Jacob Botoshansky, Yekheskel, Bronstein, Haim Bass, Moshe Gross-Zimmerman, Abraham Lis, I. C. Biletzky, L. Domankevitch, Samuel Margoshes, Chaim Lieberman, I. Silberg-Cholewa, S. D. Singer, A. Tabachnik, S. Tenenbaum, Jacob Patt, Abraham Patt, Baruch Zuckerman, J. Rapaport, I. Turkov-Grundberg, C. S. Kazdan, G. Sapozhnikov, Moshe Laks, Moshe Shulstein, I. Kahn, I. Goldkorn, I. Spiegel, Mordecai Tsanin, Chaim Sloves. These books had a limited and ever dwindling audience.

The critics aged and no longer reached out to the Jewish generation that came to dominance in the 1970's. The readers that still treasured Yiddish literature in the original tongue also aged and preferred the classics that satisfied their nostalgia for a vanished Jewish world.

11

SOVIET YIDDISH LITERATURE

Impact of Revolution • Hegemony of Kiev • Bergelson • Der Nister • Kvitko • Hofstein • Markish • Shteinman • Shvartsman • Khashchevatsky • Challenge of Minsk • Axelrod • Charik • Kulbak • Dominance of Moscow • Litvakov • Fefer • Kushnirov • Halkin • Persov • Gildin • Teitsh • Teif • Fininberg • Gurshtein • Godiner • Zeldin • Rossin • Wendroff • Kipnis

JEWISH LITERARY CREATIVITY in revolutionary and post-revolutionary Russia was largely centered in the three cities of Kiev, intellectual capital of the Ukraine, Minsk, capital of White Russia, and Moscow, into which Jews began to stream once the Czarist restrictions were lifted.

Intoxication gripped Jewish youth when the hour of emancipation from centuries-old disabilities came in 1917. A galaxy of radiant and courageous poets, whose creative energy was released after the war years of enforced silence, trumpeted forth their joy at the new order which promised them guarantees of freedom and equality. Their holiday mood was, however, short-lived. The incursion of pogrom hordes, led by Denikin, Petlura, Machno and other counter-revolutionaries, into the provinces of the Pale inhabited by most Jews, brought death and tragedy to hundreds of thousands.

The Yiddish poets then took up sword and pen to preserve the newly gained and once more imperiled freedom. Two of them, Osher Shvartzman and Beinish Shteinman, fell at the front in their twenties before their lyric talent had a chance to ripen. When victory finally came after a hard struggle that decimated dozens of Jewish townlets, hunger set in throughout the devastated provinces. The severe and probably necessary restrictions of military communism were supplanted by the New Economic Policy, which gave greater leeway to individual initiative not only in business and industry but also in literature and journalism.

During the years of the N.E.P., Kiev exercised hegemony over Yiddish literature in Russia, since the Warsaw and Vilna centers had been severed from Soviet territory; Moscow and Minsk were not yet sufficiently articulate to offer a serious challenge; and the Wise Men of Odessa, who had used Hebrew far more than Yiddish as their literary medium, were either silent or had emigrated to New York, Berlin and Palestine.

Three alternatives faced Russian Jews during the first post-Revolutionary decade. After the Balfour Declaration of 1917, they could answer the call of Zion; leave legally or, more often, illegally for the promised Jewish homeland. There they could continue their Hassidic or Rabbinic traditions, immerse themselves in biblical learning, or as secularists develop a neo-Hebrew culture. Thousands chose this path, joined kibbutzim, buttressed Jewish national and religious institutions, and paved the way for the establishment of an independent Jewish state.

Another alternative, once freedom of movement was vouchsafed to Jews, was to leave the cramped towns and townlets of the Pale for the cities and provinces of the vast Soviet realm, especially for the great metropolitan centers of Moscow and Leningrad. There they could slough their ghetto characteristics, intermarry, and assimilate into the Slavic majority. Hundreds of thousands chose this path.

A third alternative favored not Jewish disappearance, whether through emigration or assimilation, but rather an intensification of Jewish belongingness and the reconstruction of the Jewish nationality on Soviet soil, either in their existing communities or in new concentrations in Crimea or some other Jewish autonomous region. This was the alternative chosen by millions and at first supported by the government. For these millions, Yiddish was the chief unifying factor.

Religion was on the decline, since Marxists had dubbed it opium for the masses and good Communists were expected to espouse atheism. Zionism was looked at askance as a form of alien nationalism and its leaders were imprisoned or exiled. The dense concentration of Jews in Ukrainian towns was especially favorable for the growth of Yiddish cultural institutions and the Communist regime generously subsidized schools, libraries, press, scholarly and literary groups. The Kiev Group then forged to the van. The mentors of this group were David Bergelson and Der Nister, talented writers whose reputation was already well established before the Revolution.

Bergelson, who was born in 1884 at Sarne, a small town in the province of Kiev, first attracted attention in 1909 with his novelette *Railroad Station (Arum Vokzal)*. His earliest long novel *After All (Nokh Alemen)* was hailed in 1913 as the tenderest masterpiece of impressionistic writing. Thereafter he continued to enrich Yiddish literature with plays and narratives of enduring value.

From the work of this post-classical writer, more than from the blatant noises of partisan propagandists, one can gain a good insight into the transformations that swept over the millions of Jews between the Dnieper and the Dniester, the Baltic and the Black Seas, during the first half of the twentieth century. Their spiritual distress and their unflagging idealism, their decadent moods and their unrealized hopes for a Messianic morrow live on in his prose epics and dramas.

Two literary strains commingle and merge in this novelist of Ukrainian Jewry. His Russian lineage goes back to Goncharov, Turgenev and Chekhov. His Jewishness owes more to the folklore of the Pale and to the Yiddish revival launched by Mendele and Peretz than to the Bible and the sages of the Talmud.

Bergelson is not of the giants of the pen and his voice does not ring out in stentorian tones demanding attention and allegiance. His is the almost inaudible voice of the wayfarer on the abandoned by-paths and forgotten lanes of dying towns. Silence hovers about his characters, silence and loneliness, loneliness and melancholy. Though young in years, his heroes and heroines are old in their moods. Their faces are pale and colorless. Their eyes are deep sunken. They are prematurely tired. They resemble tender autumnal flowers that have been nipped by the first frost and that can never regain the energy to blossom in full flowing October. They lower their heads in mild resignation and wait patiently for their dreary end.

Mirel Hurwitz, the heroine of Bergelson's finest novel, *After All*, and his most carefully drawn character, best illustrates his pre-Soviet types. As the only child of a well-to-do and highly respected merchant, she lives in daydreams and indulges in vague longing for some indefinable arena of action larger than the few streets of her little town. At seventeen she drifts into an engagement with a nice young man of the neighborhood, a young man acceptable to her parents, her relatives and public opinion in general. But when she gets to the provincial capital on a visit and when she sees wider horizons than she has hitherto known, she becomes utterly dissatisfied with her narrow circle and its traditional, intolerant views. She breaks off her engagement and resumes her passive reveling in nebulous visions of freedom, in misty dreams of vast panoramas. Day follows day with unvarying routine, with activities that are not too meaningful. Months come and go. They unite to years and the years meander on lazily.

Mirel's melancholy smile turns ironic. Her tiredness turns to utter indifference to the few joys or sorrows that might fall into her lap. She drifts into a practical marriage without any real desire and without overmuch resistance. The eternal sameness saps what remains of her youth and rebelliousness. Her mind and her feelings become dulled. From a kindhearted, hard-working, slow-witted husband who bores her, she seeks relief by returning to her parents. But there everything is as petty and as empty as before. The same people are still engaged in the same talk as in all the preceding years. The best of her acquaintances are still dissatisfied with life, but not a single one of them does anything concrete to overcome this dissatisfaction. They get together at each other's homes and over a cup of tea they lament the passing of time and the barrenness of their world. Then each of them goes back to his own hearth and resumes his monotonous activities and undeviating habits. Their today does not really differ from their yesterday or yesteryear, nor will their tomorrow be any different because of their exertions. They will continue to vegetate on and on, unless an unexpected catastrophe intervenes. And yet, they are all the time conscious that somehow, somewhere, storms must be brewing and that the almost universal urge for a dramatic change must be materializing into action.

Young Bergelson is aware of the teeming activity of the large metropolitan centers in which slumber the forces of the future. But in his pre-Revolutionary tales, he is primarily the chronicler of the little towns whose past, though never too bright or too glorious, was incomparably better than their hopeless present: "I am sitting so long at the gate of the town into which nobody enters and which no one leaves. All that I once knew, I have long ago forgotten and only a single thought remains in my mind, the thought that all, all have died and that I alone have survived. Hence, I am really no longer waiting for anybody. And when I look about me again and when I feel the energy and the power that slumber in me, I do not even sigh any more. I merely think that I am the guardian of a dead town."

Bergelson is an Impressionist. He describes not events themselves but rather the echo of events in the souls of human beings. He is a painter of twilight moods, of late autumn landscapes, of withering hopes, of chronic unhappiness, of ineffectual yearning for the unexpected and the dramatic.

The Revolution of 1917 galvanized the lethargic villages and towns of the Ukraine. The Jewish middle class, whose dying had been the main theme of Bergelson's writing was, however, beyond recovery. Catastrophe followed catastrophe. During the years of civil strife and of military communism, the formerly respected burghers of hundreds of communities between the Dnieper and the Dniester were, on the one hand, hounded and massacred because of their Jewishness by the followers of Petlura and Denikin and, on the other hand, despoiled and degraded because of their bourgeois origin by the Bolshevik conquerors. The slight alleviation of their fundamentally hopeless status during the period of the N.E.P. did not long endure. Starvation and exile, economic decay and migration to the interior provinces of Russia decimated their ranks throughout the 1930's, and the Nazi avalanche of the early 1940's annihilated the survivors and engulfed whatever remained of their cultural institutions and their traditional way of life.

Bergelson had early voiced his faith in the new Russia that was arising out of the ruins of Czardom, feudalism and foreign exploitation. He participated in the Yiddish publications and cultural activities of revolutionary Kiev from 1917 to 1919. His few years in Berlin during the period of the N.E.P., and his trip to the United States in 1929, merely confirmed him in his preference for Soviet society. In the short stories of *Biro-Bidjaner* (1934) and in his long novels of the 1930's, *Penek* and *Dnieper,* he depicted the painful transition to the new order. Despite his affirmation of the dominant Communist regime, there is, however, even in these works, unmistakable nostalgia for a world that is no more, the world of his childhood, its unhurried pace, its shabby respectability, its wasteful aimlessness. There is also the recognition that, in the Communist state even as in the capitalist state, assimilation of Jewish culture to the cultural patterns of non-Jewish neighbors is still a long way off.

During the Second World War, Bergelson enriched Soviet Jewry with finely chiselled short stories, of which the best is *Between*

Mountains (Tsvishen Berg). His last novel, *Two Worlds (Tsvei Veltn)* was being published in Moscow in 1948, when all news of him ceased. Throughout the next decade, every question about him addressed to Soviet authorities and to Soviet writers was answered with silence. After the death of Stalin, this silence was broken and his liquidation on August 12, 1952 was confirmed as a miscarriage of justice.

The same purge to which Bergelson fell a victim also removed from the literary scene in 1948 the finest of the symbolist novelists and poets, Der Nister, pseudonym of Pinchas Kahanovitch, who was born in 1884 in the city of Berdchev and who perished in a Soviet prison two years before the firing squad blotted out the lives of his Kiev associates.

The Yiddish-Hebrew pseudonym, Der Nister, which may be translated as the Hidden One or the Occult Person, is an apt characterization of the outstanding representative of Neo-romanticism among the Yiddish writers of the Ukraine.

Der Nister began in 1907 with prose poems, dream images, in which Jewish, Christian and Olympian supernatural creatures were intermingled. He continued in 1912 and 1918 with songs, odes, versified prayers, allegories of God and Satan, mystic visions that spanned heaven and earth and dissolved in nebulous melancholy, ballads which were meant to delight children but which also hinted at meanings beyond their grasp. Thus, the tree that resists the peasant's axe and is as reluctant to die as the horse pursued by the bear, the white goat that lulls the infant to sleep, the sprites that dwell in abandoned ruins, the gnome that bestows wealth, the cat that feeds its playmate the mouse, the rooster that is the sole companion and nurse of the sick grandmother—all have traits and feelings not unlike those of human beings and yet they are at the same time symbols of abstractions and qualities. What Marc Chagall sought to express in color, Der Nister attempted in verse and poetic prose.

As the translator into Yiddish of Hans Christian Andersen's fairy tales and as a student of cabalistic lore, Der Nister succeeded in combining European and Hebraic elements in his tales. He also felt strongly the influence of Rabbi Nachman Bratslaver, the most talented of the Hassidic weavers of stories. Forests alternate with deserts, enchanters and witches with angels, demons and Nazarites, bears of the north with lions of the South. Amidst the whirl of events that traverse earth and moon and starry constellations, the loneliness of the individual peers through as he roams far and wide in search of holiness and ultimate wisdom. Unhappy with his own age and powerless to change it, such a person attempts to break out of it. He wanders on and on beyond any specific time or clearly defined realm. Now and then he encounters a hermit or a graybeard who is even further removed from normal pleasures and mundane pursuits and therefore closer to the source of essential insight. They help him to overcome demonic temptations. They find for him a track through seemingly trackless wastes. They accompany him for a while through the darkest mazes of forests. They weave their tales into his tales.

Der Nister's reputation as a leading member of the Kiev Group was already well established when the Russian Revolution broke out. As a non-political writer, he felt ever more and more isolated amidst the contending ideological coteries and left for Berlin. There he published two volumes of *Contemplations* (*Gedakht*, 1922), stories that followed the model of Nachman Bratslaver. In one story, he made a beggar the savior of kings. In others, he introduced magic stones, a healing mirror, a wolf that travelled faster than the wind. Transported on the back of the wolf, the hero of the *Bovo-Maisse* could quickly reach the remote land where his betrothed, a paralyzed princess, was awaiting his coming to bring about her recovery from a baneful spell.

After returning to the Ukraine, Der Nister was silent for several years and, when he resumed publishing in 1929, his volume *From My Treasures* (*Fun Meine Giter*) betrayed a pessimism not evident earlier. The opening narrative was put in the mouth of a madman in a madhouse. This madman related his experiences in converting mud to gold until he became the supreme lord of the land and arrogant beyond all mortals. Then Der Nister sketched the downfall and degradation of this plutocrat, who, in his final extremity, after exhausting all other means of feeding ten hungry bears, had to offer them his own ten fingers and his heart to gnaw at. Beyond the apparent meaning of these changes of fortune, the reader senses the author's hints of intense anguish and spiritual distress but hints so deeply veiled that their true import still defies clarification. Perhaps such labyrinthean mystification was necessary if the romantic writer wished to remain true to his inner self and yet to survive at a time when anti-Romanticism and Socialist Realism were the prescribed slogans for literature.

A decade later, however, the pressure upon Der Nister was too great to be successfully resisted. In his major work *Family Mashber*, the first volume of which appeared in 1939, he adopted the realistic style of writing demanded of all Soviet novelists. However, he applied it not to contemporary life, but to an era which was already historic and to a social order of which only vestiges remained: Berdichev of the 1870's.

Caught between his sympathy for his tradition-rooted characters and the necessity of following the anti-religious Communist party line, he added an apologetic preface. In it, he explained that he deemed it artistically more desirable not to pronounce the doom of his characters in advance but rather to portray them proceeding slowly and inevitably to their historic destiny, the abyss. He wanted to let them unfold their glamorous traits no less than their ugly ones and then to show how the logic of their further inner development would drive them unalterably to decay and damnation. He promised that, together with the still uncompleted later volumes, his work would put the finishing touches to an old generation which was steeped in medievalism and would also trace the tragic beginning of a more enlightened way of life which would gradually ripen into revolutionary activities and sweep away the accumulated rot of centuries.

The city depicted by Der Nister developed in the form of three concentric circles. The innermost circle, the market district, was the heart of all business activities. The second circle embraced the residential area, in which were concentrated the religious and cultural activities of the Jewish community. The third circle, suburbia, was inhabited by the poorest of the poor, criminals, cranks, prostitutes, the subversive and revolutionary elements that would later topple the entire social edifice.

The Mashbers belong to the patricians of the city. Luzi, the oldest brother, faces a spiritual crisis when the Hassidic rabbi in whom he found sustenance and guidance passes away. Ultimately he discovers the genuineness he seeks; he joins the despised, poor, ardent Bratslaver Hassidim. Among them, he comes to understand and to appreciate the true humanity in the town's third circle.

Moshe Mashber, the second brother, puts his faith solely in business and lives primarily in order to accumulate wealth. By experiencing a business crisis and a decline of fortune, he is humbled in his pride and is saved from despair by a saintly pseudo-beggar, a *Lamedvovnik*.

Alter Mashber, the youngest brother, has to overcome pain and illness. When his clouded mind recovers, he accepts the equality of all human beings and is happy to marry the maid of the Mashber household. The stratified social structure, as exemplified by this well-to-do family, begins to show fissures and its ultimate collapse can be predicted.

This collapse occurs in the second volume, which was published in 1948 in the United States but not in Russia: in that year all Yiddish publications ceased in the Soviet Union, not to be resumed until after Stalin's death. Moshe Mashber's wealth disintegrates, he is forced into bankruptcy, he is imprisoned for fraud, and on his release he dies a broken man. Meanwhile, Luzi Mashber continues his quiet acts of kindness and love in behalf of the despised and oppressed members of the Jewish community, as befits an adherent of Bratslav Hassidism. He is joined by Sruli, a saint in tatters, and by Michael Bukier, whose eternal questioning leads to excessive scepticism and, as a result, to unmerited persecution on the part of the town's religious fanatics. In these three characters, but especially in Luzi Mashber, the author depicts himself and his kind, silent, self-effacing approach.

Only once does Luzi break out in eloquence. Then he expresses his undying hope and unshakeable faith in his Jewish people. His words spring from the heart of the author, who otherwise had to masquerade his feelings: "Israel is beloved. Neither the pains of Galut nor his expulsion from his father's table stops him from feeling himself to be God's child, chosen to reign in the future. Let not the nations of the earth rejoice in the rich portion allotted to them now and let them not look down upon Israel, which is now black as are the tents of Kedar. Israel is indeed divided and left at the mercy of many swords which hang above his head and compel him to beg for life's sustenance of all the cruel murderers in this world. Let not the nations rejoice and mock Israel, who appears strange, disunited, an outcast stepchild among them. The curse upon Israel is only temporary, no matter how long it lasts. His lot, to be an unhappy beggar on accursed roads, will ultimately end. He will be the light and salvation predicted and promised by the Prophets. Yet even now and in all generations when catastrophes overwhelm Israel, saints arise who fathom the meaning of Israel's destiny, who accompany him on his thorny road with love and compassion, and who gladly receive the arrows meant for him. They and their followers are fortunate enough to feel Israel's sublime pain, the pain of the insulted, injured and tortured heart of the world. Israel is God's beloved, an example to mankind of the fortitude and dignity with which one bears suffering even when the knife is at one's throat. Beloved is Israel, who even in darkest moments still retains a shimmer of hope in salvation, salvation not alone for himself but for all mankind, for whom he is the blessed victim and also herald of the Messianic promise of a time when all tears will be wiped away from all faces. Yes, a time will come when to the Holy Mountain there will troop, as to a wedding, sages and crowned light-bearing saints with the Anointed One in their midst and the whole world following them—man, woman and child, not only of the human species but also of beasts and cattle and birds, all of whom will be lifted up and filled with knowledge of that day of universal rejoicing, every sage with his admirers, every prophet with his followers, every saint with his disciples, everyone who guarded the Holy Flame amidst storms and prevented its extinction. My brothers, guard this Flame bequeathed to you, guard it until the Messianic era when all knees will bend before the Savior and all heads of all living creatures in which there is a living soul will ask His blessing. Guard the Flame, my brothers!"

Luzi's ardent words of hope and comfort were rudely interrupted by a stone hurled at him through a window. Even so was this valedictory of Der Nister, upon which he worked for more than a decade, rudely interrupted by the Soviet secret police who came to arrest him. His first words on that occasion are reported to have been: "Thank God, you came at last. I have waited for you so long." Thereafter silence engulfed him and he died in prison on June 4, 1950.

Premonitions of his end filled the second volume of Der Nister's masterpiece, upon which he continued to work while one after another of his friends, colleagues and followers were vanishing from the public eye and terror stalked the survivors. The final chapters, therefore, overemphasized scenes of dying and bared the long hidden suffering of a tortured soul.

The author was expected to revile a people and a tradition which he loved so fervently in his heart of hearts and he had no way of knowing whether this love, concealed beneath an outer veneer of apparent dislike and locked up in not easily decipherable symbolic language, would ever penetrate to readers in later years or be intelligible to them. In the morass in which he was forced to move in his last years, he remained a hidden saint, the noblest personality among the Soviet Yiddish writers.

The most talented disciple of Der Nister was Leib Kvitko (1890-1952), who together with David Hofstein and Peretz Markish formed the lyric triumvirate of the Kiev Group. These poets came to the fore during the period of revolution and military communism, 1917 to 1921. They were tragically stirred by the Ukrainian pograms which followed the initial wave of liberation. They left the communities that were drenched in Jewish blood and found a temporary asylum in Berlin of the early Weimar Republic. They returned to Kiev during the thaw of the New Economic Policy in the mid-1920's. There, as well as in Kharkov and Moscow, they devoted the next two decades to directing literary, educational and cultural activities in the Yiddish tongue and to hymning the glory of Soviet achievements in war and peace. Despite their patriotic submission to every aspect of Soviet policy, all three were imprisoned in 1948 during Stalin's purge of Jewish intellectuals and, after four years of interrogation, torture and suspense, perished in 1952.

Kvitko stemmed from an impoverished rabbinical family of Podolia and was orphaned at an early age. Wandering from town to town, he eked out a bare living at various trades. When the Revolution broke out, he welcomed it as ushering in an era of justice and equality.

In a lyric of 1917, he bade farewell to the old, joyless, flowerless, songless world. After the gun and the sword will have destroyed the yoke of ages, he was certain that peace would sprout and a healthy youth, with fiery blood in its veins, would march on and on, free and strong.

In another lyric, Kvitko described Red Youth, radiant and intoxicated with the new freedom, streaming and storming onward, while parents stood on the sidelines and looked on horrified. The rift between the generation of mice and the generation of wrath was unbridgeable. "Though my father dies of hunger and calls me to his couch, I try not to hear. I must belong to the storm of destruction, to the hammers that build a new structure. I become more young, more free. Our East is afire at dawn and a new day begins."

During the following two years, however, Kvitko experienced Petlura's reign of terror in Ukrainian Jewish communities. He then composed lyrics full of hatred toward a foe who smashed cradles and hanged infants, and full of love for his long suffering Jewish people. In an unforgettable lyric in the volume *1919*, he depicted Jesus, the Jewish child worshiped by the perpetrators of pogroms, as going about from place to place, bloodstained and crucified, with Jewish pain in his eyes and Jewish patience in his veins. As Jesus passed houses where Jewish children once frolicked, he dared not look into them. He paused on roads where his image was displayed, tore it down, and bowed his head in shame. Stopping before every priest's home, he scratched on the walls in embittered silence deep black crosses of shame.

In another lyric, Kvitko saw his ancestors pleading with him not to curse the murderers but to forgive them. "Was not every murderer once a child? Does not every murderer laugh and smile at his own child? Forgive, forgive!" But young blood seethed in the poet's veins and, viewing the aftermath of slaughtered communities, he rather prayed for the strength to hate, strength which, as a Jew, he did not possess.

In the lyric anthology *Youth* (*Yugend*), which appeared early in 1922 after the defeat of the counter-revolutionary forces, Kvitko reverted to his earlier enthusiastic mood, glorying in Soviet achievements, in the war of youth against parental authority, in the burning of the old rags of the defunct order. "I am as young as the dawn and as fresh as the dew. I'll build a new temple in the sun-blest day. Go away, you oldsters, depart with the day. Your heart is an old fiddle whose song is long ended. We are the blood-and-fire youngsters who paint with clear colors a new life and a bright panorama."

Kvitko's volume *Green Grass,* which appeared in 1922, after his arrival in Berlin, reprinted the poems of his earlier volume *Steps* (*Tritt,* 1919) and added others full of joy in his youthful exuberance, radiant in dreams, treasuring memories, delighting in hopes. After his return to the Ukraine in 1925, he resumed writing tales for children of Yiddish elementary classes and lyrics to be sung in nursery schools and kindergartens. Some of these emphasized social responsibility, Communist reconstruction, the need for agricultural pioneering; but most spoke joyously to the hearts of children about ponies and calves, fishermen's dancing skiffs, fiddles that enchanted birds and bees and hens. Kvitko was undoubtedly Soviet Russia's greatest master of the juvenile lyric.

Kvitko's tales, on the other hand, lack originality. They follow faithfully the approved formula for Soviet narrators. They feature Soviet heroes who engage in underground activities, unmask traitors, and succeed in conspiratorial work abroad. Such a hero is Presber in the novel *Rio Grande Furs* (*Riogrander Fel,* 1928). Presber aids Hamburg's proletarian rebels in 1923. He participates in the capture of a ship after it leaves the German harbor for the high seas, and in the diversion of its cargo to revolutionary China. Despite a smashed hand and the loss of an ear, he is back in

Hamburg from the Far East within a year and helps to lure a traitorous Soviet agent back to Russia for proper punishment.

Kvitko's *Selected Works* (*Geklibene Verk,* 1937) were dedicated to Stalin and abounded in flattery to him. Stalin was clothed with the divine attributes of omniscience and omnipotence, in a lullaby sung by a child to its mother. The child dreamed that it went to a forest to cut tree-trunks to build a ship which would float over seas and catch golden fish. The child was able to frighten off an intruding hare and to ward off a fox, but then there came a pack of wolves that wanted to tear it to pieces. Stalin heard what was going on and he sent a tank to the rescue. The tank shot up the wolves and brought the child back to its mother. In another dream, the child sailed on the ship. Rains came and a great wind which capsized the ship. Stalin heard the cries of the child as it was being swallowed by the waves and he sent a hydroplane which scattered the storm and brought the child back to the Kremlin. In a third dream, the child heard the door open. Someone entered, picked it up and talked to it like a loving father. "Well, guess who it was. Surely you know!" The same volume also included tributes to Voroshilov, Marshal Budenny, war heroes of the Red Army, and sailors of the Red Fleet, all of whom were absolutely fearless and were furthering the victory of the proletariat and the liberation of the world.

Kvitko's last volume, *Songs of My Moods* (*Gezang Fun Mein Gemiet,* 1947), contained the poems he composed after the Nazi attacks upon Russia in 1941. They abounded in invective against German barbarism and in praise of Soviet heroism and self-sacrifice. They also made mention of Jewish fighters and Jewish fliers who avenged German misdeeds. A little over a year after the appearance of this patriotic poetic collection, Kvitko was imprisoned on charges trumped up by the secret police upon Stalin's urging. Together with other Jewish poets and novelists, he was shot on August 12, 1952. Two years later, he was rehabilitated as another innocent victim of miscarried justice and hailed as the great poet who united in his art the destinies of the Jewish, Russian and Ukrainian cultural groups.

David Hofstein (1889-1952) was only a year older than Kvitko, but he began to write much earlier. He grew up in a Volynian village at the edge of a forest as the oldest of eleven children, and his first lyrics reflected his intimate contact with nature in its various aspects. They were united into poetic cycles entitled "Fields," "Mountains," "Forest." These idyllic songs of nature, begun in

1911, continued until his cycle "Snow" in 1919. They breathe the freshness of youth and the joy of early love. He speaks of himself as a young branch of an old tree, as gathering young strength from the old trunk. He sings of young brows, young knees, young days, young hearts, young joy. He is ecstatic with wild joy, pristine joy, sun-joy, hot joy, new joy.

Meanwhile, the Revolution of 1917 broke in upon his gentle moods and stirred him to rapturous acceptance of the new socialist reality. Ten years earlier he had been refused admission to the University of Kiev because of the restricted quota for Jewish students. He then had to acquire his higher education by himself without the guidance of teachers. Now he was elevated to the position of a lecturer in Moscow and he could head the Yiddish Cultural League in Kiev. He felt himself to be at last a free individual, the equal of all proletarians within the Soviet realm. His verses welcomed the dawned day of revolution, the glories of October and May, the rainbow colors that flooded the world, the brotherhood of peoples. He was happy to take his place in the vanguard of advancing mankind, marching proudly in step with millions of toilers. He called himself a bit of resounding copper that wakened the tired and drowned out the feeble-hearted, so that the procession under the Red Flag should not falter or retreat. His songs hailing the achievements of the Revolution established his popularity not only in his own land but also in radical Jewish circles beyond its borders.

Hofstein's elegies, in which he mourned for the Ukrainian Jewish communities devastated by Petlura, Denikin and counter-revolutionary hordes, appeared in 1922, with illustrations by Marc Chagall. Passing through ruined towns, Hofstein wondered whether anything could compensate for a single drop of a child's innocent blood. He noted that for generations the Ukrainian market-places had echoed with the drunken songs and the boots of bandits, and that the shadow of shame was still lingering on Ukrainian highways.

Brave in the exercise of his new freedom, Hofstein protested against the dominant sector of the Jewish Communist movement, the *Yevsektsie*, for its endorsement of the banning of Hebrew and the persecution of Hebrew writers. He then discovered that he too was suspect and subject to persecution for daring to speak up. He thereupon left Russia in 1923. For a time he lived in Leipzig and in Berlin, then he moved on to Palestine. In the Jewish homeland he contributed Hebrew songs, chiefly to periodicals of the Labor Zionists. Seeking inspiration in the Bible and in Jewish legends, he completed a dramatic poem, *Saul*, in 1924, and an Expressionistic spectacle, *Messianic Times (Moshiakhs Tsaiten)*, in 1925.

The former work depicted the first king of Israel at the beginning and at the end of his troubled reign. The real hero, however, was the populace rather than this tragic ruler. In the first scene, the people of Israel are faced with the aggression of their Ammonite neighbors. They realize that the corrupt sons of the prophet Samuel are incompetent, unable to protect them, and they therefore demand a strong monarch to lead them. Despite Samuel's warning not to accept the yoke of a monarchy, they proceed to acclaim Saul as king.

The second scene then shows the aftermath of this unwise decision: Saul in his last moments at Gilboa. Wielding absolute power, his character has deteriorated. Moody, depressed, consorting with witches, he has become unpopular with his subjects. When these again find themselves harrassed by enemies on all sides, they rise up in revolt against the capricious ruler. After his children are slain and the trapped monarch falls upon his own sword, there is general acclamation: "The King is dead, long live the People!" Free once more, the masses live on, fight, create, eternally strong, forever rejuvenated.

Parallels between the dramatized events and contemporary Russian events were not difficult to discover and afforded an insight into the poet's thinking while abroad.

When restrictions upon individual initiative were temporarily loosened during the period of the N.E.P., writers began to feel a thawing also of oppressive measures imposed upon literary expression and publishing during the earlier period of military communism. After Kvitko and Markish returned to Kiev, Hofstein too was overcome by longing for Russia, especially for his children who had remained there. Confessing his heresies and promising atonement, he was permitted to resume his lecturing, editing, writing and translating.

In the preface to his *Songs (Lieder, 1935)*, he referred to the labyrinthian road on which he travelled before he became a militant Marxist. He recalled his early religious upbringing, the idyllic delusions of his childhood, his contentment with admiring phenomena as a mere onlooker, his gradual questioning of essences, until his final abandonment of his position on the sidelines and his becoming a participant in the struggle for a better world.

After his return to Russia in 1926, Hofstein had to follow faithfully prescribed patterns of thinking and creating, and the various gyrations of the party line. He had to sing optimistically of a freedom he no longer saw about him and of a future he no longer believed in unreservedly. As a result, the quality of his poems declined while the quantity kept on increasing. The subdued idyllic tone of his genuinely beautiful early poems gave way to a raucous overidealization of Soviet achievements in all fields. He even sang of "dear Soviet writing paper." In 1930, he wrote a hymn to the tractor as the tender-limbed steel horse of the free earth. In 1931, he hailed the construction of a dam along the Dnieper. In 1932, he was supposedly inspired by the launching of an Arctic icebreaker. In 1935, he eulogized aluminum as the Socialist metal. In 1936, he sang out again and again and again his gratitude to Stalin as the leader and friend of all free peoples. In 1937, he put into verse his worship of the Hammer and the Sickle. He glorified the restoration of Kiev as the Ukrainian capital. He saw Birobidjan as the promised home for the Jewish proletariat of all lands. Not in the desolate wastes of Palestine but in the seething steppes and primeval forests of the Jewish autonomous region in Siberia would Jewish genius flourish and great deeds be done.

Never again did Hofstein treat a biblical theme or refer to Jewish historic events. In a poem on woman as the alluring wonder in the ethereal world, he did mention that naive grandfathers related that woman first ate of the sweet fruit of knowledge. He hesitated, however, to betray the fact that his true source was the Book of Genesis. Nevertheless, now and then an ambiguous verse for a moment revealed like a lightning-flash a corner of his soul inaccessible to casual readers. Thus, he prophesied a deluge of pitch and sulphur which would descend upon all lands. He hinted that, though eyes looked up through tears of blood to cruel gods of destruction, everyone must still continue to execute a fervent dance of supreme joy on the edge of a sword. He compared conscience to a dog torn from its leash. He felt that it was good to be bitten suddenly by its sharp teeth in the midst of too much servility and constantly calculating steps. Conscience enabled a person, after a thousand years, to utter at least a single bitter growl of nay.

After years of pretended prescribed joy, a moment of true joyous enthusiasm broke forth from him in 1948 when the new state of Israel came into existence with the blessing of Russia.

He could then hail the young Jewish democracy without fear of retribution: "May the joy hidden in me reach out to all of you. I stand at my window and tell the world Good Morning." He gave assurance that the thin thread which linked him to his beginning had not torn.

Before the year was over, Hofstein was made to realize that he had revealed too loudly and too soon his joy at Israel's rebirth. The Soviet attitude towards Israel was changing, and what had been permitted at the beginning of the year was condemned as heretical before the end of the year. Hofstein was seized along with the other Jewish intellectuals of the Kiev Group. He was transported to Moscow for more severe interrogation of his purported deviationism, then condemned to a tortured existence in remote Siberian Tomsk, and finally shot on August 12, 1952, together with his prison mate David Bergelson. He also was later rehabilitated as a victim of the so-called personality cult.

Peretz Markish (1895-1952), the youngest of the Kiev triumvirate, published his first lyrics in 1917 and participated in the anthology *Eigens* of the following year, a combined venture of the Kiev Group, which then included not only Kvitko and Hofstein but also Bergelson, Der Nister, Yekheskel Dobrushin, Nachman Maisel and Kadia Molodowsky. This anthology gave expression to the general enthusiasm at the fall of Czarism and the liberation of the Jewish people along with the Ukrainian and Russian masses.

Markish's first volume, *Thresholds (Shveln)*, appeared in 1919, the same year as Kvitko's first volume, *Steps (Trit)*, and Hofstein's, *Along Roads (Bei Vegn)*. Revolutionary romanticism gripped him no less than others of his circle. The past was over and gone. The future was veiled. The present was exciting and heroic. Lyrics burst from the heart of young Markish like an avalanche and were gathered in eight collections between 1919 and 1922. The best of these, *The Mound (Die Kupe,* 1922), has been compared to Chaim Nachman Bialik's powerful elegies following the Kishinev pogrom of 1903, especially in the vigorous protest against God, a God who permitted the massacre of his faithful people.

During the following years, Markish lived in Warsaw and was the recognized leader of an Expressionistic group of young poets whom Hillel Zeitlin, editor of the influential Warsaw daily *Moment,* attacked as "The Gang"—*Khaliastre*—and who then adopted this name as a badge of honor and used it as the title of two anthologies. The first of these appeared in Warsaw in 1922 under the editorship of Markish and I. J. Singer. The second appeared in Paris two years later under the editorship of Markish and Oizer Varshavsky, with illustrations by Marc Chagall.

As the idol of Yiddish avant-garde writers, Markish was triumphantly received in London, Berlin and Paris. His extraordinarily handsome features, his melodious voice and his powerful gestures added to the effectiveness of his poems, which he recited and chanted to large, applauding audiences. Maturer critics, however, voiced the hope that the poet's feverish fermentation and Expressionistic hysteria would subside with greater maturity and would be replaced by more disciplined artistry. S. Niger characterized him in 1922 as a firebrand hurled forth from the revolutionary flame and as Pegasus on the run whirling around in a chaotic tornado, without goal or direction.

Throughout his entire odyssey, which led him as far as Jerusalem, Markish never slackened in his enthusiasm for the achievements of the Communist revolution. He defended the new Yiddish poets of Kiev as superior to the Yiddish lyricists of other lands. In his view, a spring torrent had descended upon the Jewish Pale and had swept away the idyllic, sweet, Sabbath melancholy which had characterized the entire inter-revolutionary period between 1905 and 1917. A world had been destroyed and a new one had been created. Yiddish poetry should, therefore, no longer be nostalgic and funereal but forward-looking and joyous. It should mirror the storm and stress of the new Soviet reality. Markish saw no contradiction between being a good Communist and a good Jew.

When he returned to Russia in 1926, he had no deviationary past to regret or to atone for. He was accepted in Kiev and in Moscow as the literary spokesman of revolutionary youth. In his hymn *My Generation* (*Mein Dor*, 1927), he eulogized the red dawn spreading from Russia, rousing, kindling, dazzling, liberating the remaining five-sixths of the globe that were not yet communistic. His marching song for May Day, 1928 roared and boomed and thundered and called for a united effort to break the workers' chains in all lands.

Markish's first novel, *Generation Follows Generation* (*Dor Ein, Dor Ois*, 1929), presented in two volumes the liberation of the multi-racial Ukraine from reactionary forces. The hero of the first volume was Mendel, the representative of the older, tradition-bound Jewish generation. The hero of the second volume was his son Ezra, who was caught up in Bolshevist enthusiasm and eager to build a better order. Both father and son sacrificed their lives for their fellow men, but each did so for a different objective and in a different way. The Orthodox father sought to ensure the survival of the Jewish community by bending before the havoc-wreaking, incited pogromists and hoping to minimize the damage. His was a passive martyrdom because any other form of resistance by a minority group, which had been denied weapons for self-defense, was unthinkable. The Communist son could plan and execute active resistance because the revolution liberated the Ukraine's Jews and enabled them to participate on equal terms with others in fighting political and social injustice.

Markish's second novel, *One Plus One* (*Eins Oif Eins*, 1934), presented as its central figure a Jewish bricklayer who left America after twenty-eight years of toil in order to lay bricks for socialism in the Soviet state and who gradually came to understand that, despite certain hardships and an apparent lack of efficiency, Russian ways of working, creating and living were, on the whole, superior to American ways.

Markish's overlong poem in thirty cantos, *Brothers* (*Brieder.* 1929), concentrated once more on the theme of revolution. It chronicled the heroism of young Jewish proletarians, two brothers in a Ukrainian townlet, who sacrificed their lives for the triumph of their Communist ideal.

The poet's adoration of the dominant regime reached its climax in his epic *On Stalin* (*Poeme Vegn Stalinen*, 1940). In bombastic rhetoric, he sang of the great Stalin to whom all persons stretched out their hands in gratitude, Stalin from whose eyes lightning flashed and at whose feet thunders prostrated themselves, Stalin who covered Russia with light and clothed it with a coat of steel so that it could become the foremost fortress of this planet, the foremost homeland of thought. It is doubtful whether these hollow phrases, devoid of any lyric felicity, sprang from the heart of the poet. They probably had to be penned because all Yiddish poets who had been at the forefront of the struggle against the Nazi philosophy in the 1930's were suspected of not being too enthusiastic about the Molotov-Ribbentrop Pact which in 1939 pointed to an alliance between Stalin's Russia and Hitler's Germany.

Then came Hitler's betrayal of Stalin and the Nazi invasion of Russia. Markish then began his last and greatest poem, *War* (*Milkhome*), an epic in 162 cantos, upon which he worked throughout the war and post-war years and which was published in 1948, shortly before he was forever silenced by prison entombment. The poem covers the events that followed the invasion. Its

main emphasis is on the suffering and heroism of Jewish individuals.

Unforgettable is the figure of Gur-Arye, the sole survivor of a
slaughtered community. In a magnificent scene, he arises at night
from the pit of the murdered Jews, feels himself miraculously still
alive, escapes to a forest and ultimately reaches a peasant's hut.
As he collapses on the threshold, he sees an image of Jesus on the
wall. In a visionary trance he then talks to Jesus as one crucified
Jew to another, asking him whether he also came from the pit
and whether he would now be going again to the suffering Jews
still surviving in ghettos, to be with them at another crucifixion.
Would Jesus still preach non-resistance? Would he let widows
and orphans be handed over to the Nazi murderers? Foxes,
smelling recently living limbs around the pits, have already left
their forest lairs in anticipation of a promising feast. "Go, Jesus!
Let those at the ghetto gates know that nobody ascended to
heaven from the Cross, that you too are hiding in a peasant's hut.
You have served the hangsmen far more than the liberators by
turning your other cheek. Throw away your crown of thorns, step
on it, pulverize it! Go to the ghetto! There you will meet innumerable crucified children who are holier and purer than you, the
Nazarene."

Despite Markish's faithful services to the Soviet regime, he did
not escape four years of torture in a Moscow prison on the usual
trumped up charges and a firing squad on August 12, 1952. He
was, however, rehabilitated soon after the death of his adored
Stalin. In 1957 his poems reappeared, but in a Russian rendering
prepared by forty-two different translators. This attested to the
fact that he had at least forty-two literary admirers with a
thorough mastery of Yiddish, and yet the official explanation for
the non-appearance of his works in Yiddish was that there no
longer seemed to be any interest in Yiddish. In 1959, his uncompleted poetic epic, *Heritage (Yerusha)*, was published in Buenos
Aires in the original Yiddish but not in Moscow or Kiev, where
Yiddish continued to be frowned on. In 1964, his prose epic,
Generation Follows Generation (Dor Ois, Dor Ein), was reprinted
abroad but not in Russia, the land he loved and for which he
agonized.

The apex of the literary creativity concentrated in post-revolutionary Kiev was reached in the second anthology of *Eigens*, in
1920. Here were included major tales of Bergelson and Der Nister
and poems by all three of the lyric triumvirate. Symbolist abstrac-

tions and universal moods still dominated and proletarian tones were muted. Beinish Shteinman (1897-1919) and Osher Shvartz- man (1890-1919), two young poets who had met their end a few months earlier while fighting with the Red Army in the Ukraine, were represented by works only remotely connected with their heroic deeds.

Shteinman, in his dramatic poem *Moshiakh ben Yosef*, depicted a gloomy world over which Lilith, Queen of the Night, had ruled for a thousand years. When Moshiakh ben Yosef appeared amidst thunder, lightning and a reemerging sun, the enslaved populace hailed him as the long-yearned-for redeemer. Lilith, seeing her reign threatened, tried to calm her subjects and to lure the Mes- siah into her arms. When he disdained her overtures, she then tried her last stratagem. She pretended to join in the universal enthusiasm at the coming of the radiant Messiah who, as she explained, would bring happiness to innumerable later generations but not to the generation of transition. The present night-born generation was destined to fertilize with its blood the millennium to be. The disappointed populace then turned angrily upon the Messiah and stoned him. Again Lilith had triumphed, but her Dominion of Night would not endure forever. While the chorus joined in her outcry: "Messiah will not arise, he will not come," three little stars, fading away in the gathering gloom, sang tremu- lously: "Yet will he come, yet will he come," thus hinting that the premature, inadequate Messiah, son of Joseph, would be followed in the fulness of time by the true Messiah, son of David, who would usher in the genuine Messianic Age.

Osher Shvartzman's songs in *Eigens*, though written at the front lines from 1914 on, dealt with twilight moods when the sun poured its last yellow upon quiet fields, and with summer evenings when the cattle returned to recline on the dewy grass. In a lyric prayer from the battlefield, he begged God not to delay any longer his mercy to those upon whom he poured out wrath but to bring back lit windows and abundant bread from plowed fields to the dark, hungry townlets.

Shvartzman left as his legacy hardly more than sixty lyrics, but these sufficed to put him in the foremost rank of the Kiev Group. From 1911 he served in the Russian cavalry, experienced humiliations because of his Jewish origin and was demobilized only after the Bolsheviks seized power. Then he returned to Kiev and participated in the publications of the Yiddish Communists.

He felt closest to his cousin David Hofstein, who later edited his poems.

Despite the influence of Heine's *Weltschmerz*, Lermontov's Russian melancholy, and Bialik's tragic pathos, Shvartzman retained a sunny outlook and sang enthusiastic hymns to love and nature, freedom and joy, friendship and youth. Life in barracks from 1911 to 1914 and at the front from 1914 to 1917 was not easy for a sensitive poet and often he fled from drunken, carousing comrades to commune with himself and to record his feelings in verse. Most of his preserved songs, though, were composed in his last two years. When Kiev fell into the hands of Petlura and Ukrainian bands, he joined the Communist underground and, when pogroms on a large scale were perpetrated in town after town, he enlisted in the Red Army to avenge the innocent blood of his kinsmen and to safeguard the fruits of the Revolution. In one of his last poems he wrote: "I shall not return to the land until I shall hear the full word of redemption." He did not return. His heroic death in battle, however, lent an aura to his personality and gave rise to lyric tributes by Hofstein, Kvitko, Itzik Fefer, Aaron Kushnirov, Ezra Fininberg, Aaron Vergelis, Moshe Khashtchevatsky and many other poets. His deeds were recounted and his poems studied in Soviet Yiddish schools until the last school was closed and the Kiev Group was liquidated.

Moshe Khashtchevatsky (1897-1943), who wrote Shvartzman's biography and who had idealized him ever since their first meeting in 1917, also died a hero's death in the Red Army, fighting in a later war to save Moscow from the Nazis, but by then Yiddish poets could no longer be held up as models for Soviet youth, Jewish or non-Jewish. A pall of silence descended upon him and not a single one of his many volumes of verse and prose has been reprinted since his death.

Khashtchevatsky's best lyrics were the early ones of his Kiev period, when the N.E.P. still permitted considerable freedom of expression. David Hofstein then compared him to the Russian Symbolist Fedor Sologub. In an introduction to Khashtchevatsky's first volume of verse, *Thirst* (*Durst*, 1922), he characterized the young poet as the cheerful portraitist of life's heaviness and his poems as sweet magic, pure joy hovering over foaming poisons, red sunrays above the green mold of swamps.

Though caught up in the fast moving events, Khashtchevatsky could not easily dissociate himself from the old ways of the Ukrainian townlet. His symbolic name for the Jewish townlet was "The

Swamp." The twenty-year-old poet set out to search for the lost days of his youth and found that these had retreated to the swamp, where they sat brooding in an ever aging circle. He wanted to forget gray, gloomy yesterdays and to turn his face to the morrow. But he could not. Byronic tones infiltrated his lyric cries. "My cries go up to heaven but heaven is covered with clouds. Or perhaps there is no heaven and all my efforts are vain. I am lost in the world even as Hagar in the parched desert. No miracle is in sight, no water to fill my pitcher. I am destined to feel my way blindly in the dark wilderness."

Khashtchevatsky compared his songs to raindrops that came too late and to letters sent to friends who were already dead. He longed for tranquility, for a roof above his head, for a haven of peace within his four walls.

With the ending of the N.E.P., he had to stop singing of his own sorrows and joys. He then followed the prescribed party line. He rhapsodized Lenin, Stalin, industrial enterprises, Birobidjan, the Red Army and the Black Sea Fleet. His poetic epic *Lenin* (1937) consisted of seven cantos. It began with Lenin's birth, recorded the various stages of his revolutionary career, and ended with a requiem upon his death and with Stalin taking up Lenin's heritage: to guard the achievements of Communism. During the Second World War, however, Khashtchevatsky's last poems, *Once and Now (Amol Un Haint, 1943)*, reverted to biblical imagery. he stressed the Jewish aspects of the conflict no less than the Russian. He saw the Jewish struggle against Hitler as a continuation of David's struggle against Goliath, Samson's against the Philistines, and the Maccabeans against the Syrians. When the war ended and such sentiments were punishable as evidences of Jewish nationalism, the poet was no longer among the living.

The decade from the Revolution to the end of the N.E.P. was the most productive decade of Soviet Yiddish literature and the Kiev Group harbored the greatest concentration of Yiddish literary talent. Despite the increasingly harsh restrictions of the following decades, the Kiev writers were able to maintain themselves as a viable group until they were decimated by war and imprisonment and their leaders executed by the firing squad on August 12, 1952.

The hegemony of Kiev was supported by the significant Yiddish literary center of Kharkov, the capital of the Ukraine after the Revolution, but was challenged by the large White Russian center of Minsk and, above all, by the ever growing Jewish center in the

Soviet capital, Moscow. The literary critics of the latter two aspiring Yiddish centers scented heresies in the Kiev Group and contrasted the proletarian realism and Communist patriotism of their own writers with the decadent symbolism and apparent lack of Communist fervor among the Ukrainian Yiddish writers, with the single exception of Itzig Fefer. The attacks increased as the comparative freedom of the N.E.P. gave way to the stricter party control introduced in the early 1930's.

The Minsk critics were especially vehement in their denunciation. They flaunted their own superpatriotism and their own unflinching adherence to the party line, yet their end came earlier and the liquidation of their center was more thorough.

In the Czarist Empire, Minsk had been unable to rival its neighbors, Vilna and Warsaw, and after the Revolution it vainly sought to equal the achievements of Kiev and Moscow. The worker-poets, who came to the fore in its newly founded periodicals during the period of military communism, were rich in optimism but poor in talent, full of enthusiasm for the new freedom but unable to embody this enthusiasm in works of distinction. They vociferously called upon the Jewish masses to battle for eternal peace and universal justice. They appealed to Jewish youth to destroy the traditional religious values and institutions and to forge a brighter future for all peoples in an earthly paradise. But their versified calls and dramatized appeals had far more propagandistic than artistic worth.

When the civil war ended and greater economic and political stability was established during the N.E.P. years, higher literary standards were demanded of writers. With the founding of the Yiddish organ *Shtern* in 1925, the Minsk Group became more significant. In its columns, essayists of distinction laid down rules for Yiddish proletarian literature and meted out stern rebukes to all who dared to deviate from these rules. Considerable authority was wielded by Ber Orshansky (1883-1945), who headed a Yiddish section in the Institute for White Russian Culture, by Yashe Bronshtein (1906-1937), who despite his youth pontificated as professor of Yiddish literature until he was liquidated as an enemy of the people, and by Khatzkl Dunietz, who as editor of the Yiddish daily *Oktiaber* faithfully interpreted the party line in literature as well as in politics until his arrest in 1935 by the secret police and his liquidation as a counterrevolutionary Trotzkyite soon thereafter.

To the Minsk group belonged Mordecai Veinger (1890-1929),

whose ideas on the phonetic spelling of Yiddish were accepted in Soviet Russia, though not in the non-Communist lands. He lectured in Yiddish and Germanic philology at the Minsk University and supervised research projects in the Yiddish department of the White Russian Academy until his suicide.

In 1928, Moshe Kulbak (1896-1940), who had lived in Vilna and Berlin, joined the Minsk Group. He was followed in 1929 by Max Erik (1898-1937), who directed Yiddish literary research both in Minsk and in Kiev until his arrest and death in a prison camp.

Of the Minsk poets, only Selig Axelrod (1904-1941) and Izzie Charik (1898-1937) commanded attention far beyond the borders of White Russia—until the former was shot for the crime of Jewish nationalism and the latter tortured to death in Russian prisons for as yet unrevealed heresies.

Axelrod had spent his youth in a Yeshiva and was deeply immersed in Jewish tradition when the Revolution broke out. In the five volumes of his lyrics, published between 1922 and 1938, he combined acceptance of the new revolutionary regime with nostalgic sadness at the disintegration of the warm hearth of his father and grandfather. In his lyric cycle "Old Home," he described the hopeless, emaciated faces of his graying parents, who remained behind in their lonely, decaying rooms while their three sons scattered in diverse directions, each occupied with his own destiny.

Axelrod confessed that he could not soar beyond his own individual emotions, that preoccupation with himself often made him forget the common weal. His subjectivity, his melancholy, his alternating between fear and hope made him suspect at a time when objectivity, optimism and unquestioning obedience to party programs were prescribed. He was accused of overemphasizing the bourgeois "I" and failing to stress the proletarian "We," of brooding Hamlet-like over the meaning of existence while profoundly dramatic events surged all about him, of following the decadent example of Sergei Yessenin, the Russian peasant-poet who proved incapable of adjusting to the Soviet reality and who committed suicide in 1925. Despite Axelrod's efforts to rehabilitate himself with songs of the glory of the Red Army, he was adjudged to be too Jewish-minded in his general outlook and was executed on June 26, 1941, two days before the German invaders entered Minsk.

The story of Axelrod's execution was revealed by a fellow-prisoner, the Yiddish writer, Herschel Weinrauch, author of *Blood on the Sun (Blit Uf Der Zun,* 1950). Before the Germans approached the White Russian capital, bombs from their planes set fire to the prison. When the prisoners clamored to be let out, the guards and secret police opened the bars and asked the prisoners to arrange themselves in rows, the political prisoners on one side and the criminals on the other. Since the records had been destroyed in the conflagration, some political prisoners, including Weinrauch, preferred to take their chances with the thieves and murderers. Axelrod, truthful to the end, joined the column of political offenders. These were marched off to a nearby forest clearing and shot without further ado. The hardened criminals were set free when their guards, fearful for their own lives, disappeared as the Germans came ever nearer. Weinrauch, who soon found himself behind the front, joined a partisan group, succeeded in finding his way to a Russian outpost, was evacuated to Samarkand, enlisted in the Soviet army, fought bravely against the Nazis, won officer's rank, was wounded in battle, and finally, after perilous adventures and utmost disillusionment with Soviet ideals, escaped to Palestine.

Izzie Charik rose like a meteor, flared brightly for a decade and a half on the literary horizon, and disappeared into the silence of an unknown grave at the age of thirty-nine.

As the son of a cobbler, Charik experienced early privations. He joined the Red Army in 1919 as a young revolutionist, and was accepted into the Communist Party as a most devoted member. When his first lyrics appeared in 1920, his talent was immediately recognized and he was sent to Moscow to study literature and art. His lyric volume, *On the Earth (Uf der Erd,* 1926), earned him the title of "singer of the muds of Minsk." As editor of the literary periodical *Shtern,* he became the most influential member of the Minsk Group. In 1935 he was honored by a book of eulogies, in which noted critics paid tribute to his poetic genius and to his political reliability. Nevertheless, two years later while at the height of his fame, he too fell a victim to a Stalinist purge.

As though he had a premonition of his early death, he expressed his eagerness to drain life of its experiences quickly and in the raw. "I care not if I am unknown to posterity and if nobody preserves my footsteps; now, now, I arrive with fists in my song." He longed for storm-filled days and restless nights. "My restlessness whirls like the wings of a windmill." His main subject matter was the galvanization of the dormant Jewish townlet, the transformation of bearded idlers to creative tillers of the good earth. He felt that there was no need for Jews to tarry any longer amidst the muds of Minsk at a time when the Urals and the Crimea beckoned and the vast spaces of all European and Asiatic Russia were open to them. The attachment to parents must be severed. "Pass away, pass away, you melancholy sires with frightened, snow-braided beards. From the last tragic collapse, you remain as the last witnesses. Pass away, pass away, you melancholy sires." Lenin's dictum that Soviet power plus electricity equals Communism was illustrated by Charik in a poetic narrative in which a simple, obedient Jewish worker participated in the building of an electricity station and by his vigilance helped to thwart attempted sabotage. After three years of colossal exertion, electric blood finally streamed from city to city and Communism had scored another magnificent victory.

Charik included in this narrative a hymn of adoration to the G.P.U., the secret police that stood on guard everywhere and that came at midnight to shatter the nests of the dissident. One midnight in 1937, the police came for the adoring poet and he was silenced forever. Two decades after his disappearance, he was rehabilitated as an innocent victim of Stalin's personality cult and his poems were published in translation.

Moshe Kulbak's literary career spanned two decades, of which the first was spent in Kovno, Vilna and Berlin, and the second in Minsk. He began to write poems in 1916 in the Neo-romantic tradition, some of them in Hebrew under the influence of Ahad-Haam. Typical of his early period was the symbolist poem "Lamed-Vov" (1920). Its hero was the chimney-sweep Shmuel Itze, the eternally wandering Jew, who swept the ashes from a thousand chimneys but who could not clean out the ashes from his own soul. Mired in pain and darkness, he yearned for light and holiness, even as did Samael, the pain-filled, infernal counterpart of the Lord of Heaven. Only after he faced, understood and overcame the chaotic, negative, ugly force of Samael did Shmuel Itze attain to salvation.

Kulbak resided in Berlin from 1920 to 1923, when German Expressionism was at its height. The influence of this literary movement interpenetrated the grotesque episodes of his prose narratives *Moshiakh Ben Ephraim* (1924) and *Monday* (*Montag*, 1926). These rambling tales alternated between the realm of reality and a metaphysical world beyond reality, a world where *Lamedvovniks* roamed and where man, escaping from self, became one with the bird of the forest, the cow on the meadow, and the loam of the earth.

Kulbak's Expressionistic lyrics were full of the joy of life. His earlier, tired receptivity gave way to an active grasping of sensations. He wanted to embrace the entire earth, to dissolve into song, to be drunk with laughter and ecstasy. He saw in Soviet Russia the radiant sun of renewal, the splendid realm of social justice, a giant bearing golden tablets of universal liberation. He hailed Russia's bronze youths who responded to the ringing of the bells of freedom, who left the feeble-hearted oldsters behind them and marched forth to a more vigorous future.

Kulbak's Expressionistic period ended in 1928, when he cast in his lot with the Minsk Group. He found that Expressionism was condemned by the Soviet literary spokesmen as heretical and that he would have to confine himself to write in accordance with the requirements of Socialist Realism. He did so in his novel *Zelmenianer* (I, 1931; II, 1935).

In the two volumes of this novel Kulbak portrayed a Jewish family whose members had vegetated for seventy years in a decaying district and who discovered, after the Bolshevist Revolution, that their material and cultural structure was built on a rotting foundation. Despite their Oblomovism, inertia, resistance to progress, they had to accept electrification of their district and the erection of new, bright, tall buildings in place of their antiquated, spider-encrusted, loam houses. Kulbak's crotchety characters, steeped in Jewish traditional behavior, were the heirs of Mendele's and Sholom Aleichem's *Luftmenshen*. But even his young Bolshevik innovators did not entirely slough their family characteristics. Their creator could not avoid smiling at them once in a while. Because of his mildly ironic approach, he fell afoul of the grimly serious Soviet critics who could not tolerate his laughter and his apparent unwillingness to depict the representatives of the post-Revolutionary youth as flawlessly heroic. They were somewhat mollified a few years later by his *Disner Childe Harold* (1933), a satirical epic based on his experiences in Berlin during the early years of the Weimar Republic. There his humor was directed against the degenerate German bourgeoisie, a welcome target in the year of Hitler's ascent to power. While the title was reminiscent of Byron, the influence of Heine's comic epic *Germany, A Winter's Tale* was even more obvious.

In 1937, at the height of Kulbak's success, while his poems were being sung, his *Zelmenianer* widely read and his last play performed in Moscow to the accompaniment of good reviews, the secret police swooped down upon him, forbade further performances of his plays and banned all mention of his books. After his transportation to a Siberian prison camp, silence enveloped him. He dragged on a slave laborer's existence until 1940. Sixteen years after he perished, he was rehabilitated as another innocent victim of Stalin's personality cult.

After the liquidation of the Minsk writers in 1936 and 1937, only the Moscow center continued to function as a rival to Kiev. Before long, the rigid discipline and strict uniformity imposed by the Stalin dictatorship effaced any distinction between the literary centers. Writers became party functionaries, and literature a useful tool of the state in molding a Soviet type of being. The Yiddish language was still tolerated, but the content was restricted to non-Jewish themes in so far as possible. The proclaimed slogan was: "Soviet in content, Yiddish in form." But content and form could not always be easily wrenched apart, since words and phrases, especially those derived from the Hebrew, were laden with Jewish historic associations. Writers, therefore, had to exercise extreme caution in their use of language, avoiding Hebraisms and biblical expressions whenever possible. Because they often faltered and stumbled, they exposed themselves to Communist heresy hunting and political inquisitions. They were repeatedly forced to repent unpremeditated sins and lived in a constant state of insecurity. Besides, the ever shifting party line resulted in works that were hailed as Soviet literary achievements at one time being labelled subversive at a later time. With writers distraught and confused, the quality of their publications declined even before all Yiddish writing was suppressed during Stalin's last years.

The main organ of the Yiddish Communists from 1918 on, was *Emes,* published in Moscow. Its editor, Moshe Litvakov (1875-1937), was the chief spokesman for the Soviet party line in literature until his liquidation. In his young years he had been a leader of the Labor Zionists and had written in Russian, Hebrew and Yiddish on social, philosophic and literary problems. Upon the outbreak of the Revolution, he became active in the Kiev Group and participated in its journals and anthologies. In 1921 he left for Moscow and the following year he entered upon his career as editor of *Emes.*

Thereupon, this scion of a religious family, who until his seventeenth year had himself been immersed in Talmudic studies and who until his fortieth year had preached Zionism, undertook a vigorous campaign to uproot Jewish religious observances and Jewish national aspirations. He flaunted his godlessness and raged against Jewish petrifaction and Zionist chauvinism. However, in his critical articles, and as a Professor of Yiddish Literature and History, he often could not avoid touching on the Jewish past. Indeed, the two volumes which contained his best literary essays, *Amidst Unrest* (*In Umruh*, I, 1918; II, 1926), called attention to the cultural heritage which proletarian writers inherited from Morris Rosenfeld, Abraham Reisen, Sholom Aleichem and Peretz.

When the American Yiddish poet H. Leivick visited Moscow in 1925 and rebuked its Jewish men of letters for their isolationism and their complete break with the past, Litvakov, in an essay entitled "Heritage and Hegemony," replied that Soviet writers were prepared to accept some aspects of the Jewish cultural heritage, aspects which contained desirable values for the working masses, but that they must insist on the hegemony of Soviet Yiddish literature in the contemporary world.

Litvakov pointed out that, unlike Russian literature which was revolutionary throughout the century since Pushkin, Yiddish literature was chiefly rooted in religious tradition and mirrored reactionary, nationalistic aspirations. Created by bourgeois intellectuals, it was more at home in the house of prayer, the kitchen or the business office than amidst political demonstrations, strikes and riots. Except for the Kiev Group of poets, it was caught unprepared for a society and a culture based on the dictatorship of the proletariat. A new beginning had to be made and was being made by poets such as Lipe Resnik, Itzig Fefer, Ezra Fininberg, Aaron Kushnirov, Shmuel Halkin and Izzie Charik. While these poets were revolutionizing Yiddish vocabulary and filling Yiddish literature with new content, Yiddish writers in America, Poland and elsewhere were sinking into the slough of decadence, nationalist clericalism and Zionist chauvinism. They could only hope to emerge from esthetic fogginess to the bright sun of revolutionary creativity by following the example of the Russian Yiddish writers and by recognizing the superiority of the planned Soviet literature. Only Moscow could teach them to curb their capricious intuition and to create according to well-defined proletarian regulations. They could then become the vanguard and trumpeters of the coming social revolutions in their lands. The choice was between orientation toward Jerusalem, symbol of a decayed past, or orientation toward Moscow, symbol of a sunlit future. "When

Yiddish literature abroad will proceed on the road to Moscow and attain to momentous results, we shall rejoice with it and, if it be worthy, we shall not contend with it for hegemony. But until then hegemony belongs to us, to Moscow."

Despite Litvakov's militant assertion of Soviet superiority in literature as well as in all other fields of endeavor, he was not spared attacks by even more fanatical followers of Stalin who professed to see in his essays fragmentary remnants of Jewish nationalism and separatism. By counterattacking his opponents, he was able to outmaneuver efforts to purge him in 1931 and 1932. He continued his anti-religious campaign and his editing of *Emes* until 1937. In the major purge of that year, he too was arrested as an enemy of the people and perished in prison within a few weeks.

The power Litvakov had wielded passed into younger hands. In the decade after Litvakov's fall from grace, Itzig Fefer (1900-1952) dominated the literary scene. His rise can be ascribed to three factors: his proletarian orthodoxy, his power of invective, his lyric talent.

As a youth of nineteen, Fefer fought with the Bolsheviks against Denikin. When Kiev was captured by Denikin, he remained in the city and engaged in underground activities. He was caught and imprisoned. When his mother learned that her son was in danger of being shot, she set out from her townlet of Shpole for Kiev. Though Denikin's underlings threw her out of the train when they discovered that she was a Jewess, she continued on foot. The typhus epidemic then raging in the devastated city chained both mother and son to hospital beds. Fefer recovered and was liberated by the Red Army shortly thereafter but she, who came to comfort him, was borne to her grave. Twenty years later, Fefer paid moving tribute to her in a poem which stressed both the loving care with which she surrounded him and her courage in sending him forth to fight against the foes of the Revolution.

Fefer's finest songs dealt with the civil war, his leaving Shpole, his taking part in battles, the storming of Kiev, pogroms, hunger, and, despite all, joy atop ruins. His emphasis was not on the cruel events themselves but rather on his emotional reaction to them, the moods they evoked, above all, the mood of exhilaration. "When the blood is fresh and young, then the road is fresh and young."

Fefer trod the narrow road of strict party conformity. His power of invective helped him to down opponents and to rise ever higher in the Soviet literary hierarchy. His study on *Yiddish Literature in the Capitalist Lands,* published in Kiev in 1933, displayed his mastery of the vocabulary of literary derogation. For him, Bialik was an agent provocateur and propagandist, Aaron Zeitlin a Fascist, I. J. Singer a rabbinical pornographer, Aaron Glanz-Leyeles a nonsensical reactionary, Leivick an ape-romanticist who dreamed of returning to the savage era of the orangutan, Shimon Dubnow a clerical chauvinist who committed the crime of accusing the Ukrainians of organizing pogroms. "Calm down, worthy historian, Mr. Dubnow! We know who organized the pogroms. We remember well your comrade and Jabotinsky's comrade: the pogromist Simon Petlura, as well as his predecessors of all the three hundred years about which you babble."

Fefer derided Asch, Zhitlowsky, Bialik, David Einhorn, Jacob Leshtchinsky, Abraham Cahan, Max Weinreich and Old Dubnow as incompetent assistants of the ailing bourgeoisie. He called them literary physicians who were themselves sick and unable to stop the march of the Revolution to world ascendancy. He held out hope only for a few fellow-travelling petit-bourgeois writers who had become confused because of the economic depression in the land of prosperity, America, and who were jumping from the Fascist swamp onto the bandwagon of Socialist reconstruction.

During the Second World War, Fefer rose to the rank of lieutenant colonel and in 1943 he was sent to the United States and Canada together with the Soviet's best Yiddish actor, Shlomo Michoels (1890-1948), in order to win Jewish support for the Soviet struggle against the Nazis. It was then that he penned his proud lyric affirming his joy in belonging to the Jewish group, to the people of Samson, the Maccabeans, Spinoza, Marx and Heine.

This affirmation was soon to cost him dearly. Despite his many services to the Soviet cause, this feared spokesman for the party line in Yiddish literature also fell a victim to Stalin's axe. Arrested in 1948, he too was tortured for four years and finally shot on the tragic August 12, 1952, together with his friends and foes.

Aaron Kushnirov (1890-1949) was one of Fefer's earliest and staunchest supporters. In a lyric "Epistle to Fefer," he hailed the latter in 1930 as a comrade-in-arms in the struggle against Symbolism and Romanticism and for Socialist Realism. Kushnirov too was glad to load his own lyrics with gunpowder and to encase them in steel. According to him, the times were calling for metallic hammering and not for the filigree work of jewelled images. Every esthetic cat could file and polish. Veiled hints, abstractions, impartial objectivity must be replaced by clarity, concreteness, party-mindedness.

Fefer, in his reply, welcomed Kushnirov into the marching shock-brigade of poets. En route to electric days, the tempo must be forced and whosoever tarried must be shoved aside. Poetry was not a tickling of rhymes but a weapon in the class struggle. It must pierce with the spear of satire and be as vitriolic as a pasquil. Poets must be prepared to fight with both song and shrapnel when the country called them.

Kushnirov had begun in 1921 with a volume of lyrics, *Walls* (*Vent*), to which David Hofstein had written a glowing introduction. The title poem was a stirring outcry of the Walls. These had been condemned for thousands of years to listen but not to speak out. At last, relief from their enforced silence was granted them. The echo of iron steps was penetrating to them. Revolutionary power was compelling even the haughty granite to bend and kneel before it. Plastered with placards and posters, the Walls recovered their voices. They too could blare forth: "We hear the firm, heavy, triumphant marching."

Moving to Moscow in 1922, Kushnirov immediately became involved in the literary projects of the Yiddish section of the Moscow Association of Proletarian Writers. His short stories *Children of the People* (*Kinder Fun Folk,* 1928) were welcomed as models of good Soviet prose. He was invited in 1928 to co-edit the Minsk Yiddish organ *Shtern,* but soon returned to Moscow, where his plays were to be staged and where the star of his friend Fefer was in the ascendancy. He thus escaped the bloody purge which overwhelmed the Minsk Group a few years later.

When the Germans invaded Russia, Kushnirov, at the age of fifty-four, volunteered for the front. He fought like a hero, won medals and distinctions as an officer, and published battle lyrics. The most moving of these lyrics was "Father-Commander," composed in 1944. He described himself peering at night into the tired faces of the eighteen-year-old soldiers under his command, the fledglings who had just learned to take wing. Before dawn he might have to send these young eagles into battle. Many would fall, perhaps he himself. But, if he should manage to escape bullet or shrapnel, he would have difficulty after the battle in recalling the smiles or the names of the missing—even as other officers were unable to recall his own eighteen-year-old son, who had also been sent into battle and was never heard from again.

Despite Kushnirov's services to his Soviet fatherland, he too did not survive Stalin's dictatorship. During the war, which called for a maximum effort of all nationalities, he too found the courage, as did Fefer, to proclaim his love for his bleeding but unbowed Jewish people, which had survived the ravages of four thousand years. The poem "Through This World" contained the stanza: "With my face, with my fate, I belong to my people, eternally trodden under foot but never crushed, eternally threshed but never annihilated."

Kushnirov's last public appearance took place in October 1948, soon after the Moscow Anti-Fascist Committee had been liquidated as a nest of traitors. By that time Shlomo Michoels had been mysteriously murdered and almost all the other leading members were under arrest. The Moscow organization of Soviet writers called a special meeting to discuss the problem of Yiddish literature, obviously a subversive literature, as proved by the fact that its outstanding representatives had been imprisoned. Kushnirov was delegated to speak at this meeting and, as a faithful party member, to vilify Yiddish literature, the fate of which had already been sealed by the highest authorities. The gathering was to give expression to public indignation. The guilt of the accused was taken for granted, since in a Soviet state innocent persons would not have been hailed away and kept under arrest. As a good Communist, Kushnirov was chosen to castigate the writers who had fallen from grace. He was at his seat waiting for the chairman to call him to mount the platform. At this moment, one of his friends walked up to him quietly and whispered in his ear that during the preceding night the aged, ailing literary critic Yekheskel Dobrushin (1883-1953), to whom he had dedicated a poem from the battlefront, had been arrested. He then heard his own name called as the next speaker. Trembling and glassy-eyed, he arose, walked onto the platform, tried to speak, but could not utter a sound. His lips moved, his body was distorted in pain. Minutes passed. An uncomfortable silence spread among the audience, then he was helped from the hall. Another Communist stalwart substituted for him with the prescribed vituperation. There then followed the arrest of the Yiddish writers of Kiev, Minsk, Odessa, Kishinev, Czernovitz, and other cities. Kushnirov did not recover from this experience. Illness chained him to his bed and he passed away in his own home six months later.

Another poet whose liquidation was averted by illness was Shmuel Halkin (1897-1960). Stemming from a large family rooted in traditional Jewishness, he never lost his love for the Jewish people, even though he was forced to sublimate this love during the Stalin era. His early religious training had taught him that the purpose of human existence was moral perfection, that every individual was a microcosm which bore responsibility for the macrocosm, and that every evil deed increased the evil content of the world.

Halkin long vacillated between painting and literature. The decision was made for him when he came to Kiev in 1921 and Peretz Markish accepted his first short lyric for publication, Its eight lines contained Halkin's basic theme: the striving to retain the Sabbath mood and to bring the holiday tone to weekdays.

In 1922, he left for Moscow. There David Hofstein helped him to publish his first lyric booklet. Nevertheless, though living in the Soviet capital, he still contemplated settling in Palestine and until 1924 he even belonged to a Zionist circle. A Hebrew song, "Shir Hachalutza," written at this time, gave expression to his Zionist longing. It was not published until after his death and then it appeared only in Israel. A Yiddish poem, entitled "Russia," lamented that every one in Russia who had a bit of land could plant a tree on it and wait for the fruit; only "we," after so many years of horror, must still seek a new earth. Halkin, in his autobiographic sketch, listed among the poets who influenced him most throughout his life the medieval Sephardic poets Yehuda Halevi and Solomon ibn Gabirol.

No wonder, therefore, that Halkin's poems of the 1920's were attacked by critics as voicing nostalgic despair and falling outside of the new requirements for proletarian art. In 1932, he was compelled to confess his errors and to repudiate his Jewish nationalistic heresies. He promised to "give Soviet literature at least one book worthy of the time." However, *Shulamis,* a dramatic poem based on Goldfaden's musical drama, hardly fulfilled this promise. *Bar Kochba,* another verse drama, did so only partly. Both were produced in Yiddish theaters. Halkin preferred to devote his lyric gift to the non-controversial task of translating into Yiddish foreign classics such as Shakespeare, Longfellow, Kipling, and older Russian classics such as Pushkin and Tyutchev. During the Second World War he wrote a dramatic poem on the Warsaw ghetto uprising. It was to have been staged by the Moscow Yiddish Theater, but when the liquidation of Yiddish culture set in, the theater was shut down and Halkin was arrested. When his health broke down in prison, he spent a year and a half in the prison hospital and was then released because of his impaired heart. He survived longer than most of his Jewish literary colleagues, long enough to experience rehabilitation in 1958. After his death in 1960, his birthplace Rogatchov in White Russia named a street after him, a rare honor for a Soviet Jewish poet. In 1966, the poems and ballads of his post-Stalin years were published in Moscow.

Rehabilitation also came to Shmuel Persov (1890-1952), the talented Moscow novelist, five years after his liquidation. A rebel against Czarist authority in his boyhood, Persov escaped to America at the age of sixteen, when the Revolution of 1905 ended in disaster, but returned to Russia in 1917, filled with enthusiasm for the Communist regime. As an official in a Moscow cooperative, he wrote on economics for Russian journals, but his original sketches and short stories appeared in Yiddish organs from 1918. He was a founder and pillar of the *Yevsektsie*, the Yiddish Section of the Moscow Association of Proletarian Writers.

Persov's short story *Derelicts* (*Sherblekh*, 1922) anticipated the method of Socialist Realism and was enthusiastically received by his Moscow literary colleagues. It described the broken remnants of social groups which had been formerly dominant: a Greek Orthodox priest, a tubercular Czarist officer, a Jewish merchant. These derelicts are huddled together in a prison cell, alternating between fear of liquidation by the Bolshevik masters of the town and hope of liberation by counter-revolutionary peasant hordes. This story was later incorporated in the volume *Corn Bread* (*Kornbroit*, 1928), narratives of the bitter struggle between adherents and saboteurs of the revolutionary order.

Persov avoided the black-and-white technique of less talented Communist storytellers and propagandists. He peered into the tortured souls of former petty Jewish tradesmen and he laid bare the psychological difficulties which they faced in adjusting to a new way of life. He had sympathetic understanding for the declassed storekeepers whose windowless, doorless trading booths looked out upon the market place like open mouths from which the teeth had been drawn. He realized that such impoverished Jews were not enemies of society but rather bewildered persons whose standard of values had been too suddenly upset and who could not yet grasp the greater desirability of productive toil as peasants or as factory workers. In the final story of *Corn Bread*, Persov mirrored himself in the figure of the government agent who set out to collect overdue taxes from Jews still clinging to their decaying homes, dramshops, market hovels, and who did not have the heart to attach their last possessions as payment.

In the tales of *Day and Night* (*Tog Un Nakht*, 1933), Persov again documented his love for Jews as Jews. He had a leading character of the title story inveigh against sending the declassed Jews of a deteriorating townlet to work in the factories and mines in the heart of Russia, because these Jews in their loneliness and uprootedness would quickly lose their precious Jewish uniqueness and would assimilate to the overwhelming majority of non-Jewish fellow workers. He preferred to see them settled in Birobidjan, Crimea, and other agricultural colonies that were predominantly Jewish, so that they could retain their own language and cultural associations because "The Russian Bolsheviks know that the Jewish people is an homogeneous people." Such sentiments, tolerated in the young years of the Communist regime, were later denounced as Jewish nationalist deviationism and their author had to pay with his life for having voiced them.

When the Germans invaded Russia, Persov wrote a series of stories about Jewish heroes of the Red Army and the role of Jewish partisans behind the various fronts. His pride in specifically Jewish patriotism and in the contributions of Jews to the victory of the Soviet forces found expression in his book *Your Name is Folk* (*Dein Nomen Is Folk*, 1944). This book was regarded as additional confirmation of the accusation leveled against him that he was espousing Jewish separatism. He was arrested together with the other Jewish proletarian writers of Moscow and shot in 1952. Five years later he was rehabilitated as yet another innocent victim of the Stalin cult. A selection of his works appeared in 1957 in a Russian translation. Not until a decade after his liquidation did a fragment of his unpublished prose appear in Russia's only Yiddish periodical *Sovetish Heimland*.

Chaim Gildin (1884-1944) also perished in a Stalinist purge despite his devotion to Soviet ideology. He had participated in the Revolution of 1905. He had suffered two years imprisonment under the Czar's regime. He had attained to influence in the 1920's as editor of the Kharkov Yiddish monthly *Roite Velt*. Five booklets of his poems appeared between 1921 and 1932 and were followed by his *Collected Works* (*Gezamelte Verk*, 1932), which included his short stories and critical articles. Despite his absolute loyalty to the Communist Party Line in literature and politics, he was nevertheless arrested during the purge of 1937 and perished after seven years of hard labor in a Siberian camp.

Moishe Teitsh (1882-1935) survived an early purge by the Moscow Communist Party in 1922, was rehabilitated as a faithful Soviet journalist, poet and novelist, and died a natural death two years before the major purge of 1937. Stemming from Vilna, he had joined the Bund in his youth, had been imprisoned at nineteen for anti-Czarist activities and had aroused attention with his sad, autumnal lyrics and short stories written under the influence of Abraham Reisen. After the Revolution of 1917 he wrote juveniles, proletarian lyrics and tales, and the biblical drama *David and Bathsheba* (1920). He reached the height of his popularity with his novel *The Death of Comrade Volya* (*Der Toit Fun Chaver Volya*, 1928).

Moishe Teif (1904-1966), a native of Minsk, escaped the purge of the Minsk group with whom he had been associated since 1924, having moved to Moscow in 1928. There he worked for the Yiddish organ *Emes*. A protege of Kushnirov and Dobrushin, he translated Friedrich Schiller, Walter Scott, Ernst Toller and Maxim Gorky, and published poems and short stories for children and a collection of lyrics for adults. His *War Songs* (*Milkhome Lieder*, 1947) mirrored his experiences at the front. He was spared during the second purge of Yiddish writers in 1948. After Stalin's death, a selection of his poems appeared in a Russian translation in 1958, a second selection in 1964, and finally a selection in the original Yiddish in 1966. His translation of *The Song of Songs* and his autobiography appeared posthumously in 1967.

The literary beginnings of Ezra Fininberg (1899-1946) go back to the revolutionary year. In his early poems, although they were written under the Communist regime, he cannot tear himself away from the Jewish past. In a poem on his grandfather's "Wednesday," he sees this past, with its worm rot and cancerous petrifaction, continuing into the new era and attaching its prongs into his soul. High above his grandfather's "Wednesday," the Milky Way leads to a marble home, where trees of purest gold spread their giant foliage. He, however, still feels the crippling effect of the decaying townlets and the hoary traditions which link him to the Jewish ancestors.

Fininberg's muse does not shout. It pleads for more mildness, less anger, more tolerance, less coldness. In the 1920's, he sings of personal aches and joys, tender love and childhood innocence. In the 1930's, his verses are less genuine. They lost freshness and picturesqueness. Jewish themes and references disappear and expressions that might arouse religious reminiscences are excised.

He has to sublimate whatever love he may have for the Jewish people.

The Jewish tone reappears, however, in the songs *From the Battlefield* (*Fun Shlakhtfeld*, 1943). After two years at the front, facing death daily, defending the Soviet fatherland against the Nazi invaders, he returns on furlough to Moscow and finds poisoned glances directed upon him by his own countrymen. In the lyric, "My Report" (*Mein Barikht*), he proudly retorts to those Moscovites who look upon him, the Jewish defender of Moscow, as an alien. He tells them that he is indeed Semitic in his features, in his gait, in his heart, but nevertheless no more of a stranger than the Russian, the Ukrainian, the Soviet warriors of other ethnic origins. He invokes the spirit of the Yiddish writers, his comrades, who died at the front during the preceding two years. There was Buzi Olievsky (1908-1941), who composed Yiddish songs for children, lyrics of Soviet prowess in the air, tales of Birobidjan.

There was Meir Viner (1893-1941), the Galician philosopher and critic, who gave up a promising career in Berlin and freely cast in his lot with the Soviets in 1926. He edited *Die Roite Velt* in Kharkov in 1927, he lectured on Yiddish and Western European literatures in Kiev. He enriched literary history with valuable studies on folklore, Aksenfeld, Mendele and Sholom Aleichem. He wrote a history of nineteenth century Yiddish literature from the Marxist viewpoint. But when Russia was in danger, he exchanged the pen for the gun and fell in defense of the city of Vyazma in the early months of the conflict.

There was Fininberg's best friend, Aaron Gurshtein (1895-1941), who collaborated with Viner on problems of literary criticism, who taught literature at the University of Moscow and at pedagogical institutes of Kiev and Odessa, and whose career was cut short when he fell resisting the Nazi foe.

There was Shmuel Nissan Godiner (1893-1942), a skilled narrator who followed in the footsteps of David Bergelson and Der Nister. His first short stories dealt with the Russian civil war. They were Impressionistic and did not eschew symbolism. His later stories, however, followed the requirements of Socialist Realism. His most popular novel was *The Man With the Gun* (*Der Mentsh Mit Der Biks*, 1928). In the very first month of the German invasion, he left Moscow in order to fight with the partisans in the occupied region and died a hero's death a year later.

There was Yashe Zeldin (1901-1941), the first Yiddish poet to write songs of the Russian fleet, songs based upon his own experi-

ences in the Soviet navy from 1923. He translated Vladimir
Mayakovsky and Lermontov into Yiddish and collaborated with
Godiner and Kushnirov in dramatic playlets. He too volunteered
for military action and lost his life in battle.

There was Shmuel Rossin (1890-1941), poet, narrator, dramatist,
who was among the first casualties of the war. Fininberg himself
would soon be returning to the flaming front, where he would be
battling for Jewish honor as well as for the Soviet fatherland. "My
people, my Jewish people, you it was that gave me the glow, the
pain, the radiance, the deep courage. . . . You accompanied me,
the soldier, every night. You stood at my side every morn. You
are not impure, my people. Your foe is filth and impurity. You are
pure, my Jewish people, and holy is your blood."

When Fininberg in his last poems mentions his people, he means
the Jewish people. He no longer eschews biblical imagery. Marching westward with the advancing troops to liberate Ukrainian
towns formerly inhabited mainly by Jews, he laments that no
familiar Jewish tones greet him and that no Jewish breath is
visible anywhere. Slaughtered are the millions, buried in swamps
and ditches, and he himself is bereft of his Jewish friends and
relatives. But the blood of the Jewish martyrs calls for retribution
and his martial stanzas in his beloved Yiddish tongue will echo the
call.

Fininberg's last collection of lyrics, In Gigantic Fire (In Rizikn
Feier, 1946), includes hymns of triumph. Berlin has fallen, the
insolent city that sought to rule over all lands. The guns are silent.
The blood-encrusted fields are turning green. The poet can again
dream of children who will be born on a peaceful earth under a
milder sky.

Shmuel Rossin, whom Fininberg included among the Jewish
heroes who fell in battle, was a gentle-voiced poet who found it
difficult to join the optimistic chorus that hailed every event that
occurred in Soviet Russia as a stupendous achievement. During
the stormy revolutionary period, he was content to versify fairy
tales for children. His Grandmother Tales (Bobe Maisses, 1919)
were specifically Jewish in atmosphere and imagery. The savior, for
example, who helped the blind Mirele to escape death and who
restored her sight, was not Lenin but the Prophet Elijah.

In Moscow, Rossin felt lonely and estranged from his neighbors.
He longed for the warm Jewish atmosphere of his youth. He was
certain that, if he could be united with his own ethnic kinsmen
and share his songs with them, then he would attain to heights of

inspiration now beyond his reach. Fresh streams rushing from the depths of his being would hurl him upward to ever loftier peaks. Apparently, however, the past was over and gone. He had been wrenched from it; he had been severed from his roots. "I feel, I feel that here my head, my heart, my hands are superfluous."

To those who asked him to turn his face to the future and to sing joyously of reconstruction, he replied, as early as 1924, that it was not easy to silence one's woes. Perhaps sadness and longing were not desirable subjects for the poet in the new era, but one could not compel the heart to march in step like a soldier. A heart sometimes cried out in pain, even though it should know that this was no time for individual sorrow. But a heart was only a heart and the joy encompassing all others could not shield it from its own woe.

Rossin continued, therefore, in his lyric booklets of the 1920's, to sing of love's longing and fulfillment, of tears and kisses, of the blossoming of lips in spring and the pain of parting in autumn. Such love lyrics were rare among the Yiddish poets of Moscow. Even in his translations, Rossin chose not lyrics of social protest or of proletarian heroes but rather such love lyrics as Heinrich Heine's "Asra" and Richard Wagner's "Song to the Evening Star" from *Tannhäuser*.

Shortly before the Second World War, Rossin's last booklet appeared, *Songs About My Father (Lieder Vegn Taten*, 1939). His father, whom he had lost at thirteen, became for him the symbol of all Jewish fathers. He remembered him as restless, joyless, careworn, wandering from village to village with pack on back, trying to eke out a bare living for his family.

Rossin's pure, melancholy lyrics could not be used to advance any party cause and were allowed to lapse into oblivion after their author's death.

The war against the Nazis exacted a proportionately larger toll of the Jewish population than of any other ethnic group in Russia, because extermination of Jews was proclaimed as official German policy—the so-called Final Solution—and was carried out ruthlessly in all the temporarily occupied provinces. The toll of Jewish writers was also proportionately larger. Twenty years after the Soviet victory, *Sovetish Heimland* paid tribute to forty Yiddish writers—twenty-one talented in verse and nineteen in prose—who perished while battling the foe.

To these great losses must be added the still greater casualties which followed in the post-War years when Stalin undertook to root out Yiddish literature and its creators. The last issue of the sole Moscow Yiddish newspaper, *Einigkeit,* appeared on November 20, 1948. The last Jewish organization, the Jewish Anti-Fascist Committee, was then dissolved and its principal members carted off to prison cells. The last publishing house, "Emes," ceased all publication. With the closing of the last theaters and Yiddish schools, and with the execution of the Yiddish literary élite on trumped-up charges, for which Beria, the head of Stalin's secret police was afterward blamed, a pall of silence descended upon all Yiddish activities. All inquiries about the fate of individuals and groups went unanswered. Not until after the death of Stalin did word of the secret trials and executions leak out.

By mid-century, Yiddish literature in Russia seemed doomed to extinction. After sixty Yiddish books were published in 1948, not a single book appeared during the entire following decade. However, when the full extent of the cultural genocide directed against the Jews by the supreme Communist hierarchy of the Stalin era became known, a revulsion set in and the Soviet authorities were compelled to loosen somewhat the imposed strictures against Yiddish culture and to rehabilitate the innocent victims of Stalin's purges. Although most of the rehabilitated writers were no longer among the living, a few who had survived harrowing experiences in prisons and labor camps returned to Moscow and Kiev during the Khrushchev thaw. These included the novelists Zalman Wendroff (1877-1971) and Itzik Kipnis (b. 1896), both of whom were unbroken in spirit.

Wendroff began his literary career in Lodz in 1900. He participated in Anarchist journals during his London years until 1905, returned to Russia during the revolutionary ferment of that year and escaped to America when the revolution failed, but was back in his native land a few years later as correspondent for American Yiddish journals. When the Communists came to power, he stayed on in Moscow, avoiding involvement in party politics. He continued to write humorous sketches and tales, some of which were reprinted on the eve of the Second World War in the volume *On the Threshold of Life (Ofn Shvel Fun Leben,* 1941). When Moscow was threatened by the Nazi invaders a few months later, he volunteered to fight at the front even though he was in his mid-sixties. In the 1948 purge of Yiddish writers, he was accused of cosmopolitanism and of communicating with agents of hostile powers. Though tortured night after night and deprived of sleep for seven full months, he remained steadfast in his refusal to confess to imaginary crimes. Nevertheless he was sentenced to ten years imprisonment. Shortly before his eightieth birthday, he was released. A volume of his narratives was again published but in a Russian translation. Only ten years later did his tales become available in Yiddish. His ninetieth birthday was celebrated in 1967 both in Russia and abroad. His courage and his faith in Yiddish cultural survival were stressed in many tributes.

Similar courage and faith in dark hours were displayed by Kipnis. Like Wendroff, he too tried to steer clear of politics. His lack of Communist party-mindedness made him the subject of virulent attacks, but his popularity among Yiddish readers did not decline. He had begun his literary career in 1923 with a booklet of lyrics and in 1924 with tales for children. In his best-selling narrative *Months and Days (Khadoshim Un Teg,* 1926), he unfolded a kind, idyllic picture of Jewish life in his native Volynian townlet, which retained traditional charm despite pogroms and civil strife. Evacuated from Kiev during World War II, he returned in 1944 and penned his tragically moving sketch *Babi-Yar,* which dealt with the Nazi massacre of Kiev's Jews three years earlier and was filled with love for his martyred coreligionists. In 1948 he was arrested as a criminal Jewish nationalist and spent the years until Stalin's death in a remote, forced labor camp. After his rehabilitation, his works reappeared but only in a Russian translation in his native land. In New York, however, his autobiographic novel *En Route (Untervegns,* 1960) was published in the original Yiddish.

In 1962 permission was granted for the publication of the first and only post-Stalin literary periodical in Yiddish, the bimonthly *Sovetish Heimland.* The editor-in-chief was Aaron Vergelis (b. 1918), a lyricist who had grown up in Birobidjan and who was ever prepared to do the bidding of the Soviet authorities without murmuring. He was not harassed during the dark days of Stalin's rule. After Stalin's death, he published his own poems in Russian in 1956 and edited Russian translations of Soviet Yiddish writers. He gathered about him the writers who had survived the terror of Nazism and Stalinism. Within the limitations imposed by Communist doctrine, these writers were permitted to resume literary expression in Yiddish. Though they were restricted to but a single organ, they were able in 1966 to effect the expansion of the bimonthly to a monthly. They also succeeded in prying ajar somewhat the ban upon the publication of Yiddish books. However, the Soviet capital could not, with this meager literary fare, again challenge the hegemony of New York, nor rival the rising Yiddish center of Tel Aviv. The Soviet Yiddish writers aged. New, young writers did not arise.

12

GALICIAN NEOROMANTICISM

The Lemberg Center • S. J. Imber • Königsberg •
Chmelnitzky • Mestel • Neugröschel • Ber Schnaper
• Ber Horowitz • Moshe Zilburg • Gross-Zimmer-
mann • Ravitch • Naftoli Gross

THE YEARS 1904 to 1909 were the birthyears of Yiddish Neo-
romanticism in Galicia. The central figure of this movement was
Shmuel Jacob Imber (1889-1942), son of the minor Hebrew writer
Shmarya Imber (1868-1950) and nephew of the Hebrew minstrel
Naftali Herz Imber (1856-1909), author of *Hatikvah,* the hymn
of the Zionist movement and of the State of Israel.

In 1904, Gershom Bader (1868-1953) founded the first Yiddish
daily in Galicia, the *Lemberg Tageblatt.* In the same year Melech
Chmelnitzky (1885-1946) made his debut in Yiddish, abandoning
Polish completely. Soon thereafter he became the literary editor of
the *Tageblatt* and opened its columns to aspiring young writers.
It was in this daily that Jacob Mestel (1884-1958), who later was
celebrated on three continents as actor, theatrical manager and innovator, published his first, dream-drenched lyrics. But it was not
until Imber appeared upon the Lemberg literary scene in 1909,
and was joined by his youthful disciple Melech Ravitch (b. 1893),
that Lemberg forged ahead as an important center of Yiddish
Neoromanticism.

Lemberg had always looked to Vienna for its inspiration, and
in Vienna anti-Naturalistic trends had been dominant since the
turn of the century. *Jungwien,* allied to the Symbolist movement,
claimed the allegiance of Jewish writers in the German tongue far
more than of non-Jewish writers. The former included Arthur
Schnitzler (1862-1931), a physician specializing in psychotherapy,
who delved into subconscious strata of the soul and in his literary

works unlocked infinite possibilities dormant within each person; Richard Beer-Hofmann (1866-1945), whose dignified affirmation of Jewishness found expression in biblical plays, classics of German literature and landmarks in the Jewish cultural renascence; Peter Altenberg (1859-1919), author of witty, impressionistic sketches and melancholy aphorisms; Felix Salten (1869-1945), feuilletonist of the influential daily *Neue Freie Presse*, author of humorous, satiric, erotic novels and plays, later best remembered for *Bambi*, a children's classic; Karl Kraus (1874-1936), essayist and dramatist who broke away early from the group and founded his own satiric, critical periodical, *Die Fackel* (1899-1936), as an influential weapon in the struggle against intellectual hypocrisy and social corruption; and, youngest of the group, Stefan Zweig (1881-1942), who excelled in poetry, drama, short stories, essays, biographies, who strove to be a Good European and to effect a synthesis of Germanic and Hebraic culture, and who ended as a refugee in Brazil and a suicide.

The Yiddish poets of Lemberg were magnetically drawn to Vienna and, when the First World War broke out, most of them found their way to the Hapsburg capital. Included in this group were Imber, David Königsberg and Melech Ravitch.

Imber was a gentle poet who reached out toward lyric perfection but could not attain it. He sang in simple, melodious quatrains and traditional stanzaic forms about uncomplicated emotions, timid longings, the pain of unfulfilled love, attachment to Palestine's holy soil, romantic nature far removed from his urban abode. Often he imitated Heine, whom he translated but whose complex personality was beyond his grasp. His lyrics abounded in echoes of Heine's doves and nightingales, reluctant damsels and gallant, lovelorn knights. Like young Heine, he opened his bleeding heart to the world, he flirted with death and the grave, he dissolved in tears at the slightest pretext, but the profundity of the martyr of Montmartre eluded him.

In the poetic romance *Estherke* (1911), Imber retold with lachrymose sentimentalism a fourteenth-century legend which the folklore of Polish Jewry still retained: the love of Esther, the beautiful daughter of a Jewish blacksmith, and Kasimir, the chivalrous King of Poland. Imber depicted the Jew of the centuries of exile as a powerless giant, preserved by God but scorned by man. This giant would regain pristine strength only by returning to Zion.

Imber visited the Holy Land in 1912 and wrote many songs of

Zion. These were translated into Russian by the Hebrew-Russian poetess Elisheva in 1916 but they were, unfortunately, never set to music as was the case with the *Hatikvah* of his uncle. They stemmed from the longing of his heart for Jewish resurgence in Palestine far more than from his actual observations there. Though he looked upon real scenes and met real pioneers, he saw them with eyes of wonder and through a colorful veil of traditional folklore, even as Eliakum Zunser and Abraham Mapu envisaged them half a century earlier without stepping upon the sacred land.

There was a song of the Matriarch Rachel who could not be comforted after the exile of her children. Every night she arose from her grave and wandered forth in search of them. But now her tears of sorrow were giving way to tears of joy as she saw them beginning to stream homeward to her. Another lyric voiced Imber's renewed faith in a divine purpose, ever since he came in contact with the toiling pioneers on the God-kissed earth. He called on his contemporaries who were still waiting on the sidelines to join in the blessed labor of redemption, to dig up the parched, long-neglected soil, to bring into blossom the desolate banks of the Jordan. The sweat of Jewish exertion would wash away the accumulated stains of millennia. He thanked God for having brought him into this world in the generation of his people's glorious rebirth rather than in the preceding generations of decay, and for letting him witness the dawn of the splendor that would in later years envelop his entire people.

Not long after the publication of his poems of a Jewish homeland, Imber was drafted into the army to fight for the Austro-Hungarian homeland. In the midst of war, however, he continued to write poems in which he sought to tie the golden threads of an idyllic Jewish life of the past to the innocent life of an idealized Jewish future.

These poems were included in the volume *Inter Arma* (1918), which he edited and which also contained contributions by his former Lemberg associates Uri Zvi Greenberg, Jacob Mestel, David Königsberg and Melech Ravitch, all of whom were then involved in the war effort. These poets also participated in the literary monthly *Nayland* (1918-1919), which Imber founded immediately after the war. In this periodical, his predilection for Neoromantic and Impressionistic literary trends came to the fore in the foreign authors whom he introduced to Yiddish readers. These included Rabindranath Tagore, Selma Lagerlöf, Oscar Wilde and Knut Hamsun. His own associates, however, were gradually being

weaned away from Impressionism toward the Expressionism of
Franz Werfel, Elsa Lasker-Schüler and other stormy disciples. Uri
Zvi Greenberg and Melech Ravitch left for Warsaw. Jacob Mestel
left for America. Imber himself also left for the United States in
1921 but he was not happy there. Five years later he returned to
Lemberg, where he felt most at home. There he continued to write
his Neoromantic ballads, songs and critical articles, until he was
murdered by his Ukrainian neighbors during a purge of Galician
Jews in 1942.

David Königsberg (1889-1942) once referred to Imber as the
head of "Young Galicia" and to himself as its heart. He was one
of the ablest sonneteers in the Yiddish tongue. Although his translation of Heine's *Book of Songs* (*Buch der Lieder*) was never
published, the influence of this German poet upon him was no
less enduring than upon Imber. This influence was most strongly
felt in Königsberg's first volume, simply entitled *Songs* (*Lieder,*
1912). In this volume, the only one in which quatrains and not
sonnets predominate, he sings of his preference for silent joys, far
from the excitement of raging competitiveness. He compares himself to a bird that builds itself a nest on a tall tree and pours out
its heart in melodies that seep down to other hearts. He does not
delude himself that his gentle tones of a culture which is being
wafted away by the winds of change can affect the course of
people's lives, but he hopes that these tones can bring a bit of
delight to leisure hours. Let others sow and reap and harvest ripe
corn for daily bread; he is content to meander among the many-
colored flowers that grow in his fields, even if these flowers cannot
be put to practical use. Let others follow the guidance of reason,
but not he, the lover of dreams. In his eyes, reason is a sharp
sword which cuts through the beautiful threads of golden days. As
a romantic poet, he would rather dispense with it, indulge in sweet
sorrows, recapture fading memories, garland himself with lyric
pearls, and hearken to night's deep mysteries.

Königsberg's love sonnets were composed after he left Lemberg
and came under Viennese influence. His language became encrusted
with Germanisms. His sonnets abounded in antiquated imagery
of damsels, knights and nightingales. He no longer gave frank,
intimate expression to his feelings but rather compressed them
into artificial molds. The young Galician poet lost his naiveté
during his years of fighting in the Austro-Hungarian army for a
cause in which he did not believe, and during his sojourn in Vienna,
recovering from a wound he received at the front. He toyed with

Weltschmerz, serenaded imaginary maidens, flirted with death, but he failed to reflect genuinely his own experiences in the mud of the trenches and in the daily struggle to ward off starvation. Only when he touched national Jewish chords did he rise above mediocrity. Then he called upon the Supreme Judge to pour out righteous wrath upon those who seared the sons of Israel with pogroms. Then he portrayed Jews as exiled princes who had never lost their aristocratic bearing in all their harried wanderings and who still dreamed royal dreams of a homecoming to their historic land and heritage.

After the Balfour Declaration of 1917, Königsberg felt that the hour had struck for the end of the Galut, the horn of redemption had sounded and all the sleepers among his people must now arise to welcome the Messiah who came to lead them forth from millennial woe. As for himself, he was content to be a bridge over which others could cross into the Promised Land. He never did get beyond Lemberg's horizon in his later years. He lived in a village in its vicinity and perished at the hands of the Nazis in the Janow extermination camp.

Melech Chmelnitzky (1885-1946) came to Galicia from Kiev at the age of twelve and grew up in Lemberg. He then went on to study at the University of Vienna and remained in this city as a practicing physician until the Nazi occupation compelled him to flee to the United States in 1939.

In his youth, under the influence of the decadent, satanic Polish novelist Stanislaw Przybyszewski (1868-1927), he wrote in Polish and translated Yiddish poetry into Polish, but with the founding of the *Lemberger Tageblatt* in 1904, he turned to Yiddish and translated Polish and German poets into Yiddish. Although he was widely known as a writer of popular articles on medical subjects for more than a third of a century, his most original work was contained in three lyric booklets filled with sad, tired, decadent moods and nostalgic recollections of childhood years. Sitting at the bedside of patients, cooling their feverish brows and comforting them, he often obtained insight into hidden recesses of their souls and became ever gentler, ever sadder, ever more resigned, ever more aware of the dream-life that consciousness suppressed. He became the singer of night, of the ripples made by subterranean forces that rose to the surface in unguarded moments. His best verses, those of his Viennese period, were melodic, abounding in assonances, undulating with gentle rhythms at a time when Expressionistic, explosive, jagged outcries were more fashionable in

Austrian and Yiddish circles. He had to reconcile himself to being little read, and his lyric productivity therefore dwindled after the early 1920's.

Jacob Mestel (1884-1958) was primarily an actor and theater-director. However, he began as a Yiddish Neoromantic poet while still a student at the University of Lemberg. His first lyrics appeared in 1906 in the Lemberg *Tageblatt*, which had been founded by Gershom Bader but which was then being edited by Moshe Kleinman. Under the influence of the early Galician Zionist agitator Jacob Kenner, and of Zerubabel, who arrived in Lemberg in 1908, Mestel became interested in Labor Zionism. His first lyric volume, *Visionary Hours* (*Farkholemte Shoen*, 1909), appeared in the same year as Imber's first volume and confirmed the rise of "Young Galicia" as a distinct literary group. In his early writing, Mestel's diction suffered from excessive Germanisms, which he discarded as he matured. In his love poetry he aped the young Heine and the sensuous intensity of Richard Dehmel. In his poems espousing Jewish nationalism, he lamented his people's pale ghetto existence and called for regeneration in Zion.

In Vienna after 1910, his main interest shifted to the theater. He acted in German and Yiddish plays and founded a Yiddish dramatic school. After emigrating to the United States in 1920, he joined the Yiddish Art Theater and cooperated with Maurice Schwartz in raising the standard of Yiddish dramatic productions. When ARTEF, abbreviated name for Arbeiter Teater Farband, a workers' theater group, came into existence in the mid-1920's, he was its director. He trained its actors in studios and experimented with bold innovations in staging. ARTEF sought to combine proletarian ideology with Jewish traditional heritage and won devoted adherents among Yiddish Leftists. In his last years, Mestel wrote valuable memoirs and studies of the Yiddish theater and co-edited with Zalman Zylbercweig the first three volumes of the *Lexicon of the Yiddish Theater*.

Galician Neo-romanticism in the Imber mood was continued by Mendl Neugröschel (1903-1965), the biographer of Melech Chmelnitsky. In the lyrics of Neugröschel's *Tents* (*Gezelten*, 1930), a sweet tiredness pervaded existence as in the Viennese poems of young Hofmannsthal. The elegiac mood of autumn, the constant awareness of the transitoriness of youth and love, the emphasis upon the pain of existence and upon the holiness of dying—all pointed to an oversensitive, non-viable generation that was heading towards a final debacle. Neugröschel, a lawyer by profession, experienced the death throes of the Danubian republic and Nazi brutality in Dachau and Buchenwald, but was able to get to Brazil before World War II and later on to the United States.

In New York, he felt forlorn and desolate, especially after the war. In one of his saddest lyrics, he described himself walking along Norfolk Street and Henry Street in the heart of the Jewish East Side, as if he were walking among exotic tribes of Haiti. "Is this my people? My destiny? My language? O, gray words, long withered!" He wondered for whom he was still penning his verses and reasoned that perhaps, when he would be laid to rest in the poet's corner of a Brooklyn Jewish cemetery near his fellow Romanticists Mani-Leib and Moshe Leib Halpern, he would there help to guard the last bastion of the Yiddish word.

Ber Schnaper (1903-1943) was no less pessimistic in his outlook upon life than was Neugröschel. The son of a cobbler, he grew up on the outskirts of Lemberg. In a poem dedicated to Neugröschel, he characterized himself and his entire group of Galician poets as singers of pale, melancholy, unobtrusive songs, as lyric birds who fly and fly without knowing whither. His entire literary career spanned but a single decade. His first book of verse *Scum* (*Upshoym*) appeared in 1927 and his last one, *Blue Words* (*Bloe Verter*), in 1937. In these, the mood of decay predominates. His milieu is the little townlet or the poor district on the edge of the big city. His Jews know only hunger and need. They lead useless lives in their old, crumbling houses. These houses are so dark and filthy that, if an erring ray of light were to find its way into their interior through the tear-stained windows, it would blush for shame at what it saw. The women he describes know neither joy nor plenitude. They are worked to exhaustion during the day and bitten and flayed at night by savage husbands. They are constantly pregnant and always angry at the world. They wait for the redeeming hour when they will hear the quiet footsteps of Death the Reaper who will come to claim them. Their anemic children sleep on rags in cellar nooks in which spiders walk about as lords. The hands of these children are like dry branches and they rummage for bits of moldy bread which the teeming mice may have left over.

Life is for Schnaper a pus-filled wound. His typical characters are the old prostitute, the street urchin, the blind beggar, the lonely spinster. He is weary of his human lot, since human beings are handicapped by their structure as reasoning creatures. He would prefer an existence which is all feeling and all instinct, an existence like that of a bug or a bee.

Nevertheless, when Schnaper finally succeeded in exchanging his Galician townlet for the metropolises of Vienna and Warsaw, he was even more unhappy. He then glanced back upon the wretched townlet, which in his childhood was still mired in medieval petrifaction, as a grandmother might look back upon her dream-filled past. He described this townlet in the lyrics of *My Town* (*Mein Shtot,* 1932) as peaceful, pious, modest, gilded with sunlight and silvered with moonlight. Its Jews were engaged in discussions with God, who might otherwise have felt very lonely amongst the stars. God's countenance was mirrored in their faces and God's kindness in their hearts.

The poet lamented that the transformation which war and industrialization brought to the Jewish townlet banished beauty and poetry from its streets. The crooked houses were straightened and now stood on parade in long rows like soldiers at attention. Each settlement was naked, exposed, devoid of individuality, and he, the Yiddish poet, walked about among the dull, renovated lanes like an unburied corpse waiting for the final rites.

In contrast to Ber Schnaper, Ber Horowitz (1895-1942) entered upon the Yiddish scene full of the joy of life, overflowing with health and energy. Born in a Galician village in the Carpathian Mountains, he barely completed a Polish Gymnasium in Stanislaw when he was called to serve in the Austrian army. His early lyric "Galicia 1914" recorded the mood of the multinational recruits among whom he was thrown. While the Poles of Galicia went to battle singing of the coming redemption of Poland, and the Ukrainians of the liberation of the Ukraine, the Jewish soldiers sang songs that dripped tears of futility, not understanding why they were required to kill or be killed.

Horowitz saw war not as a glorious field for heroism but as a senseless slaughter of God's creatures. He depicted war through the tired eyes of the one-armed, one-legged invalid in the hospital who watched the rhythmic march of the battalions that were leaving Vienna for the front. On the drill field with three hundred companions who were practicing sharpshooting, the young poet wandered in imagination to the Caucasus and to Naples, distant places where mothers were at the same time bidding farewell to sons who would ere long fall as victims to the more accurately fired bullets of the three hundred so-called enemies or patriots.

He depicted mothers as the principal sufferers and their sons as helpless pawns of a military machine.

In his post-war lyrics, Horowitz glorified the Jewish villagers of the Carpathian range. His Jewish peasants could catch a bull by the horns and wrestle it down. His village children intoned Hebrew and Yiddish tunes and their games simulated jousts between Turks and Palestinian *shomrim,* or watchmen. Idyllic poems conveyed the shudder experienced by the lonely wanderer in the forest at night, the melodious magic of the birds who disported themselves in their free realm between the green treetops and the blue sky.

Horowitz's prose tales were designed not only to entertain but also to convey a moral. They often centered about the Baal Shem, founder of Hassidism. In one of them, a Carpathian Robin Hood came under the influence of the Baal Shem, who had retired to a forest in the mountains in order to meditate on God's wonders. In another story, the Baal Shem exorcized an evil spirit that had found entry into a young man's body at birth. He then substituted the righteous soul which properly belonged there but that had until then not been able to enter the occupied body. In Horowitz's best narrative, "The Legend of the Madonna," he intermingled Jewish and Christian folklore. He had the Madonna descend from her pedestal in a forest chapel and hand over the jewels with which she was bedecked to a poor, aged widow as dowry for a marriageable daughter.

Horowitz's first volume of verse, *From My Home In the Mountains (Fun Mein Heym In Die Berg,* 1919), was followed by his only other book of original poems, *Smell of Earth (Reyekh Fun Erd,* 1930), in which he continued his joyous hymns to life, his sensuous grasp of nature and love. In contrast to the uprooted, melancholy, Neoromantic poets who yearned for the big cities, he returned from a temporary sojourn in Vienna to his native Galician village like a sick bird to its old nest. There he recuperated from sophistication and rationalization; there he sang lullabies to his child, Piniele with the golden hair; there his verses proclaimed how lovely was this earth and how good it was to be a human being on it.

In 1938, Horowitz published a volume of translations of Jewish poems by non-Jewish Polish poets. These were to document his faith in the possibility of a peaceful coexistence of Jews and non-Jews on the soil of Poland. Four years later his life was cut short when the Nazis, unhindered, if not actually assisted by his Polish and Ukrainian neighbors, massacred nine thousand Jews of Stanislaw in a single day.

Though Horowitz's robust, joyous affirmation of life distinguished him from most Galician Neoromanticists, he was nevertheless closely connected with this group, which centered about Imber. It was Imber who first discovered Horowitz as a poet and printed his lyrics in *Nayland*, the literary monthly he edited in Lemberg. When most members of this group found their way to Vienna, *Nayland* was succeeded in February 1920 by the more militant quarterly *Kritik*, which fought against the rising tide of Expressionism.

The editor of this organ was Moshe Zilburg (1884-1942), who had been compelled to leave his native Vilna because of revolutionary activities and who had settled in Lemberg before the First World War and in Vienna at its conclusion. He took over the leadership of the Galician group when Imber left for the United States. He succeeded in winning the allegiance to his quarterly of Melech Ravitch, Melech Chmelnitzky, Moshe Gross-Zimmermann, Ber Horowitz, David Königsberg, Mendel Singer, A. M. Fuchs, and others.

In an opening manifesto, the declaration was made that *Kritik* was to serve the youth of Lemberg, Warsaw, New York and Vilna. It was to be the link binding all Jews who recognized that without the living Yiddish word Jewish life could not flourish. A series of articles by Zilburg attacked Martin Buber, Max Brod, Simon Bernfeld, and all Zionist and communal leaders who wrote in German or Polish. Zilburg accused them of undermining Jewish existence by their arrogance towards the East European Jews. These writers had become estranged from the townlets in which the Jewish masses dwelt. They had acquired so-called higher education in the large centers of Central and Western Europe, but, having experienced rejection by the outsiders whom they courted, they had returned to elevate their benighted brethren with the superior alien wisdom imbibed from strangers. Zilburg ironically expressed his gratitude for the praise that these rediscoverers of the Eastern Jews bestowed upon them. There was Max Brod, an admirer of the half-assimilated Jewish girls, who grafted intellectualism upon a religious base. There was Hermann Cohen, who tried to convince Eastern Jews that they were close relatives of Kaiser Wilhelm's subjects. There was young Nahum Goldmann, whose Lithuanian soul had experienced transmutation to a Western one. All of them were seeking to erase the true features of the

Jewish face so that it would become as pale and expressionless as their own. They were flooding the orphaned Yiddish youth with German-Jewish periodicals such as *Jüdische Rundschau* and *Der Jude*. One of them was even Germanizing the Bible with a new translation reminiscent of his reforming predecessor Moses Mendelssohn. With biting satire, Zilburg castigated the neo-intellectuals who professed to believe in religion but did not practice it, who espoused Zionism but continued to live in Berlin and Warsaw, who sympathized with Socialism but did not work for it, who endorsed Jewish nationalism but sank ever deeper in the slough of assimilationism. As the antithesis to these neo-intellecuals, Zilburg hailed the genuine ghetto Jew, relatively healthy in body and soul, normal in his Jewish reactions, rooted in the language and folkways of Jewish traditions. He, therefore, advocated the slogan: "Back to the Ghetto!"—not the medieval ghetto with its yellow badge but the ghetto type of cultural autonomy, the retention of Jewish uniqueness in speech and habits of thought, the transformation of outside influences and spiritual forces into Jewish forms.

Zilburg was followed by Moshe Gross-Zimmermann with articles on "Problems of Form in Yiddish Literature." The latter attacked Expressionism as a formless, chaotic movement, and defended the Galician group's Impressionism as aiming at perfection of form. Moshe Livshitz (1894-1940) countered with a defense of Expressionism, especially as practiced by Moshe Broderzon, a newly risen star over the Yiddish horizon. Livshitz's approach foreshadowed the gradual disintegration of the unity which had bound the young writers of Vienna under the aegis of Imber, who did not return from America until 1925. Expressionism was luring away strong pillars of the original Neoromantic group, including Melech Ravitch and Uri Zvi Greenberg.

Melech Ravitch (b. 1893) is primarily a poet, even though his travel sketches, critical essays, philosophical discourses and autobiographic volumes far exceed his lyrics in quantity.

Stemming from a family long rooted in Eastern Galicia, his has been a life of uprootedness spanning five continents. His wandering began at fourteen when he left his native townlet, Redom, for the larger town of Stanislaw and two years later for the still larger town of Lemberg. His twenties were spent in the capital of the Austro-Hungarian dual monarchy as a bank clerk and at various fronts during World War I. His thirties were spent in the capital of the new Poland as secretary of the Yiddish Authors'

League. Then followed still longer odysseys, which swept the restless poet on to Australia, South America, Canada and Israel. Not
until the end of his sixties did he reconcile himself to a stable
domicile in Montreal.

Peretz, passing thrugh Stanislaw in 1908 after the conclusion
of the Czernovitz Yiddish Conference, made an indelible impression upon the fifteen-year-old lad who was trained in a commercial
academy for a business career. Despite a better mastery of Polish
and German, Ravitch then decided to become a Yiddish poet. His
earliest lyrics, composed between his sixteenth and his nineteenth
year, appeared in 1912 and were followed by twelve more volumes
of verse during the next four decades. In 1954, Ravitch made a
selection of his best poems under the title *The Songs of My Songs*
(*Die Lieder Fun Meine Lieder*). From these poems, as well as
from the autobiographic volumes *The Story of My Life* (*Dos
Maase-Bukh Fun Mein Leben*, I, 1962; II, 1964) and the essays of
the volume *Jewish Thought in the Twentieth Century* (*Einems
Yiedishe Makhshoves in 20. Yorhundert*, 1949), the literary personality of Ravitch can be reconstructed.

The first literary circle in which he found a congenial atmosphere
and encouragement for his creative striving was the Lemberg
Group, which in 1910 included not only the poets S. J. Imber and
David Königsberg but also the realistic novelist A. M. Fuchs
(b. 1890), the Zionist editor Berl Locker (1887-1972), the Hebrew
poets Gershon Schofman (b. 1880) and Uri Zvi Greenberg (b.
1894), and the Yiddish actor Ludwig Satz (1891-1944). Ravitch
and Imber roomed together, hungered together, and in Imber,
Ravitch found a severe critic who stimulated him to his utmost
efforts and who collaborated with him in the search for lyric
perfection.

Ravitch's youthful verses *At the Threshold* (*Oif Der Shvel*,
1912) betray the influence of Imber and of Heinrich Heine, Imber's
master. They are full of *Weltschmerz*, sweet melancholy, and
overflow with sentimental love for all mankind. Ravitch sings of
dawning dreams, tender friendships, regret at the loss of childhood
innocence, and wonder at the blossoming of his heart in first love.

The poems of Ravitch's Vienna decade, which followed the
Galician period, are more cheerful, even though they were com-
posed in the midst of war and the crash of the Hapsburg Empire.
During free hours in military barracks, between 1916 and 1918,
Ravitch completed his cycle *Spinoza*, a lyric tribute to the lonely
philosopher in whom he found the embodiment of absolute truth

and goodness. In this cycle there was already revealed the poet's inclination to versify ideological questions, to concretize thoughts, emotions, intuitions in vivid images. He depicted the life and death of Spinoza as anchored in calmness and devoid of sadness, despite persecution and excommunication. He showed Death curt-seying before the sage, offering him the bread and salt of hos-pitality, the keys to the City Beyond Life, and begging him to enter. "And the sage assented with a smile and with a gallant bow, and took the hand of Death." Spinoza's system of thought re-mained a principal inspiration for Ravitch's own thinking through-out all later years. Indeed, he ranked Spinoza with Moses and Jesus.

In Vienna, Ravitch came into contact not only with the Yiddish poets who had fled from his native Galicia when it was overrun by the Russian army but also with poets whose medium was German. He was especially drawn to Stefan Zweig, and to Uriel Birnbaum (1894-1956), the younger son of the Zionist pioneer Nathan Birnbaum (1864-1937). He joined in the prevailing admira-tion for early expressionists such as Else Lasker-Schüler (1869-1945) and Franz Werfel (1890-1945). He was invited by Albert Ehrenstein (1886-1950) to translate into Yiddish the poetry of the New Germany. Soon his fame spread to New York, where the Yiddish writers of "Die Yunge" commended his verses. Reuben Iceland called him a great luminary on the poetic horizon and David Ignatoff welcomed him as a comrade-in-arms.

With the appearance of *Naked Songs* (*Nakte Lieder,* 1921), Ravitch forsook rhyme, regular metric lines and stanzas, and followed the Expressionistic tide in subject matter and in rebellious exhilaration. He now saw the poet's mission as being the con-science of the world, as a comforter amidst adversity, as the voice of the silent, suffering creatures, man, woman, child, beast and plant. His elegy "Mother Earth," written under the impact of his older brother's suicide, ascended from outbursts of pain to a pantheistic acceptance of human destiny in its mysterious passage from the womb of the individual mother to the womb of the universal mother, Mother Earth.

In 1921, Ravitch gave up his comfortable position in a bank and his stable existence in the cosmopolitan capital of the Austrian Republic in order to escape from the assimilationist conflagration which he saw raging there among Jews. As an antidote to the poison of decay which he felt was eroding Viennese Jewish intel-lectual circles, he developed a love for Polish, Lithuanian and

Ukrainian Jewry. Though he himself had moved far from religious orthodoxy, he still viewed religiously oriented Eastern European Jewry as basically sound and healthy. He was, however, even more impressed by the Yiddish revival. Warsaw beckoned to him as the main Yiddish literary center. A brief visit there convinced him that he should make his home in this city, which then contained the greatest concentration of Yiddish writers.

Soon after his arrival, Ravitch found himself in the midst of increasing activity as editor, as poet, as a key figure in various artistic projects, and as General Secretary of the Jewish Writers' Association, which had a membership of 250 authors. From 1921 to 1923, he was associated with Peretz Markish and Uri Zvi Greenberg in the struggle against realism in art. The triumvirate adapted the innovations of German Expressionism and Russian Futurism. They succeeded in outraging public opinion and were branded as the *Khaliastre* or "Gang." They accepted this designation as a badge of honor and termed their literary anthologies *Khaliastre*. They succeeded in attracting as contributors David Hofstein, I. Kipnis, Moshe Khashchevatsky, Israel Stern, I. J. Singer, and Oizer Varshavsky. Not all of these writers were in sympathy with the striving of the *Khaliastre*, but they were impressed by the vitality of the triumvirate.

Ravitch's *Naked Songs* had already anticipated Uri Zvi Greenberg's call for the free, naked human expression, for the chaotic outcry of the blood. Ravitch's "Song to the Human Body" (1922) called for the dethronement of mind and proclaimed the autonomous sovereignty of every limb in the confederation of the human frame. His "Song to the Sun" (1923) was an ecstatic, rhythmic yell to the radiant source out of which arose the earth and all life. Rocks, plants, whales, elephants, eagles, apes and humans were characterized as but torn bits of sun, eternally whirling in orbits, dancing around the solar God.

Ravitch no longer wished to fixate momentary impressions as in his earlier poems. He rather sought to discover essences, absolutes. He wanted to ascend from personal moods to universal moods, to become the lyric spokesman of a super-individual collective. In his "Song of Hate and Love for the Jewish People" (1924), he spoke out as the voice of the pogromized, post-war generation. He pleaded with Jehovah to wrap the *tallit* of chosenness about another people, since the Jewish people had already paid with enough blood for the many centuries of chosenness. In the world of today, he held, there was no longer any need for the moral, intellectual people of Moses, Jesus, and Spinoza. "Lord of Being and non-Being, we give you back our eternal existence. Give us eternal non-existence."

The climax of the *Khaliastre*'s striving was reached in the issues of *Albatross,* edited by Greenberg in 1922. This periodical of the New Poetry proclaimed itself as the organ of convulsive individualism. It preached exaltation, renovation, revolution of the spirit. It saw its cruel, chaotic songs as the honest expression of the naked, dishevelled, uprooted, blood-drenched generation, a generation in transition between the twilight of one world and the dawn of another.

The Yiddish Expressionists of the *Khaliastre* set out to fragmentize the language of Peretz and Mendele and to rebuild it anew, even as Vladimir Mayakovsky was then attempting with the Russian language. They preferred rhythmic tautness and explosiveness to the rounded, melodious verse. Greenberg compared the Yiddish of the time with its exhausted clichés to a street harlot with whom everybody had slept and who had become ripe for death. Ravitch referred to the new poetry of himself and his colleagues as naked poetry pulsating between the two poles of love and death and appealing to the instincts rather than to the mind. "Poetry communicates from nerve to nerve, from heart to heart, from sex to sex, from sadness to sadness, from laughter to laughter. It is an elemental outcry in which are commingled water and fire, earth and gold, word and blood." Greenberg's verse-epic *Mephisto* (1922) presented the spirit of negation which reigned over our world. Of the forces that stirred throughout the universe, nine-tenths paid allegiance to Mephisto and only one-tenth remained faithful to God. As for our specific mortal realm, the Deity did not bother with what went on there, while Mephisto was eternally awake and exercising his suzerainty.

The revolutionary excitement of the *Khaliastre* was short-lived. The poetic triumvirate scattered in three widely divergent directions, physically and ideologically. Markish stormed into the Soviet capital singing hymns to Communism. Greenberg abandoned Yiddish for Hebrew and became in Israel an extreme exponent of Zionist Revisionism. Ravitch migrated to Australia and continued to wrestle with ethical questions and with the meaning of Diaspora existence.

Ravitch's moods and experiences of restless years until his settling in Melbourne in 1936 were reflected in the songs and ballads of the volume *Continents and Oceans (Kontinenten un Okeanen,*

1937). With greater maturity, he gave up efforts to shock readers. Turning from Expressionism, he aimed at maximum clarity and intelligibility. Walt Whitman, the bard of pure humanity, became his ideal. He proclaimed himself to be a citizen of the world, an a-national poet. Yet, though his themes ranged over all continents, his treatment of these themes was always unmistakably Jewish. Poems of Harbin, Peking and Singapore alternated with dramatic ballads of Johannesburg, Moscow and New York. His Whitmanesque hymns to New York visualized the restless, light-flooded American metropolis as reaching up to cosmic heights, as the crucible of races, cultures, tongues, as the womb of the new man of coming millennia. The poet paid lyric tribute to this generous city which offered freedom and hospitality to two million of his pale, frightened, despairing Jewish brothers and sisters, who had been forced to flee from modern Pharaonic oppression.

In 1937, Ravitch left Australia and resumed his wandering over the face of the globe. He sojourned a year in Buenos Aires and two years in New York. In 1941, he finally decided to make Montreal the center of his activities, a center from which he set out for other lands whenever the lure of wandering overcame him but to which he always returned. Not even Israel, which he visited in 1950 and where he stayed from 1954 to 1956, could wean him away from the Canadian metropolis. There he succeeded in unfolding rich activities as educator, literary mentor and publicist. From this vantage point, he could survey and react to the ever changing Jewish scene and record his impressions in four additional volumes of verse. His book of essays, *Jewish Thought in the Twentieth Century* (1949), created a considerable stir in the Jewish press. It voiced his faith in the unity of the Jewish people as a world people and his wish that the post-biblical thinking, feeling, prophetic vision and historical creativity of this people be canonized in a volume comparable to the Bible. A similar suggestion had been made by Abraham Coralnik in 1928 without arousing much attention. Ravitch's passionate espousal of the idea after the Nazi holocaust and during the birth struggles of the Jewish homeland was better timed. Like Coralnik, he wrote not from a partisan viewpoint but as an eclectic who respected all shades of commitments from extreme Zionism to extreme Communism. Affirming Jewish unity in space and time, he urged that the wisdom of all groups, all generations and all languages should form the basis for careful winnowing by the best minds before inclusion in such a definitive volume.

Ravitch saw the original Book of Books, in all its kaleidoscopic variety of subjects, styles and moods, revolving about a single idea, the idea of the oneness of God. He believed that the new, additional Book of Books should revolve about the oneness of Man—an idea which first dawned among the ancient Prophets as a longing for an individual redeemer of all mankind, the Messiah, and which then developed into the concept of a people of redeemers, the Jewish people as the bearers of Messianism.

Ravitch's later writings culminated in his autobiographic volumes *The Tale of My Life* (*Dos Maase-Bukh Fun Main Leben,* I, 1962; II, 1964), in which the cultural life of Galicia since the closing nineteenth century was vividly depicted and in which the writers of his generation, friends and foes, were delineated sympathetically, generously, and picturesquely. In these volumes as well as in the three volumes of *My Encyclopedia* (*Mein Leksikon,* I, 1945; II, 1947; III, 1958), Ravitch, the impressionistic chronicler, performed a service for Yiddish literature of no less value than his earlier services as lyricist and as catalyst of the Galician and Warsaw poets.

Lemberg as the center of Galician Yiddish resurgence exerted a strong influence upon other thriving Jewish communities. Among these the town of Kolomea felt the pull both of Lemberg and Czernovitz. It was in Kolomea that Naftoli Gross (1897-1956) was born and Shlome Bickel (1896-1969) grew up.

Although Gross left his east Galician birthplace at the age of sixteen and spent his entire adult life in New York, he never really freed himself from the spell of Kolomea and of the surrounding Carpathian foothills. In his father's house at the edge of a forest, he heard folk tales of long, long ago, and they brought a flush of joy to him. He was especially fascinated by the legendary deeds of Dobush, the Robin Hood of the Carpathians, and by the humble saintliness of the Baal Shem, who also roamed this mountain range. In this he was following the precedent set by Ber Horowitz.

In the poems composed on American soil, Gross romanticized old Jews of Kolomea, who studied Torah and walked in God's ways, and young Jews, whose laughter and tears streamed from a genuine, uncorrupted heart. Though the weekdays of such Jews might be full of restless toil, their Sabbaths were blessed with holiness and contentment. It was this Sabbath mood that Gross sought to recapture in verse.

Picturesque characters of Galicia and not of New York predominated in his verses. There was the Maggid, whose comforting oratory brought near to every listener patriarchs and prophets of a distant past, mystics and hidden saints of more recent days, and Messiah, who was expected to come riding into town and to put an end to all troubles. There was the cabalist who had renounced all worldly pleasures and was eagerly awaiting the blessed hour of mankind's final redemption. There was the town rabbi, who never smiled because he bore upon his shoulders the burdens of the entire religious community as its respected spokesman to the reigning duke in the silent castle. There was the pious Jew, who sought to execute God's will in every act and thought, no matter how trivial. There was the merchant, who was no less tempestuous than was the Sambatyon River until Friday noon; just as this fabled river ceased its raging and whirling on the eve of the Sabbath, so too did the harried tradesman relax then in the midst of his family and intone sweet melodies of the Song of Songs.

Gross called his Galician Jews "a people of pure dreamers and poets." In their dreams they sated themselves with what they lacked in real life; their poor huts became palaces and their humble turrets golden minarets. The girl of marriageable age likened herself to Rachel waiting at the well for her Jacob and to Shulamith soon to be wooed by King Solomon, her beloved. The red-bearded, silent, fearless drayman felt closer to stones and trees, cattle and wild beasts, than to mere mortals. The water-carrier brought to poor and rich God's gift of water but he was most solicitous that men of learning be copiously supplied. Yossel Klezmer, to whom Gross devoted a dozen lyrics and ballads, entranced and uplifted as he fiddled away at the market-place and at festive assemblies, assisted by his partner on the pipe, with Berl Blinder bimbamming on the bassviol and the Marshalik pouring out merry rhymes.

The first mature volume of lyrics, Jews (Yiedn, 1929), brought all of these types to the fore, especially in their gayer moods, and also heroes and heroines of biblical vintage, such as Samuel and Daniel, Yael and Bathsheva. The second volume, however, which appeared under the same title in 1938, reflected the harsher reality experienced by the poet during the decade of the Great Depression in America and the rise of Hitler in Europe. He then linked his own individual fate to that of the hungry, defiant masses. He lamented the waste of his life among asphalt pavements, grimy subways, and skies gray with smoke. He depicted the lean operator bent over a sewing machine hour after hour, day after day; the unemployed outcast, homeless save for a bench in Hester Street; the tens of thousands demonstrating at Union Square on May Day. He sang a ballad of Sacco and Vanzetti, two idealists who fought for their vision of freedom in the land of golden idols and whose death earned them a seat at the table of the immortal just. Old Kolomea of the poet's dream-filled youth, however, continued to break through his contemporary themes. Yossel Klezmer reappeared and so did Dobush and Elijah. Gross painted the joy of Jewish children on Passover night. He conjured up again the Purim that he had celebrated with masquerades and the exchange of sweets in the house of his father before he and his artist brother, Chaim Gross, departed for distant shores.

The poet's images and moods, usually so colorful and joyous, turned tragic and black when the Nazis wiped out the Jewish settlements of Galicia. The strings on Yossel Klezmer's fiddle snapped amidst the ruins and were silenced forever. The singer of Kolomea on America's soil became the mourner of Kolomea. Never did he curse the murderers who desecrated the human species with their vile deeds. He merely bewailed the end of a Jewish community that had flourished so long and to whose spirit he, the poet, could only give the inadequate tribute of his verses.

The Galician Neoromanticists did not include any titans of Yiddish literature but they did enrich it with lyrics of value; they did give expression, in talented Yiddish works, to their love of their cultural heritage; they did lessen the attractiveness of alien lures, German and Polish; they did help to maintain the quality of Jewish living during a period of war, revolutionary disturbances and increasing anti-Jewish pressures.

13

NOVELISTS OF POLAND

The Warsaw Center • Weissenberg • Oizer Varshavsky
• Horonchik • Kacyzne • Justman • Trunk •
I. J. Singer • Bashevis-Singer

IN WARSAW, Peretz reigned supreme until his death in 1915. In the decade before World War I, his dominant position in Yiddish literature was unquestioned. From all of Eastern Europe, young men, talented and untalented, trekked to his home and brought him the first products of their pen. A word of encouragement from him opened the doors for them to publishers and editors. His first disciples, David Pinski, Sholem Asch, Peretz Hirshbein, expanded the range of Yiddish in directions in which he had pioneered. Their plays were produced on the stages of Europe and America and their narratives were translated into German, English, Russian and Polish. Only I. M. Weissenberg (1881-1938), the consistent exponent of pure Naturalism, still awaited recognition, comparable to theirs, which he felt was his due but which was being withheld from him.

The death of Peretz left an hiatus in Yiddish letters which was not easily filled. In the Polish capital, Weissenberg laid claim to the vacant throne and gathered about him a group of young novelists who followed in his Naturalistic footsteps. The most gifted among them were Oizer Varshavsky (1898-1944) and Shimon Horonchik (1889-1939). Weissenberg furthered their vogue during the early years of the Polish Republic in the periodicals he edited and through the publishing venture he founded. In the long run, however, the negative, analytical or purely descriptive creed of Naturalism could not retain the allegiance of readers, since it offered no guidance out of the impasse in which Polish Jews found themselves in an ever deteriorating situation. Only in the realm of the Soviets, where Socialist Realism dominated during the Stalin Era, did the works of the Polish Naturalists continue to find favor with critics and educators.

Encouraged by Peretz, Weissenberg had begun with short tales in 1904, but it was his novelette *A Townlet* (*A Shtetl*, 1906) which first attracted general interest. In contrast to Sholem Asch's romantic idealization of small town Jewish life, Weissenberg painted this life as far from idyllic. As early as the 1860's, Mendele Mokher Sforim had already uncovered the excrescences which had attached themselves to the long dormant Jewish communities far from the mainstream of new ideas and revolutionary currents. But it was Weissenberg, four decades later, who first stressed the impact of the new revolutionary doctrines upon the townlets, rousing them from their lethargy and shattering their foundations.

Workers, in his stories, were becoming class conscious. Emissaries of the Bund and of Polish Socialist parties were infiltrating the townlets, fomenting strikes, organizing demonstrations against local and imperial authorities. Youths rebelled against fathers and mothers, apprentices against master-craftsmen, the unbelievers who trusted the power of pistols against the chanters of psalms who put their faith in God. The restless spirit of 1905 permeated the political scene. The harsh cry of the underprivileged resounded from such narratives as *The Mad Village Lass* (*Die Meshuggene In Dorf*, 1906), a pathetic tale of a young girl who desperately resisted her mother's efforts to compel her submission to an imposed, unloved husband, or *One Generation Goes and Another Comes* (*Dor Holekh Vdor Ba*, 1904), a short story of an overworked, undernourished father who collapsed in a shoe establishment and of his eighteen-year-old son who was expected to replace him immediately and to continue to grind out profits for the boss.

In fighting fanatically and vitriolically for his ultra-realistic approach, Weissenberg succeeded in raising up many antagonists. These embittered his later years and gave him a feeling of frustration and undeserved persecution. His barbed polemics wounded many, but they inflicted far more harm upon himself by deflecting him from more positive creative achievements. The promise of his early years was not fulfilled. Nevertheless, he did stimulate believing followers and he did bring excitement to the Warsaw literary scene.

Oizer Varshavsky's best novel, *Smugglers* (*Shmugler*, 1920), appeared under the aegis of Weissenberg and did not deviate in the slightest from Weissenberg's Naturalistic creed. Its theme was the demoralization of the Jewish townlet during the years of German occupation of Poland, 1915 to 1918. The younger residents, who were healthy in body and mind, had by then been conscripted to fight in the Czar's army. Psychopaths, cripples, invalids, graybeards, underworld figures and women were left, and these somehow had to shift for themselves. Smuggling became their principal occupation and enabled them to survive. Fathers, in Varshavsky's novel, gave their daughters as bribes to the German occupying authorities. Pious patriarchs became informers for the sake of a petty monetary reward. Husbands replaced their wives with female smuggling assistants who could be useful as decoys. In the synagogue, worshipers interrupted prayers with mutual recriminations and brutal melées. Fists decided disputes even in the presence of the rabbi and were more effective than appeals to decency.

Varshavsky's novel had no central figure or main plot. It offered a rich assortment of society's lower depths. His thieves, prostitutes, liquor distillers, social outcasts, lawbreakers lived by their wits, courage and unscrupulousness. Rarely did moments of tenderness break in upon harsh, cruel days and only at the edge of the abyss. Such a moment came to the smuggling team of Pantel and Mendel, father and son, after they had flayed each other in the cellar of a hunchbacked panderer. Another such moment came to Pantel after he kicked his pregnant wife and brought her near unto death. But the tenderest scenes took place between the dangerously ill Mendel and the prostitute Nache, who nursed him back to health. These scenes, in which pain purified him and pity renovated her, were reminiscent of Dostoevsky, Varshavsky's model.

The Jewish townlet emerged from World War I critically ill, according to Varshavsky, and without hope of convalescence. Uprooted from tradition, it had no ideals to fight for, no moral values to live by, no principles that could tame lust or avarice. The cynical novelist seemed to gloat at the passing of holiness from the dying Jewish communities and to mock at the rituals and folkways of pre-war vintage, outmoded in the post-war era.

The first significant novel of Shimon Horonchik *Confused Ways* (*Farplonterte Vegn*, 1924) also appeared under the sponsorship of Weissenberg and also portrayed the physical and moral disintegration of the Polish-Jewish townlet during the years of German military occupation. This novel was followed by other Naturalistic narratives, such as *Whirr of Machines* (*Geroish Fun Mashi-*

nen, 1928), which was based on the author's observations and experiences in a Polish lace factory, *1905* (1929), which depicted the struggle of Jewish workers during the year of the unsuccessful revolt against the Czarist regime, and *Swamp* (*Sump,* 1931), in which Horonchik's rich relatives served as models of hard-hearted exploiters.

The rise of factories during the first quarter of the century and the substitution of machine production for the individual handiwork of independent craftsmen resulted in a migration from villages and townlets to the larger cities and brought to the fore unscrupulous parvenus and class-conscious wage-earners. Strikes, riots, fear of pogroms darkened the Jewish scene and were reflected in Horonchik's tales. Rarely did a gleam of sunlight break through his gloomy descriptions of Jewish life, probably because he himself was constantly haunted by fear, poverty and loneliness.

When in 1915 the German military authorities occupied the town of Kalish, which had been set afire by the retreating Russians, they corralled its male inhabitants, all of whom were Jews, lined them up in rows, and shot every fifteenth person. This was done to instill fear into the trapped community. Horonchik was the fourteenth in line. The shock he was subjected to on that day reverberated in him as an undefinable terror throughout his later years. After his wife, who was his main support, left him, he became ever more gloomy, more cynical, more restless. In 1934, he moved to Warsaw. There he witnessed the rising tide of Polish anti-Semitism and sensed the gathering of even more destructive forces against which Jews were powerless. When the German army in 1939 again attacked Poland, he fled from the Warsaw conflagration. But his will to live was undermined. Arriving at the conclusion that the entire world had become one vast swamp, he did not want to wait to be engulfed in its mire. He gave up further flight, cut his veins and let his life's blood ooze out.

Despite the keen observation of the Naturalistic writers and their faithful reproduction of the fading of old traditions, the disintegration of long established communal institutions, and the emergence of new, unhappy types and conflicts, they could not command popularity beyond the first few years of their literary innovations; they offered no gleam of cheer, no hope of a better tomorrow either on earth or in the afterworld. They were therefore soon eclipsed by Neoromantic and mystical writers whose works could bring some solace by conjuring up visions of a glorious Jewish past and of a future redemption both on earth and in an imagined heaven.

The Neoromantic, mystic drama *Dybbuk* by the folklorist S. Anski (1863-1920), which remained unperformed during his lifetime, proved a phenomenal success at its first performance in Warsaw on December 9, 1920, and held the stage for two decades thereafter.

Alter Kacyzne (1885-1941) was the literary heir of Anski, whose folklore collection enriched him with fascinating themes and whose fragmentary, final play, *Day and Night* (*Tog Un Nakht*), he completed and brought to the Yiddish stage after the latter's death. His own early poetic drama *Prometheus* (1920) suffered from an overabundance of allegorical mysticism and could not be staged. However, he did attain a theatrical triumph in 1925 with *The Duke* (*Der Dukus*), a drama based on the legend of the Polish nobleman Potocki who embraced Judaism and was burned at the stake. It was followed in 1926 by the historical tragedy *Herod,* which dramatized the rise to power and the disintegration of a strong personality who had to wade in blood in order to maintain himself on Judea's throne.

Kacyzne acknowledged himself to be also a pupil of Peretz, a pupil and not an imitator. The influence of this classical master was most evident in the ballads and grotesques published in 1936. In these the world of reality merged into a ghostly, surrealist realm and tragic happenings were lightened by an infusion of sad, tolerant humor.

Kacyzne's only full length novel, *The Strong and the Weak* (*Shtarke Un Shvakhe,* 1929), portrayed Poland's disillusioned Jewish intellectuals of his generation. The finest gem of his narrative art, however, was *Sick Pearls* (*Kranke Perl,* 1922), his short tale of Shulamith and the Queen of Sheba, both beloved of Solomon, a tale breathing the freshness and vigor of young, wild love against the background of Jerusalem's romantic nights.

Kacyzne's originality as lyricist, dramatist, novelist and essayist was only fully appreciated after his *Collected Works* (*Gezamelte Verk*) began to appear in 1967, more than a quarter of a century after he was clubbed to death by Ukrainian collaborators of the Nazis when he sought refuge in the Galician town of Tarnopol after escaping from Warsaw.

The warm splendor of Hassidism shone through the nostalgic tales of the Warsaw novelist Moshe Justman (1889-1942), who wrote under the psudonym of B. Jeuschsohn. His articles in the Warsaw daily *Moment* until 1925, and his column in the rival Warsaw daily *Haint* from 1925 until his flight to Israel in 1939, won him a large following especially among troubled Hassidic youth, which was then torn between traditionalism and the lure of modernism. His earliest novel, *At the Hassidic Court (Inm Rebbins Hoif,* 1911), stressed the joyous fervor prevailing in Hassidic circles. But it also depicted the infiltration of the doctrines of the Maskilim even among the children of the most stalwart Hassidim. The novelist loved the old order but recognized the inevitability of its further decline. For many years he immersed himself in the study of Jewish folklore and he retold tales of old with reverence and humor. His eight volumes, *From Our Old Treasure (Fun Undzer Alten Oitzer,* 1932), were eagerly devoured by readers, both Orthodox and non-Orthodox.

Folklore material also supplied the basis for much of the best work of I. J. Trunk (1887-1961). Descended from rich patricians and famed rabbis, he enjoyed a carefree youth in his native village on the outskirts of Warsaw and then the finest secular and religious education under private tutors in the industrial city of Lodz. Coming under the influence of Peretz, he sought a synthesis of European rationalism and Jewish mysticism. Travels throughout Europe, Asia and Africa in his twenties gave him a background broad and deep, unsurpassed by any of his contemporaries at so early an age. On the eve of the First World War he lived in Palestine and his early tales, *Fig Trees (Feigenboimer,* 1922), reflected his observations of its landscape and picturesque figures. The volume also included an artistic retelling of the Babylonian epic of Gilgamesh.

After spending the war years in Switzerland, Trunk returned to his native Poland, settled in a palatial home in Lodz and devoted himself to a life of study and contemplation. Admiring the Neo-romanticism of Knut Hamsun, the iconoclasm of Friedrich Nietzsche and the estheticism of Oscar Wilde, he made these writers better known to Yiddish readers through meticulous essays and discerning critical comments. But he owed his greatest literary debt to the romanticism of the later Peretz. He saw in the realistic, satiric works of Peretz a temporary aberration and in the mystical, Hassidic tales and dramas of Peretz a profound thinker's search for absolute truth transcending mere reason, flashes of ultimate insights, premonitions of spiritual values that emanated from the divine source of all knowledge. Despite his patrician background, his wealth and his leaning towards mysticism, Trunk became an adherent of the Bund and a supporter of its Socialist aspirations and its Diaspora nationalism.

His polemic essay, *Yiddishism and Jewish History* (1930), was an extreme formulation of Shimon Dubnow's view that history and language were more important than territory in keeping Jews together as a distinct cultural group. History was not for him, however, pious ancestor worship, but the heart of contemporary Jewish reality, the fountain from which the Jewish people drew the water of life, the national treasure from which Jews brought their unique contributions to mankind. To sever the Jews from the legacy of the past meant undermining their living roots. This past included Poland as well as Palestine, and Yiddish far more than Hebrew.

Negation of Yiddish, the tongue of the Jewish group personality in its densest concentration in Eastern Europe, meant reducing Jews to museum-fossils, to epigones who survived merely as ruminating, rachitic descendants of a once vigorous historic entity. Jews must not let themselves be linguistically crippled, mummified, tied to the Procrustus bed of Hebrew. They should rather step out upon the world arena with their richly developed vernacular even as Dante had done when he composed his *Divine Comedy* in his Italian vernacular rather than in the sacred tongue of Catholicism. To seek a Jewish renaissance by means of two languages was, in Trunk's opinion, as absurd as a body trying to think with two heads or to feel with two hearts. In order to forestall national schizophrenia, he suggested retaining Hebrew as the Latin of the Jews, as the medium for religious services, but to base Jewish nationalism on Yiddish.

By 1936, however, when Trunk reprinted his essay on Yiddishism in the volume *Near and Strange (Noent Un Fremd)*, he was forced to acknowledge that the prospects for a Jewish Humanism based on Yiddish were growing ever dimmer. The Polish bastion of Yiddishism was crumbling; three years later it collapsed. Trunk himself barely managed to escape via the Orient to the United States. The *grand seigneur* of Yiddish letters arrived in New York penniless. For the last two decades of his life he was engaged in a daily, difficult struggle for bread. Yet these proved to be his most creative years.

As Trunk looked back upon them during his final days, he saw them as the climax of his lifelong search for the harmony of diversities, for unity amidst multiplicity, for Jewish integration in the cosmos. At first he had sought to find himself in nature, in the landscape of Poland, where he was born and reared. Then he had discovered that contemporary life was rooted in history, in the thoughts and deeds of the many preceding generations, and so he turned to write historical novels. His autobiographic, nostalgic prose epic in seven volumes, *Poland* (*Poilen,* 1944-1953), occupied his main attention during his first years in America. It was a family chronicle but it also painted a warm, faithful portrait of Polish Jewry at the apex of its creative development and splendor. Then, in his final stage, he had freed himself from his infatuation with a Poland that was no longer the center of Jewishness and he sought in surviving myths, folklore, and folk tales the answer to the questions: how does the world look through Jewish eyes? how is it mirrored in the Jewish subconscious? how does Jewish history live in the imagination of the unsophisticated, unalienated Jew?

In his romance of a Jewish Don Quixote, *Simkhe Plakhte* (1951), Trunk combined two antithetical aspects of the Jewish soul. On the one hand, the inarticulate, Golem-like Simkhe reacted instinctively and unconsciously to the events happening around him. On the other hand, his Sancho Panza, the Lithuanian rationalist Feivel, reacted with the subtle, refined irony of pure Jewish intellectualism. Simkhe, a water carrier of limited intelligence in a Polish townlet, found himself catapulted into ever higher social strata. Without being able to read or write, he ended up, against his own will, as a revered rabbi and as the chief advisor to the Polish nobility and even to the king himself. Feivke, the sharp-witted sceptic who was able to push the simpleton Simkhe up the ladder of worldly success, remained ever aware of the fickleness of fortune and stayed out of its clutches, content with a piece of bread, a bit of onion, and an ever deepening insight into the follies of a transient world.

Trunk followed this comic romance with a narrative of the early adventures of Hershele Ostropoler, entitled *The World's Merriest Jew* (*Der Frehlekhster Yied in Der Velt,* 1953). The stories dealt with Hershele's years of apprenticeship. In this wag, Jewish folklore had created a figure who alternated between hope and disappointment and who finally reached the stage of laughing at the world and getting others to join in his laughter. According to Trunk, Jews could surmount the tragedies with which their past and present so richly endowed them throughout their wandering over the globe because they possessed the gift of laughter. Instead of becoming the world's greatest pessimists, they managed to retain ineradicable faith in the ultimate triumph of goodness over evil. Their optimistic tales told of their waiting for the coming of Messiah and of the intervention meanwhile of his precursor Elijah and of one or another of the thirty-six *Lamedvovniks* or Hidden Saints to reverse direst ill fortune.

Undaunted by adversity, Trunk completed as his next romance *The World Is Full of Miracles (Die Velt Is Ful Mit Nissim,* 1955), and devoted his last year to composing tales about the founder of Hassidism, the Baal Shem of Mezhbish, whom popular imagination had endowed with clairvoyance and the power of working miracles. Eleven of these tales were completed and were appended to his historical novel of the Messianic claimant Sabbatai Zvi, entitled *Messianic Storm (Moshiakh-Gevitter,* 1961).

Two other Polish novelists, I. J. Singer (1893-1944) and his younger brother I. Bashevis Singer (b. 1904) were, like Trunk, the offspring of Polish rabbinical families and deeply immersed in the folklore of Hassidism. The rise to fame of I. J. Singer beyond the boundaries of his native land must be ascribed in large measure to the dramatization of his novels by Maurice Schwartz, who achieved phenomenal box-office successes with them, both in New York's Yiddish Art Theater and wherever he included them in his guest performances.

Yoshe Kalb (1932), a novel which Maurice Samuel translated into English under the title *The Sinner* (1953), presented a far less flattering picture of a prominent Hassidic Court than had Trunk in his tales. Singer's Rabbi of Nyesheve is a powerful but temperamental and unascetic leader of thousands of Hassidim throughout Galicia and Russia. He is able to bully and cajole followers and opponents until he gets his way. After burying three wives, he is determined, in his sixties, to take young Malke as his fourth mate, but first he must marry off his youngest daughter, Serele. He succeeds in negotiating a match between Serele and the adolescent, God-seeking Nahum, despite the latter's resistance. When Nahum later catches sight of Malke, however, he is more attracted to her than to his own wife. In a moment of weakness he succumbs to her longing for him and thereafter he seeks to atone by a life of ascetic, penitent wandering. Always he strives for the purification of his soul. Nevertheless, he becomes involved in complicated situations. These reach a climax when he returns to Nyesheve after an absence of fifteen years and is put on trial by a Sanhedrin of seventy rabbis, who attempt to untangle the ramifications of his dual personality: saint and sinner,

Yoshe Kalb the simpleton and Nahum the learned cabalist. The final court scene is tensely dramatic and accounts to a large extent for the success of the stage version of the novel.

Singer's finest prose epic is *The Brothers Ashkenazi* (1935), which an enthusiastic critic ranked with Tolstoy's great epics. It spans a century of Jewish life in Lodz, from the post-Napoleonic era to the Polish Republic of the 1920's. In three volumes, it depicts the rapid rise of Lodz from an insignificant village to a large metropolis, its efflorescence as a main textile center during the reign of the last Czars, and its decline when it was cut off from its hinterland, the vast Russian market, after the Revolution of 1917.

The German and Moravian master weavers and their followers, who brought this industry to the Polish settlement, encountered keen competition from Jewish importers, smugglers, peddlers and the miscellaneous dealers who swarmed into the developing town. Soon Jews proved themselves to be indispensable as general agents also for the larger German firms. In the course of decades of patient, unremitting initiative, they were able to gain control of the industry.

Most successful was Max Ashkenazi, whose passion for hard work was inexhaustible. Despite repeated setbacks, he was able to amass wealth and to retain it. He became known as the King of Lodz. His principal rival was his twin brother, Jacob. Through the interlocking fate of the two brothers, their divergent characters, their feuds, their reconciliations, the author unfolded a rich panorama of flourishing Jewish activity in the midst of a hostile majority population of Poles, Russians and Germans. Jews managed to surmount ever changing varieties of discrimination and oppression, including Cossack pogroms, German occupancy, revolutionary expropriation and Polish chauvinism. They participated in all liberal and radical movements, only to be thrust aside when these movements attained to victory. They bled on all fronts and still somehow survived. In the virulently anti-Semitic New Poland, however, Lodz was doomed; it crumbled and putrefied. With the extinction of its last glimmer of industrial vitality, the Jew Max Ashkenazi, who had acquired the title of King of Lodz, also closed his eyes. Meanwhile, Zionist pioneers set out from the dying Polish city for Palestine and other Jews for America. They sought a new life and they left behind them the desolate and alien city where everything they had built in the course of a century was built on shifting sand.

The basic theme underlying Singer's narratives is the loneliness of the individual who can never be understood in his uniqueness and who is fated to be trodden under the heel of the conformist masses. In *Chaver Nachman* (1938), translated by Maurice Samuel under the title *East of Eden* (1939), the novelist, who had himself experienced the harsh reality of Soviet Russia, voiced his disillusionment with the Communist panacea. In *Family Carnovsky* (1943), he let three centers of Jewish life pass in review—Poland, Germany, America—and arrived at pessimistic conclusions concerning all of them. Three generations were projected on a broad canvas. The earliest was that of the enlightened Polish Jew, David Carnovsky. The second was that of his son, the successful German-Jewish physician Dr. Georg Carnovsky. The third was that of his grandson, the semi-Aryan Yego Carnovsky, who even on American soil was still infatuated with Nazi ideology and suffered from Jewish self-hatred. All experience rejection by non-Jewish groups but none can find a way that might lead to salvation.

Singer himself concluded sadly, in an essay of October 1942, that efforts of Jews to live peacefully and happily among non-Jews constituted a two-thousand-year-old error, which should be rectified by the return of Jews to a territory of their own. Ever since Judea's defeat by the Romans, Jews had sought to retain their group identity in lands of the Diaspora, and in almost every generation attempts to annihilate them were renewed. On the one hand, most Jews persisted in their refusal to submerge themselves in the dominant group. On the other hand, most non-Jews would not admit them to brotherhood save at the price of the obliteration of their group distinctiveness. The war between Rome and Jerusalem was still being waged, though under different slogans. Numerous explanations for this antagonism between Esau and Jacob were offered. These included religious fanaticism, economic rivalry, psychological incompatibility, racial, metaphysical and mystical theories. But the bitter fact remained that there was no peace between Jews and non-Jews crowded together on the same soil. In Singer's view, the evidence of twenty centuries, culminating in Hitlerism, should suffice to convince the wildest optimists that a symbiosis of Jews and their non-Jewish compatriots was unattainable, that Jews could not live as a people on other peoples' territories without arousing antagonism. Why then renew illusions which had always ended in disappointment? "The people of Israel must again be taken out of Egypt just like three thousand years ago. The thornbush is burning in the fire and is calling to Moses, the shepherd, who is busy feeding alien sheep in the desert."

I. J. Singer was the mentor of his younger brother, who wrote under the name of "I. Bashevis." While the former strove to veer from Neoromanticism to ever more transparent Realism, the latter preferred in his narratives to revel in romantic visions that verged on the grotesque and to move in the direction of the Expressionists and Surrealists.

The world of Bashevis abounds in evil, sickness, harshness, anger, beatings, tortures and horror. It is a strange world in which wicked spirits tempt all creatures of flesh and blood and in which demons wrestle with *Lamedvovniks*. The weak among mortals succumb and end tragically. The strong battle allurements, overcome temptations, seek atonement after initial missteps, and emerge as radiant personalities, a blessing to their fellows.

Bashevis cannot reconcile himself to the existence of undeserved suffering, especially the undeserved suffering which befell God's so-called chosen people. He is depressed by the cruelties inflicted upon innocent children and saintly graybeards at the hands of the most enlightened people in the heart of contemporary Europe. The wounds of our century are, however, too vividly present and the catastrophe too immense for him to be able to structure them within the framework of an objective, artistic narrative. He, therefore, prefers to go back in his imagination to tragedies on a more manageable scale, suffered by Polish Jewry in earlier generations, from the massacres of Hetman Chmelnitzky's hordes in the mid-seventeenth century to the pogroms perpetrated by the conquerors and the conquered of World War I. Yet, even these tragedies, as narrated in chronicles of survivors, are too horrible for him to describe directly and he wisely limits himself to the after-effects of the crushing events. Thus, the novels *Satan in Goray* (1935), *The Slave* (1962), and numerous short stories, bring to life the post-1648 era in grotesque images and mangled characters.

The former novel takes place in the townlet of Goray in 1665 and 1666. Although sixteen years have passed since Chmelnitzky's destructive raid, the community has not yet recovered. It lives in constant dread of another Cossack incursion. Its main hope is centered on the coming of Messiah, whose imminent appearance cabalists have predicted on the basis of mystic calculations. Ba-

shevis reproduces the grim atmosphere of the terrorized, superstition-ridden Jews who are ripe for religious hysteria. When the
satanic Gedalia arrives in Goray, he takes advantage of the community's longing to escape from despair and desolation. He
announces that salvation is at hand: Messiah has already appeared on earth and has already revealed himself in distant Turkey
in the figure of Sabbatai Zvi. He finds in the half-demented
Rechele a prophetess whom he can mold to his purposes. Rechele,
daughter of a patrician who was ruined in 1648, has been raised
by a century-old, deaf hag, her uncle's mother-in-law. This uncle,
a slaughterer with black beard and red eyes, let the hag maltreat
the sensitive child. Rechele was never allowed to leave her room
to play outdoors. Her senile guardian hissed at her like a snake,
cursed her with blood-curdling curses, tore out her hair, dunked
her head in boiling water, beat her with bony hands, with a log,
or with a moistened cat-o'-nine-tails. Psychological tortures included bedtime tales of dragons and wild beasts, dead souls that
flew about incessantly, dybbuks that sought to enter into living
bodies, murderers who lived in caves and consorted with witches,
cannibals who roasted children on spits, a one-eyed savage on
the lookout for a mate. As a result of such treatment, Rechele
succumbed to fits of panic.

Gedaliah, playing upon the willingness of Goray's Jews to
believe in miracles, proclaims the girl's hysterical visions to be
prophecies. As the new, self-appointed mentor of the inspired
prophetess, he is able to manipulate himself into a position of
dominance in the community. He has Rechele divorced from her
ascetic husband so that he himself can marry her. He then institutes a reign of vice and moral degradation in the formerly pious
townlet, on the theory that the world must be completely sunk
in sin before the Messiah can arrive to purify it.

Bashevis delights in depicting Goray's sensual orgies, the wallowing of men and women in uncleanliness of spirit and flesh. He
spares only a single character from the rampant degeneracy,
Rabbi Beinish; but this aged, sympathetic communal leader is
shown as helpless to stem the madness gripping all the inhabitants. Mortally ill, he begs to be taken to Lublin so as not to die
in his native Goray, which has fallen under the domination of
satanic forces.

A variation of *The Satan of Goray,* Bashevis' earliest novel
of mass hysteria, is the short story "The Ball," in which the arch-
devil Samael himself takes a hand and debauches an entire town.

He tempts its poor, pious Jews with the glitter of gold. He prom-
ises a chain of pearls and a thousand ducats to all unmarried
persons who will marry before the crowing of the cock at dawn.
This offer proves to be irresistible. Young and old are caught in
the devil's net, participate in the black weddings, become mired
in sensuality, and would have perished utterly in swamps of filth
if not for the rabbi's vehement adjurations. The town's rabbi
persists in calls to repentance and in quoting apt precepts of the
Torah. Bit by bit, individuals emerge from the slough and find
their way back to moral sobriety. Although many generations
have passed since the night of orgy and black weddings, the
memory of the devilish temptation lingers on and renders the
descendants immune to the lure of wealth and indecency.

The Slave is a novel dealing with a survivor of Chmelnitzky's
massacres. Having fled from the Cossack murderers, Jacob had
been dragged away by Polish marauders and sold as a slave to a
Polish landowner. Throughout lonely years among depraved peasants, enduring great hardships, and in constant danger of being
killed, he nevertheless retained his Jewish morals and religious
observances. He even infected the Polish peasant girl Wanda with
a longing for the Jewish faith. Ultimately, he was ransomed from
his savage environment and escorted back to his native town.
Wanda's image lived on in him, however, and he undertook to
rescue her from her semi-pagan, semi-Christian village. During
this period of upheavals and persecutions, Jews were constantly
on the move. The ex-slave Jacob found his way to a ravaged town
which was being rebuilt by returning survivors. Wanda became
an exemplary Jewish wife. But misfortune dogged the couple.
After Wanda, renamed Sarah after her conversion, died in childbirth, Jacob fled with the infant to the Holy Land and raised his
son to become a learned and pious son of Israel. He himself returned, after the Sabbatai Zvi debacle, to end his days and to be
buried near his adored mate of alien stock.

Bashevis frequently breaks down the boundaries between the
natural and the supernatural, between the living and the dead.
In one tale, the beloved, deceased wife of a rabbi enters the body
of a young girl, lives there as Esther Kreindel the Second, remarries the widowed rabbi, and continues her interrupted earthly
existence in the borrowed body. In another tale, a devil persuades
a man and a woman to deviate ever more from the truth until
they become so mired in falsehoods that he has them completely
in his toils. They end on the gallows in this world and are directed

to hell in the next. A third tale, "The Mirror," is a monologue of a demon.

In "Taibele and Her Demon," a *badchen* overhears Taibele tell a story of a woman who was forced to consort with a demon. He thereupon impersonates this demon in the darkness of night and forces Taibele to submit to him, at first unwillingly and under horrible threats but before long most gladly.

In the gruesome tale "Blood," a woman and a *Shochet* find their carnal ecstasy increasing as the steaming blood of the butchered animals gurgles about them and as the death rattles supply tonal accompaniment. Ultimately, she becomes so ravenous and so passionately unrestrained that she prowls as a were-wolf through the nights. Her escort, however, does at the end find a way to repent and atone.

Despite the infatuation of Bashevis with the horrible, he also composes now and then tender, idyllic tales in the tradition of Peretz. Such a narrative is *Short Friday,* the story of the simple tailor Shmul-Leibele and his good wife, Shoshe. Their life of piety is symbolized by the holiness with which they usher in the Sabbath. Both pray that they might leave this world on the same day. Their prayer is granted when they are asphyxiated by the fumes from the Sabbath stove and awaken to find themselves in their graves, side by side. The story ends with the author's concluding remarks: "Yes, the brief years of turmoil and temptation had come to an end. Shmul-Leibele and Shoshe had reached the true world. Man and wife grew silent. In the stillness they heard the flapping of wings, a quiet singing. An angel of God had come to guide Shmul-Leibele the tailor and his wife Shoshe into Paradise."

In *Gimpel the Fool* (1957), Bashevis portrays with loving kindness, but also with gentle satire, a pure simpleton who believes everything he is told. He assumes that all others are like himself, utterly without guile or malice. He is married off to a woman chosen for him by the community, lives with her for twenty years, and believes unquestioningly in her faithfulness. On her deathbed, she confesses to him that not a single one of their six children has been fathered by him. Yet, though everyone deceives him, he cannot bring himself to the point of repaying in like coin. This world may be a tissue of lies but beyond it is the world of truth toward which he heads by leading a blameless life. He hopes to reach that better world as soon as he passes the bourne of the grave.

The hero of the narrative *Spinoza of Market Street* (1961) is also a pure simpleton, despite a doctorate in philosophy and a lifelong exposure to the wisdom of great thinkers. Dr. Nahum Fishelson, an abstemious scholar, lives alone in a Warsaw garret and devotes twenty-five years to the writing of a commentary on his idol Spinoza. Events pass him by as he thinks his solitary thoughts and communes with the pantheistic deity, the lord of logic and pure reason. Finally, however, the disturbances of the First World War also penetrate to the retreat of the Warsaw philosopher. A neighbor comes to nurse the sick man who has already reconciled himself to death. She manages to restore him to health. He marries her and comes to understand that the cosmic forces which operate in the macrocosm also stream within him, that the whirl of universes which are forever in flux also embraces the emotional transformations to which he is being subjected. "Pardon me, Spinoza, I have become a fool!" he finally exclaims.

The Magician of Lublin (1959) is a novel of Jewish life in late nineteenth-century Poland. Its hero, the Jewish juggler and acrobatic performer Yasha Mazur, has become famous as the Magician of Lublin. In the course of his journeying from place to place, he has sloughed his religious habits and has hurled himself into the pleasures of the flesh. These lead him to ever greater excesses and bring him to the verge of an abyss of crime. At the last moment, however, he retreats from evil and seeks self-purification. He realizes that there must be an accounting for every deed, every word, every thought, and that, in the final reckoning, good must triumph over evil. He concludes that each good act increases the goodness content of the universe and that each transgression delays the day of Messianic deliverance. Yasha the Magician thereupon becomes transformed into Reb Jacob the Penitent. He immures himself as a hermit in a small, doorless house, four cubits long and four cubits wide, with a tiny aperture through which he receives his daily food. He puts himself under this rigorous restraint, since otherwise he, the libertine with strong appetites, would be unable to resist the temptations of this world.

The most ambitious novel of Bashevis is *Family Moskat* (1950), a chronicle of the decline of a patrician family of Warsaw from its height in the first decade of the twentieth century to its final debacle in the Hitler period. The patriarch of the family, Reb Meshulam Moskat, combined Hassidic piety and shrewd business sense. In the course of fifty years, he accumulated considerable wealth. At eighty, he married a third wife and was still the chief support of his seven children, their mates, and his many grand-children. After his death, the strong bonds uniting the various members of this large family were weakened. Religious observances fell into disuse. Traditional standards of conduct were discarded. Divorces increased, a few children drifted to apostasy, others embraced epicureanism, still others Zionism. Most led unhappy lives, devoid of meaningful values. The First World War hastened the process of decay and, by the time the Second World War broke out, the surviving descendants were ripe for the end. Death took over. The final words were spoken while Warsaw was under Nazi bombardment and all routes of escape were cut off: "The Messiah will soon come. . . . Death is the Messiah. That's the real truth."

If Meshulam Moskat stood out as the symbol of the stable old order that was able to maintain itself until our century, Asa Heshel Bannet came to the fore as the symbol of the younger generation that set out in search of new wisdom and that was whirled about as driftwood by the storms that rocked Eastern European Jewish existence to its foundations. Coming to Warsaw at the age of nineteen, with a glowing letter of recommendation to the Moskats and with a copy of Spinoza's *Ethics,* this young prodigy of a distinguished rabbinical family sought to acquire knowledge of ultimate reality, to synthesize Torah and Enlightenment, but never got far in his studies. He became involved in emotional entanglements, married the wrong woman in a moment of despair, divorced her, then married the right woman only to make her unhappy also. Drafted into the Russian army to fight for the Czarist regime which persecuted Jews, he experienced revolutions and pogroms, and returned to Poland in time to be drafted into Pilsudski's army in which anti-Semitism also prevailed. Finally, he saw the rearisen Poland perish at the hands of Hitler's cohorts, while he, the symbolic contemporary Jew, continued to be the preferred victim of man's bestiality to man.

Bashevis abuses his literary talent by straining far too often for sensational effects, by indulging in exaggerations, by emphasizing sadistic aspects. Instead of a balanced view of Jewish life, he offers a distorted, demonic view. Though his fame in the 1960's and 1970's exceeded that of any Jewish novelist since Sholem Asch, it was not likely to be as enduring as that of his older brother, I. J. Singer, whose novels presented a sounder insight into Polish-Jewish reality before its extinction.

14

POETS OF WARSAW

Circle of Hillel Zeitlin • Aaron Zeitlin • Einhorn •
Segalowitch • Kadia Molodowsky

LITTLE MORE than two decades elapsed between the liberation
of Poland from the Czarist yoke and its partition between Nazi
Germany and Communist Russia as a result of the Molotov-
Ribbentrop Pact. These years did not bring about an abatement
of anti-Semitism in the newly independent state. Nevertheless,
Jewish energy was sufficiently released by the acquisition of certain rights guaranteed to ethnic and linguistic minorities so that
an upsurge of creativeness could manifest itself in many fields,
including literature.

Though Peretz, the chief inspirer of the Yiddish renascence,
passed away in 1915, the seeds he had planted matured in the
works of his many disciples both in Poland and across the Atlantic. Besides, other literary circles in the Polish capital continued to function until cut short by Hitler's invasion. The most
influential of these was the circle centering about Hillel Zeitlin
(1872-1943) and his two talented sons Ahron (b. 1898) and
Elchanan (1900-1943).

Already before Hillel Zeitlin came to Warsaw in 1908, his home
in Homel and then in Vilna attracted publicists, poets and thinkers
of different shades of opinion, who admired his religious sincerity
and philosophical acumen. Frequent visitors included Z. I. Onochi
(1878-1947), Zalman Schneour (1887-1959), Peretz Hirshbein
(1880-1948), Yeshaihu Bershadski (1871-1908), and I. D. Berkovitch (1885-1967). In Warsaw the circle about this influential
editor and sage expanded to include Mordecai Spector (1858-
1925), Yone Rosenfeld (1880-1944), Yoel Mastboim (1884-1957),
Jacob Steinberg (1887-1947), Yitzhok Katzenelson (1886-1944),

Jacob Fichman (1881-1958), Shlome Gilbert (1885-1942), Zysman Segalowitch (1884-1949), Menahem Boraisha (1888-1949), A. Almi (1892-1963), Moshe Teitsh (1882-1935), Joseph Tunkel (1881-1949), Moshe Justman (1889-1942), A. Mukdoni (1878-1958), Baal Makhshoves (1873-1924), and Eliezer Shteinman (1890-1970).

Elchanan Zeitlin, in the first volume of his memoirs, *In a Literary House* (*In a Literarishe Shtub,* 1938), paints a broad panorama of the Vilna years but covers the Warsaw years only until 1914. A projected second volume never appeared, since the author died of hunger in the Warsaw Ghetto shortly after his father was shot by the Nazis. Fortunately, his brother Aaron survived, having been stranded in America while on a visit before the outbreak of hostilities.

Although Aaron Zeitlin stayed on in New York and was no less prolific during his three decades there as a journalist and poet than he had been during his earlier decades in Warsaw, his literary personality did not change appreciably throughout his American period. He merely added themes of the Holocaust and of the new Israel and merely refined the Symbolist technique and the mystic strain which had characterized him since his first poetic epic, *Metatron,* was published in 1922.

Critics spoke of Zeitlin's lyrics as reasoned products, as ideas incorporated in images and rhythmic patterns, but he himself maintained that the original lyric impulse was somnambulistic and stemmed from the subconscious. This impulse produced the raw material upon which the poet's consciousness then acted and which he laboriously fashioned into an artistic whole. With greater maturity, a poet should therefore rework earlier versions until in time the poem approached perfection. He himself did not hesitate to revise lyrics even decades after their first appearance. The version of *Metatron* in the third volume of his *Complete Lyrics* (*Gezamelte Lieder,* 1957) was completely different from the one he composed thirty-six years earlier. Indeed, when this third volume appeared, ten years after the first two volumes, he reprinted several lyrics in a revised form and begged the reader to look upon earlier texts not as variants but as non-existent. He preferred that his poems should be read and considered not chronologically as stages in his growth but rather thematically as expressions of his basic poetic configuration, as his lifelong wrestling with God for an ultimate understanding of essences.

Zeitlin is a religious poet, deeply steeped in the Cabala and in

Jewish mysticism. Devils, doubles, demons, dybbuks, ghosts, astral emanations, transmigrated souls, angels and archangels abound in his lyrics, ballads and dramas. The struggle between spirits of negation and pious followers of God is at times treated with delightful humor, as in the long poems *Jewish Demons* (*Yiedishe Shedim*, 1948) and *Shmuel Rosh Medina*. More often, however, there are serious encounters between personified forces of good and evil, between doubters and believers, between satanic emissaries and saintly personalities. In the end, goodness triumphs over evil, souls of sinners attain salvation, falsehood becomes manifest as but the shadow of truth, and death is revealed as a mere boundary between this life and a life hereafter. Even after Maidanek and the cruel end of his family, Zeitlin proclaims his trust in the God of his fathers, a God who destroys and recreates. To be a Jew means to be eternally running toward God, even if God is ultimately unreachable. It means waiting for the trumpet of the Messiah, even if the coming of the Messiah is so long delayed.

Zeitlin's Messiahs, true and false, range from Messiah ben David, Messiah ben Joseph, to Sabbatai Zvi and Jacob Frank. In addition, he brings to the fore many legendary figures who dream of bringing Messiah down from his heavenly abode to offer salvation to the suffering human race. Some of his legendary heroes ascend to upper realms of being and seek there to counteract the machinations of diabolical spirits. Such memorable, saintly, wonder-working Jews are the Baal Shem, Nachman Bratslaver, Leib Sores and Joseph della Rina.

The mystic mood and the Messianic visions, which overhang so many of Zeitlin's lyrics, also hover over his drama *Jacob Frank* (1929). This drama deals with two antithetical approaches to God, that of Frank, the most devoted disciple of Sabbatai Zvi, and that of the Baal Shem, Frank's contemporary and the exponent of a more spiritual doctrine. Frank, though a God-seeker, wades through the complexities of sin, lust and darkness, in the belief that only after the world is saturated with evil will the pendulum of the universe swing back toward spirit, purity and radiance. The Baal Shem, on the other hand, is the God-finder. He discerns God's presence everywhere. He sings hymns to all of God's creation. He lives simply, works hard and steers clear of overmuch questioning and brooding. Frank, with the aid of demonic powers, can create the body of a Golem but only the Baal Shem, by invoking the Ineffable Name, can imbue it with life and feeling. In the end, the followers of Frank, the false Messiah, become confused and disillusioned. They grope in darkness and scatter in all directions. The Baal Shem, on the other hand, lights the way for a self-effacing, God-intoxicated, life-giving, religious movement, Hassidism.

Zeitlin's drama *Brenner* (1929) appeared in the same year as *Jacob Frank*. Its hero was Joseph Chaim Brenner, the Hebrew poet who had been killed in the Jaffe pogrom of 1921. Brenner had, in his youth, come under the influence of the dramatist's father. He had then experienced imprisonment in Russia and had escaped to London, where he became active in Zionist circles, Under the impact of A. D. Gordon's "back to the soil" philosophy, he had worked as an agricultural laborer in Palestine until his violent death. Zeitlin, who had been in Palestine during the unrest of 1921, transferred to his dramatic hero much of his own stormy striving and pain-filled visions.

Brenner, as portrayed by Zeitlin, could not endure seeing the Jewish people sleeping on its bundle of troubles or hiding in garrets while other peoples walked freely on their own soil under their own skies. He therefore sought to help his people through the power of his pen and through the example of his own physical labor, repeatedly exposing himself to danger and martyrdom. Through pain to salvation was his motto. Courageously adhering to his convictions, he neither fled from nor did he resist actively the incited, knife-wielding Arab who slew him. Brenner saw himself as the Jewish Abel who looked fearlessly into the eyes of the non-Jewish Cain. Thereafter the victim's blood cried out for atonement, not vengeance but atonement, and the fratricide recoiled branded and terror-ridden, pursued by his own awakened conscience.

Palestine was also the scene of Zeitlin's novel *Burning Earth* (*Brenendike Erd*, 1937). The theme of the novel was the Nili Affair of the First World War, the espionage group centered about the Aaronson Family of Zichron Yaakov which hoped to gain Palestine for the Jews by helping the British win the war against the Turks. Zeitlin's was the first fictional treatment of this theme, which Michael Blankfort later brought to wider attention through his novel *Behold the Fire* (1965) and especially through the motion picture based upon the novel.

Zysman Segalowitch (1884-1949) was only briefly associated with the Zeitlin circle and David Einhorn (b. 1886) not at all. Both poets rose to popularity on the eve of the First World War because their romantic, sentimental lyrics spoke to the heart of longing youth in the awakening townlets.

Einhorn's first booklets, *Silent Songs* (*Shtile Gezangen*, 1910) and *My Songs* (*Meine Lieder*, 1912), captured the rhythm of sad, still moments, the mysteries of words that tamed moods. He sang of his young days and nights spent among the four walls of a House of Learning, far removed from the world's turmoil, when dreams were reality and reality but a dream, when eyes were turned inward and ears cradled with *Gemara*-melodies, when eternal verities were prized more than temporary illusions. Einhorn also offered to the denizens huddled in townlets escape in imagination to enchanted forests in which nightingales abounded, to old castles inhabited by bold knights and pale damsels, to sweet and tender sorrows such as Eichendoff, Mörike and Heine had conjured up for the romantic European youth of an earlier generation. In the land of his day-dreams, apples were always golden, the sand glittered like diamonds, the silken sound of a sighing beloved dissolved the habitual melancholy about lovelorn hearts, the poet was an exiled prince made clairvoyant by innocent suffering and hence responsive to the pain of others.

In his later poems, Einhorn continued to yearn for the God of his boyhood whom he lost when he left the Vilna Yeshiva and began his wandering which led him to Bern, Geneva, Berlin, Paris and Warsaw, until he found a late home in New York. His sentimental melancholy turned to bitterness as he witnessed the tragedy that overtook the Bundist fellowship to which he had devoted his years between the two world wars. He then condemned God's work as wicked and pitiable. Why dream and strive for a better order, if every peace was but a prelude to war and every revolt brought new distress? The poet saw all about him wrath, hate and tears, the seed of death in every living being and a bitter kernel inside every fruit. In the end, however, he found no refuge save in God and he concluded his *Collected Songs* (*Gezamelte Lieder*, 1952) with the credo: "O God, I know you are with me. You are with me when I think of you. You are with me even when I deny you."

Segalowitch, too, experienced the metamorphosis from early romantic sentimentalism to later, bitter anger at God's world, but, unlike Einhorn, he never reverted to God as his final anchor in his sea of troubles. Segalowitch stemmed from Bialystok, a center of the Jewish textile industry. The pogrom of 1905 drove him forth from his native town and, despite his yearning for rootedness, he was constantly uprooted. Lodz, Warsaw, Odessa, Kiev, Moscow, Tel Aviv and New York were some of his way-stations and each left its impress upon his restless personality.

Young Segalowitch began under the spell of Byronism and Heine's *Weltschmerz*. His poem, *Kazmerzh* (1912), brought him early fame. It wove a tender web of colorful fantasy about an old townlet where piety and only slightly mellowing traditions prevailed. There, the tired soul of the poet dreamed of forest nymphs and the great God Pan. There it longed for the freedom of the open spaces, the loveliness of dew-drunk flowers and the gaiety of singing, laughing Wanda, the Hassid's daughter. But girls like Wanda, full of the joy of life, run off with light-hearted Polish strangers, while Jewish young men, lacking the courage to defy religious taboos, remain with romantic daydreams, nebulous mirages, and the sadness of ages in exile.

Reisele, the shochet's daughter and the heroine of Segalowitch's most popular ballad, also has a carefree, dancing, loving heart like Wanda. However, she lacks the wild courage to resist her angry father, who wants to mate her with a rabbi's son rather than with Motele, the sturdy, gay watchman with whom she shared happy hours. When her father learns of her enchantment with Motele, he cuts off the beautiful curls which make her so entrancing. She can then only muster the pathetic courage to drown herself in the cold waters of the Vistula.

Segalowitch's sentimental poems of love's ebb and flow, of joy seasoned with melancholy, of spring's white blossoms and autumn's golden charm, reach a climax in *Regina* (1915), the idyllic tale of the proud, elegant, mysterious woman, desired, found, lost, retrieved, and forever vanished, but leaving behind her evanescent fragrances and grateful memories. Such a woman arises out of a poet's dreams in the springtime of life, bubbles with overflowing vitality in the glow of summer, and dissolves with the snows of winter.

In the poetic drama *The Wall* (*Die Vant*, 1915), Segalowitch combines militancy with sentimentalism. He condemns the weeping and futile lamenting with which some Jews react to wrongs inflicted upon them. He advocates resistance no matter what the consequences. Though the Jewish hero of this drama dies, he does so sword in hand and thereby rouses the admiration of his aristocratic Polish adversary, who had until then looked upon Jewish girls as free game and who despised Jewish men as cowards and money-grubbers.

The militant tone of Segalowitch, however, did not long endure. He remembered that the Revolution of 1905, in which he participated, ended in anti-Jewish outbreaks. Nor could he wax enthusiastic about the Communist Revolution. Unlike his younger brother Wolf-Hirsh Segalowitch (1890-1937), who cast in his lot with the Soviets, served them faithfully, and was shot by them when the Minsk group of Jewish intellectuals was liquidated, the poet chose in 1919 to exchange Kiev and Moscow for Warsaw, where he survived for an additional three decades.

His years in the Polish capital were his happiest. There he continued to compose lucid, singable lyrics and sentimental stories. There he was idolized by Jewish youth and especially by his women readers. There he presided over the Association of Yiddish Writers and Journalists.

In his book of memoirs, *Tlomazke 13* (1946), he gave a moving, somewhat idealized portrait of the home of this Association, a center of Yiddish culture for more than two decades, before it was reduced to rubble by the Nazis and most of its members burnt to ashes at Maidanek and Treblinka. "Toward evening at a table, sat a group discussing philosophy, poetry, Cabala, and other matters—a little world severed from the great world outside. . . . Often the discussions reached a very high level. Nobody wanted to budge from his seat or to be disturbed by the street's tumult. It might appear as though this were a consultation of conspirators, but actually these people were passive toward all conflicts. They lived in the world and felt the need of discussing everything that went on—everything. And though we ironically called one another idlers, the Association was for us a sort of university where we learned from each other. There was not a theme of contemporary or eternal problems which was not debated at our table."

The writer's club at Tlomazke 13 offered a forum and an audience not only for the Warsaw group but also for visitors from all lands, for poets, actors, sculptors, painters, composers. Non-Jewish writers were received at banquets and brought news of literary events abroad. They came from France and Norway, from Japan and India, from Communist and non-Communist lands.

The first product of Segalowitch's Warsaw period was the lyric cycle *Ripe Grapes* (*Tseitike Troiben*, 1920), in which he converted his delight in passionate love into melodious verses. In these verses there is no thought of yesterday and no fear of a tomorrow; there is only today, or rather tonight, for the enjoyment of the stars in heaven and the women on earth. The poet's ideal is to sing, to drink deep, to burn with love's intense flame until he is entirely consumed.

Within a few years, however, the poet was emptied of his dreams and his ecstasies. Sadness came with its light wings and descended upon him with leaden heaviness. Youth and beauty were gone. The tabernacle he built for earthly divinities was empty. The moments he sought to sanctify through song were unblessed and unanointed. Nevertheless, he still preferred to meander along his own zigzag way, singing of the green earth in springtime and hating nobody, while others were carrying red banners and sharpening swords. At the same time, he feared that the harsh clash of steel would soon drown out his tender tunes. Like all who still lived with sentiments, he was becoming prematurely old, he was growing tired, he was only half-awake.

Segalowitch's forebodings were realized in 1939, when the Germans descended upon Warsaw and he had to run before their battalions. He fled from Warsaw to Lublin, from Lublin to Rovno, from Rovno to Vilna, from Vilna to Kovno. He experienced terror and hopelessness, cruelty and hard-heartedness, or at best indifference. Only fellow Jews, even while themselves in the shadow of death, shared with him their hearts, their blankets, their bits of bread, thus enabling him to survive his many ordeals and ultimately to make his way to Tel Aviv. Then he came to love his Jewish people with an ardor that no longer permitted satiric mocking of their feelings. Then he grew to hate the efficient, cultured Teutonic barbarians with a hatred he never knew earlier.

Segalowitch's wanderings during the first years of the conflict until his coming to the land of his Jewish kinsmen were described by him in the volume *Burning Steps* (*Gebrente Trit*, 1947). But even in the comparative safety of Tel Aviv, he was haunted by the terror of the less fortunate Jews trapped in the Nazi cauldron. Visions of Treblinka pursued him by day and by night until he found emotional release in penning the heart-rending stanzas of the elegy *There* (*Dorten*, 1944). By "there" he meant the hell in which his Jews were being burned, not figuratively but literally, burned by other human beings who were fashioned not in the image of God but in the image of devils.

The elegy is dedicated to Arthur Zygelboim (1895-1943), the heroic Bundist leader who committed suicide in London in order to awaken the world's conscience to the Jewish tragedy in Poland.

In all the poetry of the Holocaust there is no poem, except "The

Song of the Murdered Jewish People" by Yitzkhok Katzenelson (1886-1944), that can compare with Segalowitch's elegy in sheer power and intensity. The sentimental esthete is no longer sentimental and he is sick of estheticism.

After the opening stanzas, in which Jewish life before the Holocaust is nostalgically surveyed, there follow stanzas portraying the heroic three weeks when Warsaw's Jews fought with other Polish citizens to hold off the Nazi avalanche. With the fall of Warsaw, the Jews were at the mercy of gorillas in well-tailored suits, orangutans in uniforms, cravat-wearing tigers. Jews were caged in stifling ghettos, decimated by hunger and typhoid, yellow-badged and branded like cattle. Some fled, only to perish on icy roads, in swamps, at impassable borders, in compulsory labor camps, along the frozen taigas.

The poet poured searing curses upon all who sharpened knives for Jewish throats or who made living a hell for Jews, because of a need for scapegoats. The time of apologies for Jewish mistakes was over. All languages and all dialects needed to be scanned for sufficient maledictions to hurl upon German hangmen, the beasts in human shape who slaughtered their fellow men with the newest slaughter machines. The poet could not understand how stars still continued to shine in silent beauty upon such a world or why a deluge did not wipe out the entire unworthy human race. Talk of victory was in the air, but of what avail would victory be for the millions of Jews whose voices had been silenced for ever? "I plead not to the robber for pity. I weep not before the cold murderer. But I still have a spark of faith and so I ask of a higher power: how can we cross the abyss? How can we forgive ourselves for living on? How can we still talk of humanity and of love? O, Lord of Mercy, have compassion upon us, the mourners. How can we, the lonely, the weak, mourn for so many victims, our brothers and sisters? Let our last prayer be: descend, O Lord, from on high and help us bury our dead, help us weep for them. By the dew of the living grass, by the light of pure dawns, we beg of you, O Lord of Mercy, don't have us say Kaddish for you!"

Segalowitch, in his last years, walked about as a silent skeleton, tall and emaciated, afflicted with tragic memories, having the will but lacking the strength to slap the world in the face. He saw yesterday's torturers attending picture-galleries and listening to symphonic music, and he averted his eyes from them. He wished the entire human race to be annulled, because a race which did not avenge the millions innocently martyred, the children gassed with their mothers, did not deserve to survive. He himself was glad not to have to live on much longer on this planet and was no doubt grateful when death came to him in 1949.

The unanswered cry of Segalowitch as to why such a catastrophic fate was meted out to Jews resounded in the Yiddish poems of martyrs and survivors. Kadia Molodowsky raised this question most poignantly in the introduction to her anthology *Songs of Destruction (Lieder Fun Khurban,* 1962). She, however, found refuge in faith. Above the abyss of pain and despite the incursion of critical reasoning, she continued to intone the words that comforted Jews even on their last walk to the gas chambers: "*Ani maamin,* I believe." Flames could not destroy this eternal faith. She was certain that Jews who had once rearisen from the Valley of Dead Bones, as Ezekiel had foreseen, would also arise from the Valley of Ashes and reconstitute themselves, a free, viable, God-trusting people.

Kadia Molodowsky is generally regarded as the most talented Yiddish poetess. Although she was creative in fiction, drama and criticism, and as editor of the Yiddish literary quarterly *Sviva,* her main contribution has been to the treasure of Yiddish poetry. Her early lyrics and tales in verse were sung in the Yiddish schools of Eastern Europe until these schools and their pupils ceased to be. They were sung in Yiddish classrooms in North and South America. They resounded in excellent Hebrew rendering not only in Israel's kindergartens and elementary schools but also in Ulpanim where they delighted and rejuvenated oldsters. Her later lyrics probed deeper levels of lacerated Jewish hearts.

Born in 1894 in a Lithuanian townlet, the poetess received her first education from her father, who was a Hebrew teacher. She then went on to Warsaw and Odessa in order to prepare herself for a teaching career, which she then practiced for many years.

Her earliest lyrics, begun in 1920 and published in 1927 under the title *November Days (Kheshvendike Teg),* touched the hearts of women, for she sang of their sorrows and motherly tenderness, of cold rainy evenings when children offered comforting warmth, and of sleepless nights when tiny hands dispelled gloomy thoughts. Yet, while her women readers cradled infants and nourished them with full naked breasts, she herself cradled verses in lonely midnights and the children she nourished with her maternal love were the shouting, unruly pupils of her school. She tamed their wildness with the verses of her *Kindermaaselekh,* which were set to music when published in 1930 and which won her widest acclaim.

The uniqueness of these simple poetic tales, full of humor and apparent naiveté, lay in the vivid personification of objects. For her barefooted tots she penned a ballad of a pair of little shoes which a shoemaker hammered into life and sent out into the world to fetch him bread and salt and other necessities. One day the shoes stopped before a door, knocked and entered. There sat a child alone, barefoot, naked, unhappy. There the shoes remained, unwilling to proceed further, and the shoemaker is still waiting for them to return. For her coatless boys and girls, the poetess sang a ballad of a coat that was handed down from Shmulik to Yossel-Behr, to Beele, to Hindel, until it reached Pantel, the youngest child. Unlike his older brothers and sisters, who wore it three years, he proceeded to dismember it piece by piece within a few days. When only the holes were left, he pranced about, happy in his nakedness. For her emaciated pupils, who had to assist their parents with household chores, the lyricist intoned the merry ballad of Olke with the Parasolke, a six-year-old who was constantly called away from play in order to wash, scrub, darn, and mind the baby, but who always managed to get back to imagined flights over radiant roads to far-off places.

Kadia Molodowsky animates the inanimate as do most romantic poets. She gives a voice to things; plates and pots and bottles talk, make demands upon each other, engage in quarrels, suffer casualties. The sun combs Berele's head with a golden comb. A letter journeys to various addresses by train and ship in response to a mother's request for news of her son. A washtub rolls up and down from floor to floor to offer laundering services to a different tenant each day. The poetess is always aware that no adult can fathom, as can a child, what a stone tells the listening sky above it or what the grass in springtime tries to communicate to its graying boss, the gardener.

In 1931, Kadia Molodowsky completed the maturer lyrics of *Dzike Gass,* a Warsaw street inhabited by the poor, the unemployed, the rebels against the social order whose children she taught. She was torn between her conviction that she ought to join the march of the radical sansculottes and her longing for the carefree, joyous spirit of blossoming spring, moonlit fragrances and the green woods beyond the street's horizon. She tried to ensconce herself in an ivory tower. In vain! The call of her starving neighbors penetrated to her. She had to answer their call.

In the poems of *Fraidke* (1935), she depicted the proud, class-conscious laboring men and women of Warsaw, their strikes, their illegal activities, their enforced emigration from their native land. She herself left Poland in 1935. Her odyssey through European countries and on to the United States found poetic expression in the volume *My Native Land* (*In Land Fun Mein Gebein,* 1937). A mood of tiredness was beginning to creep into her exuberant personality as she was forced to learn ever new tongues and to face hate and woe. "There'll be so much to tell: how all the streams are bitter and how all, all yearn to be sweet."

Disappointment awaited her in New York. In the metropolis which had been through the Great Depression, she found sickening commercialism, exploitation and decadence similar to what she had left behind. Without a roof over her head and without a secure haven against hunger, she retreated to the rich fairyland of her dreams. In her verses drawn from the realm of memory, the suffering and cruelty of her Polish past were as effectively erased as are the sting and poison of the bee in the final product of honey. Only beauty, kindness and the warmth of shared friendships remained.

This approach is reflected in her dramatic poem *All Windows to the Sun* (*Alle Fentster Tsu der Zun,* 1938). The eleven scenes center about a child-hero, Boom, and his playmates. Their vivid imaginations transformed little spools to immense railroad trains on which they could travel to romantic lands, far, far away. When Boom grew up, the same inventive talent let him construct a time machine in the form of a tower. This tower enabled its owner to relive historic happenings of earlier years. A demonstration before Sholom Aleichem's broker, Menachem Mendel, and the latter's multimillionaire client, Rothschildowitch, unlocked the injustices of the past. At one moment it showed Copernicus accused of rebellion against God's order by maintaining that the earth was not the stationary center and anchor of the universe, at another it showed Hirsh Lekert's execution in 1902 for his terrorist act in avenging the lashing of Jewish demonstrators in Vilna. Though Rothschildowitch refused to invest in this invention which talked to the conscience of man, salvation would come from other sources.

In 1942, the first novel of the famed lyricist appeared. Entitled *From Lublin to New York* (*Fun Lublin Biz New York*), it was ostensibly the diary of a refugee who had arrived in New York soon after the outbreak of World War II. It included many incidents and observations based upon the author's own privations during her early years of adjustment to the American scene. It was the weakest product of her pen and not until two decades later did she again experiment with the literary medium of the long novel. Her strength lay elsewhere.

The poems of *Only King David Remained* (*Der Melekh David Allein Is Gebliben*, 1946), were mostly written under the tragic impact of the war and the Holocaust. She often dreamed of her Sorolekh and Berelekh, the children trapped in the ghettos. She felt their searing tears, she heard their suppressed moaning. The ghosts of the slaughtered floated before her. In a moving psalm, she implored the God of Mercy to choose another people as victims of his blessings. The desolated house of Israel needed a respite. Every letter of the Ten Commandments had been paid for over and over again by the blood of infants and graybeards. It was time for others to be God's emissaries and for Jews to become simple shepherds, tanners, smiths.

With the founding of the Jewish state, the poetess left for Israel. Her play of 1949 bore the symbolic title *Toward the God of the Desert* (*Nokhn Gott Fun Midbar*). Its heroine was Donna Gracia Mendes, the sixteenth-century Marrano who found her way back to the faith of Israel and who, together with her nephew, the Duke of Naxos, helped settle persecuted Jews of Italy in the Holy Land. In Tel Aviv she edited the periodical *Heim* from 1950 to 1952. Her songs of joy at the restoration of Zion appeared in 1952 under the title *Angels Come to Jerusalem* (*In Yerushalaim Kumen Malokhim*). Now that the dead bones of her people had taken on flesh again, she saw angels helping them lift the stones and drag the sand for the upbuilding of the new Jerusalem. Holy again was the abode of her forefathers, holy the gravel and the earth, the lamb and the goat. All life was blessed once more. The parched, starved, wounded mourners were feeling the sweetness of water, the fatness of corn, the renewed kindness of God.

Returning to the United States, she noted that Jewish children were growing up in a milieu no longer saturated with yearning for Zion, for whom ancestral glories were not alive during waking hours, and whose dreams were not infiltrated with Jewish aspirations for a unique future. She, therefore, undertook in her volume *On the Roads to Zion* (*Oif Die Vegn Fun Zion*, 1957) to retell the tales of Jews who in all eras and from many lands tried to make their way to Israel. Her homecoming heroes ranged from Obadiah of Bertinoro, who in 1488 set out from Italy, to David

Ben Gurion, who arrived in 1906 to till the Palestinian soil and who later became Israel's first prime minister.

In 1957, the poetess collected her narratives, written during the preceding fifteen years, under the title *A House With Seven Windows* (*A Shtub Mit Zibn Fentster*). These fifty-eight short stories may be grouped into tales of the Old Country, tales of immigrants in America, and tales that reach their climax in Israel. Those with an Eastern European background are filled with nostalgia for a vanished world: its devoutness, its integrity, its spirit of mutual help. The American narratives are more critical. They stress the substitution of superficial glamor for traditional values, the erosion of religious habits by materialistic concepts, the loosening of communal and family ties in the relentless drive for personal success. Nevertheless, even in America, the kindness of the Jewish heart reasserts itself. The residue of former, more pious generations dispels the spiritual indolence that darkens the lives of immigrants. A happy ending is generally effected. The author's disillusioned insight into human weakness is brightened by forgiveness and gentleness.

Kadia Molodowsky's ripe lyrics *Lights of the Thornbush* (*Likht Fun Dornboim,* 1965), are characterized by brevity, simplicity and tender suggestiveness. They stir the imagination but calm the emotions. They breathe contentment with God and man. Even death holds no terror for her; she invokes it again and again as a welcome release from the burdens of existence that weigh so heavily. Since the Divine Potter created the human vessel and determined how much of life's foaming wine it may hold, of what avail are protests against one's lot? Let us accept with equal love roses and thorns, praise and blame. In her Jerusalem lyrics, the *Shechina* or Divine Presence spreads its light from the holy city over the entire earth; angels descend from heaven to awaken the dead and to teach children love of Torah; the very stones diffuse grace and light in all directions because they have been washed by tears and purified by suffering. These lyrics were often sung, recited and broadcast over Kol Israel radio, especially after the reunification of Jerusalem in 1967.

In her novel of life in Israel, *At the Gate* (*Baym Toyer,* 1967), the poetess embodied her observations of the idealism and spirit of self-sacrifice which interpenetrated the simple activities of ordinary men and women.

In the 1960's a group of congenial writers and admirers gathered about her. Upon their urging she revived *Sviva,* the organ of prose and verse which she had originally founded in 1943. In its quarterly issues, poets of America and Israel, old masters and young beginners, found a common platform for the discussion of literary problems and for the publication of original literary products.

New York had replaced Warsaw as the center of Yiddish creativity.

15

NEW LYRIC
VOICES IN AMERICA

Menahem Boraisha • Auerbach • Leivick

THE MASS EXODUS of Jews from Eastern European, Yiddish-speaking townlets to North American metropolises, which set in since the 1880's, included at first only a minute proportion of intellectuals. Even most of these were subjected to the purgatory of sweatshops and could devote themselves to literary pursuits merely during periods of unemployment and in spare moments after long, wearisome hours of service to machines. Not until the decade preceding the First World War did "Die Yunge" offer a congenial home and platform for the creative products of young writers and not until after this war did a second group of Yiddish writers, the "Insichisten," join in a manifesto outlining a common literary striving.

There were, however, other writers who kept aloof from coteries and who trod a lonely way through the labyrinth of ideas. They peered into their inner souls and found original modes of expressing what they saw within themselves. Such lyricists were Menahem Boraisha (1888-1949), Ephraim Auerbach (b. 1892) and H. Leivick (1888-1962).

Born in Brest-Litovsk as the son of a Hebrew teacher, Menahem Goldberg came to Warsaw in 1905 and was encouraged by Peretz to publish his first lyrics in Yiddish rather than in Russian. He did so under the name of Menahem, and only much later did he add his mother's maiden name of Boraisha as his adopted name.

These early poems consisted mainly of rhapsodic odes filled with longing for God and Holiness. Some were in the form of prayers in which he wrestled with the Creator of the Universe and begged for a revelation that would make comprehensible the mysteries of heaven and earth, life and death. Others sensed the presence of God in the fire of passion consuming men and women. Still others emphasized the ancestral roots and the tradition-drenched earth that gave sustenance to the poet.

Peretz reminded the aspiring young man that the God of the Jews could not be forcibly dragged down to earth nor exhibited on wooden beams along village roads. Menahem, however, continued to wrestle with God throughout all later years. He never accepted the doctrine of art for art's sake nor could he envisage lyric beauty as an end in itself. Poetry was for him inseparable from religion, philosophy, history. It was for him primarily intuitive apprehension of truth in contrast to the logical apprehension sought by the exact sciences. It was cosmic knowledge welling up from the subconscious in contrast to factual knowledge based on minute observation. It was recovery of the Greater Memory possessed before birth and persisting outside of time—a concept basic to Platonic philosophy.

Menahem did not, however, invoke Plato, Wordsworth or Shelley as his forerunners and allies in this approach to the function of poetry. He found his inspiration in Jewish sources. His symbol for the supreme poet was Moses, to whom the Infinite was first revealed in the Burning Bush. Maintaining that revelation was as legitimate a gate to the realm of the Absolute as were the calculations of reason, Menahem held that in Moses, the most creative of poets, were embodied the powers of revelation, national vision, Messianic faith and the urge to holiness. Menahem's dramatic poem *Moses,* posthumously published in 1950, was the final expression of his religious, philosophic and poetic insight.

Meanwhile, the aspiring lyricist had gone through many disappointments with transitory ideals. The seventeen-year-old youth, who came to the Polish metropolis from Lithuania, was dazzled by the cultural life of Warsaw. He saw in the Poles an ethnic group oppressed by the Russians even as were the Jews. He equated the melancholy of the Poles, which stemmed from a loss of national independence, with his own sadness and that of his coreligionists who were forced to be homeless wanderers. He therefore dreamed of a symbiosis of Poles and Jews. But this dream did not last long. He discovered that the Poles were engaged in an economic boycott against Jews in order to compel the emigration of this unwanted minority. In blistering verses he then hurled lacerating accusations against every sector of the Polish population, until his mentor Peretz had to remind him that it was unseemly to talk to an entire people in such bitter tones. After the appearance of his poem *Poland* in 1914, he left that land.

He arrived in the United States shortly after the outbreak of the First World War. Here too he suffered keen disappointment. Though surrounded by two million Jews in the largest American metropolis, he felt repelled by the growth of secularism among his coreligionists, by their abandonment of long-preserved traditions, by their acceptance of the tinsel values of a commercial, industrial order. For more than a third of a century he was active as a journalist in Yiddish dailies and English weeklies. He participated in Jewish cultural organizations and occupied an influential position in the Joint Distribution Committee and later in the American Jewish Congress. Nevertheless, he remained a lonely wayfarer, ever in search of deepest insight and ever dissatisfied with the fragmentary wisdom within his reach.

To the poems he published in 1920, he gave the symbolic title *Sand,* because he held that Jews were dispersed everywhere like the sand on the seashores. Apparently, it was their fate to wander on and on, buffeted by storms of hate throughout the Old World. Yet, their fate was no less tragic in the New World, even though they did manage to escape from hate and to pioneer successfully. There the mild sun of freedom and the warmth of prosperity melted away and dissolved their Jewishness. Ultimately, as depicted in his poem "By the Sea," only a fenced-in tombstone with a half-faded inscription remained as testimony of a Jew's former presence in an American frontier community. The Jew's Americanized Christian descendants knew him no more. The poet concluded: "At your lone tomb I stand and ask: who will come after us and who will revive our heritage?"

Menahem is melancholy but not pessimistic. He is sad but not nihilistic. He never doubts that there is purpose and direction in this universe of which we human beings are an integral part, but he experiences difficulty in ferreting out the precise meaning implicit in our existence. His main philosophic verse epic, upon which he worked for nine years and in which he recorded his adventures in the realm of ideas, was *The Wayfarer (Der Geher,* 1943). Its motto was taken from a Hassidic dictum: "A saint falls seven times and rises again each time. Man is a wayfarer and not a stationary bit of creation. He must go on from level to level."

Menahem relates the ascent from level to level of Noah, a nineteenth-century Jewish wayfarer, who combines traits and experiences both of the poet and the poet's brooding father.

The odyssey of Noah, the Jewish Faust, begins at infancy. His mother dies at childbirth and his nineteen-year-old father puts him into a knapsack and goes forth with him into the strange world. When the father remarries, the child, unwanted by the stepmother, is shunted back to an uncle. At thirteen, Noah is on his own and resumes his wandering. Thirsting for knowledge of God and all creation, the poor youth must content himself with black bread at charitable tables and with a hard bench at a synagogue for his weary head. In his dreams, however, he consorts with the angels who ascend and descend the ladder that leads to heaven. At sixteen he gets to the court of the Habad Hassidim and immerses himself in cabalistic lore. But he does not drown in this ocean of mysticism.

In the midst of his studies, temptations of the flesh assail him and he escapes from them by marrying, at twenty, a bride of the finest lineage of scholars. His father finds the long-lost son and urges him to settle down as a rabbi in some community and interpret the Jewish law to parishioners. Noah, however, seeks not stability but learning without end. He therefore leaves his wife and child and as a wandering scholar continues to adventure in the realm of reason and then beyond reason. He makes his way past Maimonides and Aristotle. He ascends ever higher on the ladder that leads to perfection.

When the realization comes to him that he ought not to evade family responsibilities, he returns from his distant roaming. He teaches Torah to the children of his pious community but is unable to make a living and suffers from the injustice of the rich and the powerful. Employed as a night watchman, he acquires a better understanding of nature. Creatures of air and earth, who were mute for him hitherto, voice to him their pain, their terror, their joy, their wisdom. Lilith tries to convince him that the flame she kindles in man is not sin but redemption, that she too fulfills God's command, that through her body a path also leads to unity, salvation, eternity.

Noah continues his wayfaring, his questioning, his searching for clarity of perception, for the key that will unlock eternal mysteries and resolve all his doubts. As a salesman, he gains access to homes of the rich and the poor, the virtuous and the sinful, the kind and the hard-hearted, the normal and the abnormal, the dissident and the submissive. His insight grows and deepens but is still inadequate to pierce the mystery at the heart of things.

After reaching an abyss of poverty and after burying his emaciated child, he temporarily experiences a change of fortune and becomes a storekeeper. He makes contact with the Men of Enlightenment, the Russian followers of Moses Mendelssohn. They teach him that Jews must live in harmony with their neighbors, must make concessions, must leave isolation, must interchange ideas. This approach of Mendelssohn, who sought to fashion peace between *tallit* and Cross, loses its glamor, however, when he learns that this philosopher's children ended by embracing the Cross. In a vision he witnesses a similar, earlier approach by Elisha ben Abuya to mediate between the Hebraic and the Roman ways in the days of Bar Kochba, an approach which also failed utterly. When Noah's teacher ends as a convert to the Russian Church, he recognizes the danger of the manna of Enlightenment and betakes himself back to the synagogue and the Talmud.

To the argument of his friends, the Maskilim, that their mentor Mendelssohn did not reject the yoke of the Torah but rather that he brought the Torah with him from the ghetto of provincial Dessau to the intellectual metropolis of Prussia, Noah counters with the question: why then are Mendelssohn's descendants today to be found in non-Jewish cemeteries? His own explanation is that the German reformer did indeed bring the Torah to Berlin but that he left the Jews behind in Dessau. Torah without Jews dies even as Jews cannot survive as Jews without Torah.

Noah's wayfaring again brings him to Hassidic circles. His debate with a widely adored Hassidic *rebbe* does not resolve his doubts. Just as he could not accept the reasoned wisdom of the Maskilim which was not grounded in faith, so too he cannot accept the faith of the Hassidim that is not grounded in reasoned wisdom.

A brief encounter with a Christian missionary leads him to study the New Testament. He finds its insistence upon blind belief in an intermediary between man and God even more distasteful than Hassidic efforts to interpose the *Tzaddik* as such an intermediary. He wants to break through directly to God, who is for him absolute truth and absolute righteousness.

Pursuing his life's quest, he consorts with Socialists and with peasants, the supposedly unspoiled natural creatures. Under the spell of Rousseauism, he seeks salvation in physical labor as a woodcutter. At the hands of his rough fellow workers, he experiences cruelty, beatings, brutality. He learns that whosoever seeks truth must be able to endure torments. Soon thereafter he sees remorse assailing his tormentors and he arrives at the conclusion that, just as the righteous are not wholly righteous, so too the wicked are not entirely evil.

When Czar Alexander II is murdered, Jews are sought as scapegoats. Although the hanged conspirators all bear Russian names, the incited masses are most easily appeased with Jewish blood. Pogroms spread like an epidemic. Noah wonders whether it is a tradition since time immemorial that the robbers remain with their booty and the victims with their hurt. Or whether there is indeed retribution and expiation.

Meanwhile, as a reaction to the massacres, Zionist ideology finds receptive ears in Noah's town. The call of Daniel Deronda for a reconstitution of the Jewish nation on its historic soil of Palestine reaches him. It is followed by Lawrence Oliphant's call to the people of the Bible to return to the land of the Bible. The Jewish magnates fear that endorsement of a Jewish exodus from the pogrom-ridden land might cast doubt upon their own loyalty to their Russian fatherland. Although Oliphant fails to win the rich and the influential Jews to his vision, young Jewish idealists do set out for the Promised Land under the banner of Bilu. Noah joins such a group and gets as far as Istambul. In the course of his weeks of traveling and waiting, however, he has a change of heart. He becomes conscience-stricken when he recalls his abandoned wife and children. He is not as free as his companions of Bilu. They may proceed to carve out a national Jewish existence in the Holy Land. He has no right to shed his responsibilities toward his family; he must return. Nevertheless, this return is not a retreat or a descent. It too is a dedication and a service to his people.

Just as the earth returns every morning to its position of previous mornings and just as the sun returns every spring to its spring location of earlier years, and yet with each return a new day and a new year is born, so too the wayfarer, completing his round of duties and accepting normal responsibilities, was venturing ever further and further on the road to holiness and to an understanding of God's universal order. Noah, the Jewish Faust, who set out in search of knowledge without limit and righteousness without any trace of wickedness, thus ends by accepting the fact that there is a boundary to human knowledge and that there is no righteousness without some taint of evil, or wickedness without some kernel of goodness. A superior power does exist. We must bow to it and do its bidding, even if we do not entirely comprehend its design or purpose.

Menahem Boraisha's philosophic and religious brooding reaches its climax in this epic of a simple individual's efforts to rise to moral eminence and to obtain a glimpse of pure essential truths. During the poet's last years, two other major poems were completed. These reflected new doubts that arose in him during the years of the Holocaust and they reaffirmed his hard-won faith in the meaningfulness of Jewish and human existence.

In one poem, Menahem attempted a moral stocktaking of his own generation. Above the ashes of Warsaw's ruined ghetto, he engaged in a dialogue with his mentor I. L. Peretz, whom he invoked from the Beyond. Both relive scenes of horror, moral degradation, extermination and desperate heroism. They emerge with faith in God and man unshaken.

In *Moses*, a dramatic poem not entirely completed at the time of Menahem's death in 1949, the poet was still engaged in reaching out to God. His Moses had caught a glimpse of the nameless, eternal "I Am" and it became his task to raise his people from slavery in Egypt to holiness in their Promised Land. This task required superhuman patience and fortitude, since physical enslavement had also resulted in moral decay. Though Moses succeeded in bringing his people out of the land of the Pharaohs and in having them sense the nearness of God at Sinai, he could not eradicate their longing for Egyptian fleshpots nor prevent their relapsing into defilement again and again. Besides, in the very effort to uproot evil in their midst, he had to exercise utmost severity and wade in blood. Even the God-intoxicated Moses could not always scourge with the fire of wrath. As a human being he made concessions to human frailties. He yielded on occasion to his people's weaknesses, though less so than his gentler brother, Aaron, for he too was blood of their blood and bone of their bone. The process of evolving a group of liberated slaves into a holy people, God's people, was a gradual process and, after forty years in the wilderness, Moses had only begun it. His successor, Joshua, would continue it and the hundred generations after Joshua would still not succeed in completing it. Yet Moses had set his people on the right path and they would march on and on as the moral vanguard of the human species.

Menahem lived to see the founding of Israel and hailed enthusiastically this historic event. But he also recognized that many physical pitfalls and many moral temptations faced this young state of an old people. Would it strive for normalcy and an end of wayfaring? Or would it continue to pioneer on the road set for

God's people by Moses, the Prophets, and all the later seekers of a moral realm on earth?

These questions were also asked during the same time by Ephraim Auerbach, a poet of no less distinction and originality than Menahem. He also found inspiration in the past of his people and in the present of the reborn Jewish homeland. His longing for Israel was intense throughout half a century of lyric creativity and found repeated expression in his works. But only on rare occasions could he sate this longing by temporarily sojourning there.

Auerbach began as the singer of Bessarabian Jewry. Born in 1892 in the town of Beltz, he could trace his paternal ancestry back to the family of Rashi, the famous biblical commentator. The Auerbach home resounded with song and dance on Sabbaths and holidays. In his youngest years, Ephraim chanted portions of the Bible and Talmud. Soon he learned to insert his own words into rhythmic molds and to find joy and emotional release in creating lyrics. From the age of seventeen, his Yiddish verses and tales were published in Vilna, Warsaw and Odessa.

Auerbach's ancestors had been the town's ritual slaughterers —*shochtim*—for several generations. His father had to yield to family pressure and continued the profession, despite his distaste for it, since it conferred social prestige upon its practitioners in that Orthodox community.

The sensitive poet, however, succeeded in escaping. In his lyrics in *The Red Thread* (*Der Roiter Fodem,* 1927), he wrote how, as a child, he felt the pain of the gentle doves whose throats were slit to provide meat. He heard the moaning of the oxen when the red river of life flowed out of their necks, and he saw their terror-frozen eyes fixed upon him with mute questioning. His joy in dancing with the calf in the springtime was tempered by awareness of the gory end destined for it at the hands of his father.

In 1911, Auerbach left for Warsaw, and a year later, fascinated by Zionist idealism, he joined the pioneers who set out for Palestine. He worked there in Judean colonies until the Turks compelled the evacuation of the young Russian Jewish immigrants to Egypt. He then joined the newly formed Jewish Legion and fought under Josef Trumpeldor at Gallipoli. When he fell ill, he was sent back to Alexandria and from there, in 1915, made his way to the United States, which became his home.

Caravans (*Karavanen*), his first volume of verse, appeared in 1918. A few of its lyrics harked back to idyllic moods of early years along the Dniester, but most dealt with his impressions of Palestine. Included is his farewell to his mother, whom he comforts with the thought that he is leaving a realm of frost and ice for a warm and verdant land, a land always remembered in her devotional prayers, a land where he would not have to trade and haggle but could plant and harvest the almonds about which she sang in her lullabies. An unbreakable thread led from the distant, desolated land of his forefathers to his longing heart. This thread tugged at him until it brought him to Judean shores, caves and hills, well-known to him from dreams and *cheder* memories.

The poet saw the Palestinian landscape with romantic eyes: a shepherd playing on a flute while grazing his flock; the brown Yemenite maiden bearing her earthenware jar to the well; the chanting cameleer swinging past along figtrees; the Arab lover serenading the beautiful Fatima. But Auerbach also sang of the joy of physical labor, his delight in reaping golden barley, cutting grape-clusters from vines, planting saplings for a new forest, and accompanying them with hope and love and a prayer for dew and rain. A youthful freshness permeated these verses, with the word "joy" constantly repeated.

Throughout Auerbach's long career as a poet, he sought out themes, images and thought-associations based on Jewish sources. His subjects ranged from Adam and Cain to contemporary Jewish events. In his early lyrics, the landscape and picturesque figures of Bessarabian Jewish communities fascinated him. In his middle period, the American Jewish experience became important. In his later period, the European Jewish catastrophe and the rise of the Jewish State became an obsession. In his last lyrics, he reverted to Bessarabian Jewry, now annihilated, but which once teemed with vitality and continued to live in his imagination. Despite half-a-century on American soil, he was haunted by the melodies of Beltz. As late as 1963, his poems in the volume *The Steppe Is Awake* (*Vakh Is Der Step*) still dealt exclusively with the cultural milieu of his childhood years in Bessarabia.

Auerbach accepted the basic doctrine of Hassidism that to be a Jew was good per se, and that goodness was synonymous with happiness. In *Pure Is the Old Source* (*Loiter Is Der Alter Kval*, 1940), he contrasted the joy of goodness with the sadness of evil. He held that just as trees obtained their vital essence from deep roots in good earth, so too man derived his sustenance from deep-rooted optimistic faith in justice and goodness. Happy were those who sat in the dwellings of goodness and were warmed by the light of God. Pure was the biblical source and it supplied him with ever new inspiration. Beyond the ageless biblical figures, Auerbach also recalled to life legendary figures ranging from Baal Shem, father of Hassidism, to Hershele Ostropoler, the Jewish Till Eulenspiegel, as well as such picturesque figures of his native Beltz as the Red Flutist and Pusi the Water Carrier.

Auerbach's most cheerful volume of verse was *Ada's Songbook* (*Ada's Liederbukh,* 1934). It consisted of songs composed for his six-year-old daughter Ada and featured as characters the dog Hintl-Vintil, the cat Kitzele-Ketzele, the goat Tzigele-Migele, and the horse Ferdl-Berdl. The poet animated the inanimate: windowpanes smiled, raindrops danced with glee and were scolded by a child for not waiting with their dance until she got home. A halfbaked, half-burned loaf of bread suffered rejection all day long but found appreciation at the hands of a poor, little girl at the close of the day. The girl bought it for a pittance and shared it with her brothers and sisters, all of them singing as they sated themselves with its goodness before dropping off to sleep.

Auerbach's lyrics of the American scene centered about New York. In the volume *The Red Thread,* he sang of the immigrant quarters in more cheerful tones than did his predecessors, Yiddish social poets like David Edelstadt or Morris Rosenfeld. In Orchard Street, located in the heart of New York's Lower East Side, it was not the filth and poverty that he observed but the merry mingling of peddlers and customers, the glances and colorful phrases of man and maid, the play of a bit of sunlight on tousled heads and eloquent beards. In a cycle of fifteen sonnets, he reproduced the mood of the Bowery and its tramps. The denizens of the gutter and sidewalks lived truthfully even if shabbily. Theirs was lucid pain, naked honesty, disillusioned understanding, strange charm. Wallowing in dirt, at the edge of the abyss, they fathomed the deep, pure meaning of human existence.

Under the influence of the European catastrophe, Auerbach composed religious lyrics. In the volume *The Tents of Jacob* (*Yakov's Getseltn,* 1945), he comforted the survivors of the Holocaust and beseeched the mercy of heaven for the Jews, living and dead, all of whom had been purified by their unfathomable suffering. He lamented with his coreligionists who were weeping by the waters of the Vistula and with those who were penned within ghetto walls. He recalled the heroism of the Jewish of Tulchin who, almost three centuries before the revolt of Warsaw's ghetto dwellers, defended Jewish honor against Cossack hordes and died for the sanctification of God's name.

During the War years, sadness engulfed this lyricist of joy, a recurrent weeping in the stillness of the night, a moaning for a generation prematurely cut off from life. Never did he yield to despair, however, or question that all creation was imbued with the Creator's will. As an antidote to despair, he invoked the spirit of Rabbi Nachman of Bratslav from the Beyond and he had this Hassidic sage and storyteller fortify the faith of contemporary disciples by relating to them a still untold tale: the redemption of the Land of Evil by contact with the Land of Goodness.

The Tents of Jacob also contained an adaptation of the Song of Songs, interpreted, in accordance with tradition, as an allegorical dialogue between God and Israel, God's beloved people. In addition, there was a poetic drama based on a legend of Beltz. During the Turkish occupation, cells has been chiseled into the walls of a cave in this town so that it might serve as a prison. Jews regarded this cave with awe and whispered that it led on and on, coming to the surface in the land of Israel. In the first two scenes of the poetic drama, Auerbach depicted the privations of the surviving Jews who escaped annihilation by taking refuge in the dark, damp, dreary cave. But in the final scene, they found the far exit in the land where vines and almonds grew. They emerged from the darkness in which they had long been entombed to the sunlit radiance of the Holy Land, where a new life could blossom for them. There, on their own soil, the remnants of Israel would again plow and sow and reap.

After the founding of the Jewish State, the poet revisited the land which he had first experienced as a young pioneer on the eve of the First World War. His rapture in witnessing in Tel Aviv the first anniversary celebration of Israel's independence was reflected in *The White City*, composed in 1949 and published in a Hebrew-Yiddish bilingual edition in 1960. He recalled the days in 1913 when, barefoot and hungry, he trod the sandy dunes of Tel Aviv, kneaded the loam, and planted the cool shade for the first boulevards. Now the proud, white metropolis was full grown, its colorful populace, drawn from all tribes, was dancing in the streets, and its veterans were heading a Jewish government.

A decade later, in the volume *Golden Sunset* (*Gildene Shkiye*, 1959), he sang a song beyond all his songs, a hymn to his people's return from the thorny roads of exile. He saw the new life blossoming in redeemed towns and villages and he blessed his Bessarabian contemporaries who had found their way to the Emek, Galilee, Jerusalem. He saw himself as the chronicler of the desert generation, doomed to die in the wilderness en route to the Promised Land. Yet, it had been granted him to catch a vision of his reinvigorated, rejuvenated people. "It is evening. I sit beside the Mediterranean. Waves with foaming lips kiss the stones. Here I am a guest, soon to leave. How shall I tie together my here with my there?"

As a late reaper in the Yiddish field, Auerbach was well aware that his rhymes would not set many spirits afire or change the course of galloping events, but perhaps they would brighten a thought in an individual mind or send a moment's thrill through a human heart. This sufficed him in his seventies when, sated with slogans, he sipped sadness drop by drop and found compensation in mating moods to words, ever quieter moods to ever lower-toned words.

After his seventy-fifth year the poet collected the best of his poems in the volume *A Life Between Covers* (*A Lebn Tsvishn Tovlen*, 1968). It included many new poems inspired by Israel. In 1970, he finally came to the Jewish land no longer merely as a guest. He made his home in Tel Aviv. His long odyssey had come to a desired end.

H. Leivick, who was four years older than Auerbach, was the most revered Yiddish poet on the American scene by the mid-twentieth century. He was born as Leivick Halpern in a townlet of Minsk Province. In America he changed his name to H. Leivick upon the publication of his first book in 1918 in order to avoid being confused in the minds of readers with M. L. Halpern, poet of "Die Yunge," then at the crest of fame.

Leivick was the oldest of nine children. His parents, who could barely eke out a living, sent him forth at the age of ten to study at a Yeshiva away from home and to provide for himself as best he could. During the next four years he experienced hunger, sickness, and dependence upon the good graces of kind householders who provided him with meals several days each week. But in these maturing years he also acquired a vast store of knowledge, traditional and secular, and was infected with forbidden, socialist ideas. He was seventeen when the Revolution of 1905 broke out and he joined the Bund. When this Jewish socialist organization fell under the Czarist ban after the suppression of the Revolution, he continued to participate in its illegal demonstrations and conspiratorial activities. He suffered his first arrest early in 1906 and his second arrest later in the same year. There followed three months of solitary confinement in his birthplace and two years of imprisonment in Minsk while awaiting trial. He endured chains, lashings, a hunger strike lasting seven days, but his spirit was unbroken. At his trial, he refused to defend himself. When the judge asked him if he wanted to make any statement before sentence was pronounced, he asserted that he was fully aware of what he was doing when he joined the Jewish revolutionary Bund and that he would continue to do everything in his power to overthrow the Czarist tyranny and its bloody judges and hangmen. The judge silenced him and condemned him to four years imprisonment with hard labor and lifelong exile to Siberia.

While in jail, witnessing the mistreatment and hanging of fellow prisoners, he wrote his first rebellious and compassionate drama, *The Chains of Messiah (Die Kehten Fun Moshiakh, 1908)*, in which he voiced his longing for a savior who would redeem mankind. According to Jewish folklore, the Messiah was chained by angels upon the command of God in the third night after the destruction of Jerusalem's Temple. In Leivick's version, the angel Azriel revolted against this command. He refused to join the other angels in carrying it out and in singing hymns of praise to the Almighty, while the desolated earth was groaning under the burden of suffering. He was prepared to forfeit heaven's bliss for the deeper experience of sharing in man's woe. Defiantly he hurled back his angelic wings and accepted a human lot: to roam through the earthly sphere and to work for the liberation of the Messiah. He was joined by the prophet Elijah, who had once ascended to heaven on a chariot of fire but who also returned to earth in order to comfort man during generations of suffering with the assurance of glorious salvation as soon as the human heart would be cleansed of evil. Leivick stressed in this early Messianic drama that, if all the dispersed of Israel would continue to call for Messiah, they would ultimately succeed in freeing him from his chains and usher in the Messianic age.

After Leivick's four years of hard labor came to an end, he was attached to a transport of convicts and forced to march for months through steppes and wild forests until he arrived in a village of Eastern Siberia, along the banks of the Lena River. Escape seemed impossible from a region more than a thousand miles from a railroad. There winters lasted more than nine months and admitted but a few hours of daylight. Nevertheless, young Leivick managed to escape by evading the authorities, acquiring a horse and sled, and traversing the frozen Siberian tundra until he reached a railroad station. He was then helped to get out of Russia.

He arrived in New York penniless in the summer of 1913. His first years as an unskilled immigrant were difficult. He spent almost two decades toiling throughout the day with brush and paste as a paper-hanger in New York's apartments, until tuberculosis compelled him to give up this work. But his evenings were devoted to poetry and the writers of "Die Yunge" hailed him as one of their adherents.

His first published volume of lyrics, *Locked In* (*Hintern Schloss,* 1918), dealt with his harrowing experiences abroad and his first years in the land of political freedom and economic exploitation. In these poems his perennial themes came to the fore: the universal prevalence of pain and the expectation of purification through pain; the silence that accompanied sorrow and the joy that inhered in self-sacrifice; the loneliness of each creature and the need to reconcile oneself to this loneliness; the radiance in every human heart and the search for a key to unlock this radiance.

In four long poems, written under the impact of the pogroms that followed the Russian Revolution, Leivick raged at man's inhumanity to man. In one poem, entitled *He* (*Er,* 1918), the author was visited by an unexpected guest, obviously Jesus, who complained about his mother behaving unmotherly, insisting upon her virginity, and worshipping her own son as if he were an idol. Temples were being built to him as the savior, and yet he felt more at home in cellar-dwellings. His brow was being crowned with diamonds and he was being stifled with incense. He cannot stand this idolatry. He does not want to be exceptional in a world filled with pogroms and with commands to murder. He is tempted to prove he is human by cutting the throat of his own mother. The poem voiced Leivick's despair of the Christian world and he depicted its symbol as sick, epileptic, blood-intoxicated, spiritually paralyzed.

In another long poem, *The Wolf* (*Der Volf,* 1920), Leivick has a rabbi arise from a mound of ashes as the sole survivor of a massacred Jewish community. Looking about him the rabbi sees neither victims nor victors. The victims have perished and the victors have moved on. Only ashes, smouldering chimneys, and uncanny silence surround him. He burrows in the mound to find the limbs of the perished Jews so that he could bury them in a Jewish cemetery. In vain! Naught is left of them but coal and ashes. When night descends upon the ravaged, deserted town, the Rabbi creeps away to the forest and is gradually transformed into a werewolf. Later on, when Jews, expelled from other communities, find their way to this town and seek to rebuild the devastated houses and the synagogue of which only bare walls remain standing, they ask the rabbi, when he reappears, to resume religious services. But he insists that the ruins be retained as a memorial for his dead generation and that the synagogue be not rebuilt. He himself does not want to live on. He howls as a wolf through the nights and terrorizes the new inhabitants. On Yom Kippur he invades the synagogue as a werewolf and finds release from his suffering when he is beaten to death. Then the newcomers need no longer fear this last survivor whose existence was bound up with his murdered generation. They can resume the reconstruction of a new communal life. This poem was regarded, after the Hitler catastrophe, not as Leivick's reaction to Petlura's pogroms but as a prophetic vision of the later and greater extermination of Jews by their Christian neighbors.

The bloody deeds of the revolutionary and post-revolutionary years, the degradation of his socialist ideal by the Bolsheviks' use of brutal means, filled the poet's heart with sadness. Messiah obviously had not yet come; the world was in the grip of a Golem. From 1917 to 1920, Leivick worked on his most famous poetic drama, *The Golem.*

The Golem, a robot, automaton or homunculus, recurring in Jewish folklore since biblical times, became, for Leivick, the symbolic personification of the physical force that sought to bring about a Messianic order in an age when the human spirit was still impure and unready. The legend of the Golem as the physical protector of the Jews against their assailants was associated with sixteenth-century Prague and with Rabbi Loew, better known as the Maharal (1513-1609). The helplessness of the Jewish minority, entrapped in the midst of hostile populations, led it to imagine a savior who could have the power to strike back effectively in an hour of the greatest need. Such an hour came to Prague when a false accusation of ritual murder threatened to wipe out the entire community. Then the revered rabbi, well versed in cabalistic conjuring, was believed to have brought the clay image of the Golem to life and to have sent it forth to discover and punish the real murderer and the maligners of the Jews.

Leivick's *Golem* does not aim so much at vivifying a past era as rather to use an historical legend in order to cast light upon his contemporary world with its Utopian and apocalyptic overtones, its efforts at mass redemption and its responsibility for mass tragedies. His Golem is the dull, inert body, into whom the life of the spirit has been injected by the Maharal. During the many generations while the clay was dormant, the spirit had wandered about lost in space. Nevertheless, when the hour of its entry into the body arrived, the spirit begged to be allowed to remain in the shadowy realm. It feared to exchange the calm dark stillness of the unborn for the restless turbulence of streets and people. It forewarned that, wherever its powerful foot would tread, desolation might ensue and that, whenever it would let its mighty fist descend on things, these might turn to dust and ashes. To animate the Golem meant to unleash brute force. The Maharal, however, thought that the time was not yet ripe for the true Messiah whom Elijah was ready to bring forward. The Messiah was too gentle for the harsh tasks which still had to be completed in the pressing emergency. The iron strength of the Golem was more suitable for repelling the peril that threatened the Jewish community. He soon learned, however, that no living creature could be used merely as a means to an end. The rabbi wanted a robot who dwelt in darkness and brought light to others, a servant who obeyed every command and asked no questions. But the moment a robot was granted a soul, it could not be prevented from developing a will of its own or from experiencing sadness, restlessness, loneliness, and a yearning for love. Others might need it solely as a temporary savior able to answer force with greater force. But once it had been taught to strike with its axe and to spread havoc, it continued on a wild rampage, killing friends and foes, and even threatening the Maharal himself, until it had to be stopped in its thoughtless frenzy. The Maharal, who had hoped to undo injustice, saw his emissary and creature cause new injustice. In the end, he had to deprive the Golem of the breath of life and return its limbs to inertness.

Leivick was horrified at the cost in blood and cruelty exacted by the Communist Revolution. He could not reconcile himself to the revolutionary Golem as the long anticipated Messiah. He therefore had the true Messiah appear in the play as a young beggar in the company of Elijah, an older beggar. Both roamed about unheeded and, when recognized by the Maharal, were chased away by him. Their age had not yet dawned, their love was still unwanted and undeserved. Human hearts were not yet cleansed of evil, suffering had not yet reached sufficient magnitude to renovate the human species.

Leivick's symbolic drama was followed by more realistic plays during the 1920's. Maurice Schwartz successfully staged *Rags* (*Shmattes*) in 1921, a social drama which reached a climax in the strike of ragged Jews in a shop where rags were being collected and cleaned. The great actor was less successful a year later when he brought to the stage of the Yiddish Art Theater Leivick's play *Otherwise* (*Andersh*).

After a trip to the Soviet Union in 1925, during which Leivick was welcomed by its Communist writers as a Fellow Traveler, he completed the social drama *Shop* (1926), in which Jacob Ben Ami starred, and the revolutionary drama *Hirsh Lekert* (1927), which was produced on the Yiddish stages of Moscow, Odessa, and Kharkov, as well as in Poland and South America. The hero of the latter play was a Vilna shoemaker who was hanged for attempting to assassinate the Governor of Vilna Province in 1902. Hirsh Lekert's deed was immortalized in a widely sung folk ballad and was also dramatized by the Soviet writer Aaron Kushnirov.

In 1929, at the height of Leivick's popularity with the Communists, he broke with them, because they justified the Arab massacre of the defenseless Jews of Hebron as an act of liberation from colonialism and imperialism. His Leftist admirers then labelled him a traitor to their cause. He reacted by writing the psychological drama *Chains* (*Kehten*, 1929), in which he questioned whether any desirable end justified the use of ignoble means and whether the desire to further the general good justified inflicting hurt upon individuals.

The hardships to which the poet was subjected during the following years of economic depression and mass unemployment aggravated his incipient tuberculosis and compelled him to spend the years 1932 to 1936 in the Denver Jewish Sanatorium. These were years of intense physical pain and highest spiritual elevation. Being cut off from all distractions and disturbances, he could concentrate purely on essentials of the spirit. Looking death in the face daily, he overcame its terrors. In his *Ballad of Denver Sanatorium* (1934), he sang of the holiness and heroism of a fellow patient who came there at sixteen and who remained cheerful and considerate throughout fifteen years of deteriorating health. In Denver he completed his *Comedy of Salvation* (*Geula-Komedia*), his *Songs of Paradise* (*Lieder Fun Gan-Eden*), his biblical dramas

Sacrifice (*Die Akede*) and *Sodom,* and his medieval drama of martyred love *Abelard and Heloise.*

The *Comedy of Salvation* may be regarded as a sequel to the *Golem.* Though it deals with tragic dilemmas, it bears the appellation "Comedy," because, like Dante's *Divine Comedy,* it ascends from an inferno to a happier state of being.

The inferno is our earth in its pre-Messianic state. Though the action takes place in the remote future, bloodshed and warfare still darken our planet. The Golem, who was lying in the Prague attic for centuries after the Maharal had deprived him of motion and vitality, finally aroused himself from the paralysis of inertness. He yearned for a Messiah who would release him from his dull Golem condition and transform him to a pure human being. But the earth was still in the grip of evil. It was the battleground for the forces of Gog and Magog. Two Messiahs appear upon the scene, the power-hungry, unholy Messiah of the House of Joseph and the pure-hearted, love-imbued, holy Messiah, offspring of David. Both aim at a better world but the former seeks to achieve it by the methods of a Stalin and the latter by the methods of a Gandhi. The former leads the underprivileged masses in the battle against Magog, but hardly is he victorious when again there arises out of the midst of his followers a division between the newly sated individuals and the still hungry hordes, between the sycophants who know how to exploit the new opportunities and the less adroit persons who have to submit to further restrictions. The savior of the House of Joseph becomes drunk with achieved power. He who was hailed as the apostle of a social revolution that promised justice to all persons fails to carry out his promise. He who proclaimed salvation from bloodshed continues to shed blood. He ends by persecuting his gentler ally, the Messiah of the House of David. The latter alone feels the pain and the terror of the tortured and the slain, whether of the righteous or the unrighteous camp. For, is not the blood of Gog and Magog also blood? Though the entire world may condone liquidation of opponents as a political necessity, the longed-for, true Messiah cannot. The true savior embodies the conscience of the world and bears responsibility for all that happens everywhere. The true redeemer will, therefore, be the last to be redeemed, when man will be truly human and not merely animated matter.

Abelard and Heloise (1934) dramatized martyred love, ascetic love that endured faithful through the years, pain-filled love that paved the way for liberation from the corporeal and for ascent to pure compassion and moral responsibility.

This compassion and moral responsibility seemed to have been swept away during the Hitler-years when an avalanche of terror and horror descended upon Europe. Apparently Satan had seized God's throne, and a poet in his helplessness could merely weep for the victims and curse their executioners. He wondered that God was not ashamed to want to live on after man had become hitlerized. The poems of the war years were collected by Leivick in the volume *I Was Not in Treblinka (In Treblinka Bin Ikh Nit Geven*, 1945). He felt guilty for not having been among the tortured and gassed in this death-factory. He was still alive while his own sister, his brothers, their families and six million other Jews had perished. What poem of his could reproduce the agony and the last throes of the men, women and children locked in gas-chambers? Every day was bringing news of additional atrocities and increasing horror. The poet could do nothing to lessen the suffering of the doomed Jews. He could at best identify with them and agonize with them from a safe distance. But was that enough? Was it not sinful on his part to seek comfort in words and rhymes? Perhaps the time had come for singers like himself to be mute. Their muteness might make a greater impact. God too had been struck dumb after Maidanek and Treblinka. In a vision the poet saw God enter his room at night in the figure of a tired, mute beggar from whose brow dripped red drops and whose mien was that of a suppliant pleading for forgiveness after having let human dogs devour Israel's progeny. But the poet could find no word of pardon for such a God. The Nazis were merely tools in the hands of the Creator and the real accounting for amassed guilt must be made with the Creator himself. But, alas, the witnesses that could call the Lord of the Universe to account were now mounds of ashes. Noting the indifference of other peoples to the continuing slaughter of the Jewish people, he despaired of arousing the conscience of the world. It was up to the Jews themselves to organize resistance and to avenge the blood of the innocent.

In his poetic drama *Maharam of Rothenburg*, completed in 1944, Leivick drew parallels between German persecutions of Jews in the fourteenth century and similar events of the twentieth. The Maharam (1220-1293), a famed rabbinical authority and head of a Yeshiva, was thrown into a dungeon and a high ransom was demanded for his release. Though his community was prepared to accede to the demands of the extortioners, the Maharam refused to let them do so in order not to set a precedent for the seizure of other rabbis and holding them for ransom. He remained in prison for seven years and died there. Leivick saw in the resistance of this medieval martyr to German mistreatment the Jewish pattern that should prevail in Nazi Germany. The drama opened in Dachau's concentration camp but the following six scenes took place in thirteenth century Mayence. The poet let Ahasver, the immortal Wandering Jew, transport Daniel, the Dachau prisoner, to the medieval German Jewish community and had this young Jew participate in the happenings of the earlier era. In the meeting of the tortured contemporary prisoner and the Maharam, the continuity of Jewish martyrdom and Jewish self-sacrificing resistance was stressed. When the Maharam was asked what status should be assigned to teachers who taught Jewish children swordsmanship, he replied: "The same status as those who teach them Torah." Jewish children must learn to defend Jewish honor and must prove to enemies that wickedness shall not prevail.

When the war ended, Leivick was delegated to visit the surviving Jews in Displaced Persons' Camps in the American Zone of Germany. He made a tremendous impression upon them. His own reaction to this encounter with newly liberated inmates of Maidanek, Treblinka and Fernwald was recorded in a prose volume of 1947, in the lyrics of the cycle *In Fire,* and in the dramas *A Wedding in Fernwald (A Khassene in Fernvald,* 1949) and *In the Days of Job (In Die Teg Fun Iov,* 1953).

The theme of the former play was the first Jewish wedding in the refugee camp at Fernwald. In the marriage of two liberated survivors whose earlier mates had been dragged away to death, Leivick sought to symbolize the beginning of a new Jewish existence that would again flourish over the ruins of the old. In the latter play, he reverted to his perennial theme of the meaningfulness of martyrdom. Job, who was upright and eschewed evil, but who nevertheless was made to suffer far more than the wicked, was seen by Leivick to be the forerunner of all later Jewish martyrs. The dramatist was struck by a Talmudic passage which asserted that Job might have lived in the days of Isaac. This passage gave Leivick the inspiration to bring together these two victims of God's testing.

The radiant deity, who directed Satan to test Job, was seemingly unmoved by the victim's suffering and expected the pious man to endure without whimpering. Satan, however, did not relish the role assigned to him. He had been at Moriah when

Isaac lay on the altar gazing with horrified eyes upon the knife
wielded by Abraham in religious frenzy. Was not such a deed
commanded by God more reprehensible even than his own more
recent mangling of Job's healthy body? Moreover, even if Isaac's
flesh was miraculously spared at the last moment, would not his
soul forever bear the scars of this agonizing experience? Leivick
had seen many scarred souls among the survivors who had been
redeemed from death at the last moment at Treblinka. They had
relived Isaac's ordeal.

The dramatist, therefore, had Isaac leave Abraham's peaceful
tent in Beersheba upon hearing of Job's suffering in the distant
land of Uz. Together with the blind, the lame, the crippled and
the leprous, Isaac made his way to the afflicted crier in the night
who was demanding a reckoning of God. Job became the spokesman of all the misshapen, underprivileged, beaten creatures. He
wanted the supreme overlord to justify himself. If their suffering
was indeed punishment for guilt, then God was at least equally
guilty for subjecting them to temptation and leading them on to
sin. If God's omnipotent will ruled the world, then God also willed
sin, cruelty, misery and bloodshed. Once the question which Isaac
had not dared to ask on Moriah was opened up by Job, others
joined in, from the sick and disabled human beings to the over-
burdened camel and the becudgelled donkey. The sacrificial ram
whose throat had been slit in lieu of Isaac's throat asked this son
of Abraham how it was possible for one who had just seen the
knife poised above his own throat to sacrifice gleefully another
creature soon thereafter. Must not each of us feel some sort of
responsibility not alone for the pain we ourselves caused but also
for the pain inherent in all existence and whose author was God?

Leivick refused to accept the facile answer that in the long run
the Lord requited all pain with joy and compensated for all the
wrong that he seemingly caused. For, not even God could undo
what had once been done. Assuming that the Lord of Heaven and
Earth could resurrect children who had been hurled into the
flames and reduced to ashes, there was no way for him to obliter-
ate the agony they experienced as they were being consumed in
the fire.

Satan, the eternal critic, was not satisfied with the answer that
God, speaking out of the whirlwind, gave to Job. The Lord's recital
of the grandeur of natural phenomena sidestepped and did not
really refute the powerful accusations hurled against the moral
structure of the world he created. Perhaps there was no answer

that was logically supportable. However, beyond the realm of logic and beyond the spirit of scepticism personified by Satan, lay the realm of faith and the spirit of trust.

The dramatist, therefore, had Satan in the end bow before the Lord and plead for his own annihilation, thus leaving the field to Isaac and Job, both of whom had been seared but not broken by pain. These sufferers were prepared to bind up each other's wounds, to rebuild their lives on the basis of faith and love, to plow and to sow again the desolated earth so that it might bear more wholesome fruit for less turbulent generations.

After this drama of Job's tribulations and retention of faith, Leivick wrote no more plays but he did succeed in completing two volumes of verse before he himself was afflicted by paralysis and physical pain which kept him on an invalid's bed for four years until he was released by death in 1962.

A Leaf on an Apple Tree (*A Blat Oif An Epelboim*, 1955) contained a selection of the lyrics he wrote between 1946 and 1954. The title stemmed from his vision of a tree rich in apples and leaves. He imagined its saying to them: do not be afraid at the end of the summer when you have to fall away; you will come back again next year. The volume was filled with verse meditations on the destiny of man and of man's common bonds with nature and all that lived, yearned, suffered and vibrated with mysteries. It also included repercussions of his second trip to Israel in 1950. The poet had been there for the first time in 1937 and had then composed a cycle of lyrics under the title *There Where the Cedars* (*Dortn Vo Die Tseder*). He came for the third and last time in 1957 to participate in the Ideological Conference convoked by Ben Gurion in Jerusalem. His address on that occasion was greeted by a tremendous ovation. It gave rise to animated discussion in the Yiddish and Hebrew press everywhere. It was included in the posthumous volume *Essays and Orations* (*Essaien Un Reden*, 1963). While hailing the miracle of Israel's sovereignty on its ancient soil, he warned against the negation of the Galut and its millennial achievements. The State of Israel was not the beginning but the continuation of Jewish historic experience. A Jew who returned to Israel from exile lived at peace with himself but he had no right to claim moral superiority over his fellow Jews who remained in other lands. A Jew who spoke Hebrew should not downgrade the Yiddish of his kinsmen, the language of the Baal Shem, Nachman Bratslaver, the heroes of the Warsaw Ghetto Uprising, the radiant martyrs of Hitler's gas chambers, the creative writers who erected through their precious works the strongest bulwark against assimilation.

During this final trip to Israel, the elegiac singer struck up cheerful melodies. He dreamed in the golden silence of Jerusalem's dawning and in the blue silence of its nights about the long lost paradise of his people which could again be won. In the City of Holiness, the white-haired, tired wanderer at last experienced peace, joy, supreme beauty, and a new youth. His last poems of Israel were included in the volume *Songs to Eternity* (*Lieder Tsum Eybikn,* 1959). In these twilight poems, the poet curbed his earlier rebellion against the destiny allotted to him and his people. He sought refuge in the faith that good would somehow be the final end of evil, a faith that did not come easily to him. As the greatest Yiddish poet and dramatist of his generation, Leivick absorbed and expressed its tragic reality, its dream of salvation, and its emergence to new hope. He helped to shield the Jewish personality from decay.

16

INTROSPECTIVISM

Insichism • Glanz-Leyeles • Glatstein • Minkoff •
Lewis • Ludwig • Blum-Alquit • Stodolsky • Kurz
• Shloime Schwartz • Licht • Heisler • Alef Katz

THE INTROSPECTIVE movement in poetry, for which the Yiddish designation is "Insichism," arose in 1919, when the three young poets Aaron Glanz-Leyeles (1889-1966), Jacob Glatstein (1896-1971) and N. B. Minkoff (1898-1958) agreed upon a common program and upon the founding of the literary organ *In Sich* for the propagation of their credo and the publication of their works and those of allied spirits.

Older poets, such as Yehoash and H. Leivick encouraged them. Soon there rallied to their standard the young immigrant poets Eliezer Blum-Alquit (1896-1963), Bernard Lewis (1889-1925), Kalman Heisler (1899-1966), Reuben Ludwig (1895-1926), Jacob Stodolsky (1890-1962) and Alef Katz (1898-1969). Contributors to later issues of *In Sich* included the poets J. I. Segal (1896-1954), Michel Licht (1893-1953), Eliezer Greenberg (b. 1896), A. Lutzky (1894-1957), Aaron Kurtz (1891-1964), Shloime Schwartz (b. 1912), Celia Drapkin (1888-1956), Esther Shumiacher-Hirshbein (b. 1899) and Anna Margolin (1887-1952). Shortly before *In Sich* ceased publication in 1940, the first writers of a still newer group known as "Young Vilna," Abraham Sutzkever (b. 1913) and Leiser Wolf (1910-1943), made their American debut in its monthly issues. By then, the original founders of the movement had matured, had discarded flamboyant proclamations, and were engaged in defending their non-political devotion to art against the onslaughts of aggressive so-called proletarian poets.

The American Yiddish lyric had been in a state of revolt against

311

traditionalism since 1907, when "Die Yunge" had challenged the social and moralizing poets dominant during the pioneering generation and had succeeded in emancipating the Yiddish muse from servitude to anarchist and socialist causes and in replacing utopian visions, calls to revolution and sweatshop elegies with the reproduction of individual moods and longings. Now a lyric group, younger than the "youngsters" of a dozen years earlier, was demanding attention.

In contrast to "Die Yunge," who had emphasized art for art's sake and who had sought to communicate faithfully impressions that impinged upon them from the world without, the new group of Insichism stressed poetry as the expression of emotionalized thought or intellectualized emotion and sought to reshape and to reinterpret the environment in accordance with the individual's *Gestalt* or psychic configuration.

Introspectivism meant peering into oneself. The Insichists wished to give a structure to the chaotic multiplicity of phenomena, an organic form based upon their own uniqueness. Their earliest manifesto of January 1920 proclaimed: "The world exists for us only insofar as it is mirrored in us, insofar as it touches us. The world is a non-existent category, a fiction, if it is not related to us. It becomes a reality only in us and through us."

Leyeles questioned the existence of an objective world. Even if such a world did exist in some chaotic, amorphic way, we could not possibly know it. All we know is ourselves. It is our soul that organizes the chaos. We operate or recreate the world in our image. In us are all worlds, past, present and future. What we see within ourselves is the only truth for us.

Minkoff, too, despaired of objective reality. He did not trust facts. He sought the truth behind and beyond the facts. "All that we see with our eyes has deceived us. We no longer believe in the reality of the world about us. We believe only in what our inner will can create. This is our true world." He therefore called upon poets to find their way through the chaos of apparent facts to the absolute, dazzling, creative clarity which pulsated in their innermost being.

The Insichist concept of poetry as the expression of a poet's inner panorama, no matter how kaleidoscopic, contradictory or unclear it might be, paralleled the egocentric formulation of the Expressionists dominant in Central Europe during and after World War I. Like the Expressionist poets, the Yiddish group found existing metrical and stanzaic patterns too confining. The inner

melody of a poem was for them the essential element. They therefore preferred to experiment with free verse as practiced in American poetry from Walt Whitman to Amy Lowell. They felt that
every lyric must have its own individual rhythm.

If a poet wrote about a subway, about the sand of the sea in
summer, and about his love for a girl in the same rhythm or meter,
then at least two of his poems must be false, probably all three.
Without entirely rejecting the straitjacket of regular rhythms, the
Insichists believed that free verse could better reproduce the
accelerated, irregular, noisy tempo of the metropolis and the
machine civilization. Seeking to narrow the boundary between
prose and verse, they refused to accept rhyme as an essential
ingredient, but they were willing to use it for special effects in
combination with free verse, even as Vachel Lindsay, whom they
admired, was using it.

Although the Insichists called also for a widening of the lyric
horizon to include any and every subject, and although they
claimed the urbanization of the Yiddish lyric as one of their
supreme achievements, their chief contribution resided in innovations of style and not of content: their creation of ever newer and
subtler rhythms, their concentration on essential traits rather than
heaping of detail upon detail, their emphasis on the simple word
rather than the decorative one, their stress on the exact, sculptured
phrase and the concrete, sharply delineated image rather than the
dreamy diffusiveness preferred by their Impressionist forerunners.

Aaron Glanz, who in 1914 adopted the pseudonym of A. Leyeles
for his verse but not for his prose, was the oldest member of the
Insichists. In 1905, at the age of sixteen, he emigrated from
Poland to London in search of higher education and four years
later he continued on to New York. During his student years at
Columbia University, from 1910 to 1913, he obtained a thorough
knowledge of American literature. Afterwards he proved, by his
superb renderings of Edgar Allan Poe's "The Raven," "Annabel
Lee," and other lyrics, his ability to translate complex English
rhythms into equally effective Yiddish rhythms.

His first original volume, *Labyrinth* (1918), showed the influence of the American Modernists but also his mastery of intricate
traditional forms. It preceded the founding of Insichism and did
not spurn Impressionistic effects. In one poem, "Rain," he aimed
at imitating in trochaic dimeters the harsh fall of heavy raindrops.
In another poem, "Snow," he sought to reproduce in trochaic
stanzas of varying lengths the soft fall of snowflakes. In "Noc-

turne," he tried to convey through an accumulation of adjectives the mood of night—a mood of weariness, satiety, melancholy, uncanniness, ghostliness. In "Rest" he joined various colors from pale blue and pale violet to orange and tender rose, and various images from a soft sofa with silversilken cover to dying flowers and medieval magic, in order to create a unitary impression of autumnal tiredness.

Leyeles, however, also sang in strident tones of the sights and sounds of New York, its haste and confusion, its Bowery figures and asphalt pavements, its streetcars and granite skyscrapers. His subject-matter was universal rather than specifically Jewish, with the single exception of his final poem, "Yehuda Halevi." This poem related the story of the medieval Sephardic minstrel's longing for his ideally envisaged Zion and his death at the gates of Jerusalem when he attempted to realize his dream.

In the lyrics of *Young Autumn* (*Yungharbst,* 1922), the Introspectivism of Leyeles was full grown. When he now composed a new poem on "Snow," he sought to capture in images the essence of a mound of snow and not the temporary mood it evoked. As he compressed the frosty whiteness of the snow in his hand, he felt its soul running down in cold tears. This evoked the image of an expired infant whose mother was still wiping the last tears from its pale, chilled cheeks. When he now composed a 'Nocturne," the emphasis was on images and thought associations that spanned many years and not on the immediate impression of a New York night under the cold shimmer of an electric lamp. The subjects of Leyeles now ranged from cats and worms, chaos, madness and pogroms, to maidens with musical, exotic names by the shores of the Ganges, along the sands of the desert, and within the harems of fabled Samarkand. Free verse was now his normal medium.

As the chief theoretician of Insichism, Leyeles continued throughout later decades to battle for his concept of poetry as rhythmically disciplined thinking, feeling, experiencing. He prefaced his lyric volume *Fabius Lind* (1937) with a vigorous restatement of his creed.

Fabius Lind, the title hero, is Leyeles. In him are commingled two main streams which had their origins in Lodz and in New York. His ancestry and childhood experiences molded him into a Jewish personality to whom every aspect of his people's past and present was precious. But his adult years were spent in the American metropolis. Hence New York also became his spiritual no less than his physical home. He loves and sings of its teeming life from the Battery and Bowery to Crotona Park and Bronx Park. If he reacts in anger and in sadness to Hitler's anti-Jewishness, he reacts no less intensely to the hurt inflicted upon America by reactionary forces. He cannot cavort in the roundelay of carefree life as do others. He dreams throughout his days and nights of a non-existent utopian land and of human beings as they should be and not as they are.

Jews, whom others despise and drag through horrors, come closest to his ideal of man because amidst their suffering they still scorn the might of their oppressors. For a brief moment he puts his faith in the Birobidjan pioneers as symbols of Jewish rejuvenation in the land of the Soviets. But he is quickly disillusioned by Stalinist reality. He is no less shocked by American injustice and laments the fate of Sacco and Vanzetti in a poem of 1927, the year of their execution. His disappointment with America, however, is only temporary and he emerges with renewed faith in America's historic ideals, a faith he documents most eloquently in the lyrics of *America and I* (*Amerika Un Ich*, 1963).

The lyrics of *A Jew at Sea* (*A Yied Oifn Yam*, 1947) were composed mainly under the impact of the Jewish catastrophe in Eastern Europe. This catastrophe cries out in him. He is ashamed to walk in the sunlight along the banks of the Hudson while his kinsmen were being ground to dung along the Vistula. He is pursued by nightmares of the horror being perpetrated at Maidanek and Treblinka. After a moment of weakness in calling for vengeance upon those who desecrated the face of man, he recovers and calls upon the surviving Jews to react rather in typically Jewish fashion to the evil which has spread over the globe—by becoming better, purer, holier.

A verse preface to this volume opens with the line: "In the beginning was the melody." Only a person who has an ear for a poem's inner cadence is at home in the mystic land of poesy. A decade later, in the introduction to the lyrics of *At the Foot of the Mountain* (*Beim Fuss Fun Barg*, 1957), Leyeles restates his opposition both to pure abstract poetry stripped of emotional content, and to poetry as the expression of untamed feeling utterly devoid of ideas. He continues to insist that poetry is always concrete, the direct or indirect expression of a real experience in which thought and feeling, feeling and thought rise together at the same time like two leaves from a single root. He holds that the best Jewish poets have always sung of the meaning and purpose of life, the omnipresence and splendor of God, the destiny of the Jewish people, and, above all, man's submission to a higher entity. Non-Jews might content themselves with songs of unbridled emotions and unfettered instincts. Jews believe in the taming of emotions and in the fettering of instincts by reason.

Of Leyeles's experiments in poetic drama, only *Shlomo Molcho* (1926) aroused considerable interest. This drama centers about the Portuguese Marrano of the early sixteenth century who returned to Judaism and who was regarded by many as the Messiah. The drama is over-rich in ideas. It moves from the royal palace at Lisbon and the synagogue of Joseph Caro in Safed to the ghetto of Rome, the chambers of the Pope, and the Emperor's court at Regensburg. The basic conflict of ideas rages between the two Messianic aspirants, David Reubeni and Shlomo Molcho.

Reubeni wants to redeem the Jewish people by the power of the sword and to restore them to a normal existence on their ancient soil. Molcho, a disciple of cabalistic lore, wants the Jews to remain in the Diaspora and to become the self-sacrificing redeemers of all mankind. In this ideological conflict, Molcho triumphs over Reubeni, his teacher who becomes his follower. But other dramatic conflicts also come to the fore in which Molcho becomes the victim. In one scene the extreme demands of young Molcho for absolute sincerity and holiness in word and deed are opposed by a wise, aged Marrano who has become a Prince of the Church and the king's confessor and who uses his influence to mitigate somewhat Jewish suffering and to ward off threatening, more stringent anti-Jewish decrees. In another scene, Molcho's efforts to convince Jews and non-Jews of an impending Messianic salvation are opposed by the Jewish leaders along the Tiber, who bear responsibility for the survival of the endangered, oppressed community and who fear that his arousal of unjustified and unrealizable Jewish hopes might lead to an irreparable catastrophe. In still another scene the intense otherworldly faith of the Jewish visionary is juxtaposed with the lack of faith of the all-too-worldly Pope Clement VII, scion of the House of Medici.

The climactic scene, in which Molcho the Jew calls upon Emperor Charles V, mightiest ruler of Christendom, to give up illusions of temporal power, to dissolve the empire, and to initiate the return of man to God, is strongly reminiscent of Friedrich Schiller's climax in *Don Carlos*, when Marquis Posa calls upon King Philip of Spain to establish a reign of religious tolerance, freedom of thought, and human fraternity in all his realms. In both plays the monarch is deeply moved for a moment by the splendor of the grandiose vision, but both conclude by turning over the Messianic dreamers to the Inquisition.

The most memorable performance of the drama took place in the doomed ghetto of Vilna towards the close of 1941 before an audience of *morituri*. The poet Abraham Sutzkever, who composed a prologue for this occasion, reported that he saw the performance through a veil of tears.

Leyeles also deals with Jewish Messianic longing in a second drama, *Asher Lemlen* (1928). On the eve of the Lutheran Reformation, when a peasant revolt threatens, Messianic visions come to the Jew Asher Lemlen. These visions help to fan the rebellion. However, when Lemlen's followers wish to join in the struggle against oppressive aristocrats and landowners, he opposes the use of brute force. He counsels delay until God's will is made more manifest. He opposes bloodshed under any circumstances. He cannot face reality, in which pure and impure ingredients are tangled. He can only sacrifice himself and fall a victim.

In his seventy-fifth year, Leyeles visited Israel for the first time and was stimulated to a new burst of lyric creativity. The poet, who had been entranced throughout his life by beauty as a goal, saw in Israel a free, sovereign Jewish community to which, as in days of old, beauty came, if at all, only as a byproduct and not as an objective of group activity.

In a poem *Joseph and Judah*, penned in Israel, he contrasted the dazzling beauty of Joseph with the earthbound virility of Judah. Joseph, the favorite of Jacob, saw in dream-visions lords bowing low before him and peoples subjected to his will; but now Joseph's descendants, even as those of Reuben and Simeon, have disappeared from the face of the globe, and Joseph himself is but a legend of beauty, sad and nostalgic. Judah, on the other hand, less beloved by his father and less intent on dominating others, still lives a life of service. His descendants still wander over the earth bearing his burden of pain and memories, and are still attached to his heaven and his inward vision of service to his fellowmen. Now and then Judah betakes himself to his old home, kisses its soil, builds anew structures of stone and loam, but soon thereafter he resumes his roaming over the world. He is, he exists, he carries on.

A similar refrain "We are here, we are here," concluded Leyeles's cycle of poems on *En Gedi*, composed after his visit to this Israel outpost on the Dead Sea. He described his rapture in the new vineyards of En Gedi, vineyards that recalled memories of Saul, David and Solomon, that looked out upon the heroic ramparts of

Massada, and now re-echo the sound of cymbals, tambourines and the gay songs of youths and maidens.

Leyeles' songs of Israel appeared in the Israel quarterly *Di Goldene Keyt* shortly before and after his death. Its editor, Abraham Sutzkever, called them miracles of poetic renewal, fresh, clairvoyant, melodious, even though composed in the poet's late seventies, reminiscent of the young pure rhythms of the earliest songs, but more symphonic and more Jewish.

Far more intense than in the case of Leyeles was the transformation of his Introspectivist co-founder Jacob Glatstein from a beauty-intoxicated cosmopolite to a lyric spokesman of Jewish tragedy and Jewish rebirth.

Glatstein, too, ranks among the finest lyricists in the Yiddish tongue. His earliest book of verse appeared in 1921, seven years after his arrival in the United States from his native Lublin, in Poland. He had begun to write at thirteen and published his first short story soon after landing in New York in 1914. Fascinated by the unlimited opportunities for higher education which were open to immigrants, he quickly acquired a knowledge of English and was admitted to the Law School of New York University. There he struck up a friendship with a fellow-student, N. B. Minkoff, and soon both came under the influence of Leyeles, slightly older, who had already attracted wide attention with his lyric volume *Labyrinth* (1918).

In 1921, a year after the three poets published their credo of Introspectivism, Glatstein's first volume, applying this credo, appeared. The book bore no title but only the name of the young author. Seeking to avoid parochialism in the choice of subject-matter, he preferred to invoke Buddha and Brahma rather than Jehovah, and to sing of Nirvana and of proud monarchs who rode victoriously into conquered towns at the head of sword-flashing warriors. He delighted in original sound effects. He replaced rhyme and metrical stanzas with complex assonances, alliteration and onomatopoeia.

Free Verses (*Freie Fersen*, 1926) was the title of Glatstein's second volume. Jewish themes were still muted but did break through now and then. The poet spoke not only through the voice of King Canute, who vainly bade the waves of time to stand still, but also through the voice of King Saul, who would gladly have exchanged his care-filled throne for the earlier carefree guardianship of his father's flocks. The poet bewailed the poor lot of a Chinese family and also the mournful end of King David over whose dying nights Abishag, the young Shunamite, maintained vigil.

Two other booklets of verse followed, in which the poet's mastery of Yiddish ripened. But it was not until tragedy broke upon the Jewish people that he became the lyric interpreter of their woe and grandeur.

In 1934, after an absence of two decades, Glatstein revisited his native Lublin. His trip from New York until his arrival in Poland was recorded in the prose volume *When Yash Set Out (Venn Yash Is Gefuhrn*, 1938). Most of the chapters dealt with his five days on board ship and the international assortment of travelers he encountered. Some were returning to their permanent home in Europe while others were vacationing abroad, but all were released from normal inhibitions as they floated between heaven and the watery depths. They readily communicated memories and emotions, even such as were usually kept out of sight when on solid land. Their revelations provided insight into the various currents of thought, national and social stratification, as well as individual yearnings and ambitions in the 1930's.

The later chapters dealt with the train trip across the European continent, over which the shadow of Hitlerism was then spreading. While non-Jews made their way to pleasure-resorts in France, Italy, Spain and Switzerland, Jews were en route to relatives in Poland, Rumania, Lithuania and Soviet Russia. "I look upon their darkened faces and the thought occurs to me that twenty-five years from now, this type of traveler will have disappeared completely. The last survivors of an older generation are on their way to ancestral graves. Almost all their fathers and grandfathers have already passed away and soon the sons will also be gone. When grandsons will later travel to Soviet Russia, Poland, Lithuania or Rumania, it will be for them a summer resort like Paris, Switzerland, or Italy. For none of them will it constitute a homecoming. They will be journeying to those distant lands in order to affix foreign tags to their valises. They will not be seeking their old roots. The Poland which was will have died and the longing or hatred for that Poland will also have faded. They will be touring and not hastening to dying or dead fathers and mothers. In a quarter of a century something will be missing on these train-carriages."

Homecoming at Twilight (Venn Yash Is Gekumen, 1940), a second volume, mirrored Glatstein's impressions during his stay in Poland and the reactions of the Polish Jews toward this visitor

from a happier clime. In Buchlerner's rest home he created a Jewish parallel to Thomas Mann's Magic Mountain sanitarium. Here
the Jewish sick arrive in various stages of physical decay and
spiritual dissolution. They have a foreboding that their days are
numbered and that death will overtake them ere long, as indeed
it does overtake Steinman, the lustiest character among them.

The mood of the novel is autumnal throughout. The melancholy
guests are aware, even in the midst of their open-air waltzing, that
winter is on the way, the winter of the year as well as of their
lives. They reminisce about the past, when Jews were supposedly
of a stronger mettle—great personalities who saw themselves as
God's emissaries on earth. In Poland between two world wars,
however, even Hassidic *rebbes* were embittered, taciturn, worried
about the increasing impoverishment of the Jewish flock. Every
Jew sensed the accumulated hatred of his Polish neighbors. "They
hate us for observing the Sabbath and they hate us for violating
the Sabbath. They hate pious Jews and they hate free-thinking
Jews who eat lobster. They hate our capitalists and they hate our
beggars. They hate our reactionaries and they hate our radicals.
They hate Jews who earn their bread and those who die three
times a day from starvation."

Steinman, who in his childhood survived a pogrom by hiding
in a synagogue book closet, interpreted this hatred as a continuation of Cain's hatred of Abel, an enduring hatred beyond logical
explanation. To escape it, he once dreamed of joining the movement
to build a Jewish state. He recalled Herzl's appearance upon the
Jewish scene, when Jewish backs straightened and Messianic visions
floated before ghetto eyes. Jewish misery lingered on, however,
and was intensified decade after decade, while the state was still
unborn.

This misery paraded before Glatstein's eyes: a steady stream of
the poor who saw in him the messenger from a mythical paradise,
a messenger holding out the possibility of salvation from crushing
penury. Each of the supplicants was described with his past history, his present aches, his dreary future. Only a miracle could
save the Jewish masses in Poland from deepening despair. This
miracle was not forthcoming: Hitler's march into Eastern Europe
ended their hopes and their lives.

In the post-Hitler period Glatstein concentrated on specifically
Jewish themes. He was not averse to Jewish lyricists joining in all
battles for a better humanity but he felt that their position in
such battles should be on the Jewish barricades. They should sing

out their faith in a moral tomorrow in Jewish tones and should trust that these tones would reach beyond their own borders.

In his *Memorial Songs* (*Gedenklieder,* 1943), Glatstein sought to recapture the simple Sabbath holiness of the Jew rooted in tradition, the melody of the Yiddish word that blossomed on the lips of grandmothers, the awesome mood of the *shofar* and the comforting delight of a Goldfaden melody. The poet bade farewell to the "wide, great, stinking world," even to the effete democracies with their cold sympathy-compresses. He put on the yellow badge as his emblem, and he groped his way back to the narrow, dust-covered lanes of his bearded coreligionists locked in ghettos.

Glatstein sang of these coreligionists in his cycle *Radiant Jews* (*Shtralendike Yidn,* 1946), after the Holocaust. At night in a vision he saw millions of outstretched dead hands imploring him to cry out the Jewish pain, to be the intermediary between martyred sires and their living descendants. He no longer defined the Jews as a people, a race, a religion. They had become a sect of mourners bearing mute urns, a legion of survivors marching in an unending funeral procession memorializing their perished relatives. The Torah which Jews received at Sinai from the Lord of heaven and earth and with which they lived for millennia was returned by them at Lublin when they died in the gas-chambers; the dead could no longer praise God.

Enveloping himself in the cloak of Rabbi Nachman of Bratzlav, the poet begged God to let him share in the punishment being meted out to Jews. Why should he be spared when so many of his coreligionists endured so much? After seven years of mourning, however, his lamentations subsided and he turned his attention to comforting his people.

In the cycle *Father's Shadow* (*Dem Tatens Shutn,* 1953), Glatstein held that the time had come both for the maimed God as well as his surviving bard to give up pretensions of universality and for both to betake themselves from the seven continents to the tiny land of their origin. For it was far better to be the intimate deity of a *minyan* of Jews than to be the mighty God of countless brigands. It was far better to dwell in the tabernacle of Israel than to be Lord of the world, especially such a world. When Jehovah set out from His people's tent and became international, His Jews followed suit and became a world-shaking, world-inflaming group. Now they were sick of that world and of their role in it. "Save yourself, O God, return with us to our little land, become once more the Jewish God." A people that was convalescing and regaining its youth would also help its God to rejuvenate Himself. In many variations Glatstein reiterated his preference to be remembered in the small vineyard of the Jewish people rather than on the broad highways of the non-Jewish world. Let others emphasize their cosmopolitanism, his emphasis would continue to be on his Jewishness. He illustrated this in his last lyric volumes *The Joy of the Yiddish Word* (*Die Freid Fun Yidishen Vort*, 1961) and *A Jew of Lublin* (*A Yid Fun Lublin*, 1966).

The former volume begins with memorial verses for departed poets of his circle, elegies for the souls of ravaged cities, satiric jibes at tired humanity. Then the poet bursts forth with joyous hymns to the re-arisen Jewish homeland whose flags flutter in the free air, a state built on the basis of shared poverty, cooperative fraternity, and warm with hope of redemption. Through thunder and lightning, out of the ashes of the recent conflagration, a new beginning has emerged. After commemorating so many tragic events of the past, the old people of wanderers can at last celebrate on *Yom Ha-atzmaut* a young holiday of rejoicing, a new holiness.

Despite affirmation of the dynamic Jewish reality symbolized by Israel, Glatstein nevertheless cannot tear himself away in his creative imagination from the vanished world of his youth. In *A Jew of Lublin*, published in his seventieth year, he continues to revert to his native Lublin and its more moral civilization. He dips his pen in misanthropic gall when he writes of the present coarse, wicked, oversexed Occident. He lashes out sardonically at the wild insanities of the avant-garde literature which interprets it, which crashes the privacy of the bedroom and which dissects and embalms the still living flesh. He sees in the Beatnik a caricature of the filthy, obnoxious, contemporary man, an angry nihilistic protester against sick, false respectability. He can understand such negative characters even though he does not sympathize with them. His own preference is to escape from maledictions, unbelief, and scepticism even to a Hassidic booth, if necessary. There he can at least pray with a handful of genuine, old-fashioned Jews and sense a breath of God's nearness.

Looking back upon a life of service as a guardian of the shrinking Yiddish heritage, Glatstein finds his chief joy in the Yiddish word and he wishes to continue with it until his last hour. His verses are magnificent tributes to the richness of Yiddish as a linguistic medium.

The third of the founders of Insichism was N. B. Minkoff, who began as a poet but who was more influential as editor, literary critic, scholar and lecturer.

Raised in Warsaw, in a home where Russian and Polish were esteemed far more than Yiddish, it was not until after he emigrated to the United States in 1914 and came into contact with Yiddish writers, actors and composers, that he began to write Yiddish songs. Leyeles, his mentor, and Glatstein, his classmate at New York University's Law School, roused his interest in the Insichist movement they were about to launch, and he joined them from 1920 on in common literary ventures.

Minkoff remained faithful to the Insichist credo. His poetry is indeed intellectualized emotion. He rarely permits the cry that wells up from the heart to find untamed expression, and even the dream-visions that float up from his subconscious are filtered through the clear logic of thought before they are compressed into words and tangible images. Nevertheless, not all his mystic insights emerge unshrouded by obscurity despite his straining for clarity.

As a trained musician, Minkoff has an impeccable ear for tonal effects and he experiments with subtle rhythms of free verse, as do all Insichist poets. But, like Leyeles, he too likes equally well the discipline imposed upon his roving imagination by the sonnet. His first volume, *Songs* (*Lieder,* 1924), reaches its climax in the wreath of sonnets "Alone Am I." A tired melancholy whispers in him, but it never descends to the depth of cynicism. He often invokes the concept of joy, but his longing for joy fails to find fulfillment and he lacks real cheerfulness. The shadowy domain of night is more congenial to him than the glare of daylight. Typical titles of the poems in the first volume are: "Autumn," "November Nights," "The Weeping of Winterland," "Weeping of Pure Reason," "Sleepless Nights."

Minkoff's second lyric volume, *At the Edge* (*Beim Rand,* 1945), is even more thoroughly saturated with the imagery of death and desolation. It is written under the impact of the Hitler years. But the finest lyric of this mature volume deals with the thought-associations and conjectures that come upon him "Upon Hearing Beethoven's *For Elise.*" The music impinging upon his ear and penetrating into his heart of hearts evokes a mood of reverie. In this dream state he has an awareness that his journey betwixt birth and death is merely half the road that his soul travels and that there is another half between death and rebirth which he must have traversed earlier and which he will traverse later. There come to him intimations of immortality, a feeling that he has been

here before, though when or how he cannot tell, a possibility that
there is no end to the renewal of lives, a wondering whether his
previous, lost existences do not stream back to him in his semi-
conscious reveries as last spasms of recollections beyond space
and time.

Minkoff seeks and fails to find a meaning in the suffering imposed upon his people. He wants to retain his faith in God but
finds it most difficult to do so amidst war and catastrophe. Yet,
even as he drives God from himself, God returns as creator and
renewer, and the poet's heart, tired of raging and rebelling, finally
accepts Him, though without hope of ever comprehending His
mysterious ways.

Minkoff, who stresses subjectivity in his verse, is a most objective critic and scholar in his prose. His studies, *Eliahu Bocher*
(1950), dealing with the sixteenth century Yiddish minstrel, and
Glickl Hamel (1952), dealing with the matronly memoirist of the
early eighteenth century, display great erudition and meticulous
accuracy in interpretation. His books of essays, *Yiddish Classical
Poets* (1937), and *Six Yiddish Critics* (1954), show his understanding and tolerance of widely different attitudes to life and
letters. His main contribution to literary scholarship, however,
consists in the three volumes *Pioneers of Yiddish Poetry in America* (1956). These volumes trace the growth and development of
the social lyric, dominant in America during the closing decades
of the nineteenth century.

Although Minkoff as a poet fought for pure poetry undiluted
by propaganda or party programs, nevertheless as a literary historian, he appreciates the value of the Yiddish lyric pioneers who
placed their talent at the service of socialistic, anarchistic and
revolutionary causes. He correctly recognizes that Yiddish literature from its very origin was oriented toward the common man and
on the whole rejected the "art for art's sake" philosophy. If the
Jewish immigrants who faced exploitation in sweatshops, or near
starvation as peddlers and small shopkeepers, were saved from
despair and moral disintegration by faith in a better tomorrow,
they owed this faith to a large extent to the social poets whose
verses ranged over a wide field, from naturalistic depiction of contemporary evils to romantic, Messianic visions of a classless utopia.
Minkoff is at his best in tracing the intellectual growth and the
literary characteristics of Morris Vinchevsky, David Edelstadt and
Joseph Bovshover, the three most gifted and most popular poets
who pioneered in singing of the sorrows and hopes of the working

masses, even though they themselves were not of proletarian origin. But Minkoff also revivifies, both as writers and as human beings, nineteen other social poets who have become in the course of half a century shadowy figures. Some of these fervent idealists and sombre cynics he knew in his early years, when in the exuberance of youth he fought for Insichism and against their excessive didacticism.

According to Minkoff, the most erratic and extreme follower of Insichism was Bernard Lewis, who began with English verses but whose chief claim to fame lies in the Yiddish lyrics of his Insichist year, 1920. Minkoff describes him as a Byronic type, pessimistic but not resigned, dynamic in his hatred and scorn, theatrical in his speech and behavior.

Before Lewis came to America in 1906, at the age of seventeen, he had already participated in the Jewish self-defense organization which resisted the perpetrators of a pogrom in Odessa and he had joined a revolutionary cell which planned and executed the assassination of a Czarist official in Slonim. After escaping to America, he continued an adventurous existence, roaming as a hobo over the entire continent, impressing vagabonds with his bravado, and hatching impractical, idealistic castles in the air.

In Insichism, Lewis found a movement which apparently endorsed his egocentrism and let him give vent to his self-glorification and to indulge in eccentricities. Yet, before a year had passed, he took leave of his fellow poets in a misanthropic poem in which Nietzschean tones are audible. He told them that his Asiatic blood could not stand their inferior species. He disclaimed communion with them on the ground that they were born to be servile and would soon pass away. He, on the other hand, would watch their disappearance from his lofty pedestal and would sing a hymn of triumph.

Lewis's versified phantasmagorias often bordered on the absurd and the insane, but they did show flashes of greatness. In the imaginary land of his "own madness," which he called Flamtalin, he let the skeletons of his thoughts dance their infernal dance on the edge of the abyss, until he sickened of himself, "his wretched, wild blood," his aimless wandering. He then let mocking laughter resound in his lyrics. "My heart rattles towards the lawless grass, the decaying rocks and the red orgy of death, as a snake rattles to its prey."

After spending his last years in a sanitarium for consumptives and denying premature reports of death's arrival, death caught up with him in Colorado Springs at the age of thirty-six. Two years later his poems were collected in the slender volume *Flamtalin* (1927), with an introductory tribute by Leyeles.

Reuben Ludwig also made a meteoric appearance among the Insichists with poems that emphasized the imminence of death. However, before death claimed this consumptive poet in his thirty-first year, he sought to escape the deterioration of his health by sojourning in dry areas of New Mexico, Arizona and California. His few well-constructed lyrics dealt with the Far West. He discovered the silence of the snow-covered Rockies and the desolation of the yellow Southwestern deserts. Throughout his lyrics there coursed the refrain that for him there would soon be darkness and nothing more. His three short stories also dealt with the sick who yearned for the sun and for whom the damp, cold grave was waiting.

Ludwig experienced America, to which he came at fifteen, as his own and yet not his own. His sympathy was with the old Indian who had given way to white intruders, the Negro torn from the wilds of Africa to serve white masters, the melancholy, guitar-playing Mexican, the exotic Chinaman, and other underprivileged characters. The poet was prematurely sad, pale and stripped of hope, even while his heart ached for joy, robustness and the intoxication of love and glorious adventuring. A single volume, containing his *Collected Poems* (*Gezamelte Lieder*), appeared posthumously in 1927.

The quietest of the Insichists was Eliezer Blum, who wrote under the pseudonym of B. Alquit and who was one of the editors of *In Sich*. Orphaned at an early age, he left his native Chelm in Poland at twelve, wandered on to Lublin, Warsaw, Vienna, and at seventeen arrived in New York. There he experienced the grueling fate of a sweatshop worker.

A posthumous, slender volume, *Songs* (*Lieder*, 1964), contains the sum total of his lyric efforts of forty years, and a collection of short stories, *En Route to Peretz Square* (1958), contains his best narratives. His lyrics are compassionate and gentle, lucid and barely audible. They express the eternal melancholy that, in his opinion, hovers over shadows of nothingness. His metaphors are startling, his imagery is grotesque, his thought-associations are bold and original, his melodious verses with their subtle assonances drift gently onto the inner ear. He concretizes abstractions. His themes range from memories and figures of Chelm, the town of his childhood, to recurring premonitions of death. He sings of the silence of night, the sadness of the earth, the loneliness of the sea, the fading of dreams, the ebbing of desire, the autumn of life, the coolness of the grave. He does not struggle against adversity or resist the encroachment of age. His characters do not find much meaning in existence. He fathoms the fruitless longing of the girl who sees her youth wasting away in the factory, and he peers into the withering eyes and hearts of middle-aged ladies who frequent picture galleries. These frustrated beings understand far better than the sixteen-year-olds the transitoriness of all existence and that even God has become tired of fruitless activity and is therefore resting in the clouds.

Alquit belongs neither to the victors nor to the defeated but rather to those who stand on the sidelines and observe the passing scene. From the wine of life, he sips drops of melancholy; from the parade of the years, he extracts verses of haunting loveliness.

Jacob Stodolsky, publisher, bookseller, editor and poet, participated in the publications of the Insichists, but left only few lyrics of value. His volume of free verse bears the symbolic title *Will-O'-The Wisp* (*Irrlicht*, 1966). In it, he, the son of a Hassid, describes himself as having pursued deceptive lights before finally returning with Hassidic fervor to the God of his fathers and accepting a humble role as a guardian of his people's traditions. The will-o'-the-wisp he refers to is the anarchist philosophy which he followed in his earlier years in Warsaw and Paris before coming to New York in 1912. He wants to atone for former blasphemies by devoting himself entirely to the Yiddish word. He captures in verse the uniqueness of Jewish boulevards, such as Manhattan's Second Avenue and Brooklyn's Ocean Parkway. He sometimes dazzles the mind with his heaping of colorful image upon colorful image, but he rarely succeeds in moving the heart, a common failing of the minor Insichist poets who, in seeking to combine intellectualism with emotional sensitivity, lose themselves in artificial, barren abstractions from which the emotions have oozed away.

Aaron Kurtz came from a Hassidic home in a Vitebsk townlet. He began his wandering and struggling for a livelihood at thirteen. He arrived in the United States in 1911, worked in factories and wrote poetry. When the Insichist Movement arose, he was at first attracted by it and contributed to its journals, but before long he felt drawn more closely to the proletarian writers who sought to change America's social and economic structure. Insichism did not involve its followers in the struggle between capital and labor and Kurtz felt that poets should take their place at the vanguard of this struggle, inspiring, conjuring, suffering with the underprivileged masses. In *Placard* (1927), he introduced an original poetic style, which he designated as "placard style." Its dynamic rhythms were designed to reproduce the kaleidoscopic metropolis, the raw, chaotic manifestations of industrial capitalism, the striving of the red-hearted, black-breaded plebeians. In *The Golden City* (*Die Goldene Shtot*, 1935), he sang of strikers, mass protests, the Negro slums of New York's Harlem, the derelicts of its Bowery, the angry rebels of its Union Square. In *No Pasarán* (1938), he identified himself with the Spanish Republicans in their desperate struggle against Fascism. In *Marc Chagal* (1947), he paid lyric tribute to the painter of the phantastic whose soul, even as his own, was rooted in Jewish Vitebsk, and who placed his talent at the disposal of all fighters for freedom. Like Chagall, he too was battling for a world of social justice and pure love, but used the rhythmic word rather than the brush as his weapon.

Shloime Schwartz identified himself with the Insichists in the preface to his first volume *Blue Monday* (*Bloimontik*, 1938). Indeed, most of the lyrics in this volume originally appeared in their organs. These lyrics are consciously conceived, and then draped in images and besprinkled with emotions. In the title poem, for example, Sunday sighs out its holidayness and only burnt-out tallow is left of its festive light; the blueness of Monday ushers in the tower-high, spiralling problems which wrap themselves around the weekdays. Schwartz prefers melancholy moods and autumnal visions. He reproduces the nuances of various months but his preference is for October, November and December. Even in his New Year's poem, he emphasizes the loss of the faded year rather than the promise of the coming one. His love poems forfeit immediacy of feeling as his emotions are intellectualized and frozen into crystalline images.

In his second volume, *America* (1940), Schwartz frees himself to some extent from dogmatic adherence to Insichist theories, and his artificial straining for original word combinations is less marked. The poet of Chicago sings of sights and sounds in his mid-Western metropolis and discovers in the ranges of Wyoming and the deserts of Arizona scenes and figures new to Yiddish poetry. But the worsening Jewish situation on the eve of the Second World War compels him to take cognizance of Jewish woes earlier untouched by him. Poetry cannot any longer remain for him merely playful variations on exotic and impersonal themes. Flaming ghettos and ships with unwanted Jewish refugees adrift on the high seas recall him to his poeople's destiny, to biblical subjects, and to legends of his grandfather.

In *Golden Exile* (*Goldener Golus*, 1971), Schwartz, three decades later, laments the twilight of the Yiddish song as he sits by the waters of Lake Michigan and recalls the once aspiring poets of "Young Chicago," who have aged or faded from life. He alone is left with his Jewish sadness in the golden exile of the mid-Western metropolis.

Michel Licht contributed to *In Sich* and edited literary journals in 1925 and 1926 together with Jacob Glatstein and N. B. Minkoff. His earliest lyrics, which go back to 1917, show Impressionistic characteristics in their emphasis on the communication of moods and in their vague symbolism. His preference then is for the echoes of sounds, cool shadows, gentle reveries, twilight and demi-night. He lets paintings, symphonies, the gyrations of dancers and acrobats, the movements of birds and swanlike maidens, impinge upon the senses. He tries to reproduce the effect in words, but soon he becomes dissatisfied with the mere reproduction of impressions and feelings. Under the influence of the Insichists, he filters these through his intellect and dissolves them in irony. His metaphors become too refined, his neologisms not entirely comprehensible. He assimilates influences from avant-garde French and American poetry and adores Ezra Pound. His cerebral rhythms astound with their virtuosity but leave the reader unmoved. He revolts against the concept that art should mirror life and that the Jewish artist should mirror Jewish reality. He prefers universal themes, often far removed from his own immediate experiences. He loses himself in abstractions and versifies pure ideas. He is rationally sober even in the midst of dreams. He pacifies his turbulently beating heart with the cold medicine of logic.

After publishing three volumes of lyrics during the decade 1922-1932, Licht was chained by illness for twenty years and, only after his death in 1953, did his *Collected Poems* (*Gezamelte Lieder*) appear. By then his tamed ecstasies and allegorical chimeras were even less intelligible to his few readers.

Kalman Heisler stemmed from Kymarno, Eastern Galicia, and experienced the First World War in Prague. He arrived in New York in 1921, when the Insichists were propounding their new literary insights, and he attracted the attention of Jacob Glatstein. In 1927, he published his first lyric booklet *People* (*Mentshen*), with an introduction by Glatstein, who compared Heisler's gallery of Galician characters to Edgar Lee Masters' unheroic heroes of *Spoon River Anthology.*

The young poet sketched portraits of his ancestors and his townsmen with nostalgic affection and with subtle humor. There was his great-grandfather, who tailored before the days of specialization and mechanization, singing and humming as he worked, content with God and man, and with his most precious possessions: children and grandchildren, needles and scissors, *tallit* and *tefillin.* There was his grandfather, also skilled in tailoring but no longer disdaining the help of the new machines, a reputable master who brought the latest Parisian styles to the Galician outpost and who retained the pious, stable habits bequeathed to him by tradition. There were his father and mother, who still accepted, as apparently God-ordained, their status on a low rung of the social ladder. In his own generation, however, the tailor lads were infected with doctrines of class struggles and hoped for a social revolution. They proudly evaluated their profession as superior to that of the idle bourgeoisie. After adolescence, many of them made their way to American shops, even as did their poetic chronicler, but they retained the traits of their native Kymarno.

In the lyrics of a subsequent volume, *Kymarno Types* (*Kymarno Parshoinen,* 1930), Heisler continued to delineate the townsmen he had known in his boyhood years, each an individual with unique characteristics but all enveloped in an east Galician Jewish atmosphere. Under the influence of Moshe Nadir, a satiric undertone accompanied these crotchety types with their picturesque nicknames. This satiric tone subsided, however, when a quarter of a century later he reverted to lyric sketches of additional townsmen in the booklet *Alas, My Kymarno* (*Meine Kymarner Nebikh,* 1953). By then, this centuries-old Jewish settlement survived only in his memory, since its men had been machine-gunned in 1941 and its women and children set afire in 1942.

Alef Katz, a far more versatile poet than Heisler, also was encouraged by Glatstein and also had his early poems published in the organ of the Insichists. His first lyric volume, *A Tale of the Sea* (*A Mayse Fun Yam,* 1925) incorporated Insichist innovations. The opening poem, "A Leaf," lets us view in lucid images the movement of a leaf from the instant it parts from its branch, even as a dream from a sleeper's brain, until it finally touches the earth and comes to rest. Other poems, in the manner of the American Imagists, let us experience New York by directing our gaze to single specific objects which are delineated with utmost clarity. Katz shows not a mass of skyscrapers but the single Woolworth Building, not a multiplicity of streets but the Bowery only, not the majesty of rivers but the Hudson River as perceived from a definite point on the Upper Manhattan bank where street lamps cast braids of light upon the water.

In his second volume, *Plowing Time* (*Akertzeit*, 1929), the poet still emphasizes New York subjects. He is again fascinated by the picturesqueness of the Bowery. In the manner of Edwin Markham's *Man With the Hoe*, he describes the man of the Bowery, cast out by society, unable to find his way back or to advance forward to respectability, a severed link of the human chain, a derelict devoured by hatred, his burning brain cooled by the sad melody of nighing death.

In the poetic booklet *Heavenly Saucer* (*Dos Tellerl Fun Himl*, 1934), Katz emancipates himself from Imagism and Insichism, only to fall under the spell of the then fashionable proletarian practices. He shows starving workers becoming class conscious and revolting against their sated plunderers.

Not until the lyrics of *Once There Was a Story* (*Amol Is Geven A Mayse*, 1944), written under the impact of the European Jewish tragedy, does Katz find his own, original tone and the subject-matter closest to his heart. He tells of his disillusionment with the proletarian panaceas. The eagles he followed to the desired land of pure humanity turned into terrifying, wild, screeching bats. He was left lonely and bereft of his wings. Recovery from his temporary paralysis came when he linked himself again to the healthy trunk of the Jewish generations, past and future. "My father is in me and I am in my father. We are all one, in a single, complex truth."

Katz then pens children's poems, playlets, stories for the coming generation and finds real happiness in this activity, because these are sung, played and recited in Yiddish schools and thrill young Jewish hearts. A playlet, *Good Morning, Alef* (1946) has as its dramatis personae the letters of the Hebrew alphabet. These letters are indestructible. When Houses of Learning went up in flames in the Hitler decade, the letters floated up and wandered about in the air. *Alef* and *Bet* set out in search of their dispersed comrades and, when all of them were found, the question arose as to who could use them after the conflagration. A child was discovered that survived the night of the long knives, and Elijah descended on earth to teach it the alphabet. Jewish learning was thus resumed and the Hebrew letters again had a home and a new lease of life in

Jewish hearts. This dramatic poem was produced in camps of post-war survivors and brought much needed cheer.

The lyrics and playlets of the following volumes—*Dreams Be with You* (*Cholem Aleichem*, 1958) and *Quite a Wedding* (*Die Emesse Khassene*, 1964)—are singable and playful, a delight for adults and children. The best of the poetic tales are based on stories of the Hassidic Rabbi Nachman Bratslaver.

"An Old Portrait," with its suggestive symbolism, is typical of Katz's mature style in his last volume. After years of silence, a portrait in a museum suddenly begins to talk. It recalls the moment when it was created, the painter who created it, and the whole world that once was. Now it looks out of its frame upon an entirely strange world in which the painter and the subject portrayed are no more. As the solitary hero of a wordless drama, as the shadowy survivor of a faded era, it alone lives on. In this apparently simple lyric of a portrait, there obviously peers through the face of the aging poet and of his entire Yiddish-speaking generation. This is Alef Katz at his best.

His uniqueness, late arrived at, lies in his ability to bridge with laughter life's yawning abysses and tragic canyons. Amidst the maze of symbols, the ever changing rhythmic patterns, the virtuosity of startling rhymes, the capricious whirl of metaphors, serious meaning trickles through or is hinted at. The poet's weeping becomes music; his tears dissolve into songs; his sad memories skirt along the edge of humor; he hides behind supernatural creatures and animated objects. He is aware that words alone are inadequate to express a reality beyond observed phenomena and he even entitles one of his mystic poems "What Cannot Be Uttered in Words." But he hopes that this reality can be hinted at through allegorical symbols.

Insichism was primarily an American movement of young Yiddish poets. It flourished in the 1920's and brought excitement and experimentation. Its vogue receded in the 1930s. Some of its followers returned to traditionalism; others became infatuated with proletarian poetry as practiced in Kiev, Minsk and Moscow. Still others discovered their own uniqueness and followed a lonely path, removed from the main currents. But all had been enriched by the temporary enthusiasm which Insichist striving had called forth.

17

AMERICAN ECLECTICS

Lutzky ● Eliezer Greenberg ● *Getzeltn* ● Weinstein
● Nissenson ● Bialostotsky ● Schweid ● Tkatch
● Stolzenberg ● Tabachnik ● Stiker ● Krull ● J. I.
Segal ● Feinberg ● Almi ● Esselin

THE YIDDISH WRITERS active on the American scene between
the two world wars were almost all of Eastern European origin.
Torn from their native roots and transplanted across the Atlantic,
they still continued to reflect in their poems, dramas and novels
the attitudes and ideologies of the Old World, even when they expanded their horizon to include subject-matter based on their
experiences in the New World.

Attempts begun by "Die Yunge" before the First World War
and by the Insichists after the war to bring about indigenous
American movements were not sustained by their successors who
arrived during later decades. Indeed, after the 1920's there was
not a single Yiddish group which could properly be designated as
a literary movement with an original approach. There were only
individual writers of greater or lesser talent who enriched the
stream of Yiddish literature without modifying its direction. New
poets could come to the attention of large audiences only through
the medium of the daily press. This necessitated submission to the
authority of influential editors. Rebels against such authority faced
years of frustration before they won a hearing.

The most revered and most feared editor was Abraham Cahan.
He introduced controversial material and experimented with entertaining features calculated to attract men and women who had
not previously been accustomed to reading dailies. He insisted on
his associates using the simplest vocabulary, even English words
current in the speech of his New York readers. Difficult concepts

were to be avoided or else presented in a most elementary manner. Cahan's ardent devotion to the cause of trade unionism, and his leadership in the struggle for the amelioration of sweatshop conditions, soon made his newspaper the most influential voice of the Jewish immigrants, most of whom still lived in slums and abject poverty and whose knowledge of English was scant. He educated them and tried to help them make their integration into American ways less painful. But he also castigated them for their bad manners and their tendency to change from exploited to exploiters when material success beckoned. His discovery of new talented writers decade after decade was not the least of his achievements.

It was to Cahan that A. Lutzky (1894-1957) owed his early reputation as well as his pseudonym. He had arrived as Aaron Zucker from Lutzk in Volynia in 1914. Not until three years later were his first poems accepted by the New York dailies *Tageblatt* and *Tog.* When Abraham Cahan was then alerted to the rise of a new poetic talent who was beginning to appear in rival dailies, he immediately engaged him to write a weekly poem for his organ and changed the poet's name to A. Lutzky. After a year, Lutzky had to sail overseas to fight with the American forces in France. When he returned, after harrowing experiences in the trenches before Verdun, he astonished and perturbed readers with his strange new style.

Lutzky was a bizarre poet, adept at lyric acrobatics, a juggler of capricious word combinations which needed to be read aloud in order to be fully grasped. Animating the inanimate, he erased the distinction between immobile nature and mobile organisms. Water, rain, wind, fire, sunlight, come to life, leap, dance and sing. A match rides on the back of a stream and thrills to the sight of ever new landscapes. A piece of paper, overwhelmed by the pain of existence, decides to commit suicide; it lies down on a railroad track, but when the locomotive nighs, it regrets its hasty decision and flutters away, back to life. Another piece of paper is panic-stricken because rain threatens and it dreads becoming disintegrated by the wetness; but then the clouds pass away, the sun comes out, and the paper, relieved of fear, laughs a hearty laugh. Pennies meet in the pocket of a beggar and exchange stories of their past migrations. Waters run about the earth foaming with delight. A button weighs the merits of single loneliness versus marital unitedness. A pea and a bean, cooking in separate pots and facing their final moments before disintegration, still argue about their relative importance, until the pots begin to boil and then both are silenced and cease their individual existences.

Lutzky encircles his trembling woes with magic syllables until these woes are transformed into music and rhythmic movement. He is a humorist who smiles at the vanity of existence, a pessimist who cloaks with gaiety his disillusionment with the human merry-go-round. He acts the clown, though his heart bleeds because of the imperfections about him.

Lutzky's first volume, *Take It! It's Good for You!* (*Nemt Es! S'is Gut Far Aikh!*, 1927), begins with the lyric collections "Joyous and Vivacious" and "Songs and Dances," but merges into the collection "Somewhat Sad." In his second volume, entitled *The Beginning Is the Middle* (*Bereshis-Inmitten*, 1932), he finds relief from pessimism by atomizing time, space and other fundamental concepts. In his third volume, *Portraits* (*Portretn*, 1945), he attempts to sketch in words the silhouettes of Jewish contemporaries, writers, editors, trade-union leaders and public figures. His final volume, *A Book for Life* (*A Bukh Tsum Leben*, 1948), contains his most mature lyrics.

Lutzky heightened the effect of his verses by dramatic impersonations, acting out through facial expressions, gestures and bodily contortions what his words only hinted at. These impersonations have been imitated by leading actors and entertainers and have entered into the lasting Yiddish repertoire.

In contrast to Lutzky's explosive intensity and theatrical showmanship, Eliezer Greenberg (b. 1896) is restrained, contemplative, suggesting rather than expressing emotions. While Lutzky sublimates tears under a veneer of laughter, Greenberg transmutes even ecstasy into sadness. His imagination is tamed by censoring reason and his measured lines are of severe brevity.

Born in Lipkan, Bessarabia, Greenberg came in his youth under the influence of his literary townsmen Eliezer Steinbarg, Jacob Sternberg and Moshe Altman. Though he left for America in 1913 at the age of sixteen, he retained affectionate memories of this center of traditional Jewishness. However, his earliest songs already deal with New York's streets and avenues, houses and bridges. The Woolworth Tower symbolizes for him the vaulting ambition of twentieth century man. Brooklyn Bridge's miracle of iron and steel testifies to the majestic victory of mind over matter. But New York also harbors crippled tenements where toilers suffer while laboring from dawn to dusk. The poet senses the travail of the workers, the monotony of their days when they are fully employed and their hunger when they are unemployed, as in the years of the Great Depression. The social tone then comes to the fore in his verses.

When tragedy strikes the Jewish people, however, the poet lays aside proletarian protests, individual sorrows and universal themes. He senses his kinsmen's danger. He sits by the waters of the Hudson, as his ancestors sat by the waters of Babylon; he weeps as he remembers the Jewish woe in the unfree lands and notes the indifference of the free lands to Jewish extermination. In a poetic monologue, he speaks through the voice of the dying Heine, who asks his ex-Jewish friend Karl Marx: "O Marx, how could we flee from our own stricken people and purchase our safety with baptismal water?" In another poem, Peretz meets Bontsie Schweig, the silent Jew, in the ruins of Warsaw's ghetto. As the sole survivor, when the Jews were set afire on all the world's scaffolds, he can no longer remain silent; he begs his creator Peretz to give him a tongue so that he can bear witness to the world's muteness, while the Jews, children and graybeards, poor and rich, were being exterminated. Elsewhere, the poet, grown rich in disillusionment, voices his refusal to march alongside of the triumphant democracies in the victory parades, for were not these democracies partners through their silence in the murder of his six million Jewish brothers?

In *Night Dialogue (Banakhtiker Dialog,* 1953), Greenberg communes with himself in silent hours of the night and reverts to his earlier, calmer, more meditative moods. He again drinks in with all his senses the loveliness of his limited world and forgoes the desire to roam beyond New York's horizon. He is at peace with himself, content to convert memories of man and tree and earth into lyric perfection.

In his sixth lyric volume, *Eternal Thirst (Eybiker Dorsht,* 1968), Greenberg sings of his thirst for a just and moral world in his "bloody, godless century." While others jump on the bandwagon of the victors, he weeps with the victims. The dove and the lamb are closer to him than the rapacious tiger and the roaring lion. The aging poet becomes more sensitive to the pain of autumnal withering, the defoliation of nature, which presages winter and death. Indeed, death emerges as his most frequent theme: the death of a tree with which he shared experiences of a quarter of a century; the death of a dog that was a cheerful friend and a loyal guardian; the death of a doomed woman whose ever present smile defied extinction even in the hour when she was lowered into the grave. He pens elegies for writers whom death tore away from a creative life in young years: the Yiddish poet Nochum Bomze, the English poet Isaac Rosenfeld, the Prague novelist Franz Kafka. He laments his native city of Lipkan, whose Jewish figures live on only in his imagination and in his verses. He writes a dirge for New York's Second Avenue, once the rendezvous of Yiddish poets and actors and later haunted by their ghosts. Despite the apparent omnipresence of death and decay, the poet cannot reconcile himself to the thought that he is merely a transient guest in God's mysterious world. Though doubts assail him, he cannot exist without faith and, in poem after poem, he struggles to ferret out meaning in seemingly meaningless happenings.

Greenberg devoted critical studies to Moshe Leib Halpern, the poet of "Die Yunge," Jacob Glatstein, the poet of Insichism, and H. Leivick, the poet of Jewish Messianism. He was influenced by these and other older contemporaries but he did not follow in their footsteps. In the literary magazine, *Getseltn*, which he coedited with Elias Schulman from 1945 to 1949, he welcomed poets of every description. Eclectic in his own judgments, he encouraged them to follow their inner voice and not to give in to momentary lyric fashions.

Alongside of the works of major, long-recognized Yiddish writers, such as Jacob Glatstein, David Ignatoff, Itzik Manger, Melech Ravitch, I. J. Trunk and Reuben Iceland, there appeared in the columns of *Getseltn* lyrics of many minor poets, some of whom were not welcomed in less eclectic literary organs. There was Jeremiah Hescheles, a virtuoso of the Yiddish language, whose verbal innovations were daring and original, whose imagery was rich and plastic, and whose themes, encased in sonnets, ranged from the Talmud, Buddha and Socrates to Albert Einstein, entropy and the new biology. These sonnets were later published in book form as *Sonnets of Chaos (Soneten Fun Tohu Vavohu* (1957). There was Herman Gold (1888-1953), who had begun to write in 1907, two years after his arrival in New York from Brisk in Lithuania, but who never attracted much atention. There was Alter Esselin (b. 1889), who maintained a lonely outpost of Yiddish culture in Milwaukee. There was Selik Heller (1894-1970), a Chicago poet who began in 1916 but whose chief contribution was the lyric volume *Sabbath (Shabbes,* 1953), in which he hymned the glory of heaven and earth, God and the Jewish people, sanctified by the weekly day of rest. There was Mattes Deitch (1894-1966), another Chicago poet who was also active from 1916 in the Yiddish cultural life of the mid-Western metropolis. There was Israel Goichberg (b. 1894), whose songs for children were often set to music by Jewish composers. There was Celia Drapkin (1888-1956), whose poem "The Boundary" in one of the last issues of *Getseltn* summed up her contentment with having lived a full life and in which she extended her hand without fear across the thin boundary that separated her from the enchanted land of death. Only a single volume of her lyrics appeared during her lifetime and only a single volume of her collected poems and stories posthumously. Both bore the same title *In Hot Wind* (*In Haisen Vint*, 1935, 1959).

In young years at Kiev, Celia Drapkin wrote in Russian and was encouraged to continue by A. N. Gnessin (1879-1913), the Hebrew narrator. After her coming to America in 1912, Abraham Liessin recognized her talent and influenced her to change from Russian to Yiddish. "Die Yunge" welcomed her in their periodicals and the Insichists opened the columns of *In Sich* to her lyrics.

These lyrics were characterized by intense feeling, pure longing and passionate fulfillment. She compressed uncomplicated experiences in rhymed quatrains: the submission of a wife to a beloved husband, the happiness of a mother, the blessedness of living without pain or guilt. Her lullabies to her infant children delighted with their simple charm, and her songs for her more grown-up sons and daughters expressed motherly care and tenderness.

Among the frequent contributors to *Getseltn* was Berish Weinstein (1905-1967), whom critics called the most American of the Yiddish poets. After an adventurous youth in Galicia, Bohemia and Vienna, during which he accumulated a basic knowledge of Polish, German, Hebrew and Yiddish, he arrived in New York at the age of nineteen and was enriched by English and American influences. He began his Yiddish literary career in 1927. His lyric volume *Fragmentation* (*Bruchvarg*, 1936) was hailed as a significant achievement in Yiddish letters by S. Niger, A. Mukdoni, S. Margoshes and Moshe Nadir. This volume was later incorporated in the more important collection *Songs and Poems* (*Lieder Un Poemes*, 1949). Weinstein's chief claim to fame, however, was the trilogy which unfolded in colorful imagery and grand rhythmic panoramas the three stages of his inner evolution: *Raishe* (1947), *America* (1955) and *In King Davids' Domains* (*In Duvid Ameilekhs Giter*, 1960).

In Weinstein's earliest lyrics non-Jewish subjects were dominant and much use was made of Christian symbolism. Several poems dealt with Negro toil and Negro suffering. Others sang of sad-robed, soft-treading nuns who never felt the touch of a man's hand. Still others centered about Sheepshead Bay, a harbor district in Brooklyn, where salt-blown fishermen anchored their ships and through whose streets sailors sauntered in search of pleasures and female company.

The opening lyric of *Fragmentation,* entitled "Beethoven's Bust," revealed Weinstein's early virtuosity. Just as a physicist converts one form of physical energy into another, and the second into a third, so, said the poet, the emotional and spiritual energy which found expression in Beethoven's musical accords could be transmitted first by a sculptor's hand to inert bronze, until the metal became vibrant with it, and then by the poet into verbal imagery, ultimately living on again in rhythmic stanzas.

Although Weinstein attempted to reproduce in lyrics the moods of Brahms, Tchaikovsky, Sibelius, César Franck and Dvorak, his chief love continued to be Beethoven. In a series of poems, he reviewed the various stages of this composer's career, his abysmal loneliness, his cosmic sadness and his one moment of supreme ecstasy when he wanted to embrace millions and kiss the macrocosm.

With the rise of Hitlerism, Jewish themes came to the fore. Repercussions of 1933 are to be found in lyrics such as "Hangmen" and "Hakenkreuz." In the poem "Jews," Weinstein recalls tensions in his own Polish town, a pogrom he had witnessed, a desecrated Sabbath when Jewish children with dazzling white Sabbath loaves in their hands were set upon by stone-hurling neighbors and when churchgoers wielding canes caused blood to flow from wise Hassidic brows upon Sabbath robes of velvet and satin.

When reports of Maidanek and other extermination camps reached the poet, he felt that the martyred sons and daughters of his Jewish people had prior claim upon his muse. In tones reminiscent of the biblical *Lamentations,* he bewailed his slaughtered kinsmen and all the holy ones of Israel whom God deserted in years of wrath. Maidanek was for Weinstein not only the altar upon which Jews went up in flames but also the gallows upon which God himself was hanged.

To expiate his own guilt in not having been with the victims in their hours of agony, the poet devoted his volume *Raishe* to a reconstruction of their vanished world, the world he had known in his childhood. An entire civilization parades before our eyes. Shadowy figures are quickened into being and move about in work-a-day and in holiday moods. The streets and market-places

of the Galician town come to life and hum with activity. His
Raishe becomes symbolic of every town in which East European
Jews dwelt in tolerable security and semi-poverty for many generations until they were overtaken by ever increasing pressures.
He stresses the experiences of his own contemporaries who were
uprooted from traditional ways and forced to set out on endless
wanderings along the highways and bylanes of this globe. A few
of them managed to get to Palestine and to pioneer a new life for
themselves and their people. More got to America, even as he himself did. With his crossing of the Atlantic, the first epic of his
trilogy comes to an end. By not continuing the narrative to the
final catastrophe, the almost total liquidation of the many who
remained behind in Raishe or on the European way-stations, the
poet leaves the reader sad but not crushed, unhappy but not bitter.

Weinstein's second epic, *America*, begins with the landing of
the young immigrant upon the strange new soil and describes his
gradual integration into American culture. At first the loneliness,
indifference and cruelty of New York fill him with longing to
return to the warm hearth of his childhood. He comes in contact
with the crushed victims of the sweatshops, the flotsam and jet-
sam of the Bowery, the bankrupt souls of the Great Depression.
These pass before him, each with a grim tale of frustrated hopes.
After his first difficult decade of adjustment, however, he responds
to the resurgent ideals instilled by Franklin D. Roosevelt's New
Deal and he establishes new roots. In Whitmanesque verses, he
sings of America's vast spaces, rich history, pioneers of freedom.
The idealism of Lincoln, the Great Emancipator, fills his soul,
displaces older dreams, and gives him temporarily the feeling of
being truly at home. Standing on the once blood-drenched field of
Gettysburg, he accepts the ringing phrases of the Gettysburg
Address as the genuine voice of democratic America, the blessed
land of his children though not of his forefathers.

As for himself, the yearning for a complete Jewish life, such
as he knew in his pre-American youth, still lingers with him.
Israel reborn draws him irresistibly. In the third epic of his trilogy,
In King David's Domains, he records the impact of his first visit
to the land beside the Jordan. Cabalist Safed is not strange to
him, nor is Tiberias by the Sea of Galilee; he remembers them
from tales of his grandmother and from legends of his grand-uncle.
To stand on Mt. Carmel is to relive childhood dreams of Elijah
which were submerged for many years. In the orchards and vineyards of Zion he finds his classmate Sanya, who tended them

while he himself was busy tending alien orchards and vineyards. He realizes that Raishe and America were long way-stations. In the domains of King David is his yearned-for home. There the stones talk to him and the trees whisper to him reminiscences of ancestral deeds and daring.

With a reiteration of the biblical vow "If I forget thee, Jerusalem, may my right hand wither," and with the annually repeated hope "Next year in Jerusalem," Weinstein ends his poetic trilogy, the main achievement of his life-long wrestling to find himself and to attain a stable relationship to his people's past and present.

His epic *Homeriade* (1964) sought to capture in dactylic hexameters the sunny spirit of carefree Hellas, but his Jewish heart was with the conquered and despoiled Trojans such as Hector, Priam and Hecuba, far more than with the wily Odysseus, the fleet-footed Achilles and the other well-greaved Achaians. In three cantos, he recreated Homeric legends of the "Radiant Helen," the "Wrath of Achilles," and the "Homecoming of Odysseus." But by far the finest legend retold was that of the blind bard Homer, with whom the contemporary poet identified himself.

In the volume *Songs Granted Me* (*Basherte Lieder*, 1965), American themes were again dominant, especially New York with its subway scenes, wharfs, beaches, parks, avenues, saloons. The poet's characters ranged from sailors and drunkards to Hassidim and visionaries; bronze, yellow, black and white human beings of all social strata. But there were also repercussions of his trip to Israel in 1952, verses of the fields of Galilee and the tents of Jacob. In every European city en route to Israel he felt himself a stranger and longed for the sight of a Jewish face. He recalled how in his younger years he had wished to walk along the boulevards of Basel, Bern, Brussels, Paris. Now these cites were for him merely foreign places leading on to the land of his heart's desire. It was not granted him, however, to tarry long in Israel. "In New York I shall always be sad with yearning for you, Jerusalem; I shall never forgive myself for leaving you, Jerusalem, for leaving only a tear in you."

Weinstein belongs to the epigones of Yiddish literature. He opened no great new vistas. He did, however, reduce to rhythmic utterance and vivid imagery the physical and spiritual migration of his Yiddish-speaking generation from its origins in Eastern Europe through the squalor and glamor of America onto an autumnal rejuvenation in Israel.

To this generation belonged Aaron Nissenson (1898-1964), who was brought to the United States at the age of thirteen and who in his personality combined Lithuanian melancholy and New York's turbulent joy.

In his first volume, *One Hundred Songs* (*Hundert Lieder*, 1920), he described his final moments in the townlet of his birth, his young friends asking him not to forget them in the distant trans-Atlantic continent, his last view of a golden-haired maiden at the well. Thereafter, memories of an idyllic, lost boyhood paradise accompanied him and he tried to recover this paradise in poetic visions. In the storm of restless days, he yearned for simplicity and kindness. In the depths of the Great Depression, he composed his dramatic poem *The Road to Man* (*Der Veg Tsu Mentsh*, 1934), in which the central hero was the Socialist leader Eugene V. Debs, symbol of immaculate man. Amidst the barbarity of the Hitler years, he sang of a coming reign of pure goodness. In twelve scenes of *The Promised Land* (*Dos Tsugesogte Land*, 1937), he depicted man's efforts to evolve toward moral perfection. Beginning with Pharaoh and Moses, in whom antithetical forces of evil and goodness, matter and spirit, were embodied, the poet traced the struggle of these forces in various transformations throughout historic times and voiced his faith that science would soon end man's schizophrenic tendencies and would bring him closer to the radiance of God.

While the Second World War was at its height, Nissenson entitled his lyric volume *Life Sings Even In Death* (*Dos Leben Zingt Afile In Toit*, 1943) and, after the war, he entitled his last volume *In the Footsteps of the Righteous* (*In Tzaddiks Trit*, 1950), thus continuing to voice optimism in the triumph of life over death and of righteousness over wickedness, despite temporary horrors and bloodshed. Instead of blasphemous accusations against God, he pointed to the wondrous structure of God's universe and to the most recent scientific achievements that could pave the way for compassionate, just human beings who would evolve from the imperfect creatures of the past and the present.

Benjamin Jacob Bialostotsky (1893-1962) came to America in the same year as Nissenson and also retained throughout his life an abiding faith in man's inevitable progress and perfectibility. Though memories of his childhood in a Lithuanian townlet were reflected in his poetry, he preferred to direct his gaze more often upon the American metropolis. He felt that Jews must accept the fact that they had outgrown the townlets which cradled Yiddish culture and that they had become to the largest extent city

dwellers. The task of a Yiddish poet should be, therefore, to reproduce the sights and rhythms of urban, industrialized civilization.
He should be forward-looking, sensitive to the new era in which he
lived, without letting himself be entirely consumed by it.

Bialostotsky's early model was Morris Rosenfeld, to whom he
dedicated adoring essays and whose influence was paramount in the
social songs of *Along the Highway* (*Beim Breiten Veg*, 1920).
These songs depicted the poverty and sadness of the immigrant
generation. He too sang of the sallow, white-bearded operator who
sat bent over a machine day and night, the mother who sewed
a shroud for her only child, the homeless drunkard asleep on a
park bench, the blind beggar, the Bowery vagabond, the bleary-
eyed derelict.

In his later lyrics, the picturesqueness of New York's East Side
came more to the fore, but also its rebellious mood. The old house
on Cherry Street, doomed to demolition, reminded him of the
toiling tenants of earlier decades who chanted Morris Rosenfeld's
pathetic lyrics and whose eyes glowed with visions of a juster
world for which they were prepared to strike and to hunger. In
Ludlow Street, the poet still found bearded Jewish pushcart-ped-
dlers and aging Jewesses who spoke the earthy, unadulterated
Yiddish of Vilna, and he enclosed in rhymes their honest efforts
to earn their bread by their own labor. The lyrics, which allied
him to the proletarian poets of the 1920's and 1930's, failed to
survive the ravages of time. His simple children's songs, however,
set to music by Solomon Golub and Michel Gelbart, continued to
be sung in Yiddish elementary schools and his poetic tales of
Noah, Moses, Elijah and Chelm long fascinated young audiences.
His masterpiece for children, however, was *Bienele* (1940), the
story of a little boy who set out in search of the land of the
eternal holiday and who, after many adventures past the river of
tears, the maelstrom of blood and the mountain of dead bones,
finally arrived at the terrestrial paradise, where people worked
and enjoyed the full products of their labor and where sadness,
distress and death were unknown. Only three days were granted
to Bienele to be there, but the memory of the experience remained
with him ever thereafter and his days were irradiated by his faith
in the inevitable nighing of such a utopia for all the inhabitants
of this globe.

In his last years Bialostotsky retold for adults Jewish tales and
legends from Babylon and Rome, parables of the famed Maggid
of Dubnow and jests of legendary merrymakers and contemporary

humorists. Though originally written for newspaper readers, they were based on thorough research as well as memories retained from the folklore with which his father, a famed preacher, regaled audiences during the poet's youth.

Mark Schweid (1891-1969), an actor by profession and a poet by inclination, began under the influence of Peretz in Warsaw. At twenty he arrived in New York from Vienna and began an illustrious career on the Yiddish and English stage. He also translated and adapted German, Polish, Russian and English dramatists, but his original contribution was in the lyric. Using simple words, pure rhymes and traditional metrical stanzas, he stressed the need for drinking deep of momentary joy even though pain was more universal and enduring. He found joy in the transitory fragrance of a flower, in the loaf of bread earned by the sweat of one's brow, in a bit of love that glowed for an instant, in Jewish festivals that infused bright colors into gray seasons.

While Schweid's early, Viennese, romantic poems betrayed the influence of the young Heine, his later, more realistic, American poems were lightened by humor and deepened by contemplation. The sonnet became his favorite vehicle for expressing immediate insights and rcollections of past moments. For decades there recurred in his verses the longing for his parental home and his native townlet where he did not feel himself to be a superfluous, lonely individual but a vibrant Jewish cell functioning within a living Jewish communal organism. After the Nazi destruction of his Polish-Jewish birthplace, he recognized the futility of nostalgia, vented his anger at the destroyers of his kin, and contented himself with expressing in verse his ripe autumnal experiences and distilled impressions. Under the title of *Complete Poems* (*Ale Lieder Un Poemes*, 1951), he included in a single volume all his poems which he cared to preserve.

Meir Zimel Tkatch (b. 1894), a native of the Ukraine, began as a Russian poet in New York on the eve of the First World War and did not publish his first book of Yiddish songs and fables until 1927. Eight additional volumes followed. The best of his verse narratives, fables, parables, sonnets, triolets, serious and humorous lyrics, songs for children and translations of Russian and American poetry were collected in the two volumes of *My Possession and Gift* (*Mein Hob un Gob*, 1963).

Tkatch is at his best in his fables. These are superb miniature dramas. Each teaches a lesson by means of a vivid, verbal encounter between animals or things. Their dialogues afford bitter insight into motivations. Tkatch does not indulge in moral abstractions, but a moral code fit for creatures endowed with reason emerges from watching the behavior and listening to the conversations of things and beasts not so endowed. The tree that wants to reach up to heaven rebukes the roots that hold it fast to earth and is then accused of ingratitude by the roots, for is it not by sucking at their juice that the tree has the strength to aspire to the heights? When the sour Miss Lemon turns green with chagrin because Mr. Orange does not call her by the more aristocratic name of Citrus, she receives the answer that the fairer name will not change sour to sweet. The neutralist hyena steers clear of the combat that rages between its neighbors, but when the battle is over it feeds leisurely, with the appetite of a neutral, on the casualties left on the field.

Tkatch loves earth and sky, man and worm, and he sings in happy tones of this love. He says yea to life, though it be a tangled skein of good and bad. He wants to weed this earth of its noxious growths and convert it into a paradise. The optimist is shocked, however, as he becomes aware of his people's tragedy during the years of conflagration. His light verses are then tear-stained as he demands a reckoning of God for Jewish blood that cries up from the ground. Tkatch's mastery of his verse medium comes to the fore also in his sonnet-sequences and in his translations of Robert Frost, Sergei Yessenin and Yevtuchenko.

Aba Stolzenberg (1905-1941) arrived in New York from Eastern Galicia in 1923. His first poems appeared during the following year. A friendship with Meyer Stiker (b. 1905) and Abraham Tabachnik (1901-1970) led to a common literary striving. This found expression in the journal *Feilen,* published between 1928 and 1931. Although Stolzenberg in his earliest poems sought to follow the example of the undisciplined Khaliastre poets then in fashion, he soon came under the influence of their antipode, the poet Reuben Iceland, a pillar of "Die Yunge." Iceland taught him to tame his exuberant imagination, to eschew Expressionism and to encase his strong emotions in few words and carefully chiseled lines which produce a unitary mood.

Stolzenberg tried to curb his restlessness and to control the fire that burned within himself, but his heart continued to yearn for storms and raging billows. Chained to poverty, he turned his eyes to his Galician past, irretrievable save for idealizing, dream-drenched memories. He sang of young hopes no longer realizable, of first love whose flaming breath once seared him, of beauty that faded all too soon, of cold autumnal rains that fell upon gray days. Romantic melancholy enveloped him. Compassion filled him for bankrupt souls, for girls with extinguished eyes, for women with bent shoulders, sad and obedient under the yoke of unending toil, for a Yiddish poet who had hanged himself and an Irish drunkard clubbed by police.

In the largely autobiographic poetic cycle "The Diary of the Straw Knight," Stolzenberg set out to recount the evolution of a Galician Jewish intellectual of his generation. The twenty-four lyrics and ballads of this cycle bore dates from January 1, 1900, until March 14, 1909. Had he been able to complete this work, upon which he labored until his death, it would have given a colorful panorama of a typical Galician townlet both before and after World War I. According to his fellow poet Abraham Tabachnik, to whom he confided his innermost thoughts, the cane-twirling Straw Knight, who went forth to adventure in the wide world, would have wandered among many ideologies and would have returned at the end, exhausted and disillusioned, to die on the soil of his Galician birthplace.

Tabachnik, who wrote the finest evaluation of Stolzenberg, was primarily a literary critic and essayist, even though he contributed to poetic journals and published two volumes of lyrics. In his first volume of 1936, he let his songs dance like painted puppets on a string and used rhythmic words to build castles in the air. He toyed with concepts ranging from God to estheticism and was eclectic in his choice of subjects and forms. He characterized himself as a cup full of wine that poured itself out before every swine. However, this wine was pressed from a mixture of grapes of varying quality.

In his second volume of 1949, Tabachnik again immersed himself in the essence of other poets and sought to reproduce their uniqueness in lyric portraits. By selecting poets to whom he reacted sympathetically, such as Morris Rosenfeld, Joseph Rolnick, Mani-Leib, Zishe Landau and Aba Stolzenberg, he was able to blend his own emotions with theirs. Lacking naiveté and endowed with fine taste, he recognized his limitations as a poet. Nevertheless, he did create a few lasting poems as in "God's Bunker-Weeping," in which he presented the beaten God fleeing from heaven and finding refuge in a ghetto bunker among a dozen Jewish children. For them He was father and mother, grandfather and grandmother. He began to teach them the alphabet and He regaled them with wonder tales of heaven. But before He got to the end of the alphabet, all the children had perished. God alone survived and His weeping in the bunker resounded throughout the universe.

The best of Tabachnik's essays were collected under the title *Poets and Poetry* (*Dichter Un Dichtung,* 1965), a volume of discerning insights in impeccable prose.

Meyer Stiker was the third of the closely knit poets who appeared as a group in the issues of *Feilen.* Unlike Stolzenberg and Tabachnik, who only rarely included American themes in their verses, Stiker was not indifferent to his New World environment. Although his first volume, *Songs* (*Lieder,* 1945), sought to rescue from oblivion types and scenes of his native Galician townlet before its destruction, his more significant second volume, *Yiddish Landscape* (*Yiddishe Landshaft,* 1958), roamed across the entire range of contemporary Jewish life, from Eastern Europe to Israel and America. But it also touched on eternal problems, on the lure of life and the inevitability of death, on the alternation of the seasons with their varying moods, on the reality of dreams and the dreamlike quality of even trivial, normal experiences. Like Tabachnik, he too lacked naive freshness and compensated for this lack by subtlety of language and utmost refinement of verse. He was well acquainted with the most modern currents of German, French, English and American literatures, but preferred rhymed quatrains and severe traditional forms to free verse and undisciplined rhythms.

Chaim Krull (1892-1946) stood under the shadow of death for many years. As a result, the theme of death predominated in his poems, which included elegies to a dead child, to a deceased friend, to his mother to whom he was deeply attached and who passed away at a young age. Death was welcomed by him as the redeemer from life's pain and loneliness.

A single, unhappy love left its impact upon him, saddening him prematurely. In short, impressionistic verses, he reproduced a rich variety of sensations, emotions and nervous excitations which this love, more longing than fulfillment, aroused in him. *About Myself* (*Arum Sich,* 1930) contained not only cycles of love poems but also a prose romance about this girl of his adolescent dreams who left for America before he could win her in reality and whose traces he could not find when he landed in New York. The volume also included essays on Yiddish writers in which he, the Impressionist, displayed less interest in facts than in the atmosphere about each of his subjects.

Krull's closest affinity was for J. I. Segal (1896-1954), the Montreal poet, who also invoked death in many a poem, following upon the loss of his young daughter. Indeed, the literary critic Baruch Rivkin characterized them as two poets who prayed from the same *siddur*.

While Krull was economical in his use of words and left but a modest literary legacy, J. I. Segal was extremely prolific and only a part of his prose and verse has been collected in the dozen published volumes. Through most of them there resounded the mournful refrain of the fading of beauty along with the fading of the traditional Yiddish way of life. He undertook the task of preserving in his own poetic idiom whatever could be preserved of the liturgical style of Tkhines, and to make retrospectively fascinating whatever could be retained of the folk habits of the Yiddish townlets. He averted his face from the Canadian metropolis in which he spent his post-adolescent decades. He preferred to mingle in imagination with simple, quiet, silver-bearded Jews who walked in the paths of piety. He sang of the holiness of the Sabbath in Podolian Jewish communities where God's spirit hovered closely over a chosen, obedient people. He retold tales of the Prophet Elijah, the Baal Shem, and less well-known, humble, saintly personalities. The poet's mother was for him the symbol of the goodness that inhered in poor, hard-working, uncomplicated souls and he repeatedly invoked her in his lyrics.

While Segal spent his mature years in Montreal, Leon Feinberg roamed over lands and languages and ideologies before he attained to stability as a person and as a poet. Born in 1897 as the youngest child of an impoverished cabalist in a Podolian townlet, he was reared in traditional learning, but began his literary career as a Russian lyricist under the name of Leonid Grebniov. He dreamed of becoming another Pushkin, or at least another Soloviev or Yessenin, poets whom he admired. When the Revolution of 1917 broke out, he exchanged the pen for the gun and fought for three years against the anti-Semitic Ukrainian bands. Then followed restless wandering from Bombay to Jerusalem, through North Africa and Europe, until he landed in 1923 in New York, his more enduring home. He then made Yiddish his primary linguistic medium and continued with Russian as his secondary medium.

In the poems of *Metropolis* (*Groisshtut*, 1928), he groped his way to original perceptions through a vast variety of literary influences with which he had come in contact. He assimilated Russian mystic and revolutionary strains, American Imagism and

Yiddish Insichism. He alternated between warm reminiscences of his pious heritage and a desire to help the forward march of the new redeemers. The epic "Bolsheviks" in the volume *Light and Bread (Likht Un Broit,* 1931) represented the climax of his proletarian poetry. In the ballads of *Comrade Life (Khaver Leben,* 1938), he still prided himself on being a class-conscious, belligerent poet. He still wove a ring of sonnets about Soviet Russia, the motherland he loved with an unabating love. Then came the Stalin-Hitler Pact of 1939 which brought him sobering disillusionment. In the volume, *The Inheritors of the Earth (Die Yorshim Fun Der Erd,* 1941), his infatuation with Soviet Russia was replaced by an ardent affection for the Jewish people. He felt that forces of destruction had overwhelmed the creative revolutionary forces which had once sought to bring salvation to Adam's children, and he found new comfort in the Bible and its teaching that the wicked would ultimately be destroyed and that those who put their trust in God would inherit the earth. In his poem *Yiddish* (1950), he drew his self-portrait. From the alien idols he had formerly served so faithfully, he had escaped back to his own fold. Thereafter he would guard his own vineyard; he would seek his inspiration in the Hebrew prophets; he would be the harpist of Jehovah; he would be the guardian of the Yiddish tongue and heritage.

There then followed four novels in verse, each of them autobiographical, illuminating under various disguises the poet's inner conflicts. *The Doomed Generation (Der Farmishpeter Dor,* 1954) portrayed a hero who was disappointed with the Communist ideal. *The God of Wrath (Der Gott Fun Zorn,* 1957) showed the heretic Elisha Ben Abuya vacillating between Hebraism and Hellenism, seeking a synthesis between Greek beauty and Jewish ethics under Roman power. But, Apollo, Shaddai and Jupiter were mutually contradictory forces and could not be reconciled. The heretic, who opposed the revolt of Bar Kochba, could not witness the martyrdom of his people at the hands of the conquering Romans without repenting his heresies and returning to them in their hour of affliction. *The Blessed Generation (Der Gebentshter Dor,* 1962) reverted again to Feinberg's own generation, which achieved maturity in the decade between the abortive Russian Revolution of 1905 and the First World War. In the hero Lulik Adler, the poet relived the events of his early years—the pogrom by the Black Hundreds in Kiev in 1906, the feverish weeks of liberation in 1917, the visions and emotional ecstasy of his youthful striving for the laurels of a Russian lyricist, his struggle for survival in communities ravaged by Denikin and Petlura, his escape from chaos, epidemics, massacres and the horror of Odessa in 1920, his unsuccessful attempt to adjust to the hard realities of the re-Promised Land where the heroic pioneers were shepherds and kibbutz tractorists. Finding himself mute and useless among the Jewish colonists, Feinberg's hero resumed his odyssey, experienced Parisian loves and hells, and shed the non-Jewish layers of his soul. However, unlike his author, he resisted the temptation to settle in America. Tired of wandering, he returned to kibbutz life in the Emek. The bankrupt Jewish Don Quixote, erstwhile worshiper of Apollo and the Muses, finally found happiness and fulfillment as a tiller of the soil in the land of his forefathers but still dreaming vivid Messianic dreams, a creative member of the blessed first generation of Jewish redemption. The final cantos of this verse epic were filled with yearning for a world which the author could not make his own, for an Israel Feinberg could only experience in glowing verses that stirred imagination, mind and heart in the autumn of his life.

The last of Feinberg's poetic epics of the Russian Jewish intellectuals with whom he shared his early years was *The Ruined Generation (Der Khorever Dor, 1967)*. In this work, which followed the pattern and the stanzaic form of Pushkin's *Eugene Onegin,* he dealt with the Communist idealists who did not leave their native land, since they had faith in the vistas of freedom and equality apparently opened up by the Revolution of 1917. These Jews fought, even as Feinberg did, in the ranks of the Bolsheviks against the pogrom bands of counter-revolutionists. During the early years when Lenin held sway, some rose to high rank in the Soviet hierarchy. However, their Jewish origin, which they sought to forget, continued to render them vulnerable and, under the Stalin dictatorship, the Kremlin realists wreaked havoc among them. Some perished before firing squads, others languished and died in Siberian labor camps. In the Jewish youth Pinie Yolles, who rose to the rank of Marshal of the Red Army and who was then liquidated, Feinberg drew a sympathetic portrait of Jan Gamarik, who was his friend and a brother-in-law of Chaim Nachman Bialik and who in 1937 received an order from Stalin's secret police to shoot himself. Only a single survivor of the Ruined Generation, the poet's alter ego, succeeded, thirty years after the Revolution, in escaping from Russia and in penning a fierce condemnation of the entire oppressive system. The tortured lives and unsung death of the Jews who remained found late expression in Feinberg's poetic laments.

The most controversial figure among the American Yiddish poets was Elihu Chaim Sheps, who wrote under the adopted name of A. Almi (1892-1963). Born in Warsaw and experiencing a difficult childhood amidst poverty and misunderstanding, he early attracted the attention of I. L. Peretz, H. D. Nomberg and Abraham Reisen. He published his first lyrics at fifteen. After sojourning in Cracow and Vienna, he returned to Warsaw and wrote for its influential daily *Moment*. At twenty he left for the United States. In New York he was welcomed by editors and literary colleagues and reached the height of his popularity during the following decade when he published more than a dozen books of prose and verse. He translated the sayings of Buddha, introduced Yiddish readers to the poetry and philosophy of China and made the mythology of Japan and India intelligible to wider audiences. However, his non-conformism and his bitter humor estranged friends and nurtured antagonists. He had keen insight into Jewish life and, since he did not hesitate to call attention to social ills, literary shams and religious hypocrisy, he was constantly engaged in feuds, in the course of which he inflicted many wounds and received more in return.

In his two autobiographic volumes, *Moments of a Life (Momenten Fun A Leben*, 1948) and *Spiritual Balance (Kheshbon Un Sakh-Hakol*, 1959), he detailed his spiritual odyssey, his espousal of anarchism, spiritualism, vegetarianism and various esoteric doctrines, his suicidal tendencies and his quarrels with his fellow men, whose weaknesses he had a talent for ferreting out. As he aged, loneliness gathered about him. Reacting against neglect, he found relief in sardonic outbursts against God and man, dominant ideologies and popular idols.

On Almi's seventieth birthday, a volume of appreciations by critics who admired him appeared, but by then his mood had become thoroughly nihilistic and his self-destructive urge could no longer be arrested. A decade before his self-willed end, he took leave of the lyric muse in his volume *Last Songs (Letzte Gezangen*, 1954), in which his cosmic despair found raging expression. He felt that God's show would go on interminably but he did not want to be part of it. The role of a marionette dancing to the whimsical tunes of a supreme puppeteer did not appeal to him. He looked up to the stars and saw them smiling, while human beings squirmed here below. The heavens were praising the Lord, while hearts bled on earth and fists were raised in vain protest against a callous Almighty. The faith of the pious, the verses of the poets, the destiny of the entire human race, the pain of all species, mattered nothing in the wild whirl of galaxies. With all our weeping and imprecations, we still remained insignificant dust in the vast expanse of time and space. The God was dead who had once proclaimed "Let there be Light!" and we were groping with blind fingers in a blacked-out universe. The poet hurled curses at the cosmic slaughterer who led the Jewish people to the sacrificial altar and had them go up in flames. He repeatedly called Him to judgement and proclaimed Him guilty.

Almi's principal theme was death. He invoked it in a thousand shapes. Death was final wisdom and ultimate truth, while life was folly and illusion. He toasted death and faced it fearlessly—"Only a fool fears death." What did worry him, however, was the possibility that souls might survive physical extinction, as his cherished Oriental philosophers asserted. In that case, he prayed that an exception might be made for him and that his bruised soul might share total extinction together with his body.

Death and pessimistic insight also permeated the poetry of Alter Esselin (b. 1889), the Yiddish lyricist of Milwaukee, Wisconsin. His best elegy was on the death of a tree, his companion for eighteen years, his sympathetic friend that peered into his window, listened to his verses, shared his melancholy on wintry nights, and let him partake of its joy in blossoming April days. Another unforgettable poem portrayed the death of an ox in the snow, its impotent rage, its struggle against the implacable Almighty, its last roar of despair before it sank into the whirling, white heap.

Esselin described himself in a poetic epitaph as a lyricist who poisoned himself with songs in which honey and arsenic were mixed. He was born in Chernigov, Ukraine. At ten he lost his father and, as the oldest of five children, he had to face mature responsibilities. He worked as a carpenter's apprentice. At sixteen he emigrated to America and labored in several mid-western communities before settling in Milwaukee. His poems, beginning with *Knots* (*Kneitn*, 1927), and continuing with *Songs* (*Lieder*, 1936) and *Songs of a Desert Poet* (*Lieder Fun A Midbernik*, 1954), voiced his pride that he was earning his bread with saw and hammer and that he was endowed with the physical stamina to stand up against all the blows of fate. He wrote stirring social poetry and boasted of his proletarian uncouthness. Nevertheless, he could not mask his tender sensitivity. He felt the pain of all creatures, the pain of the hungry dog and the frost-bitten cat no less than of the drunkard in the gutter and the Negro beaten to death in a lynching. In sick dawns and solitary nights, he raged at God through tears. In his loneliness he found companionship in the realm of dreams, and in his poverty he found wealth in the silver of the moon and the diamonds of the stars.

The American epigones and eclectic poets suffered from the fact that they were uprooted from their Yiddish base in Eastern Europe at an early age and were compelled to spend most of their years in an English speaking environment. They witnessed the gradual aging and diminution of their reading public and they were plagued with doubts as to the meaningfulness of their literary creativity in Yiddish. These doubts arose at a time when Yiddish had attained a richness of vocabulary, a flexibility in syntax and a stylistic artistry all of which enabled it to express the subtlest thoughts and feelings with utmost refinement.

18

MINOR EUROPEAN CENTERS

Rumanian Center ● Psanter ● Groper ● Botoshansky
● Steinbarg ● Sternberg ● Altman ● Manger ●
Younger Poets ● English Center ● Pioneer Writers
● Gaster ● Morris Myer ● Oved ● Leftwich ●
● Stencl ● A. M. Fuchs ● Paris Center ● Elie
Wiesel ● Efroykin ● Finer ● Sloves ● Shulstein
● Dluznowsky ● Domankiewicz

WHILE THE THREE principal centers of Yiddish creativity in the twentieth century were the United States, Poland, and Soviet Russia, the immigration of Yiddish-speaking Jews to Western Europe, Latin America, South Africa and Australia resulted in the rise of new centers for Yiddish cultural activities. But even older Jewish settlements such as Rumania experienced new vitality because of shifting national boundaries and greater population mobility.

Rumania entered upon the Yiddish literary scene in 1876 when the folksinger and wedding bard Velvel Zbarzher Ehrenkranz (1826-1883), who stemmed from Galicia, sang and acted out his dramatic verses in Rumanian towns, and when Abraham Goldfaden (1840-1908), who came from Russia, began in Jassy his first experiments in Yiddish dramatic performances. The enthusiastic reception given to Goldfaden in Rumania prompted him to expand his dialogues and scenarios into full-length comedies and his two or three acting assistants into large troupes that wandered throughout Eastern Europe.

Of Yiddish poets indigenous to Rumania, the best known was Yakov Psanter (1820-1900), who was born in Botoshani and reared in Jassy. Self-educated and talented in music, he became a wedding bard, adapting the verses of famed *Badchonim* to his

Rumanian audiences. For years he roamed with a gypsy band and performed on cymbals at non-Jewish festivities. Compelled to listen in aristocratic homes to constant slurs against Jews as foreigners and undesirable intruders, he wrote a two-volume history in their defense. This history set out to prove that Jews had lived in Rumania since the days of Nebuchadnezzar and that a large contingent had arrived while the provinces that later became Rumania were still under Roman rule. The first volume, published in 1871, ended with the fall of the Byzantine Empire in 1453. The second volume, published in 1873, continued the narrative until Psanter's own generation. Psanter's history is no longer accepted as an authentic source, but it performed a valuable service during the decades of the struggle for Jewish rights in Rumania, from the Berlin Peace Conference of 1878 to the First World War. It was often quoted as evidence of the antiquity of Rumania's Jews.

The Czernovitz Language Conference of 1908 stimulated Yiddish cultural activities throughout Eastern Europe, and had repercussions in Rumania. Among the pioneers of Yiddish letters on the eve of World War I were Jacob Groper (1890-1966) and Jacob Botoshansky (1892-1964). They were the most talented contributors to the first Rumanian Yiddish literary journal, *Licht,* published in Jassy during the two years preceding Rumania's entrance into the War in 1916.

Groper began to write Yiddish poetry while still a student of law at Jassy University and while serving in the Balkan War in 1913. His poems appeared in periodicals and anthologies from 1914 on, but not until twenty years later were they collected in a slender volume, *In the Shadow of a Stone (In Shutn Fun A Shtein,* 1934). The poems are romantic in tone and replete with youthful melancholy. The poet wants to grasp the glad moments of spring's blossoming because he is aware that cold winds will soon nip the blossoms and it will be too late to be glad. He sees his bright dreams dissolving and his heart becoming filled with pain, but he is still young enough to wait for the flowering of new dreams and for the heart to recapture its buoyancy. Groper's lyrics, once on the lips of Rumanian Jewish youth both in the Yiddish original and in Rumanian translation, are today forgotten. They did, however, help to raise the prestige of Yiddish. His admirer, the literary critic Shlomo Bickel, said of him: "As a creator of Yiddish, Jacob Groper was in Rumania the start; as a Jewish intellectual he was the zenith; as a spiritual personality he was the full day of the Old Rumanian Jewish community."

Jacob Botoshansky participated in the upsurge of Yiddish in Rumania from 1914 to 1926 as critic, essayist, journalist and dramatist before emigrating to Buenos Aires. There he edited Argentina's most influential Yiddish daily, *Die Presse*, and for more than a third of a century he was a central figure in Jewish cultural activities. His survey of Rumanian Yiddish literature in the volume *Mother Yiddish* (*Mame Yiddish*, 1949) anticipated the more detailed analysis in Shlomo Bickel's *Rumania* (1961).

After World War I, Bessarabia, Bukovina and Transylvania, with their large Yiddish-speaking populations, were added to Rumania. Only then did a reading public arise of sufficient magnitude to support quality journals and Yiddish publishing ventures. From these newer provinces, rather than from Old Rumania, stemmed the majority of the Yiddish writers of the next half century. The single town of Lipcani, in Northern Bessarabia, was the birthplace of the fabulist Eliezer Steinbarg (1880-1932), the dramatist Jacob Sternberg (b. 1890) and the novelist Moishe Altman (b. 1890).

Steinbarg, the most original writer of fables in Yiddish, attained international fame only after his death. His fables, which had appeared solely in periodicals during his lifetime, were collected in a posthumous Yiddish volume. It had a large vogue, and was translated into Hebrew and into half a dozen European languages. Steinbarg was an educator in Lipcani, Rio de Janeiro, and Cernauti. His *Tales for Children* (*Meiselekh*, 1936), combining Yiddish folk treasures, imaginative animal lore, light humor and simple vocabulary, furnished attractive reading material for Yiddish schools.

His fables are generally in the form of dialogues and the characters are inanimate objects more often than animals or plants. To all of them he assigns human traits and has them engage in disputes as to proper behavior. Each object experiences far more suffering than joy; through each the author emphasizes the tragedy and the injustice inherent in the structure of the world.

Steinbarg is pessimistic, yet compassionate. He holds that heaven may perhaps punish sinners, but that earth certainly punishes the virtuous. He illustrates this conclusion in the fable of the good-natured piece of soap which cleanses and purifies, but is penalized for this virtue by becoming ever thinner and nearer to dissolution. In another fable, that of the knife and the saw, he points out that on the imperfect planet the *shochet's* knife is blessed, strutting about as a glistening aristocrat because its function is to cut living throats, while the saw is looked upon as an ugly plebeian because it busies itself with the menial task of sawing dull, wooden blocks.

Steinbarg opposes docile submission to the dominant order, which he regards as an evil order. He advocates resistance to it under all circumstances. He illustrates this view by means of the fable of the cow that appears before heaven's judgment seat as complainant against the butcher Shloime Zalman, murderer of the cow and its offspring, the young, innocent calves. The court's decision is in favor of the defendant. It is the cow, not the butcher, which has horns, teeth, hooves, and yet lets itself be milked and slaughtered; the cow deserves to be sent to Gehenna because by not resisting it tempted this servant of God, the butcher, to apply the knife to its throat. In the fable of the hammer and the iron, Steinbarg agrees that there may perhaps be no way of escape from being beaten if one is caught between hammer and anvil, but one should at least cry out at such a merciless destiny. The unctuous hammer advises the bar of iron to be patient under the undeserved blows. It is true that the striking hammer and the struck iron are both God's children fashioned of the same metal, but God has assigned a different function to each. The hammer is carrying out its divinely ordained assignment by hammering its brothers until the sparks fly. It bears no malice. It is acting under compulsion, under the command of the smith, who is himself merely doing his duty as a craftsman, restoring to health a wagon's broken axle. The wagon too acts under compulsion, since it is enslaved to the horse that compels it to turn the wheels unceasingly. But the horse also cannot be blamed, for it is lashed by the whip which in turn carried out the orders of a higher authority, the driver—and so on *ad infinitum*. Despite the logical reasoning of the aggressive hammer, the iron, writhing in agony, still cries out, as it properly should, against its apparent fate.

Steinbarg makes use of all the riches of Yiddish, the spoken idioms as well as the written word. He borrows phrases from the Hebrew prayer book and the Talmud and adapts them in startling, original combinations. Nor does he hesitate to invent a multitude of neologisms whose meaning evolves from their strange sound effects. He ranks with Itzik Manger as Rumania's greatest master of Yiddish.

Jacob Sternberg, who edited Steinbarg's *Fables*, began in 1908 with lyrics and short stories that immediately won recognition. Toward the end of World War I he wrote and produced, in collaboration with Jacob Botoshansky, nine playlets and satiric revues for the Bucharest Yiddish Theater. During the following two decades he forged ahead as the most popular theater director of Rumania. His lyrics gradually eschewed Neoromantic, Symbolistic characteristics and evolved into the grotesque Expressionism of his volume *Profile of a City* (*Shtot in Profil*, 1935). Fleeing from the Nazis in 1941, he spent his later years in Soviet Russia. Until 1945 he was a refugee in the Asiatic province of Uzbekistan. After World War II, he directed Yiddish plays in Kishinev. He served as the most prominent Rumanian member of the Jewish Anti-Fascist Committee in Moscow until its liquidation in 1948. He spent the following five years in a Siberian labor camp. After Stalin's death, he was rehabilitated as an innocent sufferer and became a much respected contributor to *Sovetish Heimland*. His poems were translated into Russian in 1950, and his critical articles of the 1960's carried great weight with the younger Soviet Yiddish writers. His memoirs resurrected for them the pre-Revolutionary period that had already become historic.

Moishe Altman, a townsman of Sternberg and born in the same year, excelled in the 1920's with short stories that had a moral undertone. He also wrote two novels of Bessarabian Jewish life in the 1930's. The chronicler in both novels is Mottel Unruh, his alter ego, who experiences many disappointments and little joy. While most of Altman's characters, including Mottel himself, are but vaguely delineated, a few are so clearly etched that they captivate the imagination for a long time. There is the beautiful, robust, sophisticated, honey-voiced, sex-driven peasant girl Marianna, whose body exudes fragrant magic like a tree in blossom and who is prepared to outrage her family and to marry the Jew Yosef, if there is no other way to satisfy her longing for him. There is her rival and antipode, the dutiful, virtuous, silent, brooding Jewish maiden Rita, whose calmness is ruffled when Yosef appears upon the scene. And there is Yosef himself, the emaciated, tubercular young Jew, whose ascetic saintliness seeps like a poison into the veins of the women about him, inflaming them, even while his own thoughts and dreams still bear the scars of the pogroms which killed his wife and child and hurled him far from his native Ukrainian province.

Altman's love for Bessarabia's earth, its toiling Jews and rugged peasants, led him to remain there when it was occupied by Soviet forces in 1940. The following year, however, he was forced to flee before the German invaders. After the war he returned and resumed his writing of tales glorifying the tillers of the soil. Despite his proletarian proclivities, he was not spared years of hardship in a Siberian camp beginning in 1948. After Stalin's death, he was rehabilitated and permitted to publish again, but the only available periodical in the post-Stalin era was *Sovetish Heimland*. In it appeared his story *A Tale with a Name* (*A Mayse mit a Nomen*, 1968), in which the principal character is again a restless Mottel who possesses many skills and is helpful to his fellow men, Jews and non-Jews, but who has learned to be silent, undemanding and unobtrusive. Like his author who had undergone many trials in the course of a difficult life, Mottel has become an enigma to every person with whom he is in contact.

Rumania's greatest gift to Yiddish literature was Itzik Manger (1901-1969). Although he was born in Czernovitz, the capital of Bukovina, when this province was still part of the Austro-Hungarian Empire and when its name had not yet been transmuted to Cernauti, and although his family stemmed from Kolomea, Galicia, he is nevertheless generally associated with the Rumanian literary group because he grew up in Jassy, the important Jewish center of Old Rumania, and also because the Rumanian editors were the first to recognize his talent and to publish his poems and essays in their periodicals. Warsaw, Paris, London, New York and Tel Aviv were other waystations in the creative experience of this last and greatest of Yiddish troubadours.

From his father, a master-tailor who dabbled in Yiddish verse, Manger imbibed Yiddish folklore from childhood on. At the secular high school in Czernovitz, which he attended until he was expelled for his pranks, he acquired a knowledge of German literature. At Jassy, he worked at several callings without much success. The founding of several Yiddish journals in Greater Rumania after World War I supplied the young craftsman with an opportunity to publish his early lyrics and ballads. The first of these appeared in 1921, but it was not until he arrived in Warsaw seven years later and published his earliest book of poems, *Stars On the Roof* (*Shtern Oifn Dakh*, 1929), that he was recognized as more than a regional poet.

Manger's last venture in Czernowitz was *Getsehlte Verter*, a short-lived journal for literature, theater and art. The first issue of August 2, 1929 contained a grotesque manifesto outlining his poetic credo: "We trumpet reform. . . . At the cradle of our project stands Don Quixote, the father of all illusion. . . . Our program: to crack loudly the lice that have implanted themselves in the dimples of Yiddish literature. Our specially manicured nails are ready. We mobilize all fighting troubadours in East, West, North and South—hither to us. Literature too necessitates barricades at times. Help us to clear away the false and harmful elements which distort the true literary picture, which tangle the threads and make more difficult the path of those who are arriving and those who are yet to come. . . . Song is everything for us. It flutters over the cradle and the child, it trembles in love and fevers within the bridal veil, it is a companion on the march, it weeps in solitude, it exults in bread and wine, it storms amidst hunger and thirst. . . . Ripe prose is merely a colossal detour to song."

In his early lyrics, Manger succeeds in combining the simplicity of folksongs and folk ballads with the sophisticated structures derived from German classical and romantic poets. Quatrains alternate with sonnets. Echoes of popular Galician bards like Velvel Zbarzher, Berl Broder, and of the theatrical innovator Abraham Goldfaden, resound alongside reminiscences of Bürger's *Lenore*, Goethe's *Erlkönig*, and the young Heine's ghostly ballads. Monks, nuns and gypsies appear alongside of pious Jewish maidens and the biblical figures of Rebecca, Joseph and David. Jesus is invoked, but far less often than the Baal Shem. Unlike the Christian Messiah, who bears the pain of the world, the Baal Shem hymns the joy of all creation and proclaims: "The world is holy and threefold beautiful." The poet joins in this refrain. He too sings out his joy on all occasions and seeks to get to God over the bridge of ecstasy. "My song is my gold," he proclaims in a poem that bears the characteristic title "Happiness" (*Glik*), and in which he likens himself to rich Croesus because whatever he touches turns to lyric gold. Elsewhere he speaks of himself as a simple tailor's wildly lost son whose young years wandered in the wind until he found the thin golden ray that lit up the dark alleys. It was the ray of joyous poesy which revealed to him beauty in every nook and corner, which converted reality to fantasy, and which made of dreams reality. Looking at the world through the blue lantern of illusion, he finds everything beautiful and good and holy, delight in every tear, a spark of love in every eye, a bright end to every road.

In Manger's second book of poems, *Lanterns in the Wind* (*Lamtern in Vint*, 1933), the troubadour of light and joy matures to perfection. All nature is personified and throbs with vitality. The cloud becomes a wanderer who visits him in ever new attire and talks to him throughout the night about adventures amidst stars and winds. The bird brings him greetings of the world's crossroads and of the changing seasons which return more lovely each year.

The rain that knocks at his window is an enchanted prince who can resume youthful charm when greeted with a smile.

In most poems gaiety mingles with ironic wisdom. But there also creep upon him sad and tired moods when he is emptied of lyric intoxication, when he feels that he has frivolously squandered golden youth, when he becomes aware of loneliness amidst adulation, when he weeps for the God of his fathers toward whom he yearns but whom he cannot grasp.

In those moods Manger turns to the Book of Books, the eternal text of his people, and it lives for him again as intimately as in his childhood imagination. Just as a child in its daydreams and night fantasies envisages characters of long ago and far-off places in terms of immediate family relationships and familiar childhood experiences, so too does Manger read into the souls of biblical figures from Adam and Eve to David and Abishag, thoughts, feelings and motives which might indeed have been theirs, had they lived in his generation in East European townlets still permeated with traditional lore.

In Manger's biblical songs, published in 1935 and 1936, patriarchal figures become contemporary Jews, with all their foibles and all their charm. The mythical figures are no longer embalmed and enshrined in Torah scrolls, they are flesh of our flesh, our grandfathers and grandmothers, our brothers and sisters. We lose our awe of them but we love them even more. Father Abraham scolds his nephew Lot for getting drunk every night in the tavern, thus ruining the family's reputation and making it impossible for the two grown-up daughters to get decent husbands. Hagar, the maid, washes the kitchen dishes during her last evening in the house of her boss Abraham and laments the faithlessness of men, whose love floats away like the smoke of a railroad engine. On the following morning, Abraham sees her off on her journey into the unknown after haggling with the coachman who has come to drive her to the railroad station. Hagar comforts her crying baby Ishmael by telling him that he will have to learn to adjust to the ways of the world: "That's how patriarchs with long, pious beards behave." Fortunately for her, the Turkish Sultan, passing by with his caravan, recognizes little Ishmael as the ancestor from whom Allah's worshippers and even he himself stem.

When Joseph walks in his silk blouse along the boulevard, girls with blue parasols and May fragrance walk past him smiling, casting sly glances, and wondering how they could entice him as husband or lover. Samuel, the lonely old bachelor who claims to be wedded to prophecy, foresees for the shepherd lad David a crown, a sword and a collection of psalms. He asks Reb Jesse to pack a valise for David, the youngest son, who is to be taken to the train and brought to King Saul's court.

The peasant girl Abishag of the village of Shunam dreams of silks, muslins, golden chariots, awaiting her in the marble palace of the legendary David, whose portrait hangs over her mother's bed. However, when she comes to live in the vicinity of the old king, she is miserable and bewails her lot as his hot-water bottle. She find no comfort in learned men's assurances that she will earn a line in the Bible. An inked line on parchment cannot compensate for her wasted years and her misused young body. By heaping anachronisms upon anachronisms, Manger constantly moves from the biblical to the contemporary level and produces original poetic effects, a combination of religious reverence, sceptical satire and sly folk humor. He is a superb master of romantic irony.

As the last Yiddish troubadour, Manger has an affinity for earlier minstrels. He penned penetrating sketches of Berl Broder, Yakov Psanter, Velvel Zbarzher, Eliakum Zunser and Abraham Goldfaden. To Zbarzher he devoted a cycle of twelve songs in the form of lyric letters which this bard supposedly wrote to Malkele the Beautiful expressing the sad longing of the roaming Galician minstrel for his idolized beloved in far-off Constintinople. Zbarzher's golden dreams of her are transmuted into song. He is aware that golden dreams end in illusions. While they last, however, they warm the heart and should not be lightly discarded.

Manger voices in these Zbarzher letters his own personality, his own feeling that everything wants to become song, everything which breathes, laughs and blossoms, wind, bird and cloud, teardrop and winedrop, chimney sweep and blind beggar, mother and child, milkman and flower maiden, above all, the longing that can find no other form of fulfillment.

When Manger lived in Jassy, the tradition of Velvel Zbarzher, who had acted out his songs in its wine cellars, was still alive in the memory of its inhabitants. Folk plays, especially Purim plays written and directed by amateurs, still delighted Yiddish audiences. Manger recalled that his own father, the master tailor, once assembled the tailor apprentices and led them to put on a performance of the Esther story at Purim festivities. Manger's *Megilla Songs* (*Megilla-Lieder*, 1936) retell the Purim episodes in the form of dramatic lyrics to be sung and acted out by various biblical characters. But the poet also introduces characters and incidents which are not found in the original source, such as the unhappy love of a tailor apprentice named Fastrigassa for Queen Esther, both before and after her coronation, and his attempt to assassinate his rival, King Ahasuerus, an attempt for which he paid with his life. These lyrics were produced as a tragi-comedy thirty years later in Israel and were eminently successful, reviving in Israeli towns the almost extinct tradition of the Purim plays.

As the ablest successor of the folk dramatists, Manger was invited by a Warsaw theater to adapt Goldfaden's plays for a post-Goldfaden generation. These adaptations proved to be theatrically successful. Indeed, he reworked one play, *Koldunia*, so completely as a comedy in three acts and fourteen tableaux that he afterwards published it as his own work, *Hotzmach* (1947), giving Goldfaden credit for the theme and inspiration. To the original characters which had delighted audiences for half a century, Bobbe Yakhne, Hotzmach, Mirele and Eliakum, he added others of his own creation, and to popular Goldfaden arias and duets he added new ones of his own composition.

Manger paid eloquent tribute to Goldfaden in a narrative depicting the final hour of the creator of the Yiddish theater. He let pass before Goldfaden's dying eyes for the last time colorful scenes of an eventful life, and stage characters from the hilarious Shmendrik and Kuni-Leml to the tragic Shulamith and the heroic Bar Kochba. The Angel of Death appeared to the theatrical pioneer in a theatrical mask and carried on a stylized conversation that, in Goldfaden's opinion, would have guaranteed success on any Yiddish stage.

Manger also paid tribute to other predecessors in the volume *Endeared Figures (Noente Geshtalten, 1938)*. He showed Eliakum Zunser, the famed bard of Vilna, moving wedding guests to laughter and tears with rhymed improvisations. He showed Berl Broder intoning at an inn sweet, sad melodies and verses about poor craftsmen who toiled for a pittance and retained unwavering faith in God, the ultimate bringer of light to this dark world in which they were enshrouded. He showed the impact made by the wise jester Hershele Ostropoler upon the masses who adored him for his merry anecdotes and who, even while accompanying him to his grave, recalled his cheerful, comforting aphorisms in which he castigated the hard-hearted rich and the respected leaders of the community. In the various portraits painted by Manger, his own features, his own experiences, and his own love for the common man peered through.

Manger's most charming, fantastic, grotesque tales were, however, those he told about authentic life in the Garden of Eden.
These tales were published in Warsaw in 1939, a few months before bombs rained down upon this city and destroyed Jewish light-
heartedness. He put these stories in the mouth of the newborn
babe Shmuel-Aba Aberval.

According to Jewish lore, when children have to leave their
heavenly home in order to be born on earth, they are shorn of
their angelic wings and are given a fillip on the upper lip or nose
which causes them to forget their former existence. The clever
and impish Shmuel-Aba of Manger's narrative succeeds in eluding
the drunken angel who is to administer this fillip and he therefore
retains, after birth, memories of his experiences in the Jewish paradise and even of a temporary excursion into the Christian sector
of heaven. Night after night the precocious baby Shmuel-Aba
regales his earthly parents and their three invited guests with
his adventures among the patriarchs and saints in the realm of the
immortals. All of these immortals retain, in their super-terrestrial
home, the traits and interests they displayed before their terrestrial
death. Their quarrels and reconciliations, their appetites and expectations, their escapades and flirtations, their tragedies and
amusements are portrayed in most vivid colors by the artistic
conjurer, Manger, at the height of his creative power.

The author planned more than a single volume of these stories
but was interrupted by the war, which caught up with him in
France. He succeeded in escaping to London, which became his
temporary home for a decade and which he exchanged for New
York in 1951 and for Israel in 1967.

In 1967, two years before his death, Manger took leave of his
readers in the volume Stars in the Dust (Shteren in Shtoyb).
The title was meant to be symbolic. The stars that once sparkled
on the roof were now rolling in the dust and the last promenaders
on the dusty road were not even stopping for them. These last
songs, in what he called "the murdered language," were indeed
sad. He felt the shadows lengthening about him and the night
coming on. In a world of woe and weeping, his sole consolation at
life's twilight was the mirage of past days which shimmered in his
verses.

Throughout the post-war period, Manger's songs of joy and wine
and his ballads of love and death continued to be chanted by
Yiddish survivors of the Holocaust as an antidote to nightmarish
memories. His triumphant appearances in Warsaw, New York and

Tel Aviv were holidays for overflow audiences that flocked to hear him. He remained in the post-war decades as in the pre-war years the poet of his people in their gay moods, even as he alleviated with his playful, yet sophisticated humor their tragic moods. He was their bridge to joy, beauty and a strange kind of holiness.

In the wake of Rumania's Yiddish pioneers, a galaxy of aspiring writers arose on the eve of the Second World War. Many of them perished during the catastrophic years when Rumania became involved in this war. The survivors scattered in all directions. Among the surviving young poets were Jacob Friedman, Chaim Rabinsohn, Freed-Weininger and Motl Sakzier. Prose writers included the historian and editor Joseph Kisman, the literary critic and essayist Yitzkhak Paner, the narrator of Hassidic tales Baruch Hager, and the philologist Chaim Gininger.

Jacob Friedman (b. 1910), a descendant of the Hassidic dynasty of Rizhin, began writing in 1934, spent the war years in a Transnistrian camp, attained artistic maturity in Israel, and was awarded the Itzik Manger Prize for poetry in 1970.

Chaim Rabinsohn (b. 1910), also of rabbinic descent, began with Yiddish lyrics in the same year as Friedman, but after his arrival in Israel, he gradually changed over to Hebrew. His collected songs, Earthly Days (Yemai Haadamah, 1966), revealed that he had mastered the nuances of Hebrew style to an even greater extent than Yiddish.

Freed-Weininger (b. 1915) also began with lyric contributions in 1934. He was encouraged by Shlomo Bickel and, like Bickel, was able to reach the United States shortly before the Holocaust. His poetic collections Evening Along the Prut (Ovent Baim Prut, 1942) and Along the Prut, the La Plata and the Jordan (Baim Prut, La Plata Un Yarden, 1966) ranged in content from themes of Bukovina, North and South America and Israel, to cosmic visions and philosophic meditations, and in style from restrained sonnets to meandering free rhythms. In 1969 he too found a lasting home in Israel.

Motl Sakzier (b. 1907), son of a Bessarabian tailor, wrote primarily social poetry. In his verses he often recalled his father, who sewed new clothes for rich customers but remained poor and yet content with dreams of a nighing Messianic salvation. He himself escaped from a stifling workshop to a Parisian garret and then to Vienna and Bucharest. His elegies of his attic existence, Therefore (Derfar, 1936), mingled sentimentalism and irony. They showed him in languid, melancholy moods, drinking of love wherever he could find it. Nevertheless, this spinner of dreams about Parisian boulevards and Viennese streets could not liberate himself from images of Jewish tailor lads in his native Bessarabia who went to their martyrdom singing hymns of the Bund and songs of freedom penned by Vinchevsky, Bovshover and Edelstadt, the adored poets of tailor workshops. After years in Asiatic Labor Camps, he survived Stalin's purges, returned to Kishinev and continued to pen proletarian poems there in the 1960's.

Yitzkhak Paner (b. 1890) was influential as editor, feuilletonist and poet in Bukovina before the Second World War. He spent the war years in Transnistrian exile. Upon returning to Rumania, he edited two anthologies of the new Yiddish poetry. Seeking to make his way to Palestine with the Illegals, he was interned in Cyprus and released after Israel was established. He then lived in close proximity to Sholem Asch, about whose last years he wrote a penetrating study in 1959. His essays on Rumanian writers offered valuable material about this Yiddish center. His two books of sketches and miniatures, *Sun and Shadow* (*Zun Un Shotn,* 1964) and *In My Own Port* (*In Eigenem Hafn,* 1970), contained largely themes of Israel, recorded in melancholy and happy moods.

Baruch Hager (b. 1896) also spent the war years in Transnistria. As the descendant of Hassidic rabbis, he was unhappy in Communist Bucharest after the war and left for France in 1947. Five years later, he emigrated to Argentina. His Hassidic tales, climaxing in the volume, *The Kingdom of Hassidism* (*Malkus Hassidus,* 1955), won wide recognition. His allegorical tale *The Palace* (*Der Palatz,* 1969) treated in a most original style the theme of the rich man who faced the inevitability of death. Without an heir to whom he could bequeath his palace and wealth, he realized that all his acquisitions were but vanity of vanities—unless he could use them for charitable deeds that would win him a permanent palatial dwelling in heaven. In his insatiable ambition to accumulate sufficient good deeds, however, he misused the power that his treasures bestowed upon him and ended unblessed and in mortal terror of death.

Soviet Kishinev, in the post-Stalin era, remained as the home of Yiddish writers, such as Yekhiel Shreibman, who excelled in short sketches, and Yankel Yakir, who wrote longer stories of Bessarabian Jewish life. At the same time, Cernauti harbored not only Moshe Altman after his liberation but also the younger writers Meyer Kharatz, Hirsh Bloshtein and Chaim Melamed. Their contributions were published in the 1960's in *Sovetish Heimland.*

In the truncated Rumania of the post-Holocaust decades, the quantity and quality of Yiddish literary activity continued to decline. The severance of Bessarabia and Bukovina from Rumania, the migration of Jewish intellectuals to other Soviet centers, the large *aliya* to Israel, the pressure for integration into the culture of the majority population, the decrease of the Yiddish reading public—these were major factors accounting for this decline. Though some literary activity was still being maintained in the 1970's and a Yiddish theatrical company was still functioning and even undertaking guest performances in Israel in 1968, the outlook for a Yiddish resurgence, such as Rumania experienced a generation earlier, was bleak.

At the other end of the European continent, a decline was also evident in the Yiddish literary creativity of England and France. London had been an important Yiddish center since the large immigration of Eastern European Jews which set in during the 1870's. The first writers used Yiddish primarily as a linguistic medium through which they could spread their socialist or anarchist doctrines among the newcomers. Such writers were Aaron Lieberman (1845-1880), who arrived in London in 1875, and Morris Vinchevsky (1856-1932), who followed in 1879.

Lieberman founded the first organization of Yiddish-speaking workers in the British capital. Though he himself wrote far more in Russian and in Hebrew than in Yiddish, he did pave the way for the Yiddish socialist publicists who succeeded him. By 1884 there were sufficient readers of Yiddish in England for the first weekly, *Der Poilisher Yingel,* and a year later for the second and longer lasting weekly, *Der Arbeiter Freind.*

Vinchevsky, who edited the former journal, wrote not only propaganda articles and timely editorials but also short stories, feuilletons, and above all sentimental and inflammatory poems. These poems were included in his first verse booklet of 1885. They aroused sympathy for the victims of an oppressive economic system and called for a revolt of the proletarians under the banner of socialism. Vinchevsky also participated with political lyrics, social satires and philosophical meditations in *Der Arbeiter Freind,* which was the principal organ of the Jewish Socialists of England from 1885 to 1891. In the latter year it was taken over by the Anarchists. Its first editor was Vinchevsky's associate Philip Krantz (1858-1922).

Krantz had arrived in London in 1883 after having participated in revolutionary activities against the Czarist regime. He numbered among his friends the assassins of Czar Alexander II, but escaped from Russia before he could be implicated. In England he attracted to his organ a group of dedicated political journalists, pamphleteers and poets, who sought to organize the Jewish immigrants to battle for an amelioration of their wretched lot. Strangely enough, however, he rejected as of little value the poems of the most talented social lyricist of London, Morris Rosenfeld, and it was only after the latter left for America at the end of 1886 and Kranz followed in 1890 that the editor atoned and became the first biographer of the poet. Krantz was for more than a third of a century the most prolific Yiddish popularizer of science, social science and cultural history. His books included a survey of astronomy, a history of the French Revolution, a history of socialism, a description of pre-Columbian America and an analysis of the Exodus from Egypt which led to the formation of the Jewish people. These books helped to educate Jewish immigrants who had not yet acquired a sufficient knowledge of English.

Associated with Krantz in his London period were the journalist David Goldblatt (1866-1945), who became a militant fighter for Yiddish in South Africa after arriving in Capetown in 1898, and the pamphleteer, atheist and Socialist agitator Benjamin Feigenbaum (1860-1922), who spent half a century writing, lecturing and campaigning against God, religious observances and capitalism.

For many Jewish emigrants from Eastern Europe, England was but a temporary abode, especially since the British government, becoming increasingly alarmed at the influx of the impoverished Jewish victims of Russian pogroms, encouraged them to leave for overseas. With the westward movement of the Yiddish masses to the United States in the 1890's, Vinchevsky, Krantz, Feigenbaum and other Yiddish intellectuals followed.

Yiddish actors and theater directors had already begun to leave somewhat earlier. Jacob P. Adler, who had arrived with his troupe from Russia in 1882 and who played to enthusiastic audiences for five years, left hurriedly in 1887 as a result of a mass tragedy, a panic that broke out during his last performance when someone in the audience called out "Fire"; in the ensuing mad rush seventeen persons were trampled under foot. Among prominent actors who exchanged London for New York were David Kessler, Samuel Goldenberg, Ludwig Satz, Maurice Moscowitch, and the actress Kenie Liptzin.

In the new century London could no longer vie with New York

as a Yiddish literary and theatrical center. Indeed, from 1898 until the First World War, the influential weekly *Der Arbeiter Freind* was under the editorship of the German Anarchist and non-Jew Rudolf Rocker (1873-1958), who had acquired a knowledge of Yiddish in the course of his agitating for his libertarian cause among the Jews of Whitechapel. Rocker translated into Yiddish Anarchist classics and wrote Yiddish studies on Anarchist pioneers such as Michael Bakunin, Peter Kropotkin and Francisco Ferrer.

London was also a waystation for Solomon Dingol (1887-1961), who edited three periodicals there, all of them short-lived, before leaving in 1916 for New York, where he reached the pinnacle of his influence as editor of the daily *Der Tog*.

There were, of course, Yiddish writers and scholars who came to England at the turn of the century and who remained there, leaving a lasting impact upon its Jews. They included Moses Gaster, Morris Myer, Moshe Oved and Joseph Leftwich.

Moses Gaster (1856-1939) was expelled from his native Rumania in 1885 because of his unrelenting struggle against Jewish discrimination by the government. In London he became, in 1887, the Haham (Chief Rabbi) of the Sephardic community and the leader of the budding Zionist movement, but his interest in Yiddish manifested itself in his research into Yiddish dialects and in his meticulous translation and interpretation of the *Maase-Bukh* of 1602.

Morris Myer (1879-1944) was also a native of Rumania. He arrived in London in 1902 and participated in many Yiddish publications, beginning with his editorship of *Der Arbeiter Freind*. He was most influential as editor of the London daily *Die Zeit,* founded in 1913. He raised the level of Yiddish journalism by attracting Sholem Asch, Abraham Reisen and Baal-Makshoves as his collaborators on this daily. He furthered Yiddish theatrical enterprises as literary advisor and as Yiddish translator of English, German and Rumanian plays.

Moshe Oved (1885-1958) arrived in England from Poland in the same year as Myer. Although poetry was his keenest interest, he became better known as a connoisseur of art than as a literary figure. His Cameo Corner near the British Museum attracted famed literary personalities such as Sholem Asch and George Bernard Shaw, the English dramatist whom he sought to interest in Yiddish. Oved's first book, *Out of Chaos (Arois Fun Chaos,* 1917) contained prose poems, psalms, prophetic visions, lamentations at the suffering of Jews in exile, verses of comfort at the dawning of hope for their return to Zion, visions of a Messianic era of truth and beauty that would replace the age of sin and ugliness. Seven additional booklets of prose and verse followed. His last work, *Prayers and Songs* (*Tkhines Un Gezangen*, 1955), appeared in his seventieth year and contained a selection of his best poems, including his hymn to Yiddish, penned in 1919. Despite the Holocaust, Oved's tone remained to the end ecstatic, rhapsodic, full of faith in a coming redemption for all mankind.

Joseph Leftwich (b. 1892), the finest interpreter of Yiddish literature for English readers, was brought to London at the age of seven and grew up in a bilingual environment. He was strongly influenced by Israel Zangwill (1864-1926), the best English narrator of the tragedies and comedies of the ghetto dwellers. He translated Zangwill's tales into Yiddish. In addition to his own poems and essays in Yiddish, he was a prolific translator of Yiddish prose and verse into impeccable English. His anthologies *Yisroel* (1933) and *The Golden Peacock* (1939) were bestsellers and called attention to rich treasures of Yiddish. His study *Abraham Sutzkever* (1971) was the finest English tribute to the poet of "Young Vilna," whose greatness he was among the first to recognize.

I. M. Sochaczewski (1889-1958) settled in London in 1913 and participated for thirty-five years in the daily journalistic tasks of *Die Zeit*, before he founded and edited his own weekly, *Die Yiddishe Shtimme*, in 1951. His poems, essays, dramas and novels, products of his facile pen, were of little enduring value.

Leo Koenig (1889-1970) lived in London from the First World War until he left for Israel in 1952. His essays on art and artists were his most original contribution but he also displayed profound insight into Yiddish and European literary phenomena.

The first third of the twentieth century was a lean period in London's Yiddish creativeness, when compared with the period preceding or following. After Hitler's rise to power, however, Yiddish writers and scholars, fleeing from Nazi tyranny, found a refuge in England and helped to arrest the decline of Yiddish. They included the Yiddish linguist and grammarian Shlomo Birnbaum, the folklorist and literary historian Jacob Meitlis, the poet Abraham Nochem Stencl, the narrator A. M. Fuchs and his brother, the journalist and short story writer who preferred the pseudonym of J. A. Liski. In the literary booklets *Yiddish London* (1938-1939), their contributions appeared alongside those by the earlier Londoners, Oved, Myer, Leftwich and Koenig. During the war years, London was also the home of Itzik Manger and of the Bundist leader and journalist Arthur Zygelboim. The latter's suicide in 1943, in order to arouse the conscience of the world by calling attention to the Nazi liquidation of Polish Jewry, was the subject of elegies by Zalman Schneour, Glanz-Leyeles, Z. Segalowitch, Chava Rosenfarb and H. Leivick.

In 1941 Stencl (b. 1898) founded and edited *Loshen Un Leben*, a literary periodical which became the main guardian of Yiddish creativity in post-war England. Stencl was born in Poland and participated with Expressionistic lyrics in Germany when Expressionism was at its highest vogue. He won the admiration of Elsa Lasker-Schüler and Thomas Mann before he fled to England in 1936. In his first booklet on British soil, *London Lyrics* (*London Lyrik*, 1940), he caught the mood of the great metropolis, from the lanes of Whitechapel to the mighty turrets renowned in history, from the lanterns that pierced the foggy gloom to the proud trees of the famous parks. His poems were translated into Hebrew, German and English. In 1943 he founded the London "Friends of Yiddish" as a spiritual haven for lovers of Yiddish. After 1948, Israel became the main theme of his poetry. He hymned the uniqueness of Jerusalem in the volume *Jerusalem* (1948), when the Jewish state came into existence, and he continued to sing exultantly of this city ten years later in his volume *Exile and Redemption* (*Galut Un Geula*, 1958).

A. M. Fuchs (b. 1890) began his literary career in 1911 as a writer of realistic short stories in Lemberg. Neoromanticism was then fashionable both in this Galician metropolis and in Vienna to which he moved in 1912. However, he resisted this fashion and portrayed the poor Jewish villagers of his native Galicia without any embellishments. Because of his Naturalistic style, he was dubbed a modern Mendele Mokher Sforim. Thieves, prostitutes, cripples, bankrupt actors and perverse characters abounded in his tales. When the Nazis overwhelmed Austria in 1938, he made his way to England and remained there until 1950, when he found a lasting home in Israel. His last stories portrayed Israeli characters and Israeli landscape.

Despite the intensification of Jewishness in England after the founding of Israel, Yiddish literature continued to decline in the post-mid-century decades. The children of immigrants were English-speaking, and in most schools devoted to Jewish studies Hebrew rather than Yiddish was preferred. The audiences for Yiddish plays were aging and diminishing in numbers. They could no longer support a permanent theater and after 1961 only rare guest performances could still attract sufficient theatergoers. Yiddish writers felt ever more isolated and unread. Some left for Israel but even those who remained in England looked to Israel for inspiration. English and not Hebrew or Yiddish became the exclusive literary medium for all British-born Jews.

France did not become a Yiddish literary center until after the First World War. The main stream of immigrants from Eastern Europe coursed through England and continued on to the United States, Canada, and South Africa. The first Yiddish writer to settle in Paris was Israel Aksenfeld, the pioneer of Yiddish drama. He came to the French capital in 1864 in order to join his son, a physician who had been appointed a professor at the Sorbonne. He died there two years later.

The first significant group of Eastern European Jews attracted to France were the radicals and socialists who had to leave Russia after the failure of the Revolution in 1905. These political refugees were largely Russian-speaking. They were joined by hundreds of Yiddish-speaking Jews in flight from pogroms and lacking the means to continue on overseas. Soon these hundreds increased to thousands and by 1912 there was a large enough audience to support theatrical performances in Yiddish.

After the First World War, guest performances became more frequent, the most notable being those of the Vilna Troupe in 1922, of New York's Yiddish Art Theater under the direction of Maurice Schwartz in 1924, and of the Moscow Yiddish Kammertheater directed by Alexander Granovsky, with Shlomo Michoels as star, in 1928. Local theater ventures began on a small scale in 1929 and on a larger scale in 1935, when PIAT—Pariser Yiddisher Arbeiter Teater—was founded. Four years later the war ended these ventures; but hardly was the war over in 1945, when Yiddish performances resumed. In that year Aaron Poliakov founded the Yiddish Folksteater. He also published, from 1953 on, an illustrated theater journal, Der Teatershpiegel, of which forty-three issues appeared. However by 1960 Paris was sharing the fate of larger communities such as New York and London in that it could no longer support a permanent Yiddish theater but only rare performances by visiting actors.

Post-Holocaust Paris still boasted of two Yiddish dailies, the Zionist-oriented Unzer Vort and the Communist-oriented Freie Presse, as well as several weeklies and monthlies. The writers did not include a single Jew born in France. They were recruited from the ranks of Eastern European Jews who had survived the war in hiding, or had immigrated from Displaced Persons' Camps. But even these soon discovered that they could reach far larger audiences by writing in French rather than in Yiddish. The most distinguished among them were André Schwartz-Bart, whose masterpiece, *The Last of the Just,* received worldwide acclaim and was translated into most European tongues, and Elie Wiesel, who was bilingual, but whose great trilogy *Night, Dawn,* and *Day* was written in French and then translated into other tongues.

Israel Efroykin (1884-1954), who settled in Paris in 1920, was a central figure in its Jewish communal and intellectual activities but did not publish his four books of basic literary and historic research until the last decade of his life. Other Yiddish scholars followed him when the Yiddish Encyclopedia project was transferred from Berlin to Paris in 1933. They included the editor Ben Adir (1878-1942) and the historian Elias Tcherikover (1881-1943), both of whom succeeded in escaping to the United States when the Germans invaded France.

I. Finer (b. 1908), who left Warsaw for Paris in 1935, remained in France throughout the war and fought with the resistance groups in forests and mountain hideouts. The stories of his first book, *The Twilight Hour (Die Shoe Fun Bein-Hashmoshes,* 1951), were based upon his observations and experiences during the years of occupation. The twenty-one stories of his second book, *The Four Seasons (Die Fier Tsaiten,* 1966), dealt mainly with post-War Jewish life in France. Finer's characters, survivors of the Holocaust, could not erase the scars of the Hitler-years. Always there welled up, from their subconscious, memories of persecutions, tortures, underground resistance, the daily imminence of death. Events of the present and recollections of the past intermingled vividly. The narrator moved with great skill between the world of facts and the world of hallucinations, treating both as aspects of reality, though at different levels of the soul.

Finer has a French lightness of touch which makes the tragic events he narrates emotionally bearable. He lets a schizophrenic victim of Auschwitz experience moments of release from inner terror through the compassionate understanding of a nurse. He calls attention to self-sacrificing deeds of Frenchmen when Jews were imperilled, and no less heroic deeds of Jews in helping the French to harass the Nazis. Only a few stories take place in a non-French milieu. One such story, "A Jew En Route to Israel," contrasts the romantic, religious longing for Israel, alive in a Jewish family for generations, and the sober fulfillment of this longing, when the last descendant lands on the soil of the new Israel and finds settlers engaged in normal activities and reluctant to devote themselves to romantic memories of their pre-Israel years and relationships.

The dramatist Chaim Sloves (b. 1905), a native of Bialystok and in France since 1926, was also active in the French underground during the war. His postwar plays included *Avengers* (*Nekome-Nemer,* 1947), *Haman's Defeat* (*Hamans Mapole,* 1949), and *Baruch of Amsterdam* (1956), a drama which concentrated on the soul-wrestling of the young philosopher Spinoza. Sloves made the intensest impact with his symbolic drama of the last Jews in the Warsaw Ghetto, *We Were Ten Brothers* (*Tsen Brieder Zeinen Mir Geven,* 1965). His plays were staged not only in Paris but also in New York, Buenos Aires, Rio de Janeiro, Bucharest, Tel Aviv, Johannesburg and other Yiddish centers. David Licht, Yonas Turkov, Jacob Weisslitz and Ida Kaminska were among the directors and actors who brought his plays to Yiddish audiences. Sloves was a founder of YKUF and a propagandist for its leftist approach. His essays, *In and Around* (*In Un Arum,* 1970), interpreted Yiddish literature from the viewpoint of the radical left. They were filled with sadness at the Soviet liquidation of a virile literary generation but retained hope in the revival of Yiddish in Russia.

Moshe Shulstein (b. 1911), the most prolific Yiddish poet of Paris also stemmed from Poland, where his first lyric booklets appeared in 1934 and 1936. His songs of the Carpathians were characterized by love for the peasants and shepherds who toiled along the mountain slopes. The war years found repercussion in his verse booklets *On the Ashes of My Home* (*Oifn Ash Fun Mein Haim,* 1945), and *A Tree Amidst Ruins* (*A Boim Tvishen Khurves,* 1947). But it was with his dramatic poem in nine scenes, *The Melody of Generations* (*Der Nigun Fun Doires,* 1950), that his talent ripened. The dramatic action began in the summer of 1939 when the wedding of a patrician Jewish couple of Paris was interrupted by news of the German attack on Poland. It continued with increasing Nazi outrages against the Jews. It concluded with the liberation of Paris and the reunion of the surviving couple in their ransacked apartment.

Until the mid-1950's Shulstein's poems idealized Soviet achievements and Communist aspirations, but in the poetic volume *Flowers of Regret* (*Blumen Fun Badoier,* 1959), dedicated to the martyred Soviet Yiddish writers, his disillusionment with the Soviet panacea was expressed. His ballad on Peretz Markish and his poems on David Bergelson and Der Nister lamented their undeserved fate. Shulstein's new hopes were concentrated on Israel and he was certain that the Jewish state would not disappoint him as had Moscow. His eleventh book, *Gold and Fire* (*Gold un Feier*, 1962), consisted largely of versified fables but in his dramatic vision *At the Chronicle of Lublin* (*Beim Pinkas Fun Lublin*, 1966) he reverted to the theme of the Holocaust, confronting the great Jews of Lublin's former generations with the witnesses of the final catastrophe.

In the stories of *Above the Roofs of Paris* (*Iber Die Dekher Fun Paris*, 1968), Shulstein dealt largely with the reconstructed lives of Jewish survivors who returned to Paris from camps and from underground resistance. Having been in contact with evil and brutality, they treasure goodness and kindness and are considerate in their relations with their fellow men.

Shulstein's critical essays *Before My Vision* (*Geshtaltn Far Meine Oigen*, 1971) dealt primarily with writers who rose to prominence between the two World Wars and were based largely on personal reminiscences of his meeting with them in Warsaw, Paris and Jerusalem.

Moshe Dluznowsky (b. 1906) emigrated from Poland to Paris in 1930. As a travelling salesman, he came to know French and Jewish life of all social strata and described it in short stories and sketches. In 1939 he fled to Morocco before the invading Nazis and discovered in its Mellahs a still unexplored field for Yiddish literature. In his stories, and especially in his novels *Windmills* (*Vint-Miln*, 1963), and *The Guest from Afar* (*Der Oirakh Fun A Veitn Veg*, 1971), he reproduced the sights, sounds, smells and bustling activities of impoverished Berber-Arab-Jewish settlements. Above the noise, stench and filth, he perceived beauty enthroned and kindness peering through. He held that to experience beauty and kindness a person needed merely the will to turn his eyes aloft and his heart heavenward.

The hero of his earlier novel, a young physician from Paris about to begin medical practice in a Mellah, was taught this wisdom by an itinerant *lamedvovnik* of the Atlas Mountains. He was then thrown into emotional conflicts and experienced much sorrow. Nevertheless, his years tending the sick and comforting the heavy-hearted were well spent, even if the grateful tears of a pogrom-ridden community were his only reward. To the heroine, who escaped from the Mellah to a glamorous Parisian career, this wisdom

came much later in life and led her to return to her people in the
hour of desperate need. Other characters, Jews, Arabs, Frenchmen,
left their mark upon this strife-torn region between the sea and
the Atlas Range. In the hearts of all, God and the Devil were
shown to be contending for mastery.

Dluznowsky succeeded in getting to the United States in 1941.
He wrote stories and fiction serials for Yiddish newspapers, primarily for the New York *Forverts*. His works included several
plays for stage and radio, the novel *As a Tree in a Field* (*Vie a
Boim In Feld*, 1958), the juvenile *The Chariot* (*Der Reitvogn*
1958), and the collections of short stories *The Wheel of Fortune*
(*Dos Rod Fun Mazel*, 1949), *A Well Along the Road* (*A Brunem
Beim Veg*, 1953), *Doors and Windows* (*Tirn Un Fenster*, 1966),
as well as other fascinating, informative tales, which were of considerable cultural value.

A realistic appraisal of the possibilities for Yiddish in France
and elsewhere during coming years was attempted by Leiser
Domankiewicz (b. 1899), Parisian literary critic and editor of the
Paris Yiddish daily *Unzer Vort*, in his essay "From Quantity to
Quality," first published in 1960 and later included in his book
Words and Values (*Verter Un Vertn*, 1965). He warned against
both optimists and defeatists. The former were stressing that, after
all the wounds inflicted upon Yiddish, it was still an international
tongue, spoken by Jews from New York to Johannesburg, from
Paris to Melbourne, from Buenos Aires to Moscow. These optimists cherished the illusion that Yiddish would continue to survive on the lips of millions. They refused to face the obvious
truth that the speakers of Yiddish belonged to an aging generation
and that this tongue was no longer one in which youth felt at
home. The defeatists, on the other hand, saw the demise of Yiddish
as inevitable and, by their proclamations of doom, were hastening
its end. Domankiewicz accepted as a fact the quantitative decline
of Yiddish from year to year. He urged that efforts should be
directed to retain the high quality it had attained since the classical era and to transform it into a sacred tongue even as Aramaic
had been thus transformed after ceasing to be a spoken language
of the Jews. Yiddish could then continue for centuries as the
linguistic medium not of the masses but of tens of thousands of
the academic and literary elite throughout the world. Cabalistic
works were composed in Aramaic for a long time, and in traditional
Jewish homes, Aramaic songs were still sung at Sabbath feasts.
Yiddish too could be conserved in similar fashion.

19

YIDDISH IN SOUTH AFRICA
AND AUSTRALIA

Yiddish Pioneers in South Africa • Hoffmann • Gold-
blatt • Polsky • Morris Hoffman • J. M. Sherman
• Feldman • Ben Moshe • Ehrlich • Fram •
Yiddish Journals • Tabachnik • Playwrights • Mel-
bourne Center • Goldhar • Bunim Varshavsky •
Rubenstein • Birshtein • Mintz • Rapoport • Ber I.
Rosen • Y. Kahn • Bergner

JEWS DID NOT EMIGRATE to South Africa in significant
numbers before the second half of the nineteenth century. The
requirement of the Dutch East India Company that all settlers
must be Protestants prevented Jews from coming there at all
during the first century and a half of European colonization. The
earliest Jewish settlers were mainly from England, Holland or
Germany. They established congregations in Capetown, Grahams-
town, Port Elizabeth and Kimberley. While a few Jews of Eastern
European origin whose mother tongue was Yiddish arrived in the
1870's in the Cape Colony, it was not until after the Russian
pogroms of the early 1880's that such Jews began to stream to
South Africa, attracted by tales of freedom and prosperity. During
the following thirty years, about thirty thousand Jewish immigrants arrived, most of them from Lithuania. To meet their needs
a Yiddish press arose during the quarter of a century before World
War I and a Yiddish literature began to flourish soon thereafter.

The earliest pioneer of Yiddish journalism was Nehemiah Dov
Baer Hoffmann (1857 or 1860-1928), who founded the short-lived
Der Afrikaner Israelit in 1890. When this weekly ceased publica-
tion, he successively launched four other weeklies and a monthly.
His book of memoirs, *Sefer Hazikhronos* (1916), was the first book

printed in South Africa and ushered in the most productive period of Yiddish literature in this southern outpost.

Hoffmann was a picturesque, talented personality. He stemmed from a townlet of Kovno Province. In his youth he came in contact in Vilna with the pillars of enlightenment, the *Maskilim* Abraham Ber Gottlober, Shmuel Joseph Finn and Abraham Baer Lebensohn. Kalman Schulman and Zvi Nissun Golomb encouraged him to write, and in 1879, Michel Levi Radkinson, editor of the Hebrew weekly *Hakol* and the Yiddish weekly *Kol l'Am*, invited him to Koenigsberg as editorial assistant. Although he remained under Radkinson's tutelage for less than half a year, he acquired literary and journalistic experience which was useful to him in subsequent years.

Hoffmann's first books were in Hebrew. When Golomb and the Vilna publisher Matz suggested to him that he try his skill at writing story booklets in Yiddish for the less sophisticated readers, he completed about twenty such booklets in a few months. These followed the tradition established by Isaac Meir Dick and Shomer, the most popular narrators of the early 1880's, and bore sensational titles such as *Life in a Harem, Poisoned Love, Innocently Convicted, To the Gallows*. In 1882 he was engaged by the Hebrew editor Haim Zelig Slonimsky to write for the Warsaw journal *Hatzfira*. Three years later Kasriel Zvi Sarasohn brought him to New York to work for the Yiddish weekly *Yiedishe Gazetn* and the newly founded first Yiddish daily, *Tageblatt*. After nine months in the United States, however, longing for his wife and children caused him to return to Europe. In 1886 he was called upon to edit the Hebrew weekly *Hamagid*.

When the Jews of his native Lithuania began to emigrate to South Africa, he too was persuaded by his brother-in-law, Barnett Millin, to exchange Czarist Russia for a freer life in Capetown. But when he arrived there in 1889, he at first experienced the hardships to which most Jewish immigrants were subjected. Unacquainted with the language of the Boers, he yet took to peddling among them, travelling from farm to farm with horse and wagon. Despite Millin's encouragement, he was singularly unsuccessful.

In 1890, Hoffmann brought over the first Hebrew-Yiddish type to South Africa and was thus able to print the first Yiddish weekly, *Der Afrikaner Israelit*. While this periodical lasted only half a year, his second weekly, *Ha-Or*, lasted from April 11, 1895 to July 5, 1897 and his third weekly, *Der Yiedisher Herold*, an additional two years. His fourth weekly venture was *Der Afrikaner*

Telegraph, 1898 to 1902; his fifth venture was the weekly *Yiedishe Folkszeitung,* which suspended publication after only two months in 1905; his final venture was the monthly *Der Afrikaner,* from January 1909 to April 1914.

In his articles and, above all, in his book of memoirs, Hoffmann gave a colorful picture of the pioneering generation of Lithuanian Jews in South Africa. In his *Sefer Hazikhronos,* whenever he refers to a friend or acquaintance—and these included outstanding personalities on three continents—he adds a biographic sketch and a subjective evaluation. His facts are not always accurate, but his pen portraits are vivid and illuminating. He writes with great facility in a popular but somewhat archaic style and retains the interest of his readers, despite a moralizing tendency which constantly interrupts his narration of events in his own life and in the life of others.

David Goldblatt (1866-1945), who was co-editor and co-owner with Hoffmann of *Der Afrikaner Telegraph,* was another early pioneer of South African Yiddish journalism and a most ardent champion of the Yiddish language and literature. He had grown up in Radom, Poland, and had lived in Warsaw, Berlin and London, before emigrating to South Africa. In London he had mingled in the circles of the Russian revolutionary writer Prince Peter Kropotkin, the English socialist idealist William Morris and the Yiddish poet Morris Vinchevsky. In the British capital he acquired his first journalistic experience as a writer for the Yiddish organ *Der Arbeiter Freind.*

In 1898, Goldblatt arrived in Capetown and was invited by Hoffmann to write for *Ha-Or,* the only existing Yiddish weekly. The following year he founded the first Yiddish daily, *Der Kriegstaphet.* It appeared from October 16 to December 13, 1899. Each issue consisted of a single page and brought reports of the Boer War, an editorial and news of interest to Jews.

Goldblatt's most successful journalistic venture, however, was the weekly *Der Yiedisher Advokat,* which appeared regularly from 1904 until 1914, when he left for the United States. In South Africa Goldblatt is best remembered for his struggle to gain recognition for Yiddish as a European language. The immigration law of 1902 restricted admission to the Cape Province and Natal to persons who could pass a written examination in a European language. Jews whose mother tongue was Yiddish were in danger of being refused admission. Authorities claimed that Yiddish was a jargon and not a language, that it was not the national language of any

European country, and that it was written in Oriental characters, from right to left. Goldblatt and the eloquent advocate Morris Alexander were the leading figures in the successful struggle for Yiddish. Goldblatt's pamphlet *Yiddish, Is It A European Language?* marshaled the arguments for Yiddish and influenced the legislators of the Cape House of Assembly to accord it equal legal status with the other European languages.

During World War I, Goldblatt came to the United States in order to gain support for a projected twenty-volume Yiddish Encyclopedia on which he worked for thirty years. He succeeded in completing and publishing the first volume in 1920 and the second volume in 1923, but the unfavorable reaction of the Yiddish press and insufficient financial backing forced him to abandon the project. Nevertheless, his militant advocacy of Yiddish continued unabated until the end of his long life and found expression in many essays and also in the Yiddish volume *In the Struggle for Yiddish* (*In Kamf Far Der Yiddisher Shprakh,* 1942) and in the English volume *The Jew and His Language Problem* (1943).

Hyman Polsky (1871-1944) was five years younger than Goldblatt. He grew up in a townlet near Grodno. To avoid impressment in the Czarist army, he left for London in 1891 where he became a successful photographer. It was not until his fortieth year that he emigrated to South Africa. In order to make a living at his profession of photography, he travelled through many towns and villages and had an opportunity to observe Jewish life in its many varied aspects. He recorded his impressions in sketches for Yiddish periodicals. He was a regular contributor to the Johannesburg Yiddish weekly *Der Afrikaner* and was its editor from 1920 to 1923, when it was merged with the *Afrikaner Yiddishe Zeitung.*

Unlike the militant Goldblatt, Polsky avoided controversy and shunned loud, sensational effects. He was at his best in sketching the transformation of the character of Lithuanian Jewish immigrants under the impact of the harsh struggle for survival in pioneering communities. These immigrants usually arrived with illusions of golden opportunities awaiting them in the land of gold mining. Having no experience in any trade and knowing neither English nor Afrikaans, they had to begin as peddlers of miscellaneous wares. When they did acquire a sufficient knowledge of the spoken languages, they opened little country stores, trading with the Boers and more often with the natives. Years passed before a new immigrant could save enough money to bring over his wife and children from the Old Country. Often, when they finally did come, estrangement had set in because of the long separation and this led to many domestic tragedies. Polsky wrote of these tragedies with a deep understanding of all the human frailties involved. Kindness permeated his depiction of Jewish men and women. He reproved their failings but without bitter denunciation.

Polsky is most compassionate in portraying the Jewish woman as mother, wife or beloved. As mother, she takes pride in giving her children the best moral education at home and tries against great odds to inculcate in them respect for traditional Jewish customs and values. As wife, she waits patiently through interminably long years in the Lithuanian townlet until her husband is in a position to send for her. Meanwhile she works hard to raise children of whom he can be proud. In her new home, she is a faithful helpmate, comforting her husband when he despairs, assisting him in his country store or farm, joining him in scrimping and saving for a better tomorrow, understanding him even in his aberrations. As beloved, she seeks to bring happiness to her man, even if he is an old bachelor who had already spent his younger years in the bush or semi-desert, toiling to gain an economic foothold which would enable him to marry. Often she marries him in order to help support her poor parents or needy brothers and sisters in the Old Country. She finds contentment in living for others and bringing a bit of sunshine to the aging, much-tried man who has chosen her.

Polsky is less tolerant of the more prosperous, assimilated Jewish men who flaunt their newly gained wealth. He castigates the vice of card-playing to which many of them are addicted. He has no sympathy for the Jewish pseudo-Boer or the would-be English sportsman who sheds his Yeshiva values, or the son who is ashamed of his father, the cobbler, and his uneducated mother, after these had toiled for years to see him complete medical school and gain a respected social position as a doctor.

Polsky's satire is mild. He prefers the happy ending. He rewards the good even if only at the end of their sad, wearisome years. He punishes the wicked but not too severely. A son who brings his old father to South Africa and then unwittingly hurts him by abandoning traditional piety, thus forcing him to seek refuge and understanding in an old-age home, is himself punished by discovering his own children becoming estranged from him.

Morris Hoffman (1885-1940) was another keen-eyed observer and talented chronicler of the immigrant generation. Born in Preil, near Vitebsk, he emigrated to South Africa in 1906 and lived for many years in the Karu, a semi-desert of Cape Province. After eight years of loneliness and hardships, during which he was buoyed by his romantic dream of the youthful beloved left behind in Europe, he voyaged to her on the eve of World War I, married her and settled to a happier existence as a storekeeper in De Aar. She encouraged him to record his pioneering experiences and he did so in the poetic volume *Chants of a Wanderer* (*Voglungsklangen*, 1935) and in short stories which appeared posthumously under the title *Under Africa's Sun*, (*Unter Afrikaner Zun*, 1957).

The best poems of the former volume were the early ones that deal with Malpenheim—"Monkeyhome"—his designation for Hopetown, his first home in Cape Province. Hoffman emphasizes the tragedy of idealistic young Lithuanian Jews who succumb to primitive African conditions which reward the strong, the brutal and the unscrupulous and which crush the gentle-hearted, the visionaries and the intellectuals. He depicts the decay of morals in an inhospitable environment, the desecration of love, the mad life of the newly rich. When his immigrants attain to affluence, they generally take on the values of their Boer neighbors, but a last vestige of Jewishness still clings to them and makes them sensitive to the pain of their servants and employees. They are on the whole more humane in their dealing with their customers of darker hue. The daughters of immigrants are often fascinated by the robust, earthbound, Bible-loving Boer youths among whom they grow up. However, when these youths embrace Nazi doctrines, they recover from their assimilationist delusions and revert to the Jewishness of their parents. There is a moral tone in Hoffman's tales as in those of most South African Yiddish writers.

Jacob Mordecai Sherman (1885-1958), who came to the Transvaal in 1903, began with sad poems that reflected his early hardships. More than half a century later, when he collected his poems in the volume *In Quiet Hours* (*In Shtile Shtunden*, 1957), he recalled his years of stress, wandering and changing callings. He was *shochet*, storekeeper, farmer, bookkeeper, before he attained stability and maturity and accepted his fate. A poem of the nineteen-year-old, entitled *Lonely* (*Elent*, 1904), reveals him in a despairing mood, wondering how much longer he can survive the all-encompassing loneliness. In another poem of the same year, he dreams of the poor but warm home he left behind; this old-fashioned Jewish home takes on the hues of a paradise when compared to his wretchedness in his new, strange abode. In still another melancholy poem, he wonders what happened to the ideals he once nurtured, and he replies that they remained with his real self when he sailed forth on the Atlantic and that only a shadow of himself survives in the land of his present exile.

Sherman participated in many Yiddish publications and edited several Yiddish periodicals, including the bi-weekly *Dorem Afrike*.

He was the author of the first Yiddish novel in South Africa, *Land of Gold and Sunshine* (*Land Fun Gold Un Zunshein*, 1956), as well as of a volume of tales and lyrics *On Transvaal's Soil* (*Oif Transvaler Erd*, 1949).

Sherman's novel is largely autobiographic. His hero, Meir, comes to South Africa in the same year as did the author himself and goes through a similar metamorphosis from butcher's assistant to storekeeper before finally integrating completely into his strange environment and living as a farmer on his own soil. Stress is laid on the friendly relations between Boers and Jews, the respect of the religiously oriented Afrikaner for the Jews as the people of the Bible. By answering the needs of the non-Jewish farmers and plantation owners, the Jews prosper as traders in outposts far from the large towns and in the course of years help to develop these outposts into viable communities. Sherman gives detailed, sympathetic consideration to the problem of mixed marriages between Jew and Afrikaner. He recognizes that the paucity of Jewish girls among the immigrants faced young men with the dilemma of marriage outside of their faith or no marriage at all. Though Jews as Whites were associated with the dominating sector of the population, they are portrayed by the novelist as extremely solicitous of the welfare of the Blacks, who formed a majority of the population.

The relations between Blacks and Whites formed the main subject of Richard Feldman's narratives. Feldman (1897-1968) was brought by his parents from Lithuania to South Africa at the age of thirteen, He played a prominent role in the liberal and labor movements of the Transvaal. For eleven years he served as a Labor member in the Transvaal Provincial Council. His book of short stories, *Black and White* (*Shvarts Un Vays*), was first published in 1937 and was republished twenty years later, the only Yiddish work in South Africa which experienced a second edition.

Feldman stresses the dignity, the warmheartedness, the cheerfulness of the Blacks. He shows their exploitation for the sake of gold and diamonds and their physical and moral decay when detribalized. He depicts the suffering and the ostracism meted out to the so-called White Kaffirs, the few Whites who intermarry with the Blacks and raise families in Zulu villages. Feldman also calls attention to the precarious position of the Jewish settlers in cities in which racial strife was reaching a climax after World War I. The volume includes a playlet about Jewish hawkers whose livelihood depended upon the good will of all racial groups and who, when subjected to crucial tests in the racial conflict, remained true to the Jewish values inculcated in them in pre-African years by the Bible and the Talmud.

In the writings of Leibel Feldman (b. 1896), the older brother of Richard Feldman, there is also a tendency to depict the "noble savage" as somehow more moral than the civilized European, a romantic tendency which harks back to Rousseau and his idealization of the natural man. This tendency comes to the fore in his impressionistic sketch of a temporary sojourn among the Bechuanas in the village of Mochudi and in his narrative of his brief experience as a diamond-digger.

Leibel Feldman recounted the economic, social and cultural development of the Yiddish-speaking pioneering generation in his early study *Jews in South Africa* (*Yiedn in Dorem Afrike,* 1937), and in his study of 1941 on the rise and decline of the Jewish community of Oudshoorn, once famed as the Jerusalem of South Africa and until World War I a most important center of ostrich-breeding and of a flourishing trade in ostrich feathers. His later studies dealt with the Jews of Johannesburg (1960), the Indians of South Africa (1961), Israel (1965) and an analytical survey *My View of History* (*Mein Kuk Oif Geshikhte,* 1967).

With the founding of the Yiddish Cultural Federation in 1947, its monthly organ *Dorem Afrike* in 1948, and the publishing venture Kayor in 1949, South African Yiddish literature reached its crest.

Kayor began with the lyric volume of Michel Ben Moshe (b. 1911). A journalist by profession, Ben Moshe arrived in South Africa in 1931, wrote for Hebrew periodicals, coedited the Hebrew monthly *Basad* in 1932, changed to Yiddish in 1936, and collected his Yiddish poems under the title *Fragment* (*Opris,* 1949). These were impressionistic lyrics full of despair, with only now and then a glimmer of a distant light beyond the encompassing gloom.

In 1971 the best poems of his autumnal years appeared under the symbolic title *Twilight* (*In Likht Fun Ovent*). These poems were laden with ripe wisdom and deepest melancholy. Some were full of longing suffering biblical figures such as King David, lonely on his throne, and Job moaning to God amidst ashes. Still others reflected African scenes: the heavy tread of elephants in the vast bush, the smoke curling above kraals, the dark glow of bronze bodies in the veldt, the dawn of hope among young toilers fettered to their locations. Only in his final hymn to Jerusalem was Ben Moshe's basic pessimism dissipated.

Kayor also published the sketches of Hyman Ehrlich, *Dankere* (1956), and his verses for children, *Grow, Flowers, Grow (Vaksen, Vaksen, Bliemelekh,* 1964), as well as the epic poem on Johannesburg by Nathan Berger, *The Golden Rand (Beim Rand Fun Gold,* 1966).

Ehrlich, who was born in Dankere in 1888, revivified in his sketches this Latvian townlet which bordered on the three provinces of Vitebsk, Courland and Lifland and whose Jewish inhabitants remained poor, pious and picturesque, generation after generation.

He described their weddings and funerals, their superstitions and their stubborn resistance to change. By means of a single characteristic episode or anecdote, he illustrated the uniqueness of each figure. The cobbler, the tailor, the grave-digger, the thief emerged as more sympathetic human beings than the town's only patrician or the reputedly miracle-working rabbi.

Although Ehrlich came to South Africa in 1906 and spent most of his mature years in Johannesburg, his prose and verse did not reflect the slightest influence of this land and its largest metropolis. Nathan Berger (b. 1910), on the other hand, was enamored of the Rand. His epic poem on Johannesburg consisted of two cantos in rhymed quatrains. In the first canto, he sang of his beloved Transvaal metropolis which arose from the bush eighty years earlier and which became ever more resplendent in luxury and ever more troubled in spirit. This canto ended with the dream-musing of an old Swazi watchman, who transversed in imagination the long road from his former tribal kraal to his present detribalized, lonely vigil far from his kinsmen. In the second canto, the poet gave a composite picture of Johannesburg's Jews, their rise to affluence, their transmigrated culture, their gradual yielding to the assimilationist forces of their glamorous environment. He concluded sadly that this much-tried Jewish community, which fought long and stubbornly to retain its own group personality, was becoming ever more alienated from healthy, traditional roots and was giving up long-defended cultural positions—"because life so demanded." The Jewish bard of the second canto was not unlike the Swazi watchman of the first canto. He too was nostalgically recalling the

shtetl which he exchanged in his youth for the glittering South
African metropolis and he too felt emptied of his earlier radiant
dreams and was also now holding a lonely vigil surrounded by
mountains of dead sand from which the gold had long since been
extracted.

South Africa's finest Yiddish poet was David Fram (b. 1903),
who began in 1923 with idyllic poems of Jewish life in Lithuania,
before emigrating to Johannesburg in 1927 and moving on later
to Salisbury in Rhodesia. His *Songs and Poems (Lieder Un
Poemes,* 1931) was the first lyric collection by a recognized poet
based in part on South African experiences. His later poems, however, reverted to the vanished world of his Eastern European
childhood and youth. Two decades after the end of World War
II, he still raged at God and could not reconcile himself to the
Almighty who let His most faithful followers go up in flames.

Among South African Yiddish writers of considerable significance after World War II were Levi Shalit (b. 1916), editor of
the *Afrikaner Yiddishe Zeitung* since 1953 and author of a study
on H. Leivick's Messianism (1947) and of memoirs recalling his
ghetto years and concentration camp experiences, *Thus We Died
(Azoi Zeinen Mir Geshtorben,* 1948); Hersh Shishler (b. 1903),
author of four volumes of humorous sketches; Bernard Mirwish,
author of the satirical tales *The Glory Seekers (Die Koved Zukher,*
1946); Sarah Aizen, lyricist of Capetown, whose *Selected Songs
and Poems (Geklibene Lieder Un Poemes,* 1965) ranged in subject
matter from Kovno to Israel and Africa but who was at her best
in her simple verses of woman's longing and tender sadness; David
Wolpe, poet, essayist, narrator, and editor of *Dorem Afrike;* and
Zalman Levi, his successor as editor of this literary monthly in
1970 and a pillar of the Yiddish Cultural Federation.

Mendl Tabachnik (b. 1894), poet and dramatist, matured late.
He was past seventy when his first book of songs and poems, *In
Late Hours (In Shpete Shtunden,* 1965) appeared. He then began
a three-volume fictionalized autobiography, *Kalman Bulan* (I,
1968; II, 1970; III, 1971). The first volume dealt with the experiences of the hero, Kalman, in a Lithuanian townlet, his impressment in the Czarist army, his escape across the Russian
border after having gotten into trouble with his anti-Semitic
superiors and his arrival in Capetown shortly before the First
World War. The second volume encompassed the hero's early
years of adjustment to South African reality. This reality was
especially harsh for an immigrant who arrived penniless and with-

YIDDISH IN SOUTH AFRICA AND AUSTRALIA 387

out any special skills. But every Jewish immigrant to Johannesburg could reckon with the help of a family member, or a *landsman*, who had preceded him. Hard work from dawn to sunset,
and scrupulously honest dealing with the natives of the Transvaal
settlement in whose midst Kalman found himself, enabled him
to make headway quickly. His greatest asset was his steadfast
moral personality, the product of his Eastern European Jewish
heritage. It did not deteriorate despite the pressures and temptations of his new environment. The third volume dealt with Kalman's later and less stormy years.

The author, in his late seventies, was at peace with the world.
He painted difficult situations in the relations between man and
woman, boss and employee, White overlords and Black underlings,
but he resolved them before they reached tragic proportions by
effecting mutual understanding between opposing individuals. In
his mild, kind, tolerant, compassionate approach to human conflicts, he followed the tradition of South African Yiddish fiction
begun by Hyman Polsky and continued by J. M. Sherman and
Richard Feldman.

Yiddish plays were staged in South Africa since 1895 but they
were generally written by dramatists from other lands, of whom
the most popular was Abraham Goldfaden. American Yiddish
actors frequently toured South Africa both before the Boer War
and throughout the twentieth century. The dramatist Peretz
Hirshbein spent several months there in the course of his world
tour, 1920-1922, and aroused great interest with his lectures and
dramatic readings.

South African playwrights whose Yiddish dramas and comedies
were published between the two World Wars included David
Fram, I. M. Sewitz (1896-1939), Hersch Bril (1891-1925), Mendel
Tabachnik and Shlomo Kartun (b. 1895). The demand for Yiddish
plays subsided with each decade and only guest performances by
visiting actors and amateur productions now and then still attracted significant audiences after the mid-century.

Because of the negligible immigration of Jews to South Africa
after the founding of Israel and because of the aging of the pioneering generation, Yiddish literature could no longer thrive with
its former intensity and vigor. Jews born and reared south of the
Zambezi were English-speaking and, to a lesser extent, Afrikaans-
speaking. In the 1960's the best Yiddish poems about the South
African landscape were written not by indigenous poets but by
Abraham Sutzkever, the poet of Vilna and Tel Aviv. The out-

standing Jewish novelists of South Africa, Sara Gertrude Millen, Nadine Gordimer, Lewis Sowden and Dan Jacobson, wrote in English and the finest lyricist, Olga Kirsch, wrote in Afrikaans before her settling in Israel. By 1970 South Africa's Jews numbered 115,000 but the number of Yiddish readers was barely sufficient to support a single weekly and a single monthly.

While the Yiddish-speaking Jews of South Africa stemmed from Lithuania, those of Australia came to the largest extent from Poland and for a long time retained nostalgia for the communities from which they had been uprooted. There was a trickle of such immigrants before the First World War, a flurry in the 1920's which was immediately arrested by restrictions imposed by the Australian authorities, and a comparatively large influx after the Second World War.

The early immigrants from Eastern Europe, who found themselves among a white population whose ethnic background was almost entirely British, suffered from loneliness and the dissipation of their hope for a vigorous continuation of their Jewish communal ties. Their loneliness was not lessened by the presence of British Jews who had preceded them and who had attained superior social and economic status.

In 1907, when the Jewish Colonization Association published a Yiddish booklet with information for Jews who might wish to emigrate to Australia, it estimated the number of Jews already there at 20,000. Only few were of Eastern European origin. Though the economic level of Australian Jews was described as satisfactory, their cultural level was conceded to be low and opportunities for educating children in Jewishness to be extremely limited.

Not until the close of the 1920's were the Yiddish immigrants sufficiently numerous to be able to set up cultural institutions of any significance. Their travails and moods were best described in the *Australian Tales* (*Dertsehlungen Fun Australian,* 1939) by Pinchas Goldhar (1901-1947), the pioneer of Yiddish literature on this southern continent.

Goldhar stemmed from Lodz and immigrated to Australia in 1928. As a Yiddish journalist, he could not at first continue his profession. There were Jewish journals as early as 1842 but they catered to English-speaking Jews. The most significant were the bi-weekly *Jewish Herald* of Melbourne, founded in 1879, and the weekly *Hebrew Standard* of Sidney, founded in 1896. The Yiddish press began in 1928, the year of Goldhar's arrival, with a single page supplement to the *Jewish Herald,* and offered local and general news. It was not a literary medium. In 1931 the Yiddish weekly *Australier Leben* was founded with Goldhar as its editor. His was a lonely outpost of Yiddish and he felt keenly his isolation from the mainstream of Yiddish creativity in Europe and America.

Loneliness and uprootedness became the main theme of his Australian tales. He dissected the characters of the Yiddish pioneers in minute detail and with ruthless honesty. Most of them were hopeless and helpless, frittering away their lives in the pursuit of wealth which eluded them or which offered them no lasting satisfaction if obtained. In his story "Old Friends," two aging bachelors spend their days accumulating petty profits, one from a pawnshop and the other from real estate, and their evenings playing cards with each other. Thus the years pass by and finally, after one of them dies, the other continues playing both sides when evening sets in, for there is nothing else he can do with himself, a lonely, dull, flabby, useless creature on this vast globe.

In another story, "A Funeral," the sadness and alienation of the Yiddish immigrants are illustrated when one of them dies and is buried in the Jewish sector of the Christian cemetery. The Yiddish-speaking mourners who come to the funeral find themselves out of place and unwanted. They become keenly aware that in death as well as in life they are intruders whose foreign ways are intolerable to the older settlers and devoid of content even to themselves.

In the story, "Mandel, the Restauranteur," Goldhar unlocks the pain of a Jew who cannot and does not want to live Jewishly and who is yet constantly reminded of his Jewish origin. Mandel, the owner of a Kosher restaurant in Berlin's Grenadierstrasse, suffered as an "Ostjude," even though he tried to ape German ways. Forced to flee when the Nazis came to power, he tried to grow new roots in Australia by opening up a fashionable restaurant, but soon found that there too he could not escape his ancestry. Non-Jewish clientele kept away and neighborhood children chalked a Hakenkreuz on his door.

In his best stories Goldhar depicted stronger, more attractive personalities who tried to stem the deterioration of Jewishness, but who also ultimately failed. "On a Farm" presents Sam Rothman, a hard-working, lonely Jewish farmer who wants to prove that Jews can survive and prosper as tillers of the soil. He hopes that his example will encourage others to follow and that ere long a purely Jewish colony would arise far from the temptations and perils of the alien culture of the big town. He is even willing to marry the unlovely daughter of the Jewish immigrant Zelman rather than the more attractive daughter of the Irishman O'Brien, because with the former he could have a Jewish home and raise Jewish children. But when he comes to woo her, he discovers that she and her family are preparing to move to the big town. The embittered, disappointed idealist has to abandon his grandiose Jewish vision and he yields to the lure of O'Brien's daughter.

In "The Last Minyan," Goldhar projects as his strongest character an old rabbi who stubbornly clings to the synagogue which he helped to erect in his young days when he came to a pioneering community, then in the midst of a gold rush, and to which Jewish storekeepers streamed to service the gold-diggers. When the veins of gold were exhausted and the town took on a ghostly appearance, most of the Jews also left. The rabbi remained with the last *minyan*, and even thereafter. At the end he is a lonely, tragic figure, continuing religious services with but a single follower, for Judaism must not be abandoned.

Goldhar was at work in the 1940's upon a prose epic of his Jewish generation in Australia but was able to complete only two precious fragments when death overtook him at the age of forty-six. By then he was no longer the solitary Yiddish pioneer. Melech Ravitch had joined him in 1937, and edited the first anthology of Australian Yiddish writing. Bunim Varshavsky (1893-1956) arrived in 1939, after a literary career of three decades in Poland as poet, journalist and translator. He became co-editor of the second Australian anthology, which appeared in 1942. Two years later, he published his romance *The Lost Princess* (*Die Farlorene Bas-Malke*, 1944), in which he retold in verse one of the best tales of Rabbi Nachman Bratslaver.

Chaim Rubenstein (1870-1948), who came to Melbourne in 1934, succeeded Goldhar as editor of *Australish Yiedishe Neies* and edited five literary booklets in 1938.

Yossl Birshtein (b. 1920) emigrated from Poland in 1939, participated in Australian publications for a decade, primarily with Yiddish lyrics, but left for Israel after publishing in Melbourne his poetic collection *Beneath Alien Skies* (*Unter Fremde Himeln*, 1949).

Hersh Mintz (b. 1906), essayist and historian, arrived in Australia from Poland in 1928. He wrote with equal fluency in English and Yiddish and headed the research activities of the Melbourne section of YIVO.

The Warsaw essayist Joshua Rapoport (1895-1971) arrived in 1946, after having spent the war years in Shanghai and was immediately hailed as a literary critic of vast knowledge and sensitive insight. Rapoport was a native of Bialystok. In Poland he had participated in Zionist agitation and had edited weeklies of the Labor Zionists. A connoisseur of world literature, he translated into Yiddish works by Rabindranath Tagore, Maurice Maeterlinck, Waldemar Bonsels, Romain Rolland, Boris Pilnyak and Martin Anderson-Nexo. Upon his arrival in Melbourne, he was for a time editor of the newspaper *Australish Yiedishe Neies,* but he exerted greater influence as columnist for the *Australishe Yiedishe Post.* In his column "To the Point" (*In Pintel Herein*), he wielded a sharp, satiric pen. His comments on books and cultural phenomena were often resented, since he was no respector of authorities and insisted on making judgments on the basis of the highest esthetic and moral standards. The best of his essays on literary problems and personalities were collected in seven volumes which roamed over a vast area and which helped to educate Australian readers and to shape their literary taste.

Like Rapoport, Ber I. Rosen (1899-1954) had escaped from Poland to Shanghai upon the outbreak of the war and then moved on to Australia when the war ended. In his early years he was associated with S. Anski. After the latter's death, he devoted five years to editing the fifteen volume edition of Anski's works. He then turned to acting, journalism, poetry and agitation for the Bund. His first book was the collection of short stories *Raw Earth* (*Roye Erd,* 1926), descriptions of Polish Jews in a naturalistic style reminiscent of his admired I. M. Weissenberg. During his seven years in Melbourne, nostalgia overcame him for the vanished Polish-Jewish culture and in his *Tlomatzki 13* (1950), and in the posthumously published *Portraits* (1956), he revivified scenes and personalities of earlier decades. His pen portraits of Anski, Weissenberg, Nomberg and Hillel Zeitlin were based on intimate knowledge and were especially valuable.

Yitzchok Kahn, who wrote the introduction to Rosen's *Selected Works* (*Geklibene Shriften,* 1957), also had his early roots in Poland but only matured after his arrival in Melbourne in 1937. Not until 1964 did his first collection of essays, sketches and critical articles appear under the symbolic title *Sparks and Flames* (*Funken Un Flammen*). It was followed by his later essays *On the Crossroads (Oyfn Tzesheidveg,* 1971). He had an affinity for biblical and historical themes. In his analysis of Richard Beer-Hofman's biblical drama *Jacob's Dream* and Thomas Mann's Joseph-trilogy, he showed how biblical sparks were fanned into flaming masterpieces. In the historical novels of Moshe Shamir, Lion Feuchtwanger and Joseph Opatoshu, he traced the revolt of the Jewish spirit against the rule of brute force. In essays on Walter Rathenau, Benjamin Disraeli and Stefan Zweig, he showed talented Jews in tragic estrangement from their heritage and yet glorying in it.

The most talented narrator of the post-Goldhar decades in Australia was Herz Bergner (1907-1969), younger brother of Melech Ravitch. Bergner had already attracted attention in Poland with his short stories. In Melbourne, to which he came in 1938, he continued Goldhar's tradition of literary realism with four volumes of narratives. His were the first Australian Yiddish novels to be translated into English: *Between Sky and Sea (Tsvishen Himmel Un Vasser,* 1947), which dealt with a boatload of refugees and their destinies, and *Light and Shadow (Likht Un Shoten,* 1960), the moving story of a Jewish family struggling for acceptance in an Australian community.

Bergner's short stories, culminating in the volume *Where the Truth Lies (Vo Der Emes Shteht Ein,* 1966), mirror faithfully the life of the post-Holocaust immigrants. Most of these immigrants, mindful of their own suffering before their escape to the distant continent, are filled with compassionate understanding for their fellow mortals. The novelist shows them reconstructing their shattered existences and adjusting fairly well to new mates, new callings and a new reality. But the shadow of the past always accompanies them and they are never as lighthearted or gay as their neighbors who did not experience the Hitler years.

Bergner does not shock. He soothes and heals. He emphasizes little deeds of kindness that draw people to each other, last flickerings of love before extinction, common bonds that strangers discover in each other after overcoming mutual suspicions, golden sunlight that seeps into gray days in hospitals and old age homes, goodness that seeks to efface past cruelties.

Melbourne continued to be the citadel of Yiddish culture in Australia. As early as 1921, Peretz Hirshbein contrasted the warm, vibrant Yiddish atmosphere he sensed there with the coldness and indifference of Sydney whose Jews were already then thoroughly assimilated to English speech and customs. Zerubabel, who visited

Melbourne thirty years later, dubbed it the Jerusalem of Australia. Mendl Mann, who tarried there a decade after Zerubabel, paid tribute to its Yiddish vitality. However, the transition of the sons of the Yiddish-speaking immigrants to the dominant English tongue could not be arrested. Though the Jewish population of Australia in the 1970's had increased to more than 70,000, Yiddish literature there, as in South Africa, served only the needs of an ever aging, ever dwindling group.

20

YIDDISH IN LATIN AMERICA

Argentine Center ● Alperson ● Prose Pioneers ● Aba Kliger ● Leib Malach ● Giser ● Zhitnitzky ● Rozhansky ● Granitstein ● Suskovich ● Grynberg ● Sapozhnikov ● Kehos Kliger ● Pinson ● Post-Holocaust Writers ● Zak ● Chilean Writers ● Brazilian Writers ● Kishinovsky ● Leibush Singer ● Lipiner ● Raizman ● Hersh Schwartz ● Kutchinsky ● Palatnik ● Mexican Writers ● Jacob Glantz ● Berliner ● Vinetzky ● Berebicez ● Weisbaum ● Salomon Kahan ● Corona ● Young Cuba ● Dubelman ● Berniker

A MAJORITY OF THE JEWS in Latin American countries live in Argentina and most of them immigrated from Yiddish-speaking communities of Eastern Europe or are descendants of such immigrants. Argentina entered upon the world Jewish scene as a significant center after the large-scale efforts of Baron de Hirsch, beginning in 1889, to settle Jews in agricultural colonies there. By 1900 the Jewish population surpassed 30,000. Differences between the Baron's administrators and the new settlers led to a migration from farms to cities, especially to the capital, Buenos Aires. There Yiddish schools arose after the First World War, a Yiddish press flourished, which included the dailies *Die Yiedishe Zeitung,* founded in 1914, and *Die Presse,* founded in 1918. Yiddish actors found large audiences and Yiddish writers a growing reading public. By 1944 an anthology of Yiddish literature could bring contributions by ninety Argentine Yiddish writers.

Enriched by an influx of Yiddish intellectuals who survived the European catastrophe of the Hitler years, Argentina was surpassed in the 1950's and 1960's only by the United States and Israel in the number of Yiddish books published. These included more than 150 volumes of the series *Dos Poilishe Yiedentum* and an ever increasing number of volumes of Yiddish literary masters, edited by Shmuel Rozhansky. By 1970, the Jewish population of Argentina was close to half a million, with about 300,000 of them concentrated in Buenos Aires.

The earliest Argentine Yiddish writer was the narrator Mordecai Alperson (1860-1947). He came to the new land in 1891, along with the first wave of colonists. Among his fifteen volumes, the most important was his narration of three decades of pioneering Jewish life, *Memoirs of a Jewish Colonist* (*Memoiren Fun A Yiedishen Kolonist*, I, 1922; II, 1926; III, 1928).

Early pioneers of Yiddish prose included Michel Hacohen Sinai (1877-1958), who founded, in 1898, the first Yiddish periodical, *The Echo* (*Der Viederkol*); Y. S. Liachovitzky (1874-1937), the first editor of *Die Yiedishe Zeitung;* Baruch Bendersky (1880-1951), who wrote sketches about Jewish colonists following his arrival in Argentina in 1894; Aaron Brodsky (1878-1925), dramatist and novelist of Buenos Aires, his home since 1904; Israel Helfman (1886-1935), journalist and writer of short stories and sketches; Noah Vital (1889-1961), novelist of Argentina since 1905 and of Chile since 1926; Pinchas Wald (b. 1886), active as educator, journalist and essayist; Joseph Mendelson (b. 1891), editor of *Die Yiedishe Zeitung* and of literary journals; and Pinie Katz (1882-1959), who came to Buenos Aires in 1906 and, as editor of *Die Presse,* influenced the Yiddish literary scene. Ten volumes of his own essays attested to his prolific pen but his most noteworthy achievement was his translation of the Spanish classic *Don Quixote*.

Pioneers of Yiddish poetry in Argentina included Aba Kliger (b. 1893), who wrote lyrics of the Andes Mountains and of the La Plata during his Argentine period, 1913-1921, before emigrating to the United States, and his friend, Moshe Pinchevsky (1894-1955), who stemmed from Bessarabia and came to Argentina in 1913 but was caught up by enthusiasm for the Russian Revolution and continued his poetic career in Russia. There, his tales for children were read in Yiddish schools, his poems published, and his dramas acted on Yiddish stages, until the fateful year 1948 when he was arrested during Stalin's liquidation of Yiddish writers and spent his remaining years in a Siberian Labor Camp.

The pioneering period ended during World War I. Among the best known writers of the 1920's were Leib Malach (1894-1936) and Moshe David Giser (1893-1952). The former, a protegé of H. D. Nomberg, stayed in Argentina only from 1922 to 1926, but his travel sketches and tales of Latin America were widely read and his dramas produced in Buenos Aires, New York, Warsaw and Paris. The latter was in Argentina from 1924 to 1933. There he published poems, ballads, songs for children, literary essays, and edited literary journals. After his death, the best products of his pen were collected in *The Song of Life* (*Dos Gezang Fun A Leben,* 1953). Jacob Botoshansky (1892-1964) matured in Rumania as dramatist and literary critic before arriving in Argentina in 1926, where he was most influential as co-editor of *Die Presse* and as a literary historian and critic. Pinchas Eliezer Zhitnitzky (1894-1967), also co-editor of *Die Presse,* was a central figure in Argentine Yiddish cultural activities for four decades. Shmuel Rozhansky (b. 1902), columnist, theater-critic, and literary historian, began in Buenos Aires in 1922 but became best known in the 1960's as editor of many volumes of Yiddish classics and as the dynamic director of Argentine's YIVO projects. His anthology of poetry, fiction and essays, *From Argentina* (*Fun Argentina,* 1960), drew attention to the many Yiddish writers in that land. Moshe Granitstein (1897-1956) began his literary career in Warsaw in 1922 but left for Argentina five years later and continued for almost three decades to publish booklets of poetry, essays, short stories and three volumes of recollections of his native Volynia. Shlome Suskovitch (b. 1906) was first known as a writer of humorous sketches for *Die Presse;* he compiled the most comprehensive anthology of Argentine Yiddish literature in 1944 and edited the literary-philosophical quarterly *Davke* from 1949. His philosophical work *The Two Sources of Ethics* (*Die Tsvai Kvalen Fun Moral,* 1963) received the award of the Argentine Section of the Congress for Jewish Culture.

Berl Grynberg (1906-1961) combined realistic and romantic traits in his short stories, which attracted attention far beyond Argentine borders. There was hardly a tale of his which did not have a kind character whose goodness dispelled pain, greed, and sadness. His anger at human folly always dissolved into a compassionate understanding of human fallibility. In two stories of the collection *The Blue Ship* (*Dos Bloe Shifele,* 1948), he presented two mothers with contrasting attitudes toward their Jewish heritage. One felt lonely and dejected because her children, like many of their young peers, were imbued with Jewish self-hatred. The other gloried that she had three daughters who married into fine Christian families. She could not understand why her fourth daughter refused to escape the burden of Jewishness by also intermarrying. This daughter was, however, fascinated by the holiness and warmth of Friday evenings at the traditional home of her pious aunt. The light of the Sabbath candles reminded her that in Jewishness there was Sabbath joy to compensate for gray weekdays and there were holy rituals that linked her to a millennial past.

The finest story of Grynberg's collection *Affection* (*Liebshaft*, 1953) presented a wealthy but paralyzed Jew who was visited by a friend. In the course of their exciting conversation this friend was also overtaken by a paralytic stroke. Both realized that, when they at long last wanted to begin to enjoy life, it was too late. "Both sick friends were silent. They looked into each other's eyes and read in these eyes the hopeless inevitability of the course of human existence, extinguished dreams, fading hopes, senseless, eternally senseless travails."

Nachman Mizheritzki (1900-1956) was a physician who wrote short stories since 1929. His posthumously published *Selected Tales* (*Geklibene Dertzehlungen*, 1956) dealt mainly with sick characters. Critics compared them to Dostoevsky-types.

Gershon Sapozhnikov (b. 1907), editor, educator and essayist, revealed in his two books of literary criticism, published in 1958 and 1969, profound insight into the psychological wrestling of creative Yiddish writers. His adoration of Sholom Aleichem led him in a series of essays to stress the universal quality of this humorist and to rank him above Mark Twain and Anton Chekhov, the other great humorists of that generation who sought escape from the tragedy of human existence through laughter.

Kehos Kliger (b. 1908), who immigrated to Argentina in 1937, a decade after Sapozhnikov, was a poet whose lyric volumes since 1941 dealt mainly with his new home. However, in addition to ballads of the pampas and of mistreated and disadvantaged characters—prostitutes, vagabonds, chimney-sweeps—for whom he displayed great sympathy, he also wrote songs full of nostalgia for his Volynian birthplace, especially in the volume *Song of Earth* (*Gezang Oif Der Erd,* 1941). His poems and poetic tales of the years during and immediately after World War II, in the volume *The World Invites Me to Die* (*Die Velt Farbet Mikh Shtarben,* 1950), reflected his disillusionment with the cruel species which tolerated the annihilation of his kin just because of their Jewish birth. The volume ended with his ballad on Shmuel Balaban (1877-1942), a long elegy on this historian of Polish Jewry who continued his research even while in Warsaw's doomed ghetto. In Kliger's final poetic collection *I and the Sea* (*Ikh Un Der Yam*, 1961), he emphasized the lure and silence of the sea far more than its menace and rage.

Boleslav Levin (b. 1908) came from Poland and Uruguay. As Professor of Argentine History at universities, he wrote Spanish studies on Latin American marranos, but he also participated with Yiddish studies in YIVO's publications and in other Yiddish periodicals.

Mimi Pinson (b. 1910) came to Argentina as a child of four and, despite her growing up in a Spanish-speaking environment, wrote Yiddish stories in a pure, idiomatic style. Her volume *The Windowless Courtyard* (*Der Hoif Ohn Fenster*, 1965) allied her to the proletarian storytellers.

Chaim Finkelstein (b. 1911), educator, orator and Labor Zionist leader, wrote chiefly on pedagogical themes. A selection of his best essays, *Vision, Word, Reality* (*Vizie, Vort, Vor*), appeared in 1967 two years before he was called to Jerusalem to head the education department of the Jewish Agency.

Of Yiddish writers who found refuge in Argentina after World War II, the most prominent was Shmerke Kaczerginski (1903-1954), a pillar of "Young Vilna," a partisan fighter with rifle and pen, a chronicler of Jewish martyrdom during the Holocaust.

I. J. Yonasovitch (b. 1909) experienced a long odyssey, from Siberia through Russia, Poland, France and Israel, before settling in Buenos Aires in 1952. His poems, playlets and journalistic articles aroused less attention than did his pen portraits of Soviet writers in his book *With Yiddish Writers in Russia* (*Mit Yiddishe Shreiber in Russland,* 1959).

Abraham Zak (b. 1891) experienced a similar odyssey from a labor camp in the Polar region of the Soviets through Siberia, Poland, France and Israel before arriving in Argentina in the same year as Yonasovitch. He had begun as a poet in Grodno, Poland, under the influence of his townsman Leib Naidus, had served as literary editor of the Warsaw daily *Moment,* had published collections of his lyrics since 1918 and of short stories since 1922, but it was on Argentine soil that he composed his most important work, an epic trilogy, *A World in Dissolution* (*Eine Velt Geht Unter,* I, 1954; II, 1956; III, 1958). This was followed by a volume of essays on literary figures whom he had known, *The Kingdom of the Word* (*In Kenigreikh Fun Vort,* 1966).

Moshe Knapheim (b. 1910) also came from war years in Soviet

Russia and post-war years in Poland and France. In Argentina he resumed his interrupted writing of Yiddish lyrics.

Mordecai Bernstein (1905-1966) lived in Argentina after his repatriation from Soviet Labor Camps and participated in YIVO's research projects in Yiddish linguistics and folklore.

Baruch Hager (b. 1898) arrived in Buenos Aires in 1952 and completed there his Hassidic tales, *The Kingdom of Hassidism* (*Malkhus Hassidos*, 1955).

Israel Ashendorf (1909-1956) came to Argentina a year after Hager. A native of the Ukraine and educated in Lemberg, he spent the war years in Russia and was repatriated to Poland. In Warsaw he edited *Yiedishe Shriften* in 1948, but soon thereafter he left for Paris and five years later for Argentina. His three booklets of lyrics before the war were unnoticed, but after the war he reached a wider audience with his play *King Saul* (*Melekh Shaul*, 1948), and his short stories *Partners of Fate* (*Shutfim Fun Goirel*, 1953).

Mark Turkov (b. 1904) was involved in Poland in the struggle against the Hitler menace and escaped to Argentina in 1939. There he edited the many volumes of the series *Dos Poilishe Yiedentum*. He was joined in 1940 by his older brother Zygmund Turkov (1896-1970), a distinguished actor and regisseur, who stimulated and directed Yiddish theatrical performances in Buenos Aires and Rio de Janeiro, and who published five volumes of memoirs about his colorful career on the stage and his contacts with literary circles.

Despite the heroic efforts of Argentine Jewish educators, editors and communal leaders to maintain Buenos Aires as a bastion of Yiddish culture, the transition of the younger Jewish population to Spanish and the exodus of Yiddish intellectuals to Israel, especially after the Six Day War, brought about a constant decline in the number of Yiddish readers, theatergoers and writers, so that by 1970 Yiddish creativity was at a far lower ebb than a decade or two earlier.

Chile's Jews numbered about 35,000 in 1970, less than one-tenth of the Argentine Jewish population. Yiddish literature was closely linked with neighboring trends in Argentina. The most talented Yiddish poet of Chile, Moshe David Giser (1893-1952), had spent nine years in Argentina before settling in Santiago in 1933, where he edited the bi-weekly *Zied-Amerike* and the weekly *Chilener Yiedishes Vochenblat*. His co-editor, the novelist Noah Vital (1886-1961), spent more than two decades in Argentina before coming to Chile in 1926 and was equally prominent in the Yiddish literature of both lands. Yitzkhok Blumstein (b. 1897) was the Yiddish poet of the Argentine Andes before he embarked in 1936 upon his career as editor of Yiddish periodicals in Chile. Falik Lerner (b. 1903) was a prominent Argentine editor and was active in Chile only during 1944-1946, when he edited the journal *Dos Yiedishe Vort*. His articles in the volume *Persons and Landscapes* (*Mentshen Un Landshaften,* 1951) mirrored Jewish life in Chile, Argentina and Uruguay. Pinchas Bizberg (b. 1898) was an agronomist in a Jewish colony near Buenos Aires since 1927 and made his reputation in Argentina as a Yiddish dramatist before settling in the Chilean capital in 1953. Only Jacob Pilovsky (1898-1969), son of a Vilna rabbi, immigrated directly to Chile as a young man in 1924 and for decades occupied a prominent position in Santiago's literary and journalistic activities. He completed three volumes that afforded an insight into Chile's life. His last six years were spent in Israel and there his final collection of short stories, *By the Way* (*In Gang,* 1967), appeared, as well as his fascinating autobiography, *A Jew in the World* (*A Yied Oif Der Velt,* 1970).

The first Yiddish newspaper in Chile, *Idishe Presse,* was founded in Santiago in 1930. Seven years later the Yiddish weekly *Dos Vort* began to appear as the organ of the Yiddish-speaking community. This community, small in numbers, continued to draw its cultural sustenance from the far larger Jewish community of Buenos Aires. However, the considerable Jewish emigration, which set in since 1970, hastened the decline of Yiddish productivity.

The Jewish population of Brazil numbered only about 5,000 on the eve of World War I, but increased tenfold during the quarter of a century thereafter and to 150,000 by 1970. Most of the new immigrants were from Central and Eastern Europe and to meet their needs Jewish schools were founded and a Yiddish press arose. The first Yiddish weekly was launched during the war in Ponto Allegro in 1915 by Joseph Halevy but ceased publication the following year. In the Brazilian capital of Rio de Janeiro, the first Yiddish weekly, *Dos Idishe Vochenblat,* was founded in 1923 and survived for six years. *Idishe Folkszeitung* came into existence as a semi-weekly in 1927 and was expanded into a daily in 1935. *Idishe Presse* followed in 1930. Both newspapers had to suspend publication as a result of a government prohibition of all the foreign language press. After the prohibition was lifted, the latter organ resumed publication in 1947 under its original editor Aaron

Bergman (1890-1953). Bergman had written for Russian periodicals and had edited a Zionist weekly in Lemberg before migrating
to Rio de Janeiro in 1927. For two decades he continued as editor
and as a champion of Yiddish in Brazil. I. Z. Raizman (b.
1901), who taught in a Yiddish school of Ponte Allegro in the 1920's and
wrote for Brazil's Yiddish journals, published in 1968 a survey
of the Yiddish press from its beginnings until it was banned during the Second World War.

The first Yiddish book by a Brazilian writer was *New Homes*
(*Neie Heimen,* 1932) by Adolph Kishinovsky (1891-1935), a collection of short stories about immigrant life. The author had come
to Rio de Janeiro in 1918 after nine years in Argentina. He was
for a short time editor of *Dos Idishe Vochenblat* and founded a
short-lived monthly *Die Neie Velt* in 1927.

Other early pioneers of Yiddish letters in Brazil were Aaron
Koifman (b. 1892), who settled in Rio de Janeiro in 1921 and
who was co-editor of *Dos Idishe Vochenblat,* and Menashe Halpern
(1871-1960), whose literary career in Russia went back to 1899.
After settling in Rio de Janeiro in 1926, he published *From the Old
Source* (*Oisn Alten Brunen,* 1934) and in his eighty-eighth year his
lyrics, *Lieder* (1959). Far more important was his book of memoirs
Parchments (*Parmetn,* 1952).

The lyrics and short stories of Leibush Singer (1906-1939) did
not appear in book form until after his early death. They were
entitled *Quiet Chords* (*Akkorden in der Shtil,* 1939). Those of his
contemporary Joseph Lande (b. 1905), poet and narrator of San
Paolo, *Bright Dawns* (*Lichtike Kayoren,* 1959), were not published
until two decades later. In San Paolo, Elkana Harmatz (b. 1910)
was active since 1946 as journalist and short story writer.

Elihu Lipiner (b. 1916), editor of San Paolo's *Idishe Zeitung*
in the 1930's and of *Der Neier Moment* since 1950, became better
known as the author of *By the Waters of Portugal* (*Bei Die Teik-
hen Fun Portugal,* 1949), a scholarly work on the Jews of Portugal.

Raizman, also an editor of San Paolo's *Idishe Zeitung,* published in 1935 a history of the Israelites in Brazil from the beginning until the end of the Dutch occupation, and a novel about
the first Jewish settlers in the colonies established by the Jewish
Colonization Association, ICA. His second novel, *Stormy Lives*
(*Lebens In Shturm,* 1965), which appeared after he settled in
Israel, dealt with a difficult period in Brazilian Jewish life, the
early twentieth century, when white slavers, posing as rich ranchers and plantation-owners, brought beautiful girls from impov-

erished Jewish homes overseas and imposed upon them a life of sin. The central characters of the novel were a glamorous girl, who was caught in a net of vice and yet managed to remain pure-hearted amidst her degrading surroundings, and the young man of her dreams, who found his way from their *shtetl* to Rio de Janeiro but who failed to extricate her from her sinful realm while she was still alive. He did, however, gain insight into her tragedy and into the moral and social problems of the poor immigrant outcasts, men and women, peddlers and harlots, unscrupulous go-getters and socially conscious individuals. A high pitch of suspense was maintained throughout the narrative and stark tragedy was mitigated at the edge of the abyss by deeds of kindness.

Hersh Schwartz, who came to Brazil from Buenos Aires in 1926, emphasized in his collections of tales, *The Beginning* (*Der Onheib*, 1954), and *Green-Golden Home* (*Haim, Grin-Goldene*, 1960), the difficulties that faced the immigrant generation during the early years of adjustment and the loss of cherished Jewish ideals in the course of the hard daily struggle for bread. In the story, *The Beginning*, a nineteen-year-old immigrant from Bessarabia summed up his initial experiences in a letter to his father in his native townlet: "I've arrived on the new earth. Though the sun burns and my body is bathed in sweat while earning a living, my heart glows as never before. The earth of this vast land is primitive and so are its people. They suffer and sing of life passionately, without hate. Indeed, there is enough of love for natives and newcomers. But my conscience troubles me: will the Torah and the dreams of my earlier years leave me and fly away. I've seen my fellow-Jews who once nourished dreams and, my God, how they've changed. Will I too change? No, I'll struggle. It's worth it."

Meir Kutchinski, in the realistic stories of *The Brazil Version* (*Nusakh Brazil*, 1963), also pointed out that for newcomers who had to wander with pack on back, unfamiliar with the language of their customers, and in constant fear of tax collectors and licensing officials, book learning and devotion to intellectual avocations proved a hindrance. Nevertheless, even in the remotest hamlets such individuals were to be found who kept the sparks of Jewish culture, morals and group responsibility glimmering. When Europe's Jews were endangered, and when Israel fought for independence and survival, Brazil's Jews responded magnificently with aid and devotion to common causes and were themselves invigorated in their Jewishness.

The short story writer Rosa Palatnik (b. 1904) first attracted attention with her volume *Krasnik-Rio* (1953), narratives of her birthplace Krasnik in Poland and of the Brazilian metropolis, her home after 1936. It was followed by other collections of short stories about Brazil: *Along the Atlantic* (*Beim Geroish Fun Atlantic*, 1957), *Thirteen Tales* (*Dreizehn Dertsehlungen*, 1961), and *Selected Tales* (*Geklibene Dertzehlungen*, 1966).

The typical Palatnik story centers about a moment of truth in the life of Jews apparently successfully integrated in Brazil. There is a flashback to youthful years in the Old Country. There follow reminiscences of immigrant years of hard work until bread is assured and then increasing growth in affluence, a gradual realization that in the pursuit of wealth precious Jewish values were tossed aside, an effort, generally but not always successful, to return to the Jewish idealism still glimmering at subconscious levels of the soul.

In one story, a boy and a girl, who engaged in subversive activities in their Eastern European townlet in order to bring about a juster social and economic order, become *allrightniks* in the Brazilian city to which they immigrated. They slough their moral idealism and their Jewish observances. They raise their son and daughter to be well-mannered, pseudo-aristocratic Brazilians but become remorse-ridden when both children fall in love with non-Jews. Fortunately, surviving sparks of Jewishness can still be rekindled in the heart of these children, especially when news of the Holocaust in which European kinsmen were gassed reaches Brazilian shores. Then these children refrain from taking the final step of intermarriage and thus cutting themselves off from the Jewish group. Parents and children regain moral and spiritual health by working for the regeneration of the Jewish people from which they had been estranged.

In another story, a father who is ready to go to extremes to prevent his daughter from marrying a non-Jewish Brazilian wins the latter's admiration for Jewish tenacity. The story ends with the young man converting before marriage and with the father proudly entering the synagogue with his son-in-law for Yom Kippur services.

Another story depicts a hard-working immigrant who is despised by his *landsleit* because they remember that in the Old Country he was nicknamed Mechel the Golem. But when this immigrant in the course of years attains to wealth, then these *landsleit* want to marry off their daughters to him. The aging bachelor rejects these mates, however, and chooses as his wife a poor, old-maidish

orphan who came to ask him for a job and whose simple, un-
tarnished decency impresses him. She was more likely to make his
cold, palatial villa into a warm, cosy home.

Not all of Palatnik's stories have such happy endings. In one
of her Brazilian narratives, a father who built up a big business
and brought his educated son into it soon found that old-fashioned
Jewish ways and Yiddish speech irritated this son. The latter, on
taking charge of the business, contributed a large sum of money to
have an Old Age Home built in which his father could be kept
occupied and happy as the director. But when the father once
came to visit his former villa and saw the transformation that had
been made so that nothing remained of Jewish objects and atmosphere he held so dear, then he suffered a heart attack and died.

The thirteenth of Palatnik's *Thirteen Tales* deals with Jewish
survivors of the Holocaust who found life difficult in Israel and
were tempted by glowing reports of their wealthy Brazilian relatives to leave for Brazil. But they soon discovered that there too
they were regarded as rootless strangers by the natives who had
Brazilian earth under their feet and Brazilian sky above their
heads. The *Yordim* ended by returning to Israel, which alone
could be home for them. "On disembarking, all of them put happy,
firm steps on the sunny earth and felt that their tired, long
wandering feet kissed fervently the awakening earth of the land
of Israel."

Yiddish literature in Mexico dates back to 1927, when the three
poets Yitzkhok Berliner (1899-1957), Jacob Glantz (b. 1902) and
Moshe Glikovsky (b. 1904) united to publish a volume of their
poetry under the title *Three Ways (Drei Vegn)*. Glikovsky had
arrived from Poland in 1921 and had participated in the earliest
Mexican Yiddish journals. He later published a volume of lyrics,
Erring Spirits (Blondzhendike Geister, 1929) and a novel in two
volumes, *Daniel Stapler* (1946). Berliner arrived in Mexico a
year after Glikovsky and won renown beyond Mexico's borders
with the lyrics of his volume *City of Palaces (Shtot Fun Palatzen*,
1936), a volume that was illustrated by Mexico's most famous
painter, Diego Rivero. His fifth lyric volume, *Song of Man
(Gezang Fun Mentsh*, 1954), was his profoundest. Composed during months of illness, it wrestled with the meaning of death and
found consolation in a cosmic faith.

Glantz came to Mexico in 1925. As a lyricist he experimented
with ever new forms and as essayist and literary editor of *Der*

Weg, 1936 to 1946, the newspaper founded in 1930 by the pioneering journalist Moshe Rosenberg, he stimulated esthetic sensibility in the young Jewish community. The poems of his first Mexican decade, *Step Onto the Mountains* (*Trit In Die Berg*, 1939), included recollections of idyllic boyhood years, unfortunately terrorized by pogromists; Mexican scenes observed in the capital, in Indian villages and along Xochimilko's canals; and melancholy contemplations of the threatening European catastrophe. Glantz's most creative period was the decade 1936-1946, when he published three volumes of eclectic verses. In *A Bit of Earth* (*A Kezais Erd*, 1950), he again cast a remote halo about his native Ukrainian village, then surviving only as memory. His last poems were influenced by avant garde trends in Occidental poetry.

Joseph Vinetzky (b. 1900), a pioneering journalist and editor, arrived in Mexico in 1921. His poems on biblical themes made little impact but his novel *Beginnings* (*Beginen*, 1941), which described Jewish immigrant life, was more widely read.

Abraham Zebulun Berebicez (b. 1902) arrived in 1926 and distinguished himself primarily as a columnist of *Der Weg*. Kalman Landau (b. 1912) edited the Zionist bi-weekly *Dos Vort* since 1947. Moshe Rubinstein became best known as the editor of the semi-weekly newspaper *Die Shtimme*. However, his narrative *A Life in Mexico* (*A Lebn In Mexico*, 1952) aroused interest and controversy because of its realistic depiction of the rapid rise to affluence of the Jewish imigrants in their new environment.

The theme of the Jewish nouveau-riche in Mexico was especially popular with the humorist and feuilletonist Abraham Weisbaum (1895-1970) in his two books *Mexican Zig-zag* (*Mexicaner Zigzagn*, 1947) and *Mexican Paradise* (*In Mexicaner Gan-Eden*, 1959). Weisbaum was a keen and witty observer of Mexican Jewish life following his arrival in the capital in 1925. The characters which he created—Yente Tinifotsky, Yankel Feifer, and their children—became proverbial among Jews south of the Rio Grande. To the new class of *allrightniks* he presented a mirror of its foibles and shortcomings but he did so without malice and with genuine faith in its moral regeneration. His language eschewed eloquence. It reproduced the daily speech of the harried businessman, the ostentatious matron, the over-indulged young fop and the flighty Jewish senorita. His situations were real and not contrived, depicting the decay of the immigrant generation under the impact of too sudden prosperity and the brave struggle of the Yiddish intellectuals, few in number, to stem the tide of assimilation. Weisbaum's impressions of Israel, *Under Israel's Sky* (*Unter Israel-Himl*, 1959), steered clear of the satiric tone that dominated his sketches of Mexico and Los Angeles, and combined lyric sentimentalism, nostalgic romanticism and good-natured humor.

The severest critic of Mexican Jewry, especially of the younger generation that grew up in affluence and that lacked the dynamic vitality of the immigrant fathers, was Salomon Kahan (1897-1965), who came to Mexico in 1921. Kahan was creative in two languages. He published five volumes in Spanish dealing almost exclusively with music, and five volumes of Yiddish essays covering the entire range of Jewish cultural development both in Mexico and in other lands. He also translated into Spanish Graetz's *History of the Jews.*

Meir Corona (1890-1965) grew up in Poland, pioneered in Palestine from 1920 to 1925, and spent his last four decades in Mexico writing tales of its Jewish immigrants, the difficulties of their adjustment to Mexico and the gradual disintegration of their Jewish personalities. His humor was overlaid with sadness and his keen insight was enriched by ironic contemplation. His stories were collected in five volumes between 1939 and 1965. Of these, *Lost Roads* (*Farlorene Vegn*, 1953) aroused most interest when translated into Spanish, the language of the estranged children of the Yiddish-speaking immigrants. His younger brother, Mordecai Corona, was the editor of *Freind*, Mexican organ of Labor Zionism.

The youngest of Mexican Yiddish writers is Sholem Lokier (b. 1921), who came to Mexico at the age of eight and was assistant editor of *Der Weg* at seventeen. He is a philosopher and essayist in search of Jewish meaningfulness.

With two newspapers, several weeklies and monthlies and with patrons subsidizing Yiddish publishing and offering prizes for Yiddish literary achievements, Mexico continues to be a significant center of Yiddish creativity in the 1970's. But its Yiddish writers are aging and its Yiddish readers are becoming ever fewer.

Until 1881 Jews were not permitted to reside in Cuba and until the First World War the few that did settle in this largest Caribbean island were either Americans or Sephardim. However, after 1920, when the United States introduced immigration restrictions based upon a racial quota, Eastern European Jews left for Cuba in the belief that from there admission to the barred mainland would be easier. For most of them the temporary asylum became a long lasting home, especially when the Great Depression of 1929 set in and the United States imposed still stricter quotas. At first the young immigrants worked in sugar mills, as stevedores, and above all as peddlers. Before long the peddlers opened country stories and the laborers small factories. Within two decades after the coming of the first European Jews, their number swelled to ten thousand, almost all of them engaged in commerce and industry. Their cultural needs were met when the first center for Yiddish-speaking Jews, Centro Hebreo, was opened in Havana in 1924 and when Yiddish journals made their appearance in 1925. In 1926 a second center arose. On November 11, 1932, the semiweekly *Havaner Leben* began publication and offered a lasting medium for Yiddish literary expression. Other Yiddish literary journals of the 1930's, such as *Dos Yiddishe Vort* and *Kubaner Bleter*, had fewer readers and were short-lived. The first editors of *Havaner Leben* included Y. O. Pines and Eliezer Aronowsky, pioneer poets who, together with N. D. Korman, formed the core of a literary group which called itself "Young Cuba" and which was most active in the 1930's before several of its leading figures left for continental America.

"Young Cuba" began in 1927 with Korman's book of verse, *Island Earth (Oif Inzelsher Erd)*, and in 1928 with Aronowsky's *Cuban Songs (Kubaner Lieder)*. Korman toiled in a shoe factory all day for a pittance but his poems resounded with joy and hymned hopes for a bright future. After settling in the United States, he continued to write lyrics idealizing proletarian types. In his last volume, *Days and Years (Teg Un Yorn, 1970)*, he also sang optimistically of his love for Israel as the land of freedom and productive labor. Aronowsky, on the other hand, was more sceptical, and the prevailing tone of his four lyric booklets was deeply pessimistic. Pines published the poetic epic *Hatuey* in 1931 and the versified tales for children, *The Golden Fountain (Der Goldener Fontan)* in 1934. The former idealized the freedom-loving spirit of primitive man. This spirit was personified in the Haitian leader, Hatuey, who fought the invading Spaniards, who fled to Cuba after the conquest of Haiti in 1511, and who led the Siboneyean Indians in their brave but hopeless struggle until he was captured and burned at the stake in 1512. Hatuey, the noble savage, and his followers were contrasted with civilized, gold-greedy white men under Velasquez. Scorning a last minute offer to convert him to the conqueror's God of love, in whose name bloody deeds were being perpetrated, Hatuey foretold, even while the flames were licking his limbs, that a renewal of freedom was inevitable in days to come because love of freedom was imperishable in the human heart.

Yiddish books of prose were not published before 1935. In that year there appeared the tales of Abraham Josef Dubelman, *On Cuban Soil* (*Oif Kubaner Erd*), and of Pinchas Berniker, *Silent Lives* (*Shtille Lebens*).

Dubelman, who arrived in Havana in 1925 at the age of seventeen, depicted the lonely, tragic struggles of the first newcomers, their eking out a bare living in distant Cuban provinces, their spiritual decay far from their fellow-Jews, their succumbing to the temptations of the flesh in the hot, tropical climate. Discovering that Cuban villagers who had never seen Jews envisaged them as wicked-hearted, horned, diabolical monsters, some Jewish peddlers tried to pass as Germans or at least as "Polacks." They sold ikons and crosses as well as articles of clothing. In others, Jewish pride manifested itself and they stressed their Jewishness both to their neighbors and to their non-Jewish wives and children. In one of Dubelman's earliest stories, a missionary tried to persuade a Jewish peddler to confess his sins against the Christian savior in order to attain redemption. The peddler did confess that, when in pre-immigrant days he witnessed his parents being butchered and his sister raped and stifled by cross-bearing pogromists, he did cry out against Jesus, their God. The paling of the priest led the peddler to suspect that the missionary priest must have been a *meshumad*.

Dubelman's second volume of short stories, *The Balance* (*Der Balans*, 1953), was of finer literary texture. The title story won for him the much coveted *Zukunft*-Award and high praise from the severe critic Shmuel Niger. The characters depicted were no longer recent immigrants in pursuit of bread and love but rather older settlers who had prospered and raised up a new generation far removed from Jewishness. The conflict of parents and children then assumed greater dimensions. A father who toiled so that his only son might become a doctor found that this assimilated, successful physician no longer had anything in common with him. A peddler in remote Oriente Province, who had established a profitable business and married into a Christian family, discovered too late that his wife and children looked upon his Jewish origin as something uncanny and disreputable. Annually he made a financial inventory but only after twenty-five years did he make an inventory of his soul. He then discovered that he was spiritually bankrupt and he extorted from his wife a promise that on his death he would be transported to Havana's Jewish cemetery. There the lonely Jewish businessman would at long last be surrounded by his own people.

Pinchas Berniker (b. 1908) came to Cuba in 1925 and remained there only six years before leaving for the United States. His Jewish characters too were lonely peddlers and storekeepers who yearned for Jewish companionship. In his best story, two solitary Jews in a remote Cuban village competed fiercely with each other. However, when one of them felt his final hour approaching, he felt the need to call his hated competitor to his bedside so that he might have the consolation of a Jew nearby. After his death, the surviving competitor came to the recognition that the amassing of wealth was insufficient compensation for the loneliness of living far from his fellow Jews. He therefore fled from his village to the Cuban capital in order to spend his remaining years among his coreligionists.

The banning of Jewish immigration to Cuba on the eve of World War II, the exodus of Jews to continental America during and after the war, and to a lesser extent to Israel after the founding of the Jewish State, the flight of the more prosperous Jews after Castro's communist regime came to power, the increased use of Spanish among the remaining Jews—all these factors depleted the ranks of the bearers of Yiddish culture and brought about a precipitous decline of Yiddish writing.

21

YOUNG VILNA

Forerunners • Zalman Reisen • Leiser Wolf • Hirsh
Glick • Shimshon Kahn • Moshe Levin • Kaczer-
ginski • Wogler • Miranski • Karpinovitch • Grade
• Sutzkever

YOUNG VILNA was the youngest and most promising Yiddish
literary group on the eve of the Second World War and from its
ranks stemmed writers who influenced the Yiddish scene in the
United States, Argentina, France and Israel during the post-
Holocaust decades.

Vilna was known as the Jerusalem of Lithuania before the
destruction of its Jewish community. During and after the First
World War it changed hands repeatedly before ending under
Polish jurisdiction. Its population contained Russians, White Russians, Poles and Lithuanians, but the Jews predominated. By 1939
they numbered more than 200,000.

Vilna could look back upon a century of Hebrew and Yiddish
Enlightenment. It harbored magnificent library collections, the
best of which was that of Mathias Strashun (1817-1885), deeded to
the Jewish community after his death. Pioneers of Yiddish literature in Vilna included Isaac Meir Dick (1814-1893), the storyteller
with the largest reading audience of his generation, Michel Gordon
(1823-1890), the militant lyricist of the Haskalah, and Eliakum
Zunser (1836-1913), the most popular bard or *badchen*. From
Vilna stemmed also Abraham Cahan (1860-1951), who became the
most influential Yiddish editor in the United States, Abraham
Reisen (1876-1953), the poet of the poor and the narrator of
Jewish sorrow, and Shmuel Niger (1883-1955), the literary critic
famed throughout the Yiddish world.

During World War I and under the German occupation, Yid-

dish writers continued their literary activities. A notable product
of those years were the two volumes of *Vilner Zamelbukh* (I,
1916; II, 1918), edited by the physician and communal leader
Zemach Shabad (1864-1935) and the critic Moshe Shalit (1885-
1941).

Hardly was the war over, when plans were set afoot for more
ambitious literary projects. The dramatist A. Veiter (1878-1919),
liberated from Siberia by the Russian Revolution, the folklorist S.
Anski (1863-1920), the historian S. M. Zitron (1860-1930) and
the critic S. Niger were among the dynamic figures in the reorgan-
ization and co-ordination of Yiddish literary activities. Unfortunately, Veiter was shot in April 1919 by Polish legionnaires during
their rampage when they recaptured Vilna from the Bolsheviks,
Niger emigrated to the United States a few months later, and
Anski died the following year. However, their efforts, brief but
intense, bore fruit in several directions. The Yiddish daily *Der Tog*
was founded under the editorship of Niger from May to August
1919 and of Zalman Reisen thereafter. Within a few years Vilna
could boast of five Yiddish dailies. The Vilna publishing house of
Boris Kletzkin (1875-1937) eclipsed the century old Vilna publishing firm of the Romm family, whose Yiddish booklets had
reached hundreds of thousands of readers. The Vilna troupe of
actors, first organized in 1916, attained its artistic peak with the
performance of Anski's *Der Dybbuk* in Warsaw in 1920 and then
went on to celebrate triumphs in other communities. In Vilna's
Yiddish schools and Teachers' Seminary, youth was inspired by
the literary historian Max Erik (1898-1937), the poet Moshe Kulbak (1896-1940) and the educators Falk Heilperin (1876-1945)
and Abraham Golomb (b. 1888). After 1928, YIVO offered an
hospitable home for aspiring intellectuals who streamed to Vilna
to be trained by YIVO's scholars under the direction of Max
Weinreich, Zelig Kalmanovitch and Zalman Reisen.

Reisen, journalist, scholar, editor of the Vilna *Tog*, is generally
credited with being the discoverer and inspirer of Young Vilna.
On October 11, 1929, he introduced the group to the readers of his
daily under the headline "Young Vilna Marches Into Yiddish Literature" and during the following years he encouraged beginners
by printing their poems, which were often immature but which
contained sparks of talent. Soon the group, constantly augmented,
gained confidence and published its united efforts in periodicals
and individually in books of verse and fiction.

The writers associated with Young Vilna had no common plat-

form and issued no manifestos. What united them was a common
cultural background, youthful enthusiasm, a love of Yiddish and
a desire to use it as a medium for self-expression. Leiser Ron and
Elias Schulman, two members of the group who later chronicled
its achievements, listed more than three dozen adherents who participated to a greater or a lesser extent in its publications. However, the only ones among them who matured to perfection were
Chaim Grade (b. 1910) and Abraham Sutzkever (b. 1913). Others
perished during the Second World War or soon thereafter, while
still others, deprived of the Yiddish-saturated atmosphere of Vilna,
failed to fulfill adequately the promise of their first years. Among
the former, the most talented were Leiser Wolf (1910-1943), Hirsh
Glick (1922-1944), Shimshon Kahan (1915-1941), Moshe Levin
(1907-1942) and Schmerke Kaczerginski (1908-1954).

Wolf was a protegé of Zalman Reisen. He contributed to all
three annuals of *Yung Vilna*, 1934-1936. His first verse booklet,
Eviningo, was printed in Latin characters in 1936. It consisted of
sixteen pages and imitated the sonorous rhythms and the picturesque imagery of Longfellow's *Hiawatha*. Far more important
was the selection of his lyrics, *Black Pearls* (*Shvartse Perl*, 1939),
which appeared just before the outbreak of the war. Wolf succeeded in escaping to Soviet Russia, where his third poetic booklet,
Lyric and Satire (*Lyrik Un Satire*, 1940), was published with an
introduction by the Moscow Yiddish poet Aaron Kushnirov. When
the Germans invaded Russia in 1941, he was evacuated to
Uzbekistan. Enduring hardships in this Asiatic region and undernourished month after month, his health deteriorated and led to
his death at the age of 32. Shortly before his end he was hailed by
Peretz Markish as the Yiddish Heine. In his mingling of melancholy sentimentalism, romantic irony and social satire, he did
indeed resemble the German poet. Besides, he often modelled his
early lyrics after Heine, as in "The Weavers" ("Die Veber," 1935),
an anti-Nazi song in which the members of the Underground were
depicted as weaving amidst curses a net to enshroud the "Brown
Vampire."

In a poem of 1936, Wolf described with subtle irony the only
meeting of Heine and Goethe, and identified himself with the
young singer of sorrows rather than with the old Olympian sage
of Weimar. Wolf's Heine resented Goethe's patronizing tone and
coldness of spirit, his smug pursuit of sweet calmness, his dwelling
in a palace of fortune, his insufficient familiarity with pain. Wolf's
Goethe, on the other hand, saw in Heine a young upstart, a

borrower of artificial pain, a dispenser of hate, a poet of little talent. When Goethe politely inquired: "What are you now creating, my dear?" Heine answered in hot anger: "A Faust!" And both eyed each other, sensing themselves to be worlds apart.

Wolf assimilated influences from German, Russian and American poets. He felt a kinship to Byron, Pushkin, Nietzsche, Spinoza, literary rebels and heretical philosophers. But the Jewish heritage meant far more to him and he was well versed in Yiddish literature of preceding generations. Above all, Vilna scenes, figures and incidents supplied him with rich subject-matter. In one poem, he contrasted the Vilna Gaon with the Baal Shem. In a verse dialogue, the aged Vilna storyteller Isaac Meir Dick came to life. In a poetic tribute to the Yiddish classical triumvirate, he showed them seated on golden thrones in paradise, with silver-haired, steel-eyed Mendele in the center, flanked by Peretz of the mighty brow and fiery dark eyes and Sholom Aleichem with the brown curls, resplendent blue eyes and the open mouth always laughing, laughing, laughing.

In 1939 Wolf headed a group of very young Vilna writers who collaborated in publishing the modest journal *Yungwald*. The war ended this venture and dispersed the group. Wolf left for Dniepropetrovsk and there penned anti-Nazi lyrics. Moshe Gurin (b. 1921), who participated in all four issues of *Yungwald*, survived the liquidation of Vilna's ghetto and Latvian concentration camps and reached Israel in 1947, where he continued with lyrics of the new landscape. Hirsh Glick, a cousin of Gurin and the youngest member of Young Vilna, was only seventeen when he joined the *Yungwald* group and only twenty-two when he died fighting with the partisans after escaping from Vilna's ghetto and from an Esthonian concentration camp. Nevertheless, he succeeded in attaining immortality with a single lyric, his *Song of the Partisans* (*Partizanerlied*, 1943). This stirring song, set to the melody of a Cossack march, instantly won the hearts of resistance groups. Its five stanzas lent courage in darkest hours and instilled faith that the struggle of the doomed would not be vain. It began with the admonition not to despair: "Say not, you're going on the last road, even if leaden skies obscure blue days." It continued with the assurance that the longed-for hour of deliverance would yet come, the golden sun would dissipate the gloom, and the song of heroism of the Jewish people, fighting amidst tumbling ghetto walls, would resound from generation to generation. Translated into the principal languages spoken by Jews, this song has been sung at memorial meetings for the Nazi victims year after year. The young author was the subject for poems by Peretz Markish, Abraham Sutzkever, Shmerke Kaczerginski, Moshe Gurin and Peretz Miranski.

Shimshon Kahan belonged to the original group discovered by Reisen in 1929. He earned a living as a teacher in a village near Vilna, as a toiler of the soil, as a prompter with a troupe of wandering actors. He associated with gypsies, learned their language and translated their songs into Yiddish. His own lyrics were generally shrouded in sadness and appeared only in periodicals.

Moshe Levin was a portrait painter and storyteller. He participated with naturalistic tales in all three annuals of *Yung Vilna*, 1934-1936. His volume *Spring in a Cellar Den* (*Frihling in a Kellershtub*, 1937) contained gloomy sketches of honest craftsmen who suffered from chronic unemployment, anti-Jewish discrimination, filth and vermin. While his pious characters accepted their apparently God-given destiny, which condemned them to hunger, sickness and anti-Semitism, his younger characters revolted against poverty and social degradation and engaged in Socialist activities to undermine the existing regime. As the son of a glazier, Levin wrote a moving story of the unfair competition to which Jewish but not Christian glaziers were exposed. *In Motie Droshke* he chose as the representative of the older, tradition-bound generation a driver of a droshke, who was dull-witted, good-natured and submissive to authority. The driver's younger daughter, however, rebelled against tradition, read Marx and Engels, fought against the reactionary Polish regime and endured arrest with a smile.

When the Soviets overran Vilna, Levin contributed to Communist publications. When the Nazis later captured the town, he escaped to Minsk and was active in the underground of the Minsk ghetto. When Jews in 1942 were led to the Minsk prison courtyard to be liquidated, the German commander offered to spare Levin's life because of his usefulness as a painter, but he preferred to share the fate of his coreligionists and was shot together with them.

Shmerke Kaczerginski began with militant proletarian lyrics and sketches, participated in the annuals *Yung Vilna* under the pseudonym of C. Shmerke, and survived the horrors of the Vilna ghetto and the dangers of a partisan behind the battlefront, only to perish in an airplane accident on a flight from Argentina. During the early years of the war he was employed by the Nazis to classify YIVO's collection of books and manuscripts so that the

most valuable items could be transported to Germany and used
for anti-Semitic studies after the war. In the process of making
the selection, he succeeded, with the assistance of Abraham Sutzkever, in hiding and burying many precious items. When the
work neared its end and his liquidation seemed imminent, he fled
with Sutzkever to the surrounding forests. There the poets fought,
gun in hand, until the day of liberation. At the same time Kaczerginski kept a diary of his experiences, while Sutzkever reduced the
group's perilous deeds to flaming verses. After the war both returned to Vilna. They succeeded in finding and digging up the
hidden YIVO material amidst the rubble of the destroyed ghetto.
Kaczerginski found a temporary refuge in France and a permanent
one in Argentina before his fatal accident. His post-war volumes
of Vilna's ruined community and of the partisan struggles chronicled Jewish heroism and Jewish martyrdom. These volumes are
among the most moving, authentic sources for the Holocaust years.

Among the survivors of Young Vilna was the symbolist poet
Elchanan Rozhansky (1907-1969), who wrote under the pseudonym of Elchanan Wogler. He chose this pseudonym because
wogler is the Yiddish word for wanderer and it symbolized his
homelessness ever since he was orphaned at an early age. While
earning his meager bread as a sign-painter, Wogler came under
the influence of Moshe Kulbak but soon developed his own original
lyric style. In his first booklet, *A Leaf in the Wind* (*A Bletl in
Vint,* 1935), he animated natural phenomena. The theme of this
idyl in rhyming quatrains was the poet's marriage to the Plum
Orchard. This marriage took place after he fell in love in the
spring. It flourished throughout the summer and ended in red
autumn, when the beloved died of tuberculosis, leaving her orphaned children, the plums, at the mercy of cannibalistic humans.
The road beside the orchard was depicted as an old, withered
bachelor, who moaned whenever a heavily laden truck passed over
him. The neighboring rose garden was personified as a beautiful
young maiden who was wooed by many attractive birds and bees.
When she was caught at a rendezvous with a male butterfly, the
jealous bees challenged the latter to a duel, which ended fatally
for him. They then proceeded to bite the maiden's lips, to tear
her silken dress and to rape her. The wind was portrayed as a
happy fiddler. When his yellow wife, the grain, passed away, he
mourned her for seven full days and then set out in search of a
new mate. He played a tearful elegy for his orchestral comrades,

the rivers, before they were locked up in an icy prison for the winter.

Wogler was shaken out of his poetic allegories when the Nazis neared Vilna in June 1941. He fled to Alma Ata, in the Asiatic region of Kazakhstan. After the war, he was permitted to return to Poland, and from there he emigrated to France. In Paris he felt lonely and lost. There he wrote his nostalgic recollections of young Vilna and published his collected lyrics *Spring On Earth* (*Frihling Oifn Trakt*, 1954). Some of these lyrics harked back to pre-war scenes, to idyllic characters such as the bearded drayman Moshe, who disputed with God while driving along the village road, or the Lithuanian shepherd Nikite, who reigned over an empire of sheep, commanding their obedience with the sounds of a flute. The poet still personified phenomena of nature as, for example, the Old Wind who survived three wives, was wooing a fourth wife, and was raging at his son, the Young Wind, who was no less amorous. In Wogler's war and post-war verses, new tones came to the fore: elegies on the poet Shmuel Rossin and on the martyred Vilna hero Itzik Wittenberg, laments for the children of Vilna's ghetto, sad echoes of his Lithuanian homeland lost to him forever, pessimistic images of Parisian garrets where painters, musicians and poets consorted.

Another survivor of Young Vilna was the poet Peretz Miranski (b. 1908), a cousin of Hirsh Glick. He joined the group in 1934 and participated in its annuals with fables and parables in the manner of Eliezer Steinbarg but with a grimmer undertone of social satire. Fleeing before the Nazi invaders, he reached Samarkand in Central Asia. There he wrote in 1943 his apocalyptic poem "War," depicting a city at night as it waited with darkened eyes for its doom. Then death flew over it on silvery, icy wings and sealed the streets with blood. The terror-stricken houses collapsed under thunderclaps and fiery rain. When pale morning dawned, the smoke-filled city lay in ruins, its trees corpses, its windowless, roofless dwellings mounds of fresh graves. In the ballad "The Gaon and the Partisan," the poet let the Vilna Gaon arise from the Old Cemetery and encounter a Jewish partisan who came to avenge murdered kin. Despite the Gaon's compassion for man and beast, he blessed the avenger, since such monstrous crimes as the Nazis had perpetrated must be atoned for.

Returning to Vilna in 1945, Miranski saw his own house in ruins while the house of his non-Jewish neighbor stood intact. His own father, mother, sister were dead, but this neighbor enjoyed their few belongings. Then the latter's preferred glass of water seemed to drip drops of blood and the cherries in the garden seemed to have been reddened by his sister's life when it oozed away. He could no longer stay on in post-war Vilna and fled to a German Displaced Persons' Camp. In 1949 he reached Canada where his only volume, *A Candle for a Penny* (*A Likht Far A Groshen*, 1951), appeared. It included the fables of his Vilna period, the lyrics of his war years, and the poems of his post-war impressions in Berlin, Paris and Montreal.

Abraham Lev (1910-1970) participated in the earliest publications of the Vilna group but emigrated to Palestine as early as 1932 and later became one of Israel's finest lyricists.

Abraham Karpinovitch (b. 1918) also began in Vilna in the pre-war decade, but did not succeed in getting to Israel until 1950. He was the son of Moshe Karpinovitch, the director of Vilna's *Folksteater* and the brother of Melech Karpinovitch, co-editor of Israel's literary quarterly *Die Goldene Keyt*. In his volume *In Vilna's Courtyard* (*Beim Vilner Durkhhoif*, 1967), he recreated Vilna's Jewish types before the city's destruction, especially the underprivileged characters, the outcasts such as the gangster girl whose feelings were not blunted, the prostitute who behaved with greater kindness than did the more respectable maidens, the actor who fell on evil days but did not lose his humane disposition, the fishwife who was fascinated by an YIVO researcher, the deranged person who received and requited genuine affection. A final story recounted the reunion of the underworld survivors in Israel where their energy was directed to the upbuilding of a land, at last their own.

The spirit of Jewish Vilna also emerged from the poems and novels of Chaim Grade (b. 1910), and the poems of Abraham Sutzkever (b. 1913).

Grade stemmed from a family that was long rooted in Vilna. In a poem of 1936, "The Cry of Generations," he portrayed the three generations that preceded his own: his great-grandfather of pre-Napoleonic days who still suffered from medieval disabilities imposed by a fanatical church; his grandfather, who hailed Napoleon as the world liberator; his father, a Hebrew teacher who turned from the mysticism of the Cabala to the rationalism of Moses Mendelssohn, who became a social incendiary, hating the pious patrician whose children he taught, and who died prematurely. Grade inherited from his father a shelf of books and a rebellious temperament. His mother insisted that the seventeen-year-old orphaned lad continue to study at Yeshivot, while she eked out a bare living for herself, peddling fruit in Vilna's marketplace.

Grade was most influenced in his adolescence by a great and saintly teacher, the Hazon-Ish, under whom he studied for seven years. What this sage meant for him he later recorded in an elegy composed in 1954 after his teacher's death in Israel. He called him an angel who hid his wings while among mortals, a pillar of radiance who shed the light of compassion upon his pupils. "Though he did not want to bless my way of life, yet do I shine by the reflection of his great love."

While dreaming of beauty, young Grade consorted with the adherents of the Musar movement, whose ideal was spiritual purity and who despised the pursuit of beauty as sinful, seductive, vanity of vanities, time ill-spent. This movement was originally launched by Rabbi Israel Salanter in the nineteenth century and its tenets continued to be practiced with great zeal and severity between the two World Wars in the Navaredker Yeshivot. Grade depicted his experiences in such a Yeshiva in his epic poem *Musarnikes* (1939). He emphasized the disputations of his classmates who strove for moral perfection. He mirrored himself in the figure of Chaim Vilner, a twenty-year-old, pale, emaciated, grimly serious student, who conducted himself like a person long past his youth. He was perpetually hounded by a sense of guilt, a fear that he had sunk into a morass of moral impurity, and he tried desperately to work his way out of this morass. He felt himself attracted to secular books rather than to ethical tracts. The former books were taboo in this ultra-religious institution and yet he could not resist the temptation to peer into their forbidden contents. For a time he joined in the self-flagellation and the constant confessions indulged in by the Musar youths, but finally he gave up his unsuccessful straining for extra-mundane holiness. The bird that sang in the sunlight enchanted him and the wind that rustled in the forest tore him away from his Talmudic tomes. He became aware of social injustice. He began to resent economic inequality. He threw himself into the struggle for political renovation, as did so many poets of Young Vilna.

From 1932 he joined these poets in their publications. His first lyric booklet, *Yea* (*Yo*, 1936), gave expression to his affirmation of active striving, after he had torn himself away from the pursuit of contemplative asceticism. The volume began with tributes to his mother who was still supporting herself by marketing her basket of apples each day. He idealized her in many lyrics as a model of integrity, self-effacing, deeply devoted to her God and her children. Various aspects of her personality also emerged from the poetic volume *My Mother's Testament* (*Der Mames Tsvue*, 1949), and from his prose volume *My Mother's Sabbaths* (*Der Mames Shabosim*, 1955). When the Nazis entered Vilna, she remained and perished together with many of her townsmen on the Day of Atonement, 1941. The poet succeeded in escaping by joining the refugees who streamed eastward. He found safety throughout the war years in towns of Asiatic Russia. From there he launched poems of hatred against the invaders and calls for vengeance. Some of these were included in the volume *Generations* (*Doires*, 1945), and others in the lyric collection *Refugees* (*Pleitim*, 1947). However, far more numerous than the accusations he hurled against the Nazi foe, were the poems of love and comfort he directed toward his own people. The Yellow Badge had united Jews. Common wandering and common suffering had obliterated the dissensions long raging between Jewish groups. The fratricidal strife between Hebraists and Yiddishists was over. The language of the Bible was being rejuvenated in the ancestral Holy Land and the Yiddish speech of the masses was being sanctified by their martyrdom. Grade prayed for prophets to arise in both tongues to uplift the hearts of Jews who would survive the Holocaust.

Grade survived the difficult war years in Central Asia. In 1945 he trekked westward to Moscow, then on to ruined Vilna after its liberation from the Nazis. In the early chapters of *My Mother's Sabbaths*, he gave the finest literary description of pre-War Vilna as seen through the eyes of his mother's generation and his own, and in the closing chapters a most moving narration of his postwar homecoming to Vilna's empty houses and full graves. When he learned that his wife, a nurse in the Vilna ghetto, had been led to her death together with the last Jews when the ghetto was liquidated in September 1943, he could no longer linger amidst Vilna's ghostly memories and he continued on to Paris. In Paris he was active among the surviving Yiddish writers but, when most of them left their temporary French asylum for more permanent homes in Israel and the Americas, he too left for New York to rebuild his shattered existence.

In the United States, Grade found admirers of his poetry, audiences for his lectures and readings, publishers for his narratives of the Vilna he had experienced but which had already become historic. The three novelettes of *The Synagogue Courtyard* (*Der Shulhoif*, 1958) brought back to life the narrow, teeming streets of Vilna's poorest district in which his early years had been spent. Though the houses had turned to rubble and their inhabitants had been exterminated, they were still vivid in his memory and he fixed them for posterity in beautiful narrative prose.

The longest novelette is *The Well*. It narrates the efforts of the district's water-carrier, Mende, to get the well of the courtyard repaired so that the poor inhabitants would not have to trudge to a distant part of the town for their water or to pay the monastery, which had the nearest functioning well, for the precious liquid needed to sustain their lives. In addition, there was the constant danger that the whole neighborhood might go up in flames if a fire were to break out and no water be available in the courtyard to extinguish it.

Most chapters deal with Mende's experiences, successes and reverses as he tries to scrape together from the townsmen the sums needed for this repair job. His chief ally in his solicitations is the ascetic Reb Bunim, who continues throughout the narrative to mourn his two children who perished of hunger during the war and his oldest son who succumbed soon after the war. Bunim wants desperately to absolve God of guilt in their death. He seeks an answer in studying the Book of Job and pondering the destiny of this biblical father whose reverses paralleled his own and who yet remained faithful to the Lord. Mende shows him how to find consolation by joining in the charitable project of gathering funds for the well.

Grade depicts these crochety, good-natured, trusting characters and their more practical wives with sympathy and sly humor. The townspeople with whom they come in contact range from superstitious old women to rebellious workmen, from an attractive merry widow and a robust, red-cheeked merchant, her suitor, to the widow's pale daughter, who hovers between three suitors, an aging Torah scribe, a youthful, dreamy-eyed sceptic and an immature, irreligious apostle of revolution.

The novelette reached its climax in the assembly of the Polish rabbis convoked by a saintly sage, the revered, ninety-year-old Chofetz Chaim. Each rabbi is portrayed in his individual traits and carefully differentiated from the others. This great assembly is brought to a pause in its deliberations of weighty political and religious problems in order to help the humble water-carrier in his simple, charitable deed. At the dedication of the repaired well, the principal characters are brought together in a final scene of rejoicing and festive dancing. The author's kindness constantly leads him to mitigate stark tragedies by deflecting attention to acts of moral greatness by those whom God afflicted. He feels that trust in a divine order helps one to bear adversity and to retain an optimistic attitude amidst all the ups and downs of fortune.

Grade's longest and most significant narratives, composed at the height of his creativity in the United States, are *The Agunah* (*Die Agune,* 1961) and *Tsemakh Atlas* (1967).

An *agunah,* in Jewish law, is a woman who is legally barred from entering into a new marriage because she has not been granted a *get,* a bill of divorcement, by her husband. Though the husband may have disappeared during the sinking of a ship on which he was sailing or in the course of a pogrom or in the midst of battle, Jewish law considers him alive unless there are credible witnesses and adequate testimony establishing his death beyond the possibility of doubt. The unmerited, cruel fate of living widows always aroused sympathy. Down the centuries rabbis have, therefore, differed in the strictness of their interpretation as to the amount and quality of evidence necessary to establish the fact of certain death.

Grade's novel deals with the struggle of two schools of rabbinical thought in the case of a woman of Vilna whose husband did not return from the First World War and whose entire squadron was reported to have been wiped out. Though nobody actually saw him die, yet fifteen years passed since his squadron came under fire and not a single one of its soldiers was known to have survived. It could therefore be presumed that he was killed in action, but presumption was not sufficient proof in the opinion of most rabbis to justify freeing the woman so that she could remarry. A compassionate religious judge was found, however, who was prepared to take upon himself the responsibility of giving the Vilna *agunah* a *get* in order to mitigate her loneliness and suffering and to let her wed a pious *hazzan.* As a result, this dissenter was haled before a *Bet-Din,* a rabbinical judicial assembly, and was subjected to persecution by the more literal-minded rabbis and Jewish officials.

Grade unrolls a rich panorama of Jewish religious life in Vilna and the struggle between traditionalists and innovators in the 1930's, the final decade of Vilna's eminence as a center of Jewish learning. The further this city receded in time, the more did the novelist discover a kaleidoscope of attractive colors in its apparent grayness, the more beauty did he ferret out in its simple, poor Jews, the more tolerance did he display toward the religious extremists, whose fanaticism he deplores with ever increasing mildness.

Grade's poems of the post-Holocaust period, The Man of Fire (Der Mentsh Fun Fayer, 1962), continued to revolve about his people's tragedy. In the silence of nights he was haunted by visitors who had long since been turned to smoke, dust and ashes. They called upon him to resurrect them in people's memories by writing about them. Since he saw the hill of shoes at Maidanek and the heaped ashes that were once the feet to which these shoes belonged, he went about with bowed head and felt that he must pen epitaphs for the burned victims. In the course of years, however, as the poet became rooted in his new home beyond the Atlantic, he also included joyous New World themes. He sang odes to the Grand Canyon, Yosemite, Niagara, the mountains of California, the desert of Arizona and the islands of the Pacific. But when confirmation reached him that the Russian Yiddish writers with whom he had consorted in Moscow had been liquidated by Stalin's hangmen, he again reverted to his earlier mournful tones. In his magnificent elegy "I Weep for You in All the Letters of the Aleph-Beth," he paid tribute to these martyred friends: Bergelson, Der Nister, Kushnirov, Hofstein, Kvitko, Michoels, Dobrushin, Fefer and, above all, Peretz Markish. He likened his dearest friend Markish to Jonathan, David's dearest friend, and he lamented him in biblical tones reminiscent of David's dirge for the prince who fell at Mt. Gilboa. Even in Grade's happiest moments, shudders would come over him, reminiscences of destroyed Vilna and he reverted to the scenes, the moods and the figures of his youth, embodying them in poignant images and unforgettable stanzas.

Abraham Sutzkever was only twenty-six when the idyllic period of Young Vilna came to an end. His more important works were written after 1939 in the Vilna Ghetto under Nazi surveillance, among the Partisans behind the Front after his escape from the Ghetto, and above all in his creative decades in Israel after his arrival in 1947. However, the roots of his personality were laid in the vast spaces of Siberia, to which he was brought from Smargon in White Russia as a two-year-old, when his family fled before the German invasion of World War I. Then came his years of storm and stress during which he matured. These were spent in

Vilna, to which he returned with his mother following his father's death in 1920.

The Siberian landscape and childhood experiences found poetic repercussion in the lyrics collected under the title *Siberia* (*Sibir*, 1936). The city of Omsk, the Irtish River, the vast expanse of snow-covered forests lived on in his memory and imagination long after his carefree boyhood had come to an end and he was confined to the cramped quarters of Vilna's Jewish district. His early lyrics reflected the joy of life and the longing for liberty which were implanted in him during the Siberian years close to nature. He recalled that he often drove with his father to fetch wood from the forest. Then he came to know fox and wolf, the setting sun in fiery fur and the harp of the moon that accompanied his homeward-bound sled.

In the dank quarters of Vilna he yearned for light, beauty and freedom. Failing to find these in reality, he sought to conjure them into being through the magic of rhythmic incantation. In his verses, the grass babbled, the roots laughed, the skies brightened, the dewdrops kissed. He was like a freshet gushing forth young, joyous lyrics. He wove legends of the changing seasons, from intoxicating spring and star-studded summer to fading autumn and chilly winter. In these legends were intertwined visions of the ethereal beloved, who also blossomed, changed, ripened and faded with the seasons. In forest, field and brook he did not yet sense fear or hostility. The passing cloud implanted kisses on the forest. The village lass dreamed beside her sickle which rested in the field. Trees slept peacefully. The poet embraced with his loving glance a twig of ripe cherries and a fiery blond apple until he entered into the essence of each. Life to him was rhythm and cosmic fire. He wanted to drain his earthly time to the last drop, to soar like an eagle in the wind, released from taboos and conventions, to peer into all animate and inanimate objects with pristine, wondering eyes like Adam when he first set out upon his terrestrial adventure.

Suzkever's optimism was irrepressible. He felt sunny music in his veins and sparks of joy impinging upon all his senses. "Ecstasies" was the title he gave to a series of twenty-eight lyrics because their dominant mood was ecstatic. What if clouds and storms at times obscured bright sunlight! What if earth also contained gray steppes and stinging thorns! The poet came, even as did the rainbow after the thunder and the lightning, to color the steppes with rosy hue and to feed the thorns with beauty. The poet harmonized discords and brought a holiday mood to the dreariest days.

Then came the war. It locked the poet in the Vilna Ghetto and gave the lie to his optimistic faith. During his two years of living entombment, 1942-1943, his utopian dreams went up in smoke and his light-hearted verses gave way to elegies for the dead and the doomed. He sang of the self-sacrificing courage of the teacher, Mire, who continued to brighten the school hours of her pupils with the humor of Sholom Aleichem, with melodies of spring and hope and with preparations for a dramatic pageant, even while their number dwindled from day to day until she and her last wards were liquidated. He sang of the ghetto Orpheus who dug up his buried fiddle and awakened the dead with his playing. He gave a rhythmic description of a wagonload of shoes transported by rail from Vilna to Berlin: bridal shoes, children's shoes and his own mother's Sabbath shoes. These shoes twitched and rattled, though the feet and bodies to which they had adhered were no longer alive.

In February 1943, Sutzkever composed the poetic monologue *Kol Nidre,* which ranks with Katzenelson's *Song of the Murdered Jewish People* and Segalowitch's *There* among the most memorable verse records of the Holocaust years. It described the raid of an extermination squad on Yom Kippur eve, when the Jews of Vilna were assembled for the Kol Nidre prayer in the synagogue. The worshippers are dragged off to prison pens for final processing on the following day. Among them is an old man whose father, wife, five sons and grandson preceded him in death. He is ready for the end, since he has nobody to live for and nobody who will miss him save perhaps his oldest son who left home twenty years earlier and who may still be alive. During the night the old man encounters a wounded Red Army prisoner who has been brought in to share the fate of the Jews and whom he comes to recognize as his long lost son. When a Gestapo officer mocks and humiliates the doomed Jews, this prisoner revolts against such treatment and hurls a stone at the brown-shirted tormentor. To save the son from torture and Nazi vengeance, the father stabs him. When the death wagons lead forth the Jews and the bullets mow them down, the old man somehow survives the hail of bullets and tells his tale of woe to the poet on the following Yom Kippur.

By the spring of 1943 the elegiac verses of the mild-mannered poet were being replaced by cries of defiance and calls for vengeance. No longer was he willing to wait for miracles. The time had come to rely on weapons of iron and not merely on prayers to

God for deliverance from the oppressor. He felt that every hand must hurl itself against the annihilating foe. Revolt was in the air. In September 1943, on the eve of the final liquidation of Vilna's Jews, when the last men were being transported to Esthonian camps and the women and children to the Auschwitz crematoria, the poet, along with a few survivors, fought his way, weapon in hand, to a forest beyond the doomed town and joined the partisans. He participated in the military activities of a Jewish group, "The Avengers," until March 1944, when a Soviet military airplane brought him from his forest base to the Russian capital. Over the Moscow radio he broadcast first-hand information about German atrocities in the Vilna area. In Moscow he also began his longest epic poem, *Secret City* (*Geheimshtot*, 1948), in which he described the struggle for survival of a group of ten Jews in the city sewage canals, a dark realm of mice and mud, but irradiated by the will of these Jews to remain moral personalities and to preserve their group identity.

In 1946 Sutzkever returned to Poland. He testified at the Nuremberg Trial of the Nazi war criminals and then went on to Paris and to Switzerland. With his arrival in Palestine in 1947, his period of storm and stress came to an end. A new creative period began for him. Themes of the Holocaust gradually gave way to Israeli themes based on his experiences in the Jewish homeland and on his observations during Israel's three wars for survival. His search for lyric perfection continued and his creative vitality was undiminished during the following decades. In him as well as in Chaim Grade, the generation of "Young Vilna" reached its apex.

"Young Vilna" is gradually becoming a legend. It is a legend of the dynamic striving of a Yiddish-speaking youth that was born before World War I, that matured during the post-war struggle for the retention of Jewish minority rights in Eastern Europe and that was filled with enthusiasm for the new literary medium forged to perfection by the classical Yiddish triumvirate and standardized by the scholars of YIVO. This youth, endowed by an abundance of talent and united by a common will to express its subtlest emotions and deepest insight in Yiddish, was rich in fulfillment and richer in promise. It never fully ripened because most of its members perished during the Holocaust. The survivors, uprooted from their native soil in the Jerusalem of Lithuania, continued against overwhelming odds a valiant struggle to arrest the decline of Yiddish and to retain a reading public for the products of their pen. In their prose and verse Yiddish still bears fruit of fine literary flavor.

22

THE HOLOCAUST

Forebodings ● Gebirtig ● Katzenelson ● Shaiewitch
● Ulianover ● Hershele ● Israel Stern ● Yekhiel
Lerer ● Perle ● Gilbert ● Kalman Lis ● Kacyzne
● Bursztyn ● Rachel Auerbach ● Kviatkovsky-Pincha-
sik ● Rosenfarb ● Bryks ● Rochman ● Broderzon
● Moshe Grossman ● Bomze ● Emiot ● Rubinstein
● Mendel Mann ● Smoliar ● Sfard ● Heller ●
Repercussions

DURING THE PERIOD between the two World Wars, Yiddish
literature matured and became a refined instrument for the expression of the profoundest thoughts and the subtlest moods of the
Jewish people. While the transition from Yiddish to the dominant
tongues of Europe and America was proceeding at an increasingly
rapid pace, it did not yet reach catastrophic proportions. The survival of Yiddish was not endangered so long as its base in the
heartland between the Vistula and the Dnieper was sound. There,
forces of decline were countered by forces of regeneration. Catastrophe struck when the Germans invaded Poland in 1939 and
Soviet Russia in 1941 and the Final Solution, total Jewish extermination, was set in motion by the Nazis. Yiddish writers, along
with the other Jews, were crammed into ghettos and concentration
camps. While awaiting imminent death, they continued to pen
their verses, stories and memoirs in order to keep up the spirit
of hope and resistance among their people and to leave to future
generations a record of their martyrdom.

Symbolic of the mood on the eve of the war was a poetic premonition of doom by Mordecai Gebirtig (1877-1942) entitled *The
Townlet Is Afire (Dos Shtetele Brent)*. Gebirtig was a folksinger
of Western Galicia, the ablest troubadour between Mark Varshav-

sky and Itzik Manger. While working at his bench as a carpenter in the 1920's and 1930's, he hummed his songs of Hershele, Motele, Moishele, Kievele and Reisele. These songs spread quickly from mouth to mouth and were brought by popular Yiddish performers such as Menachem Kipnis, Molly Picon and Chayele Gruber to audiences of the Old and the New World. However, it was Gebirtig's single lyric of the burning townlet which became best known. Composed in 1938, after the Polish pogrom of Pshytik, it sounded a call of alarm and warned his coreligionists of a coming apocalypse. It foretold that the Jewish settlements might go up in flames, their inhabitants reduced to ashes, and only empty, blackened walls would remain. It adjured Jews not to stand with folded arms while the conflagration raged but rather to take action to extinguish the fire, with their own blood if necessary.

Locked up in Cracow's ghetto, Gebirtig continued to write folksongs until his last day. Some of these voiced despair but others predicted a coming hour of retribution. In a lyric of October 1940, he called upon the Jews to hold out until war's end. Though the foe was driving Jews from their dwellings and cutting off Jewish beards, his end would be that of Haman and he would never wash the mark of Cain from his brow. In May 1941, Gebirtig still dreamed a sweet dream of peace spreading over the entire world, children and graybeards dancing on all roads, foes becoming friends again, and Jews experiencing a Messianic era of kindness toward them on the part of their oppressors. However, in one of his last songs, penned a month before his death, the mood had changed to deepest gloom. The verses described the sleepless nights of the ghetto denizens who never knew when their final hour would toll. Through the interminably long nights, they lay awake, listening to the slightest sound, sensing imminent danger when the wind rustled or when a hungry mouse pounced upon a piece of paper. When the Jews of his street were collected for their final march to an extermination camp, the sixty-five-year-old poet could not move fast enough and was shot together with the other stragglers.

Though most of the literature created during the war years perished together with the authors, enough survived to provide an insight into the tragic and resistance moods of the doomed Jews.

Among the stirring songs of resistance groups, the best known was Hirsh Glick's *Song of the Partisans* (*Dos Partizenerlied,* 1943), and among the laments for the slaughtered Jews the most outstanding elegy was *The Song of the Murdered Jewish People*

(*Dos Lied Fun Oisgehargeten Yiedishen Folk*) written by Yitzkhak Katzenelson (1886-1944) shortly before he was deported to Auschwitz's death camp.

Katzenelson was primarily a Hebrew poet and dramatist although also famed as an educator. For the Hebrew school which he founded and directed at Lodz, he wrote textbooks which were widely used throughout Poland and the Baltic States. His early Yiddish fame rested upon his elegy *The Setting Sun* (*Die Zun Fargeht In Flammen*) and upon a few one-act plays.

When the Germans invaded Poland, Katzenelson fled from Lodz to Warsaw and was an eyewitness to the decimation of his coreligionists there. Because of his claim of Honduran citizenship, he was temporarily spared the fate of Warsaw's Jews and was transferred in May 1943 to a French internment camp to await the war's end. On April 29, 1944, however, he was included in a transport of Jews that left the French camp at Drancy for final liquidation at Auschwitz. His great elegy was composed between October 1943 and January 1944, hermetically sealed in three bottles, and buried under a tree of the camp. When France was liberated, the poem was unearthed and was published in 1945. Its impact was enormous. It was immediately reprinted in the United States and extracts were included in most anthologies of Yiddish verse.

The elegy was a lament for the millions of perished Jews. The poet saw flitting about him the shades of his murdered wife and sons and the many Jews reduced to heaps of ashes or cakes of soap. His jeremiad voiced the pain of the silenced victims. He felt that if Jews beyond the Atlantic would know the horror inflicted upon their European kinsmen, their world would be darkened and poisoned. He described scenes he had himself looked upon in Warsaw's streets: the zealous search for hidden Jews, the driving of the becudgelled men, women and children to the death wagons, until the houses were emptied of them, the transportation to waiting trains. These trains would return empty on the morrow, with opened, hungry mouths eager for more Jews, never satiated with the banquets of fresh living bodies dished up to them daily. The first to be devoured were the helpless children, who were hurled into the death wagons like heaps of garbage. The threnodist wanted to know of God: why such agony for innocent tots? He portrayed in searing images the terrible efficiency of the Germans, the increasing speed of processing Jews, from six thousand a day to ten thousand, the suicide of Adam Cherniakov when asked to meet the higher quotas, the preparation for resistance, the uprising in the ghetto, the spreading conflagration and the burning of the trapped Jews, the end in smoke, ashes and eerie silence. Thus perished Europe's Jews while their neighbors assisted in the slaughter or pretended not to know what was happening. These neighbors would soon be taking over the abandoned houses and would carry on trades and crafts. But no Jew would any more be visible at market-places or fairs, and no Jewish child would ever again awaken to a bright morning, attend school or play in the sand.

The elegy ended with the lines: "Woe is me, none left. A people was and is no more. A tale begun with the Bible and continued until now, a tale so sad—and is it really over?—a tale of Amalek and one worse than Amalek, the German. O wide heaven, broad earth, great seas, don't lump together to annihilate the wicked, let them destroy themselves!"

The lyrics of the martyred poets were immeasurably sad and yet irradiated by pride. The poet of Lodz, Simcha Bunim Shaiewitch, who perished in Auschwitz in 1944, penned a lyric to his little daughter before their transportation to the death camp in which he implored her not to weep or lament but to defy the enemies by smiling, smiling on their final march. In all generations Jews went steadfast to their *akeda*. Despite physical fear difficult to suppress, the effort must be made to look death in the face with flaming eyes and to walk as proudly as did their father to the scaffold. In another poem, he described the coming of his last spring. The trees were again forming new roots and the birds were again building new nests, but he and his ghetto-brothers were being uprooted from their homes and dragged day by day and night by night to the assembly-pens like sheep to the slaughter.

Another lyricist of the Lodz ghetto, Miriam Ulianover (1890-1944), continued to write poems until she was deported to Auschwitz. She perished there together with her daughter and granddaughter four months after Katzenelson. Her fame was based upon her only published volume, *My Grandmother's Treasure* (*Mein Bobes Oitzer*, 1922). Her second volume was being prepared for publication when the war intervened and only extracts of these ripe poems have survived. Her songs combined the simplicity of folksongs with tender romantic mysticism and nostalgia for the lost traditional world of her grandmother and great-grandmother in the Polish townlets. Her room in the ghetto was a meeting place for poets who sought her approval for their works even while death lurked all about them. These included Shaiewitch, Bryks, Chava Rosenfarb and Rivke Kviatkovsky. The novelist, Isaiah Spiegel, who saw her until the spring of 1944, compared her to the legendary Sarah Bas Tovim.

Jewish books were treasured and read in the ghettos and literary creativity continued despite all hardships. As long as libraries and bookstores were permitted to function, Jews flocked to them to read Yiddish and Hebrew publications and to learn about Jewish history, the long record of past martyrdom and glory. Such books gave spiritual nourishment, made the present more bearable, and nullified the efforts of the Nazis to impose upon Jews a feeling of inferiority.

In the ghetto of Warsaw an illegal press flourished and cultural activities were carried on uninterruptedly until the Revolt of April 1943, when the ghetto was reduced to rubble and its inmates to ashes. Periodicals and leaflets were printed clandestinely and their distributors, if caught, risked torture and execution by the Gestapo. Nevertheless, Zionist, Bundist and Communist cells found ways of keeping up the morale of the entrapped Jews through the written word. They printed information about transports to the death camps and acts of sabotage and Jewish resistance. They encouraged faith in the ultimate defeat of the oppressors.

Yiddish writers who participated in the underground press included Hershele Danielewitz, Israel Stern, Yekhiel Lerer, and Joshua Perle, none of whom survived the Holocaust.

Hershele Danielewitz (1882-1941) was the most talented of the folkpoets who created the folksongs and grim folk-humor which spread throughout the ghetto. During the First World War, he had already experienced the cruelty of the Germans when he was lined up by them to be shot together with a large number of Jews in the occupied town of Kalish. At that time he succeeded in escaping. Throughout the following years he composed and collected many folksongs which circulated from mouth to mouth and were printed in several collections. But during the Second World War he succumbed to hunger in Warsaw's ghetto.

Israel Stern (1894-1942) also starved in the ghetto. A legend spread that he lay down on the stone pavement of a ruined courtyard and did not budge for days until he died of hunger. Based upon this legend, H. Leivick composed in 1943 the moving lyric "My Brother, Israel Stern," in which he compared the self-sacrifice of this religious poet to the *akeda* of the patriarch Isaac.

Though no ram appeared to save Stern, the dying poet accepted his martyrdom as God-ordained, even as he had accepted pain and poverty throughout the years, without ever doubting that justice would ultimately prevail, that all sins would be atoned for, and that all suffering would find compensation. Rachel Auerbach, who escaped from the ghetto, reported that Stern, on the brink of death from starvation, was saved at the last moment by Jewish community leaders and nursed back to health, only to be seized by the Germans a short while afterwards and transported to Treblinka's gas chambers. After his death, his poems and essays, which had appeared in periodicals since 1919, were published in book form in 1955.

Yekhiel Lerer (1910-1943) perished in Treblinka. He too was a religious poet like Stern. In his twenties he had been hailed by I. M. Weissenberg as a Yiddish Tagore and his poem *My Home* (*Mein Haim*, 1937) had been praised by Sholem Asch as divinely inspired. It was later characterized by the critic Joshua Rapoport as the finest work of the decade before the Holocaust. Some of Lerer's poems of the ghetto years were recovered after the war and included in the volume *Songs and Poems* (*Lieder Un Poemen*, 1948).

Joshua Perle (1888-1943) was primarily a novelist. His autobiographic prose epic, *Normal Jews* (*Yiedn Fun A Gants Yor*, 1935), was regarded as his greatest achievement. In Warsaw's ghetto he was working on a novel when transported to the Bergen-Belsen camp. But even there he continued his literary activity until he perished in Birkenau, near Auschwitz.

In Warsaw's ghetto Emanuel Ringelblum (1897-1944) wrote detailed memoirs for posterity. Shmuel Lehman (1886-1941) collected folk lore material until his dying day. Yakir Varshavsky (1885-1942), novelist of Hassidic life, continued to write vivid short stories until deported for extermination. Shlomo Gilbert (1885-1942), author of poetic dramas and realistic tales, maintained his faith in the value of his work for God and man until he perished in Treblinka's death-camp. Kalman Lis (1903-1942), a poet of great sensitivity, remained at his post as director of an institution for retarded children and wrote lyrics of the tragic Nazi years until all the children were shot and he soon thereafter. His last poem "Why Are You Silent, O World?" was unearthed after the war. Alter Kacyzne (1885-1941), poet, dramatist, and writer of short stories, succeeded in escaping from Warsaw to Russian-occupied Lvov in 1939 but, when the Germans approached this Galician city two years later and he again fled, he was clubbed to death by Ukrainian allies of the Nazis. His collected works began to appear in 1967. In one of his last poems he lamented the tragedy of the homeless Jews whose days were desolate and whose nights were black, who were driven from place to place, amidst snow and wicked storms, unpitied and unwarmed. The novelist Michal Bursztyn (1897-1945) also escaped from Warsaw but was trapped in Kovno, when the Germans overran Lithuania. He perished in Dachau just as the war was nearing its end. In the midst of hunger, horror and calamity, ghetto writers called for hope, trust and resistance. On the edge of the abyss, they had faith that the eternal people would rearise even from the ashes and they implored coreligionists who would survive and greet a new radiant dawn not to forget the woes inflicted upon the innocent who did not survive.

In the ghetto of Vilna, the writers of "Young Vilna" tried to keep morale at a high level. They organized dramatic performances and composed poems of pain, longing and defiance. When final liquidation of the ghetto loomed, members of the group, including Abraham Sutzkever and Shmerke Kaczerginski, succeeded in escaping to the surrounding forest and in organizing a Jewish partisan section behind the war front. They fought with guns and bombs but also with lyrics of righteous wrath and brotherly love.

In the Soviet sector of Poland, a flurry of literary activity was evident during the two years after the partitioning of this country between Germany and Russia. A considerable number of fleeing Warsaw writers found refuge in Bialystok. They were tolerated by their Soviet hosts so long as they sang the praises of Stalin and did not disparage his German ally. A few of the literary refugees were able to make their way from Russia to Israel after perilous adventures, others were trapped by the eastward surge of the invading Nazis in 1941, still others were evacuated to Caucasian provinces and to Siberian labor camps.

The most prominent poet of the first group was Zysman Segalowitch, who left a record of his desperate flight in the powerful elegiac poems of There (Dortn, 1944), and in the prose volume Burning Steps (Gebrente Trit, 1947).

To the second group belonged the Galician poets Shmuel Jacob Imber, who was slain by Ukrainian collaborators of the Nazis, David Koenigsberg, who ended at the Yavne extermination camp, and Ber Horowitz, who was killed during the massacre of Stanislaw's Jews. All of these poets perished in 1942.

A few writers, trapped during the invasion of 1939 and the later invasion of 1941, survived the war and the Holocaust and ultimately found a refuge in Israel. They included Rachel Auerbach, whose hiding place on the Aryan side of Warsaw was not discovered by the Nazis and who recorded the underground activities of heroic Jews on both sides of Warsaw's ghetto walls; Isaiah Spiegel, who experienced the ghetto of Lodz and the concentration camps of Auschwitz and Teresienstadt; Rivke Kviakovsky-Pinchasik, who in the ghetto of Lodz composed, in 1942, a deeply moving poetic prayer begging God to take from her the designation of human being, since it was easier to endure existence as an ox, a horse, a dog, or a stone than to carry on as a member of the human species. In another poem, "The Song of an Entire Loaf," written in the Stuthof Concentration Camp in 1944, she recalled her mother's radiant face when cutting the last loaf of bread into small slices. Being together, even if hungry, was a joy. Now, however, the poetess alone was left of the entire family and, though she obtained an entire loaf for herself, she could not touch it. Death and terror reigned around her and there was no longer a mother or a sister with whom to share the fresh, brown bread or on whose tender, warm bosom she could weep. Her book of short stories, *In Faithful Hands* (*In Zikhere Hent*, 1965), was based on tragic incidents of the Lodz ghetto and of various concentration camps, incidents narrated with tenderest compassion. The title story centered about the last days of a girl of nine who was handed over by her mother into the apparently safe hands of a Polish policeman who took her out of the ghetto. However, the policeman's wife robbed her of her last belongings and then left her at the gate of the Gestapo headquarters.

Chava Rosenfarb was brought to the Lodz ghetto on her seventeenth birthday and wrote her first poems there. Four years later, on the day she was deported to an extermination camp upon the liquidation of the ghetto in September 1944, she began her poem with the title and the refrain "We perish, We perish." It included the stanza: "Nameless our last day wanes. A spider will remain. Who will remember father's last sigh or mother's last cry? We perish, we perish. Who will gaze in awe on sister's braids disheveled by the wind on her last march? We perish, we perish." At Auschwitz her poems were taken from her, as she was being processed for extermination. Miraculously she escaped death at the final moment and was able later to reconstruct some of her verses from memory.

In her "Ballad of Yesterday's Forest," dedicated to her teachers, Arthur Zygelboim and Simcha Bunim Shaiewitch, she compared the Jews to sturdy trees of a forest overwhelmed by a conflagration. Only singed stumps remained and, at the edge of the forest, a lonely pine survived, surrounded by a bit of grass. The forest craved for renewal. The ashes of the destroyed trees would nourish new growth.

In her *Song of the Jewish Waiter Abram* (*Dos Lied Fun Dem Yiedishen Kelner Abram*, 1948), she paid tribute to her father who survived the harsh Nazi years, only to perish at war's end while his camp was being liberated in April 1945.

In her tragedy, *The Bird of the Ghetto* (*Der Foigl Fun Geto*, 1958), Itzik Wittenberg, the commander of the Vilna ghetto fighters, emerged as the symbol of Jewish heroism and self-sacrifice. When Wittenberg was arrested by the Gestapo, and then rescued from his captors by the freedom fighters, the Germans issued an order that he be returned alive to them, otherwise the entire ghetto and its inhabitants would be destroyed. At first the general staff of the underground hesitated to hand over the commander and prepared for resistance to the end. However, when dissension broke out within the ghetto because of this decision, Wittenberg gave himself up to save the shedding of Jewish blood and was tortured to death by the Germans on July 18, 1943. The drama depicted with glaring vividness the tragic dilemma in which ghetto Jews found themselves during the closing years of the war, whether to raise the banner of revolt and to go down fighting against hopeless odds, as did the Jews of Warsaw, or whether to submit to cruel German demands for ever more victims in the hope that some Jews would remain alive until the hour of liberation.

The poetess was among the few who remained alive. After her liberation from her last camp, Bergen-Belsen, she was chilled by the indifference of the non-Jewish world to the remnants of her people. She then called upon her co-sufferers, who had been singed but not destroyed by the conflagration, to take up the holy mission of teaching others loving-kindness and the sanctity of human life. In her second collection of lyrics, *Out of Eden* (*Arois Fun Gan-Eden*, 1965), her melancholy was milder. However, the vision of the knife long poised above her throat still haunted her. Not until three decades after her ghetto experiences was she able to complete her novel of the life and death of the Jews of Lodz and thereby attain equanimity. She entitled it *The Tree of Life* (*Der Boim Fun Leben*, 1971).

Rachmil Bryks, who also experienced the horrors of the Lodz Ghetto and who also survived Auschwitz, dealt with the inner life of the harried and doomed Jews in three volumes of short stories and two volumes of verse. While not minimizing negative manifestations, he stressed the spiritual heroism of the ghetto inmates, their will to outlive their oppressors, their wisdom in nullifying ever harsher decrees. His long poem *Ghetto Factory 76* (*Geto Fabrik 76*) was completed in 1944. When he recited it before a ghetto audience, he was placed on the list of those to be deported to the gas chambers but was liberated at the last moment when troops of the Allies reached Auschwitz. The manuscript was discovered in the ruins of the ghetto after the war and was published in 1967. The best known tale of Bryks, *A Cat in the Ghetto* (*A Katz In Geto*, 1959), interlaced a realistic description of grim ghetto life with sardonic humor. It was staged as a tragi-comedy in the 1960's and was filmed in 1970. His narratives *The Emperor of the Ghetto* (*Der Kaiser in Geto*, 1961) and *The Paper Crown* (*Die Papierne Krone*, 1961) centered about Mordecai Haim Rumkovsky, who reigned in the Lodz ghetto by grace of the Gestapo as head of the Judenrat and who, in the last stage of the ghetto's liquidation, discovered that his crown was only a paper crown. Rumkovsky, who sent tens of thousands of his coreligionists to their deaths, was depicted by the compassionate novelist to have been finally overwhelmed by nightmares and crushed by the weight of conscience, so that he added his own name to the list of Jews to be sent to the crematoria.

The glaringly vivid narratives of Bryks were based on authentic facts and made a profound emotional impact. They provided a satiric commentary on the behavior of the human species under stress. His ironic laughter was born of the need to maintain spiritual equilibrium in a world apparently gone mad. He believed that intensest artistic effects were attained not by generalizing about the martyrdom of millions but rather by a simple, honest narration of the suffering, feeling and thinking of specific individuals. The single man, woman, child, or family could serve as a symbol of all. Through the mask of his kindest character, the poet Blaustein, Bryks reviewed the pain, despair, heroism and indestructible hope of the ghetto Jews. He revealed that in Lodz, too, there were protest demonstrations and social struggles, battles for culture and education at the very edge of the grave, insistence on justice and decency among the doomed, even if a revolt of the magnitude of the Warsaw ghetto was impossible.

Bryks' constant obsession with his ghetto past throughout his post-war, New York decades found creative expression as late as 1972 in the novelette of his native Polish townlet Skarzhisko, *The Non-Survivors (Die Vos Zeinen Nisht Gebliben)*, and in his novel *Escapers (Antloifers)*.

A vast material chronicling events in the ghettos and death camps was published by survivors, including works by Hillel Zeidman, Tsivia Lubetkin and Bernard Goldstein on the Warsaw ghetto, Herman Kruk and Mark Dvorzecki on the Vilna ghetto. Shlome Frank and Israel Tabaksblat on the Lodz ghetto, Simcha Polakevitch and Vassili Grossman on Treblinka, Mordecai Strigler on Maidanek, Philip Friedman and Katzetnik on Auschwitz. Katzetnik's *House of Dolls,* dealt in fictional form with the degradation and suffering of the most beautiful Jewish girls who were selected for the use of German soldiers before they were sent to the Russian Front. The novel was translated into most European tongues and had a tremendous vogue.

Leib Rochman, one of the few survivors of the Jewish community of Minsk-Mazowiecki in Poland, kept a diary during his fourteen months of agony between June 1943, when the last Jews of the ghetto were shot by Nazi liquidation squads, and August 1944, when he was saved by the Red Army from his living entombment in the hollows of walls and in ditches and pits. This diary was later published under the title *And In Your Blood Shall You Live (Un In Dein Blut Zolstu Lebn,* 1949). Of far greater literary value was his autobiographical novel, *With Blind Steps Over the Earth (Mit Blinde Trit Iber Der Erd,* 1968), which dealt with the years immediately following his liberation. His hero, the sole survivor of an extinguished Jewish town whose painful dying he witnessed, arises from his hiding place in the Valley of the Dead at the end of the war and walks again among his fellow men. Haunted by the ghosts of his decimated coreligionists who claim him as rightfully belonging to them, and resented by the still hostile Poles as another shade from the Beyond, he revisits his community as the only visible Jew; he walks among the ruins of the Jewish streets and houses picked bare by non-Jewish scavengers; he sojourns for a single night in the home, once his own and now occupied by anti-Semitic neighbors; he makes his way to Lodz, the center to which survivors trek in the hope of finding kinsmen; then on to Amsterdam, Lausanne, Offenbach, until he arrives in a Swiss mountain sanitorium where the maimed in body and crippled in soul are gradually rehabilitated.

During his three years in this Magic Mountain resort, reminiscent of Thomas Mann's tubercular asylum, he comes in contact with a motley assortment of post-Holocaust victims who came up from the Valley in various stages of physical disintegration and spiritual distress. Each patient is described with his past history, his present aches and his future hopes. By this device, the author gives a cross-section of European Jewry of the immediate post-War years.

Rochman's chronicle of decay and dissolution is comparable to Thomas Mann's *Magic Mountain* and Hermann Broch's *The Death of Virgil,* but despite Kafkaesque overtones it ends on a happy note: the hero ultimately makes his way to Rome and from there with the Illegals to Palestine, where a new vitality begins to stream through the emaciated bones and starved souls of the remnants of the Jewish people.

The largest group of survivors among the Yiddish writers of Poland were those who fled eastward to the land of the Soviets. There too they were not welcomed with open arms. They endured hunger and humiliations and, nevertheless, were expected to sing the praises of Stalin. Suspected of inadequate loyalty to the Soviet regime, many were condemned on trumped-up charges and sentenced to hard labor in Arctic lumber camps and in Siberian mines. The more trustworthy found refuge in Caucasian and Asiatic towns and somehow managed to keep body and soul together while waiting for the war's end and liberation from their Communist saviors. After the war, Yiddish writers began to trickle back to their native Poland but not a few had to complete their long terms of hard labor and were not released until after the death of Stalin and after their health had been undermined.

The Expressionistic poet and dramatist Moshe Broderzon (1890-1956), founder and director of little theaters in Poland, spent seven years in Siberian work-camps before he was released in 1955 and allowed to return to Lodz and Warsaw. There he was received with great ovations, only to die soon thereafter. The story of his sixteen years of suffering under the Soviets was described by his wife, the actress Shene-Miriam Broderzon, in the book *My Tragic Road with Moshe Broderzon (Mein Leidensveg Mit Moshe Broderzon,* 1960).

Moshe Grossman (1904-1961), the author of novels on Karl Marx and on Rosa Luxemburg, escaped from Warsaw in 1939 to Bialystok in the Soviet-occupied zone of Poland, expecting to find a utopian regime of happy brotherhood. His first short stories published in the Yiddish journal of Bialystok gave expression to his enthusiasm for the Communist regime. But deportation to an Arctic work camp on suspicion of spying, and seven years of torture and suffering, disillusioned him. These years were recorded by him in his intensely felt, well-structured book, *In the Enchanted Land of Dzugashvili* (*In Farkishiftn Land Fun Dzugashvili*, 1949), after he was repatriated to Poland and then left for Paris. Dzugashvili was the middle name of Joseph Dzugashvili Stalin.

Nochum Bomze (1906-1954), a Galician poet who began his literary career in Lvov with his volume of verse *On Weekdays* (*In Die Teg Fun Der Vokh*, 1929), was living in Warsaw when the war began and succeeded in getting back to the Galician metropolis which was in the Russian zone. There his fourth book of lyrics, *Transition* (*Ibergang*, 1941), left the press a few days before the Germans bombarded the town. He was mobilized in the Soviet army and demobilized a few months later. Then began his painful odyssey which took him to Uzbekistan and Bukhara and which found repercussions in the lyrics of "Woe and Wandering," later included in the definitive collection of his selected poems *Wedding in Autumn* (*A Khassene In Harbst*, 1949). When he was permitted to return to Poland at war's end, he imagined that the green grass was reddened with the blood of his kinsmen and that the bread he ate had grown out of his brother's corpse. He therefore continued on to New York, where his weakened body brought him to an early death. His last poems were filled with romantic longing for the lost world of his youth and expressed in exquisite imagery his unending loneliness and melancholy.

Israel Emiot (b. 1909), who completed four volumes of verse before the war, escaped to the Russian zone of Poland after the Nazis shot his mother. He was filled with enthusiasm for the promised autonomous Jewish region of Birobidjan and worked as a journalist in the main city of this region until 1948 when its Jewish intellectuals were liquidated by the Stalin regime. He then spent seven years in an isolated Siberian labor camp, one of whose inmates was Moshe Broderzon. After Stalin's death, he was amnestied and made his way to Poland and finally to the United States. But the scars of his years of entombment remained with him and he often referred to himself as one rearisen from the dead. In his lyric volume *In Melody Absorbed* (*In Nign Aingehert*, 1961), filled with visions of his own sufferings and those of his fellow-prisoners, there was no word of anger or outrage at all the evil and cruelty he had seen and experienced, but only sadness in many variations. From the coldness, harshness and loneliness of post-war reality he fled in search of what little warmth he could find in the embers of the almost extinguished pre-war world, and what little gentleness and communion he could find among the surviving Jews. Though Jewish Lublin and Warsaw were no more, nevertheless, when he laid his ear to their walls, he still heard millions of echoes of sighing, wailing and weeping. His book *In Middle Years* (*In Mitele Yorn*, 1963) contained essays, short stories, feuilletons, lyrics, translations, memoirs of experiences in Soviet provinces and of meetings with leading Yiddish writers before they were purged, and elegies on the passing from the Jewish scene of Poland's Yiddish literary elite. Though never light-hearted or gay, Emiot was also never bitter. From all his sad narratives of man's inhumanity to man, there radiated warm sympathy for every living creature and he constantly called attention to little, unremembered acts of kindness and love amidst tragedy. In the lyric cycle "Siberia," included in the volume *Before I Am Extinguished* (*Eider Du Leshst Mikh Ois*, 1966), he contrasted the loveliness of the Siberian landscape with the brutal ugliness to which human beings were subjected there. He was grateful, during his years of agony, for a day when the white snow was not discolored by the bloodstains of persons shot. Suffering under the misdeeds of his fellow-men, the poet put his trust in God and implored Him again and again to right the wrongs inflicted by His creatures here on earth. Emiot's keen observation, sad longing, religious sensitiveness and tolerant kindness also emerged from the short stories, lyrics and pen portraits of his volume *For the Sake of Ten* (*Tsulib di Tsen Unshuldike*, 1969). The title stemmed from Abraham's plea to God to save Sodom for the sake of ten righteous persons, if such could be found there.

Soon after the first book of verse of Joseph Rubinstein (b. 1900) appeared in Warsaw in 1939, this gentle poet was forced to flee before the Nazis and found temporary asylum in Bialystok. In 1941 he was again in panic flight eastward as the Nazi hordes advanced upon Russia. He traversed thousands of miles in search of safety and bread. Everywhere he encountered Jews with hunted looks, contemporary marranos. By the waters of Central Asia and at the foothills of the Himalayas, they sat in fear. Beside strange shores they wept hot tears when they recalled the horror that was overwhelming their people. But amidst hunger and filth and homelessness, the dispersed men and women retained their stubborn faith in Jewish survival. "We Shall Endure" became their slogan. And they endured. Reason could not fathom nor logic explain the unity among these individuals without a state or territory or language of their own, without a Sabbath or a holiday celebration, without a *minyan* or a *kheder*, without a book, newspaper, or other means of communication. Nevertheless, they recognized one another at a glance and somehow sensed their common destiny and the common hostility of their neighbors. Before his repatriation to Poland, Rubinstein was implored by the muted Soviet Yiddish writers to sing out the pain of Russia's Jews and their undying devotion to their imperilled historic and religious heritage. This mission he fulfilled in the elegiac verses of his epic *Scroll of Woe of a Polish Jew in Russia* (*Megilat Russland*, 1960).

In his second poetic epic, *Polish Jewry—A Lament* (*Khurban Poiln*, 1964), Rubinstein described his repatriation to Poland in the spring of 1946, his parting scenes with the Yiddish writers later liquidated by Stalin, his memories of NKVD gruelling and of nameless friends who enabled him to survive his ordeals. In his most moving lyric, he described his last Passover evening on Russian soil. To ward off all suspicion, the Jewish marranos arranged a seemingly joyous party together with their non-Jewish neighbors. Beer and vodka flowed and brotherhood was toasted. However, the moment these neighbors left, the scene was changed at the midnight hour as if by magic. The door was bolted, the drapes were drawn, the festive candles were lit, red wine, a single *matzo* and a single Haggadah made their appearance. The eight remaining Jews began to intone the traditional words of an ancient exodus, tear-stained passages that were filled with a new content, legends that presaged their enslavement and their hope for ultimate redemption from contemporary Pharaohs. Rubinstein's poetic scroll described in vivid images his homecoming to his native land, the first greetings of "Zhid" at the border station and on his arrival in Warsaw, the first looks of hate and scorn that darted from old and young Poles, from peasant girls and city elders, from the heirs of Jewish homes and shops, all of whom had in their hearts offered thanks to the Germans for ridding the area of Jews and who were most unhappy to see a few stragglers returning. As the poet hobbled across the blood-drenched ruins of Warsaw's ghetto, he recalled his young bright dreams of freedom, hope and fraternity, dreams that turned to nightmares all too quickly. Nevertheless, caught in the maelstrom of the war's aftermath, he sought to rebuild his shattered existence in Poland. In vain! The

Kielce Pogrom, when the city fathers offered the Polish populace an opportunity to murder and pillage the repatriated Jews, convinced him that the old method of using Jews as scapegoats for the sins of an unpopular regime would continue unabated. There seemed to be no other course open to the Jewish poet save to resume his wandering. Once again he bade farewell to the soil where peasants were already busy plowing up and covering with dung the graves of his fathers.

Exodus from Europe (*Yetsiat Europa,* 1970), the concluding volume of Rubinstein's poetic trilogy, dealt with his wanderings and temporary havens in Europe and ended with his taking permanent root in New York. Everywhere memories of the Holocaust pursued him. He suffered from a *khurban*-complex. The smoke and ashes belched by railroad engines reminded him of the smoke and ashes that emanated from the crematoria of Auschwitz and Maidanek. In Sweden he was not only grateful for the asylum granted him but also envious of the calm and carefree people who had carried on their normal pursuits in that neutral land while his coreligionists were a hunted group that lived in daily fear of extermination. As he crossed the Rhine, he realized that the bombed German cities along this river would soon be rebuilt and German songs would again resound loud and boisterous. In Warsaw and in towns along the Vistula, however, Jewish voices and Jewish melodies would not again be heard. When he asked himself the question why all the pain and horror inflicted upon Jews, he found a slight comfort in the knowledge that a worse fate could have been theirs: God could have created them as Germans, a people from whose ranks stemmed the S.S. murderers. In France, Rubinstein caught sight of the Illegals, who were being transported to camouflaged ships waiting to break through the British sea blockade and to bring them to their longed-for and much promised Jewish homeland. He himself, tired of wandering, took the less perilous road to the New World. But visions of Jewish martyrdom in Nazi and Communist Europe continued to haunt him and were incorporated in his poetic epics.

Mendel Mann (b. 1916) ranks among the finest novelists of the Holocaust generation. He was at the beginning of his career as a painter on canvas and a painter in words when the war broke out and forced him to flee from Warsaw. He found a refuge in Russia where he was drafted into the Red Army and participated in the defense of Moscow in 1941 and in the battles which cul-

minated in the Soviet army's entry into Berlin in 1945. At war's
end, he resumed his literary work with the booklet of songs and
ballads *Silence Demands* (*Die Shtilkeit Mont,* 1945). This was the
first literary publication to appear in Poland in the very year of
that country's liberation from the Nazis. The poet saw silence
all about him. He walked along the streets of Plonsk, the ruined
townlet where he was born. Through these streets his kinsmen
were driven to their death. A few Jews had survived but they were
silent. Their Polish neighbors too were silent. But the silence cried
out and made demands. The poet begged God, who had chosen
the Jewish people, to take back this chosenness with its burdens
and to give Jews the quietness that was the lot of every simple,
unchosen peasant who plowed ancestral earth generation after
generation.

The Polish pogrom of Kielce in 1946, when returning Jewish
survivors were murdered by their Polish townsmen, compelled
Mann to resume his wandering. A second volume of his poems,
Heritage (*Yerusha,* 1947), appeared in Germany, when he edited
a Yiddish weekly for displaced persons in the American zone.
After Israel's gates were opened in 1948, he settled there and
wrote his great trilogy of the war on the Eastern Front as seen
through the eyes of a Jewish recruit. These volumes *At the Gates
of Moscow* (*Bei Die Toiren Fun Moscow,* 1956), *At the Vistula*
(*Bei Der Veisl,* 1958), *The Fall of Berlin* (*Dos Faln Fun Berlin,*
1960), constituted a grandiose poetic epic which was immediately
translated into English, French, Spanish and other tongues and
was compared by reviewers to Tolstoy's *War and Peace.*

The central hero was Menachem, a Jewish refugee from Poland
who found himself deep in the heart of Russia among villagers
with a way of life at first utterly strange to him but soon as dear
to him as that of his own Polish homeland. He joined these villagers when they were mobilized for the struggle against the Germans, he fought with them in the desperate defence of the Soviet
capital, he reached with them the banks of the Vistula, he participated in the triumphal march into Berlin. Nevertheless, at every
level of command, he came in contact with distrust of Jews. No
matter how self-sacrificing and super-courageous he and other
Jews were, the legend of Jewish cowardice could not be dislodged
and deeply embedded anti-Semitic prejudices could not be effaced.
Menachem was subjected to constant slights, affronts and unjust
suffering just because of his origin. When he was required to in-

terrogate German prisoners, one of them refused to answer questions because they were put by a Jew. Menachem was so aroused at this impudence that he could not proceed with the questioning. He was then accused of disobedience and was court-martialed.

Enduring hardships as a forced laborer in the coal mines of the Urals, he again volunteered for the Front. Fighting with his contingent along the banks of the Vistula, he witnessed the agony of Warsaw and the tragedy of the remnants of its Jewish population which was still being hunted as free game, not only by the retreating Germans, but also by Polish compatriots and by renegade Russians and Ukrainians. When the Soviet army finally reached the heart of Berlin and the Nazis were in their last throes, the friendliest of Russian officers confided to a Jewish fellow-officer: "The Germans have not only murdered your people, they have also disturbed the stability of every surviving Jew. It will be impossible for a non-Jew to live with you. You are filled with suspicion, hostility, distrust, anguish and feelings of vengeance. Not only individuals who lose a lot of blood remain sick for the rest of their lives but also a people that bled so profusely in the war will be sick for many generations. You Jews are now a sick people, and I belong to those who are sorry for you." Hardly had Berlin been taken, when the attitude of Russians toward Germans changed. The latter were accepted as allies in socialist reconstruction and in a looming confrontation with the capitalist West. The Jews, on the other hand, including their heroic fighters in the Soviet ranks, were eyed with suspicion. They were accused of blindly hating the Germans, of seeking to fraternize with non-Soviet Jews, and were shipped back to unknown destinations to atone for imaginary crimes. For the much tried Menachem, who helped in the storming of Berlin, this intensified anti-Semitism came as the final shock. There was no way out for him except to leave the accursed soil and to resume his wandering. The war-trilogy ended with the words: "He left this sad earth forever, the earth of his ancestors. He took with him nothing save his tired body and a great heart filled with pain, anger, and love."

While Mendel Mann, Rubinstein, Emiot, Bomze, Grossman, Rochman and other Yiddish writers repatriated to Poland soon left this land which had become the graveyard of millions of their coreligionists and which was drenched with hatred of the survivors, other writers still retained hope that Jewish cultural life could somehow still flourish there and they undertook its reconstruction. They included Hersh Smoliar (b. 1905), who worked in the Polish Communist underground before the war, escaped from the Minsk ghetto in 1944, fought with the Partisans in the forests, headed the Culture Department of Polish Jewry since 1946, and edited the only post-War Yiddish newspaper in Warsaw, *Folksshtimme,* whose circulation decreased from year to year until by 1970 it had less than 3,000 readers, including subscribers from abroad; David Sfard (b. 1905), poet and essayist, who occupied a prominent position in Jewish cultural life after returning to Warsaw in 1946, founding *Farlag Idishbukh,* and supervising the publication and editing of more than two hundred volumes before he was forced to leave Poland during the intenser anti-Semitic wave that swept over this Communist-governed land in 1969; Binem Heller (b. 1908), the most prolific Yiddish poet of post-Holocaust Warsaw, who suffered disillusionment with the Communist panacea he had so enthusiastically hailed in his early verses and who then left for Israel in 1956 in a repentant mood; and I. Grudberg-Turkov (b. 1906), who attempted to restore the Yiddish theater under the new regime but had to give up the attempt. With the emigration of Ida Kaminska to the United States in 1969, the last great star of the Yiddish stage left Poland and its ever dwindling Jews.

As the greatest Jewish catastrophe of modern times, the Holocaust made the profoundest impact upon Jews of all continents and was reflected in soul-stirring works by Yiddish writers far removed from the grim events. Writers on American soil who incorporated the theme of the Holocaust in memorable lyrics, stories and dramas included Sholem Asch, David Pinski, Joseph Opatoshu, H. Leivick, Jacob Glatstein, Abraham Reisen, Ephraim Auerbach, Aaron Zeitlin, Itzik Manger, I. I. Schwartz, Zishe Weinper, Mani-Leib, Glanz-Leyeles, Melech Ravitch, Kadia Molodowsky, David Einhorn, Menachem Boraisha, B. J. Bialostotsky, Naftoli Gross, Eliezer Greenberg, Berish Weinstein, Abraham Tabachnik, Meir Stiker, A. Almi, M. Z. Tkatch, J. I. Segal, Gabriel Preil, Leon Feinberg. Indeed, it would be difficult to find any Yiddish writer of stature on any continent who did not mirror in his creative work the death of the Jewish people in the Holocaust and their resurrection in Israel. Death and rebirth were the two themes dominant in the literature of the post-war decades.

When Aaron Zeitlin entitled the initial volume of his collected poems *Poems of the Holocaust and Poems of Faith* (*Lieder Fun Khurban Un Lieder Fun Gloibn,* 1967), he was summing up not only his own late poetry, which alternated between apocalyptic and Messianic visions, but also the literature of his generation. He was also expressing in his opening verses its conviction that, as long as a single Jew would survive on earth, his heart would bleed for the murdered millions of the martyred people and, if he believed that there was meaning to existence, then he would believe that there must be some mystic connection between the night of the Holocaust and the dawn of Israel. Elegies of Auschwitz, Maidanek and Treblinka were succeeded by hymns to the heroic warriors and pioneering builders of a new life on Israel's resuscitated soil. Out of despair new hopes blossomed.

23

AGING OF YIDDISH

Polish Finale • Post-Stalin Russia • Aftermath of Six
Day War • Joseph Kerler • Yizkor Books • American
Novelists • Dramatists • Humorists • Lyricists •
Women Writers • Literary Critics • Essayists • Mid-
western Writers • Montreal Center • Rochel Korn •
Los Angeles Center

OF THE THREE PRINCIPAL CENTERS of Yiddish literary
activity before the Second World War—Poland, Russia, America
—only the American center continued to be of importance after
the Holocaust.

When the bulk of the Jewish population in Poland was destroyed, the Polish center was deprived of most Yiddish writers
and readers. It was, nevertheless, able to maintain itself at a low
level of vitality for another quarter of a century. Before the end
of the 1960's however, even the surviving writers were forced to
emigrate by a hostile political regime which removed Jews from
all sensitive areas of activity. By 1968 the only Yiddish daily
Folksshtimme was converted to a weekly because of the negligible
number of readers. Its editor Hersh Smoliar, a veteran Communist
who enjoyed the full confidence of the Polish government until the
Six Day War, was dismissed on charges of Jewish nationalism. In
July 1971 he arrived in Israel disillusioned with the Communist
regime. By then, the élite of Poland's Yiddish writers, including
those who had followed the Communist Party line most faithfully,
abandoned hope of reviving Yiddish culture in the intensely anti-
Semitic environment and left Poland.

In Soviet Russia, Yiddish men-of-letters continued to write and
to publish significant works until 1948, despite increasing difficulties imposed by the totalitarian regime that did not tolerate any

deviation from Communist Party directives. But in 1948, Yiddish literature was completely silenced and its most talented representatives entombed in prisons and labor camps or liquidated by firing squads. A slight recovery occurred during the Khrushchev era. The single literary periodical *Sovetish Heimland* was tolerated since 1962 and a few Yiddish books again became available.

In 1960 only one book appeared. It dealt with the Jewish autonomous region of Birobidjan. The following year there were republished in Moscow the poems of Osher Shvartzman and selected tales of David Bergelson. Except for a book of Yiddish folksongs in 1962, there were no further publications until the prose anthology *This Is How We Live* (*Azoi Lebn Mir*, 1964). In 1965 a slight thaw set in which permitted the publication of four Yiddish books: *Heaven and Earth* (*Himl Un Erd*) by Nota Luria, *I Must Tell* (*Ikh Muss Dertseiln*) by Masha Rolnik, selected poems by Moishe Teif, and an anthology of Soviet Yiddish poetry. Two books were published in 1966: Peretz Markish's novel of World War II, *Steps of Generations* (*Trit Fun Doires*), which he completed in 1947, a year before he was imprisoned, and Shmuel Halkin's *My Treasure* (*Mein Oitser*), containing poems completed before his death five years earlier. In 1967 Zalman Wendroff was honored on his ninetieth birthday by the publication of his tales, *Our Street* (*Undzer Gass*); Itzik Fefer's songs and ballads were reprinted, fifteen years after he was shot; Mendel Lifshitz's poems *At Home* (*Bei Sikh In Der Heim*) appeared. In 1968 a second anthology of Soviet Yiddish prose was published and also a collection of poems by Ziame Telesin. The total of books by Soviet writers published in Yiddish during the two decades after the tragic year 1948 was indeed meager when compared with books by Yiddish writers which were permitted to appear in translation. In the single decade 1955 to 1964, 282 books by ninety Yiddish authors were translated into fifteen languages of Soviet Russia and totalled twenty-six million copies. The official explanation for the paucity of Yiddish books was that there was a negligible demand for them.

The harder anti-Israel line taken by the Soviet government after the Six Day War did not discourage Jews from expressing identity with the Jewish people. Indeed, a renaissance of Jewishness was evident among youth in cities from the Baltic to the Black Sea. However, this resurgent Jewish youth was Russian-speaking and Russian-writing. Fifty years after the revolution,

its understanding of Yiddish was extremely limited. It demonstrated its yearning for its Jewish heritage by assembling in the
thousands before Moscow's Great Synagogue on the eve of Sim-
chat Torah, singing and dancing from sundown to dawn.

The Moscow poet Joseph Kerler (b. 1918) described these young
men and women in a Yiddish poem of 1970 as assembling like
little puppies looking blindly for the breast of their mother. They
came from universities, from factories and from homes long estranged from Jewishness. Like submarines that suddenly emerged
to the surface, proud, blossoming Jewish heads appeared before
the well-worn, gray temple-steps.

The Jews of Silence, as Elie Wiesel dubbed them, were no
longer silent. They knocked at all official doors pleading for an
opportunity to leave the land where they were denied the right to
live their ancient heritage and to transmit it to coming generations
through Jewish educational and cultural institutions. When their
pleas went unheeded, they undertook steps for Jewish self-emancipation. They formed Hebrew-speaking circles and sought to educate themselves in Jewish subjects. Though their efforts were
frowned upon by the Soviet regime and though their boldest
spokesmen were subjected to secret trials and condemned to long
terms of imprisonment at hard labor, they were not intimidated
and in the 1970's their plight was arousing international attention
and concern.

Israel was the land of their heart's desire and the sole Yiddish
organ, which was subservient to the Kremlin's whims, did not
meet their need. The narratives, poems and essays in Sovetish
Heimland, and the pitifully few, carefully winnowed Yiddish books
published in the 1960's and 1970's, were written by ever aging
authors for ever aging readers. The contents alternated between
reminiscences of the Holocaust and pre-Holocaust past on the
one hand, and a glorification of Soviet achievements and vituperation of capitalist, bourgeois behavior abroad on the other hand.

Aaron Vergelis, editor-in-chief of the Yiddish monthly, continued to function as the faithful spokesman for Soviet policies
toward Jews and was repeatedly sent abroad until 1971 to defend
the regime against charges of anti-Semitism leveled in many quarters, Jewish and non-Jewish. The other editors, of whom the most
talented were the novelists Yekhiel Falikman (b. 1911) and Note
Luria (b. 1906), were equally meticulous in following the prescribed party line in literature. Elie Gordon (b. 1907) continued

to pen, in the style of socialist realism, narratives of Jewish peasants and workers who integrated successfully into the collectivist villages of the Ukraine. Liuba Wasserman (b. 1905) continued to sketch, in prose, colorful portraits of Birobidjan Jewish women and, in verse, the loveliness of the landscape along the Biro River. She had begun her literary career in Palestine with the poems of *Twilight* (*Farnakhten,* 1931), six years after she had come as a young, idealistic *chalutza.* Disappointment with the mandatory regime and longing for an envisaged Communist Jewish utopia led her to return to Russia and to join the pioneers in the much heralded Siberian Jewish autonomous region. She survived the Stalin purges without becoming embittered. The Jewish types she described in the autumn of her life were kind professionals, the woman-physician who was entirely devoted to patients, the school teacher adored by all pupils, the kindergartener who hummed Shmuel Halkin's poems while moving along with light, quick steps after a day's playing with children. Her poetry, too, mirrored joyful scenes and moods. She hailed the first snow of winter and was enchanted by the melodies of spring. "May happy childhood flourish and fields ripen, O Heart, what more would you want of life? If only there were peace in the world!"

A plea to the Jewish writers of the world to strive for peace and friendship between the peoples of the Middle East—Jews and Arabs—was issued by fifty-nine Soviet Yiddish writers in September 1970. At the same time the urgent and repeated efforts of Soviet Jews to leave for Israel also infected some writers. When the poet Ziame Telesin (b. 1907) and his wife, the narrator Rochel Boimvol (b. 1913), asked to be allowed to leave for Israel, they were expelled from the Writers' Union because of such heretical behavior. In the poems of the volume *My Responsibility* (*Oif Meine Akhrais,* 1968), Telesin avoided the usual Soviet themes and concentrated on his responsibility toward his resurrected people and its holy ashes in Auschwitz. He ended his poem "Resurrection" with the verse: "Enough to be without a bit of light! Arise for the resurrection of the dead!" In the poem "The Ship," he described a ship that sought to break out of its moorings and to escape into the distance, but was always hurled back by a rope tied to a pillar. In April 1971, Telesin and Boimvol succeeded in getting to Israel.

When the poet Joseph Kerler applied for permission to emigrate to Israel in 1970, *Sovetish Heimland,* which had lavished extravagant praise upon him only two years earlier, reviled him as a completely untalented scribbler. Kerler had participated in Russia's war against the Nazis and had published in 1943 a volume of lyrics composed on the battlefields. He had then shared the fate of other Yiddish writers who were immured in Siberian labor camps in 1948. In 1956 he was liberated and two of his lyric collections appeared in a Russian translation. But, by 1970, his poems could no longer be printed in Moscow. Some reached Israel, however, and were published in *Di Goldene Keyt*. He dared to say to the Russians in the concluding stanza of the poem "Accounts": "The land is yours, the earth is yours, and everything on this earth belongs to you, everything except me. Me—let go. Me—don't detain. We are quits." In his song to the Ukraine, he voiced his longing for his birthplace, the hate-filled step-land Ukraine, but he also expressed the hope that his descendants would no longer know such longing. He ended his poem to Israel, entitled "June 5, 1967," the first day of the Six Day War, with the stanzas: "I do not know whether you need me, but I need you, even as eyes need light, lungs air, a fish water, and a poor table cornbread. Wherever I turn, wherever I am, you are my only star, my only light, my only joy, my only pain. To You I belong. With you I'll be." In March 1971, he was finally permitted to depart for Israel but had to leave all his manuscripts in Moscow. He was received with great enthusiasm in Jerusalem, and in Tel Aviv he was awarded the much-coveted Itzik Manger Prize for 1971.

The rebirth of Jewish consciousness in the Soviet realm was in full swing in the 1970's. For Soviet Yiddish literature, however, this rebirth came too late. While *Sovetish Heimland* sought, since January 1969, to acquire new readers for Yiddish by including in each issue two pages of elementary grammar and basic vocabulary with Russian transcriptions and translation, such an effort was woefully inadequate to raise up a younger generation of readers and certainly could not produce writers. The Yiddish men-of-letters who somehow still participated in this waning literature were, with rare exceptions, in the age range of sixty to ninety-five and so were their readers.

In the United States, the decline of Yiddish was not as precipitous as in Russia or Poland. Indeed, literature was temporarily strengthened by the arrival of Eastern European writers who escaped the Holocaust and found refuge on America's hospitable shores. Yiddish scholarship benefitted from the transfer to New York of the rich library and archival treasures of YIVO and by the arrival of YIVO's surviving scholars, as well as by the introduction of Yiddish studies in American universities.

Books of individual memoirs and of collective memoirs in the form of Yizkor-volumes forged to the fore quantitatively. The latter sought to perpetuate the record of Jewish life in ruined and vanished communities, and often involved a cooperative effort of American and Israeli writers under the auspices of YIVO in New York and YAD VASHEM in Jerusalem, as well as of *Landsmanshaften* on all continents. Such volumes numbered more than 500 during the quarter of a century between 1945 and 1970.

Fiction also dealt extensively with the Holocaust and the period preceding it. However, many novelists preferred to retreat in their imagination to a remoter past of Jewish suffering and heroism. The historical novel flourished and covered a vast range of generations. Novels of biblical times included Sholem Asch's *Moses* (1951), and Izban's *Jezebel* (1960) and *Jericho* (1966). Mendl Osherowitz (1888-1965), in *Queen Marianne* (*Kenigin Miriam,* 1957), dealt with Jewish tragedy in Herodian days and Joseph Opatoshu, in *Rabbi Akiva* (1948), with the Bar-Kochba Revolt. Zalman Schneour's historical novel *Emperor and Rabbi* (*Kaiser Un Rabbi*) appeared in five volumes from 1944 to 1952. Historical tales with the greatest popular appeal were those of Bashevis Singer, who took as his fictional domain the period from the Chmelnitzky massacres of the mid-seventeenth century up to the First World War. The American scene became increasingly a theme for Yiddish narrators, including Sholem Asch, Baruch Glasman, S. Miller, Chaim Pet and B. Alquit.

Drama declined rapidly during the post-war decades. The Yiddish theater ceased to be a major factor in the cultural life of America's Jews. With the closing of Maurice Schwartz's Yiddish Art Theater in New York in 1950, the last theatrical bastion in the New World fell. Actors were left homeless and dramatists had to turn to other literary media or to content themselves with writing book-dramas, with ever waning hope of seeing them staged. Dramatists who continued to create in this declining medium included H. Leivick, Fishel Bimko, Ossip Dymov, Leiser Treister and Zvi Kahn.

Yiddish humor, satire and sardonic wit, so prominent since the tales of Chelm, the exploits of Hershele Ostropoler and the chanting of the Badchonim, reached its apex in America in the first quarter of the twentieth century with *Der Kibbetzer* and the far more popular *Der Groisser Kundus,* founded in 1909. The lat-

ter's co-founder and editor for almost two decades was the poet
Jacob Marinov (1869-1964), who had migrated to New York in
1893. The contributors to this journal of humor, wit and satire
included Sholom Aleichem, Yehoash, Lutzky, Moshe Nadir, Abraham Reisen, Moshe Leib Halpern, Jacob Adler, who wrote under
the pen-name of B. Kovner, and Chaim Gutman (1887-1961) who
was far better known as "Der Lebediker." Gaiety subsided as the
Yiddish writers aged. Besides, the post-Holocaust decades were
not propitious for the rise of humorous talents. With the death
of Marinov at the age of ninety-five and the silence of Adler after
the age of ninety-eight, the era of the humorists who were idolized
by the unsophisticated Yiddish readers and who had exposed to
laughter all unwise and improper aspects of Jewish private and
public behavior came to an end.

The lyric of the post-war period was dominated by the two
themes of the Holocaust and Israel. A sense of guilt permeated
poets who were far from the martyrdom of their European kinsmen. Longing for Israel led the poets Itzik Manger and Ephraim
Auerbach to spend their last years there, while other poets such
as Glanz-Leyeles and Kadia Molodowsky were inspired to a new
burst of creativity during aging years when they came in contact
with Israel's soil and people. Mordecai Yoffe (1899-1961) supplemented his four volumes of translations of Hebrew poetry with
his last work, an anthology of Yiddish poetry dealing with Israel,
published in 1961.

After the mid-twentieth century, however, no new major poets,
only several minor ones, made their initial appearance upon the
Yiddish scene. Hersh Leib Young (b. 1895), who came to New
York from the foothills of the Carpathians in 1914, did not publish
his first volume of verse until his sixties. This volume, *Above the
Clouds* (*Hekher Die Volkens*, 1962), was followed by two more
volumes in his seventies, *Through Light and Darkness* (*Durkh
Likht Un Finsternis*, 1967) and *Above Flaming Horizons* (*Iber
Tserflamte Horitsonten*, 1971). His poems glittered with alliterations, assonances and strange, daring neologisms. His flights to
abstractions, astral realms and cosmic seas evidenced the too persistent intrusion of the intellectual process in the structuring of
each poem. His New York was a magical, phantasmagorical sil-
houette, with sparks of gold spurting out of dark, skyscraping
palaces, glittering in the surrounding waters and reflected back in
the retina of the observer. Young lacked naiveté. He sought essences, the *Urgestalt,* or primary configuration of things, and his

odes ranged from perceptions of atomic dust to vast forays across light-years to celestial galaxies.

Leib Wasserman (b. 1915) discovered himself as a poet during his decade of suffering before he found a refuge in New York. His earliest poems appeared in 1949 while he was still in a Displaced Persons' Camp near Munich. With his second lyric booklet, *My Nights and Days* (*Meine Mes-Lesn*, 1966), he attained mature calmness. The words that recurred most frequently in his lyrics were: silence, loneliness, sadness. He loved silent people and silent moods. He thanked God for the gift of patient, luminous loneliness. He gloried in his sadness because it brought him closer to the peace of eternity. He preferred the ascetic light of the moon to the dazzling brightness of the sun, the blueness of the sky to the grayness of earth, the golden nakedness of poverty to the fatness of affluence, the secrets of mysticism to the clarity of reason. He shunned conflicts, and even activity, for these interfered with his brooding on eternity. When he invoked Israel, it was not the bustling, resurgent nation but rather the imagined Israel of its bards in exile, from Yehuda Halevi to Abraham Mapu, an Israel that was old, holy and dream-filled. In his dialogues with God, he was all submissiveness, pleading as a child with a father who was both gentle and awe-inspiring. In his lyrics on death, there was no terror, only coolness, stillness, intimate expectancy.

Women lyricists become ever more prominent on the American scene. To some of them living in peaceful, cultured homes, events of the stormy decades in Europe and Israel formed merely a background, muted and melancholy, for the reality about them: motherhood and the simple joys and sorrows of evenly evolving years.

Malke Lee, who stemmed from Eastern Galicia and whose first volume of songs appeared in 1932, reached full maturity with the poems of *In Light of Generations* (*In Likht Fun Doires*, 1961), poems full of sunshine and starlight, the delight of springtime and the gold of autumn, love's longing and rich fulfillment. She lived close to nature and sang of early years along the Dniester and later years among the thrifty farmers of New York's Catskill Range. Lyrics of her attachment to America alternated with songs of Zion and Israel's rebirth.

Bessie Pomerantz-Honigbaum, in her fine volume, *Moments of Grace* (*Reges Fun Genod*, 1957), sought escape from the reality of her "bread-and-butter existence" in the misty realm of dreams. She was aware that on other continents battles for freedom were raging and that in Israel her people were rejuvenating an ancient soil and an aged culture. Unable to participate actively in these battles and in this reinvigoration, she sent forth songs of longing from afar and verses of encouragement to others. In 1969 there appeared a selection of her four earlier verse collections with the addition of new poems which reflected the gold of her life's twilight, the warmth of nestling within her people's heritage, faith in the ultimate triumph of goodness when Messiah would burst his chains and cleanse the world of imperfections.

Esther Shumiatcher-Hirshbein (b. 1900) symbolically ended her fifth volume of *Lieder* (1956) with the poem "Twilight," which mirrored her sadness at the aging of the day amidst gathering silence and tiredness, and with a lament for the Yiddish tongue which taught her the wise lore of her people.

The poems of Hinde Zaretzky (b. 1899), in the volume *The Fourth Melody (Der Ferter Nigun,* 1960) and in the later volume *And So He Sang (Un Er Hot Gesungen,* 1968), continued to deal with characters and scenes of the White Russian townlet which she had left as an adolescent on the eve of World War I and of which she retained nostalgic memories. Her songs of New York were also based on golden recollections of earlier decades: struggles on picket lines and in sweatshops, May demonstrations and hunger pains, legendary Second Avenue and Jewish East Broadway. Her songs of Israel were blessings sent from afar, jubilations at her people's achievements in war and in reconstruction. In her autumnal moods, she was reconciled to God's world. She saw miracles everywhere, from the blade of grass that broke into life, to the tot that took its first steps toward a bright wonderland. She fought to retain her optimism, her faith in the holiness of all existence, her joy that she belonged to a moral fellowship reaching back to biblical matriarchs and embracing contemporary heroines from the martyred Hannah Senesh to the living pioneers on Zion's free soil.

Like Hinde Zaretzky, Bracha Kopstein (b. 1900) also emerged from youthful poetry of protest to autumnal poetry of reconciliation with life and society. While her lyrics of the 1930's dealt with factory scenes and proletarian rebellion, and those of the 1940's echoed Jewish tragic events under Nazi oppression, her poems of the 1950's and 1960's mirrored Israeli landscapes, characters and themes, repercussions of her temporary sojourn in the Jewish heartland. Her most moving lyrics, however, were her lullabies and children's songs. Some of Israel's finest poets, including Abraham Shlonsky, Asher Barash and Shimshon Meltzer, rendered her poems into Hebrew. Jewish composers, including Jacob Weinberg, Leib Glantz and Nachum Nardi, set them to music.

Reisl Zhichlinski (b. 1910) did not get to the United States until 1951. She began her poetic career in Warsaw with two lyric volumes, *Songs* (*Lieder,* 1936), and *The Rain Sings* (*Der Regen Zingt,* 1939). She found refuge in Russia during the Second World War but returned to Poland in 1947. There her third poetic volume, *To Pure Silent Doors* (*Shvaigendike Tiern,* 1962), contained the ripe lyrics of her American years as well as the best of her earlier poems. Critics from Itzik Manger and Moshe Broderzon to Shlome Bickel and Melech Ravitch acclaimed her originality, her intensity of feeling, her ability to communicate moods and experiences with utmost economy of words.

The art of literary criticism did not attract women to the same extent as did the art of poetry. Only Kadia Molodowsky, as editor of the quarterly *Sviva,* distinguished herself in this genre.

Significant collections of essays and articles of literary criticism were published during the post-war period by Shlome Bickel, Aaron Glanz-Leyeles, Nachman Maisel, Kalmon Marmor, N. B. Minkoff and B. Rivkin, before death removed them from the literary scene.

The best essays of Mordecai Danzis (1885-1952) appeared posthumously under the title *My Light* (*Eign Likht,* 1954) and revealed a fine stylist and a bold, original thinker. Danzis had early in life come under the influence of the Wise Men of Odessa and, above all, of Vladimir Jabotinsky. In the United States he was active since 1905 as journalist, editor and literary spokesman of the Zionist-Revisionists.

Menashe Unger (1899-1969) was a popular essayist whose favorite theme was Hassidism. Descended from a long line of Hassidic rabbis going back to Elimelech of Lizansk, he specialized in Cabala and Hassidic history at the Hebrew University before settling in New York in 1934 and joining the editorial staff of the daily *Tog.* His six volumes on the world of Hassidism and its Zaddikim appeared after the Second World War. In this subject-matter he had been preceded on the American scene by the Hassidic popularizers Yitzkhok Ewen (1861-1925) and Joseph Margoshes (1866-1955). The latter's son, Samuel Margoshes (1887-1969), was an influential Zionist journalist, essayist, editor of the *Tog* from 1926 to 1942 and its English columnist thereafter. For him, the survival and growth of the Jewish people on all continents was primary. The strengthening of the state of Israel was a necessary means to achieve this objective, but not an end in itself. Hence, he emphasized the need for Yiddish as well as Hebrew, the building of a strong American center of Jewishness as well as a viable Israel center, both interdependent and influencing each other's development, economically, politically, spiritually.

Ben Zion Goldberg (b. 1895), son-in-law of Sholom Aleichem, was another Yiddish journalist, essayist and editor of the *Tog.* For half a century he wrote on politics, social problems and literature. He often found himself involved in heated controversies because of his radical tendencies. Only late in life did he come to realize that his faith in the Soviet regime as benefactor of the Jews was misplaced.

Chaim Lieberman (1890-1963), educator, essayist and literary critic, was also a controversial figure engaging in many polemics during his later years. He had begun as a spokesman for Labor Zionism but veered ever more toward religious Zionism. His vitriolic attacks upon Sholem Asch because of the latter's Christological novels caused a sensation when published in Yiddish, Hebrew and English. This book, *The Christianity of Sholem Asch* (1953), brought much sorrow to the sensitive, esteemed novelist. Other diatribes followed against writers and movements which aroused Lieberman's ire and which he sought to demolish by the power of his pen.

Only slightly less severe in the judgment of literary figures and phenomena was Alexander Mukdoni (1878-1958), the most influential Yiddish theater critic. For half a century he fought to maintain the highest standards in acting, staging and dramatic writing, both in European countries until 1922 and in the United States until his eightieth year. After studying at German, French and Swiss universities, he had joined Peretz, Asch, Reisen, Nomberg, Dinezon and others of the classical and post-classical generations in trying to build a Yiddish theatrical tradition of highest quality in Poland. He continued his efforts in New York as literary critic of the Yiddish daily *Morning Journal,* and as editor of periodicals dealing with the theater. His four volumes of memoirs (1949-1955) cast light upon many Jewish writers, actors and theater-directors whom he had come to know in the course of his long life.

Abraham Menes (1897-1969), a leader of the Bund in Poland, Germany and France, and a founder of YIVO, succeeded in escaping to America after the German invasion of France in 1940.

Primarily a scholar, whose field of research extended from biblical themes to trends in contemporary socialism, he reached his largest audience as a writer for the New York daily *Forverts* during the two decades after 1947. His last book, *Jewish Thought in Modern Times* (*Der Yiedisher Gedank In Der Nayer Tsait*, 1957), was an important anthology of documents and essays dealing with Jewish thinking about the meaning of Galut and about the forms of redemption from Galut. Menes recognized that Galut had always been an experience of the Jewish people. It began with Abraham, the wanderer from Ur of the Chaldees, and Jacob, who ended his days in Egyptian exile. Menes emphasized the development of Jewish thought under the impact of tragic events during the past three generations, the search for the meaning of Jewish group-existence in the Diaspora both before and after the founding of Israel, the struggle for a national language or languages in which Jewish aspirations could best find embodiment, the complications caused by the uniqueness of the contemporary Jewish position outside of the Jewish homeland: a bi-cultural minority on the territories of nations who were increasingly straining toward cultural monism.

These questions also occupied the Yiddish educator and essayist Hyman B. Bass (b. 1904) in his books of essays, *Our Generation of Decision* (*Undzer Dor Mus Antsheydn*, 1963) and *Writers and Works* (*Shreiber Un Verk*, 1971). His mentors were Dubnow, Peretz and Zhitlowsky. He adapted their fruitful insights to the contemporary American scene, discarding whatever was no longer viable and emphasizing what might still be fitted into existing educational and social structures. He inveighed against the notion that a satisfactory partnership between American Jews and Israelis could be based on a differentiation of functions and obligations, with the former supplying the sinews for the upbuilding of a strong cultural center in the historic homeland and the latter alone creating and radiating Jewish spiritual values to a materially prosperous Diaspora. He maintained that culture could not be injected from abroad; it must be experienced day by day and must evolve on the basis of inner need. While American democratic values and Jewish ethical and religious traditions were not identical, they were compatible and an individual could live both at the same time, without being disloyal to either.

The educator I. Silberberg-Cholewa (b. 1898), in the essays of *Man and People* (*Mentsh Un Folk*, 1967), and the folklorist and educator Shlome Simon (1895-1970), in several of his eighteen

books, also dealt with problems of Jewish education which would
further survival in the Diaspora.

S. D. Singer (1903-1970) collected his essays on forty Yiddish
writers in the volume *Poets, Novelists and Critics* (*Dikhter Un
Prozaiker,* 1959). He sought to discover in each of them the specific Jewish tone. He found it in a quality of lamentation. Some
escaped despair by nostalgic reconstruction of the past, others
cloaked their melancholy wisdom in ironic laughter, still others
became tragically homeless after having vainly sought a spiritual
haven in Communism.

Abraham Patt (b. 1903), in the critical essays of *Light and
Shade* (*Likht Un Shotn,* 1967) sought out not only the uniqueness of contemporary Yiddish writers but also related them to
the social, political and ideological environment in which they
matured and whose approach they reflected.

In the 1950's and 1960's, the most extreme champion of Yiddish
as an essential medium for Jewish survival in America and
throughout the world was the psychologist Abraham Aaron Roback (1890-1965). Though raised in the Anglo-French environment of Montreal and though writing generally in English, Roback
was led by his unbounded love for Yiddish to overstate and over-
rate the case for Yiddish. His earlier books on Yiddish were directed
at English readers and were designed to enlighten them on the literary and folklore treasures of this language. These books were
Curiosities of Yiddish Literature (1933), *I. L. Peretz, Psychologist
of Literature* (1935) and *The Story of Yiddish Literature* (1940).
His last works were written in Yiddish and aimed to dispel the pessimism that prevailed in Jewish circles, who saw the continually
shrinking number of Yiddish readers and speakers and who therefore foretold the inevitable demise of this tongue. In his books *The
Empire of Yiddish* (*Die Imperie Yiddish,* 1958) and *The Genius of
the Yiddish Language* (*Der Folksgeist In Der Yiddisher Shprakh,*
1964), Roback mustered a vast array of facts and arguments to
counteract the Cassandra voices. He believed in the continuing vitality of Yiddish, despite its apparent aging. He insisted that its
decline could still be arrested by a more positive and more optimistic approach toward it. To some readers he appeared as the Don
Quixote of a dying Yiddish tradition and to others as the last
apostle of the Yiddishist faith earlier expounded by Zhitlowsky.

Another embattled essayist and disciple of Zhitlowsky was Isaac
Liebman (1900-1959), editor of the *New Yorker Vochenblat.* In
this literary organ he championed minor Yiddish talents and tried

to save them from complete oblivion. He assembled about himself a circle of lovers of Yiddish and, like Roback, constantly ferreted out evidence of its unspent vitality.

Liebman's most faithful collaborator was the esthete Shea Tenenbaum (b. 1910), a painter in words, a lyricist in prose, an eternally young observer of nature upon which he nevertheless imposed his own moods, a lover of sunlight, flowers and people. He too was especially attracted to writers, sculptors, painters, sensitive individuals who were wayfarers without roots anywhere. In eighteen books of delicate essays and miniatures, he sketched portraits of men and women, famous and unknown, whom he encountered in the course of his wanderings from his boyhood in Poland, his maturing decade in Antwerp, Brussels and Paris, his years of illness and slow recovery in the Denver Tubercular Sanitorium where once Edelstadt, Yehoash and Leivick stayed, and his later years in New York.

A Guest on Earth (*Bei Der Velt Tsu Gast*, 1937), the title of his earliest tales, best characterized Tenebaum himself, the temporary sojourner who observed the passing scenes from the sideline and commented on them much later, after filtering them through the haze of memory.

As a literary critic, Tenenbaum prefers to concentrate on decadent and romantic poets who suffered as victims of society's cruelties or who dwelt in the shadow of death. Constantly aware of death and decay, he accompanies these phenomena with a melancholy smile and an intense fascination for their strange beauty. Four autobiographic volumes, appearing between 1960 and 1967, contain reminiscences of his early years. The best of these, *Isaac Ashmedai* (1965) centers about a Jewish Robin Hood who lived in a Polish forest and whose exploits during and after the First World War made an indelible impression upon young Tenenbaum. In contrast to Jews of the townlets who trembled in the presence of a Polish peasant, especially when he was inflamed by liquor or religious fanaticism, Isaac Ashmedai was fearless and brutal. He fought Jewish foes and robbed prosperous Polish peasants and town-dwellers until in his old age he was set upon in the forest on a dark night by a horde of assailants incited by his own son-in-law and clubbed to death.

Personalities by My Desk (*Geshtaltn Beim Shreibtish*, 1969) contained intimate insights into literary and artistic personalities whom Tenenbaum came to know during his third-of-a-century in New York. As an impressionistic essayist, he did not aim to add new facts about their lives but rather to reproduce the moods they conveyed to him, the eager listener to their conversations, the appreciative reader of their books, the connoisseur of their paintings, the lover of their music. Eclectic in his tastes, he preferred to call attention far more to epigones and minor yet genuine creative personalities, rather than to better known giants of the pen and the brush. In his miniatures, *Hunger For The Word* (*Hunger Tsum Vort*, 1971), he embodied his observations, impressions and reflections of life and literature and, above all, of the New York scene.

Jacob Kahan (b. 1900), who also stemmed from Poland, began his literary career with a book of memoirs in 1930 and continued with essays, narratives and poems published in Warsaw, Paris, New York and Tel Aviv. The normal tenor of his life was interrupted by the Second World War. He escaped to Soviet occupied Bialystok. In the autobiography, *Under Soviet Skies* (*Unter Die Sovietishe Himlen*, 1961), he narrated in a factual, unsentimental manner his experiences of the war years in a Bialystok prison, in a Karelian Labor Camp, in Uralian, Siberian and Caucasian refugee communities. He depicted not only the daily struggle against hunger, frost and the malevolence of brutal overseers and hardened fellow-victims, but also deeds of kindness and mutual help, especially when Jew met Jew and wordless bonds of understanding were forged.

Repatriated to Poland in 1946, Kahan left for Paris two years later and, after six years of Zionist activity there, he settled in New York in 1954. The setting for his narratives, however, continued to be pre-Holocaust Poland. His novel *The Erlich Family* (*Die Mishpokhe Erlich*, 1964) portrayed a middle class Jewish family in a middle-sized town of Russian Poland during the second decade of the twentieth century. The members of this family were not unique but typical of normal Jews. The stirring events of that decade—Czarist oppression, war, German occupation, revolution, the rise of Polish nationalism—all inflicted their hurt upon the Jewish population. However, Jewish resiliency and closely knit family ties enabled the community to recover quickly and to continue its traditional ways. Only among the youth was there an incursion of Zionist ideology, chiefly of a mildly religious trend.

In Berele, the main representative of the third generation of the Erlich family, the face of the author peered through. Berele was a good, gray, unobtrusive human being. He did not rebel against his respectable clan. He merely tried to assert his individuality now and then without, however, inflicting too much hurt upon those near and dear to him. When he met with resistance, his gentle nature was not strong enough to defy convention and he retreated from intransigence. He did not marry the girl he loved when she failed to obtain his mother's approval. He espoused Zionism as a bright vision of his people's ultimate redemption but, when the gates of Palestine were opened after 1920, he did not tear up his European roots and betake himself to the land of his heart's desire.

Kahan recorded in an honest, unsentimental, realistic style, with surrealist dreams interspersed here and there in the manner of avant-garde writers. He neither indulged in the mood of nostalgia at the passing of an historic epoch, as did so many Yiddish novelists of the post-mid-century decades, nor did he stir the heart with scenes of direct tragedy. At the critical moment, tragedy was averted or compensated for and life continued placidly, unheroically, with just a few scars as reminders of inflicted wounds.

In the lyrics of *Twilight* (*Bein Hashmashot*, 1966), Kahan provided an insight into the deepest layers of his soul. His domain was the middle range of emotions, mild melancholy which never sank to the abyss of despair, restrained joy which never exploded into ecstasy. He repeatedly likened himself to a tree whose branches were cut off in the midst of blossoming. Though the trunk survived, the tree never fully recovered and was still awaiting new blossoms. Kahan's free rhythms, mirroring his moods, flowed placidly like waves with even crests and even troughs.

The essays of *In Critical Times* (*In Gerangel Fun Tsait*, 1970) continued his mature observations and philosophical reflections on ultimate Jewish goals and contemporary Jewish needs. They revealed him to be still under the spell of Jabotinsky and Peretz, whose views he sought to synthesize and to adapt to the most recent Jewish reality in Israel and the Diaspora.

With the aging of Yiddish literature, Chicago, Detroit, Philadelphia and other once flourishing Yiddish centers faced extinction. Of the twenty-four poets active in the region from Midwest to North Pacific who had participated in an anthology of Yiddish verse compiled in 1932 and edited by Mattes Deitch, Ben Sholom and Shloime Schwartz, most had by 1970 passed on to the Beyond, a few were spending their last years in the warmer climate of Los Angeles, and only the aging Ezra Korman (b. 1888) in Detroit, Shloime Schwartz in Chicago, and Alter Esselin (b. 1889) in Milwaukee remained to bear testimony to formerly vibrant Yiddish communities.

Korman lamented, in the poems of *Signs and Symbols* (*Tsaykhns Un Tsayrufim*, 1969), that mothers could no longer sing sweet and intimate Yiddish lullabies to children and that America's Yiddish heart, New York's East Broadway, was beating ever more faintly. He wrote elegy upon elegy about the poets with whom he had once participated in a common striving and he even sang a dirge for himself, the belated poet of a people which was abandoning its thousand-year-old tongue. Yet, even as a condemned person continued to hope for a reprieve and a renewal of active life, so he too hoped against hope that, though the pillars of his Jewish generation had been uprooted by a whirlwind and were being covered with the dust of oblivion, there would nevertheless arise out of the enveloping earth a new structure, somehow, sometime.

Between the Atlantic and the Pacific, only Montreal among Canadian communities, and Los Angeles in the Far West were able to maintain themselves as centers of Yiddish activity in the 1970's, though not on the same scale as New York.

In 1911, when the pioneer Yiddish poet of Canada, J. I. Segal, arrived in Montreal, there were only 75,000 Jews in the entire vast territory of the Dominion. When he died in 1954, there were close to a quarter of a million Jews there. A third of them were living in Montreal and by 1970, this city alone was the home of 125,000 Jews, but the mother tongue of most of them was no longer Yiddish.

As early as 1907, Montreal could boast of a Yiddish daily, *Canader Adler,* founded by Hirsh Wolofsky (1876-1949). Israel Rabinowitch (1894-1964), who came to Montreal in the same year as Segal, edited this daily for more than three decades. Since his main interest was in musicology and folklore, Segal took over the direction of the literary features and offered a lasting outlet for the creative efforts of Montreal's Yiddish writers. Segal's own collection of lyrics, *From My World* (*Fun Mein Velt*), appeared in 1918, and was followed by ten more volumes from his prolific pen. In addition, he edited Montreal's first Yiddish literary periodicals, ably assisted by A. Almi (1892-1963) and A. S. Skolnikov (1896-1962). Among the early Canadian journalists, Benjamin G. Sack (1889-1967) was prominent as a writer of short stories and editorials for *Canader Adler* from its beginnings in 1907, the year of his arrival in Montreal. He is best known, however, for his authoritative *History of the Jews of Canada,* which he wrote in Yiddish in 1925 and which appeared in English in 1945. Israel Midrash (1894-1964), feuilletonist of *Canader Adler* since 1922, also published a valuable historical study, *Yesterday's Montreal (Montreal Fun Nekhtn,* 1947), in which he recounted the economic and cultural development of this metropolis during preceding decades. Mordecai Ginsburg (1894-1966), who began as poet and dramatist in Lodz, in the circle of Moshe Broderzon and Yitzkhak Katzenelson, joined the staff of *Canader Adler* in 1930 and wrote informative essays on Hebrew and Yiddish literary figures. Shimshon Dunsky (b. 1899), who arrived in Montreal in 1922, wrote chiefly on pedagogical subjects, but his most outstanding contribution was his Yiddish version of the Midrashic volumes, *Ekhah Rabbah* (1956), *Esther Rabbah and Ruth Rabbah* (1962) and *Koheleth Rabbah* (1967). In his translations, he sought to blend archaic Yiddish and contemporary Yiddish, refining the archaic through the filter of the more recent vernacular and flavoring the latter with the folkloristic aroma of the archaic.

The Jewish Public Library of Montreal was founded in 1914 by the Hebrew-Yiddish publicist Reuben Brainin and the scholar Yehuda Kaufman and soon became a center of Yiddish learning, especially after the poet Melech Ravitch began to organize seminars and adult education projects in Yiddish.

By 1934, when Hananya M. Kaiserman-Vital (1884-1950) published his study *Jewish Poets in Canada (Yiedishe Dikhter in Canada),* he could include sketches and selections from more than thirty poets who wrote in Yiddish and less than a dozen whose linguistic medium was English. The lyricist Ida Maze (1893-1962), who came to Montreal at the age of fourteen, influenced the literary scene far more as a patroness of Yiddish letters than with her own elegies, poems for children and essays. She was most active during the Hitler and post-Holocaust years in aiding refugee writers to be admitted to Canada and in providing them with opportunities to reach a reading public.

Jacob Zipper (b. 1900) arrived from Poland in 1925. As director of Montreal's Peretz Schools for more than forty years, he was influential in slowing down the decline of Yiddish, even though his superhuman efforts and those of Shlomo Wiseman (b. 1899), the director of Montreal's Folksshulen, could not arrest the transition to English of the children of the Yiddish-speaking immigrants. Zipper's first book, *There Was a Man (Geven Is A Mentsh,*

1940), consisted of five tales about the Baal Shem. His novel, *On the Other Side of the Bug River* (*Oif Yener Zeit Bug,* 1946), was largely autobiographic. It was followed by the narratives of *Between Rivers and Lakes* (*Tsvishn Teikhn Un Vassern,* 1961) and the poetic elegy *I Came Again to My Devastated Home* (*Kh'bin Vider In Mein Khorever Heim Gekumen,* 1965), a lament for his native Tishevitz, whose centuries-old Jewish community was wiped out by the Nazis. Though living in Canada since his twenties, he continued to center his literary themes about the Polish *shtetl,* in which he experienced difficulties and dangers but also the glamour and warmth of traditional Jewish ways.

Zipper's younger brother, Sholem Shtern (b. 1907), who came to Montreal two years after him, preferred subjects based on his observations of the Canadian scene. Shtern's first two volumes of verse, *Dawn* (*Es Likhtikt,* 1941) and *Morning* (*In Der Frie,* 1945), commingled proletarian, national and individualistic tones. However, it was his verse novels, *In Canada* (I, 1960; II, 1963) and *The White House* (*Dos Vaisse Hois,* 1967), which made him more widely known. The former is autobiographic. Its young Jewish hero is forced to leave his native Poland and the impoverished but morally healthy and intellectually vibrant Jewish community as a result of the rising tide of anti-Semitism. He betakes himself to Montreal and there he has to struggle desperately for mere bread, while his soul aches for poetry, love, human brotherhood and Jewish culture. The various ideologies that tempted and agitated immigrant youth between the two world wars pass in review and are embodied in living characters and clashing temperaments. In the background, casting a gloomy and nostalgic pall over rapidly changing events, are the parents, sweethearts and comrades in the Old Country, over whom looms the nighing catastrophe.

Because of tightening immigration restrictions in the 1930's, fewer Yiddish writers found their way to Canada. At the beginning of this decade, Noah Isaac Gotlib (1903-1967) came from Kovno and M. M. Shaffir (b. 1909) from Bukovina, while Simcha Bunim Petrushka (1893-1950) came from Warsaw in the summer of 1939, only a few weeks before the Nazi bombardment of the Polish capital. Gotlib was the author of eight books of verse and two of prose, but found far more readers for his sketches and essays during his quarter of a century on the staff of the *Canader Adler.* His last volume, *Sixty* (*Zekhtsik,* 1965), contained not only his ripest lyrics but also evaluations of his work by his contemporaries. Shaffir published his first collection of lyrics in 1940, four more in the 1960's and his sixth in 1971. In his lyrics there is in general a rejection of the loud metropolis in which he spent his mature years and a longing for the quiet Bessarabian townlet of his boyhood. He escapes from his basic sadness and homelessness to an idealized pre-holocaust Jewish world which takes on ever more glamorous, romantic hues the further it recedes in time. He clings to Yiddish as his chief link with this past and he enriches this tongue with caressing, melodious verses which mirror his extreme sensitiveness. He feels the pain not only of all suffering human creatures but also of all things born to life and doomed to death, including the blade of grass cut down by the mower, the Siamese-twinned plums bitten apart by voracious teeth, and the watermelon whose red blood is spilled and whose flesh is cannibalized. Petrushka was an educator and scholar, who completed a two-volume Yiddish encyclopedia during his first years in Montreal. However, his supreme achievement was his Yiddish translation of the *Mishna* in six volumes (1945-1949), a translation accompanied by a detailed interpretation based on traditional authorities, medieval and modern.

The post-Holocaust exodus of Jews from Europe brought to Montreal Peretz Miranski, the poet of Young Vilna, Chava Rosenfarb, who had survived Auschwitz, Abraham Eisen (b. 1909), essayist and short-story writer who survived Vilna's ghetto and several concentration camps, Jehuda Elberg (b. 1912), a survivor of Warsaw's ghetto and author of the collection of narratives *Under Copper Skies* (*Unter Kupern Himlen,* 1951), Mordecai Hasid (b. 1909), a native of Bessarabia, who published his first volume of short stories in 1938 only to have every copy destroyed in the Vilna ghetto, and whose lyrics did not appear in book form until 1969 under the title *The Cry of Generations* (*Doyres Shrayem Mikh Ariber*). In subject-matter Hasid's lyrics ranged from biblical themes to contemporary Israel, New York, and man's landing on the moon. Their moods ranged from sadness, which never verged on despair, to joy, which did not explode into ecstasy. However, the most prominent of the narrators and poets to reach Montreal after the Holocaust was Rochel Korn (b. 1898).

Stemming from East Galicia, she felt rooted in the Polish earth and began her career with poems and novelettes in Polish. She was still under Polish literary influences when she published her first collection of Yiddish lyrics, *Village* (*Dorf,* 1828), and the realistic short stories of *Earth* (*Erd,* 1936). Seen through her eyes, the peasants of the Galician villages and the Jews who lived in their midst had a sturdy, optimistic outlook upon life, even though bread was not easily earned. However, as tensions between Jews and their neighbors increased on the eve of the Second World War, sad visions foreboding a coming catastrophe arose before her. In a lyric of January 1939 about Poland, she exclaimed: "I never knew that I was a stranger to you, a guest who came to you for a mere fifteen or twenty generations, for I grew up with your springs and summers, your forests, fruits, and harvests. . . . O Earth, if I will have to leave you for exile, every limb of mine and thine will feel the rupture, and bloodied will be you, my most beloved earth, and I and my song."

The war sent her reeling thousands of miles to the east and, in the poems composed in Soviet Asia, she became aware of her homelessness and indeed of the homelessness of every diaspora Jew. In Ufa, Fergana, and Tashkent, her lyrics wept for dear ones left behind whose fate was unknown to her. At war's end, she learned that husband, mother, brothers and all her kin, except the daughter with whom she had fled, had already perished. She could not return to the land of her birth which had been denuded of its Jews. She found a refuge in Canada. During her first decade in Montreal, her thoughts still centered about the catastrophe that had overwhelmed her people and her short stories were based on tragic incidents that had come to her attention. In her story "The Last Road," she portrayed a ghetto family which was faced with a heartbreaking decision. In the fall of 1942, each household was required to give up one member for the last road so that the quota of victims demanded of the Judenrat by the Nazis might be filled. If a family refused to cooperate, all its members would be seized. How to fulfill this cruel demand tested the mettle of each member of the family from the grandmother to the adolescent grandchild. In other stories, the long, hard road travelled by the few fortunate survivors of ghettos, camps and slavery was narrated with emphasis on the psychological states and the moral stamina of the closely knit Jewish families that were being pulverized by their oppressors.

The poems of the 1960's, *Songs of the Other Side* (*Fun Yener Zeit Lied*, 1962) and *Grace of Words* (*Die Gnad Fun Vort*, 1968), reflected calmer moods of the Canadian landscape and of Israel which she visited both before and after the Six Day War. However, sadness, silence and shadows from the past still hovered about her and infiltrated her thoughts and her dreams. Her verses were still lined with tears. She could not forget that the grain being harvested in distant Galicia grew above the ashes of her dear ones. She saw herself as Job, who had been through bitterest suffering and had been later recompensed by God. In his great travail, Job maintained his faith in his Creator. But in his restored prosperous condition, he hurled his protest against a God who, for the sake of a wager, had afflicted him so sorely and in whom he could no longer believe with his former fervor. While the poems of Canada described mainly autumnal and winter scenes and harmonized with the lyricist's aging, melancholy moods, her poems of Israel were interlaced with Messianic visions. She found divine radiance spread over the naked sands of the Negev. In the feverish glow of the desert, in the crooked, climbing lanes of Safed, and along the shores of Kinneret, she felt her poetic creativity reviving. But her sadness and her loneliness never departed from her.

Sadness and loneliness also characterized Melech Ravitch's aging poems written in Montreal in his seventies. The dynamic poet of the Khaliastre, who had stormed Parnassus together with Peretz Markish and Uri Zvi Greenberg half a century earlier, was overcome by a dominant mood of tiredness. After having warred with God and the world in searing verses, he finally sought to make peace with them. After his long probing into the mysteries of life and death, good and evil, freedom and necessity, under the guidance of his adored Spinoza and Peretz, he came to the conclusion that no answer was within his reach. He envied the stone that was silent, the blue flower which was unaware that its blueness would soon fade, the birds that flew without wondering why. He himself belonged to the only species that questioned and brooded and that could not desist from questioning and brooding. He tried to banish the terror of death by continually invoking this brother of sleep. He, who belonged to various literary groups and who was adored by readers on all continents, concluded that every individual was essentially lonely and that God was even lonelier than man, since man could escape loneliness by death but God, who was immortal, had to persist in unique solitude throughout eternity.

Montreal's eminence as a center of Yiddish creativity preceded that of Los Angeles. However, the mass immigration of Jews to the Pacific metropolis, which began with the First World War, reached a much higher crest during the following half century and attracted many more writers who wished to spend their aging

years in its mellow climate. Its Jewish population increased from
about 10,000 in 1912 to 20,000 half-a-decade later. It doubled
again during the following half decade. By the end of World War
II, the number had risen to 200,000 and by 1970 to over half-a-
million. Its Yiddish-speaking Jews teemed with vitality when they
pioneered there. However, as the immigrant generation aged and
the younger generation made the linguistic transition to English,
Yiddish creativity ebbed. By 1972 the average age of still active
Yiddish writers was about seventy and that of their readers not
much less.

Though the first Yiddish organ in California, the weekly *Yiddishe Shtime,* was founded in San Francisco in 1913, with Yekheskel Wortsman (1878-1938) as editor, it could not maintain
itself there. It was revived in Los Angeles in 1924. An attempt
was even made to convert it into a daily, with the first issue
appearing on December 11, 1927. However, after forty-seven days,
it again reverted to a weekly.

Wortsman was a talented Zionist publicist. In his student days
in Switzerland, he had joined Chaim Weizmann and Nachman
Syrkin in founding the first Zionist academic circle. In London,
he had edited in 1904 a literary monthly which propagated Zionism and, on emigrating to America, he had edited journals in New
York, Boston, Atlanta and Montreal before coming to California.
Wortsman found few writers to assist him and soon left for the
East. The journal managed to survive as *California Jewish Voice*
by becoming bi-lingual, with a single page in Yiddish, later only
a single column, and finally entirely in English.

In 1926, the Los Angeles Yiddish Culture Club was founded,
offering a platform for Yiddish writers who had settled there.
Isaac Friedland (1884-1965), one of its founders, its leading spirit
for four decades and editor of its organ *Heshbon,* a quarterly review of literary and cultural activities, had arrived in Los Angeles
in 1913 from Utah after the collapse of the cooperative Clarion
Colony which he had helped to establish. In the first part of his
book *Virgin Soil* (*Roi-Erd,* 1949), he described how a group of
idealistic sweatshop workers along the Eastern Seaboard, suffering
from the economic crisis of 1907, conceived the project of a return
to the soil. They set up the agricultural colony of Clarion in
Utah in 1910. At first they were happy to lead a life close to
nature, even though they were ill-prepared for the harsh climate,
the paucity of water and the backbreaking toil. Their enthusiasm
enabled them to survive for three years, but when a storm de-

stroyed their crops one season and a drought the following season, they had to confess failure and scattered in all directions. Friedland chose Los Angeles. His observations of Jewish life along the Pacific coast were recorded in fascinating short stories. Equally valuable were his reminiscences of pre-immigrant years contained in the volume *In Days of Struggle* (*In Teg Fun Gerangel*, 1962). The aging author recalled his youthful wandering after he had to leave his home in Russia because of the failure of the uprising of 1905. Arriving in Paris, he found himself in the midst of disillusioned ex-revolutionists who had reverted from the extreme of passionate self-sacrifice and asceticism to the opposite extreme of egocentrism and the worship of the flesh. The mood of Artzibashev's *Sanine*, the best-selling novel of the post-revolutionary years, was dominant in Parisian emigré circles no less than among the blasé intellectuals remaining in the Czarist realm. From the mood of Saninism, Friedland emerged and, after waystations in New York and Utah, found a lasting home in California.

Yiddish literary pioneers of Los Angeles included Israel Osman (1887-1951), who came there a year after Friedland. In his book *Experiences* (*Nisiones*, 1926), he retold in a warm simple style Jewish folktales he had heard in his young days in the Old Country. He was followed in 1918 by Ezekiel Brownstone (1897-1968), the editor of short-lived literary periodicals and the author of thirteen volumes of poetry, essays and literary criticism. His reminiscences, *Pro Domo* (*Fun Eign Hoiz*, 1963), written late in life, revealed him to be a keen observer and faithful chronicler of the Yiddish scene. He portrayed many Yiddish men-of-letters he had known as colorful human beings, with their striving, frustration, foibles and final loneliness.

The arrival of the poet H. Rosenblatt in 1921, and the novelists L. Shapiro and S. Miller soon thereafter, raised the prestige of Los Angeles as a Yiddish literary center and made it attractive especially as a final home for ailing or aging writers, among whom the earliest were the poet of "Die Yunge," Reuben Ludwig (1895-1926), the poet of Chicago, L. Mattes (1897-1929), who vainly tried to regain their health there, and the Hebrew-Yiddish narrator, M. M. Dolitzky (1858-1931), who turned to the writing of fables in his seventies. There Peretz Hirshbein found a congenial circle of admirers after roaming over the globe.

There Kalman Marmor (1876-1956) completed the two volumes of his memoirs which were published posthumously in 1959. There Zalmen Zylbercweig (b. 1894) compiled and edited the final volumes of his *Lexicon of the Yiddish Theater*. There the aging S. Bunyan, who landed in Galveston in 1911 in the spring of his life, spent the autumn of his life writing his memoirs *From Spring to Autumn (Fun Friling Biz Harbst,* 1965), whose most interesting chapters dealt with his experiences in the Texas Panhandle during the oil boom of World War I. There Gershon Einbinder (1900-1964), who wrote under the pseudonym of Chaver Paver, worked on his fictionalized autobiographies *Gershun Meyer dem Blindens* (1958) and *Gershun in America* (1963), in which he reviewed his early life in the Ukrainian city of Bershad, his difficulties with revolutionary and reactionary hordes who made life unbearable for Jews, his flight to America and his experiences after his arrival in the land of the free. There the educator and Yiddish ideologist, Abraham Golomb, arrived from Mexico in his seventy-sixth year and found a large group of disciples who later united to pay tribute to him in a volume of essays published on the occasion of his eightieth birthday. There Pintche Berman (b. 1892), in the poems of *Open Windows (Ofene Fenzter,* 1960) and *Soughing Wind (In Geroish Fun Vint,* 1970), turned from suffering and sorrow to hymn life's delight, beauty inexhaustible, goodness wherever found, Israel rearisen, and Diaspora Jewry convalescing. There the poet and essayist Mattes Deitsch (1894-1966), who in his younger years had helped to found "Young Chicago," a group of mid-Western Yiddish writers active in the 1920's, spent his last two decades and published his collected poems *To the Nearest Star (Tsum Noentstn Shtern,* 1959). There I. E. Ronch (b. 1889), another poet of "Young Chicago," published his twilight lyrics under the symbolic title *It's Getting Late (Es Vert Shoin Shpet,* 1970). There H. Goldowsky (1893-1948) and Sara Fel-Yellin (1895-1968) penned poems of proletarian solidarity, and Esther Shumiacher-Hirshbein and Malke Heifetz-Tusman lyrics of feminine delicacy.

There the dramatist and narrator Jacob Singer (1902-1964) wrote the novel *Young Jacobs (Der Yunger Jacobs,* 1963), in which he, the prototype of the older Jacobs, portrayed the dilemma of the young generation of California Jews who, in the Second World War, had fought side by side with other Americans and who then assumed that as Americans they were like unto their contemporaries in every respect except religious affiliation. However, they were soon compelled to realize that in the eyes of thir fellow Americans they would always remain outsiders, aliens, Jews. In the course of the hero's wrestling with his Jewishness, a vast range of problems passed in review and he finally had to conclude that not by desperately trying to efface his Jewish traits but rather by living as a Jewish personality could he uproot the dislike of his historic and ethnic group still lodged within the hearts of his non-Jewish comrades. These would then accept him as their equal, though not as kin of their kin.

In Los Angeles too, the storyteller Noah Goldberg (1902-1968) found the leisure to look back upon his young years in Russia, Argentina and New York. His three volumes of realistic short stories dealt with simple souls in the Old World and the New, their silent suffering, their patient enduring of hunger and privations, their intolerance of wrong, injustice and cruelty. Though Goldberg was aware that brutality, greed, vanity and other vicious traits often motivated human behavior, he preferred to emphasize gentleness, forbearance and self-sacrifice, noble traits which made life more bearable for everyone. He therefore let a gleam of light penetrate sad, murky, dull existences and brought warmth, cheer and brightness to chilled souls and saved them from inner emptiness and grim disillusionment. His stories were morally elevating. His characters, when exposed to critical situations, came to prefer decency to wealth, simplicity to ostentation, family loyalty to personal aggrandizement, old-fashioned Jewish living to alluring epicureanism.

Goldberg's most important work was his novel *Wild-Grass* (*Vildgros*, 1964), in which he painted on a broad canvas and with glowing colors the escape of Argentine peons from feudal oppression in the nineteenth century. Trekking to a primitive Patagonian valley under the leadership of a simple, good-natured Gaucho, they tilled the virgin earth and developed a prosperous colony on a collectivist basis. The taming of the wild region was paralleled by the taming of wild forces within the souls of these untutored human beings. But Goldberg also showed the irresistible lure that modern civilization exercised upon the children of the contented colonists when reports of glamorous city life reached the remote valley.

Heshbon, the literary quarterly founded in 1946, with H. Rosenblatt, I. Friedland and Elihu Tenenholz as its first editors, completed in 1971, under the editorship of A. Posy, a quarter of a century as the principal organ of Yiddish literature in the Far West. In the two decades before its founding, more than fifty volumes of prose and verse were published by writers of Los Angeles. During the following decade another fifty books of literary value appeared. But thereafter the decline began. Writers aged and died, with no successors in sight. Their readers also aged and declined in number. For the children of these writers and readers, Yiddish was a dimly remembered tongue and for the grandchildren it was an historical relic of which a few picturesque phrases remained with which to interlard English speech.

24

YIDDISH IN ISRAEL

Pioneers of Yiddish • Izban • Onochi • Leibl •
Papiernikov • Shamri • Lev • Mastboim • Rives
• Shargel • Biletzky • Essayists • Basok • Shen-
hod • Potash • Locker • Chain-Shimoni • Manik-
Lederman • Young Israel • Mordecai Tsanin •
Eisnman • Jungman • Shavinsky • Israel Kaplan
• Hofer • Spiegel • Olitzky • Tel Aviv Center •
Jacob Friedman • Sutzkever

IN PRE-MANDATORY PALESTINE, Yiddish was the spoken language of the Ashkenazi sector of the population and Hebrew the written medium of communication and also the oral link between Ashkenazim and Sephardim. The Zionist pioneers, in their efforts to establish Hebrew as the spoken language and the unifying force of the national revival, engaged in a crusade against German, French and Yiddish, the three rival tongues vying for the loyalty of various Jewish groups and institutions. The case for German, backed by the Hilfsverein der deutschen Juden, was lost after the battle of languages early in 1914 over the medium of instruction for Haifa's Technion and after Germany's defeat in World War I. The case for French, backed by the Alliance Israelite Universelle, was lost when the mandate for Palestine was not assigned to France. Yiddish then remained the principal target for attack by the militant Hebraists, who looked upon it as the expression of the unregenerated denizens of the Russian Pale and the Galician townlets. By 1948 the victory of Hebrew was complete and antagonism to Yiddish abated.

Symbolic of the reconciliation of Hebraists and Yiddishists in the new state was the founding under Histadrut auspices of the literary quarterly *Di Goldene Keyt* in 1949 and the establishment of a chair in Yiddish at the Hebrew University in 1951.

In the first issue of the quarterly, Yosef Shprinzak, the Speaker of the Knesset, called for an end to the antagonism between the two Jewish languages. No longer could Yiddishists, in his opinion, maintain that Hebrew was the tongue solely of intellectuals and reactionaries, and no longer could Hebraists deride Yiddish as a jargon of the Galut. The popularity of Pinski, Opatoshu, Leivick, Reisen and Kadia Molodowsky in Israel surpassed their vogue in many Yiddish-speaking centers of the Galut. Israel theaters were acquainting the young generation with the best dramas of Peretz, Sholom Aleichem, Pinski, Asch, Leivick, Hirshbein, Bergelson and I. J. Singer. With Hebrew as the firmly entrenched daily tongue in Israel, the time had come to establish there a literary base from which the Yiddish word could also resound and about which creative literary forces could gather and make their contributions to the treasury of Jewish life.

Similar calls for an end to the alienation between Hebrew and Yiddish writers were voiced by the Hebrew poet Jacob Fichman and the Yiddish dramatist H. Leivick. The former recalled that Mendele, Sholom Aleichem, Bialik, Schneour and Berkovitch attained their great literary mastery because they were organically rooted in a Jewish essence which was not split apart into segments and fragments. They were creative in both languages. His own contemporaries, Agnon, Hazaz and Tchernikhovsky, though writing in Hebrew, were nevertheless products of a bilingual tradition. Theirs was perhaps the last generation that had this bilingual base and to it they owed their timelessness as well as their contemporaneity.

Di Goldene Keyt began under the editorship of Abraham Sutzkever and Avraham Levinson. When the latter died in 1955 Eliezer Pines became co-editor. By 1972 more than seventy-five issues of this quarterly had appeared and its position was assured as the preeminent literary organ of Yiddish writers the world over.

At the inauguration ceremony of the Yiddish Department of the Hebrew University and of the first Israeli professor of Yiddish, the eminent critic and essayist Dov Sdan, Pinski recalled that twenty-four years earlier David Shapiro, publisher of the New York Yiddish daily *Der Tog,* had offered to finance the establishing of a chair in Yiddish at the Hebrew University and that the University had declined the offer. Pinski was followed by other Hebrew and Yiddish speakers, all of whom welcomed the changed atmosphere which encouraged creativity in both languages.

Before the proclamation of the Jewish state, Palestine was not an important center for Yiddish letters or for Yiddish publishing. An attempt was made as early as 1876 to publish a Yiddish journal which would minister to the needs of Jerusalem's Ashkenazim, whose knowledge of Hebrew was inadequate. The first issues of this journal, *Shaare Zion,* inaugurated on May 19, 1876, were bilingual, with Hebrew and Yiddish in alternate columns. The city's Ashkenazim were at that time divided into two feuding camps, Maskilim and Hassidim, and each had its own Hebrew organ. *Shaare Zion* sought to mediate between both extremist groups. However, after a year, the Yiddish columns were eliminated. A new Yiddish periodical made its appearance in 1877, the semi-monthly *Die Rose,* edited by Israel Dov Frumkin and Michel Hacohen. It too did not last long. Yiddish writers in Israel were a rarity before the First World War. Interest in Yiddish manifested itself mainly in translations into Hebrew of outstanding Diaspora writers. In the decade before Israel's independence, such translations included works by Leivick, Opatoshu, Bergelson, Der Nister, Kulback, Onochi, Segalowitch, Pinski, Weissenberg, I. J. Singer, Kadia Molodowsky and Moshe Nadir. The first pioneers of Yiddish found life in Palestine unpropitious for their literary efforts and generally continued on to America.

Such a pioneer was Ephraim Auerbach who came to Palestine in 1912 and whose first volume, *Caravans (Karavanen,* 1918), hymned the joy of Chalutziut. He left for America after fighting under Josef Trumpeldor in the Jewish Legion. His longing for Israel was abiding, though he could only satisfy it through brief visits, and was evidenced in the poetic volumes *Golden Sunset (Gildene Shkiye,* 1959) and *The White City (Die Vaisse Shtot,* 1960).

Auerbach's fellow-legionnaire was the poet Zishe Weinper, whose first book of lyrics, *From Our Land (Fun Undzer Land,* 1920), dealt with his experiences when he joined other young Jews to redeem Zion, then still in the hands of the Turks.

A third legionnaire, the poet, journalist and literary critic Abraham Blei (b. 1893), remained in Palestine until 1927 and helped to found the first organization of Yiddish writers and journalists. Then he too returned to New York.

Nor was the poet Yehoash any more successful in his effort to settle in the Holy Land, for which he left in 1914 and from which he returned in 1917. But the impact of these few years upon his later poetry was enduring.

After the war many Yiddish writers visited the mandated territory, wrote in glowing terms about the hardy Jewish pioneers, and left. Such writers were Sholem Asch, David Pinski, Peretz Hirshbein and Abraham Coralnik. Tolush came to Palestine twice with the intention of remaining there, but loneliness and malaria compelled him to leave. His experiences and observations gave him the rich material for the first Yiddish novel of the idealistic Zionist settlers, *The Surging Sea* (*Der Yam Roisht*, 1921). The short story writer Meir Corona (1890-1965) went through so many hardships as a laborer and road-builder during his Palestinian years, 1920-1925, that he finally left for Mexico but his enthusiasm for the ideal of Labor Zionism remained undimmed. Menashe Unger (1899-1969) came to Palestine in 1925, helped to edit the first Yiddish literary journal *Onheib* in 1928, and left for New York in 1930. There he became a popular writer on Hassidism. His six volumes on various aspects of this religious movement contained a mine of valuable information and stressed the social responsibility of Hassidic leaders. Liuba Wasserman (b. 1905) came as a pioneer in 1925. She toiled as a farmhand, as a builder of roads, as a hospital employee. She agitated for better conditions for her fellow workers and suffered imprisonment by the British authorities. She participated with poems and short stories in the earliest Yiddish publications. The lyrics of her booklet, *Twilight* (*Farnakhtn*, 1931), however, were full of longing for the Russian townlet she had left behind. Soon thereafter she returned to Soviet Russia and in 1934 settled in Birobidjan.

Shmuel Izban (b. 1905) was also animated by an ideal of *chalutziut* when he arrived from a Polish townlet in 1920. He too toiled as a laborer, building roads, planting trees and erecting buildings in Jaffa's new suburb of Tel Aviv, but in 1937 he departed for America after encountering too many difficulties. During his first year in Jaffa, his family was pillaged by rioting Arabs. At the coffee-house maintained by his father, he met artists, actors and writers, and was stimulated to compose sketches and short stories in Hebrew for local journals and in Yiddish for American and Polish newspapers. His first tales of the new land were published in 1925, but his first novel, *Masses* (*Massen*, 1929), dealt with the Russian Revolution of 1905 and his second novel, *Across the War Years* (*Kver 1914-1918*, 1936), with Poland during World War I. Apparently in his daily struggle for bread, he did not yet grasp the epic proportions of the effort to establish a Jewish homeland. Only decades later did Israel become the main theme for his long narratives.

After emigrating to New York, Izban wrote the two-volume novel of American Jewish life, *Heirs Who Arrived Too Late* (*Die Shpete Yorshim*, 1955), and nine tales of the multiracial American metropolis, *The City of Wrath* (*Die Shtut Fun Tsorn*, 1955). Only two of these tales contain Jewish characters and these characters are imbued with a sense of responsibility toward their fellow-men and rise morally beyond normal stature. In the opening story, Mr. Winter, an American Jew, cannot forget that, but for the grace of God, he too might have been among the broken survivors of the Nazi horror. He therefore takes the lead in a relief and rescue operation and is even willing to enlist the aid of a former Jew-hater in such a moral cause. In the second tale, a physician who has but tenuous ties to Jewishness, nevertheless personifies Jewish moral idealism in his practice of medicine. For thirty-five years he prefers to remain in the poor neighborhood of Williamsburg and to minister to its ever changing but always underprivileged residents. He not only lays his healing hands on their festering sores and lacerated bodies but he also shares with them his wisdom and his compassionate heart. Izban's other tales portray German denizens of Yorkville, Italians of Mulberry Street, Chinese of Pell Street. His men bear the traits of their ethnic group but his women are less differentiated as to their origin. In their youth, these women are all beautiful, adventurous, hungry for life, unafraid of danger. In their old age, they retain glamorous memories to warm them. The most precious tale presents Chance as in reality Destiny, a succession of events prearranged for human puppets by the supreme puppeteer of the universe. Two young people, unknown to each other, despair of finding lasting joy in life. Each of them, therefore, goes a-hunting for a moment's pleasure in order to dispel the melancholy that always hovers about them. They meet by chance, they seek to conceal their true intentions from each other, and yet they end by finding the unexpected: lasting joy, ultimate fulfillment.

Izban had a keen eye for details. He superimposed a romantic glaze over his realistic portraits of the underworld and the demimonde, thus commingling the strange and the exotic with the familiar and the normal.

Though remaining in America during and after the Second World War, Izban became ever more obsessed in his imagination with the events in Palestine, where the Jewish settlers were engaged in a desperate struggle for survival and for the ingathering of the refugees from the Holocaust. He aroused much attention with his stories of the Illegals who overcame seemingly insuperable difficulties, *Illegal Jews Cleave Seas (Umlegale Yiedn Shpalten Yamen,* 1948) and with his two-volume novel about an Israeli family, *Family Caro* (1949).

Izban's mastery of the historical novel of Jewish content was displayed in *Queen Jezebel* (1960) and in *Jericho* (1966). Both recreate Israel's past in vivid colors and in a style tinged with an archaic, biblical flavor. *Jericho* is an imaginative reconstruction of the fall of this ancient city to the army led by Joshua. It projects the conflict between a mighty but decaying and superstition-ridden urban civilization and the God-inspired, nomadic confederation of tribes whom Moses had hammered into a free people. Colorful mass scenes abound; individual ambitions clash with an awakened social consciousness; intense emotions are tamed by religious fervor. The novel is Izban's supreme literary achievement.

Though the 1920's were not propitious for Yiddish creativity in Palestine, some writers remained and survived all hardships. Zalman Yitzkhak Onochi (1878-1947), who had begun as a Hebrew writer in 1903 and as a Yiddish writer in 1905, tried to settle in Palestine for the first time as early as 1910 but returned to Russia before World War I. After the Revolution, he lived in Moscow, Berlin and Buenos Aires. His restless years came to an end in Tel Aviv in 1924. His decades in Palestine, however, were not as creative as his earlier ones when his monologues of *Reb Abba* established his fame and were circulated in Yiddish, Hebrew and German.

Yosef Papiernikov (b. 1899) arrived from Warsaw in 1924 and penned lyrics in Tel Aviv about his new home *In the Sunny Land (In Zuniken Land,* 1927). His friend Daniel Leibl (1891-1967) arrived in the same year as Papiernikov and Onochi and continued to fight for Yiddish, even though he wrote effective Hebrew prose for Hebrew journals. Once Leibl was even injured by demonstrators against Yiddish. He edited publications of the Literaten-Verein and the weekly *Neivelt,* sponsored by the Labor Zionists. He believed in one Jewish people and one Jewish literature. However, since Jews had been blessed or burdened with two languages in his generation, he wished to retain both, and as journalist, editor and scholar, he expressed himself with equal skill in both. It was Leibl who wrote the introduction to Papiernikov's first songs and encouraged him to persist. The latter published additional books of Yiddish verse in the 1930's and 1940's, despite the surging tide of militant Hebraism that surrounded him. "My

Yiddish song weeps in me as weeps a lonely, orphaned child that once had a home, a father, a mother, brothers, sisters, and survived alone, exposed to the storm."

Recognition finally came to Papiernikov after the new state was established. His lyric volume *The Land of a Second Beginning (Dos Land fun Tsveitn Bereshith, 1954)* was the first to win a literary award. Melech Ravitch then called attention to the jubilant spirit of this collection of songs about Israel. "One senses the joy of a Polish-Jewish Chalutz who was privileged, after thousands of years of longing, to witness the genesis of actual realization." But the volume also contained elegiac tones, because the singer could not penetrate with his warm Yiddish song to the Hebrew-speaking people of his beloved Israel. Their ears were closed to him, his world of dreams, his castles in the air, his pure poetry.

Among the early pioneers who settled in Kibbutzim, Arye Shamri (b. 1907) and Abraham Lev (1910-1970) continued decade after decade to create Yiddish lyrics of distinction in the midst of their Hebraic environment. Shamri stemmed from a pious home in Poland but was caught up in the enthusiastic, idealistic youth movement of Hashomer Hatzair. He left for Israel in 1929 and joined the Kibbutz Ein Shemer, from which he derived his new name. A tiller of the soil and a poet, he felt himself allied to the earth but not its slave. He sang of his love for nature, people, things, his nostalgia for the Hassidic atmosphere of his childhood, his longing for joy in a tear-stained world. In addition to his own books of verse, he edited the anthology *Roots (Vurtzlen, 1966)*, in which sixty Yiddish poets and narrators of Israel wrote of their rootedness in this land and of the miraculous changes effected during the half century of their travail there.

Abraham Lev stemmed from the literary group "Young Vilna," and came to Palestine in 1932. In the poems of his first volume, with the symbolic title *In Your Portals (In Dein Tor, 1937)*, he described his entering the new land like a poor man looking for a haven that could become his permanent home on life's long road. He found it in the young Kibbutz Givat Hashlosha. He was happy to carry the stones to build its first roads and to prepare the ground that would yield bread from Jewish stalks. He was proud to have become a peasant, to eat the produce of his own toil, and to dwell in the hut he had himself erected. His days were hard but purposeful and he saw the desert transformed to fruitful Jewish earth by his labor. After four decades, he, the sower of seeds and of songs, still had no regrets as he looked about him. A tree he had planted, and which inspired his early verses, had grown majestically. It offered him shade and invited him to dreams. In death he would enter into the tree's sap and emerge as a green star on its crest. In "Yoshe Ber," composed in 1946, the longest poem of his volume *In a Vise* (*In Klem,* 1967), he followed the inner and outer experiences of a typical Kibbutznik and concluded that such a person shared with his comrades common joys, festivities and dangers, but not individual sorrows. The volume also included gripping lyric laments for the poet's eighteen-year-old son who died while with Israel's defense forces. This was the most painful price which Israeli fathers were called upon to pay for Israel's survival and growth in freedom.

The novelist Yoel Mastboim (1884-1957) was among the keenest observers of the difficult pioneering years under the British mandate. He emigrated to Palestine in 1933 and wrote many stories of his experiences. Of his projected trilogy of Palestine between 1933 and 1948, only the first volume, *Power of the Earth* (*Koakh fun der Erd,* 1951), appeared, embracing the years 1933 to 1936. These were years of tremendous progress during which new communal settlements and new urban developments were started. The Arab riots of 1936 tested their viability. Mastboim contrasted the severe, dangerous, productive life of the Kibbutzim with the ragged, unproductive, urban existence of the older religious inhabitants, who were in large measure dependent upon charity from Jews abroad. In the aging Uncle Jonathan, he portrayed a traditional Jew who arrived in the Holy Land and was at first disappointed with its youth. This youth preferred hard physical toil in agricultural settlements to the easier occupations of the Galut and was subordinating individual interests to cooperative endeavors. Uncle Jonathan was more at home among the Hassidim of Mea Shearim and when a new marriage brought him sufficient capital to start a commercial enterprise which augured handsome profits, he spoke scornfully of the striving of the peasant idealists who clung tenaciously to the soil that barely gave them a meager sustenance. But when the hour of danger struck in 1936 and his wealth went up in flames, then he came to understand the new mentality and the new moral values of the Kibbutzniks.

Abraham Rives (1900-1962), who came to Palestine in 1925, also dealt in his stories with the mandatory period realistically, avoiding the temptation to sentimentalize the personalities of the early settlers. In his first collection, *Transplantation* (*Iberflants,* 1947),

he too included episodes of 1936, when Arab attacks imperilled
the peaceful development of kibbutzim, but his emphasis was on
the backbreaking daily toil which only slowly yielded fruitful
results. In his only novel, *With the Ship Tchicherin* (*Mit der
Shif Tchicherin,* 1959), he dealt unromantically with the post-
revolutionary *aliya* of young Russian Jews who had been infected
with Zionism and who came to build a new life for themselves in
a Jewish homeland. They fought for Jewish labor in orange plantations whose owners had until then employed only cheap Arab
labor. They went out to strengthen the kibbutzim along the
shores of the Sea of Galilee. They furthered trade unionism in
Tel Aviv's first factories. But disillusionment often plagued them.
Some fell afoul of the British authorities who rightly or wrongly
suspected them of Communist leanings and harassed them. The
novel ended with the deportation of the heroine on the same
ship, Tchicherin, with which she had arrived two years earlier.
In the story *Hershele's Aliya* (1949), he bared the travails of
the survivors of the Holocaust as they made their way in unsea-
worthy vessels and reached the shores of the desired land after
eluding British pursuit, their gradual recovery from haunting
memories and persistent nightmares under the influence of kibbutz
work and kibbutz compassion, the healing power of love which
augurs the return of happiness.

Jacob Zvi Shargel (b. 1905), who arrived in Palestine a few
months after Rives, was the antipode of a realist. In the poems
of his first decade, *In Blue Light* (*In Bloien Likht,* 1937), he sang
not of Petach Tikvah's orange groves, in which he toiled, but
rather of the picturesque caravan of camels which sauntered past
these groves. With youth in his veins, every day was for him a
sunlit pre-holiday. He was enraptured by the exotic beauty of the
desert and its tent-dwelling Bedouins, and his romantic sympathy
extended even to the misled, pious fellahin who was incited to
violence against the Jewish newcomers.

With Sorrow and Faith (*Fun Veh Un Gloiben,* 1959) contained
Shargel's poems of the following two decades. The poems of the
war years were filled with sorrow and those of the post-war years
reverted to his optimistic faith in a nighing hour of Jewish redemption. The lyrics of 1948 were calls to heroism in defense of
the Yishuv and those after 1948 were ecstatic expressions of
vindication of his long cherished dreams. *Sunny Thresholds*
(*Zunike Shveln,* 1968) comprised his later poems of summer and
autumn, ripeness and contentment. As Yiddish poet, Hebrew edi-

tor, administrator of Petach Tikvah's cultural department, Shargel brought enrichment to the Israel scene.

Allied to Shargel in joyous affirmation of life was Israel Haim Biletzki (b. 1914), who wrote Yiddish verse and Hebrew prose. As a twenty-year-old, he came from Poland and settled in Tel Aviv. While Shargel preferred traditional rhymed quatrains and avoided experimenting with modern, complex rhythms, Biletzky displayed impeccable artistry in sophisticated free verse and subtle stanzaic forms. His first lyric volume, *Unrest* (*Unruh*, 1935), concentrated on his restless, youthful groping, but his later volumes sought to penetrate to essences beyond himself. For him the past was no less alive than the present and in his verses he sought to preserve it. "Only he who remembers his yesterdays can kindle the light of his tomorrow. Whoever wants to find his tomorrow must tie up the sheaves of his yesterdays." His *Songs to Man* (*Lieder Tsum Mentsh,* 1967), therefore, included eloquent tributes to Yiddish predecessors who inspired him, from Peretz to Manger. In addition, his three volumes of critical essays directed attention of Hebrew readers to Yiddish masterpieces, a rich heritage to be revered even by irreverent Israeli youth.

Yiddish essayists and scholars who made Israel a growing center of Yiddish literary expression during the mandatory period included Zalman Shazar (b. 1889), who settled in 1924 and who in 1963 became the third president of Israel; Dov Sdan (b. 1902), who came in 1925 and who later headed Yiddish studies at the Hebrew University; Dov Ber Malkin (1901-1966), a distinguished literary critic who exchanged Warsaw for Tel Aviv in 1934; Zerubabel (1886-1967), a spokesman for Labor Zionism since 1904, a talented orator, essayist and editor, who made Tel Aviv the center of his activities from 1935; Abraham Lis (b. 1913), an impressionistic literary critic who arrived from Bialystok in 1936 and became increasingly influential through his sympathetic interpretation of living authors and their newest contributions; Josef Harif (b. 1901), whose miniatures of Jerusalem, his home since 1934, reprinted in his book *Alongside Days* (*Oif Rand Fun Teg,* 1969), portrayed the daily life of Jerusalemites under the Mandate, the struggle for independence of the beleaguered capital, the influx of new immigrants and their painful integration, the emotional upsurge of the Six Day War, and the romance and reality of the reunited eternal city.

Moshe Basok (1907-1966) arrived in Palestine in the midst of the Arab riots of 1936 and joined the imperilled kibbutz Ashdod

Yakov in the Jordan Valley. His poems of *Burning Days* (*Brenen-dike Teg*, 1936) dealt with the wounds then being inflicted upon the land, the setting afire of Jewish fields reclaimed from the desert, the uprooting of newly planted eucalyptus trees that helped to drain the swamps, the loss of pioneering, young lives. Nevertheless, the poet could not bring himself to hate the haters, difficult though this might be. He hoped for an ultimate reconciliation of the two peoples that dwelt on the same soil. Soon thereafter Basok changed to Hebrew as his lyric medium,

Shlomo Shenhod (b. 1912) arrived in the same year as Basok but, unlike Basok, his poems did not reflect the contemporary scene. As a romanticist he was less interested in events of his immediate environment but rather sought to penetrate to eternal truths. To him these manifested themselves in dreams that floated up from his subconscious at night and not in the vanities and preoccupations of daytime. He entitled his maturest poems *With Dream Over Abyss* (*Mit Kholem Iber Theom*, 1961). They were philosophic, mystic meditations glowing with quiet sadness.

Rikudah Potash (1906-1965) was preeminently the lyricist of Jerusalem, her home since 1934. Her early poems, published shortly before her emigration from Poland, wove a web of glamor and serenity about her native town of Czenstochov and about her traditional Jewish home. Her sadness was mild and easily faded away when she espied a beautiful creature, object or landscape. Like her admired predecessor, Miriam Ulianover, she too preferred her grandmother's world that abounded in Sabbath charm, kindness and innocent love.

The full range of Rikudah Potash's poetic domain only emerged when her posthumous collection of lyrics appeared in 1967. These included vistas of Paris, London, Athens and New York, but everywhere she longed for Jerusalem and in her verse she caught the strange beauty, uniqueness and holiness of its hills and valleys, streets and gates, old-fashioned piety and motley population. Nestling under the wings of Jerusalem and in the golden light of her loneliness, she was content to weave of words her wreaths of psalms, elegies and lyric prayers.

Jerusalem was deeply embedded in the hearts of women who invoked it in their *Tkhines* and who wept at its Western Wall for many generations. Along with Rikudah Potash, it stimulated her friends, Elsa Lasker-Schüler and Mascha Kaleko to memorable German verses, when they made their home there, and Kadia

Molodowsky and Malke Locker to Yiddish poems of enduring value.

In her lyric booklet *Yerushalaim*, which appeared soon after the Six Day War, Malke Locker collected all her earlier poems of this city, whose broad portals, massive walls and mighty turrets bore witness to ageless stability amidst the shifting sands of the Judean desert. She reproduced the moods evoked by Jerusalem's colors, from the dominant gold during sandstorms, to the kaleidoscopic hues of the normal day from dawn to midnight. Each poem was a painting in words, enriched by allusions to the city's legendary and historic past covering four millennia.

Malke Locker was both poet and essayist. In her youth in the Carpathian foothills, she imbibed German, Polish and Ukrainian as well as Hebrew and Yiddish lore. Later she acquired a thorough knowledge of French and English. Her predilection for romantic and symbolic poetry came to the fore in her biographies of Rimbaud and Baudelaire, and in her essays on European romanticists. When her husband, the Labor Zionist leader Berl Locker, left for London in 1938, she accompanied him and did not return until 1948.

The short-story writer, Leibl Chain-Shimoni (b. 1900), was active in the Zionist Labor movement of Lithuania as publicist, teacher and communal worker. After suffering imprisonment, he fled to Haifa in 1925 and served for four decades in Histadrut Councils and in the Haifa municipal administration. In 1926 he organized the Haifa dramatic circle *Unzer Vinkel*, which staged Yiddish performances until 1930. In 1928 he helped found the first Yiddish literary journal in Palestine, *Der Onheib*. His earlier book of short stories, *Up the Hill (Barg Aroif,* 1951), was followed by his novel of pioneering life, *Day In, Day Out (Tog Ein, Tog Ois,* 1954), and his reminiscences of his Lithuanian years preceding his *aliya, Yesterday (Nekhten,* 1959). Recognition came to him after the publication of *En Route (Untervegs,* 1956), realistic narratives of episodes that took place in Haifa during the final years of the British mandate, such as the efforts of immigrants, individuals and boatloads, to break through the blockade of the English navy, the attacks upon Jews by Arab neighbors with whom they had lived peacefully for generations, the erosion of goodwill between Jewish settlers and the increasingly hostile mandatory forces. The tragic ending generally preferred by the novelist reminded readers of the toll in young lives that the struggle for a Jewish homeland demanded. His later series of stories, *Onward*

(Gang, 1962) and *Basalt* (1966), stressed the continuing sacrifices and progress since 1948. The title story of the latter volume narrated the heroism in a Damascus jail of the female prisoners of Mishmar Hayarden, the only Jewish settlement overrun by the Syrians in 1948. During months of confinement, the spirit of the young girls was buoyed up by the oldest captive, Rivka, who was as tender as a mother towards them, even though she had otherwise become as hard as basalt in the course of her pioneering years and of struggles which had taken the lives of her husband and her sons. Stories of Safed traced the transformation of its religious community under the impact of recurring conflicts. In 1936 Safed's cabalists still put their faith solely in prayers and fasts, and these proved to be ineffective against Arab grenades. By 1948, however, even Safed's devout mystics combined faith in God with faith in the Palmach and helped to break the siege of their beloved city with weapons as well as with prayers. *Glowing Earth (Angeglite Erd,* 1970) included stories of the Six Day War and of Jerusalem reunited after the war. Authentic happenings were rearranged according to an artistic pattern, with flashbacks unraveling the past background of contemporary Israel.

Joshua Manik-Lederman (b. 1909) joined Chain-Shimoni in promoting Yiddish cultural activities in Haifa. He had left his Bessarabian townlet for America at the age of sixteen but, after spending five years in Chicago and five years in New York, he decided, in 1935, to cast in his lot with the Chalutzim. After seven years of physical labor on the soil of Hedera, he came to Haifa in 1942 and organized a Yiddish literary circle and a Yiddish theatrical group. At first his efforts were greeted with hostility by militant Hebraists and the group's dramatic performances were greeted with stones as well as applause, but he persisted and when, in 1970, he exchanged Haifa for Tel Aviv, his contribution as a pioneer of Yiddish in that northern gateway to Israel was generally recognized.

Manik-Lederman's poems, fables and satires were collected in five books, from 1936 to 1968. Only a few lyrics harked back to his Bessarabian childhood and his American years. Most hymned the joy of creation when he toiled to convert sand dunes to orchards and to chisel out roads through barren hills. He caught the spirit of Haifa and Safed. He sang romantically of the blue heart of the Mediterranean, of symphonic nights when the whole land appeared like a temple, of blackrobed Bedouin maidens who looked like transfigured princesses of lost empires. In his cosmic poems, he ranged through eons of time and hovered over galaxies on the edge of infinite space.

In the versified fables of *In My Glass Tower (In Mein Glezernem Turm*, 1968), he mingled humor with disillusioned wisdom, and satirized human folly by means of conversations between animate creatures and inanimate objects. Lion, fox, wolf, dog, gorilla and giraffe argued about ideals, culture, civilization, justice, decency, but all of them acted in accordance with their inborn animal nature. White spectacles and dark spectacles engaged in recrimination as to the superior value of optimism or pessimism. Human foibles and weaknesses emerged as laughable rather than as criminal.

Far sadder were the poems of the Holocaust contained in his book *Along Your Wandering (In Trit Fun Dein Vander*, 1964). In imagination he wandered along abandoned lanes of ruined Jewish townlets, with God as his companion. He had God weep with him at the sight of a synagogue from which no prayers resounded, an orphaned Torah with which nobody exulted, an old candelabrum with whose extinction all Sabbaths were extinguished. In another poem, the Creator was depicted as filled with despair because of his murdered Jews. Abdicating his heavenly throne, he roamed on earth, until caught, tortured and burned at the stake as the last Jew, thus expiating his guilt by sharing the fate of his destroyed people.

During the years of the Holocaust, few Yiddish writers were able to escape from Eastern Europe to the promised but barred Jewish national home. These included Zysman Segalowitch and Mordecai Tsanin (b. 1906). The latter had fled from Warsaw in 1939 and had made his way via Japan to Tel Aviv, where he resumed his journalistic career. With his founding and editing of *Letzte Neies,* the only Yiddish daily in Israel, he became a central figure in the struggle for Yiddish in the Jewish state. However, his literary significance is based on his deep-delving prose epic in which Jewish life down the centuries is portrayed in glamorous and tragic colors. Under the general title *Artapanos Comes Home (Artapanos Kumt Zurik Aheim,* I, 1966; II, 1968), this epic sought to probe the mystery of Jewish persistence during the two millennia from the subjection of Judea by the Romans in the days of Pompey, to its restoration as the sovereign state of Israel by the homecoming, post-Holocaust generation. Artapanos is the symbol of the wandering Jew, not accursed as Christian versions depicted him, but rather blessed by heroism and pride so that he can endure all persecutions and still retain his faith in his people and in the God of his people. The first volume embraces the period to the destruction of the Second Temple and the efforts of Rome's Jewish community to carry on despite the catastrophe that overwhelmed Judea. The second volume begins with the struggle for survival in the early middle ages of the Jews in Gaul, Burgundy and Ashkenaz, a small minority in a pagan and even more hostile Christian world, a struggle carried on with sword, faith, wisdom and learning. It ends with the martyrdom of the Jews in the Rhenish communities during the First Crusade, a martyrdom from which they emerged stripped of their wealth but strengthened in inner resources.

After the Second World War, the survivors of the Holocaust tried desperately to pry ajar Palestine's gates and to enter legally or illegally. Mendel Mann, who had fought with the Red Army up to the gates of Berlin, and Abraham Sutzkever, who had escaped from Vilna's ghetto and had emerged from the Polish forests where he had fought with the Jewish partisans, succeeded in overcoming British vigilance and arrived in 1947. In the same year came the poets Moshe Jungman (b. 1922), Moshe Gurin (b. 1921) and Rivka Basman (b. 1925). However, the poets Abraham Rinzler (b. 1923), Jacob Friedman (b. 1910), and the prose writers Yitzkhuk Paner (b. 1890), Zvi Eisnman (b. 1920) and Abraham Karpinowitch (b. 1917), were apprehended within sight of the coveted Palestinian coast and had to bide their time in a Cyprus internment camp. Other Yiddish writers were detained in European refugee camps until 1948. They included the narrator Shlome Berlinsky (1900-1959) and Yitzkhok Perlov (b. 1911), the poet Shlomo Worsoger (b. 1917), the editor Reuben Rubinstein (1889-1967) and the short story writers Israel Kaplan (b. 1902) and Joseph Shavinsky (b. 1908).

When at last the gates of Palestine were opened wide to all Jews by the newly proclaimed Jewish State, there followed such an influx of talented Yiddish writers that, within a decade, Israel became a Yiddish literary center rivalling New York and, within less than two decades, it surpassed this largest Jewish center.

The arrival from America of the revered dramatist and novelist David Pinski in 1949 was hailed as a harbinger of the coming flock of Yiddish writers who would wing their way to the new state from all continents. Pinski's home on Mount Carmel became a center for "Young Israel." Poets and storytellers brought their Yiddish works to him, as he had once brought his to Peretz, and sought his encouragement and inspiration. For his disciples Pinski proposed the slogan: Hebraism *and* Yiddish in Israel, Yiddishism *and* Hebrew in the Diaspora. He pointed out that two languages had always accompanied Jews throughout their long history: the sacred tongue of the Patriarchs and a vernacular derived from the environment in which Jews found themselves. However, Yiddish alone had developed to a degree of excellence where it could rival Hebrew. This rivalry had come to an end, but Yiddish was still the strongest bulwark against assimilation in the Diaspora. Were Yiddish to disappear, estrangement between non-Israeli and Israeli Jews would increase, because Hebrew could never replace it adequately.

H. Leivick, who visited Israel in 1950 expressed similar views in his farewell address on "The Present Role of Yiddish Literature." Leivick's poems written in Israel had a prophetic ring. He saw Elijah speeding to bring the news that the Messianic age had begun. Israel was again resting under its own tents and the biblical utterance "How goodly are thy tents, O Jacob, thy habitations, O Israel!" found repercussions in the poet's verses.

Yossl Birshtein, who arrived from Australia in 1950, suggested to young Yiddish writers who met at Kibbutz Yagur, of which Zvi Eisnman was a member, that they could overcome their difficulties in kibbutzim where little Yiddish was heard by pooling their resources of language and by stimulating each other through more frequent contacts. In issues of *Di Goldene Keyt* they frequently appeared as a group under the heading "Young Israel." Their lyricists included Rivke Basman, who survived the Vilna ghetto and concentration camps in Estonia; Benjamin Hrushovski, who wrote under the pseudonym of H. Benjamin and whose first volume, *Dust* (*Shtoiben,* 1948), appeared shortly before his arrival at nineteen to participate in Israel's War of Liberation; Abraham Rinzler, who settled in Kiryat Motzkin; Shlome Worsoger, who published his first volume, *To Be* (*Zein,* 1948), while still in a Displaced Persons' Camp in Germany; Moshe Jungman, whose first lyrics, *Coma* (*Hienerplet,* 1947), appeared in Italy on the eve of his sailing for Israel. All these poets were born in the 1920's and did indeed represent the youngest group writing in Yiddish.

An anthology of the prose and verse of "Young Israel" appeared in 1954. In the same year Jungman published his songs as the first volume of a projected Young Israel Series. Two years later Eisnman followed with the second colume of the series, entitled

The Road (*Die Bahn*, 1956), sad, idyllic tales of Poland, Russia and Israel, the three waystations on his own life's road. The critic Yitzkhak Paner characterized Eisnman's world as devoid of dynamic striving, raging passions, without dark nights or radiant days—"merely quiet breezes that rustle between falling autumnal leaves, like barely audible, mournful music which lulls into a sweet dream or into a sweet, eternal sleep. Almost all Eisnman's characters are lonely persons or persons who received severe wounds in life's battles and withdrew as invalids from the battlefront, or else persons handicapped by temperament or fate: physical and psychic cripples."

As Eisnman matured on Israeli soil, his subject-matter became increasingly Israel-oriented. The stories and sketches of his volume *Constellations* (*Mazaloth*, 1965) skirted the borderland between reality and illusion. His characters were simple, silent men and women in poor, crowded apartments, who nourished unfulfilled dreams, or children who needed so little to set their imaginations roaming beyond blue horizons. Memories of the past and expectations directed toward the future made their dull, difficult present bearable.

Jungman's poems of Israel were pervaded by a greater optimism. In *White Portals* (*Vaisse Toren*, 1964), he caught the uniqueness of Jerusalem, Safed, Tiberias, and the exuberant striving of Galilean villagers and fishermen, new settlers in Dimona and Lachish, and exotic Jewish tribesmen who had answered the call to the old-new land. His joyousness reached its apex in the poems of the Six Day War and in the volume *Smiles from the Holy Land* (*Shmekhel Fun Eretz Hakodesh*, 1969).

Joseph Shavinsky (b. 1908), a native of Lodz, published three studies on Polish-Jewish history before he was trapped in Warsaw's ghetto. Shortly before its liquidation, he fled to the surrounding forests. For twenty-seven months he endured hunger, cold, and constant danger. Liberated in 1945, he participated in the cultural activities of the refugees in the Displaced Persons' Camp of Fernwald. In 1949 he arrived in Israel and, during the following two decades, he completed several volumes of short stories dealing with Polish Jewry in its death throes and heroic resistance and with the integration of Jewish survivors in Israel. *And Then Came Man* (1970), an English translation of his best tales, dealt with God's last creation, man, in his strange moods and curious behavior. An allegorical tale, "The Whip," emphasized that every man felt the sting of a whip which urged him on and prevented his sinking back into apathy and contentment. The tale "Hemda" portrayed with great delicacy and meticulous accuracy Bedouin lore, traditions, superstitions and the restless Bedouin way of life in peace and war, in love and wrath. It centered about the concern of a Bedouin sheikh for his youngest and most beautiful wife, fourteen-year-old Hemda, when the Sinai War erupted between Israel and Egypt.

Shavinsky was able to create with absolute economy of words living characters and the unique atmosphere in which they breathed. Some were heroic, such as the Jewish partisans who harried the Nazis and the Jewish fighters in Sinai, others were silent souls suffering in anguish. Shavinsky's keen observation of human nature was also revealed in his three volumes of pen portraits of writers, artists and men of deeds.

In the 1950's, Yiddish writers continued to stream into Israel from many lands. From London came the veteran novelists A. M. Fuchs (b. 1890) and Leo Koenig (1889-1970). From Paris came Moshe Grossman (1904-1961), Leib Rochman (b. 1918) and Yekhiel Hofer (b. 1906). From Canada came the ever restless poet and essayist Melech Ravitch, but only to tarry in Tel Aviv for a few years before returning to Montreal. From Poland came the much tried novelist Isaiah Spiegel (b. 1906) to resume a creative career begun in 1930 and interrupted by a decade of great suffering. Not until 1957 did the poet Binem Heller (b. 1908) arrive from Warsaw, full of regrets for former aberrations and eager to sing songs of tender love for his new home. He was followed in 1959 by the poet Leib Olitzky (b. 1897). From New York arrived the ideologist of anarchism Abba Gordon in 1957. He edited *Problemot*, a monthly in Hebrew and Yiddish, until his death in 1964. From Philadelphia came Rochel Fishman (b. 1935), the youngest of Yiddish poets, in 1954, to settle in Kibbutz Beth Alpha. The tender freshness of her lyric collections, *Sun Above All* (*Zun Iber Alts*, 1962) and *Thorns After Rain* (*Derner Nokhn Regn*, 1966), her discovery of beauty all about her, even in the most menial tasks, her unquenchable optimism, even when sadness assailed her, were exhilarating innovations for a post-Holocaust generation. "Sweet the sky, sweet the clouds, and good as salt the earth."

Israel Kaplan, son of a Lithuanian rabbi and educated in the Lithuanian cities of Brisk, Vilna and Kovno, was seized in the midst of his teaching and literary career by the Nazi invaders and locked up in the ghettos of Kovno and Riga and in various concentration camps. He was liberated from Dachau by the American forces in 1945 and immediately set to work to record the experiences of the survivors of the Holocaust. This material was edited by him in the booklets *Fun Letzten Khurban,* which appeared from 1946 to 1948, and also formed the basis for many stories in his volumes *Byways and Detours (Shliakh un Umveg,* 1964) and *Slings (Geshleider,* 1970). Other stories emphasized the spiritual splendor of Lithuania's Jews before the Nazi era, their dignified behavior when catastrophe struck and they were subjected to the most humiliating tribulations in concentration camps, their reemergence in Displaced Persons' Camps, and their rehabilitation in Israel. For Kaplan, the ultra-religious Jews of Jerusalem had a special fascination. He portrayed the inhabitants of Jerusalem's Mea Shearim district not as exotic museum-specimens but as normal human beings whose upbringing had conditioned them to reject modern innovations and to think and behave in strict conformity to biblical and Talmudic precepts.

Yekhiel Hofer was a physician in Warsaw and became a Yiddish novelist and essayist only after his arrival in Israel in 1951. His long narratives dealt primarily with the Jews of his native city, but his best novel, *In White Remoteness (In Vaisser Farfalenkeit,* 1969), was based upon his painful experiences in Siberia during the war years. It depicted the struggle for survival of Polish Jews in a Soviet Labor Camp of the Far North, until the Russian-Polish alliance mitigated their hard lot.

Isaiah Spiegel, who was born in the same year as Hofer, spent the war years in the Lodz ghetto. His five volumes of short stories about these years portrayed not only scenes of hunger and the hallucinations evoked by hunger but also little deeds of human kindness, rays of light that illumined the abyss, flashes of resistance against Nazi bestiality, faith and hope that enabled Jews to cling to life and not to deteriorate morally.

After Spiegel's arrival in Israel, he was haunted for a long time by scenes and shades of his tormented past—his novel *Flames From the Earth (Flamen Fun Der Erd,* 1966) still dealt with the Lodz ghetto a year before its liquidation—but gradually he became absorbed also in the fate of the survivors who had found their way to Israel. In the stories of *The Bridge (Die Brik,* 1963), he depicted their rebirth in Jewish towns and villages, their last flickering memories of deluged years, the hardships and tragedies of their early readjustment, their groping for new bonds, for sunshine after gloom, for warmth after winter. Spiegel's compassion embraced all things living, the young fluttering bird and the timid little kitten no less than the forgotten spinster and the dying graybeards. He felt the suffering of the parched earth and the melodious heart-beat of the clouds in the heavens. He understood the loneliness of the remnants of his people who had looked death in the face and who recalled the horror of their recent past amidst the jubilation of a new dawn. The opening story is typical of the author's kind, calm, dignified approach. It begins with a letter received by a Polish ghetto survivor from an uncle in Israel. The winged stag on Israel's airmail is seen by the recipient as a symbol of the Jewish people rearisen from ashes and soaring onward to new national goals. Impelled by this vision to leave his native land of bitter memories, he endures in stoic silence last indignities at the Polish border station. However, when his attention is derisively called to the fact that the flying stag upon which he sets his new hope has only a single wing, he replies proudly that, though the other wing may have been broken and burnt in the Holocaust, the stag still flies upward and, phoenixlike, is experiencing another resurrection.

Spiegel's novel *Stairs to Heaven* (*Shtiegen Tsum Himel,* 1966) is autobiographic. It mirrors the world through the eyes of a Jewish boy who, like the author, grew up during the last years of the Czar's reign. Poverty was visible everywhere but also mutual help within the extended family. The first premonitions of a coming revolt sear the Jewish community. Aunt Beela goes to prison, when mistaken for the more radical Aunt Esther, in order to help the latter to escape across the border. The boy's father also submits to a term in jail for harboring Esther. Sadness dominates childhood years and a helpless awareness of mysteries which only grown-ups understand. The style of the novel alternates between naturalistic descriptions and symbolistic apprehensions of a superrational reality in which God and angels participate. Though primarily a novelist and chronicler of the Holocaust, Spiegel is also a literary critic of profound insight and tolerant sympathy. In the essays of *Figures and Profiles* (*Geshtaltn Un Profiln,* 1971, he seeks to uncover the uniqueness of thirty literary personalities, many of whom he knew intimately. Each writer is imbedded in his intellectual milieu and the original contribution of each is summed up in succinct, striking phrases. Thus, Niger is characterized as the Rashi of Yiddish literature, Lamed Shapiro as the Yiddish Kafka, Mani-Leib as the Magic Flute, and Leivick as the humane personality. But even in these essays Spiegel constantly recalls the Holocaust and he ends his volume with a call to the surviving lovers of Yiddish to carry on the legacy bequeathed to them by the martyred Yiddish writers.

Leib Olitzky (b. 1897) was the oldest of three brothers, all of whom were wrested from promising literary careers in Poland by the Nazi invaders. His younger brother, Baruch Olitzky (1907-1941), perished at the hands of the Nazis and only a single volume of his lyrics appeared posthumously under the title *My Blood Is Commingled* (*Mein Blut Is Oisgemisht*, 1951). The youngest brother, Mattes Olitzky (b. 1915), attracted attention with the poems of *In Alien Land* (*In Fremden Land*, 1948) while still in a German refugee camp before immigrating to the United States. There his *Selected Poems* (*Geklibene Lieder*, 1967) continued to revert to his Warsaw years of hunger and fear, to visions of horror and flight, to his Jewish pupils who were doomed to an early, violent death and whom he tried to comfort with false hopes of survival. Leib Olitzky succeeded in escaping from Warsaw to Soviet Russia. Repatriated to Poland in 1946, he co-edited the publications of *Idish-Bukh*, but by 1959 he despaired that Jewish cultural life could be resuscitated and made his way to Israel. His literary career had begun with short stories and the novel *In An Occupied Townlet* (*In A Okupiert Shtetl*, 1925), which dealt with Jewish life under German occupation during World War I and under the Polish Republic. During his years in Soviet Russia and in Communist Poland, he translated Pushkin and Krylov into Yiddish and wrote conformist poetry. But even while conforming to the literary requirements of the Communist party line, he found release for his hidden love of Israel by translating Hebrew poems into Yiddish. These were later published under the title *From the Golden Pitcher* (*Fun Goldenem Krug*, 1968). On Israeli soil, the poet, who had aged prematurely and had concluded that all existence was vanity of vanities, felt new fire in his veins and new inspiration as he experienced genuine meaningfulness and sanctity in each day. Four volumes of joyous verse and a novel attested to his revived creative mood. The seventy-year-old poet called his new Israeli songs *Truth and Growth* (*Vor un Veren*, 1967). In the land without frost and snow he tried to forget the Russian frosts that penetrated his bones and the blood-drenched Polish snows through which he plodded earlier. In one poem he described the temptation that came to a Jew in Israel to enjoy a more prosperous life in the Galut, but after gorging himself with worldly pleasures, the ex-Israeli heard an old melody of Yehuda

Halevi full of longing for Zion; overcome by restlessness amidst satiety, he returned for a second time to find genuineness and dream-fulfillment in the Jewish heartland, never to leave it again.

Olitzky's poetry voiced his love for Israel's every stone, tree, cloud and child. He blessed the street-cleaner who removed uncleanliness and unholiness from the cobblestones so that purity and holiness might be restored to them anew each day. He himself, through lyric admonitions, sought to cleanse his beloved Israel from excrescences of heart and spirit and therefore he combined adoration of Israel's loveliness and heroism with reproaches of sabra failings.

Olitzky's novel, *Yeshiva Folk* (*Yeshiva-Leit*, 1968), reverted in subject-matter to the teeming life of a Lithuanian Yeshiva before World War I. It drew largely upon his own adolescent experiences at the famed Slobodka Yeshiva, his first awakening to love, his wrestling between religious orthodoxy and the new learning which stimulated questioning of traditional values. In this realistic narrative, pleasant characters alternated with unpleasant ones, goodness battled viciousness without necessarily emerging triumphant, and yet there was a toning down of all harshness and a tolerance of revealed human frailties. Through all scenes moved the Rosh Yeshiva, whose saintly, unworldly spirit left its mark upon recalcitrant as well as adoring pupils. An epilogue sketched the aftermath, the decimation of this Yeshiva generation as a result of wars, revolutions and pogroms, and the renewal of shattered existences for the pitifully few survivors who reached Israel's shores.

In the 1960's Yiddish writers continued to find their way to Israel, some to seek temporary inspiration and some to make their permanent home there. Among the latter was the critic and literary historian Nachman Maisel; the California sculptor and poet Boris Dimondstein, who founded in 1961 the *Safeter Literarishe Heftn,* a quarterly review for literature, art and criticism; David Sfard, who had been a strong pillar of writing in post-war Poland; Naftali Herz Cohen who survived a quarter-of-a-century of Soviet and Polish prisons and labor camps and who recorded his ordeal of long martyrdom in the poems of *Recorded from Memory* (*Farshriben in Zikorn,* 1966); and above all, Itzik Manger, whose popularity in Israel exceeded that of any other contemporary Yiddish writer.

In the 1960's, there were available to Yiddish readers not only the daily *Letzte Naies,* edited by Mordecai Tsanin, and the aforementioned periodicals, but also the weeklies *Folksblat, Illustrirte Veltvokh, Israel Shtimme, Yiddishe Zeitung, Dos Yiddishe Likht, Frei Israel,* the fortnightly *Lebensfragen* and the bi-monthly *Eigens.* The quarterly *Di Goldene Keyt,* however, remained the principal Yiddish literary organ.

In the third volume of his *Lexicon,* Melech Ravitch in 1958 gave pen profiles of 64 Israeli Yiddish writers and 39 who wrote in both Yiddish and Hebrew. In the same year the periodical *Heimish* listed 154 Israel Yiddish writers, of whom 130 were members of the Yiddish Authors' Society as compared to nine members three decades earlier. Moshe Grossman, who founded this journal for literature, criticism and social problems, continued as its editor until his death in 1961. In 1966, Arye Shamri compiled an anthology of Yiddish poetry and prose of Israel, in which sixty writers were represented. A year later, Moshe Gross-Zimmerman, Abraham Karpinowitch and Alexander Spiglblat compiled and edited an *Almanac of Yiddish Writers in Israel,* containing fiction, poetry, essays and scholarly contributions by fifty-four writers.

In 1956 the Yiddish writers of Tel Aviv acquired their own home at Rehov Dov Hos 25. Within the following decade a Sholom Aleichem House and a Sholem Asch House became additional Yiddish cultural centers in the Tel Aviv area. These were climaxed by the Leivick House, inaugurated in May 1970 with an address by the Prime Minister Golda Meir hailing the achievements of Yiddish.

The Peretz Publishing House continued to publish about twenty-five books each year in Tel Aviv and the Hamenora Publishing House followed suit in the same city. By the mid-1960's Israel outdistanced the United States as the main center for Yiddish publishing.

When Yiddish men-of-letters met in Tel Aviv in 1965 to celebrate the appearance of the fiftieth issue of *Di Goldene Keyt,* they could look back upon a proud record of achievement and could look forward to continuing growth in prestige and influence. The editor, Sutzkever, recalled that at the quarterly's founding he had penned a poem in answer to the Cassandra voices that prophesied the quick demise of Yiddish. In this poem he foretold that in a hundred years Jews along the Jordan would still be discussing the coming death of Yiddish. One-sixth of the hundred years had already passed and the discussion was still going on. He himself was still convinced that the artistic Yiddish word would continue to resound in Israel at the end of this time limit. Sutzkever's co-editor, Eliezer Pines, felt that by becoming a home for Yiddish creativity throughout the world and by bringing, in each issue, translations of Hebrew writers, the quarterly had succeeded in its objective of furthering the unity of Jewish literature in its two Jewish languages. The fiftieth issue confirmed this conclusion by including contributions by Marc Chagall from Paris; I. D. Berkovitch, Tel Aviv; Abraham Kariv, Haifa; Chaim Grade, New York; Eliezer Shteinman, Tel Aviv; Aaron Zeitlin, New York; Ka-zetnik, Tel Aviv; Arye Shamri, Ein Shamir; Mordecai Tsanin, Tel Aviv; Jacob Glantz, Mexico; Jacob Friedman, Tel Aviv; Mordecai Strigler, New York; Rivke Basman, Tel Aviv; Binem Heller, Tel Aviv; Gabriel Preil, New York; Rachel Auerbach, Tel Aviv; Elchanan Wogler, Paris; Israel Kaplan, Tel Aviv; Melech Ravitch, Montreal; Mordecai Schechter, New York; Max Weinreich, New York; Rochel Korn, Montreal; Zerubabel, Tel Aviv; Ephraim Auerbach, New York; Moshe Gross-Zimmermann, Tel Aviv; Yekhiel Hofer, Tel Aviv; J. Z. Shargel, Petach Tikvah; L. Domankevitch, Paris; Moshe Jungman, Tivon; Shifre Verber, Tel Aviv; Mendel Mann, Paris; Moshe Basok, Ashdod Yakov; Rikuda Potash, Jerusalem; Isaiah Spiegel, Givataim; M. Waldman, Paris; Moshe Gurin, Holon; Abraham Karpinowitch, Tel Aviv; Glanz-Leyeles, New York; Bashevis Singer, New York; Abraham Sutzkever, Tel Aviv; Chone Shmeruk, Jerusalem; and Leibush Lehrer, who submitted his last article from New York shortly before his death.

The increased interest in Yiddish also manifested itself in the increased number of literary awards accorded to Yiddish writers. No award was prized more by poets than the one established in honor of Itzik Manger in 1969. It was bestowed during the initial year upon Aaron Zeitlin and Abraham Sutzkever and during the second year, 1970, upon Chaim Grade and Jacob Friedman, and during the third year, 1971, upon Joseph Kerler and Kadia Molodowsky. While four of these poets were famed wherever Yiddish books were read, Friedman's slender booklets found far fewer readers and Kerler was known only for the few poems of defiance which had been smuggled out of Moscow and published abroad.

Friedman was a descendant of the Rizhin dynasty of Hassidic rabbis. He was born in the Galician townlet of Milnitze but grew up in Czernovitz. Since his boyhood, he adored beauty and was intoxicated with verbal rhythms and ringing rhymes. His poems were published from his seventeenth year in periodicals. His lyric booklets of the 1930's gave him initial recognition among the young Rumanian poets. But it was during bitter years in a Transnistrian camp during World War II and in a Cyprus internment camp, when he tried to make his way illegally to Israel, that he was led to wrestle more profoundly with the problem of good and evil and to question God's ways with man, especially with Jews. Surely, the Jews who suffered under Nazi indignities were more righteous than their oppressors. Why then were they being punished so grievously? Would it always be their destiny to be the victims of human bestiality? Might they not fare better if they ceased to be just and moral in an apparently unjust and immoral world? The poet's skepticism, however, did not long endure. It yielded to an intensification of his deeply religious faith and to humble submission to his Creator who had vindicated Israel's trust and was restoring it to independence and glory. The poems of Friedman's first book on Israel's soil, upon which he landed in 1949, was entitled *Shepherds in Israel* (*Pastekher in Israel*, 1953). It showed him revolting against sophistication, since wisdom had become tired and sleepy. Living in the village of Beit Dagon, he envisaged himself as a shepherd whose lineage went back to Jacob and David, biblical shepherds who led simple, good lives close to nature and God's creatures. He felt that the great things were as radiantly simple as bread and salt and that only man involved himself unnecessarily in a maze of complexities. An undertone of subtle humor and mild satire pervaded the intimate, good-natured poems in which he sang of the great rabbis, his Hassidic ancestors, whose prayers exuded fervent joyous faith and who worshipped God with laughter, dance, labor and all-embracing compassion.

In the long poem, *The Legend of Noah Green* (*Die Legende Fun Noakh Green,* 1960), Friedman hailed the poet as God's mirror in which the divine spirit was reflected. "If the Creator Himself took the trouble to conceive me in His thought and then embodied this thought in the melody of flesh, veins and bones, then surely His radiant effort must have been worthwhile. . . . And I will thank Him for being what I am, not a hair's breadth otherwise, eternally unique, I."

Friedman's supreme achievement was his dramatic poem *Nefilim* (1963). The Nefilim, according to the Bible, were the sons of God who saw that the daughters of man were beautiful and they therefore descended from heaven and mated with them. The poet chose as his central characters two such sons of God who took on human bodies and lived human lives. In one of them, Nefil, the divine element remained dominant even on earth and he regretted having exchanged his lustrous wings for human limbs. His existence was filled with a constant striving for heavenly goodness, an emanation of the divine light not yet extinguished in him. In the other son of God, Yored, the earthly element took complete possession. Lust and ambition for power motivated his actions. Though an earthly crown was bestowed upon Nefil, he had little use for it and let it fall into the hands of Yored. The latter then waged victorious wars, grew ever mightier and, in his megalomania, built a tower to reach up to the sky so that he could challenge God and the heavenly hosts. The higher the tower, however, the more the sky receded and the shakier became the foundations of Yored's empire. To maintain himself, he waded in the blood of his enemies, terrorized his subjects, and even hanged the non-resisting Nefil. Nevertheless, he could not halt the collapse of his tottering tower and his own plunge into the abyss. Nefil, on the other hand, descended from the gallows unscathed, for the divine element was immortal and eternal.

Friedman's dramatic poem reflected contemporary events, the vain effort of a power-hungry dictator to erect an awesome but godless political structure and the passive resistance of a long suffering opponent who rose from apparent death to a new life. Not since Richard Beer-Hofmann's dramatic mystery *Jacob's Dream,* completed during World War I, had a comparable work been composed by a Jewish poet. Both works were products of religious poets who wrestled with skepticism and overcame it, and both Beer-Hofmann and Friedman proudly proclaimed the Jewish affirmation of the unconquerable, divine element in man.

The religious tone was not as predominant in Abraham Sutzkever as in Friedman, but his love for his people and its redeemed land was no less intense. His first cycle of lyrics in Israel, *Flaming Chariot (In Feiervogen)* contrasted the Jewish ruins he had left behind in the towns of the Holocaust with the new tents and vineyards welcoming him. He heard the land calling him: "You are mine. Blessed are you in your coming. My sheep are your sheep and my garden your garden. Plant with as much tenderness your vineyard here as you fired with cruelty your rifle there." When the Jewish world was deluged in blood, he saw no dove appear with a green olive leaf to indicate to him that the deluge was subsiding. But he did see a golden soul flying over seas to the land of his dreams. There, a new Jewish world came into being. There prophets and *Olim* walked hand in hand. There the dead in a pillar of clouds joined the living in a pillar of flames.

Wherever the poet went, images of earlier years pursued him.

Snow-covered Mt. Hermon reminded him both of the snows of Siberia, where he had spent his boyhood years, and of Lithuania, whose ghetto-enclosed Jews fell like silent snow-flakes all winter long. When he strolled on the boulevards of Tel Aviv, the faces he saw recalled to him faces that were set afire in Vilna, Kovno, Grodno. However, soon other faces interposed themselves, those of Jews that stemmed from Yemen, Kurdistan and the many tribes ingathered in the Jewish state. His poems encompassed the new landscape of the Negev and the Mediterranean and the cities of Safed and Tiberias. On ascending to Jerusalem for the first time, he felt as if he were gazing upon the Eternal face to face and he had to lower his eyes. The waters that lapped the shores of Eilat spoke to him of Solomonic ships that once brought treasures of Ophir to the ancient Jewish kingdom. In his reply to the waters, he expressed the hope that Israel's ships would again bear to the world songs of Sinai and parables of wisdom and would bring back to the tents of Jacob the pearls of friendship and the gold of peace.

As a military correspondent during the War of Independence, he accompanied Yitzkhak Sadeh, commander of the Palmach, in the conquest of the Negev and was the first Yiddish poet to sing of its strange, wild beauty in his *Songs of the Negev (Lieder Fun Negev)*. Eight years later he was with the Israel Defense forces in the Sinai campaign of 1956 and was inspired to pen his lyric cycle about Sinai.

In "Ode to the Dove," a dialogue between the poet and his muse personified as a dove, Sutzkever expressed his esthetic creed that the world needed poetry to stir it to a more sensitive awareness of beauty and to lend eternity to the fleeting moment. He himself wanted to drink passionately the wine of every minute and to create verses of timeless loveliness while in this intoxicated state. However, the completed verses bore evidence that he did not dispense with critical, sober reason. He subjected his naked, raw, elemental emotions to the discipline of classical restraint. He congealed the fiery lava from his volcanic soul in molds of sculptured perfection.

Sutzkever observed scenes intensely and described them accurately but these scenes were also significant for him because of the thought-associations they evoked and as symbols of an immaterial reality which he dimly apprehended. His outer eye caught fleeting details which his inner eye then sought to transmute to enduring verities. For him the distant past was real, the present often ghostly, the future an unfathomable abyss. Against the fading of youth and the inevitability of death, themes that constantly recur in his later poetry, he invoked the miracle of art which extended the span of life beyond allotted years.

Sutzkever is a virtuoso in his handling of verbal color, sound and imagery. His rhymes are pure and often startling, his neologisms conform to the spirit of his linguistic medium. He is equally adept in the use of traditional metrical stanzas, in the subtle cadences of free verse, and in the complicated rhythms of prose-poetry. He successfully entraps in words surrealist images comparable to those Chagall entrapped in colors. Indeed, he identifies himself with Chagall in the lyrics entitled "Chagallishe Verter." It is this perfection of form which makes him so difficult to translate into other tongues. Nevertheless, he has been translated into Hebrew, English, French and German, and his poems were included in the anthology of world poetry published by UNESCO in 1963.

In the 1970's, Yiddish literature is almost extinct in Eastern Europe where it arose and flourished. It is declining in the Diasporas of Western Europe, North and South America, Australia and South Africa. But its vitality in Israel is still unspent and in Israel are being ingathered writers, actors and educators who are enriching the Jewish homeland with Yiddish cultural treasures.

BIBLIOGRAPHY

Bibliographies of Yiddish writers are available in **Zalman** Reisen's *Lexikon Fun Der Yiddisher Literatur* (4 vols., 3 ed., Vilna, 1928) and in the more recent *Lexikon Fun Der Nayer Yiddisher Literatur,* of which seven volumes appeared since 1956 under the auspices of the Congress of Jewish Culture.

A bibliography of books on, and translations from, the Yiddish literature available in English until 1940 is appended to A. A. Roback's *Story of Yiddish Literature,* published by YIVO in New York. The *Jewish Book Annuals,* 29 vols., published by the Jewish Book Council of America from 1941 to 1972, list the more recent translations of Yiddish books. The bibliography *Yiddish Literature in English Translation* compiled by Dina Ambramowicz (New York, YIVO, 1970) lists books published since 1945.

The present bibliography serves primarily as a guide to further reading in English on Yiddish literary movements and Yiddish writers.

GENERAL REFERENCES AND ANTHOLOGIES

Basic Facts About Yiddish, YIVO, 1946.

Bellow, Saul, ed. *Great Jewish Short Stories,* New York, 1966.

Biletzky, I. C. *Essays on Yiddish Poetry and Prose,* Tel Aviv, 1969.

Block, Etta. *One Act Plays from the Yiddish,* Cincinnati, 1923.

————, *One Act Plays from the Yiddish (Second Series),* New York, 1925.

Charles, Gerda, ed. *Modern Jewish Stories,* London, 1963.

Cooperman, J. B. and S. H., eds. *America in Yiddish Poetry,* New York, 1967.

Dawidowicz, L. S., ed. *The Golden Tradition,* New York, 1967.

Doroshkin, Milton. *Yiddish in America: Social and Cultural Foundations,* Rutherford, N. J., 1970.

Frank, Helena. *Yiddish Tales,* Philadelphia, 1912.

Glatstein, J., Knox, I., Margoshes, S., Eds. *Anthology of Holocaust Literature*, Philadelphia, 1969.
Goldberg, Isaac. *Six Plays of the Yiddish Theater*, Boston, 1913.
————, *Six Plays of the Yiddish Theater (Second Series)*, Boston, 1918.
Goodman, Henry, ed. *The New Country*, New York, 1961.
Howe, Irving and Greenberg, Eliezer, eds. *A Treasury of Yiddish Stories*, New York, 1953.
————, *A Treasury of Yiddish Poetry*, New York, 1969.
Imber, S. J. *Modern Yiddish Poetry; An Anthology*, New York, 1927.
Landis, J. C., ed. *The Dybbuk and Other Great Yiddish Plays*, New York, 1966.
Leftwich, Joseph, ed. *The Golden Peacock*, New York, 1961.
————, *Yisroel*, New York, 1963.
————, *The Way We Think: Essays from the Yiddish*, New York, 1969.
Lifson, D. S. *The Yiddish Theater in America*, New York, 1965.
Liptzin, Sol. *The Flowering of Yiddish Literature*, New York, 1963.
————, *The Maturing of Yiddish Literature*, New York, 1970.
Madison, C. A. *Yiddish Literature*, New York, 1968.
Roback, A. A. *Curiosities of Yiddish Literature*, Boston, 1933.
————, *Story of Yiddish Literature*, New York, 1940.
Rosenfeld, Max, ed. *A Union for Shabbes and Other Stories of Jewish Life in America*, Philadelphia, 1967.
————, *Pushcarts and Dreamers*, New York, 1969.
Rubin, Ruth. *A Treasury of Jewish Folksong*, New York, 1950.
Samuel, Maurice. *In Praise of Yiddish*, New York, 1971.
Soltes, Mordecai. *The Yiddish Press, an Americanizing Agency*, Philadelphia, 1925.
Waxman, Meyer. *History of Jewish Literature, Vol. V.*, New York, 1960.
Weinreich, Uriel. *College Yiddish*, New York, 1949.
————, *The Field of Yiddish*, New York, 1954.
————, *Modern English-Yiddish Yiddish-English Dictionary*, New York, 1968.
White, Bessie. *Nine One-Act Plays from the Yiddish*, Boston, 1932.
Wiener, Leo. *History of Yiddish Literature in the Nineteenth Century*, New York, 1899.

OLDER YIDDISH LITERATURE

Glatt, Herman. *He Spoke in Parables; the Life and Works of the Dubnow Maggid*, New York, 1957.
Glückel of Hameln. *Life of Glückel of Hameln*, translated by B. Z. Abrahams, New York, 1963.

————, *Memoirs*, translated and edited by Marvin Lowenthal, New York, 1932.

Hassidic Anthology, edited by L. I. Newman and S. Spitz, New York, 1934; 1963.

Maase-Bukh, translated and edited by Moses Gaster, 2 vols., Philadelphia, 1934.

Maggid of Dubno, translated by Benno Heineman, New York, 1971.

Maggidim and Hassidim; a New Anthology, edited by L. I. Newman and S. Spitz, New York, 1962.

Tseno-Ureno; a Jewish Commentary of the Book of Exodus, translated by Norman C. Gore, New York, 1965.

Wise Men of Chelm and Other Merry Tales, translated by B. Bengal and S. Simon, New York, 1945.

More Wise Men of Chelm and Their Merry Tales, adapted by S. Simon, New York, 1965.

Wise Men of Chelm, adapted by S. Tenenbaum, New York, 1965.

INDIVIDUAL AUTHORS

AHAD HAAM

Selected Essays, Cleveland, 1962.

Simon, Leon. *Ahad Haam, a Biography*, London, 1960.

S. ANSKI

Dybbuk, New York, 1926; Winnipeg, 1953.

SHOLEM ASCH

Apostle, New York, 1943.

From Many Countries; The Collected Short Stories, London, 1958.

In the Beginning, New York, 1935.

Kiddush Hashem, Philadelphia, 1912.

Mary, New York, 1949.

Moses, New York, 1951.

Mother, New York, 1930.

Mottke the Thief, New York, 1935.

Mottke the Vagabond, Boston, 1917.

Nazarene, New York, 1939.

Passage in the Night, New York, 1953.

Sabbatai Zevi, Philadelphia, 1930.

Salvation, New York, 1934.

Song of the Valley, New York, 1938.

Three Cities, New York, 1933.

Three Novels, New York, 1938.

Uncle Moses, New York, 1920.

War Goes On, New York, 1936.
Lieberman, Chaim. *The Chirstianity of Sholem Asch*, New York, 1953.

HERZ BERGNER
Between Sky and Sea, Melbourne, 1946.
Light and Shadow, London, 1963.

RACHMIL BRYKS
A Cat in the Ghetto; Four Novelettes, New York, 1959.
Ghetto Factory 76, New York, 1967.

M. DLUZNOWSKY
The Potter's Daughter, London, 1959. Published under pseud. M. Dunow.

SIMON DUBNOW
History of the Jews in Russia and Poland, 3 vols., Philadelphia, 1916-20.
Jewish History; An Essay in the Philosophy of History, Philadelphia, 1903.
Nationalism and History; Essays in Old and New Judaism, New York, 1958.

ALTER ESSELIN
Poems, Chicago, 1968.

JACOB GLATSTEIN
Homecoming at Twilight, New York, 1962.
Homeward Bound, New York, 1969.
Poems, Tel Aviv, 1970.

BERNARD GOLDSTEIN
Five Years in the Warsaw Ghetto, New York, 1961.
The Stars Bear Witness, New York, 1959.

CHONE GOTTESFELD
Tales of the Old World and the New, New York, 1964.

CHAIM GRADE
The Well, Philadelphia, 1967,

CHAIM GREENBERG
The Inner Eye, 2 vols., New York, 1964.

MOSHE GROSSMAN
In the Enchanted Land; My Seven Years in Soviet Russia, Tel Aviv, 1960.

PERETZ HIRSHBEIN

The Haunted Inn, Boston, 1921.

ITZIK MANGER

The Book of Paradise, New York, 1965.

MENDELE MOKHER SFORIM

Fishke the Lame, New York, 1960.
The Nag, New York, 1954.
The Parasite, New York, 1956.
Travels and Adventures of Benjamin the Third, New York, 1949.

JOSEPH OPATOSHU

A Day in Regensburg, Philadelphia, 1968.
The Last Revolt, Philadelphia, 1952.
The Polish Woods, Philadelphia, 1938.

Y. L. PERETZ

As Once We Were; Selections from the Works of Peretz, Los Angeles, 1951.
Book of Fire, New York, 1960.
Bontche the Silent and Other Stories, Philadelphia, 1927.
In This World and the Next; Selected Writings, New York, 1958.
My Memoirs, New York, 1965.
Stories and Pictures, Philadelphia, 1906.
Stories from Peretz, New York, 1964.
Three Canopies, New York, 1948.
Three Gifts and Other Stories, New York, 1947.
Goodman, Philip. *Peretz; A Source Book on Programming,* New York, 1951.
"Guide to English Translations of Y. L. Peretz," *Field of Yiddish,* edited by Uriel Weinreich, New York, 1954, pp. 292-299.
Liptzin, Sol. *Peretz,* Bilingual Edition, YIVO, New York, 1947.
Roback, A. A. *Peretz, Psychologist of Literature,* Cambridge, Mass., 1935.
Samuel, Maurice. *Prince of the Ghetto,* Philadelphia, 1948.

DAVID PINSKI

Arnold Levenberg, New York, 1928.
Cripples, New York, 1932.
Dollars, New York, 1932.
Forgotten Souls, New York, 1932.
Generations of Noah Edon, New York, 1931.
King David and His Wives, New York, 1923.
Temptations; a Book of Short Stories, New York, 1919.
Ten Plays, New York, 1920.
Three Plays, New York, 1918.
Treasure, New York, 1915.

ISAAC RABOY
Nine Brothers, New York, 1968.

MORRIS ROSENFELD
Songs of Labor and Other Poems, Boston, 1914.
Teardrop Millionaire and Other Poems, New York, 1955.
Goldenthal, Leon, *Toil and Triumph; Life of Morris Rosenfeld,* New York, 1960.

ELYA SCHECHTMAN
Erev, New York, 1967.

ZALMAN SCHNEOUR
Noah Pandre, London, 1936.
Noah Pandre's Village, London, 1938.

JOSEPH SHAVINSKY
And Then Came Man, Tel Aviv, 1970.

SHOLOM ALEICHEM
Adventures of Menachem-Mendl, New York, 1969.
Adventures of Motel, the Cantor's Son, New York, 1953.
Great Fair; Scenes from My Childhood, New York, 1955.
Inside Kasrilevke, New York, 1948.
Jewish Children, New York, 1920.
Old Country, New York, 1946.
Selected Stories, New York, 1956.
Some Laughter, Some Tears, New York, 1968.
Stempenyu, London, 1913.
Stories and Satires, New York, 1959; 1970.
Tevye's Daughters, New York, 1949.
Tevye Stories and Others, New York, 1965.
Wandering Star, New York, 1952.
Fiddler On the Roof; Based on Sholom Aleichem's Stories, New York, 1964.
Goodman, Philip. *Sholom Aleichem; A Source Book for Programming,* New York, 1966.
"A Guide to English Translations of Sholom Aleichem," *Field of Yiddish,* edited by Uriel Weinreich, New York, 1954, pp. 285-291.
Samuel, Maurice. *The World of Sholom Aleichem,* New York, 1943.
Sholom Aleichem Panorama, edited by Melech Grafstein, London, Ontario, 1948.

I. BASHEVIS SINGER
Estate, New York, 1969.
Family Moskat, New York, 1950.
Fearsome Inn, New York, 1967.
Friend of Kafka, New York, 1970.

Gimpel the Fool, New York, 1951.
In My Father's Court, Philadelphia, 1966.
Magician of Lublin, New York, 1960.
Manor, New York, 1967.
Mazel and Shlimazel, New York, 1967.
Satan in Goray, New York, 1955.
Seance and Other Stories, New York, 1968.
Selected Short Stories, New York, 1966.
Short Friday and Other Stories, New York, 1964.
Slave, New York, 1962.
Spinoza of Market Street, New York, 1961.
Zlateh the Goat and Other Stories, New York, 1966.
Malin, Irving, *Critical Views of I. Bashevis Singer*, New York, 1969.

I. J. SINGER

Blood Harvest, London, 1935.
Brothers Ashkenazi, New York, 1933.
East of Eden, New York, 1939.
Family Carnovsky, New York, 1943; 1969.
Of a World That Is No More, New York, 1970.
River Breaks Up, New York, 1938.
Sinner, New York, 1933.
Spring and Other Stories, New York, 1937.
Steel and Iron, New York, 1969.
Yoshe Kalb, New York, 1961.

MORDECAI SPECTOR

Three Worthies of Brebendefka, New York, 1905.

ABRAHAM SUTZKEVER

Siberia, London, 1961.
Leftwich, Joseph. *Abraham Sutzkever: Partisan Poet*, New York, 1971.

TASHRAK

Marriage Broker, New York, 1960.

ZISHA WEINPER

At the Rich Man's Gate, New York, 1935.

YEHOASH

Feet of the Messenger, Philadelphia, 1923.
Poems, London, Ontario, 1952.

CHAIM ZHITLOWSKY

Future of Our Youth In This Country, Pittsburgh, 1935.

ELIAKUM ZUNSER

Selected Songs, New York, 1928.
Liptzin, Sol. *Eliakum Zunser*, New York, 1950.

INDEX